The
Chronological History
of the
Negro in America

Geo. W. Williams

the
chronological
history
of

the
negro
in
america

by PETER M. BERGMAN
assisted by a staff of compilers
under the direction of
MORT N. BERGMAN

A BERGMAN BOOK

1817

PUBLISHED IN ASSOCIATION WITH

HARPER & ROW, PUBLISHERS

NEW YORK, EVANSTON, AND LONDON

It is impossible adequately to thank all who have helped in the cooperative project of writing this book, but special acknowledgment is due to Judith Lippmann, Mark Waits and Albin Unterweger. Jean McCarroll, who among other things worked through for me more than 800 thick volumes of the *Congressional Record,* especially deserves public thanks.

—PETER BERGMAN

THE CHRONOLOGICAL HISTORY OF THE NEGRO IN AMERICA. Copyright © 1969 by Peter M. Bergman. All rights reserved. Printed in the United States of America. No part of this book may be used or reproduced in any manner whatsoever without written permission except in the case of brief quotations embodied in critical articles and reviews. For information address Harper & Row, Publishers, Incorporated, 49 East 33rd Street, New York, N.Y. 10016. Published simultaneously in Canada by Fitzhenry & Whiteside Limited, Toronto.

FIRST EDITION

LIBRARY OF CONGRESS CATALOG CARD NUMBER: 68-27434

In Memoriam
OF
GEORGE WASHINGTON WILLIAMS
A GREAT AMERICAN HISTORIAN

Table of Contents

A. SLAVERY

B. RECONSTRUCTION

C. "SEPARATE BUT EQUAL"

D. "WITH ALL DELIBERATE SPEED"

A. SLAVERY

1. The Beginning

The Negro came to America in chains. While the colonization of the New World was brought about through importation of persecuted and outlawed Europeans partly as indentured labor, the Negro came from Africa only as a slave.

Slavery, a form of human exploitation distinct from indenture and serfdom of the feudal society, was not known in the Christianized part of the world until about 50 years before Columbus sailed West. Paradoxically, slavery was introduced in the New World at exactly the same time as the dissolution of serfdom began to take place in Europe; first in mercantilistic Italy and Holland. Paradoxically also, at that same time the sovereign rulers ceased to prevent, even promoted, individual migration across the oceans—thus an act of "liberating" their subjects.

The history of the Negro in America begins with the re-discovery of Africa by the Portuguese. In 1442, Antam Gonçalvez, a captain in the realm of Henry the Navigator, captured two or three Moors of noble birth on the African coast. The Moors offered as ransom "ten blacks, male and female." The ransom was accepted, and the Negroes were brought to Lisboa; sold at the market, these legendary ten Negroes represented the beginning of the African slave trade which up till the year 1517 was, based on a Papal grant, monopolized by the Portuguese crown. Henry himself tried to stop the abuses of the slave trade and forbade the kidnaping of Negroes in 1455. Yet, in the ecclesiastical annals of Ortiz de Zuniga under the date 1474 it is related, as an astonishing experience, that Negro slaves abounded in that city and the tithes levied on them produced considerable gains for the royal revenue. In 1482, the Portuguese built the first slave-trading port, São Jorge de Mina, on the African Gold Coast.

Still, practically no countries other than the Iberian attempted to introduce Negro slavery. And even there it dwindled and would most likely have disappeared if Spain's role in the New World had not supplied the basic conditions for the historically new institution of Negro slavery. At the time of the discovery of America, Spain and Portugal were economically poor countries, i.e. without substantial manufactures. The expulsion of the Moslems and Jews which was effectuated in the same year as Columbus's voyage, deprived these countries of their most useful and active

1

*population; the great steel works of Toledo, the leather factories
of Cordoba and the intensive plantations of olive and fruit trees
were replaced by grazing land for sheep, and thereby land and
manufacture that had been fruitful before the Inquisition were
systematically ruined in order to fit the ambitions of the Grandees
and the Church. Robbery and plunder became the basic economy
of these then mightiest powers of the Christian world, "on which
the sun never set." In 1493, by a Papal Bull, the New World was
divided (without real geographic knowledge) between Spain and
Portugal. The major economic revolution was based on the gold
and silver the conquistadores had looted, and on the new system of
human exploitation that turned Africa into a warren for the
commercial hunting of black-skins.*

*Negro slavery in America was a capitalistic institution. In eco-
nomic theory it belongs, as defined by Adam Smith, to the stage of
"Previous Accumulation" (Marx calls it more correctly "Primitive
Accumulation") which began in the fifteenth and sixteenth centuries.*

*

*It is not possible to give an exact number of how many Negroes
came to America. Robert R. Kuczynski, the world-known authority
on migration statistics, estimated that a minimum of 15 million
slaves landed alive. Because of the brutal treatment on transport
and the conditions of crossing, the total number of people of which
the African continent was depleted amounted in any case to
several times more. Carter G. Woodson, in "Negro in Our History,"
estimated the total at 50 million, while W. E. Du Bois, in "The
Negro," gives the figure of 60 million.*

1492

According to legend, Pedro Alonzo Niño, one of Columbus'
crew on his first voyage to the West, was a Negro.

1493

It is most probable that on Columbus' second voyage Negro slaves were brought to Jamaica, and that they took part
in a revolt.

1498

Since the enthusiasm for the discovery had cooled off, and
not many adventurers could be found, the Spanish government
permitted Columbus to take criminals with him for his third

crossing, even robbers and murderers who were sentenced to death. In the New World they were set free, huge parcels of land were given to them, and especially the right to treat everybody who was not a Christian and European as commodity and as animal.

1501

A royal ordinance gave official sanction to introducing Negro slaves in the Spanish colonies.

Spain imported white rather than Negro slaves to Hispaniola because the Negroes were considered rebellious and difficult to manage.

1502

Queen Isabella's commission to Ovando prohibited the passage to the Indies of Jews, Moors, or recent converts, but authorized him to take over Negro slaves that had been "born in the power of Christians." Ovando set sail in February, 1502. In 1503, Ovando protested the restriction on importation because the Negro slaves ran away and often demoralized the Indians.

Portugal landed her first cargo of slaves from Africa in Hispaniola. These first slaves were carried by way of Europe where they might be "Christianized" before being sent to the colonies, and some Portuguese intermarried with the Negroes.

Between this year and 1600, 900,000 Negro slaves were brought to Latin America.

From this date to the ending of slavery in Brazil, approximately 5,000,000 African Negroes were imported for work on the sugar plantations. These Africans, considered resistant to malaria and yellow fever, were concentrated in Minas Geraes, Bahia, Rio de Janeiro and Maronhao. Most of the African slaves shipped to Latin America came from the Guinea Coast, Angola, and the Congo Basin. Each group had a distinct culture, and tribal groups were sought for their special skills. Later slaves came from Guinea and the Western Sudan.

1510

Ferdinand of Spain ordered the Casa de Contratación to send 250 Negroes to the New World. These Africans were imported to Hispaniola to work the sugar fields and the gold mines.

1511

The first 50 Negro slaves arrived in the Antilles.

1513

By this year, licenses for importing Negroes were sold by Spain, and were considered an excellent source of government revenue.

The Spanish Real Cédula of 1513 permitted the transfer of slaves to Cuba. Between 1513 and 1865, Cuba imported 527,828 Negroes from Africa as slaves, 60,000 of whom were brought in between 1513 and 1763.

When Balboa discovered the Pacific Ocean, 30 Negroes, including Nuflo de Olano, were with him. They assisted him in building the first ships made on the Pacific coast.

1514

The Spanish priest, Bartolomé de Las Casas, began his opposition to the use of Indian slaves. He condemned their treatment in his writings, and in his anxiety to help the Indians he suggested to the king that Negro slaves be used instead.

King Ferdinand of Spain restricted the importation of Negro slaves. The ratio of Spaniards to Negroes was to be three to one in the interests of security.

1517

Bartolomé de Las Casas obtained royal permission to import African Negroes into Latin America. Each settler was to be allowed 12 Negro slaves. In later years, Las Casas regretted his proposal and spoke out vehemently against Negro slavery. At the time of his death, in 1566, the annihilation of the Indians had already very far progressed and the African slave trade stood in full bloom.

1518

Emperor Charles V confirmed the legal status of the slave trade. The system was regularized as the asiento, and not more than 4,000 Negroes were to be imported each year.

The first cargo of African slaves came to the West Indies directly from Africa.

Papal permission was granted for Portuguese bishops to consecrate Ethiopians, Indians and Africans who might reach the educational and moral standards required of the priesthood.

1519

Negroes were with Cortez in his march into Mexico; they harvested the first wheat crop in the New World.

1522

There was a slave revolt in Hispaniola.

1525

Negroes saved their masters from the Indians while accompanying Almagro and Valdivia in Chile.

1526

Lucas Vásquez de Ayllón, a Spanish explorer, tried to establish a settlement in the Carolinas. Negro slaves were brought along to erect the settlement. They are considered the first Negroes to have come into what is now the United States. They fled the colony in November, however, and lived with the Indians in the interior.

1527

Estevanico, a Negro explorer, went on Navaez' expedition to Florida and the Mississippi region in 1527. He lived with Cabeza de Vaca among the Indians for several years, and then travelled with him across Texas and Mexico to the Gulf of California, finally returning to Mexico City in 1536.

There was a slave revolt in Puerto Rico.

A Spanish law of this year stated that, whenever possible, Negroes were to marry Negroes.

1530

An Englishman, William Hawkins, visited the coast of Guinea and, after capturing several Africans, sailed for Brazil. In Brazil, Hawkins sold the Negroes into slavery.

1531

There was a slave revolt in Panama.

1532

Negroes were with Pizarro in Peru. They carried Pizarro to the cathedral after he was murdered.

1533
A Negro slave revolt took place in Cuba.

1534
200 Negroes went with Alvarado on his expedition to Quito in equatorial South America.

1537
The Negro mine slaves in Mexico rebelled.

1538
Estevanico, the Negro explorer, went as a guide for Friar Marcos to look for the Seven Cities of Cibola. Leader of an advance expedition, he was killed by the Zuni Indians who did not believe him when he said that he was the emissary of two white men.

1540
By this year, the annual importation of Negro slaves to the West Indies had reached 10,000.

Negroes accompanied Alarcón and Coronado in New Mexico.

1542
Spanish law prohibited Negroes from going out at night.

1543
Charles V grants letters patent to transport slaves into the Spanish colonies.

A Flemish favorite of Charles V having obtained of his King a patent containing an exclusive right of importing four thousand Negroes into America, sold it for 25,000 ducats to some Genovese merchants, who first brought into a regular form the commerce for slaves between Africa and America.

1551
Spanish law No. 7 read: "We prohibit that free or enslaved Negroes use the services of Indians. This prohibition rises from the fact that many Negroes have mistreated their Indian mistresses. The punishment for a slave will firstly be 100 lashes; secondly, have their ears cut off. If free, they will receive 100 lashes and secondly be perpetually exiled from

the Spanish dominions. Those officials who denounce these Negroes will be given 10 pesos for their efforts."

Spanish law No. 15 stated that no Negro, slave or free, was to be allowed to carry any type of arms; that punishment for a first offense was the confiscation of the arms, a second offense 10 days in jail, a third offense 10 lashes. If free, the Negro carrying arms was to be expelled from the province.

1557

Manuel de Nóbrega, a Jesuit, denounced Indian slavery on his arrival in Brazil, but accepted Negro slavery for the colony and his own order.

1560

In Hispaniola, the ratio of Negroes to Europeans was 15 to 1.

1562

John Hawkins visited Guinea, and having loaded his ship with Negroes carried them to Hispaniola where, despite the Spanish law restricting the trade to the mother country, he sold his slaves to the planters. He returned to England with a rich cargo of ginger, hides and pearls. Hawkin's big profits from this voyage encouraged England's involvement in the slave trade.

1563

According to Spanish law, those Spaniards that had children by slaves and wished to buy them to grant them freedom, were to be given preference over other buyers.

1564

On Hawkins' voyages in this year and in 1567, he again acquired slaves in Africa, and illegally sold them in the Spanish West Indies. Although she denied approval of the English slave traffic when Spain protested, Queen Elizabeth seems to have financially participated in Hawkins' profits. She even allowed Hawkins to include in his coat of arms the figure of a bound Negro.

1565

Negro artisans and agriculturists were with Menendez when he founded the settlement of St. Augustine in Florida.

1568

Spanish law forbade mulattoes to carry arms.

1571

A French royal declaration, reconfirmed in 1607, prohibited slavery: "All persons are free in this kingdom; as soon as a slave has reached these frontiers and becomes baptized, he is free."

Spanish law listed punishments for Negro fugitive slaves: (1) absent four days from master, 50 lashes; (2) absent eight days from home city, 100 lashes and to wear on his neck for two months a ball and chain weighing 12 pounds; (3) four months absence, 200 lashes; (4) a second long absence, exile. Those finding a Negro runaway were obliged to declare his presence within three days or be fined 20 gold pieces. The principal leaders of runaways were to be put to death. Masters of runaway slaves were obliged to pay the costs of capture.

1572

In Spanish America, sons of Negro (slave or free) and Indian marriages, had to pay the same tribute as pure-blood Indians.

1573

Bartolomé de Albornoz, professor of law at the University of Mexico, wrote an attack on the methods of enslavement of Negroes and on the injustice of selling them.

1574

Spanish law required all free Negroes and mulattoes to pay tribute to the king. Provincial officials determined the amount according to the wealth of their estates.

Spanish law concerning runaway slaves provided: (1) if the apprehender was a slave, his master acquired the runaway (2) if the informer was a cimarrone, the local justice owed him a reward (3) if a fugitive was killed, the apprehender received 50 pesos (4) if the slave could prove that he went involuntarily, he was merely sent back to his master (5) a Negro who fled but brought another Negro back with him when he returned was freed; for each additional slave, he received 20 pesos (6) if a Negro or mulatto counseled a slave to hide for 4 months so as to bring him in for the reward, he was to die (7) those Negroes or mulattoes who hid Negroes received the same penalty as the runaway (8) a

Negro could be a bounty hunter with the permission of the local justice and his master.

1575

Between 1575 and 1591, 52,053 slaves were exported to Brazil from Angola.

1600

Between 1600 and 1700, 2,750,000 slaves were brought to Latin America.

1602

According to Spanish law, criminals, idle Negroes and mulattoes were to be sent to work in the mines in Latin America. Their pay was to be given to the Spanish crown.

1612

Saint Peter Claver, a Spanish Jesuit, went to Colombia. He is considered the "Friend of the Negroes" among the Saints of the Catholic church. It is said that during his stay of more than 40 years in Latin America, he baptized about 300,000 Negro slaves.

1614

Spanish law forbade the buying of goods from slaves. It was assumed that such transactions caused the slaves to rob and become unruly.

1618

In this year, the English Government granted monopolies to special companies to trade in slaves. It also granted such monopolies in 1631 and 1662.

2. *Under British Rule*

A new chapter in the history of the Negro in America started with the colonization of North America and the West Indies by the English. It is reflected by the harsh regime of these new settlers. No doubt, the general economical aim which marks the basic social relations of a society was also for the new Dutch and English settlers that the great natural resources of America were meant to be exploited as quickly and ruthlessly as possible. But under the Spanish and Portuguese the personal attitude towards the Negro was rather lax. Their juridical (and religious) system that servitude is due rather to the state (and church) than to a single master allowed therein a certain degree of freedom within assigned limits. Also baptizing and miscegenation mitigated somewhat the brutal conditions of the individual slave under Spanish rule. Even cruel treatment by slave supervising monks was somewhat paternal and not to compare with the vileness of the English and Dutch overseers. The English settlers, contrary to the Spanish, were hard-working, puritanical, self-reliant, and influenced by the then upcoming myth of race superiority—a fallacy in which even Martin Luther and Thomas More believed. These church reformers supported the idea that slavery was a necessary social institution and thus even humanitarian-minded and educated Englishmen lost shame and conscience in their views on the Negro.

The extortion of the Asiento Treaty from the Spaniards at the Peace of Utrecht was feted as the triumph of English statecraft. Now, the British did not have to smuggle anymore their slaves via the West Indies. They acquired the right of supplying also the Spanish colonies. From Liverpool alone were employed in the slave trade, in 1730, 15 ships; in 1751, 53; in 1760, 74; in 1770, 96; and in 1792, 132. Thus, Liverpool—the symbol of British economic rule in the world—became the respectable Mecca of the wretched slave-trade.

1619

At the Jamestown settlement in Virginia, John Rolfe reported in his Journal that on Aug. 20 "there came in a Dutch man-of-warre that sold us 20 negars." These first Negroes in the English North American colonies came as indentured servants. After their term of service, they were free to buy land, etc.

10

In the Spanish colonies, a summary trial could be used in actions against Negro fugitives.

1621

The Dutch West India Co. was organized, with a monopoly of both the African trade and trade with the Dutch colonies in the New World. This company then challenged the right of the Portuguese to trade on the coast of Africa, and by 1650 the Dutch had a stronghold there. Following the English Civil War, England tried to close the slave trade to the Dutch.

In Cartagena, a Spanish landing point in Colombia, Spanish law forbade Negroes or mulattoes, even if accompanied by their masters, to bear arms without a license.

1623

In Cuba, peaceful and industrious free Morenos were not to be molested or disturbed, according to Spanish law. In particular, those Morenos used by the governors for defense rather than agriculture were to be treated fairly by colonial officials.

1624

William Tucker, the first Negro born in the English North American colonies, was baptized in Jamestown.

John Phillip, a Negro, testified in a Jamestown court against a white man; his testimony was admitted. Phillip had been baptized in England 12 years before.

The Dutch in New York imported Negro workers from Angola and Brazil to work on Hudson Valley farms. Under the Dutch in New York, the children, born or unborn, of a manumitted slave were bound to slavery.

There were 23 Negroes in Virginia.

1628

According to Spanish law, no Spanish official was to give a license to any person to supply Negroes with arms.

1629

Slavery was introduced in the Connecticut Colony.

Among the freedoms and exemptions granted by the Dutch West India Co. was the first recorded promise to return fugitive slaves or bound servants.

1630

The Massachusetts Colony instituted a broad fugitive law which included runaway slaves. As in New Netherland, the law included a provision to protect those who fled because of ill treatment "till due order be taken for their relief."

In Virginia, the conduct of a white man who had violated the separation of whites and Negroes was denounced as an "abuse to the dishonor of God and shame of Christians." He received a sound whipping and was required to make a public apology.

During the period from 1630 to 1697, Negroes in Brazil attempted to organize their own state, the state of Alagoas or Palmares.

1634

Slavery was introduced in the Maryland Colony.

1636

Slavery was introduced in the Delaware Colony.

1637

Slaves were imported into Massachusetts from Barbados.

There were slaves in Boston and in New Netherland (New York).

1638

New England became involved in the slave trade. Capt. William Pierce of Salem, Mass., sailed the *Desire* to the West Indies and exchanged Pequod Indian slaves for goods and Negro slaves.

1640

Between this year and 1699, fugitive laws were instituted in the following colonies: Connecticut, Maryland, New Jersey, Virginia and South Carolina. These statutes applied primarily to indentured servants, but also to Negro slaves.

Three Virginia fugitive indentured servants were captured and tried. The Dutchman and Scotsman were sentenced to serve four extra years; the last, a Negro, had to serve "for the time of his natural life."

In Virginia, a white man who had associated with a Negro woman was compelled to do penance in church. The woman was whipped.

Negroes were first used on the tobacco plantations of the Caribbean Islands. As the European tobacco market became glutted, Caribbean planters turned to sugar as a money crop. With this development, the importation of Negroes into the Caribbean began in earnest.

As a result of sugar cultivation, the wealth of Barbados increased 40 times between 1640 and 1667. The number of slaves rose from a few hundred in 1640 to 6,000 in 1645.

1641

The Massachusetts Body of Liberties legally recognized slavery, but allowed enslavement only of "lawful" captives. Capture by "unjust violence" was illegal. This law was later incorporated into the Articles of the New England Confederation, and became law for all the New England colonies.

The French landed on Santo Domingo, and established the settlement of Port Margot. Lacking women, they brought in Negro women purchased from traders or abducted from English or Spanish settlements.

1642

The Virginia Fugitive Law of 1642 stated that people who harbored runaways of any variety were to be fined 20 pounds of tobacco for each night of sanctuary. A second escape attempt by the fugitive was to be punished with branding of the letter "R."

1643

The intercolonial agreement on fugitives of the New England Confederation formed the basis of the United States Fugitive Laws of 1787, 1793 and 1850. It made the certificate of a magistrate the only evidence necessary to convict a runaway slave.

In Virginia, before this year, servants without contracts generally became freedmen after terms of service varying from two to eight years. After 1643, the terms of service for such immigrants was fixed by law at four to seven years, the period varying somewhat with the youthfulness of the servant. The variations in the terms of service for Negro servants appear to have been greater than for white servants.

1645

Massachusetts ships returned to Boston after having picked

up slaves in Africa and then exchanged them in Barbados for cargos of wine, salt, sugar and tobacco. The profits realized encouraged the New England slave trade.

There were Negro slaves in the New Hampshire Colony.

1648

A unit of Negro soldiers under Governor Henrique Diaz participated in a battle against the Dutch, the First Battle of Guararapes, at Recife, Brazil.

1649

There were 300 African slaves in Virginia.

1650

Connecticut gave statutory recognition to slavery.

1651

To curtail the activities of the Dutch West India Co., the English Navigation Act of 1651 limited England's colonial slave trade to English merchants: "No goods or commodities . . . of Asia, Africa or America . . . or of any . . . of the English plantations . . . shall be imported or brought into this commonwealth of England . . . or any other lands, islands, plantations or territories to this commonwealth belonging . . . in any other ship or ships . . . but only such as do . . . belong only to the people of this commonwealth or the plantations thereof."

Anthony Johnson, a Negro, imported five servants and received head rights (a grant of land for each servant imported). Johnson was given 200 acres along the Puwgoteague River in North Hampton County, Virginia. Other Negroes followed Johnson and soon a community developed. At its height, this all-Negro settlement had perhaps 12 Negro homesteads with extensive holdings. Dissension plagued the community and much litigation ensued over contract infringement and property disputes.

1652

Massachusetts law obliged "Negroes, Indians and Scotchmen" to train for the militia.

Rhode Island law forbade bondage of more than ten years for both Negroes and whites. This law, however, was not strictly enforced.

The Dutch Government agreed to export Negro slaves to New Netherland. In that colony strict laws prevented the mistreatment of slaves. Whipping was forbidden unless the owner received permission from the authorities.

1656

Benjamin Doyle, a Negro, received a land grant of 300 acres in Surrey County, Va. Other Negroes also had land holdings, many in integrated communities.

1660

Connecticut barred Negroes from military service.

1661

Slavery was legally recognized in Virginia by its fugitive slave law. It stated: "In case any English servant shall run away in company with any Negroes who are incapable of making satisfaction by addition of time, be it enacted that the English so running away in company with them shall serve for the time of the said Negroes' absence as they are to do for their own by a former act."

1662

Virginia law said that children born in the colony would be bound or free according to the condition of the mother.

Colbert's mercantilist theory included the establishment of a French-controlled slave trade to rival Spain's.

1663

The Duke of York, King Charles II of England and prominent merchants organized the Company of Royal Adventures; in 1672 it was renamed the Royal African Co. It enjoyed a monopoly of the slave trade.

Governor Calvert of Maryland wrote to Lord Baltimore that the colony needed Negro slaves, but was too poor to guarantee a large annual sale to the Company of Royal Adventurers.

In Maryland, by law, all imported Negroes were to become slaves. Any free white woman who married a Negro was a slave during the life of her husband, and her children were to be slaves. This law gave legal recognition to slavery in the Maryland colony. A law of 1681 stated that the children born of white servant women and Negroes were free.

In Gloucester Co., Va., a conspiracy between white indentured servants and Negro slaves was betrayed by a house servant.

The original settlers in the Carolinas were offered 20 acres of land for every Negro male slave, and 10 acres for every Negro woman slave brought to the colony in the first year.

1664

Maryland law stated that baptism had no effect on the status of a slave. The statute was passed to end judicial decisions that had freed slaves after baptism. Similar acts were subsequently passed in North Carolina, New Jersey, New York, South Carolina and Virginia.

In September, Maryland enacted the first law prohibiting marriage between white women and Negroes.

New York and New Jersey gave statutory recognition to slavery.

An English Puritan, Richard Baxter, in his *Christian Directory,* called slave dealers "common enemies of mankind," and said it was a sin to buy their captives except to free them. He later called the slave trade "one of the worst kinds of thievery in the world."

1665

In the Spanish colonies, slaves, mestizos and mulattoes who served the government were allowed to carry arms.

1667

England passed the "Act to Regulate the Negroes on the British Plantations." It referred to Negroes as "of wild, barbarous and savage nature, to be controlled only with strict severity." Slaves were forbidden to leave the plantation without a pass; they were never allowed to leave on Sunday; they were forbidden to carry weapons. The punishment for a slave striking a Christian was severe whipping, and for a second offense, branding on the face with a hot iron. No punishment was provided for an owner who accidentally whipped a slave to death. The act also forbade slaves to possess horns or other signalling devices. The punishment for an owner's wanton killing of a slave was a £15 fine; the fine was £25 if he killed another man's slave.

1668

Josiah Child, future governor of the East India Co., argued for Negro slavery and against settlement by white laborers in the West Indies. The emigration of whites, he explained, deprived England of consumers and laborers, while with slavery a few whites could produce goods and beneficially stimulate English trade.

Virginia law said: "Negro women set free, although permitted to enjoy their freedom, yet ought not in all respects to be admitted to the full fruition of the exemptions and impunities of the English."

1670

The Body of Liberties of Massachusetts was amended to close an unintentional legal loophole that had allowed children of slaves to sue for freedom.

A Virginia law declared that "all servants not being Christians imported into this colony by shipping" were to be slaves for life, but such servants as came by land were to "serve, if boys and girls, until 30 years of age, if men and women, 12 years and no longer."

In Virginia, the principle and practice of universal suffrage was abandoned. Voting privileges were restricted to freeholders and housekeepers of certain qualifications, with the avowed purpose of disenfranchising persons recently freed from servitude.

A French royal order opened the slave trade to Frenchmen to promote "the trade in Negroes from Guinea to the Islands," as "there is nothing that does more to help the growth of those colonies . . . than the labor of Negroes."

Between this year and 1672, the French imported more than 3,000 slaves per year into their Caribbean colonies.

1671

Governor Berkeley of Virginia estimated that more than 2,000 slaves were in the colony.

A Maryland act extending the scope of the slavery law passed in 1664 declared that conversion or baptism of slaves before or after their importation did not entitle them to freedom. The act was passed to quell fears of slave owners who hesitated to import slaves for fear of losing their investment through prior or subsequent conversion, and also to encourage slave owners to convert their slaves to Christianity.

George Fox, the English Quaker, included the Negroes in Christ's martyrdom in sermons made on a missionary trip to Barbados.

1672

The King of England chartered the Royal African Co., which held a monopoly for a decade and dominated the slave trade for another 50 years. One of its contracts was to supply 3,000 slaves a year to the British West Indies.

Virginia passed a law urging and rewarding the killing of Maroons. "Maroons" was a loose description of fugitive or runaway slaves who had established camps in which they lived a primarily nomadic life. While not exclusively dependent upon banditry, the vast majority engaged in attacks upon plantations and towns. Between 1672 and 1864, there was evidence of at least 50 Maroon communities, mainly in the mountain forests and swamps of South Carolina, North Carolina, Virginia, Louisiana, Florida, Georgia, Mississippi and Alabama. The Maroon colonies established in Florida fought along with the Indians against Americans who wanted the U.S. to annex Florida. The term "Maroon" was derived from the Spanish "cimarrones," a term for runaway slaves.

1674

John Eliot, having worked to educate Indians, turned his attention to the education of Negroes.

1676

Because of the military and naval strength of the Dutch West India Co. and the English Royal African Co., the New England slave traders bypassed the west coast of Africa and began slave trading on its east coast. They were based on the Island of Madagascar.

William Edmundson, an English Quaker, sent a general letter to colonial slave holders, implying that Christian freedom and physical slavery were incompatible.

1680

Between this year and 1786, the British West Indies imported 2,130,000 slaves.

In Haiti, the Maroons formed into separate bands, raided plantations and established their own settlements in the mountains.

1681

A Maryland law declared that Negro children of white mothers and children born of free Negro mothers were to be free.

1682

After this year, persons of non-Christian nationalities could enter Virginia only as slaves.

South Carolina gave statutory recognition to slavery.

1685

The French Code Noir required baptism and religious instruction for slaves. It allowed intermarriage and forbade the working of Negro slaves on Sundays and holidays. The French colonists ignored the Code, believing that they were safer if the Negroes were ignorant, and preferring illicit relationships with Negro women. Prior to the Code Noir, French colonists in the West Indies traditionally freed their mulatto children at 21 years of age. The Code prohibited such manumission if the mother was not free. This was also ignored by the planters.

Monsieur de Cussy, the Governor of French settlements in Santo Domingo, warned the French Government that continued importation of African slaves would soon result in a Negro majority on the island. The French slaves generally came from Senegal, Sierra Leone and the Gold Coast.

1686

A law of the Carolinas forbade Negroes from engaging in any trade.

1687

During a funeral, a group of slaves on the northern neck of Virginia planned an uprising, but it was discovered before it could be carried out. A period of general disobedience and lawlessness followed.

Antoine Court, a French Huguenot traveling in New England, reported that for a small reward Indians would recapture escaped Negroes and return them to their masters.

1688

The recently settled Mennonite Quakers of Germantown, Pa., denounced slavery though at discontent of other Friends. Their leader, Franz Daniel Pastorius, addressed a petition to the Monthly Meeting, which read in part: "Here is liberty of conscience, which is right and reasonable; here ought to be likewise liberty of ye body . . . To bring men hither, or to robb and sell them against their will, we stand against. . . . In all those countries of Europe, . . . they hear off that ye Quackers doe here handel men like they handel there ye cattel. And for that reason some have no mind or inclination to come hither, and who shall maintaine this your cause or plaid for it? . . . Pray! What thing on the world can be done worse toward us, then if men should robb or steal us away, and sell us for slaves to strange countries, separating housbands from their wifes and children. Being now this is not done at that manner, we will be done at, therefore we contradict and are against this traffick of menbody. And we who profess that it is not lawful to steal, must likewise avoid to purchase such things as are stollen, but rather help to stop this robbing and stealing if possible; and such men ought to be delivered out of ye hands of ye Robbers and sett free. . . . If once these slaves . . . should join themselves, fight for their freedom and handel their masters and mastrisses as they did handel them before, will these masters and mastrisses tacke the sword at hand and warr against these poor slaves, like we are able to believe, some will not refuse to doe? Or have these Negers not as much as right to fight for their freedom, as you have to keep them slaves?" This can be considered the first recorded protest against Negro slavery in the English colonies. It came from immigrants who felt prosecuted for conscientious reasons in Holland and Germany and were therefore brought over from Crefeld (Rhine) on invitation of William Penn. Their petition to the "Monthly Meeting" of the Quakers was then referred to the "Quarterly Meeting" and finally to the "Yearly Meeting" where it was put to the files. At last, 23 years later, in 1711, the protests of these German Mennonites moved the Quakers in Pennsylvania to take a stand against the slave trade.

In this and subsequent years, the administrators of Canada begged Louis XIV to allow Negro slavery because of the acute labor shortage. The King finally gave his approval to Governor Denonville.

The slave trade from Angola to Brazil amounted from 6,000 to 7,000 Negroes yearly.

The Barbados legislature enacted Statute No. 82 for the government of Negroes. It provided no penalty for loss of life or limb by a slave under punishment by his master, £15 fine for wanton killing of a slave, £25 fine for intentional killing of another's slave and no penalty for killing a Negro caught stealing at night. The penalty for a slave striking a Christian was severe whipping, and for a second offense whipping and having the nose slit and the face branded. Negroes were not allowed to give evidence against whites.

1690

The mortality rate among Negroes on Jamaican plantations was very high. There were 40,000 slaves in 1690. Between 1690 and 1820, 800,000 were imported, but in 1820 there were only 340,000 slaves in Jamaica.

1691

By this year the free Negro class had become an object of suspicion and fear in Virginia. The preamble of a restrictive act (1691) declared that a law was necessary to prevent manumissions because "great inconvenience may happen to this country by setting Negroes and mulattoes free, by their either entertaining Negro slaves or receiving stolen goods or being grown old and bringing a change upon the country." This law charged that no Negro or mulatto was to be set free unless the person so doing paid the charges for transporting the manumitted Negro beyond the limits of the colony.

A Virginia law prescribed that "any white woman in Virginia marrying a Negro or mulatto, bond or free," was to be banished.

1692

Maryland law required seven years service of any white man who married or had a child by a Negro woman. There were penalties for white women allowing themselves to be with child by colored persons, and for free or slave Negroes guilty of sexual intercourse with such women.

1693

George Keith wrote a paper against slavery to be presented to a Quaker meeting in Philadelphia, charging Friends to free their slaves. This paper was entitled *An Exhortation and Caution to Friends Concerning Buying or Keeping Negroes.*

1696

A yearly meeting of American Quakers admonished all members against importing Negroes for slavery, with expulsion from membership as the penalty for violators.

1698

The British Parliament ended the monopoly of the Royal African Co. and allowed private traders to operate after payment of a 10% duty to the company for the maintenance of its African forts. Parliament believed the slave trade to be "highly beneficial and advantageous to this kingdom and to the Plantations and Colonies." This legally opened the trade to New England merchants.

New York had a total population of 18,067, of whom 2,170 were Negroes.

William Southeby, a Pennsylvania Quaker, addressed a letter to Friends in Barbados, asking the end of shipments of Negroes into the state. Southeby was eventually expelled from the Quaker community for his continued attacks on slavery.

1699

Virginia put a tax of 20 shillings on each slave imported into the colony.

1700

There were 27,817 slaves in the English colonies in North America. Of course, 5,206 were in the North, and 22,611 in the South.

By this date, Boston slave traders were supplying all the New England colonies, as well as Virginia, with slaves. The slave trade was almost exclusively a Massachusetts enterprise, with Boston the chief slave port. However, there were not more than 1,000 Negroes in all the New England colonies, as most of the trade was triangular. The triangular slave trade began when New England exported staple food commodities

—beans, corn, fish, horses, and dairy products—to the West Indies for rum. The rum was then taken to Africa and bartered for slaves, who were then taken to the West Indies for either sale or exchange for more rum, sugar, molasses, and cocoa. The manufacture of rum from molasses was the largest manufacturing enterprise in New England at the outbreak of the Revolutionary War. Shipbuilding and seafaring, both substantial economic undertakings in New England, were largely dependent on the slave trade. The part of the triangular trade that brought the African slaves to the West Indies was called the Middle Passage. Space of only 3 feet 10 inches for each slave was allowed on a ship between decks. The area was later reduced to 3 feet 3 inches. The slaves were packed spoon-fashion, and were not able to stand upright.

Rhode Island and Pennsylvania gave statutory recognition to slavery.

Until the close of the Seminole Wars in 1845, escaped Southern slaves found refuge with the Creek Indians and the Spanish at St. Augustine in Florida.

Judge Samuel Sewall of Massachusetts published *The Selling of Joseph* in which he advocated the end of the slave trade. He questioned the biblical interpretations used to condone slavery and the legality of the means by which Negroes were enslaved. However, he saw no hope for the amalgamation of the races if Negroes were emancipated. The book provided anti-slavery arguments well into the 19th century.

Samuel Sewall and the Boston Committee of 1700, an anti-slavery group, tried to institute a heavy duty on the importation of slaves, in the hope that this taxation would end the Massachusetts slave trade. They were unsuccessful.

The most conscientious efforts to improve conditions among the slaves were made by the Quakers. George Fox urged owners of slaves to give religious instruction to them. In this year William Penn established a monthly meeting for Negroes.

1701

In England, Rev. Thomas Bray, a former representative of the Bishop of London in Maryland, founded the Anglican Society for Promoting Christian Knowledge, better known as the Society for the Propagation of the Gospel. Its purposes were "the care and instruction of our people settled in the colonies; the conversion of the Indian savages and the conversion of the Negroes." The society was later incorporated into Dr. Bray's Associates.

1702

The French Guinea Co. contracted with Spain for the asiento. It was to deliver 38,000 Negro slaves in 10 to 12 years to the Spanish colonies, or 48,000 if the French-English war [The War of the Spanish Succession] came to an end in that period.

1704

Elias Neau, a Frenchman, started the Catechism School for Negroes at Trinity Church in New York City. Instruction was halted briefly in 1712 when a slave uprising made some New York owners suspicious of Neau's efforts.

The Boston Newsletter, the first newspaper in the American colonies, was founded, and from the very inception advertisements of slaves were a prominent part of its advertising.

1705

All officeholding by free Negroes was stopped by an act of the Virginia Assembly, declaring that "no Negro, mulatto or Indian shall presume to take upon him, act in or exercise any office, ecclesiastic, civil or military." In addition, Negroes were forbidden to be witnesses in any case whatsoever, but it was found that this disability afforded a shield for dishonest free Negroes who avoided the payment of their just debts for the reason that other free Negroes were not admitted as witnesses. Another Virginia slavery act decreed that all imported servants were to remain in lifelong servitude. Excepted were those who had been Christians in their native country or who had been free in a Christian country. This law limited slavery to Negroes and confined almost all imported Negroes to slavery.

A New York law prescribed execution for recaptured escaped slaves who had attempted to reach Canada.

Massachusetts placed a duty of £4 on imported Negroes "for the better preventing of a spurious and mixt issue."

Intermarriage between white persons and Negroes was declared illegal in Massachusetts. A minister performing such a marriage was fined £50. This prohibition remained in force until 1843, when the law was repealed.

1706

Statutes enacted in New York and Virginia established that baptism did not alter the condition of slaves.

1707

Massachusetts allowed selected free Negroes to enter the military service.

In Massachusetts, free Negroes and mulattoes could be fined 5 shillings for harboring runaway Negro servants.

1708

Virginia had 12,000 Negroes with about 1,000 Negroes being imported annually.

1709

Slavery was made legal in French Canada.

1710

There were 44,866 slaves in the British colonies in North America: 8,303 in the North, and 36,563 in the South.

The first use in Virginia of the legislative power to break the bonds of a slave was made in this year. A Negro slave named Will had been "signally serviceable in discouraging a conspiracy of divers Negroes for levying war in this colony," and in recognition and reward of the public service an act was passed conferring freedom upon him. The act of freedom read: "The said Negro, Will, is and shall be forever hereafter free from his slavery, . . . and shall enjoy and have all the liberties, privileges and immunities of or to a free Negro belonging." This act which rewarded freedom for special acts by slaves was no indication of the growth of freedom sentiment. Its real intent was a more perfect disciplining of Negroes in slavery. Freedom in the case of the Negro Will, was awarded as an example to discourage slave conspiracies.

Governor Spotswood "took measures to discourage" importation of slaves into the colony of Virginia because of colonists' alarm at the rapid increase of Negroes.

Col. Christopher Codrington willed two plantations in Barbados to the Society for the Propagation of the Gospel on condition that a college be built for the religious instruction and conversion of the Negro slaves to prove that slavery could co-exist with Christianity. The society, however, wanted to retain the profits of the estates and more or less ignored the provisions of the will. The college was finally opened for whites only in 1745. By 1761, 450 new slaves bought from traders had been added to these plantations. By 1793, only three slaves were reported as barely literate and slaves were worked on Sunday.

1711

Through the efforts of the Mennonite Quakers, the Pennsylvania Yearly Meeting finally took action, prevailing upon the colonial Legislature to ban the slave trade. The English crown vetoed the law.

A group of Maroons under the leadership of Sebastian led a reign of terror in South Carolina.

1712

In New York, 12 slaves were executed and 6 others committed suicide after participating in a slave revolt in which 9 whites were killed. As a result of the revolt, Elias Neau's school for Negroes was temporarily closed.

South Carolina's first Fugitive Slave Act mentioned mestizos as well as mulattoes, Negroes, and Indians, and implied that there were members of these classes who were free as well as members who were slaves.

South Carolina allowed manumission and appeal to the Governor and Council by illegally enslaved individuals.

1713

On March 26, by the Treaty of Utrecht, Great Britain was granted asiento or the monopoly of the slave trade with the Spanish colonial possessions. The South Sea Company, formed in 1711, was allowed to import 4,800 Negroes a year for 30 years into the Spanish colonies.

France made manumission of slaves in the Leeward Islands contingent on permission of the Governor-General. A similar ordinance existed for Guadeloupe.

1714

Gold was discovered in Brazil at the settlement of Villa Nova do Principe, which had been founded by escaped slaves from plantations in the Brazilian inland regions.

1715

The total population of the British colonies in North America was 434,600. Of these 375,750 were whites, and 58,850 Negroes. The totals were broken down this way:

	Total Population	Negroes	Negroes in % of population
New Hampshire	9,650	150	1.4
Massachusetts	96,000	2,000	2.1
Rhode Island	9,000	500	5.6
Connecticut	47,500	1,500	3.2
New York	31,000	4,000	12.7
New Jersey	22,500	1,500	6.6
Pennsylvania	45,800	2,500	5.5
Maryland	50,200	9,500	18.6
Virginia	95,000	23,000	24.2
North Carolina	11,200	3,700	33.4
South Carolina	16,750	10,500	60.0

Between 1715 and 1750, an average of 2,500 Negroes was imported to the English North American colonies each year.

A Quaker, John Hepburn, in his pamphlet *The American Defence of the Christian Golden Rule,* argued that slavery was wrong as it robbed men of freedom of choice, the only means by which an individual might pursue moral perfectability. Another pamphlet, Elihu Coleman's *A Testimony Against that Anti-Christian Practice of Making Slaves of Men,* propounded the same thesis and was officially accepted by Coleman's meeting. Both pamphlets presented numerous other arguments against slavery, including that of the spiritual damage done to Quakers themselves by accepting slavery.

A North Carolina act forbade intermarriage between whites and Negroes; another law gave statutory recognition to slavery.

1716

The first Negro slaves were introduced in French Louisiana. They were delivered by two slave ships of the Company of the West.

A tract published in Massachusetts claimed that Negro slavery impeded white immigration to the colonies by limiting occupations open to new settlers.

1717

Cotton Mather began an evening school for Indians and Negroes.

In Maryland, intermarriage of a free Negro or mulatto and a white made the former a slave.

South Carolina law forbade marriage between Negro men and white women.

1720

There were 68,839 slaves in the British colonies in North America: 14,091 in the North, and 54,748 in the South. At first, Negroes imported to the English North American colonies came primarily from the West Indies. Subsequently, however, most came directly from Africa. The majority of Negroes brought to the colonies from Africa came from a large region lying between the Gambia and Niger rivers. They came primarily from West Africa, particularly the northwest portion of the Congo. Other sources of slaves were Angola, Cameroon, Sierra Leone, the Geneglo River region, the Gold and Ivory Coasts, and Senegal.

Between 1720 and 1767 the French slave trade was handled by a monopoly, the Company of the Indies, originally organized by John Law.

Jupiter Hammon (circa 1720-1800), a Negro poet, was born a slave in the Henry Lloyd family of Lloyd's Neck, L.I. His first poems antedate by several years those of Phyllis Wheatley, generally regarded as the first Negro poet in America. Hammon's writings were largely exclamations of Methodist piety in the diction and the rhythm of Wesley and Watts. Such works as *Salvation by Christ with Penitential Cries* and *An Evening's Improvement* advocated the passive resignation of the 18th century faiths. However, Hammon personally disliked the system of slavery, and was probably instrumental in having his last master, John Lloyd Jr., include a clause in his will which provided for manumission of all his slaves upon their 28th birthdays. Little or nothing is known of Hammon after 1790. Hammon's other works include a poetical address to Phyllis Wheatley dated Aug. 4, and published in Hartford, Conn., in 1778, *A Winter Piece*, Hartford, 1782, and *An Address to the Negroes of the State of New York* presented to the members of the African Society in

New York City on Sept. 24, 1786, and printed in New York in 1787.

1721

Delaware law forbade marriages between white women and Negroes, and provided that a child of a white woman by a slave would be bound to the county court until 31 years of age.

The first smallpox inoculations in America were given by Zabdiel Boylston in Boston, Mass. He inoculated his son, Thomas, and 2 Negro slaves on the recommendation of Cotton Mather. Mather's slave, Onesimus, had previously told his master of similar inoculations administered by African tribesmen, and Mather urged Boylston to try the practice. Angry mobs stoned both Mather's and Boylston's homes when they learned of the experiment.

1722

The Pennsylvania Assembly condemned the "wicked and scandalous practice of Negroes cohabitating with white people."

1723

Free Negroes in Virginia were denied the right to vote and were discriminated against in the levying of taxes. Since 1670, voting had been restricted by property qualifications.

A Virginia act forbade free Negroes from "meeting or visiting slaves."

In Virginia, free Negroes, mulattoes and Indians were forbidden to "keep or carry any gun, powder or shot, or any club or other weapon whatsoever offensive or defensive."

In this year as in 1691, laws were enacted in Virginia which limited the increase of the free Negro class to natural means and to manumissions by special legislative acts. These laws remained in force until 1782, when there were 2,800 free Negroes in Virginia.

The Virginia Legislature delegated to the Governor and the Council the power to pass upon slaves' claims to freedom and to make judgments based on meritorious service performed by the slaves.

Rumors and certain evidence aroused the people of Boston, Mass., to take extreme precautions against a Negro plan to burn the city.

Philadelphians petitioned the colonial Assembly to do something "concerning the intermarriages of Negroes and whites."

Crispus Attucks (1723-1770), the leader of a group which precipitated the so-called Boston Massacre is described in contemporary accounts as a mulatto owned by Deacon William Browne, of Framingham, Mass. Attucks led a group of 50 to 60 men, mostly sailors, from Dock Square to State Street in Boston to harass British soldiers, on March 5, 1770. In the fray which followed, the "Boston Massacre," 3 persons were killed, including Attucks.

1725

The number of Negro slaves in the North American colonies reached 75,000.

Pennsylvania law forbade the mixture of the races.

The first Church of Colored Baptists was established in Williamsburg, Va.

1727

An early benevolent association in America, the Junto, established by Benjamin Franklin, pledged its members to oppose slavery and other forms of inhumanity to men.

The French and the Spanish colonists supported education of the Negroes insofar as it was needed to convert them to Christianity. In 1727 the Catholics in New Orleans, under the leadership of Ursuline nuns, attempted to teach Negroes and Indians.

1728

There were approximately 50,000 Negro slaves in Santo Domingo.

1729

Benjamin Franklin printed a book by Ralph Sandyford, a Philadelphia Quaker, against slavery.

The Society for the Propagation of the Gospel was reorganized as Dr. Bray's Associates. Rev. Thomas Bray had advocated the religious education of Negroes since 1701.

1730

There were 91,021 slaves in the British North American colonies: 17,323 in the North, and 73,698 in the South. The total estimated population of the British North American colonies was 654,950.

A Negro rebellion in Williamsburg, Va., was precipitated by the rumor that Governor Spotswood of Virginia had arrived with instructions to free all persons who had been baptized.

When a slave conspiracy was discovered in Norfolk and Princess Anne counties, Virginia, the government ordered white men to carry arms with them to church.

A plot by 200 Negroes in South Carolina was discovered. The plot included a raid upon a church at the mouth of the Rappahannock River in Virginia.

Aleijadinho, a mulatto and one of Brazil's greatest 18th-century architects, was born in this year.

1731

Benjamin Banneker (1731-1806), Negro astronomer, was born in Maryland of free Negro parents. He was taught to read by his maternal grandmother, Molly Welsh, who was originally an indentured servant from England. Banneker's father, Robert Banneker, an industrious and prosperous farmer with 120 acres outside Baltimore, sent his son to school. Banneker showed himself to be adept at anything mechanical. At the age of 22, he had made a clock which struck the hours. From 27 through middle age, he was occupied in running his father's farm. In 1772, Banneker was given some astronomical books by a wealthy Quaker neighbor, George Ellicot. He then read voluminously on geology, astronomy and physics, and observed the heavens with a makeshift telescope. In 1789, through the influence of Ellicot, Banneker was selected as part of a scientific team to survey and assess the Federal territory designated to become the District of Columbia. Banneker began publishing his annual almanacs in 1791; these, in addition to factual material, contained commentaries by Banneker on social problems. In the almanac, Banneker wrote a learned dissertation on bees. He was the first man to calculate the locust plague as recurrent in 17-year cycles. On Aug. 19, 1791, Banneker sent a copy of the almanac to Secretary of State Thomas Jefferson. Included in the prefatory note was an appeal to Jefferson on behalf of the Negroes' humiliating condition (slavery). In the almanac of 1793, he included an important paper, *"A Plan of Peace Office for the U.S."* Greatly influenced by the optimism of the French Revolution, William Goodwin, Thomas Paine and Richard Price, in this paper Banneker included proposals for the formation of a Department of the Interior and a League of Nations. He also opposed capital punishment. In 1802, he lost the right to vote, as did all free Negroes in Maryland. Banneker died in 1806, and unfortunately much of his manuscript work was accidentally burned 2 days later.

1732

Virginia put a 5% duty on imported slaves for 4 years. Virginia continued to impose duties on slaves, and, in 1759, a duty of 20% was put on all slaves imported into Virginia from other American colonies.

European Moravians established the first missionary settlement in Jamaica. By 1787 they had stations in Antigua, St. Christopher and Barbados to proselytize Negroes.

1733

James Oglethorpe, the founder of Georgia, owned slaves on a plantation in the Carolinas and served as Deputy Governor of the Royal African Company.

On Feb. 12, Oglethorpe founded Savannah, Ga. During this year the trustees of this experimental colony prohibited the importation or use of slaves. Gradually, these restrictions were relaxed. The prohibition of slavery in Georgia was repealed in 1749.

South Carolina's Governor offered a £20 reward for the capture of Maroons.

Spain confirmed earlier royal decrees that a slave who escaped from a Protestant colony would be considered free in Spanish lands.

1734

In Jamaica a state of warfare existed between whites and Maroons.

1735

John van Zandt, a Dutch burgher of New York, horsewhipped his Negro slave to death for having been picked up at night by the watch. A coroner's jury judged that "correction given by the master was not the cause of his death, but that it was by the visitation of God." The relations between whites and Negroes were often tense in New York. Approximately a fifth of the total population of the colony was Negro.

1736

Colonel Byrd 2d of Virginia remarked that the "saints of New England" imported so many Negroes into Virginia, that "the colony will sometime or other be confirmed by the name of New Guinea." His remarks reflected the resentment in the South toward the moral preachments of Puritans regarding slavery.

Benjamin Franklin printed an anti-slavery book by a Quaker, Benjamin Lay.

1739

Three Negro revolts broke out in South Carolina. The source of the incidents was attributed to the preaching of Spanish missionaries who allegedly created in the Negroes a false expectation of deliverance. On Sept. 9, 1739, a band of Negroes from Charleston set out for St. Augustine and freedom, slaying all whites whom they met on the way. They were themselves surrounded and massacred; 21 whites and 44 Negroes perished. The second insurrection at Stono River, S. C., was led by a slave named Cato; 30 whites were killed and even a larger number of slaves before the insurrection was put down. A third insurrection occurred at St. John's Parish in Berkeley County, S. C.

Although the Georgia trustees had been petitioned to allow slavery, another group of settlers opposed it. They claimed in their petition that slaves would endanger the colony, cause deaths and necessitate guard duty for the whites.

1740

There were 150,024 slaves in the British North American colonies: 23,958 in the North, and 126,066 in the South.

By this year, Newport, R. I., had become the hub of the triangular trade.

South Carolina's consolidated Slave Act included harsh penalties for false appeals to the Governor on the part of slaves who felt they had been illegally bonded; it forbade slaves from raising cattle, sheep, horses, etc. Any animals owned by a slave were to be forfeited.

Dr. Bray's Associates, the English philanthropic organization, founded a free school in Charleston, S.C., which had about 60 pupils.

1741

In the winter of this year, 11 Negroes were burned at the stake, 18 more hanged, along with 4 white men, when a series of incendiary fires occurred throughout the city of New York. Public suspicion fell upon Negro slaves for no other reason than that they were present in the area.

1743

Virginia had approximately 42,000 Negroes.

John Woolman began preaching on the evils of slavery to Quaker meetings throughout the colonies.

1744

A special school for Negroes was established in South Carolina by Samuel Thomas, an Anglican missionary.

A Virginia law was amended so that "any free Negro, mulatto or Indian being a Christian" should be admitted as a witness in both civil and criminal suits against any Negro, mulatto or Indian, slave or free.

Half of Liverpool's trade was in slaves.

1745

Thomas Ashley in *A New General Collection of Voyages and Travels* answered those who argued the benefits of American slavery to Negroes by saying that if slavery was so beneficial to the Negroes they should be allowed to choose it for themselves.

New Jersey had a total population of 61,383: 56,777 whites, and 4,606 Negroes.

Jean Baptiste Pointe du Sable (1745-1818), an explorer and the founder of Chicago, was born in Haiti of a French mariner and an African slave girl. He was sent by his father to a Paris boarding school, after the death of his mother. Du Sable worked as a seaman for his father's prosperous export-import business until he was shipwrecked in 1765 off New Orleans. Rescued, du Sable, fearful of being enslaved,

was hidden by friendly Jesuits at New Orleans. Du Sable and
a few companions traveled upriver to the trading post of St.
Louis. He was adopted and married into the Potwamie Indian
tribe. He traveled and explored the entire Midwest in his
capacity as a trader. Du Sable kept detailed accounts of his
business transactions and the new territories he traversed. In
1772, he opened a trading post at the southern end of Lake
Michigan. The post was lucrative due to its strategic location.
Soon a settlement grew around it. He remained a highly
respected figure of the early American frontier, and both
Chief Pontiac and Daniel Boone were his personal friends.

1746

Slaves that cost the equivalent of £4 to 5 in rum in Africa
were sold at this time in the West Indies at prices ranging
from £30 to 86, and in the Southern colonies at approximately £100 a head.

The General Assembly of the Province of New Jersey met
at Perth Amboy and authorized the president of the General
Council and Commander-in-Chief of the militia, John Hamilton, to raise a force of 500 free Negroes and Indians to serve
in Canada against the French.

Lucy Terry, a slave in Deerfield, Mass., wrote a poem
about the Deerfield Massacre. Besides being a poet, she was
a gifted story-teller. She once spoke for 3 hours before the
Board of Trustees of Williams College, trying to persuade
them to admit her son.

1747

The General Assembly of South Carolina acknowledged
that the Negro slaves had "behaved themselves with great
faithfulness and courage in repelling attacks of His Majesty's
enemies." It provided that slaves could be enlisted in the
militia up to one-third of the white men in the company, as
long as not more than one-half of all able-bodied slaves
between 16 and 60 were enlisted. In "time of general alarm
and actual invasion of this province, not otherwise, [the
slaves were] to be armed with: (a) one sufficient gun, (b) one
hatchet, (c) powder horn and shot pouch with ammunition of
powder and bullets for 20 rounds and 6 spare flints." Freedom was granted to a slave who captured or killed an enemy.

1748

Between 1748 and 1782, 127,133 slaves survived to be sold by the French in the Americas and West Indies, out of a total of 146,799 captured on 541 voyages to Africa.

The Virginia Militia Act declared that "all such free mulattoes, Negroes or Indians as are or shall be listed, as aforesaid, shall appear without arms." The above provision was, however, dropped during the Revolution to permit free Negroes to become soldiers.

1749

The Georgia Trustees' prohibition on the importation of slaves was repealed as a result of pressure from Carolinians settling in the province and the continual flaunting of the regulation by many colonists who wanted slaves for field and house hands. Negroes were to receive religious education, were protected from cruel treatment, were forbidden marriage with whites and could not be hired out. Slave owners were to have a white worker for every 4 Negroes.

1750

There were 236,420 slaves in the British colonies in North America: 30,222 in the North, and 206,198 in the South.

Maryland had 40,000 Negroes and 100,000 whites.

Father Vivier estimated 1,100 whites, 300 Negro slaves and 60 red slaves in 5 French villages in the Illinois country.

James Varick (circa 1750-1828), the founder of the African Methodist Episcopal Zion Church and its first bishop, was born near Newburgh, N.Y. He came to prominence in 1796 when certain Negro members of the Methodist Episcopal Church living in New York secured permission to hold meetings by themselves. They hired a house on Cross Street, between Mulberry and Orange Streets, and 3 years later organized a church under the laws of the State of New York. In 1820, the church declared its independence. Efforts to secure ordination from the Methodist Episcopal bishops having failed, in 1822 Varick and two others were ordained elders by three former ministers of the Methodist Church. In 1822 Varick was elected bishop of the AME Zion Church and served until his death.

In Brazil, the Jesuit Music Conservatory was established near Rio de Janiero to instruct Negro slaves in music.

By 1750, the system of coartación by which a slave might purchase his freedom at a prearranged price agreed to by his master was common in Cuba.

1751

In a pamphlet "Observations Concerning the Increase of Mankind and the Peopling of Countries," Benjamin Franklin argued that slaves would never provide such cheap labor in America as British workingmen did in England. He said, "Slaves cost 30 pounds sterling per head. Reckon then the interest of the first purchase of a slave, the insurance or risk on his life, his clothing and diet, expenses in his sickness and loss of time, loss by his neglect of business (neglect is natural to the man who is not to be benefited by his own care or diligence), expense of a driver to keep him at work, and his pilfering from time to time, almost every slave being by nature a thief, and compare the whole amount with the wages of a manufacturer of iron or wool in England, you will see that labor is much cheaper there than it ever can be by Negroes here. Why, then, will Americans purchase slaves? Because slaves may be kept as long as a man pleases, or has occasion for their labor; while hired men are continually leaving their masters (often in the midst of his business) and setting up for themselves."

In the following decade, an average of 3,500 Negroes was imported annually to the English colonies in North America.

There were 3,000 active Maroons in Haiti.

In this year, Mackandal, a leader of the Maroons in Haiti, conceived a plot to poison the white population. He was purported to be a great orator and regarded himself as a prophet. For the next six years, until he was betrayed and captured, he raided and terrorized white plantations.

1752

George Washington acquired Mount Vernon, including 18 slaves. He gradually brought the total number of slaves to approximately 200.

1753

For the next 20 years, an average of 2,800 slaves was imported annually by South Carolina colonists.

In this year the Cunliffes of Liverpool transported 1,210 slaves to the West Indies. The family amassed a sizable fortune with as many as 12 ships making 2-to-3 trips a year.

Phillis Wheatley (circa 1753-1784), Negro poet, was born in Africa and brought to America at the age of 8. She was bought by John Wheatley of Boston, a prosperous tailor, as a personal servant for his wife, who encouraged Phyllis to read and write. She learned English in 16 months, and soon afterward Latin. She was evidently a prodigy, and soon gained a considerable reputation in Boston's intellectual circles. In 1767, at 14, she published her first poem, "The University of Cambridge in New England," an ode showing the influence of her favorite poets, Gray and Pope. Over the next few years she wrote panegyrics to King George and eulogies for Boston's notables, Dr. Sewall and Rev. George Whitefield. She also published a translation from Ovid. Her ideas were poetic commonplaces of the period. In her poem *Liberty and Peace* she praised as her New England preceptors would have done freedom from "Albion's tyrants," but there was no mention of the enslavement of her own people. Very little autobiographical or personal life entered into her work. She was a minor poet, technically very competent but not extraordinary. In 1773, suffering from ill health, she traveled to Britain with her master's son. She was received by several prominent English noblemen and promptly charmed the court circles. Her book *Poems on Various Subjects, Religious and Moral,* was published, and was successful. The Wheatley family went bankrupt in 1778. Now free, she was left to shift for herself, and married John Peters, a free Negro. The hardships that befell the couple caused her health to fail, and her husband was sent to debtors' prison.

1754

The estimated total population of the English colonies, according to a report of the Board of Trade to the King of England, was 1,485,634, of which 1,192,896 were whites and 292,738 Negroes.

	Whites	Negroes	Negroes in % of population
Georgia	5,000	2,000	28.5
Maryland	104,000	44,000	29.8
New York	85,000	11,000	11.4
North Carolina	70,000	20,000	22.2
Pennsylvania	195,000	11,000	5.3
Virginia	168,000	116,000	40.9

The first clock made entirely in America was constructed by Benjamin Banneker, who had never seen a clock before. It continued to run accurately, striking all hours regularly, for 20 years.

John Woolman wrote *Some Considerations on the Keeping of Negroes*, an exhortation to convince Quakers to give up their slaves.

The population of Santo Domingo was estimated at 190,000: white, 14,000; mulatto, 4,000; Negro, 172,000.

1755

A census of Maryland described 8% of the Negroes as mulattoes. At this time Maryland had about a sixth of the total Negro population of all the colonies.

1757

Beginning in this year, Quakers in England and America took action against slave-owning members. In Philadelphia Quakers who dealt in Negroes were barred from business sessions of meetings and could not make contributions. In 1760 it became an offense among New England Quakers to import slaves. In 1761 the London Yearly Meeting asked disownment of all slave dealers.

Edmund Burke expressed his ideas on slavery in his *An Account of the European Settlements in America*. Although disapproving cruel treatment of Negroes, he believed them "stubborn and intractable." He wished their situation improved to minimize the danger of slave rebellions and to increase colonial production. Burke believed emancipation "would not always be accepted" as "slaves were often much attached to their masters."

1758

A book published in Lisbon, *The Ethiopian Ransomed,*

Indentured, Sustained, Corrected, Educated and Liberated by
Manuel Riberro de Rocha, advocated the replacement of
Negro slavery in Brazil by a system of indentured labor.

1759

Dr. Bray's Associates established a school for Negroes in
Philadelphia.

Paul Cuffe (1759-1817), the son of Negro and Indian
parents, at 16 joined a whaling vessel. On his return to Westport, Conn., he engaged in agriculture and became a ship-
owner. In 1808 he joined the Society of Friends of Westport,
and advocated Negro exodus to Africa. In 1811 he sailed in
the *Traveller* from Westport for Sierra Leone, at a personal
expense of $4,000. He made another trip in 1815 with 9
families. He planned to make a yearly voyage but his health
failed. At his death he left an estimated estate of $20,000.
Cuffe, in 1780, along with his brother, had challenged in
court the denial of suffrage to taxpayers. It was on the basis
of this claim that Cuffe secured the legal rights and privileges
of free Negroes in Massachusetts.

Between 1759 and 1803, Brazil imported 642,000 slaves
from Angola.

1760

There were 325,806 slaves in the British North American
colonies: 40,033 in the North, and 285,773 in the South.

In the next decade, an average of 7,450 slaves was imported annually to the British North American colonies.

As late as this year Rhode Island Quakers were involved in
the slave trade. Quakers of Philadelphia were not involved
after 1730; however, leading Friends were shareholders in
the Royal African Company before that year. Seven Quakers
owned slaves in the Carolinas and Virginia.

While in London, Benjamin Franklin became a member of
Dr. Bray's Associates.

George Washington wrote in his diary: "Found the new
Negro, Cupid, ill of pleurisy at Dogue Run Quarter, and had
him brought home in a cart for better care of him." Such
entries were common and showed Washington's concern for
the physical well-being of his slaves. There is little evidence,
however, of similar concern for their mental and moral
well-being.

Barzillai Lew, a Negro from Chelmsford, Mass., was listed as a member of Capt. Thomas Farrington's company. He was one of several Negroes who served as equals with whites in the French and Indian Wars.

Richard Allen (1760-1831), founder and first bishop of the African Methodist Episcopal Church, was born a slave in Philadelphia, and was sold to a farmer in Dover, Del. He became a religious worker and was converted by Methodists. They permitted him to conduct services at home, where he converted his master, who later freed Allen and his family. Allen studied privately, and preached to Negroes and whites. He traveled throughout Delaware, New Jersey, Pennsylvania, and Maryland. In 1784, at the first general conference of the Methodist Church in Baltimore, he was accepted by the hierarchy as a minister of promise. He returned to Philadelphia in 1786 and was asked to preach occasionally. He began conducting prayer meetings among Negroes and sought to establish a separate place of worship. Both Negroes and whites objected. He attracted large numbers of Negroes to the church where he preached, but whites objected to their presence and pulled them from their knees one Sunday, ordering them to the gallery. Rather than submit to the insult, Negroes withdrew and established in 1787 an independent organization, Free African Society. Some broke away to establish the Independent Bethel Church. He was ordained a deacon in 1799 and an elder in 1816. There were 16 congregations by 1816, when Allen was chosen bishop of the African Methodist Episcopal Church.

Jupiter Hammon, a Long Island slave, published *Salvation by Christ with Penitential Cries*. He was probably the first Negro poet in the U.S.

1762

Anthony Benezet's *A Short Account of that Part of Africa Inhabited by the Negroes* described African civilization and culture and included anti-slavery writings.

George Washington's contract for a new overseer specified that he "take all necessary and proper care of the Negroes, using them with proper humanity and discretion."

James Derham (1762-?), first Negro physician on record,

was born in bondage in Philadelphia, and became an assistant to his master, a doctor. Later he was sold to a New Orleans doctor whom he assisted as well. Three years later, he won his freedom and set up his own practice.

1763

By this year there were 5,214 free Negroes in Massachusetts out of a total population of 235,810. Most of the Negroes worked in menial jobs, in shipyards and as servants.

John Chavis (circa 1763-1838) was sent to Princeton to study privately under President Witherspoon, according to tradition, to demonstrate whether a Negro had the capacity for a college education. He passed successfully and became connected with the Presbyteries of Lexington and Hanover, Va. In 1801 he rode as a missionary under the direction of the General Assembly. Chavis established a classical school and prepared students for college. The sons of prominent whites were among his pupils: William P. Mangum, who was to become a U.S. Senator; Charles Manly, who was to become a Governor, and Rev. William Harris. In 1832, Chavis was advised to yield to the law of that year prohibiting Negroes from preaching.

Between this year and 1789, 30,875 Negroes came to Cuba as slaves.

1764

New England merchants objected to the passage of the Sugar Act of 1764. In their pamphlet *"A Statement of the Massachusetts Trade and Fisheries,"* they argued that sugar and molasses were essential to the slave trade which they considered the "vital commerce" of New England. The increased prices, they argued, would bring economic ruin to the area.

Abijah Prince, former slave of Rev. Benjamin Doolittle of Wallingford, Conn., owned 100 acres in Guilford, Vt. He was one of the founders of the town of Sunderland, Vt.

Benjamin Franklin related in *A Narrative of the Late Massacres in Lancaster County, etc., etc.* an anecdote of "an instance of . . . honor in a poor, unenlightened African Negro," in which a Negro named Cudjoe saved a white man's life on the coast of Guinea in 1752. Franklin quoted Captain Seagrave, from whom he heard the story: "I relate this to show that some of these dark people have a strong sense of justice and honor, and that even the most brutal among them are capable of feeling the force of reason and of being influenced by a fear of God (if the knowledge of the true God could be introduced among them) since even the fear of a false god when their rage subsided was not without its good effect."

When admirers of Samuel Adams offered to give his wife a Negro girl as a slave, Adams, though penniless, refused to have the girl enter his house except as a free woman.

James Otis, in his *Rights of the British Colonies,* stated that slaves had a right to be free.

1765

The total population of the English North American colonies was 1,750,000. About 400,000 were Negro, slightly over 20% of the total. All but 40,000 of the Negroes lived south of Pennsylvania.

In Diderot's influential *Encyclopédie,* de Jaucort, in the entry "Traité des Nègres" said of slaves: "There is not a single one of these hopeless souls . . . who does not have the right to be declared free, since he has never lost his freedom; . . . since neither his ruler nor his father nor anyone else had the right to dispose of his freedom; . . . this Negro does not divest himself, indeed cannot under any condition divest himself of his natural rights; he carries them everywhere with him, and he has the right to demand that others allow him to enjoy those rights. Therefore it is a clear case of inhumanity on the part of the judges in those free countries to which the slave is shipped not to free the slave instantly by legal declaration."

1766

John Adams reported in his diary on Nov. 5 that Massachusetts slaves brought court action of trespass against their masters to challenge the legality of slavery. The action proved futile.

Washington instructed Captain Thompson to sell his "Negro Tom" (who had been unruly and run away) for him in the West Indies for molasses, rum, limes, tamerines and sweetmeats, and "good old spirits." Captain Thompson was instructed to "keep him handcuffed till you get to sea."

1767

Denmark Vesey (circa 1767-1822), Negro leader, became the protégé of Captain Vesey, a slaver of Charleston, S.C., who traded from St. Thomas to Santo Domingo. Vesey sailed with him for the next 20 years. In 1800, he purchased his freedom and set himself up as a carpenter in Charleston. He was admitted to the Second Presbyterian Church in 1817, and joined the AME Church subsequently. Resenting slavery, Vesey spoke of rebellion on plantations from the Santee to the Guhaws, an area of over 100 miles. At meetings held at his home contributions were taken for arms. Some of the preparations made by Vesey for his uprising were instructing a blacksmith to make daggers, pikes and bayonets, and a white barber to fashion wigs and whiskers of European hair. The conspirators were betrayed and advanced the date for the uprising to June 16, but such effective precautions had been taken against the rebels that the conspiracy collapsed. Vesey was captured on June 22. He defended himself well in court, but on the testimony of informers, some of whom saved themselves, he was condemned to be hanged. On July 3, 1822, he and 35 others were executed.

Raccoon, a Negro character, appeared in Thomas Forrest's comic opera, *The Disappointment.*

1769

A petition signed by free Negroes and mulattoes to the Virginia Legislature asked that the wives and daughters of the petitioners be exempt from taxation. It met with approval and an act was passed which, after declaring that the former tax was very burdensome and derogatory to the rights of free-born subjects, "exempted from the payment of any public county or parish levies, all free Negroes, mulattoes and Indian women, and all wives other than slaves of free Negroes, mulattoes and Indians."

Emanuel Bernoon, a Negro, died leaving a house and lot and personal property valued at £539. Bernoon made his money with a catering business that he had established in Providence, R.I., in 1736, and later with an oyster house in Providence.

When Thomas Jefferson was elected to the House of Burgesses in Virginia, his first legislative action was to introduce a measure providing for emancipation of slaves. This proposal was rejected.

1770

The estimated total population of the 13 colonies was 2,312,000 of whom 462,000 were slaves.

Crispus Attucks, a slave who had escaped from his master in 1750, was one of three men killed during an attack on British soldiers in Boston. These victims of the "Boston Massacre" were given heroes' burials.

George Washington signed a resolution of the "Association for the Counteraction of Various Acts of Oppression on the Part of Great Britain," agreeing not to import into the colony or purchase slaves that had not been on the continent of North America for a year. This seems to have been inspired by the desire to retaliate against England, not by scruples against slavery or the slave trade.

Anthony Benezet and other Quakers opened the Free School for Negroes in Philadelphia under Moses Patterson. The school was later known as the Benezet House.

This year marks the birth of Joshua Johnston, Negro portrait painter.

Morris Brown (1770-1849), a bishop of the African Methodist Episcopal Church, was born to free parents in Charleston, S.C. Brown was part of a Charleston group that had such close blood relations with the aristocratic whites that they were legally or actually exempt from most of the restrictions against Negroes. Brown was ordained a deacon in 1817, an elder in 1818. He became a traveling minister. His career as a preacher came to a close when the Denmark Vesey insurrection broke out in 1822. Because of the Vesey insurrection, any Negro of influence in the Negro community was suspected of being implicated in the plot. Brown escaped and reached Philadelphia in 1823. He was made a member of the Episcopate of the church in 1828, and in 1831 a bishop. Under Brown the influence of the church was extended to states that had not been hitherto affected.

Abbé Raynal, in his *Histoire des deux Indes* argued that slavery was contrary to nature and had been introduced into America by pirates and adventurers who, because of greed, began the cultivation of sugar and the exploitation of Africa.

1771

The average number of Negroes imported each year fell to 1,700.

Vermont had only 19 Negroes in its total population of 4,669, or 0.04%.

The Connecticut Legislature forbade the slave trade.

Slavery was abolished in England by judicial decision. Somersett, a slave owned by a Mr. Stewart, was brought to England and escaped. When Mr. Stewart put the recaptured slave on a ship for Jamaica, a writ of habeas corpus was instituted on behalf of Somersett. Granville Sharp, an anti-slavery lawyer, argued the matter before the court of Lord Mansfield. Mansfield decided that since no positive law existed creating slavery, it could not be practiced in England, and that there was no legal way of taking a man's liberty by arguing that he was a slave. Somersett was freed. This became England's attitude toward fugitive slaves.

1772

New Jersey had 67,710 whites and 3,313 Negroes.

Virginia had passed 33 acts to prohibit the importation of slaves. These acts were uniformly rejected by England.

In a letter to his friend, Anthony Benezet, Benjamin Franklin wrote: "I have made a little extract of yours of April 27 of the number of slaves imported and perishing with some close remarks on the hypocrisy of this country [England] which encourages such a detestable commerce by laws for promoting the Guinea trade, while it piqued itself on its virtue, love and liberty, and the equity of its courts, in setting free a single Negro. This was inserted in the 'London Chronicle,' of the 20th of June last. . . . I am glad to hear that the disposition against keeping Negroes grows more general in North America. Several pieces have been lately printed here against the practice, and I hope in time it will be taken into consideration and suppressed by the legislative. Your labors have already been attended with great effects. I hope, therefore, you and your friends will be encouraged to proceed."

In a pamphlet published in Boston, *Oration upon the Beauties of Liberty,* Rev. Isaac Skillman demanded immediate abolition of slavery and declared that slaves had a right to rebel, conformable to the laws of nature.

A Rhode Island Negro named Aaron took part in the burning of the British revenue cutter, *Gaspee*, at Providence.

At his death, Cuffe Slocum, father of Paul Cuffe, owned 100 acres at Cuttyhunk, Mass.

George Stewart, a mulatto, was convicted of having participated in a riot in Gloucester, Mass. He was sentenced to sit on the gallows for an hour with a rope around his neck and to be given 20 lashes.

1773

South Carolina had about 110,000 slaves. It is estimated that about 25,000 escaped during the Revolution, and South Carolina's slave population did not reach 110,000 again until 1790, despite importation of thousands a year after the Revolution.

Negroes presented a petition to the Massachusetts General Court in April, asking for the right to earn money to purchase their freedom. In June, other slaves petitioned the General Court and General Gage for freedom and land.

Benjamin Franklin wrote Dean Woodward from London: "I have since had the satisfaction to learn that a disposition to abolish slavery prevails in North America; that many of the Pennsylvanians have set their slaves at liberty; and that even the Virginia Assembly have petitioned the King for permission to make a law preventing the importation of more into that Colony. This request, however, will probably not be granted, as their former laws of that kind have always been repealed, and as the interest of a few merchants here [London] has more weight with the government than that of thousands at a distance."

The first Negro Baptist church in Georgia was established by George Liste and Andrew Bryan.

Scipio Morehead (circa 1773), first American Negro painter, a contemporary of Phillis Wheatley, is known only indirectly. Phillis Wheatley wrote a poem to him, *To S.M., a Young African Painter, on Seeing His Works,* in which she described two of his classical allegorical paintings done in the style of Reynolds and Romney. The paintings were entitled *Aurora* and *Damon and Pythias*.

Poems on Various Subjects, Religious and Moral, by Phillis Wheatley, was published.

Jamaica's population included 202,787 Negro slaves, 12,737 whites and 4,093 free Negroes and mulattoes.

1774

The estimated total population of the English North American colonies was 2,600,000, of whom 2,100,000 were whites and 500,000 Negroes.

Georgia's population was almost equally divided between white and Negro, 17,000 whites and 15,000 Negroes.

There were 200,000 Negroes in Virginia.

The Continental Congress of 1774 in its "Articles of Association" called for an end to the slave trade and to stop by December next year generally all trade and manufacture with countries which keep on with the slave trade.

In his first printed work, "A Summary of the Rights of British America," Jefferson declared that the abolition of slavery is the great object of desire in the colonies.

Rhode Island law freed any slave thereafter brought into the colony, though not the slaves already there.

The Fairfax Resolves, adopted at a meeting in Virginia of which Washington was chairman, included a resolution (No. 17) stating "that it is the opinion of this meeting that during our present difficulties and distress, no slaves ought to be imported into any of the British colonies on this continent; and we take this opportunity of declaring our most earnest wishes to see an entire stop forever put to such a wicked, cruel and unnatural trade."

John Adams' wife, Abigail, wrote to her husband, on occasion of the discovery of a slave conspiracy in Boston: "I wish most sincerely there was not a slave in the province. It always appeared a most iniquitous scheme to me—fight ourselfs for what we are daily robbing and plundering from those who have as good a right to freedom as we have."

The Massachusetts General Court and General Gage received another petition by Negroes, asking for their freedom as a natural right.

The English Methodist, John Wesley, in his *Thoughts Upon Slavery* contrasted the moral and gentle relationships among Negroes recently enslaved with the insensibility and cruelty of the slavers. He called for repentance from the slaveowners and said they would continue in sin unless they emancipated their slaves.

A slave revolt in St. Andrews Parish, Ga., in December resulted in the deaths of 4 whites and the wounding of 3 before it was suppressed. The slave leaders were burned to death as a punishment.

Lemuel Haynes enlisted as a Minuteman. A Connecticut Negro, he served at Lexington and with the Ticonderoga Expedition.

The population of Cuba was 96,340 whites, and 30,847 free Negroes, 44,333 slaves, for a total Negro population of 75,180.

1775

The approximative slave population in the colonies at the beginning of the revolutionary war was more than a half a million (besides a considerable population of free Negroes); of which were in:

New Hampshire	629	Pennsylvania	10,000
Massachusetts	3,500	Maryland	80,000
Rhode Island	4,373	Virginia	165,000
Connecticut	5,000	North Carolina	75,000
New York	15,000	South Carolina	110,000
New Jersey	7,600	Georgia	16,000
Delaware	9,000		

Soon after George Washington took command of the Continental Army, he insisted that slaves not be allowed to serve. He feared that arming the slaves would lead to conspiracies and insurrections. In October, a committee made up of Benjamin Franklin, Benjamin Harrison, Thomas Kench and the deputy Governors of Rhode Island and Connecticut recommended that all Negroes be excluded from the army. Washington endorsed the decision.

Lord Dunmore, the British Governor of Virginia, offered to free male slaves who joined the British. The response was so great that General Washington in January, 1776, recommended that free Negroes be accepted into the Continental Army.

Various estimates as to the number of slaves who escaped during the Revolution exist. Several hundred obtained their freedom by serving in British armies under Lord Dunmore in Virginia, Prevost in Georgia, and Leslie in South Carolina.

In Georgia, large numbers of slaves fled to British lines or into the wilderness during the Revolution, after the British had promised freedom to fugitives.

Delancey's Rangers, who plagued New York in the Revolution, were made up of Tories and Negroes.

Virginia law allowed sale, banishment or execution of Negroes caught attempting to flee. It was enforced in 1776 when 4 runaways were hanged and 25 others were sold to the West Indies.

In the period from this year to 1783, before and after the ban on Negro service, between 8,000 and 10,000 Negroes served in the American Revolutionary armies in various capacities, approximately 5,000 as regular soldiers. Massachusetts armies had 572 Negroes in Negro and mixed regiments. There were 250 Negroes in Virginia armies. Rhode Island had 100 in one battalion and hundreds of other Negroes scattered throughout regiments. Connecticut's Second Company of the 3rd Regiment had 49 Negroes. Several hundred were in other regiments, and volunteers came from at least 47 towns in the state. Almost every Negro of military age in New Hampshire is said to have enlisted. Negroes fought in mixed companies in Pennsylvania, New York and New Jersey. New York had two battalions of Negroes in 1780, and Maryland had a regiment of 780 Negroes, as well as some in mixed ranks.

A number of Negroes from Georgia are known to have fought against the British. They received pensions and land for their service, and citations for "bravery and fortitude which would have honored a free man."

The South Carolina General Assembly provided for the use of slaves in the army for one year as pioneers, laborers, etc. Later the Assembly forbade use of slaves in the war in any capacity. The result was the freeing of some Negroes to enable them to serve.

The Negro soldiers generally fought in integrated units and were particularly effective as spies, guerilla fighters, and navy pilots.

There were 20 Negroes on the *Royal Lewis* under Capt. Stephen Decatur. Negroes saw action in many major battles in the Revolutionary War, at White Plains, Saratoga, Stony Point, Princeton, Trenton, Monmouth, and Yorktown.

Peter Salem of Framingham and Samuel Craft of Newton, Mass., both Negroes, were among the Minutemen at Concord Bridge in April. Caesar Ferrit and his son, John, of Natick; Pomp Blackman, and Lemuel Haynes of West Hartford, Conn., all Negroes, were also present. Lemuel Haynes later became a theologian.

Among the Negroes who fought at Bunker Hill in June were besides Peter Salem, Titus Coburn, Seymour Burr, Grant Cooper, Cato Howe, Charlestown Eads, Barzillai Lew, Sampson Talbert, Caesar Brown who died in battle, Caesar Basom, Alexander Eames, Caesar Jahar, Cuff Blanchard, Caesar Post, and Salem Poor. Peter Salem killed the British commander, Major Pitcairn. He later fought at Saratoga and Stony Point. Prince Hall, later a pioneer abolitionist in Massachusetts, was also at Bunker Hill.

Lemuel Haynes, Primas Black and Epheram Blackman, Negro members of the Green Mountain Boys of Vermont, took part in the capture of Fort Ticonderoga.

The American victory on Dec. 8 under Colonel Woodford against the British under Capt. Fordyce at Edenton, N.C., was largely the result of a Negro's success in persuading the British to attack hastily by convincing them that the Americans were weak and disorganized, when in fact the opposite was true.

Thomas Paine's first published article, *African Slavery in America,* appeared in a Pennsylvania newspaper. In it Paine denounced slavery, demanded its abolition and urged that Negroes be given land and economic opportunity.

The first emancipation society in the United States was organized in Philadelphia.

Negroes of Bristol and Worcester counties in Massachusetts petitioned the Worcester County Committee of Correspondence to aid them in obtaining freedom. As a result, a convention of whites in Worcester resolved to work for the emancipation of Negroes.

Slave uprising conspiracies took place in North and South Carolina. In North Carolina, severe penalties were handed out to the suspected conspirators, including 80 lashes to many.

North Carolina law forbade manumission of slaves except for meritorious service aproved by a county court.

A young German scientist, Johann Friedrich Blumenbach, came out with his dissertation *De Generis Humani Varietate Nativa* ("On the Natural Variety of Mankind") wherein he collected experimental physiological proofs showing the non-sense and fallacy of the race theories at a time when even great scientists like Linné and enlightened philosophers like Hume and Voltaire considered the Negro as half animal, approximating the orang-utan. Blumenbach was the first who demonstrated that the skull of the Negro is as the skull of the European, the capacity of the two exactly the same and their brain completely alike. Blumenbach's findings were known and discussed at the early meetings of the American Philosophical Society when Franklin and Jefferson were its respective presidents.

1776

The total population of the New England colonies was 659,446, of whom 10,034, or 2.4%, were Negroes. Massachusetts had a total population of 338,667, of whom 5,249 were Negroes.

New York had 21,993 Negroes in a population of 191,741.

The Continental Congress passed a resolution in April calling for an end of the importation of slaves.

Thomas Jefferson's original draft of the Declaration of Independence contained the following accusation against George III: "He has waged cruel war against human nature itself, violating its most sacred rights of life and liberty in the persons of a distant people who never offended him, captivating them and carrying them into slavery in another hemisphere, or to incur miserable death in their transportation thither. This piratical warfare, the opprobrium of *infidel* powers, is the warfare of the *Christian* King of Great Britain. Determined to keep open a market where MEN should be bought and sold, he has prostituted his negative for suppressing every legislative attempt to prohibit or to restrain this execrable commerce; and that this assemblage of horrors might want no fact of distinguished die, he is now exciting these very people to rise in arms among us, and to purchase that liberty of which *he* deprived them, by murdering the people on whom *he* also obtruded them; thus paying off the former crimes committed against the *liberties* of one people, with crimes he urges them to commit against the *lives* of another." At the request of delegates from South Carolina and Georgia, and some slave-trading New England states, the accusation was deleted.

In a debate in the Continental Congress on July 30, the delegate Thomas Lynch of South Carolina said: "If it is debated, whether their slaves are their property, there is an end of the confederation. Our slaves being our property, why should they be taxed more than the land, sheep, cattle, horses, etc.? Freemen cannot go to work in our Colonies; it is not the ability or inclination of freemen to do the work that the Negroes do." To which Benjamin Franklin answered: "Slaves rather weaken than strengthen the State, and there is therefore some difference between them and sheep; sheep will never make any insurrection."

Adam Smith published the "Wealth of Nations" which became the standard work of economical theory. About Negro slavery in the British colonies, he expresses the opinion that "the work done by slaves, though it appears to cost only their maintenance, is in the end the dearest of any. The work done by freemen comes cheaper in the end than that performed by slaves. It is found to be so at Boston, New York, and Philadelphia, where the wages of common labor are so very high."

In July of this year, the British Army on Staten Island included 800 former American slaves who had joined the British on the promise of freedom.

The Virginia Committee of Safety ordered the removal inland away from British forces of all slaves over 13 years of age from the eastern counties of Norfolk and Princess Anne to guard against their escape to British lines. The Congress of North Carolina ordered all male adult slaves south of Cape Fear River to be moved inland.

In November, Americans printed an appeal in a Williamsburg, Va., newspaper to Negroes urging them not to be misled by Lord Dunmore's offer of freedom, arguing that the British would sell them in the West Indies after the war was over. The flow of Negroes to the British decreased somewhat thereafter. Apparently some Negroes were in fact being sold in the West Indies instead of being used as soldiers.

In the Battle of Long Island, 140 Negro soldiers were among those who covered Washington's retreat, for which Lafayette praised them.

Two Negroes, Oliver Cromwell and Prince Whipple, were among the soldiers who crossed the Delaware River to attack the Hessians at Trenton on Christmas Day, 1776. Cromwell served 6 years and 9 months in all, and later fought at the battles of Brandywine and Monmouth. Negro troops also fought under Sullivan in successful rear guard actions at Trenton and Princeton to cover the withdrawal of Washington's troops.

The Virginia law organizing the militia provided that free mulattoes in the companies would be employed as drummers, fifers or pioneers.

Thomas Kench called for a separate detachment of Negro soldiers (white commissioned officers would be over them), saying, "We have divers of them [Negroes] in our service, mixed with white men, but I think it would be more proper to raise a body by themselves than to have them intermixed with white men." One of two such companies was formed in Massachusetts under the command of Samuel Lawrence, a white man.

An African Baptist Church was organized in Williamsburg, Va.

George Washington's letter to Phillis Wheatley upon receipt of her poem praising him, spoke of her "elegant lines" and "poetical talents." He also said, "If you ever come to Cambridge, or near headquarters, I shall be happy to see a person favored by the Muses, and to whom nature has been so liberal and beneficent in her dispensations." He addressed her as Miss Phillis, not Miss Wheatley, suggesting that he knew she was a slave.

1777

The Vermont Constitution forbade slavery. Vermont was thus the first state to abolish slavery.

North Carolina law made manumission more difficult in order to discourage "the evil and pernicious practice of freeing slaves."

The Council of Virginia gave the Governor power to move slaves wherever and whenever he thought necessary.

Massachusetts Negroes expressed "astonishment that it has never been considered that every principle from which America has acted in the course of their unhappy difficulties with Great Britain pleads stronger than a thousand arguments in favor of your petitioners," in another request to the legislature for freedom.

Connecticut raised a company of 56 Negro slaves. There were already Negro men serving with white men. This was on passage of a Connecticut law offering freedom and equal pay and bounty with white soldiers to slaves who would enlist.

There were 33 Negroes in the 2nd Regiment of Pennsylvania under Washington at the Battle of Monmouth.

A regiment of Negro troops from Rhode Island was sent to aid Washington at Valley Forge, and also fought at Monmouth and Red Bank, N.J. In Monmouth, 700 Negroes fought side by side with whites on June 28, 1778.

A Negro slave, Pompey Lamb, served as a spy for the Americans before the Battle of Stony Point, by selling vegetables to the British garrison. He also aided General Wayne and the Americans in their entrance into the fort and the capture of it.

A Negro, Prince Whipple, sometimes called Jack Sisson, was among 41 soldiers chosen by Lt. Col. William Barton for a raid on British headquarters at Newport, R. I. Whipple helped to capture General Prescott and Major Barrington so that the Americans might bargain for the release of a captured American, General Lee.

A Hessian officer, Shloezer, wrote in a letter that there was no regiment among the Americans "in which there are not Negroes in abundance, and among them are able-bodied, strong and brave fellows."

Washington, seeing his army melt away, asked the Continental Congress to approve re-enlistment of Negroes in the army. Congress agreed.

1778

The Georgia Assembly authorized the Governor to use 200 slaves from confiscated Loyalist estates as pioneers for the Continental Army in the expedition against East Florida, and 100 more to serve in the state militia.

The 2nd Maryland Brigade had 60 Negroes.

Massachusetts law permitted the enlistment of slaves as soldiers in state forces. Slaves would thus receive freedom.

On Aug. 24, the Adjutant General of the Continental

Forces reported a total of 755 Negroes in the army in New Jersey. These men represented soldiers from several states.

There were 58 Negroes in the North Carolina Brigade under General Washington.

Washington forwarded to the Governor of Rhode Island a letter from General Varnùm of Rhode Island saying that a battalion of Negroes could be easily raised; Washington also sent a letter to Congress recommending the hiring of Negroes in Carolina, Virginia, and Georgia to serve as wagoners.

A Negro battalion of 300 was formed in Rhode Island, with former slaves receiving the same compensation given to white soldiers and receiving their freedom after the war. The battalion fought in the Battle of Rhode Island in August of this year, and drove back the Hessians 3 times, killing 1,300 of them to the American loss of 211 men. Part of this battalion fought again under Colonel Greene at Ponts Bridge in New York.

Thomas Jefferson estimated that in this one year over 30,000 slaves escaped from Virginia.

In the treaties negotiated between this year and 1786 with the Indians, the U.S. included provisions for the return of fugitive slaves.

Lafayette, in writing to Henry Laurens, mentioned a report of a slave plot to set fire to Albany, N. Y.

1779

In Portsmouth, N. H., 20 Negroes petitioned the New Hampshire Legislature for freedom, arguing that "the God of nature gave them life and freedom upon the terms of most perfect equality with other men; that freedom is an inherent right of the human species, not to be surrendered but by consent."

Henry Laurens, of South Carolina, wrote to General Washington, requesting approval and arms for the raising of 3,000 Negro soldiers. Congress approved and agreed to pay full compensation to the slave owners. However, the South Carolina Legislature refused to vote for the plan.

Alexander Hamilton wrote to the President of the Congress concerning Laurens' plan to use slaves as soldiers in the South, "I have not the least doubt that the Negroes will make very excellent soldiers, with proper management. . . . I hear it frequently objected to the scheme of embodying Negroes, that they are too stupid to make soldiers. This is so far from appearing to me a valid objection, . . . for their natural faculties are as good as ours. . . . Let officers be men of sense and sentiment; and the nearer the soldiers approach to machines, perhaps the better." Hamilton continued in this letter, "The contempt we have been taught to entertain for the blacks, makes us fancy many things that are founded neither in reason nor experience; and an unwillingness to part with property of so valuable a kind, will furnish a thousand arguments to show the impracticability, or pernicious tendency of a scheme which requires such sacrifices. But it should be considered, that if we do not make use of them in this way, the enemy probably will, and that the best way to counteract the temptations they will hold out, will be to offer them ourselves. An essential part of the plan is to give them freedom with their swords. This will secure their fidelity, animate their courage, and, I believe will have a good influence upon those that remain, by opening a door to their emancipation. This circumstance, I confess, has no small weight in inducing me to wish the success of the project; for the dictates of humanity and true policy, equally interests me in favor of this unfortunate class of men." On this subject Washington, in a letter to Henry Laurens, questioned the arming of slaves on the grounds that "a discrimination" might "render slavery more irksome to those who remained in it. Most of the good and evil things in this life are judged of by comparison; and I fear a comparison in this case will be productive of much discontent in those who are held in servitude."

In Buenos Aires, of a total population of 24,000, approximately one-third were slaves. These Negroes were employed in every sort of service and occupation.

1780

There were 575,420 slaves in the U.S.: 56,796 in the North, and 518,624 in the South.

Pennsylvania passed a gradual abolition act.

Free Negroes in Dartmouth, Mass., petitioned the Massachusetts General Court for relief from taxation because they were denied the privileges of citizenship. The signers were Paul Cuffe, Adventur Childe, Paul Cuve, Samuel Gray, Pero Howland, Pero Russell and Pero Coggeshall.

Maryland law made free Negroes liable to draft, and allowed recruitment of slaves on the consent of slave or master.

South Carolina law granted a prime slave to volunteers in the Revolutionary Army as part of their bounty for enlisting.

In April, a slave named Jack of Botetourt County, Va., was sentenced to hang for attempting to lead slaves to Cornwallis' army.

In Albany, N.Y., 6 Negroes were jailed for attempting to flee to Canada.

Several slaves and 2 white men were arrested for plotting rebellion and for burning the Half-Moon Settlement outside the city of Albany, N.Y.

Lott Carry (1780-1828), a Negro Baptist missionary, was born a slave in Charles City County, Va. He began work in 1804 and purchased his freedom in 1813. He became a preacher in the First Baptist Church of Richmond, Va. On May 1, 1819, he was received for service by the Baptist Board of Foreign Missions. Before leaving, he organized the First Baptist Church of Liberia with himself as pastor. Carry sailed in the *Nautilus* from Norfolk with 28 colonists and children, sponsored by the American Colonization Society. In 1822 the group founded Liberia. He was the second agent in 1826. While defending the colony from attack, he died in 1828.

Between 1780 and 1789 the French West Indies imported 30,000 slaves a year.

1781

The New York Legislature provided for the raising of two Negro regiments in the state.

Negro soldiers were among those present at the surrender of Cornwallis at Yorktown, Va. A Rhode Island Negro, Bristol Rhodes, lost a leg and an arm in the siege.

Richard Henry Lee wrote to his brother that neighbors, Colonel Taliaferro and Colonel Travis, had lost all their slaves to the enemy, and Mr. Paradise had lost all but one.

A slave of Prince William County, Va., was hanged for leading attacks by Maroons on plantations.

Slaves in Williamsburg, Va., set fire to several buildings, including the capitol building. One white man was killed.

1782

Thomas Jefferson, writing in his *Notes on Virginia*, said,
"the whole commerce between master and slave is a perpetual
exercise of the most boisterous passions, the most unremitting
despotism on the other. Our children see this, and learn to
imitate it; for a man is an imitative animal . . . the child . . .
puts on the same airs in the circle of smaller slaves . . . and
thus nursed, educated, and daily exercised in tyranny, cannot
but be stamped by it with odious peculiarities. The man must
be a prodigy who can retain his manners and morals unde-
praved by such circumstances." Jefferson also stated his belief
that Negroes should not remain among the whites in America
after emancipation because of "deep-rooted prejudices enter-
tained by the whites," "ten thousand recollections, by the
blacks, of the injuries they have sustained," "distinctions
which nature has made; and many other circumstances,
[which] will divide us into parties, and produce convulsions,
which will probably never end but in the extermination of
our or of the other race." Jefferson considered the skin tones
of the white race, those "fine mixtures of red and white"
which lend to "the expression of every passion" superior to
the "eternal monotony . . . that immovable veil of black
which covers the emotions of the other race." He considered
the "flowing hair" and "more elegant symetry of form" of
whites superior in beauty to blacks. He wrote, "They [the
blacks] secrete less by the kidneys; and more by the glands of
the skin, which gives them a very strong and disagreeable
odor." "They seem to require less sleep." "They are at least
as brave, and perhaps more adventuresome than the whites.
But this may perhaps proceed from a want of forethought."
"They are more ardent after their female; but love seems
with them to be more an eager desire, than a tender delicate
mixture of sentiment and sensation." "Their griefs are tran-
sient." "In general, their existence appears to participate more
of sensations than reflection." "In memory they are equal to
the whites; in reason much inferior . . . in imagination they
are dull, tasteless, and anomalous." "Never yet could I find
that a black had uttered a thought above the level of plain
narration; never saw even an elementary trait of painting or
sculpture." "Among the blacks is misery enough, God knows,
but no poetry." "Religion has produced a Phillis Wheatley;

but it could not produce a poet. The compositions published under her name are below the dignity of criticism." "Whether further observation will or will not verify the conjecture, that nature has been less bountiful to them in the endowments of the head, I believe that in those of the heart she will be found to have done them justice." "I advance it . . . as a suspicion only, that the blacks, whether originally a distinct race, or made distinct by time and circumstance, are inferior to the whites in the endowment both of body and mind."

Virginia law removed restrictions on voluntary manumissions. This law was repealed 5 years later.

In Virginia a notorious integrated band, led by a white man, was active in this year.

Deborah Gannett, a Negro, served as a regular soldier under the name of Robert Shurtliff in the 4th Massachusetts Regiment of the Continental Army for 17 months, from May, 1782, to October, 1783. In 1792 she was cited by the Massachusetts Legislature for "an extraordinary instance of female heroism."

The state of Rhode Island freed a slave, Quaco Honeyman, for his services as a spy in the Revolution.

British ships leaving Savannah, Ga., carried about 5,000 escaped slaves.

1783

Slavery was abolished by judicial decision in Massachusetts. The case involved a slave, Quork Walker, who had sued for freedom on the basis of his master's verbal promise. Chief Justice William Cushing declared that slavery was altogether inconsistent with the newly adopted Massachusetts Declaration of Rights.

By court decision, Massachusetts Negroes who were subject to taxation were declared entitled to suffrage.

Virginia law gave freedom to slaves who served in the Continental Army with the consent of their masters.

Maryland prohibited the slave trade.

The Philadelphia Yearly Meeting of Quakers voted to admit a Negro to the Society of Friends.

When Lafayette wrote to George Washington, proposing that the two join in buying an estate to experiment with freeing Negroes and using them as tenants to demonstrate the practicability of emancipation, Washington replied: "The scheme . . . which you propose . . . is a striking evidence of the benevolence of your heart. I shall be happy to join you in so laudable a work, but will deter going into a detail of the business till I have the pleasure of seeing you." Lafayette later undertook this project alone.

Negroes formed the bulk of the American force which took part in an abortive march from Saratoga toward the British forces at Oswego in February. Many froze to death and the whole party was led off course.

The British ships that left New York harbor after the treaty of peace was signed contained well over 3,000 fugitive slaves; 2,997 were actually counted by the U.S. commissioners, and several ships escaped the scrutiny of the commissioners. The British ships leaving Charleston, S.C., carried about 6,500 fugitives.

Between this year and 1793 the Liverpool slave trade employed 878 ships and transported 303,737 Negroes worth £15,186,850. The gross return for the merchants was £1,700,000 a year.

The master of the Liverpool slaver, *Zong*, ordered 133 slaves to be thrown overboard and drowned. He defended the action by explaining that they were weak and likely to die on board ship. If they died at sea, the loss would be borne by the underwriters of the voyage and not the owners. The owners brought suit in Kings Bench and were awarded the verdict.

1784

Rhode Island passed a gradual abolition act.

Connecticut passed a gradual emancipation law.

Another Connecticut law forbade Negroes to serve in the militia.

New Jersey law freed all Negroes who had taken part in the Revolution.

Thomas Jefferson was chairman of the Congressional committee that recommended a plan for governing the land that was to become Kentucky, Tennessee, Mississippi, and Alabama. The committee report suggested that after 1800 there should be no slavery in the area. This clause failed of adoption by one vote.

The Methodist Church declared slavery contrary to the law of God, and gave members 12 months to free their slaves. This directive was later suspended at the demand of Virginia and other Southern states.

George Liele, a Negro born in Virginia, went to Jamaica as a missionary. By 1791 he had baptized over 400 persons there.

In the District of Montreal in Canada there were 304 slaves.

1785

The New York Manumission Society was founded with John Jay as president.

New York banned slavery.

In a letter to Edmund Randolph, James Madison wrote: "My wish is, if possible, to provide a decent and independent subsistence without encountering the difficulties which I foresee in that line. Another of my wishes is to depend as little as possible upon the labor of slaves."

A Negro Baptist Church was organized at Williamsburg, Va.

Lemuel Haynes, a Negro, became pastor of a white congregation in Torrington, Conn. He was the first Negro Congregational pastor.

David Walker (1785-1830), Negro leader and abolitionist, was born in Wilmington, N.C., of free parents. He traveled widely in the South, and at an early age acquired a deep sympathy for the enslaved members of his race. In 1827 he went to Boston and established a second-hand clothing business on Brattle Street. In 1829, Walker published *Walker's Appeal in 4 articles, together with a Preamble to the Colored Citizens of the World, but in Particular and very expressly to those of the U.S.A.* It called on Negroes to rise against their oppressors. A second edition in 1830 penetrated the South, spreading consternation among the slave holders. In a single day, after a copy was discovered in Georgia, the Legislature rushed through a law that made "the circulation of pamphlets of evil tendency among our domestics," a capital offense.

The slave code for Santo Domingo insisted on adequate food and clothing but forbade slaves' ownership of property, education and religious instruction. Whipping was allowed for contradicting a white man and Negroes were barred from artisan trades.

1786

New Jersey forbade the importation of slaves.

The state of Virginia freed James, a slave of William Armistead, for spying services for Lafayette in 1781.

A Negro, Johnson Green, was hanged at Worcester, Mass., for the "atrocious crime of burglary." Before his death he told a reporter of his thievery in New York, Massachusetts, and Rhode Island of everything from 4 cakes of gingerbread and 6 biscuits at the age of 12, to money, clothing and liquor.

Washington wrote in a letter to Lafayette: "To set the slaves afloat at once would, I believe, be productive of much inconvenience and mischief; but, by degrees it certainly might, and assuredly ought to be, effected, and that too, by legislative authority." At this writing Washington owned 216 slaves.

George Washington, writing to Robert Morris on the subject of slavery, wrote, "I can only say, that there is not a man living, who wishes more sincerely than I do, to see a plan adopted for the abolition of it; but there is only one proper and effectual mode by which it can be accomplished, and that is by legislative authority and this as far as my suffrage will go, shall never be wanting." In another letter, Washington wrote to John Mercer: "I never mean—unless some particular circumstances should compel me to it—to possess another slave by purchase; it being among my first wishes to see some plan adopted, by which slavery in this country may be abolished by slow, sure and imperceptible degrees." Two months later George Washington accepted five Negroes from Mercer in payment for some debt. Washington, in writing to Henry Lee in this same year, said, "It is not my wish to be your competitor in the purchase of any of Hunter's tradesmen; especially as I am in a great degree principled against increasing my number of slaves by purchase. . . . Yet, if you are not disposed to buy the bricklayer, which is advertised for sale, for your own use . . . and his price does not exceed 100, or a few more pounds, I shall be glad if you should buy him for me. I have much work in this way to do this summer. If he has a family, with which he is to be sold; or from whom he would reluctantly part, I decline the purchase; his feelings I would not be the means of hurting in the latter case, nor at any rate be incumbered with the former."

1787

The 6th clause of the Northwest Ordinance provided that there should be no slavery or involuntary servitude, except as punishment for a crime, in the Northwest Territory. The Ordinance also included a provision for returning fugitives who escaped into the territory.

Of the 55 delegates to the Constitutional Convention, 16 held "productive" slaves, and 9 more had at least "a few slaves around the house."

At the Constitutional Convention, Charles Cotesworth Pinckney of South Carolina declared that South Carolina and Georgia could not do without slaves. He defended slavery as justified by the examples of Greece, Rome, and modern states such as France, Holland, and England. Pinckney declared that South Carolina would not agree to any government which abolished the slave trade, but she would probably abolish it herself gradually if left to herself.

John Rutledge of South Carolina said it was in the interest of the Northern states not to oppose slavery because they would benefit by transporting the products of slave labor.

Roger Sherman said that the slave trade was "iniquitous" but he did not feel bound to oppose it.

At the convention, George Mason of Virginia, who owned 200 slaves, declared that the slave trade was brought about by the "avarice of British merchants" and that the British government had "constantly checked the attempts of Virginia to put a stop to it." He said slavery encouraged masters to be petty tyrants and discouraged arts and manufacturing. He wanted the Federal Government to have power to prevent the increase of slavery.

Madison wrote in his notebook during the Constitutional Convention: "Where slavery exists, the republican theory becomes still more fallacious." He opposed slavery and fought in the Convention against the postponement of the prohibition of the slave trade until 1808. He said in debate: "Twenty years will produce all the mischief that can be apprehended from the liberty to import slaves. So long a term will be more dishonorable to the American character than to say nothing about it in the constitution."

Gouverneur Morris called slavery "a nefarious institution, the curse of heaven on the states where it prevailed." He worried about the possibility of the North having to send militias to defend the South against slave insurrections.

The Constitutional Convention's final compromise on slavery included the provisions: that an import tax on slaves would not exceed $10 per head; that importation of slaves could not be abolished before 1808; that slaves would be counted for taxation and representation purposes for various states in the Federal Government, with 5 slaves considered equivalent to 3 free whites.

A delegate, Butler of North Carolina, proposed a fugitive slave clause at the Constitutional Convention in Philadelphia. It drew little debate and was adopted. Generally considered a practical measure, Article 4 Section 2 reads: "No person held to service or labor in one state, under the laws thereof, escaping into another, shall, in consequence of any law or regulation therein, be discharged from such service or labor, but shall be delivered up on claim of the party to whom such service or labor may be due."

Quakers and others organized the Pennsylvania Society for Promoting the Abolition of Slavery. It replaced the Abolition Society of 1775. Benjamin Franklin was elected president.

Isaac T. Hopper, of Philadelphia, had developed a plan to aid slaves escaping from the South.

Richard Allen and Absalom Jones, Negroes, organized other Philadelphia Negroes in the Free American Society which eventually became an "African Church," affiliated with the Protestant Episcopal Church.

In October, Prince Hall and other Boston Negroes petitioned the Massachusetts Legislature for equal school facilities for Negroes.

The New York Manumission Society organized the first African Free School in New York City. It began with 40 pupils.

Prince Hall, a Negro originally from Barbados and a veteran of the Revolutionary War, succeeded in obtaining a charter for a Negro Masonic lodge. This came from the Grand Lodge in England in September.

1788

North Carolina law provided for the apprehension and sale (with 20% of the sale price going to the informer) of all illegally manumitted Negroes. Many Negroes fled the state.

Jefferson wrote from Paris to a friend, Dr. Gordon, of his anger at Cornwallis' plundering in 1781 of his estate and the seizure of 30 slaves: "Had this been to give them freedom, he would have done right; but it was to consign them to inevitable death from the small pox and putrid fever, then raging in his camp."

The Negro Union of Newport, R.I. called for an exodus of free Negroes to Africa. The Philadelphia Free African Society vetoed the suggestion.

James Derham, a former slave who had purchased his freedom, was recognized as a leading doctor in New Orleans.

Andrew Bryan, a slave, founded the Bryan Baptist Church in Savannah, Ga. By 1791, his church had 200 members.

There were 15,000 slaves out of a total population of 120,000 in the Spanish portion of Santo Domingo.

1789

The Virginia Legislature freed 2 Negroes, Jack Knight and William Boush, for having "faithfully served on board the armed vessels" of Virginia. The Legislature purchased the freedom of Caesar, the slave of Mary Tarrant of Elizabeth City, for entering "very early into the service of his country and continuing to pilot the armed vessels of this state during the late war."

North Carolina put a high duty on imported slaves.

Benjamin Franklin wrote to the Pennsylvania Abolition Society, of which he was president, presenting a paper, *"Plan for Improving the Condition of the Free Blacks."* He recommended formation of a committee of 24. This committee was to be broken down into subcommittees, such as (1) a committee of inspection to "superintend the morals, general conduct and ordinary situation of the free Negroes and afford them advice and instruction, [and] protection from wrongs"; (2) a committee of guardians to "place out children and young people with suitable persons, that they may (during a moderate time of apprenticeship or servitude) learn some trade"; (3) a committee of education to "provide that the pupils may receive such learning as is necessary for their future situation in life" and to acquaint them "with the most important and generally acknowledged moral and religious principles." The committee was also to record marriages, births, and manumissions of free blacks. (4) A committee of employment to find "common labor" for Negroes to avoid "poverty, idleness and many vicious habits." In an address to the public as president of the Pennsylvania Abolition Society, Franklin said, "Slavery is such an atrocious debasement of human nature, that its very extirpation, if not performed with solicitous care, may sometimes open a source of serious evils." "The unhappy man, who has long heen treated as a brute animal, too frequently sinks beneath the common standard of the human species. The galling chains that bind his body do also fetter his intellectual faculties, and impair the social affectations of his heart. Accustomed to move like a mere machine, by the will of a master, reflection is suspended; he has not the power of choice; and reason and conscience have but little influence over his conduct, because he is chiefly governed by the passion of fear. He is poor and friendless, perhaps worn out by extreme labor, age and disease. Under such circumstances freedom may often prove a misfortune to himself and prejudicial to society." Franklin then outlined the society's work in aiding free Negroes and its need for money.

The Baptist Church declared slavery a violation of the rights of nature.

Negroes in Massachusetts established a school.

Josiah Henson (1789-1883), an escaped slave, the reputed original of Uncle Tom in *Uncle Tom's Cabin* was born in Charles County, Md., on the farm of Francis Newman. He saw his parents brutally assaulted by his master. In 1828, Henson became a preacher. When he tried to purchase his freedom he was sent to New Orleans to be sold. He then decided to escape. On Oct. 28, 1830, he crossed to Canada. Henson helped other slaves to escape and tried to start a community. He traveled to England, was honored by Lord John Russell, the Prime Minister, and invited by Lord Grey to go to India to supervise cotton raising. A quarter of a century earlier, passing through Andover, Mass., Henson had told his story to Harriet Beecher Stowe. She referred to him in *A Key to Uncle Tom's Cabin*, published in 1853. In 1849, Henson published *The Life of Josiah Henson, Formerly a Slave, Now an Inhabitant of Canada as Narrated by himself*, and in 1858 an enlarged edition appeared with an introduction by Harriet Beecher Stowe, under the title *Truth Stranger than Fiction: Father Henson's Story of his own Life*. Again in 1879, a further expanded publication under the new title *Truth is Stranger than Fiction, an Autobiography of the Rev. Josiah Henson* was published.

Charles III of Spain issued the Real Cédula which insisted on records of slaves' births, deaths, etc., and adequate food and religious instruction. It provided for punishing cruel masters and forbade branding but said slaves could be used only for agriculture. These restrictions were largely ignored by Spanish slaveowners.

1790

U.S. Census: There were 757,363 Negroes in the U.S., representing 19.3% of the population. Of these 59,466 were free, and 697,897 were slaves. The numbers of Negroes, slave and free, and percentages of state populations were:

	Negroes		In % of total
	Slaves	Free	population
Maine	none	538	.56
New Hampshire	158	630	.55
Vermont	17	255	.32
Massachusetts	none	5,463	1.44
Rhode Island	952	3,469	6.40
Connecticut	2,759	2,801	2.33
New York	21,324	4,654	7.64
New Jersey	11,423	2,762	7.70
Pennsylvania	3,737	6,537	2.37
Delaware	8,887	3,899	21.64
Maryland	103,036	8,043	34.74
Virginia	293,427	12,766	40.92
North Carolina	100,572	4,975	26.80
South Carolina	107,094	1,801	43.72
Georgia	29,264	398	35.93
Kentucky	11,830	114	16.34
Tennessee	3,417	361	10.56

Between this year and 1800, the white population of Virginia grew by 16.2%, the slave population by 17.8%, and the free Negro population by 56.4%. In North Carolina the Negro population in these same years increased by 32% (41.6% among free Negroes) while the population as a whole showed a growth of 17%. The bulk of this disproportion centered in the eastern portion of the state. Of the 174,017 white families in New England, only 1% owned slaves. The only instance of Negroes owning slaves between 1638 and 1790, in New England, was in Connecticut, where six Negro families owned slaves.

New York City had 3,252 Negroes, of whom 2,184 were slaves and 1,078 free. Philadelphia had 1,630 Negroes; 210 were slaves. Baltimore had 1,578 Negroes, of whom 323 were free. Boston had 791 Negroes, all of whom were free.

Jean Baptist Point du Sable, a French-speaking Negro from Haiti, made the first permanent settlement at Chicago.

The Pennsylvania Constitution did not explicitly deny Negroes the right to vote.

A law of Congress limited naturalization to white aliens.

Benjamin Franklin's last public act before his death was to sign the memorial to Congress of the Pennsylvania Abolition Society, opposing slavery and urging Congress to remove "this inconsistency [slavery] from the character of the American people" and to "promote mercy and justice toward this distressed race" and to discourage "every species of traffic in the persons of our fellow-men." Franklin's memorial was rebuffed by the House of Representatives, and Franklin replied in an article in the *Federal Gazette* with a parody of the pro-slavery view presented as a Muslim argument in favor of enslaving Christians.

Washington wrote to David Stuart concerning the Quaker memorial to Congress opposing slavery: "The memorial of the Quakers (and a very malapropos one it was) has at length been put to sleep, and will scarcely awaken before the year 1808."

Between 1790 and 1810 legislators in Maryland, Kentucky and Tennessee made serious attempts to pass laws permitting manumission. In 1790 in Maryland and Kentucky, efforts were made to enact laws for gradual emancipation. During this period fear of slave rebellions caused the passage of numerous regulations restricting or prohibiting the slave trade: the Federal acts of 1794 and 1800; acts in South Carolina in 1792, 1796, 1800 and 1801; in Georgia in 1793; in North Carolina in 1794; in Maryland in 1796.

Henry Evans, a Negro, organized a white Methodist Church in Fayetteville, N. C.

Charleston, S.C., free mulattoes organized the Brown Fellowship Society which admitted "brown" men of good character and had an admission fee of $50. This society provided for the education of free Negroes, assisted widows and orphans, and maintained a clubhouse and society cemetery.

The Pennsylvania Abolition Society appointed a committee to supervise the education of free Negroes and to encourage school attendance.

There were 455,000 Negroes in the West Indies, representing 86% of the population. The 260,000 Negroes in Jamaica equaled 95% of the population. Of the Negroes 97.5% were slaves.

Between 1790 and 1820 Cuba imported 225,574 slaves. By 1853, over 644,000 Negroes had been imported into Cuba.

In Haiti a society was formed to free slaves and demand political rights for mulattoes. The society was called Amis des Noirs or "Friends of the Blacks."

There were about one-half-million slaves in the French portion of Santa Domingo. It was estimated, however, that mulattoes owned at least 10% of the productive land and over 50,000 slaves. Out of the 7,000 mulatto women in Santo Domingo, 5,000 were either prostitutes or kept mistresses of white men.

1791

The revolt of Haitian slaves had a great influence on the slaves in the U.S.

Inspired by the Haitian insurrection, slaves in Louisiana attempted a similar revolt. It was badly coordinated and failed; 23 slaves were hanged as suspected participants and 3 white men involved in the plot were expelled from the colony.

Free Negroes in Charleston, S. C., protested to the State Legislature concerning the legal inequities to which they were subject. They mentioned specifically the prohibitions against Negroes testifying in court and against Negroes instituting suits in court. The memorial was rejected.

There were approximately 12 abolition societies in the U.S. from Massachusetts to Virginia.

Benjamin Banneker, Negro mathematician and astronomer, was appointed by President Washington to a commission to survey the District of Columbia. After L'Enfant left the commission appointed to plan the capital, Banneker reproduced his plans for the city.

When some of Washington's slaves were taken to Pennsylvania, Pennsylvania officials claimed that they could not be returned to Virginia. Washington instructed Tobias Lear to bring the slaves back to Virginia in a manner that would "deceive both the slaves and the public."

When Robert Pleasants wrote to James Madison asking him to present an anti-slavery petition to Congress, Madison refused so as not to give "a public wound . . . to an interest on which [his constituents] set so great a value."

St. Thomas Episcopal Church was organized in Philadelphia by Negroes, led by Absalom Jones. Jones was ordained and became the first Negro rector in the U.S.

The white population of Cuba was 153,559; the non-white population, 118,741, of whom 54,151 were free and 64,590 were slaves.

The French National Assembly granted mulattoes the right of representation in colonial assemblies. They also gave the right to vote to every mulatto in Haiti born of free parents.

1792

In Virginia, signs of slave unrest and conspiracies resulted in appeals on the part of the local militias for more arms.

Reports of slave uprisings in various counties of Virginia and neighboring North Carolina resulted in slaves being arrested and tried; some were whipped, some banished and at least 3 executed.

A law of Congress restricted enrollment in the peacetime militia to able-bodied white male citizens.

In that year, 26 acts of Parliament, encouraging and sanctioning the slave trade could be enumerated. Charters incorporating a monopoly of the importation of slaves from Africa into America were granted by James I, Charles I and Charles II.

The Rhode Island Legislature appointed a commission of 3 men to investigate conditions of ex-slaves who had fought in the Revolutionary War and were now unable to support themselves.

Virginia freed Saul, a slave of George Kelly, for "very essential services rendered to the Commonwealth during the late War."

Kentucky was admitted to the U.S. as a slave state. However, the Kentucky Constitution did not specifically deny suffrage to free Negroes.

From this year to 1806, Benjamin Banneker, a Negro published an almanac for Maryland and neighboring states.

Joshua Bishop, a Negro, became pastor of the First Baptist Church (white) in Portsmouth, Va.

The play *Yorker's Stratagem* concerned the story of a comic Yankee who married a West Indian mulatto woman and the problems this created.

Jamaican law required owners to care for disabled slaves. Regulations regarding minimal allotments of food and clothing had already been passed.

3. From the Cotton Gin to the Emancipation Proclamation

The Negro did not profit from the American Revolution. The Constitution legalized slavery. No doubt, the dominant opinion among the Founding Fathers, even from the South, was that slavery does not very much rhyme with "all men are created equal," that the conflict about slavery will one day blow-up the Union and especially that slavery from a purely economical reason became in fact more and more senseless. The utter hopelessness of making money on large slave-holding plantations (as George Washington, who was one of the biggest slaveholders, felt) was good reason to prohibit (though after a passing of 20 years) the slave trade from abroad, and even to think of abolishing slavery by colonization of the Negroes outside the boundaries of the new Federation or back to Africa.

However, the new industrial revolution changed the profitability of exploiting slave labor. And it came as Jefferson had feared: he saw, already in 1788, that there would be little hope for emancipation if industry and technical progress spread and slave labor became more productive.

1793

Eli Whitney invented the Cotton-gin and this made it possible for the Southern plantation owner to separate the fibre from the seed and export a great deal more than he had previously been able to do. The invention helped to fix economically the institution of slavery in the South.

The Federal Fugitive Law to provide for the extradition of criminals became known as the Fugitive Slave Law because it also allowed a master to seize his runaway slave in another state, take him before a magistrate and acquire authority to take him home. The law made it a crime to harbor a fugitive slave or to prevent his arrest.

Militia appeals for arms to avert rumored and actual slave uprisings reached the Governor of Virginia in August, September, and November. Officials of Richmond, Elizabeth City, and Powhatan sent such requests and prepared themselves for uprisings.

In the Presidential Ordinance of April 7, John Adams approved organizing the Mississippi territory, then belonging

73

to Georgia, now Alabama and Mississippi, in which was especially exempted therein the Anti-slavery clause of the North-Western Territory, in these words: "Exempting and Excluding the last article of the Ordinance of 1787."

In November, slaves set several fires in Albany, N.Y., that caused damages totaling a quarter-million dollars. For this, three men and two women were executed early in 1794.

Virginia law forbade free Negroes to enter the state.

Free Negroes in South Carolina protested against the state poll tax. The December, 1793, petition was signed by 23 free Negro men and women from Camden. This petition was accompanied by supportive signatures of white neighbors.

The legislature of Upper Canada abolished slavery.

1794

Congress passed a law forbidding the slave trade to foreign ports and forbidding the outfitting of foreign slave-trade vessels in U.S. ports. The purpose was to avoid spreading the Haitian Revolution to American Negroes.

North Carolina passed a law forbidding further importation of slaves.

George Washington wrote in a letter to Alexander Spotswood: "Were it not then, that I am principled against selling Negroes, as you would cattle at a market, I would not in twelve months from this date, be possessed of one as a slave. I shall be happily mistaken if they are not found to be a very troublesome species of property ere many years pass over our heads."

The American Convention of Abolition Societies was formed in Philadelphia with delegates from nine societies. Delegates came from Rhode Island, Connecticut, New York, New Jersey, Pennsylvania, Delaware, Maryland, and Virginia.

In its memorial to State Legislatures the American Convention of Abolition Societies condemned not only slavery and the slave trade, but also the legal restrictions on free Negroes: "Of what use is his hard-earned property, if the law does not spread its defence around him? . . . how is his liberty secured, if he loses little more than the name of a slave? Donations so ineffectual, and benevolence so incomplete, can only excite dissatisfaction, and suppress industry. To acquire an useful member of the community, we should hold up to his view a participation in its privileges. We promote industry by rewarding it, and encourage knowledge, by rendering it the means of perceiving happiness."

The mayor of Philadelphia, Matthew Clarkson, praised Absalom Jones and Richard Allen, who had organized Negroes in the city the previous year to aid the sick and bury the dead in the yellow fever epidemic.

Richard Allen organized the Bethel Church, a Negro Methodist Episcopal Church in Philadelphia.

The French National Assembly abolished slavery in the French colonies.

The approximate population of Haiti was 40,000 whites, 28,000 freedmen and 500,000 slaves.

Toussaint l'Ouverture attained high rank in the Spanish Army at the head of 4,000 troops. Toussaint deserted the Spanish in April of 1794, and his defection led to the surrender of the Spanish garrisons in Santo Domingo. Toussaint, Jean-Jacques Dessalines and Henri Christophe led a slave revolt in Haiti against French rule. Toussaint l'Overture issued a constitution which abolished slavery.

José de Bolonha, a Capuchin friar, was expelled from Bahia, Brazil for questioning the legality of Negro slavery.

1795

Between 1795 and 1804, 1,099 ships left Liverpool with a total of 323,770 slaves; 155 ships left London with 46,505 slaves, and 29 left Bristol with 10,718 slaves. All these English ships were bound for the America's and the West Indies. The merchants of Liverpool made large profits from these voyages. The *Lottery* made £11,039 from 305 slaves sold in Jamaica; the *Enterprise* made £6,428 on 392 slaves sold in Cuba, and the *Fortune* £1,847 on 343 slaves.

Slaves in Point Coupee Parish, La., planned a rebellion. The conspirators' lack of cooperation and inability to decide when to actually start the rebellion led to its disclosure. Militia units of the parish government were immediately pressed into service to apprehend the insurgents. Some of the Negroes resisted capture, and in the ensuing struggle about 25 Negroes were killed. Another 25 were executed and the bodies of several of the rebels were left hanging in various parts of the parish. A number of whites, probably three, were implicated in this effort and were banished from the colony. Another conspiracy was reported in the same year in St. Landry Parish, La.

In November, fires that swept through Charleston, S.C., were suspected of being set by Negro slaves.

Jeremy Belknap, one of the founders of the Massachusetts Historical Society and an anti-slavist, wrote to Judge Tucker in Virginia: "The winter here was always unfavorable to the African constitution. For this reason white laborers were preferred to blacks." He also wrote in 1795 that the white working man's opposition to slavery had much to do with abolishing slavery in the New England States.

John Adams wrote: "I have through my whole life, held the practice of slavery in such abhorrence, that I have never owned a Negro or any other slave, though I have lived for many years in times when the practice was not disgraceful; when the best men in my vicinity thought it not inconsistent with their character, and when it has cost me thousands of dollars for the labor and sustenance of free men, which I might have saved by the purchase of Negroes at times when they were very cheap."

When one of George Washington's slaves ran away, he advertised for his return, but did not allow his name to appear in the advertisement north of Virginia.

The American Convention of Abolition Societies in its *Memorial to Free Africans and other free people of color* instructed them "to act worthily of the rank you have acquired," "to do credit to yourselves, and to justify the friends and advocates of your color in the eyes of the world." The Convention suggested: "a regular attention to the important duty of public worship;" learning to read, write and do arithmetic; "useful trades" for the children; frugality and simplicity of dress and manner; temperance and avoidance of "frolicking, and amusements which lead to expense and idleness;" "civil and respectful" behavior "to prevent contention and remove every just occasion of complaint."

The Episcopal Convention voted that St. Thomas African Episcopal Church could not send a clergyman or deputies to the Annual Meeting of the Pennsylvania Diocese.

The Education Committee of the Pennsylvania Abolition Society asked the Pennsylvania Legislature to provide free schools without discrimination of color and to establish in large towns special schools for Negroes.

Amos Fortune founded the Jaffrey Social Library. Fortune was brought to the U.S. from Africa as a slave. He purchased his freedom in 1770 when he was 60 years old. He lived in Woburn, Mass., and then in Jaffrey, N.H., where he set himself up in the tanning business and became one of the town's leading citizens. A part of his bequest was used to erect a school which still exists.

In James Murdock's *The Triumph of Love*, a Negro played a Negro role that was not a comic servant for the first time. The role was a secondary romantic character.

Jose Saldanha (1795-1830), Brazilian romantic poet, was born in Recife, the son of a priest and an African woman. His verse is for the most part free of references to Negroes. One of the few exceptions is his *Ode to Henrique Dias*, the great Negro captain who defeated the Dutch. Saldanha did make reference to discrimination he suffered while in the U.S. and Venezuela in a few of his short poems. In *Henrique Dias*, the stereotype of the noble Negro or the equivalent of Chateaubriand's "Noble Savage," was created for subsequent Brazilian writers.

Out of Venezuela's population of 1,000,000, 72,000 were Negro slaves.

In Paraguay, approximately 2% of the population was of African origin.

In Chile's population of 500,000, 30,000 were Negroes and mulattoes.

Peru had 100,000 Negroes and mulattoes, Ecuador had 50,000 and Colombia 210,000.

1796

In this year a Charlotte, N.C., grand jury blamed the Quakers for slave unrest and cited as proof the unrest and the frequency of arson in North Carolina. They also cited the same conditions in Charleston; New York City; Elizabeth, N. J.; Savannah, Ga., and Baltimore, Md.

Tennessee was admitted as a slave state. However, the Tennessee Constitution did not explicitly deny suffrage to free Negroes.

The Boston African Society was organized in Boston with 44 members.

James Varick and other Negro Methodists secured permission to hold separate meetings.

The Philadelphia Yearly Meeting of Quakers resolved that prospective members should be admitted without regard to color.

Jamaican Negroes were allowed to testify against whites.

1797

Congress refused to accept the first recorded petition to Congress by American Negroes. The petition was from 4 illegally manumitted North Carolina Negroes who had fled North to avoid re-enslavement. They asked Congress to consider "our relief as a people."

Henry Clay, as a young lawyer, urged provision for gradual emancipation in the Kentucky Legislature, and frequently volunteered as a lawyer for slaves suing for their freedom.

George Washington wrote to his nephew, Laurence Washington: "I wish from my soul that the legislature of this state could see the policy of gradual abolition of slavery. It might prevent much future mischief." In a letter to another nephew, Robert Lewis, Washington said, "It is demonstrably clear that on this estate I have more working Negroes by a full moiety, than can be employed to any advantage in the farming system, and I shall never turn planter thereon. To sell the surplus I cannot, because I am principled against this kind of traffic in the human species. To hire them out is almost as bad because they could not be disposed of in families to any advantage, and to disperse the families I have an aversion. What then is to be done? Something must, or I shall be ruined; for all the money (in addition to what I raise by crops and rents) that have been received for lands sold within the last four years to the amount of $50,000 has scarcely been able to keep me afloat."

In his will, George Washington wrote: "Upon the decease of my wife, it is my will and desire that all slaves whom I hold in my own right shall receive their freedom." He provided for care of the freed slaves too old to work, and the binding out and education of freed children. He also forbade the sale or transportation out of Virginia of any of his slaves.

Washington gave immediate freedom to "my mulatto man, William, calling himself William Lee" and a life annuity of $30 to Lee.

At the meeting of the American Philosophical Society, Benjamin Rush argued that the Moss case provided proof that black skin color was a disease akin to leprosy. Previously, Samuel Stanhope Smith had argued that dark skin color was a phenomenon similar to freckles, and that white people would become Negroid with sufficient exposure to the sun. Smith illustrated the reverse process with the celebrated case of Henry Moss, a Virginia slave who appeared to have suffered a loss of pigmentation after having moved to the North.

Sojourner Truth (1797-1883), Negro abolitionist and suffragette, was born in Hurley, N.Y., as Isabella Baumfree. She lived in New York City after having been freed in 1827 by the New York State Emancipation Act. Convinced of divine revelation in 1843, she adopted the name Sojourner Truth and began traveling and speaking for emancipation and women's rights. During the Civil War she helped freedmen who had emigrated to the North and made visits to army camps. From 1865 on, she lectured and toured, urging better educational opportunities for Negroes.

George Moses Horton (1797-1883) was born a slave and lived at Chapel Hill, N.C. He worked as a janitor at the University of North Carolina where the college president was his master. He made money writing love poems for the male students; the prices ranging from 25¢ to 50¢ a lyric, depending upon the warmth desired. His first book of poems, published in 1829, was to raise funds for manumission. Unfortunately, it was a financial failure. He was well into his 60's when Union soldiers finally freed him. There are a few general statements against slavery in some of Horton's poetry, but these are too vague and mild to cause any controversy. In his second volume of poems, *Naked Genius*, published after the Civil War, Horton was a little more outspoken, as may be expected. He lampooned Jefferson Davis' attempt at escape (dressed as a woman), and in one poem, "The Slave," he expressed his true feelings on being a slave.

1798

Just after cotton became profitable, $200 was a good price for a field hand. By 1822, the average value of a slave was reported to be $300, and in 1830, $600. In 1840, prime cotton hands were worth $1,000 or more, and in 1859, at Savannah, a prime woman sold at $1,100 and a man as high as $1,300.

Georgia's Constitution made killing or maiming a slave the same as killing or maiming a white.

On March 16, Secretary of War James McHenry wrote to a Marine lieutenant on the frigate *Constellation*, "No Negro, mulatto or Indian to be enlisted, nor any description of men except natives of fair conduct, or foreigners of unequivocal character for sobriety and fidelity."

On Aug. 8, Secretary of the Navy Stoddert forbade enlistment of Negroes on men-of-war. Before this, men had been recruited without reference to race or color. This appears to have been the first Navy restriction against enlistment of Negroes. Despite this order, some Negroes did serve on American ships during engagements with French ships. Among them was William Brown, a "powder monkey" on the *Constellation*. He was wounded in an engagement with the French frigate *L'Insurgente*. He was later granted 160 acres of land for his service. George Diggs was a Negro quartermaster on the schooner *Experiment*.

The Secretaries of War and Navy also forbade Negro enlistments in the Marine Corps.

The New York delegates reported to the American Convention of Abolition Societies that in Queen's County, Long Island, "the education of children of color in the same school with white children . . . has produced great benefit to the community."

Primus Hall, a Negro, ran a school for Negroes in his Boston home. A white teacher taught the Negro pupils in this Boston school.

John C. Stanley was freed by a legislative act. He became a prosperous barber who invested heavily in plantations and bought and freed many Negroes. He was one of the wealthiest men in Craven County, N. C., and was reported at one time to be worth over $40,000.

James P. Beckwourth (1798-1867), explorer, mountain man, fur trader, was born in 1798 in Virginia of a white man and a Negro slave woman; his father was an officer in the

Revolutionary Army. In the early years of the 19th century, the Beckwourths (who had 13 children) relocated to a settlement near what is the present-day city of St. Louis, Mo. In 1816, Beckwourth, who had been apprenticed to a blacksmith, ran away to New Orleans, but soon signed up as a scout for Gen. Henry Ashley's Rocky Mountain expedition, since he could not find employment in New Orleans. Actually, one of the prime motives for Beckwourth's nomadic existence was his inability to accept the Negro's role in a white society. During the 1820's and 1830's, the heyday of mountain men and the fur trade, Beckwourth became a legendary figure, like his friends Jim Bridger and Kit Carson. He was one of the great scouts, hunters and Indian fighters of his time. The Indians respected him so highly that he was accepted into their tribes first by the Blackfeet and later the Crows. In 1848 Beckwourth became the chief scout for Frémont's exploring expedition in the Rockies. He discovered Beckwourth Pass between the Feather and Truckee rivers in California.

Half the population of Brazil was Negro, with 400,000 free and 1,350,000 as slaves in the coastal region.

On Santo Domingo, while the slave population was estimated in 1798 at 450,000 people, the number of slaves that had been imported in 100 years amounted to an estimated 1,000,000 people. The death rate was abnormally high on Santo Domingo.

1799

New York passed a gradual emancipation law.

Negroes started serious fires in Fredericksburg and Richmond, Va.

A group of Negroes in Southampton County, Va., were being transported by two whites. The slaves rebelled and the whites were killed. From four to ten slaves were executed.

James Varick's independent Negro Methodist congregation organized as a church in New York.

John Brown Russwurm (1799-1851), the first superintendent of schools in Liberia and Governor of the African colony of Maryland, was born in Port Antonio, Jamaica, of a white American father and a Negro mother. He attended school in Canada and was graduated from Bowdoin College in 1826. He settled in New York City and established a newspaper, *Freedom's Journal*. In 1829 he emigrated to Liberia, and from

1830 to 1834 he was colonial secretary and edited and published the *Liberian Herald*. In 1836 he was appointed Governor of Maryland Colony. He was instrumental in uniting the Maryland colony and Liberia.

By this year, 141,391 Negroes had come to Cuba as slaves.

A young German musician, Gottlieb Graupner, who arrived in South Carolina, in 1795, blackened his face and sang Negro songs he had heard in Charleston. He billed himself as "The Gay Negro Boy" in the Federal Street Theatre in Boston. This was the first minstrel performance on record. Graupner later organized the Boston Philharmonic Society.

1800

U.S. Census: There were 1,002,037 Negroes in the U.S., representing 18.9% of the total population. Of these Negroes 893,602 were slaves, and 108,435 or 10.8% were free. The Northern states had 36,505 slaves, located mostly in New York and New Jersey. Most Northern states had by this time abolished slavery or provided for gradual emancipation.

U.S. exports of cotton exceeded 17 million pounds.

Gabriel Prosser (1775?-1800), a Negro slave from Henrico County, Virginia, planned a slave revolt with his wife and two brothers. They organized the slaves outside Richmond, Va., and made crude swords, bayonets, and 500 bullets. They also studied the location of Richmond's arms and ammunition. Estimates of the number of slaves involved in the preparations vary. The Governor of Virginia, James Monroe, wrote: "It [the plans for revolt] embraced most of the slaves in this city [Richmond] and the neighborhood." He also stated there was good cause to believe "that knowledge of such a project pervaded other parts, if not the whole, of the state." Prosser's objective was to end slavery by seizing Richmond arsenals and killing all the whites in the city except Frenchmen, Methodists and Quakers. He planned also to attack other towns and eventually become king of Virginia. On Saturday, Aug. 30, over 1,000 slaves, some armed with scythes, bayonets and a few with guns, met outside of Richmond, Va. They disbanded, however, when they discovered that a storm the night before had made an essential bridge impassable. Governor Monroe had heard rumors of a revolt, and when two slaves betrayed Prosser's plans, he called out the military. Numerous arrests were made, and Gabriel

Prosser and between 24 and 35 others were tried and hanged
(with compensation to their owners.) Governor Monroe, who
had personally interviewed Prosser, reported: "From what he
said to me, he seemed to have made up his mind to die,
and to have resolved to say but little of the subject of the
conspiracy."

After this attempted revolt there were persistent rumors of
slave plots in North and South Carolina. In November, renewed slave unrest in Virginia resulted in the arrest of dozens
of suspected rebels.

Negro restlessness had enhanced doubts among slave
owners and Southerners concerning the wisdom of slavery.
A resident of Louisiana expressed his opposition to the pro-
jected reopening of the slave trade. He wrote: "The proposed
reopening of the slave trade was a project conceived of by
foreigners for their own profit; and that, if the planters themselves were consulted, they would raise a terrible clamor
against the measure, and would paint a fearful picture of
the disorders to which the colony is prey because of insubordination of the slaves."

A South Carolina law did not allow citizens to bring any
Negroes in from beyond the shores of the U.S. and no one
could bring in over ten slaves from any part of the nation.

The free Negroes of Philadelphia, headed by Rev. Absalom
Jones, petitioned Congress to revise Federal laws on the slave
trade, on fugitive slaves and for the gradual abolition of
slavery. Congress, by a vote of 85 to 1, stated that such
petitions ought to receive "no encouragement or countenance."

Boston authorities ordered the deportation of 240 Negroes
(natives of Rhode Island, New York, Philadelphia, and the
West Indies) on the basis of a law expelling all Negroes not
citizens of the state.

Boston Negroes asked the city to establish a Negro school.
When the request was refused, the Negroes established a
school with two Harvard men as instructors.

Secretary of State Charles Lee wrote to the Governor of
Puerto Rico, seeking honorable treatment for an American
Negro, Moses Armstead, who was being held for murder on
the high seas. A prisoner of war, he had led a revolt against
the crew of the French ship on which he was held captive.

Denmark Vesey won a lottery and purchased his freedom. Between 1800 and 1822, he was a successful carpenter in Charleston, S.C.

Nat Turner (1800-1831), the son of Nancy, a slave, and a native of Africa, was born on the plantation of his mother's owner, Benjamin Turner, in Southampton, Va. He was successively the property of Samuel Turner, Thomas Moore, and Putnam Moore, and in 1830 was hired out to Joseph Travis. Turner was a precocious child and was given the rudiments of education by one of his master's sons. A fiery preacher, he soon acquired leadership among the Negroes on the Travis plantation and believed himself chosen to lead them from bondage. With four other slaves, he plotted an uprising for July 4, 1831, but abandoned it at the last moment. On Aug. 21, 1831, with seven others, Turner attacked the Travis family and murdered them all. Securing arms and horses and enlisting other slaves, they ravaged the neighborhood. In one day and night, they killed 51 whites. The revolt collapsed on Aug. 25. Turner went into hiding for six weeks, was discovered, tried and hanged at Jerusalem, the county seat.

Between 1800 and 1900 approximately 4 million slaves were brought to Latin America.

Between 1800 and 1865 Cuba imported 386,437 Negro slaves.

1801

The American Convention of Abolition Societies wrote in its address to the Citizens of the United States that "an amelioration of the present situation of the slaves, and the adoption of a system of gradual emancipation . . . would . . . be an effectual security against revolt."

In January, Gov. James Monroe of Virginia, received more warnings of slave unrest. On Jan. 7, Monroe ordered 50 lbs. of grapeshot and 75 lbs. of powder sent to Petersburg, Va., and on the same day two slaves of Nottoway County were convicted of conspiring to rebel. They had planned to annihilate whites for, as they saw it, "if the white people were destroyed, they would be free." Both slaves were hanged.

A South Carolina act allowed no one to import over two slaves from within the U.S., and these were to be used for personal services only.

The Louisiana slave trade was reopened and flourished.

Two Negroes, Peter Williams and Francis Jacobs, obtained a charter for the African Methodist Zion Church in New York.

John Chavis, a Negro, was commissioned by the General Assembly of Presbyterians as a missionary to the Negroes.

A school was held one day a week for Negro children in Wilmington, Del., by a member of the Abolition Society.

Toussaint l'Ouverture, a Negro, captured Santo Domingo, and became the ruler of the entire island. Toussaint had been greatly influenced by Abbé Raynals' *Philosophical and Political History of the Establishments and Commerce of the Europeans in the Two Indies.*

1802

All states north of the Mason-Dixie line had by this date passed anti-slavery laws or measures for gradual emancipation, except New Jersey. New Jersey passed an anti-slavery act in 1804.

The Ohio Constitution forbade slavery and did not deny male suffrage to Negroes.

A Congressional bill to make the Fugitive Slave Law of 1793 more stringent failed to pass by a vote of 43 to 46.

South Carolina relaxed its restrictions of 1800 and 1801 on the number of slaves permitted to be imported for personal use in the state.

A bill to forbid importation for any purpose of male slaves into Mississippi was passed in the House, but was defeated by the Council by two votes.

Slave conspiracies were reported in six counties of North Carolina. In May, an outlawed Negro, Tom Cooper, was credited with a plot to lead a slave uprising in Elizabeth County, N. C. As many as 15 slaves may have been executed.

Throughout the year suspicions of slave insurrections plagued Virginia. Letters were intercepted and slaves arrested, flogged, banished or hanged for alleged conspiracies in Williamsburg, Brunswick, Halifax, Princess Anne, Norfolk, Hanover County, Richmond, King and Queen County, and Madison. It was reported that some white men participated in the slave conspiracy plan in Halifax, Va.

Napoleon sent an expeditionary force to reconquer Haiti.

Resistance was so strong that a peace treaty was agreed upon. However, Toussaint l'Ouverture was seized and deported to France, where he died in a French prison in 1803. He became a martyr to the natives of Haiti.

When Napoleon restored slavery in Martinique and Guadeloupe effective French rule in Santo Domingo, and Haiti was undermined.

1803

The House of Representatives passed a resolution "to inquire into the expediency of granting protection to such American seamen, citizens of the U.S., as are free persons of color."

South Carolina's Legislature opened the slave trade from South America and the West Indies.

The Negroes of New York planned to burn the city, and actually set fire to a number of houses, 11 of which were destroyed. Some Negroes were arrested, but other Negroes led a reign of terror for several days. Eventually 20 Negroes were convicted of arson.

The conviction of a Negro woman, Margaret Bradley, of attempting to poison 2 white people precipitated serious trouble among the Negroes in York, Pa. They made several attempts to destroy the town by fire, and succeeded within a period of three weeks in burning 11 buildings. Patrols were established, strong guards set up, the militia dispatched to the scene of the unrest at Governor McKean's orders, and a reward of $300 offered for capture of the insurrectionists.

In Haiti, Jean Jacques Dessalines, successor to Toussaint l'Ouverture, defeated the French Army.

1804

Gen. Thomas Boude, a Revolutionary officer, purchased a slave, Stephen Smith, and took him to Columbia, Pa. Smith's mother escaped and followed her son. The Boudes took her in and refused to give her up to her mistress. Some historians cite this incident as the beginning of the Underground Railroad.

New Jersey passed a gradual emancipation law.

Ohio passed the first "black laws," restricting the movement of Negroes.

In Georgia, South Carolina, and Virginia, there were arrests and imprisonments of slaves for attempted arson, and patrols against an alleged insurrection. About 20 slaves were executed for poisoning white citizens. An Englishman reported the speech of a captured Negro slave: "I have nothing more to offer [in my defense] than what General Washington would have had to offer had he been taken by the British and put to trial by them. I have adventured my life in endeavoring to obtain the liberty of my countrymen, and am a willing sacrifice to their cause: and I beg, as a favor, that I may be immediately led to execution. I know that you have predetermined to shed my blood, why then all this mockery of a trial?"

On Jan. 1, Haiti declared its independence. Dessalines was made Governor for life. He later made himself Emperor Jacques I. The white inhabitants were either killed or forced to flee. Dessalines abolished slavery, but instituted forced labor.

1805

The case of THOMPSON v. WILMOT involved a Negro taken from Maryland to Kentucky to serve a limited time. He sued when he was not set free at the appointed time. He won his freedom and $691.25 in damages. The decision was affirmed on appeal in 1809.

Maryland law forbade free Negroes to sell corn, wheat or tobacco without a license.

There were reports of slave plots or insurrections in North Carolina, Virginia, South Carolina, Maryland, and New Orleans.

The General Assembly of Virginia sent a resolution to the U.S. Government that Negroes be settled in some parts of the Louisiana Purchase.

Joseph Willis, a free Negro, established a mixed Baptist church in Mississippi.

Frederick Ira Aldridge (1805-1867), the first great Negro actor, was born in New York City. He was educated as a freeman in the African School in New York. While in his teens, Aldridge made his acting debut with an all-Negro cast in New York in Sheridan's *Pizzaro*. The young Aldridge went to Scotland to study, and in 1826 he made his London debut at the Royalty Theater, playing Othello. Aldridge played at Covent Garden and toured the English and Irish provinces. His reputation grew, and he traveled throughout the European continent. A star of the first magnitude, he was decorated by the King of Prussia and the Czar of Russia, and knighted by the King of Sweden. In Sweden, Aldridge married a Swedish baroness by whom he had three children. By 1857 he was commonly regarded as one of the two or three greatest actors in the world.

1806

Virginia law required all slaves freed after May 1 to leave the state.

Norbert Rillieux, (1806-1894), inventor and scientist, was an illegitimate son of a well-to-do white engineer and a mulatto girl. His father, Vincent Rillieux, sent him to Paris to study engineering. In 1830 Rillieux became an instructor in Paris at the L'École Centrale, where he taught applied mechanics. In this year he published a series of papers on steam engine mechanics and steam economy, and also invented the triple-effect evaporator used in sugar refining. By 1855 the Rillieux system of steam evaporation was installed in all the sugar refineries in the South, Cuba and Mexico. In 1881, Rillieux devised a system for the production of beet sugar. This also was successful and became common throughout sugar-beet plantations. Two other schemes of Rillieux were turned down because of his color: (1) a method of draining the bayous of Louisiana, and (2) a sewage system for New Orleans. Rillieux died in Paris.

One of the five battalions formed to defend Buenos Aires in Argentina against the British in this year was composed of Negroes.

On Oct. 17, Dessalines was assassinated in Haiti. Henri Christophe and Alexander Pétion established control, Christophe in the north and Pétion in the south.

1807

Congress passed a law prohibiting the importation of slaves from Africa after the end of the year. Fines were $800 for knowingly buying illegally imported Negroes, and $20,000 for equipping a slave ship. The states were allowed to dispose of imported Negroes as they saw fit. This law was widely violated.

Two boatloads of newly arrived slaves at Charleston, S. C., starved themselves to death.

By an act of the British Parliament of March 25, the slave trade was officially abolished, one year before the US law went into effect.

One of the four men the British took by force from the American frigate *Chesapeake* was David Martin, a Negro from Massachusetts.

An anti-slavery society called Friends of Humanity was formed in Kentucky.

Indiana Territory had an indenture law which provided virtual slavery. This law was repealed in 1810.

New Jersey law limited the suffrage to free white male citizens. The 1776 Constitution of New Jersey had mentioned no restrictions except age and £50 in money or property.

The first African Presbyterian Church was established in Philadelphia by John Gloucester, a Negro originally from Tennessee.

The first schoolhouse for Negroes in Washington, D.C., was built by three Negroes, George Bell, Nicholas Franklin, and Moses Liverpool.

Charles Bennett Ray (1807-1886), a Negro journalist and clergyman, was born in Falmouth, Mass. He attended school in Falmouth and worked five years on his grandfather's farm at Westerly, R.I. Ray studied at Wesleyan Seminary and Wesleyan University in Middletown, Conn. In 1832 he went to New York and opened a boot and shoe store. There he joined the anti-slavery society and helped runaway slaves. He was ordained a Methodist minister in 1837. In 1843 he became corresponding secretary of the Committee of Vigilance (for protection of those fleeing from bondage) and in 1850 a member of the executive committee of the New York State Vigilance Committee. In 1837 Ray was appointed agent of the Negro weekly, *Colored American*, and then between 1839 and 1842, he was its sole editor. Ray became pastor in 1846 of the Bethesda Congregational Church in New York.

England abolished the slave trade. It was not until 1833, however, that Parliament passed an act eliminating slavery in all British colonies. The measure was not fully enforced until 1838.

Between 1807 and 1835 Moslem Negro slaves of Bahia, Brazil, staged numerous insurrections, often led by the alufa, the Moslem priest.

Two governments were formed in Haiti, one headed by Christophe as a dictator, and the other a republic under the presidency of Pétion, the mulatto leader.

1808

The slave population in the United States stood at the million mark in this year.

On Jan. 1, a Federal law went into effect discontinuing the importation of slaves. It has been estimated that, from 1808 to 1860, approximately 250,000 slaves were imported illegally.

As early as this year, slave traders often kidnaped free Negroes, especially from the border states. They defended their actions with the 1793 Fugitive Law.

In the case of the U.S. v. MULLANY, in Washington, D. C., free-born Negroes were declared competent witnesses in all court cases.

Mississippi regulated the importation of slaves, placing a tax of $5 on each Negro brought in.

Maryland law declared evidence of slaves and free Negroes admissible for or against defendants in criminal prosecutions against free Negroes or slaves.

In Virginia, the case of SARAH v. HENRY decided that a slave owner was responsible for the court costs of the plaintiff in a suit for freedom, even if the suit was eventually decided in favor of the owner.

The Society of Friends of North Carolina began to receive slaves from masters who wished to free them but found it difficult to do so under state laws. The society gave the slaves virtual freedom and sometimes sent them to free states. In 1814, the society helped 350 Negroes.

Rev. Thomas Paul of Boston, a Negro, helped to organize in New York the congregation now known as the Abyssinian Baptist Church.

1809

Jefferson felt that the Negro slave in America "must be

removed beyond the reach of mixture" for the preservation of the "dignity" and "beauty" of the white race. In a letter to M. Grégoire, he argued: ". . . whatever be their [Negroes'] degree of talent, it is no measure of their rights."

In the case of GIROD v. LEWIS in Louisiana, it was decided that while the marriage of slaves had no civil effect while they were slaves, from the moment of emancipation the marriage had the same effect as marriage between whites.

New Orleans had a slave population of over 9,000.

Maryland law facilitated manumission. It provided, however, that children of a freed slave remained slaves unless specifically freed by the owner.

In Philadelphia, 13 Negroes established the first African Baptist church there.

Negroes in Boston established an independent Baptist church under the leadership of Rev. Thomas Paul.

The South Carolina Conference of Methodists organized the first mission of their faith among the Negroes. By 1857, 8,114 Negroes belonged to the church.

James W. C. Pennington (1809-1870), a teacher, preacher, and author, was born into slavery on the Eastern Shore of Maryland. At the age of 21 he ran away, but was soon recaptured. However, assisted by a Pennsylvania Quaker, he managed to secure his freedom. Upon leaving Maryland, he spent a brief time in Pennsylvania, and then moved to western Long Island in New York, where he worked during the day and attended night school. At the age of 26, Pennington qualified to teach in Negro schools, first at Newton, L. I., and then in New Haven, Conn. While in New Haven, he studied theology. His eloquence attracted favorable attention, and Pennington served twice as president of the Hartford Central Association of Congregational Ministers, of which he was the only Negro member. He was five times elected a member of the General Convention for the Improvement of Free People of Color, and in 1843 represented Connecticut in the world Anti-slavery Convention at London. Pennington's published works are *The Fugitive Blacksmith* (London 1849) and *Textbook of the Origin and History of the Colored People* (1841). He also contributed several articles to the *Anglo-African Magazine*.

Joseph Jenkins Roberts (1809-1876), the first President of Liberia, was born of free Negro parents in Petersburg, Va. He migrated to Liberia in 1829 with his widowed mother and younger brothers, and became a merchant. In 1842, he became the first Negro President of the colony of Liberia. The colony continued to have difficulty with former inhabitants of the area, and in an attempt to raise money, they decided to lay import duties on goods brought into Liberia. This caused international problems, because Liberia was not a sovereign country or a United States colony. Roberts visited the U.S. in 1844 in the hope of adjusting this matter, but the American government avoided taking a stand in defense of Liberia, because the annexation of Texas was forcing the slavery question to the front. The American Colonization Society gave up all claims on the Liberian colony. Roberts returned to Liberia and continued purchasing land. In 1847, he called a conference at which the new Republic of Liberia was proclaimed, and he was elected its first President. He was re-elected in 1849, 1851, and 1853. Roberts signed a commercial treaty with Britain in 1849. His visits to France and Belgium were instrumental in achieving recognition for Liberia as a sovereign country. In 1856, he was elected first president of the new College of Liberia. In another visit to the U.S. in 1869, Roberts addressed the annual meeting of the African Colonization Society at Washington. In 1871, he was again re-elected President of Liberia and served until his death in 1876.

Paul Brito (1809-1861), a Negro of Rio de Janeiro played an important role in Brazilian literature, not as a writer, but as a publisher whose bookshop became a meeting place for the leading Brazilian writers.

1810

U.S. Census: There were 1,377,808 Negroes in the U.S., representing 19% of the population. Of these, 1,191,362 were slaves, and 186,466 or 13.5% were free.

In the case of ADELLE v. BEAUREGARD in Louisiana, it was stated that "a person of color" (as opposed to blacks) was presumed to be free unless proved otherwise. A similar idea was propounded in the decision of the STATE v. CECIL in Louisiana in 1812.

Delaware law provided penalties for attempts to export a slave who was designated to be free at some future time.

In a message to Congress, President Madison said: "It appears that American citizens are instrumental in carrying on a traffic in enslaved Africans, equally in violation of the laws of humanity, and in defiance of those of their own country. The same just and benevolent motives which produced the interdiction in force against this criminal conduct will doubtless be felt by Congress, in devising further means of suppressing the evil." Madison again in 1816 asked Congress for action against violators of the anti-slave trade act of 1807.

New York law forbade residents to import slaves.

In the New York Case of the Negro Tom, a slave won his freedom on the basis of a deed of a former owner that freed him on that owner's death despite all subsequent bills of sale or wills, even though he at that time belonged to another master.

New York law required all slave owners to teach their slave children to read the Bible.

The Minor Society was organized by free Negroes in Charleston, S.C., for the education of orphans and other free Negroes.

Indiana repealed its severe indenture law.

A Congressional law excluded Negroes from carrying U.S. mails.

Georgia required incoming free Negroes to register and give full details concerning themselves and their reasons for entering the state.

Free Negroes in Maryland lost the right to vote.

During the period from 1810 to 1816, the South experienced an economic depression. It was largely induced by soil exhaustion, the embargo, the nonintercourse acts, and the War of 1812, which caused considerable devastation in eastern Maryland and Virginia. These conditions disorganized the labor force in the South and rather effectively checked exports while raising prices for imports.

In March, correspondence between slaves in North Carolina and Georgia, Tennessee, and Virginia revealed plans for slave insurrections. Rumors that in North Carolina rebels would raid Virginia resulted in a report to the Governor of Virginia, John Tyler.

In November, in Lexington, Ky., a slave conspiracy among the Negroes was discovered. Wholesale arrests followed.

Charles Lenox Remond (1810-1873), a Negro anti-slavery leader, was born a freeman in Salem, Mass. In 1838 he was appointed agent of the Massachusetts Anti-slavery Society, and canvassed Massachusetts, Rhode Island, and Maine. He was named a delegate to the American Anti-slavery Society and attended the World Anti-slavery Convention in London in 1840, and then lectured in England and Ireland on the subject of slavery. In 1841, he returned to the U.S. and continued his work. During the Civil War he recruited for the 54th Massachusetts Infantry, the first Negro regiment to be sent into action from any Northern state.

Lewis Dupré published in Charleston, S.C., a pamphlet, *An Admonitory Picture and a Solemn Warning Principally Addressed to Professing Christians in the Southern States.* It favored progressive emancipation and attempted to prove the moral wrong of slavery.

Tom Molineaux, an American Negro prizefighter, formerly a slave in Virginia, a dock-hand in Baltimore, and a porter in New York, lost a boxing match to Tom Cribb, the English boxing champion, in London.

New Granada had 210,000 Negroes in a total population of 1,400,000.

The Captaincy of Venezuela had 493,000 Negroes and mulattoes, out of a total population of approximately 900,000.

1811

On the afternoon of Jan. 9, whites fled to New Orleans from the parishes of St. Charles and St. John the Baptist, about 35 miles from New Orleans. Over 400 slaves had rebelled on the evening of Jan. 8. Armed with cane knives, axes, and clubs, and later with a few guns, they had started at the plantation of Major Andry, killed his son and then marched to other plantations. A few plantations were destroyed, and at least one other white was killed. Charles Deslondes, supposedly a free mulatto from Santo Domingo, was among the leaders of the original rebel group. Major Andry and a group of other planters pursued the slaves into the woods and indiscriminately executed them. Governor Claiborne called out the militia and forbade male Negroes to go at large in New Orleans. Brigadier General Hampton and Major Milton's Federal and state troops surrounded the rebellious Negroes on Jan. 10. Some 66 slaves were killed or executed, 16 captured and 17 were reported missing, assumed dead. Those tried in the city were executed and their heads strung aloft at intervals from New Orleans to Major Andry's plantation.

A fugitive slave community in Cabarrus County, N.C., was attacked by a force sent to recover or annihilate them. It was reported that two Negro men were killed, one wounded, and two Negro women captured.

Just before the outbreak of the War of 1812 in December, a Virginia slaveholder and Congressman, John Randolph, wrote that he would "touch this subject, the danger arising from the black population, as tenderly as possible; it was with reluctance that he touched it at all. . . . While talking of taking Canada, some of us are shuddering for our safety at home. I speak from facts when I say that the night bell never tolls for fire in Richmond, that the mother does not hug the infant more closely to her bosom. I have been a witness of some of the alarms in the capital of Virginia."

Kentucky law made conspiracy among slaves or poisoning by slaves punishable by death.

Delaware forbade the immigration of free Negroes. On entering the state they were given ten days notice to leave, after which they were to be fined $10 a week. Any native free Negro who left the state was considered a nonresident after six months' absence.

Georgia law provided that ordinary trials of slaves were to be before a justice of the peace, but for cases involving capital punishment there should be a jury trial in a county court.

In the decision of COMMONWEALTH v. DOLLY CHAPPLE in Maryland, it was held that Negroes might be witnesses against whites in cases of mayhem committed on slaves.

New York law required free Negroes to present certificates of freedom issued by a county clerk before they would be allowed to vote.

Daniel Alexander Payne (1811-1893), bishop of the Afri-

can Methodist Episcopal Church, was born of free parents
in Charleston, S. C. He mastered mathematics, English, Latin,
Greek, and French. In 1826 he joined the Methodist Episcopal Church. In 1829, he opened a school for colored children
which became the most successful institution of its kind in
Charleston. The school flourished until the South Carolina
legislature passed a law in 1834 against teaching Negroes to
read or write. Payne went to Pennsylvania and attended the
Lutheran Theological Seminary at Gettysburg, and was ordained in 1839. In 1840, he opened a school in Philadelphia,
and in 1842 he joined the AME Church. Chosen histori-
ographer of the AME Church in 1848, he traveled extensively
in the U.S. Payne was elected bishop in 1852. He purchased
Wilberforce University in 1863, and served as president for
13 years. Among his publications were *The Semi-Centenary
of the African Methodist Episcopal Church in the U.S.A.*
(1866), *A Treatise on Domestic Education* (1885), *Recollections of Seventy Years* (1888), and *The History of the
AME Church from 1816 to 1856,* published in 1891.

In Brazil, Prince Regent João issued a proclamation: "All
soldiers [for the militia] shall be drawn from the class of
whites which shall consist of those whose great-grandparents
were not black and whose parents were born free."

1812

During the War of 1812, Negroes made up a sixth of the
seamen of the U.S. Navy.

Georgia and North Carolina allowed certain free men of
color to serve in the state militia.

Louisiana was admitted to the Union as a slave state. In
its Constitution Negroes were allowed to enroll in the state
militia.

Tennessee law forbade the importation of slaves into the
state.

The General Conference of the Methodist Church met in
New York and adopted a resolution that no slave owner (if
he lived in an area where he could legally manumit his slaves)
was eligible to be an elder in any Methodist church.

The legislature of the Illinois Territory forbade the immigration of free Negroes and required registration of free
Negroes in the territory.

In various parts of the Southern states, rumored slave uprisings and rebellions caused a general repression of any slave
groups or meetings. In July, several Negroes suspected of
planning an insurrection were summarily arrested in the Mississippi territory.

Martin Robinson Delany (1812-1885), the first Negro
major in the U.S. Army, medical doctor, Negro nationalist
and writer, was born in Charlestown, Va., the son of free
Negroes, Samuel and Pati Delany. His paternal grandfather
was a prince of the Mandingo tribe who had been captured
in the Niger Valley, sold into slavery, and subsequently
brought to America. Delany studied under Rev. Louis Woodson, who was employed by a society of Negroes interested in
education. Dr. Andrew McDowell taught him medicine. In
1843 he began publishing *The Mystery* in Pittsburgh. Between
1847 and 1849 he was associated with Frederick Douglass in
bringing out The *North Star*. In 1849, he studied medicine at
Harvard University and did outstanding work in a cholera
epidemic in Pittsburgh. Delany was the first major Negro
nationalist, of whom Frederick Douglass said, "I thank God
for making me a man simply; but Delany always thanks Him
for making him a black man." In 1854, Delany issued a call
for a National Emigration Convention, which met in Cleveland in August. The second convention was in Cleveland in
1856. He moved to Chatham, Ontario, and practiced medicine. The third National Emigration Convention held at
Chatham in 1858 chose Delany as chief commissioner to
explore the Valley of the Niger. He was to make inquiries
"for the purpose of science and for general information and
without reference to, and with the Board being entirely opposed to any emigration there as such." He sailed in 1859
from New York in the *Mendi,* owned by three African merchants, and published the official report of the Niger Valley
exploring party in 1861. During the Civil War, he helped
recruit soldiers, and on Feb. 8, 1865, received a commission
as major and was ordered to Charleston as an Army physician. He served three years in the Freedmen's Bureau and
worked as a trial judge in Charleston, S.C. He was a leader
of the Honest Government League and a severe critic of the
corruption of the Reconstruction period in South Carolina.
He was nominated for Lt. Governor on the Independent Republican ticket, in 1874, but was defeated. In 1879, his

Principia of Ethnology: The Origin of Races and Color, etc.,
was published, giving his ideas on race.

The South American Catholic Church admitted mulattoes
to holy orders for the first time.

In Cuba, a conspiracy was led by Aponte with slave support. This caused the Intendant Don Alejandro Ramírez to
seek white colonization of the island.

1813

Oliver Hazard Perry won the Battle of Lake Erie against
the British. Between 10% and 25% of his 432 men were
Negroes. Commodore Chauncey wrote to Captain Perry concerning Perry's complaint at being sent Negro sailors as
reinforcements on Lake Erie: "I have yet to learn that the
color of the skin . . . can affect a man's qualifications or use-
fulness. I have nearly 50 blacks on board this ship, and many
of them are among my best men."

A large proportion of the American crew on the ship
Chesapeake in her battle with the British *Shannon* off Boston
were Negroes.

Nathaniel Shaler, commander of the *Governor Tompkins*,
praised the bravery of two Negroes in his crew, John Johnson
and John Davis. Both died in battle.

A Negro named Jeffrey leaped to a horse and rallied
Americans to fight off a British charge in the Battle of Fort
Boyer near Mobile, Ala. The rally was successful and Andrew
Jackson gave Jeffrey the title of "major" for his bravery.

In the case of the U.S. v. DOUGLASS, the U.S. Circuit Court
of Washington, D. C., decided that a free-born mulatto was
a competent witness against a white person.

James Forten, a Philadelphia Negro, sent an appeal called
"Letters from a Man of Color on a Late Bill" to the Senate of
Pennsylvania. He condemned slavery, claimed equality with
whites, and that Negroes had "inalienable rights."

Free Negroes in Virginia were required to pay a poll tax of
$1.50.

Rumors of minor slave insurrections reached the Governor
of Virginia in March, April, July and September.

Lt. Col. Thomas Smith wrote of destroying a Negro fort,
presumably of Maroons, in Florida.

Negroes in Wilmington, Del., incorporated the Union Church of Africans, the first formal, separate Negro Methodist denomination.

The Pennsylvania Abolition Society completed the building of a school for Negroes in Philadelphia at a cost of over $3,000.

James McCune Smith (1813-1865), a Negro physician and writer, was born in New York City, son of a slave who owed his liberty to the Emancipation Act of the State of New York, and of a self-emancipated bondswoman. He was educated in the African Free School, and entered the University of Glasgow in Scotland in 1832. In 1835 he received a B.A., in 1836 an M.A., and in 1837 his M.D. Returning to N.Y. to practice medicine, Smith opened a pharmacy in New York and served for 23 years on the medical staff of the Free Negro Orphan Asylum. An opponent of the American Colonization Society, he became active in the New York Underground Railroad and a contributor to *The Emancipator*. In 1839, he was made editor of the *Colored American*, to which he contributed "Abolition of Slavery and the Slave Trade in the French and British Colonies." A pamphlet of Smith's, first published in 1838, entitled *A Lecture on the Haytien Revolutions: with a Sketch of the Character of Toussaint l'Ouverture*, was issued in 1841. Other articles were "Freedom and Slavery for Africans," published in 1844 in the *New York Tribune*, and reprinted in the *Liberator* in 1844; he also contributed to the *Anglo-African Magazine*. Other articles and pamphlets of Smith's were: "Civilization: Its Dependence on Physical Circumstances," "The German Invasion," "Citizenship, a Discussion of the Dred Scott Decision," "On the 14th Query of Thomas Jefferson's Notes on Virginia." All of these were published in 1859. He contributed to *Hunt's Merchants' Magazine* an article published in 1846, "The Influence of Climate upon Longevity." Smith also contributed one essay for each of the two volumes of *Autographs for Freedom*, published in 1853 and 1854. Henry Highland Garnet thought of Smith as the most scholarly Negro of the time. He accepted an appointment as professor of anthropology at Wilberforce University in 1863, but died in 1864.

1814

Among the American troops gathered under General

Winder for the defense of Washington, D.C. against the British were Negroes such as John B. Vashon of Leesburg, Va. (who had volunteered in response to a plea for colored men to defend their country) and Louis Boulah, also a free man of Virginia. Boulah was later in the Navy. At a skirmish with the British at Bladensburg near Washington, Negroes served under Commodore Barney in the erection of earthworks and as teamsters and soldiers.

After the burning of Washington, the Vigilance Committee of Philadelphia asked James Forten, Bishop Allen and Absalom Jones to enlist Negroes in the task of building defenses for the city. Over 2,500 Negroes worked for two days on the project. A batallion of Negroes was also organized in Philadelphia, but saw no action because peace was announced.

Free Negroes, slaves and whites exempted from military service erected breastworks in Baltimore in August to defend the city against British attack.

New York law provided for the raising of two regiments of Negroes of about 1,000 men each. They were to receive the same pay as white soldiers. Slaves could enlist with permission of their masters and would be freed at the end of the war. The commissioned officers at these regiments were to be white.

A group of Negroes, including Robert Van Vranken of Albany, was attached to the victorious American force at Plattsburg, N.Y., which forced British troops numbering 14,000 to retreat.

At the Battle of Lake Champlain, many of the victorious American gunners were Negroes, including John Day, a marine on board the *Viper*. Day later went to the Mediterranean with Commander Bainbridge and served in the Navy until March, 1816. Another Negro who fought with distinction at Lake Champlain was Charles Black. He had earlier been impressed into the service of England and imprisoned in England along with 400 other Negroes and many whites when he refused to serve. Black's father had fought at Bunker Hill, and his grandfather in the French and Indian Wars.

Negroes participated in the American force at the Battle of Thames in Canada.

Andrew Jackson issued a proclamation in Mobile, Ala.,

calling on Negroes to aid in the fight against the British. A few months later, Jackson issued a proclamation in New Orleans, praising the Negro troops.

The Treaty of Ghent ending the War of 1812 included a provision of the restoration of slaves who had taken sanctuary with the British. In 1826 the U.S. Minister to the Court of St. James (Albert Gallatin of Pennsylvania) obtained $1,204,960 from the British for slaves not returned in spite of the treaty.

Free Negroes paid $8,322 in taxes in Virginia.

The Manumission Society of Tennessee was founded by Charles Osborn and others.

In the case of DAVENPORT v. the COMMONWEALTH, in Louisiana, a man who had arrested and sold a free Negro woman was fined, imprisoned and required to pay damages.

Louisiana law prohibited free Negroes from immigrating to the state. Louisiana also provided the death penalty for a slave who wilfully harmed any white. There was to be at least one white adult male present for every 30 slaves on a plantation. Parish judges were to visit plantations twice a year to enforce this law.

The legislature of Illinois Territory passed a bill which allowed the hiring of slaves from outside the territory.

1815

The first real movement of Negroes from the South to the Northwest Territory commenced. The general trend of feeling toward Negroes in the West was toleration from 1800 to 1826, persecution between 1826 and 1841, and amelioration in the years 1841 to 1861.

In the Battle of New Orleans, a battalion of about 280 New Orleans Negroes under Major Lacoste and a battalion of about 150 Negroes from Santo Domingo under Major Daquin, helped erect cotton bag breastworks for Jackson, and fought successfully against the British. A total of over 600 Negroes with Negro line officers fought under Jackson at the Battle of New Orleans.

When the British abandoned Fort Blount, on the Apalachicola Bay, Florida, about 300 fugitive slaves from Georgia who farmed in the area, and some 30 Creek Indians, drove the Seminoles from the fort and occupied it. They used the fort as a haven for runaways, and as a base for expeditions against slave owners.

George Boxley, a white man, decided to attempt to free the slaves and headed a conspiracy in Spotsylvania, and Orange County, Va. A few of the plotters obtained guns, and others swords and clubs. Rebels were to meet during harvest time at Boxley's house, to bring horses and what weapons they could, to attack Fredericksburg first, and then push on to Richmond, Va. This was known as Boxley's Conspiracy.

Louisiana law permitted a police corps of free Negroes.

Kentucky prohibited the introduction of slaves for sale.

Free Negroes in Virginia were required to pay a poll tax of $2.50.

The General Assembly of the Presbyterian Church stated that it was not strong enough as a body to take action on the slavery issue.

Henry Highland Garnet (1815-1882), educator and clergyman, was born a slave at New Market, Kent County, Maryland. He escaped in 1824 and went to New York. After finishing his education, he divided his time between preaching and abolition agitation with the American Anti-slavery Society. Garnet continued this until 1843, when he made an address at the National Convention of the Free People of Color at Buffalo, N.Y., calling upon slaves to rise and slay their masters. The Convention refused to endorse these sentiments. He was strongly opposed by Frederick Douglass. His popularity dropped and he began to devote more time to Christian work. He served as pastor of the Liberty St. Presbyterian Church in Troy, N.Y., from 1843 to 1848. In 1852, he was sent as a missionary to Jamaica. On Feb. 12, 1865, Garnet preached a sermon in the House of Representatives commemorating passage of the 13th Amendment. In 1881 he was appointed Minister to Liberia.

Edward James Roye (1815-1872), a Negro, fifth President of Liberia, was born in Newark, Ohio. He arrived in Liberia in 1846 and became a leading merchant, and the Speaker of the House of Representatives in 1849. He was Chief Justice from 1865 to 1868. Roye was elected President in January, 1871. He wished to undertake complete financial reconstruction and introduced some measures for education and an improved system of roads. In 1870, he had gone to England to negotiate a loan, and received $500,000. The very severe terms caused great resentment in Liberia. Roye was accused of embezzlement. When he attempted to extend his term of office by edict, the people rose in insurrection and deposed him from office, recalling Joseph J. Roberts from retirement. Summoned to trial, Roye escaped but he drowned in an attempt to ride breakers in a native canoe to reach an English ship.

1816

The American Colonization Society was founded in Washington, with Bushrod Washington as president, and Henry Clay, Francis Scott Key and John Randolph among those at the organization meeting. At the first meeting Clay praised the society's aim to "rid our country of a useless and pernicious, if not dangerous, portion of its population," the free Negroes.

The Virginia Assembly passed a resolution asking the U.S. Government to find a place on the northern Pacific Coast where free Negroes from Virginia could be settled.

The Manumission Society of North Carolina was formed, primarily by Quakers.

Russell Parrott, a Philadelphia Negro, addressed a celebration of the abolition of the slave trade, expressing the sympathy of free Negroes for their brethren in slavery.

John Randolph of Virginia proposed that Congress end the "infamous traffic" in slaves in the District of Columbia.

Early in 1816, a Negro woman belonging to a Spotsylvania, Va., slaveowner, betrayed George Boxley's plan to free the slaves of Virginia. Military and police measures were at once instituted, and about 30 slaves immediately arrested. Boxley, after vainly trying to organize a rescue party, fled. He finally surrendered and was imprisoned, but with the aid of his wife escaped. Though a reward of $1,000 was offered, he apparently was never recaptured. About six slaves were executed, and probably because of many appeals from white people for clemency, about six others condemned to hang were reprieved and banished.

In June, a slave of Colonel Chestnut betrayed a plot involving slaves in and around Camden, S.C., about a month

after Boxley's escape. July 4 had been selected for the outbreak, which was to start with setting fire to several houses
in Camden. The informer, his freedom purchased by the South
Carolina Legislature, was given a lifetime pension of $50.
Seven slave leaders were condemned to die, and six were
hanged, one pardoned. Another was sentenced to a year's
imprisonment in irons, at the end of which time he was to be
banished.

Major General Youngblood conducted a campaign against
armed communities of fugitive slaves in the marshes of South
Carolina. He reported that he either captured or killed every
slave.

In July, U.S. troops under Col. Duncan Clinch, together
with some friendly Indians, set out to destroy the fugitive
slave stronghold at Fort Blount, Fla. After a siege of about
ten days, and loss of four soldiers, the fort surrendered.
About 270 of the fugitives were killed.

Louisiana law provided that no slave might serve as a
witness against whites or free Negroes unless the latter was
involved in a slave plot or outbreak. Any slave who shot or
stabbed a white was to be executed, and any slave guilty of
arson or of administering poison was to be imprisoned in
chains and at hard labor for life.

Georgia law declared that inciting or attempting to incite
a slave rebellion was a capital crime.

The state of Georgia paid for the support of old or infirm
slaves abandoned by owners, and charged the owners with
the cost.

Killing or maiming of slaves or free Negroes was to carry
the same punishment as such an offense against a white person, according to Georgia law.

Georgia law also forbade the further importation of slaves.
This law was repealed in 1824, and then revived in 1829.

Indiana's Constitution forbade slavery.

South Carolina forbade the importation of slaves. This law
was repealed in 1818.

In the Louisiana case of FORSYTH *et al* v. NASH, it was
decided that a Negro could not be proved to be a slave on
the basis of a bill of sale executed in Detroit, Mich., because
no slavery was allowed in Michigan.

In South Carolina, the case of PEPEON (guardian of Phoebe) v. CLARKE, involved a person who moved to South Carolina from Maryland, bringing a slave girl with him. It was decided that the owner's admission that the girl's mother had been free was sufficient to offset the presumption of color. The girl was to be set free and was entitled to damages.

A conference of Negro Methodists organized the National African Methodist Episcopal Church in Philadelphia. They elected Daniel Coker as bishop, but he resigned in favor of Richard Allen.

Bethel Charity School was founded in Baltimore by Daniel Coker, a Negro, for the education of Negroes. He was connected with the African Methodist Episcopal Church.

In Wilmington, Del., a school and library were established for Negroes. A Negro was the teacher.

William Wells Brown (1816-1884), Negro reformer and historian, was born in Lexington, Ky. His mother was a slave; his father, a white slaveholder, George Higgins. Taken to St. Louis and hired out on a steamboat, he was next employed by Elijah P. Lovejoy, editor of the *St. Louis Times.* Hired out again on a steamboat, he escaped in 1834 to Ohio, intending to go to Canada. Sheltered by a Quaker, Brown assisted other fugitive slaves. Between 1843 and 1849, Brown worked as a lecturer for the Western New York Anti-slavery Society and the Massachusetts Anti-slavery Society. He was also interested in temperance, women's suffrage, and prison reform. In 1849, he visited England and represented the American Peace Society at the Peace Congress in Paris. He stayed abroad until 1854. Although Brown studied medicine, his reputation rests largely on his ability as an historian. His works include *Narrative of William W. Brown, a Fugitive Slave* (1847), *Three Years in Europe* (1852), *Clotel, or the President's Daughter, A Narrative of Slave Life in the U.S.,* a novel, published in 1853, and plays, *The Dough Face* and *The Escape, or a Leap for Freedom. The Black Man, His Antecedents, His Genius and His Achievements,* a history, was published in 1863. *The Negro in the American Rebellion, His Heroism and His Fidelity,* also a history, was published in 1867, and *The Rising Son, or the Antecedents and the Advancements of the Colored Race* in 1874.

William Cooper Nell (1816-1874), a Negro writer, was
born in Boston. He attended a primary school for Negro children, and read law in the office of William I. Bowditch. Nell
became affiliated with the anti-slavery movement, but concentrated on opening public schools to Negro children. In
1851, he assisted Frederick Douglass in the publication of the
North Star. His pamphlet *Services of Colored Americans in
the Wars of 1776 and 1812* was published in May of 1851.
In 1855, *Colored Patriots of the American Revolution,* with
an introduction by Harriet Beecher Stowe, was published.
Appointed clerk by John G. Palfrey, the postmaster of Boston,
Nell became the first Negro to hold a post under the Federal
Government.

1817

Philadelphia Negroes met at Bethel Church to protest the
American Colonization Society's attempts to exile Negroes
"from the land of our nativity." About 300 Negroes were
involved in the protest. They were led by Richard Allen and
James Forten.

The American Convention of Abolition Societies resolved
"that the gradual and total emancipation of all persons of
colour, and their literary and moral education, should precede
their colonization" [in Africa]. This resolution was a con-
cession to prevailing sentiments, but in principle the American
Convention was strongly opposed to colonization.

Mississippi entered the U.S. as a slave state. Its Constitution required an owner to care for his slaves and refrain
from injuring them under penalty of having them sold by the
state. It also provided for jury trial for a slave in a capital
case.

Charles Osborn, a white, began publishing *The Philanthropist,* an anti-slavery newspaper in Ohio.

New York passed a gradual Abolition Act. It provided
that on July 4, 1827, every Negro born in New York before
July 4, 1799, would be free, and all Negro males born after
that would be free at the age of 28, and all females born after
that be free at the age of 25. On July 4, 1827, 10,000 slaves
in New York were freed without compensation to their
owners.

A kidnaper of Negroes was sentenced to three years in the penitentiary in New York.

A kidnaper of Negroes arrested in Maryland was sentenced to five years in a penitentiary.

The Maryland case of BURROWS ADM. v. NEGRO ANNA decided that gifts of property by an owner to a slave entitled the slave to "freedom by implication," since the law forbade slaves to inherit or hold property.

Tennessee law forbade the selling of a slave who had brought suit for freedom.

North Carolina law declared that the killing of a slave was homicide and should be punished as homicide.

On April 7, several outbursts by slaves, possibly spontaneous, occurred in St. Mary's County, Md. Approximately 200 Negroes were involved, several whites were injured by sticks and brickbats, and two houses were sacked before police and patrols restored order.

Morris Brown, a free Negro of Charleston, S.C., was ordained a deacon in the AME Church.

John Mifflin Brown (1817-1893), bishop of the African Methodist Episcopal Church, a mulatto, was born in Odessa, Del. In 1836, he joined the Bethel African Methodist Episcopal Church. He prepared for the ministry and attended Wesleyan Academy and Oberlin College. Between 1844 and 1847, Brown served as principal of the Union Seminary, generally referred to as the original Wilberforce University, and the first educational effort of the African Methodist Episcopal Church. In 1864, Brown was chosen editor of the *Christian Recorder*, the oldest Negro newspaper in the U.S. Ordained a bishop in 1868, he is credited in 25 years of service with establishing Payne Institute, now Allen University, at Columbia, S. C., and Paul Quinn College at Waco, Tex.

Frederick Douglass (1817-1895), abolitionist, orator, journalist, was born a slave in Maryland. Given the name of Frederick Augustus Washington Bailey, he assumed the name of Douglass shortly after his escape to freedom. His father was an unknown white man; his mother, Harriet Bailey, a slave. Sent to Baltimore as a house servant, he learned to read and write. The settlement of his dead master's estate sent him back to the country as a field hand. He conspired with half a dozen of his fellows to escape, but the plan was betrayed and he was jailed. Returned to Baltimore, Douglass disguised himself as a sailor and attempted his second escape Sept. 3, 1838, and was successful. He went directly to New York City. Douglass had read Garrison's *Liberator,* and attended a convention of the Massachusetts Anti-slavery Society in Nantucket in 1841. He was employed as an agent by the society and took part in the Rhode Island campaign against the new constitution which disenfranchised Negroes. He became a central figure in the famous 100 Conventions of the New England Anti-slavery Society. In 1845, Frederick Douglass published *Narrative of the Life of Frederick Douglass* and then spent the next two years lecturing in Britain and Ireland on slavery and women's rights, thus earning enough to buy his freedom. He established a newspaper, the *North Star,* in Rochester, N.Y. He lectured, and helped Harriet Beecher Stowe establish an industrial school for young Negroes. For counseling John Brown he was outlawed by the Governor of Virginia. Douglass fled to Canada. During the Civil War, he helped to recruit the 54th and 55th Massachusetts Negro Regiments. After the War, Douglass became a member of the Territorial Legislature of Washington, D. C.; secretary of the Santo Domingo Commission; police commissioner and marshal and recorder of deeds of the District of Columbia, and finally U.S. Minister to Haiti and chargé d'affaires for Santo Domingo. The exploitation of Haiti by American businessmen caused Douglass to resign in 1891. His other works include: *My Bondage and My Freedom* (1855), *Lectures on American Slavery* (1851), and *U.S. Grant and the Colored People* (1872). By all standards, Douglass must be judged as one of the giants of the abolition movement in America.

Victor Sejour (1817-1874) was born in New Orleans. His parents (his father was white) sent him to Paris to study and avoid the handicap of his color. He frequented drama circles and knew successful dramatists such as Dumas and Emile Augier. In 1844, Le Théâtre-Français produced his first play, *Diegareas,* thus inaugurating a brilliant career for Sejour. Sejour was one of the commercially most successful dramatists of 19th century Paris.

Samuel Ringgold Ward, Negro abolitionist, author and clergyman, was born in Maryland.

Between 1817 and 1850 an estimated 3 to 5 million slaves were imported to Brazil.

The Negro population in Cuba was 339,959 or 54.0% of the total population, 115,691 Negroes being counted as free and 225,268 as slaves.

1818

Maroon activities disturbed South Carolina, Virginia, and North Carolina throughout the year. Disturbances in North Carolina became serious enough in November to evoke considerable notice from the local press, which advised patrols to keep a strict outlook. Later, an attack upon a store by Maroons led by Andy, alias Billy James, and even better known by the name Abaellino, was repulsed by armed residents.

A stricter Fugitive Slave Law was passed in the House but defeated in the Senate.

In the Mississippi case of HARVY AND OTHERS V. DECKER AND HOPKINS, it was decided that slaves taken from Virginia to Indiana in 1784, and then taken to a slave state in 1816, had been freed by the Northwest Ordinance of 1787. The judge argued that slavery could exist only where municipal regulations supported it.

In a decision of the U.S. Circuit Court of Washington, D. C., in the case of SARAH V. TAYLOR, it was stated that children born between the date of promise to manumit and the date of actual manumission were entitled to freedom at the same time as the mother.

The Illinois Constitution forbade slavery.

A law of the Missouri Territory provided death without benefit of clergy, for stealing or selling a free person as a slave, knowing him to be free.

In Delaware, two Negro women in the case of MEUNIER V. DUPERROW, were found guilty of kidnaping Negroes who were sold into slavery.

In the South Carolina case of ARTHUR V. WELLS, it was declared unlawful to kill a runaway unless the pursuer was in danger from the runaway's resistance.

South Carolina courts also decided that calling a person a mulatto was actionable as libel.

New Jersey law provided severe penalties for exportation of slaves from the state.

Connecticut disenfranchised Negroes.

Georgia law forbade free Negroes from owning real estate or slaves. The law was repealed the next year, except for Savannah, Augusta and Darien.

Andrew Jackson defeated Indians and Negroes at the Battle of Suwanee, ending the First Seminole War.

The General Assembly of the Presbyterian Church declared slavery "a gross violation of the most precious and sacred rights of human nature."

Lemuel Haynes, a Negro, became pastor of a white Congregational church in Manchester, N. H.

Free Negroes organized the Pennsylvania Augustine Society for the education of Negroes.

Public aid began to be given to schools for Negroes in Columbia and Philadelphia, Pa.

Brazil's population was estimated at 3,800,000. Of these, 1,043,000 were white, 1,930,000 Negro and 526,000 were mulatto.

1819

Charles Osborn began publication of the anti-slavery paper, *The Manumission Intelligencer,* in Tennessee.

Roger B. Taney, who in 1857 handed down the Dred Scott decision of the U.S. Supreme Court, in defending Rev. Jacob Gruber in the latter's trial for inciting insurrection among slaves, denounced slavery as an evil that must be gradually wiped out.

James Madison said that the proposition that emancipation of the Negroes "ought, like remedies for other deep rooted and widespread evils, to be gradual, is so obvious, that there seems to be no difference of opinion on that point. To be equitable and satisfactory, the consent of both the master and the slave should be obtained" and compensation should be paid to the owners. "To be consistent with existing and probably unalterable prejudices in the Unted States, the freed blacks ought to be permanently removed beyond the region occupied by, or allotted to, a white population," for example, on land in the West. "The objections to a thorough incorporation of the two people," Madison contended, "are . . . insuperable."

Alabama entered the U.S. as a slave state. Its Constitution gave the legislature the power to abolish slavery with compensation, with or without the consent of the owners. It also provided a jury trial for slaves in crimes above petty larceny, and that malicious killing or maiming of a slave was to receive the same punishment as such action would receive against a white man, and on the same proof except in cases of insurrection.

In the spring slaves in Augusta, Ga., entered into a conspiracy to burn the city. The leader of the plot, a slave named Coot or Coco, was caught and executed.

Missouri law forbade assembling of slaves or free Negroes, and forbade teaching of slaves to read.

Three white women in Philadelphia stoned a Negro woman to death.

Illinois law provided that all Negroes in the state without certificates would be considered runaways, subject to arrest, being hired out and advertised. If they were not claimed within a year, they would be given certificates and released.

1820

U.S. Census: The Negro population was 1,771,656 or 18.4% of total U.S. population. 233,634 Negroes (13.2%) were free. The City of New York had 10,886 Negroes; of these only 612 voted. The state of Pennsylvania had a free Negro population of 30,202; Philadelphia 7,582. Ohio had 4,723 Negroes. Boston's 1,690 Negroes represented 3.9% of its total population.

The Missouri Compromise admitted Missouri as a slave state, but prohibited slavery in future states north of the 36° 30' line. It also included a fugitive slave clause. The Constitution of Missouri provided trial by jury for slaves, the same punishment for slaves and whites for the same offense and court-assigned counsel for the Negroes' defense.

The Maine Constitution gave the vote and school privileges to all citizens regardless of race and color.

A white man was executed in Raleigh, N.C., for murder of a Negro, according to the law of that state which provided the death penalty for "wilful and malicious" killing of a slave.

In STATE V. ISAAC JONES in Mississippi the court ruled that the killing of a slave might be murder and that a master's rights over his slave were only those conferred by positive law.

In Kentucky the court in RANKIN V. LYDIA upheld the principle of freedom granted by removal to a free state. A similar decision was made in the case of GRIFFITH V. FANNY in Virginia.

Pennsylvania provided fines from $500 to $2,000 and imprisonment, of seven to 21 years for kidnapping of free Negroes.

New Jersey passed a law for the emancipation of slaves. It was voluntary and a few slaves remained as late as 1860.

The Delaware Legislature passed a resolution advocating Congressional prohibition of slavery in new states.

Elihu Embree, a Quaker, started in Jonesboro, Tenn., a monthly anti-slavery periodical, *Emancipator,* which ceased publication a year later, because of Embree's death.

The ship, *Mayflower of Liberia*, left New York harbor with 86 Negroes on board for Sierra Leone where through efforts of British abolitionists a settlement of liberated slaves had been started in the late 18th century.

The South was considered a high risk area for fire insurance because of fires set by rebellious slaves. An official of the American Fire Insurance Co. of Philadelphia wrote to a Savannah, Ga., man on Feb. 17: "I have received your letter of the 7th inst., respecting the insurance of your house and furniture in Savannah. In answer thereto, I am to inform you that this company, for the present, decline making insurance in any of the slave states."

Negro homes were burned in Philadelphia.

In February, an order was issued forbidding acceptance of Negroes or mulattoes in the U.S. Army.

Congress authorized citizens of Washington, D.C., to elect "white" city officials and to adopt a code governing free Negroes and slaves.

New Jersey reaffirmed denial of the right to vote to Negroes.

The African Methodist Episcopal Zion Church declared its independence from the Methodist Episcopal organization in New York. James Varick and Abraham Thompson were elected elders.

St. Phillips Church (Episcopal) was incorporated by Negroes in New York. Rev. Peter Williams, the first Negro ordained as an Episcopalian priest, held the position as rector until his death in 1840.

In Cincinnati, Ohio, the first schools for Negroes were established by Negroes.

A primary school for Negro children was established in Boston.

A 15 year old Negro, Maria Becraft, founded a school for Negro girls on Dumbarton Street in Georgetown, D.C.

The Pennsylvania Abolition Society made an unsuccessful attempt to have public school money applied to education of Negroes.

In New York, a second building was completed for the African Free School, housing 500 pupils on Mulberry Street, to supplement an 1815 building on William Street which accommodated 200 students.

Adam Hodgson, an English traveler, reported that there was an adult Negro school in Baltimore with 180 pupils.

Baltimore had 600 Negroes in Sunday school. They formed a Bible Association which was connected with the Baltimore Bible Society.

George Vashon (1820-1878), a well educated Negro, exploited Haitian subject matter for his poetry. This was not an uncommon practice, since Haiti was used by the abolitionists as proof that Negroes were responsible and could govern themselves. Vashon visited Haiti during the early 1850's and steeped himself in its culture. Out of this experience came his best poem, *Victor Ogé*, about a mulatto hero of the Haiti Revolution. *Victor Ogé* is a romantic narrative poem much in the style of Byron's *The Corsair* or Scott's *Lady of the Lake*. Its significance was twofold: it was the first

narrative, nonlyrical poem from a Negro writer, and it was
the first poetic tribute to a Negro revolutionary by a Negro.
It appeared in 1856 in Vashon's anthology, *Autographs of
Freedom*. *Victor Ogé* remains one of the best of the anti-
slavery poems.

Robert Duncanson (1820-1872), Negro artist, was born in
Cincinnati. He studied in Canada, Great Britain and Scotland,
and first became prominent in Canada with his picture after
Tennyson's *Lotus Eaters*. In 1857 he returned to Cincinnati
and painted commission portraits. Duncanson returned to
England during the Civil War, and became very successful,
enjoying the patronage of Tennyson and the Duchesses of
Sutherland and Essex. The *London Art Journal* of 1866
selected Duncanson as one of the outstanding landscapists of
his day. He also painted murals and historical sub;ects.
Among his surviving historical paintings are *Shylock and Jes-
sica, Ruins of Carthage, Lotus Eaters, Trial of Shakespeare*
and *Battleground of the Raison River*.

In the north of Haiti a revolt against the Negro king Henry
I (Christophe) broke out. Christophe, paralyzed from the
waist down, committed suicide.

1821

Thomas Jefferson wrote in his autobiography: "Nothing is
more certainly written in the book of fate, than that these
people are to be free; nor is it less certain that the two races,
equally free, cannot live in the same government. Nature,
habit, opinion have drawn indelible lines of distinction between them. It is still in our power to direct the process of
emancipation and deportation, peaceably, and in slow degree;
as that the evil will wear off insensibly."

James Madison wrote to Lafayette: "If an asylum could
be found in Africa, that would be the appropriate destination
for the unhappy race among us. Some are sanguine that the
efforts of an existing colonization society [the American
Colonization Society] will accomplish such a provision; but
a very partial success seems the most that can be expected.
Some other region must, therefore, be found for them as they
become free and willing to emigrate. The repugnance of the
whites to their continuance among them is founded on prejudices, themselves founded upon physical distinctions, which
are not likely soon, if ever, to be eradicated."

Petitions of citizens of Tennessee supporting gradual emancipation resulted in the formation of a legislative committee which recommended a law allowing manumissions and gradual emancipation, but nothing came of these proposals.

The Pennsylvania Legislature passed a law giving a more formal trial to Negroes claimed as fugitives and prohibited justices of the peace and aldermen from officiating in such cases.

When a runaway Negro was discovered in the small town of Kennett Square, Pennsylvania, by his owner and overseer, the townspeople prevented an attempt to seize the Negro. In the resulting fight the slave owner and overseer lost their lives.

A smaller proportion of Negroes than whites were chargeable to the community as paupers in Pennsylvania according to a report of the Pennsylvania Abolition Society—Negroes in Philadelphia owned $281,162 worth of real property, exclusive of church property.

In U.S. v. NEALE the Circuit Court in Washington, D.C., held that a Negro who was reputed to be free was competent to testify against a free Negro.

In HALL v. MULLIN Maryland decided that the bequest of property by an owner to his slave entitled the slave to "freedom by implication" since by law no slave could inherit or hold property.

Ohio court decisions stated that quadroons had all the rights, privileges and duties of whites.

The Massachusetts Legislature appointed a committee to inquire into the expediency of a law expelling Negroes who had come into the state.

The New York State Constitutional Convention passed higher property requirements for Negroes than for whites, longer residence requirements and a provision that a Negro who performed military service must still pay taxes in order to have the right to vote. The N.Y. Constitution of 1777 had given the vote "to every adult male."

South Carolina repealed its law of 1740 which provided a fine of £700 for willful murder of a slave, £350 for murder "on sudden heat and passion" and £100 for cutting out the tongue, putting out the eye, castrating or scalding of a slave.

Maine law declared void marriages between a white and a Negro, Indian or mulatto.

U.S. Attorney General William Wirt advised a Norfolk, Va., port official that Negroes did not legally qualify to command vessels, since acts regulating foreign and coastal trade limited command of vessels to citizens.

Benjamin Lundy, a Quaker born in New Jersey, established in Ohio *The Genius of Universal Emancipation,* the most successful anti-slavery paper of the 1820's, which subsequently moved to Greenville, Tenn., Baltimore and Washington, and finally to Philadelphia in 1834. For a short while William Lloyd Garrison assisted in publishing the *Genius,* but his views were too extreme for Lundy who was mainly interested in aiding emigration of Negroes who wished to leave the U.S. Publication of the paper ceased in 1835.

The African Methodist Episcopal Zion Church (AMEZ) was founded in New York. James Varick was district chairman of the church and became first bishop the following year. The African Methodist Episcopal Zion Church formed a conference of several churches from Philadelphia, New Haven, Long Island and New York City.

Lott Cary and Collin Teague, Negroes, formed the First Baptist Church of Monrovia and left Norfolk, Va., for Liberia as missionaries of the Baptist Triennial Convention.

In Providence, R.I., an African Union meeting and school house was completed.

A Boston school commission was established for the control of a school for Negroes meeting on the lower floor of the Colored Baptist Church on Belknap Street. This was a continuation of a Negro school founded by Primus Hall in 1798.

Mrs. Mary Billing, an Englishwoman, opened a school for Negroes on H Street in Washington, D.C., in the house of Daniel Jones, a Negro.

The First Negro Benevolent Society was founded in Baltimore.

James Forten, a Negro veteran of the Revolutionary War who became a sail manufacturer in Philadelphia and amassed a fortune of $100,000 and was a substantial contributor to the *Liberator,* was awarded a certificate for rescuing people from drowning.

Edward A. Jones, a Negro from Charleston, S.C., graduated from Amherst College, 11 days before John Russworm graduated from Bowdoin. He became an Episcopal priest, migrated to Sierra Leone and helped found Fourah Bay College there, the first institution of higher education in West Africa.

William Still (1821-1902), Negro reformer, was the son of Levin Steel, a former Maryland slave. He moved to Philadelphia in 1841, and in 1847 became a clerk in the office of the Pennsylvania Society for the Abolition of Slavery. Between 1851 and 1861 he was chairman and corresponding secretary of the Philadelphia branch of the Underground Railroad. His account of its activities, *Underground Railroad,* was published in 1872. In 1864 he was appointed post sutler at Camp William Penn for Negro soldiers near Philadelphia. He was involved in the campaign against the regulation of Philadelphia streetcar lines compelling all persons of color to ride on the front of platforms. His other works include *A Brief Narrative of the Struggle for the Rights of the Colored People of Philadelphia in the City Railway Cars* (1867), and *An Address on Voting and Laboring* (1874). In 1880, Still founded the first Negro YMCA.

Harriet Tubman (1821-1913) was born a slave on the Eastern Shore of Maryland. While working as a field hand in 1844, she was forced by her master to marry John Tubman. In 1849 she became a fugitive slave and one of the most successful leaders of the Underground Railroad, bringing slaves to the North and to Canada, sometimes even forcing the timid ahead with a loaded revolver. She later worked with John Brown and other abolitionists and then during the Civil War as cook, guide, spy and nurse. Later she was very active in establishing schools for freedmen in North Carolina. In 1869 Sarah Hopkins Bradford published *Scenes in the Life of Harriet Tubman* and then in 1886 a revised edition entitled *Harriet, the Moses of her People.*

The first all-Negro acting troupe, the African Company, started performing in a theater at Mercer Street in New York, playing Shakespearean drama, the classics and lighter popular melodrama. James Hewlett played *Othello* and *Rich-*

ard the Third. The Company performed until 1832. Ira Aldridge was an extra in this theater, while he was a student at the African Free School.

1822

The American Colonization Society purchased a site, Cape Mesurado, on the African coast and sent Jehudi Ashmun, a Congressionalist minister, to Liberia. There, Ashmun and his successor, Ralph Gurley, organized the survival of the colony of Monrovia which was beset by fever and attacks of the natives against the emigrated freed slaves from the United States.

Denmark Vesey, a Negro ship's carpenter who purchased his freedom with money he had won in a lottery, plotted an insurrection in Charleston, S.C. Vesey had been owned by a slave trader and had traveled widely and spoke several languages. Working as a skilled carpenter he acquired money and property. For several years he agitated for insurrection among the Negroes of Charleston. With Peter Poyas as his lieutenant Vesey built an organization based upon cells, each with its own leader who recruited and made assignments. Only the leaders knew the details of the whole plot. The uprising was almost a half year in preparation. The date was set for July 16, 1822. Arsenals, guardhouses, powder magazines, naval stores were to be taken and all whites were to be killed. In spite of the careful planning the insurrection was betrayed at the last moment and Vesey and 130 Negroes were arrested. Vesey and another 34 Negroes were executed.

As a result of the Denmark Vesey plot, South Carolina limited the movements and occupations of free Negroes and also enforced stricter laws against instruction of Negroes in groups. South Carolina passed a law forbidding free Negroes who had left the state to return. This law also required free Negroes to have a guardian. "Negro Seamen Acts" were passed requiring Negro seamen to remain in jail for the time their ship stayed in a South Carolina port. From one British trading vessel almost the entire crew was taken. In spite of British protests and the declaration of the U.S. Attorney General that this law was unconstitutional, South Carolina refused to repeal the law and it remained until the Civil War.

The Rhode Island Constitution disenfranchised free Negroes.

Tennessee passed a law prohibiting marriage between whites and Negroes.

In the case of MATILDA v. MASON *et al.* in Washington, D.C., the court ruled that it was not necessary to dismiss all jurors who did not favor slavery. This apparently had been the practice before.

The Genius of Universal Emancipation reported that in Virginia in that year a man was given a nominal fine for killing a slave.

In the South Carolina case of STATE v. WM. H. TAYLOR a man was fined heavily for killing a slave.

A law passed in the territory of Florida declared that for capital crimes slaves should be tried and punished like whites.

A slave taken from Washington, D.C., to reside in Pennsylvania was set free by the decision in COM. v. ROBINSON on the grounds that removal to a free state granted freedom to a slave so removed.

In the New York case OVERSEERS OF MARBLETOWN v. OVERSEERS OF KINGSTON, Judge Platt decided that in a marriage between a slave and a free person, neither party's status changed as a result of the marriage and the children of such marriage were free if the mother was free.

Negro real estate holdings in Providence, R.I., amounted to approximately $10,000.

The *Illinois Intelligencer,* an anti-slavery journal, began publication.

John Finely Crowe began to publish the *Abolition Intelligencer* in Shelby, Ky.

The Kentucky Abolition Society had 250 members and five or six branches.

The Tennessee Manumission Society sent a petition to Congress for the abolition of slavery in Washington, D.C.

Rev. John Gloucester, the first Negro minister of the Presbyterian Church, died. He was born in Kentucky about 1776.

Petersburg, Va., had two Baptist churches belonging to Negroes and an African Missionary Society composed of Negroes.

James Varick was elected bishop of the African Methodist Episcopal Zion Church.

The American Methodist Episcopal Church in Charleston, S.C., under Rev. Morris Brown had 3,000 members.

Henry Smothers built the Smothers School-House for Negroes on the corner of 14th and H Streets in Washington, D.C. The school had between 100 and 150 students.

The Bird School, later known as the James Forten, was opened on 6th Street in Philadelphia. This was the first public school for Negroes in the city.

Hiram Rhoades Revels (1822-1901), Negro Senator, was born in Fayetteville, N.C., of free parents. He attended Quaker seminaries in Indiana and Ohio, and Knox College in Illinois. Ordained a minister of the AME Church in 1845, he taught and preached in the Northwestern states. During the Civil War he helped organize Negro regiments, and was made chaplain for Negro troops in Mississippi. In 1866 he settled in Natchez, Miss., and was elected alderman in 1868. He became a State Senator in 1870. In the same year he was elected to the U.S. Senate to fill an unexpired term. After 1871, he devoted his time to religious and educational activities. Revels was president of Alcorn College, and in 1876 became editor of the *Southwestern Christian Advocate*.

1823

Negotiations between the USA and Great Britain to declare a legislative prohibition of the slave trade under the penalties of piracy led to a treaty proposal, later to be joined by other nations. It was to authorize the seizure of slavers on the "coast of Africa, America, and the West Indies." Parliament gave the approval, the Senate, however, after long debates, finally ratified the treaty but struck out the word "America." This was rejected by Britain and no treaty was concluded. A similar convention with Colombia which was planned the following year, was not ratified by the Senate even though the "coast of America" was excepted.

John Rankin published a series of letters on slavery in *The Castigator* which was edited by David Amen and published in Ripley, Ohio. Rankin became a Garrisonian and advocated immediate emancipation as early as 1817. These letters expressed his extreme hatred for slavery. Later published in book form they had a wide sale, particularly in Kentucky and Tennessee.

The Tennessee Manumission Society, which reported 20 branches with a membership of over 600, sent memorials to Congress calling for the prohibition of slavery in new states.

In the case of EX PARTE SIMMONS before the U.S. Circuit Court in Pennsylvania the principle that removal to a free state bestowed freedom was upheld.

In the case of U.S. v. BROCKETT before the U. S. Circuit Court of Washington, D.C., it was decided that "to cruelly, inhumanely, and maliciously cut, slash, beat and ill treat one's own slave is an indictable offence at common law."

In answering a question of a Dr. Morse of Liverpool, Madison wrote that free Negroes are "generally idle and depraved; appearing to retain the bad qualities of the slaves, with whom they continue to associate, without acquiring any of the good ones of the whites, from whom they continue separated by prejudices against their color, and other peculiarities."

Mississippi law prohibited meetings of more than five slaves or free Negroes. The same law also forbade any meeting of Negroes at public houses at night, and the teaching of reading and writing to Negroes. The penalty for such action was up to 39 lashes.

Negroes in Richmond, Va., petitioned the State Legislature for a permit to build a Baptist church because there was not enough room in the white church for them to attend. They were refused.

Louise Parke Costin, a 19-year-old Negro girl, established a school for free Negroes in her father's house in Washington, D.C., on A Street South. She operated the school until her death in 1831. It was later reopened by her younger sister, Martha, and existed until 1839.

The Tailor in Distress, a comedy, utilized a Negro, Edwin Forest, in the role of a Negro washerwoman. Forest was the first Negro actor to gain popular approval of a white audience.

In Brazil, José Bonifácio argued that since the 40,000 slaves imported each year hardly affected the total number of Negro slaves, because of their ill treatment, the slave trade should be abolished. Then, he reasoned, masters would have to be more careful of their property.

1824

A Missouri law enabled slaves to sue for freedom.

A Louisiana court ruled that a slave taken from Kentucky to Ohio and eventually brought to Louisiana was free, on the ground that the local Ohio laws granted freedom which could not be abrogated by return to a slave state.

The New Jersey Legislature adopted a resolution favoring gradual emancipation in the nation.

The General Assembly of Ohio urged colonization of slaves after emancipation.

A Virginia court decided that freeing a slave woman by will at a specified future date did not free any children born to her in the meantime.

The Indiana Fugitive Act allowed claimants to bring fugitive slaves before any justice of the peace for a decision. Either party had the right to appeal, and the appeal trial was to be before a jury. The act was declared unconstitutional in 1850.

The Methodist Episcopal Church felt that the abolition of slavery was impossible and instead proposed rules to govern the treatment of slaves by church members.

By this year the African Episcopal Church had a membership of 9,888, with 14 elders and 26 deacons.

Negroes in Newport, R.I., purchased a lot on Church and Division Streets and erected the first Negro church in this part of the state. It became the Colored Union Church, and its pastor was Rev. Jacon C. Perry.

In October, a fight between Negroes and whites took place in Providence, R.I. A mob of between 400 and 500 whites gathered to protest the employment of Negroes and destroyed the "Hard Scrabble" district to which Negroes had begun to move from the waterfront area. Four white men were tried for their part in the riot. Two were found guilty, but were later freed on a legal technicality.

The African Free School in New York City had an attendance of about 600 pupils and began to receive support from the New York Common Council.

The trustees of Dartmouth College reversed a decision to deny admission to a Negro applicant after a protest by the student body. It then became a permanent policy of the College to admit Negroes.

Spain freed the slaves in the United Provinces of Central America.

1825

In Providence, R.I., there were 1,414 free Negroes and four slaves.

In Kentucky, the case of BUSCH'S REP. V. WHITE AND WIFE upheld the principle that removal of a slave to a free state granted him freedom.

An advertisement appeared in *The Genius of Universal Emancipation* for eight or ten slaves and their families to be educated for freedom under the auspices of the Emancipating Labor Society of Kentucky. Frances Wright established a similar institution in West Tennessee. Both seem to have failed.

The Maryland Anti-slavery Society was founded with several hundred members in four branches. Daniel Raymond was its president and Edward Needles its secretary. For several years the society ran Raymond as an anti-slavery candidate to the Maryland General Assembly.

The Manumission Society of North Carolina investigated the opinion of people in the state and concluded that only one in 20 were "really opposed to emancipation," but that only one in 30 "desired immediate emancipation."

To promote the education and protection of Negroes an anti-slavery society was formed in New Haven, Conn., by Leonard Bacon, Luther Wright, Alexander Twining, Edward Beecher and Theodore D. Woolsey (all whites).

The new constitution of Missouri provided the same penalty for killing or dismembering a slave as for this offense against a white man.

Pennsylvania passed "personal liberty" laws to protect free Negroes living in the state.

A Negro was burned alive near Greenville, S.C.

A re-enacted Maryland law provided for the banishment of free Negroes who could not give "security for proper behavior." Any free Negro in Maryland or traveling through the state without a job had to provide security for good behavior or leave the state within 15 days. The law carried a punishment of a $30 fine or being sold into slavery for up to six months.

To sell tobacco in Maryland a free Negro needed a certificate from a justice of the peace granted on the sworn testimony of two whites.

Josiah Henson, a Negro, led a party of his master's slaves from Maryland across free territory in Ohio to Kentucky. He later became the leader of a community of escaped Negroes at Dresden, Ontario, and is the reputed original for "Uncle Tom."

A day and night school for Negroes was founded in Baltimore. The subjects taught included English, French and Latin.

Richard Harvey Cain (1825-1887), Congressman, was born of free parents in Greenbriar County, Va. He was ordained a deacon of the African Methodist Episcopal Church in 1859 and transferred to Brooklyn, N.Y., in 1862, where he was elder of the church and also published a newspaper called *The Missionary Record*. In 1865 he was sent to the South Carolina Conference and in 1868 he was a member of the Constitutional Convention. In 1868 he was a State Senator from the Charleston District. He was a U.S. Congressman from South Carolina in 1873-1875 and again in 1877-1879. Cain helped organize the Honest Government League and in 1880 was appointed Bishop of the diocese of Louisiana and Texas.

Frances E.W. Harper (1825-1911), Negro poet, was active in the abolitionist movement. Her lectures and poems were very popular. Her literary models were Longfellow, Whittier and Mrs. Hemans. In addition to anti-slavery poems such as *The Slave Mother* and *Bury Me in a Free Land,* poems noted for their simplicity and directness, she also wrote propagandist verse (e.g., *Vashti*) for the feminist movement. Her biblical narratives, such as *Truth* and *Moses,* tend to be pretentious and dull. One of her most successful works was *Sketches of a Southern Life* (1873), a series of verse portraits of Southern Negro types.

Benjamin S. Turner (1825-1894), Negro Congressman, was born a slave in Halifax, N.C. Taken to Alabama, he was freed and given a basic education. Before becoming a prosperous small businessman in Salem, Ala., he served as a tax collector and city councilman. By 1870, he was interested in politics, and was elected as a Republican to the House of Representatives. Renominated in 1872, he lost the election because of local party divisions, and retired from politics.

1826

Negroes in Boston founded the General Colored Association of Massachusetts to promote the welfare of Negroes and to work against slavery. Members included Hosea and Joshua Easton, Johny E. Scarlett, Thomas Cole, James G. Barbadoes, William C. Nell, Thomas Dalton, John T. Hilton, Fred Brimley, Coffin Pitts and Walter Lewis.

An abolition society existed at Williams College in Massachusetts. It doubted, however, the advisability of immediate emancipation.

Among the societies represented at the American Convention for Promoting the Abolition of Slavery, only the one from Sunsbury, Monroe County, Ohio, went so far as to require its members to favor complete and immediate abolition and the privileges of citizenship for freed Negroes.

In Pennsylvania, the Society for the Abolition of Slavery was influential in passing a statute which forbade taking a Negro from the state to enslave him.

Pennsylvania adopted a resolution favoring gradual emancipation in the nation.

A memorial, favoring gradual and total abolition of slavery, from Baltimore County was presented to the Maryland Legislature.

The Monthly Meeting of Friends in Delaware demanded that the Delaware Legislature immediately abolish slavery.

A reputation for freedom and proof of enjoyment of freedom for more than 20 years was considered evidence of actual freedom in the New Jersey case of Fox v. LAMBSON.

Daniel Raymond estimated that nearly 3,000 citizens of North Carolina had joined anti-slavery societies since 1824.

The Manumission Society of North Carolina reported over

40 branches and over 2,000 members. A member of the Manumission Society was elected to the State Senate.

The North Carolina Yearly Meeting of Quakers received almost $5,000 to pay for emigration of Negroes.

In his will, Thomas Jefferson freed five of his slaves, but passed the rest on to his heirs.

An anti-slavery man, the brother-in-law of Edward Coles, was elected to the Virginia Legislature.

In the South Carolina case of REAL ESTATE OF MRS. HARD-CASTLE, ADS PORCHER, ETC., free Negroes were held capable of holding real estate.

Cincinnati had 690 Negroes. In the same year a mob tried to drive these Negroes out of Cincinnati.

A study published in this year revealed that Negroes in Massachusetts made up 1/74 of the population and 1/6 of the prisoners; in New York, 1/35 of the population and 1/4 of the prisoners; in Pennsylvania, 1/34 of the population and 1/3 of the prisoners. However, Negroes were frequently arrested for minor offenses such as vagrancy overlooked for whites. They often could not obtain good legal counsel and witnesses, were often sentenced for longer terms than whites convicted of the same crimes, and usually had more difficulty securing pardons and paying fines.

North Carolina law forbade the entry of free Negroes. The penalty for such entry was $500. North Carolina law restricted free Negroes from trading in certain articles, and required a license for them to peddle outside their county of residence.

In Maryland, a free Negro, upon release from prison, was given $30 and banished from the state. If he had not left by 60 days, he could be sold into slavery for the term of his original conviction.

Delaware enacted laws making it a crime for a runaway slave to enter the state, and forbidding Negroes from leaving the state without a legal pass. Penalties for kidnaping were $1,000 or more, one hour on the pillory, 60 lashes on the bare back, imprisonment for three years or more, and servitude for seven years after imprisonment.

A Pennsylvania law required a warrant for the arrest of a Negro and the examination of the Negro before a judge.

However, officials were required to aid the owner seeking his slave, and the Negro might be kept in jail while the owner gathered more evidence against him.

A free Negro of Westchester County, N.Y., Gilbert Horton, went ashore in Washington, D.C., while the ship on which he worked was in port there. He was seized and imprisoned as a runaway. A month later the marshal of Washington advertised for his owner to claim him; otherwise he would be sold for jail fees and other expenses. Horton was freed on a letter from Gov. DeWitt Clinton of N.Y. Later in the same year, he was arrested again. The sheriff paid the court costs and fees.

In this year there were 15 schools for Negro children in the District of the Synod of Kentucky of the Presbyterian Church.

Edward A. Jones of Charleston, S.C., graduated from Amherst College. He later became an Episcopal priest and went to Sierra Leone and helped found Fourah Bay College there.

John Russworm, a native of Jamaica, was graduated from Bowdoin College. In 1829 he went to Liberia to be Superintendent of Education. He went into politics instead, and served as Governor of Maryland Settlement in Liberia from 1836 to 1851.

Henry Highland Garnet attended school in New York after his escape from slavery in Maryland. He later was to become the pastor of a white congregation in Troy, N.Y. In 1848 Garnet published *The Past and Present Condition, and the Destiny of the Colored Race*. He also published *The National Watchman* with William G. Allen.

James Madison Bell (1826-1902), Negro poet, was born in Gallipolis, Ohio. He moved in 1842 to Cincinnati and in 1854 to Canada. A personal friend of John Brown, he assisted Brown in recruiting for his raid of 1859. In 1860 Bell moved to California, and there started writing poetry. His most successful poems were *The Day and the War* and *The Progress of Liberty*. In 1868 he left California for Toledo, Ohio, where he was elected delegate to the Ohio State Convention for Lucas County. He then became a delegate-at-large from Ohio to the National Republican Convention.

The African Observer, an anti-slavery journal, began publication in Philadelphia. *The National Philanthropist,* another anti-slavery journal, was founded by Collier in Boston.

Samuel E. Cornish, a free Negro in New York, wrote *A Remonstrance Against the Abuse of the Blacks,* which was printed in newspapers. He protested against the stereotype of Negroes as uneducated and of poor conduct, and claimed that lower-class whites were often worse.

1827

New York emancipated many of its slaves by statute; 10,000 slaves were freed. The New York Abolition Society arranged after abolition: (1) for house-to-house visitation of Negro families in N.Y.; (2) for the Dorcas Society of Colored Women to sew for the needy; (3) for a refuge for the children of destitute Negro parents. Along with the Washington (D.C.) Society, it petitioned Congress for the abolition of slavery.

Of the 130 abolition societies in the U.S., 106 were in Western Virginia, Tennessee, Kentucky and the southern part of the Northwest Territory. These 106 societies had 5,125 of the 6,625 members of all abolitionist societies.

The American Colonization Society sought a Congressional appropriation for colonization of Negroes in Liberia. Georgia and South Carolina were opposed and denied the right of Congress to use public money for such a purpose. Maryland, Kentucky, Ohio and Vermont gave their support.

In the Kentucky case of HART V. FANNY ANN, the principle that children born to a slave who had already been promised freedom were free was upheld.

Most new states, especially in the old Northwest Territory, either barred Negroes or required certified proof of freedom and the posting of a bond of $500 to $1,000 guaranteeing good behavior. This was done in Illinois in 1829, in Indiana in 1831, in the Michigan Territory in 1827, in Iowa Territory in 1839.

In the case of TRUSTEES OF THE QUAKER SOCIETY OF CONTENTNEA V. DICKENSON, the highest court in North Carolina decided that Quakers could not hold slaves on the grounds that a Quaker's owning a slave was tantamount to emancipation, and since state law allowed emancipation only for meritorious service, such ownership was invalid.

The editor of the *Delaware Weekly Advertiser* of Wilmington refused to publish an advertisement offering a reward for the return of a runaway slave.

In South Carolina, a free Negro woman and her three children became slaves because she aided two fugitive children aged six and nine years.

An attempt was made to form an abolition society at Smithfield, Va. The local magistrates broke up the meeting on the ground that since there was no law authorizing such a meeting, it must be illegal.

A Florida law restricted voting to whites.

An Illinois law passed in February declared all Negroes, mulattoes and Indians incompetent to be witnesses in any court case against a white person. A mulatto was defined as one with ¼ or more Negro blood. This law was re-enacted in 1845.

Alabama law stated that a slave might be punished by whipping and branding for manslaughter, if the victim was another slave.

The Presbyterian Synod of Ohio declared slaveholding a sufficient sin to exclude a man from communion.

Between this year and 1835, the Mormon attitude toward the Negroes changed. Initially, the Mormons, many of them from New England, New York and Ohio, had abolitionist leanings and believed in racial equality, as evident from Chapter 26, 2 Nephi, of the *Book of Mormon,* which says that all men, black and white, are alike with God. In 1835, Joseph Smith in the Book of Abraham part of the Pearls of Great Price, which the Mormons recognized as divinely inspired, stated that the descendants of Ham were cursed by Noah and could therefore not enter the priesthood. The curse of Ham was considered to be black skin; the Mormons also believed that Ham married a Negress who had the mark of Cain.

The Negro Baptist Church of St. Louis was founded.

The AME Church ordained Rev. Scipio Bean to do missionary work in Haiti.

Father Vanlomen, a Catholic priest of Holy Trinity Church, established a seminary for Negro girls in Georgetown, D.C.

Run by Maria Becraft, a Negro, it had between 30 and 35 pupils.

Freedom's Journal, the first Negro newspaper, began publication in New York City. It was owned and edited by Negroes; John Russworm and Rev. Samuel E. Cornish were editors.

The Investigator was founded by William Goodell in Providence, R.I. Among the reforms this publication advocated was the abolition of slavery. In 1829 it merged with the *National Philanthropist,* and in 1830 it moved to New York City as *The Genius of Temperance.*

In Cuba, Negroes represented 55.9% of the population. Of the total, 106,494 were free, and 286,942 were enslaved.

1828

William Lloyd Garrison, editor of the *Journal of the Times,* in Bennington, Vt., began his anti-slavery career.

Garrison, in *The National Philanthropist,* denounced slavery and the South Carolina bill prohibiting the instruction of slaves.

The *Free Press,* an anti-slavery journal, began publication in Bennington. *The Liberalist,* another anti-slavery journal, began publication in New Orleans.

The New England Weekly Review, an anti-slavery periodical, began publication.

The New York Manumission Society wrote to the American Convention of Abolition Societies: "We believe it is not the *color,* abstractly considered, which causes . . . prejudice; but the *condition* in which we have been accustomed to view the unfortunate [Negroes]. And hence, by a natural association, the mind connects with the color of the skin the idea of that debasement of character which is inseparable from their condition."

William Whipper, a Philadelphia Negro, helped to found a Reading Room Society in Philadelphia for educating Negroes and developing anti-slavery sentiment. The library was supported by monthly dues and an initiation fee. It would later include works of ancient and modern history, the *Laws of Pennsylvania, The Freedom's Journal* and *The Genius of Universal Emancipation.*

Theodore S. Wright a Negro, was graduated from Princeton Theological Seminary. He became pastor of a Presbyterian Church in New York, where he worked for the anti-slavery cause.

A three-day anti-slavery convention was held in Winchester, Va. Its meetings were public, widely advertised, held in the Town Hall; there was no opposition.

The citizens of Washington, D.C., presented a memorial with 1,060 signatures to the House of Representatives proposing gradual emancipation.

The Presbyterian Synod of Indiana sent a memorial to the General Assembly expressing belief in the immorality of slaveholding.

Two Missouri cases, LA GRANGE V. CHOUTEAU, and MILLY V. STEPHEN SMITH, were decided in accordance with the principle that freedom resulted when a slave was moved to a free state.

In the Virginia case of ISAAC V. WEST'S EX, it was decided that children born to a slave mother after she had been promised her freedom became free with her.

Postmaster General of the U.S. John McLean ruled that Negroes might be used to carry mail bags from stage coaches to post offices, provided that a responsible white person supervised. Since 1810, Negroes had been forbidden by Congress to be letter carriers.

The Negro Methodist Church in Boston was organized with Rev. Samuel Snowdon as pastor.

Christopher Rush became Bishop of the African Methodist Episcopal Zion Church upon the death of James Varick.

Morris Brown became Bishop of the African Methodist Episcopal Church in Philadelphia.

The Alabama Baptist Association purchased a slave named Caesar for $625, and sent him to preach the gospel among his people. He was the companion of James McLemore, a white evangelist.

New Haven, Conn., had 800 resident Negroes and 2 schools for them. Boston, Mass., had 3 schools for its 2,000 Negroes. Portland, Md., had 900 Negroes and one school. Philadelphia had 20,000 Negroes and 3 schools, and New York 15,000 Negroes and 2 schools. Some of these schools were supported by bequests. One in New Haven for 60 students was supported by public school money for 6 months of the year and by parents of students for the rest of the year. In Pennsylvania education of Negroes was at public expense under provisions for the education of poor children.

Free Negroes of Providence, R.I., petitioned for a separate school.

Robert Bannister (1828-1901), Negro painter, was born in Nova Scotia. He studied in Boston, and then worked in Providence, R.I., becoming the first Negro to achieve recognition as a painter. Specializing in marine landscapes, he won a medal at the Philadelphia Centennial Exposition in 1876 for *Under the Oaks*. *Narragansett Bay* and *After the Storm* are among his other works.

"Jim Crow," a song and dance act, was introduced by Thomas D. Rice, a white comedian from New York, who gave the first solo performance in black face in Louisville, Ky. Rice is called "the father of American minstrelsy." The character Jim Crow, based originally on a stable boy who lived behind Rice's theater, became a stock character in minstrel shows.

A census taken in Havana, Cuba, showed that 50% of the population was white, 10% mulatto and 40% Negro; 89% of the mulattoes and 40% of the Negroes were free.

1829

A riot in Cincinnati caused 1,200 Negroes to leave the city for Canada.

Members of the Negro Methodist Episcopal Church in Cincinnati refused to join in an appeal to the Legislature to repeal the "black laws." Instead, they asked for "a continuation of the smiles of the white people as we have hitherto enjoyed them."

An anti-Negro riot in Philadelphia was set off by a personal quarrel and the abolitionist speeches early in the year by a Scottish woman, Fanny Wright Darusmont.

Charles C. Pinckney of South Carolina defended slavery as no greater an evil than poverty. Gov. Stephen D. Miller of South Carolina called slavery "not a national evil" but a "national benefit."

In the Tennessee case of FIELD V. THE STATE OF TENNES-
SEE, Judge Whyte stated that a master had unlimited power
over the life of his slave and retained all rights except those
expressly taken away by municipal or state law.

The Massachusetts Legislature stated that removal of the
Negro would be beneficial to the country and endorsed the
American Colonization Society.

In Louisiana the decision in PILIE V. LALANDE ET AL. confirmed the principle that presumption of slavery and thus
burden of proof was confined to Negroes as opposed to mulattoes and others with some white blood. In this case, actual
enjoyment of freedom was considered *prima facie* evidence of
freedom.

Georgia law provided punishment by fine and/or whipping
(the fine up to $500 and imprisonment for a white person)
for teaching a Negro, slave or free, to read or write.

Ohio law excluded Negroes from public schools, but returned to Negroes the school taxes paid on their property
holdings.

Illinois forbade marriage between Negroes and whites.

Georgia law made any ship carrying free persons of color
subject to a 40-day quarantine.

Charles Miner of Pennsylvania introduced resolutions in
the House of Representatives calling for investigation of
slavery in Washington, D.C., and for gradual abolition. These
were passed, but produced no law.

In Virginia, in HUNTER V. FULCHER, a slave who was taken
to Maryland for a number of years and then returned to
Virginia was declared free on the ground that Maryland law
forbade importation of slaves from other states.

In the Virginia case of DAVENPORT V. THE COMMON-
WEALTH, it was decided that stealing a free boy to sell him
into slavery was punishable as kidnaping, even if the offender
did not know the boy was free or even if the boy consented.

Walker's Appeal, in Four Articles by David Walker, a free
Negro of Boston, was published. This anti-slavery pamphlet
called upon slaves to revolt against their oppressors. Walker
was born in North Carolina of a free Negro woman and a
slave. He had opened a second-hand clothing store in Boston

in 1827, and died in 1830. In March, 1830, the third edition of *Walker's Appeal* was published.

Robert Alexander Young, a Negro, published a pamphlet called *An Ethiopian Manifesto*. It condemned slavery in biblical language, and prophesied the coming of a black Messiah who would forcibly liberate his people.

The New York African Clarkson Society was established by Negroes to foster anti-slavery opinions.

Freedom's Journal, after editor John Russworm left for Liberia, became *Rights of All,* under the editorship of Samuel Cornish.

William Lloyd Garrison, in *The Genius of Universal Emancipation,* declared himself for immediate emancipation.

Mississippi law provided for the care of children of poor free Negroes and mulattoes in the same way as poor white children.

Negroes established the Dixwell Avenue Congressional Church in New Haven, Conn.

The African Improvement Society in New Haven, Conn., supported a church, a Sunday school with average attendance of 80, Bible classes and an evening school.

Daniel A. Payne, a Negro, opened a school for Negro children which soon became "the most successful institution of its kind in Charleston, S.C." It was discontinued in 1834, when South Carolina law forbade free Negroes teaching slaves or free Negroes. Payne was the son of free Negroes in Charleston. He had attended Minor's Moralist Society School, established by free Negroes, had been tutored by Thomas Bonneau, and had mastered English, mathematics, Greek, Latin and French. He worked for four years in the carpentry shop where his brother-in-law was foreman. He later became a bishop of the AME Church.

St. Francis Academy for Colored Girls was founded in Baltimore, in affiliation with the Oblate Sisters of Providence Convent, and with the support of the Archbishop of Baltimore, the Most Rev. James Whitfield. The school was partly for Negro Catholic refugees from Santo Domingo who had come to Baltimore in considerable numbers in the 1790's. The Sisters of Providence was a society of Negro women dedicated to Christian education of Negro girls.

The African Free School for boys was established in Baltimore and taught between 150 and 175 students every Sunday.

Edward Mitchell, a Negro, was graduated from Dartmouth College.

Thomas B. Dalton, a Boston Negro bootblack, later became proprietor of a clothing shop on Brattle Street and left property of over $50,000 at his death.

John B. Vashon, a Negro veteran of the War of 1812, moved with his family to Pittsburgh where he helped establish the first public baths in the city.

James Theodore Holly (1829-1911), Bishop of the Protestant Episcopal Church, was born in Washington, D.C., of free Negro parents. In 1844 he moved to New York and attended school there. Between 1851 and 1853 he was associate editor of the *Voice of the Fugitive,* published in Windsor, Canada. In 1854, he was appointed as public school principal in Buffalo, N.Y. Instrumental in arranging the National Immigration Convention of Colored Men at Cleveland, Ohio, in 1854, he led a group wanting to go to Haiti. Upon returning from Haiti, he made a report to the Immigration Convention. In 1857, Holly published *A Vindication of the Capacity of the Negro Race for Self-Government and Civilized Progress,* a lecture based on the history of Haiti. Holly in 1861, again sailed for Haiti with a shipload of emigrants. They left from Philadelphia for Port-au-Prince. Of the 2,000 on board, only a third survived the trip. In the same year Holly was consecrated Bishop of Haiti.

John Mercer Langston, (1829-1897), Negro Congressman, was born a slave in Louisa County, Va. Freed on the death of his father, a white estate owner, he was sent to Ohio and educated in private schools. A graduate of Oberlin College, he also studied theology and law, and was admitted to the Ohio bar in 1854. During the Civil War he left his practice in Brownhelm, Ohio, to recruit for the USCT. He was inspector general of the Freedmen's Bureau and, from 1869 to 1876, dean of Howard University. From 1877 to 1885 he served in the diplomatic corps as Minister Resident to Haiti and chargé d'affaires to Santo Domingo. On returning to the U.S., he was chosen president of the Virginia Normal and Collegiate Institute, and elected to the House of Representatives in 1888. His works include *Freedom and Citizenship*

(1883), a collection of his speeches, and *From the Virginia Plantation to the National Capitol* (1894), an autobiography.

James Hemmenway, a Negro composer, wrote a song, "That Rest So Sweet Like Bliss Above," which was published in *Casket-Flowers of Literature, Wit and Sentiment*, a journal.

Slavery was abolished in Mexico. American pressure forced its reinstitution in Texas (which then belonged to Mexico).

1830

By this date slavery in the North had been virtually abolished by legislative, judicial, or constitutional action. (North defined as north of Mason-Dixon line). But 3,568 Negroes still remained as slaves, two-thirds of them in New Jersey.

U.S. Census: Negro population in the United States was 2,328,642 or 18.1% of the total U.S. population. 319,599 Negroes (13.7%) were free. 57% of all free Negroes lived in the Southern states and Washington, D. C. The free Negro population was distributed as follows:

Maine	1,190	Louisiana	16,710
New Hampshire	604	Tennessee	4,555
Massachusetts	7,048	Kentucky	4,917
Rhode Island	3,561	Ohio	9,568
Connecticut	8,047	Indiana	3,628
Vermont	881	Illinois	1,637
New York	44,870	Missouri	569
New Jersey	18,303	Michigan	261
Pennsylvania	37,930	Arkansas	141
Delaware	15,855	Florida	844
Maryland	52,938	Washington, D.C.	6,152
Virginia	47,348	Boston	1,875
North Carolina	19,543	New York City	14,083
South Carolina	7,921	Philadelphia	9,796
Georgia	2,486	Baltimore	14,790
Alabama	1,572	Charleston	2,106
Mississippi	519	New Orleans	11,906

Of the free Negroes in North Carolina, mostly living in the coastal counties, only about 4% lived in the nine largest towns of the state. The free Negroes amounted to 2.6% of the total state population, and Negro slaves numbered 245,601, or 33.1% of the total population.

The United States Census Bureau reported that 3,777

Negroes were heads of families who owned slaves, mostly in Louisiana, Maryland, Virginia, North Carolina and South Carolina.

In Louisiana free Negroes owned sugar and cotton plantations with slaves, had prosperous businesses, practiced many professions and trades, educated their children both in private schools and by private teachers. They also sent their children to northern and French schools. Approximately 750 free Negroes in New Orleans owned slaves. A free Negro, named McCarty, owned 32 slaves, the largest number for one individual. Martin Donato of Plaquemine Brulé, a free Negro, upon his death in 1845 left 89 slaves, 4,500 arpents of land, and personal property valued at $46,000.

James Forten helped to assemble a national convention of free Negroes, "to consider the plight of the free Negro, to plan his social redemption, and . . . to strike again at the colonization idea." Forten was attempting to shift Negro opinion from emigration to abolition. He was also influential in persuading Garrison and Weld of the racial equality of the Negro. This convention, the first national Negro convention was held in September, at the Bethel African Methodist Episcopal Church in Philadelphia. Bishop Richard Allen was chosen President; Belfast Burton of Philadelphia and Austin Seward of Rochester were Vice-Presidents. Junius C. Morell of Pennsylvania was Secretary. Each state was represented by seven delegates. A Free Produce Society was formed to encourage free labor by pledging not to use slave-produced goods. 230 people signed such an agreement.

Citizens of Maine petitioned the United States Senate, to abolish slavery in Washington, D.C.

Quakers in North Carolina owned 402 slaves, the majority of whom had been received from masters who wanted to be rid of them but could not manumit them because of the rigidity of state law. The Quakers gave the slaves virtual freedom and sent them to free states when possible, often at considerable expense. In North Carolina the process of emancipation was complicated and required a freedman to leave the state within 90 days unless he was freed for "meritorious service."

An anti-slavery publication in New Orleans, the *Liberalist*, was published by Milo Mower. Mower was imprisoned for circulating handbills advertising the paper.

William Swain of North Carolina wrote an address to the people of North Carolina on the evils of slavery. He was editor of the *Greensboro Patriot* which advocated manumission and published anti-slavery material. He also was manager of the Manumission Society of North Carolina. He had assisted Lundy in the publication of *The Genius of Universal Emancipation* for about six months in 1827 and 1828.

There were 50 Negro anti-slavery societies in the United States. After this year the number of manumissions declined because of legislation restricting manumission and because of changed slave-owner attitudes.

The Missouri case of VINCENT v. JAMES DUNCAN affirmed the principle that removal of a slave to a free state granted him freedom.

In the Kentucky case of FANNY v. BRYANT, it was decided that children of a slave mother promised freedom became free with her if they were born after the date of the promise.

Virginia exported 8,500 slaves annually at this time. The slave trade became a profitable business between 1830 and 1860; Virginia alone exported close to 300,000 slaves and South Carolina about 179,000.

In January, 80 out of 200 Negroes in Portsmouth, Ohio, were driven out of town.

Ohio law made Negroes ineligible for service in the state militia.

The President of a "Mechanical Association" in Cincinnati was publicly tried by the association for assisting a Negro boy to learn a trade.

Citizens of Philadelphia urged expulsion of Negroes from the city and state.

From 1830 to 1832 many state laws were enacted forbidding instruction of slaves, limiting Negro preachers, forbidding assembly of Negroes except when supervised by whites, limiting slave hiring, forbidding drums, whistles and musical instruments. These laws required prompt deportation of freed slaves and limited vocations and movement of freed Negroes.

Louisiana required all free Negroes except those who were there before 1825 to leave the state within 60 days. This same law provided imprisonment at hard labor for life or the death penalty for the writing, printing, publishing or distributing of "anything having a tendency to produce discontent among the free colored population, or insubordination among the slaves." It also provided a penalty of one month to one year imprisonment for teaching, or permitting, or causing to be taught, any slave to read and write.

After 1830, Louisiana protested that slaves were escaping to Mexico.

Mississippi law forbade employment of Negroes in printing offices and prohibited Negroes from keeping a house of entertainment.

A resolution in the Kentucky legislature to call a convention to amend the constitution, the avowed purpose of which was to provide for abolition, lost by one vote.

Kentucky law taxed all inhabitants of each school district, according to property, for support of common schools. However, Negroes were not allowed to vote or to use the schools although they paid taxes.

Mr. Shay, an Englishman, who ran a school for Negroes in Georgetown and later in Washington, D.C., was sent to prison for helping a slave gain his freedom.

Negroes of Hartford, Connecticut, requested a separate school because of the "intolerant spirit of the whites" which made it difficult for them to attend ordinary schools.

William Wormley, a wealthy Negro who owned the largest livery stable in Washington, built a school house for his sister, Mary Wormley, to operate. Miss Wormley however, soon became ill and died. An Englishman, Mr. Calvert, taught there for a time. In 1834, William Thomas Lee established a school in the building. In the riots of 1835 the building was sacked and partly destroyed by fire. William Wormley and Lee were forced to flee. Wormley's health and business declined under continued persecution.

James Augustine Healy (1830-1900) was the first Negro Roman Catholic priest in America and the first Negro to become a Catholic Bishop in the United States. Healy's father was an Irish planter, his mother a slave. In 1837, he was sent to a Quaker School in New York. He graduated from Holy Cross College in 1849. Healy was ordained in 1854 in Paris.

He became in 1875 Bishop of Portland, Me. His brother Patrick Francis Healy served as President of Georgetown University from 1873 to 1882.

James Whitfield (1830-1870) was born in Massachusetts but moved to Buffalo, a center of the abolitionist movement in the 1850's. With his friend and co-worker, Martin Delany, he engaged in a newspaper controversy with Frederick Douglass. In his book, *America and Other Poems*, the most successful poems were those which were blatantly propagandist. In the title poem, Whitfield pungently wrote of American hypocrisy. Stylistically, Whitfield's colorful work bears its greatest resemblance to Byron.

New York Negroes founded the New York Philomathean Society, a literary and debating society. It later developed into the Odd Fellows Lodge.

In this decade more than 400,000 Negro slaves were brought to Brazil to work on the very successful coffee plantations. Coffee production was growing so fast that 600,000 were imported in 1848 alone.

Luis Gonzaga de Pinto Gama (1830-1882), the Brazilian poet, was an ex-slave who had been taught to read by his master's friend at the age of 17. He became a lawyer, defending fugitive slaves in Brazil, and preached slave revolts. In his poetry, he is the first poet to glorify black women over white in such poems as *Junto a Estatua* and *Laura*. Gama also wrote satires about Negroes who tried to pass for white, *Pacotilha* and *Bodarrada*. Luis Gama was the first Negro writer to advocate something like negritude, or black pride.

1831

The first Annual Convention of the People of Color was held in Philadelphia June 6th to June 11th at Wesleyan Church on Lombard Street. John Bowers of Philadelphia was President, Abraham D. Shadd of Delaware and William Duncan of Virginia were Vice-Presidents. William Whipper of Philadelphia was Secretary and Thomas Jennings of New York Assistant Secretary. Delegates from five states attended. They resolved to (1) study conditions of free Negroes; (2) study settlement in Canada; (3) recommend annual conventions of free Negroes; (4) oppose the American Colonization Society; (5) approve raising of money for a proposed industrial college in New Haven, provided Negroes had a majority of at least one on the board of trustees.

The *Liberator*, edited by William Lloyd Garrison, began publication on New Year's day in Boston. The avowed purposes of the *Liberator* were abolition of slavery and the moral and intellectual elevation of the Negro. The corporation of Georgetown in Washington, D. C., passed ordinances forbidding free Negroes to take copies of the *Liberator* from the Post Office. The penalty for doing so was 25 lashes and imprisonment and possible sale into slavery.

In June William Lloyd Garrison published his *Address Delivered Before the Free People of Color in Philadelphia, New York and Other Cities* in which he urged them to sell and buy with each other in preference to whites, to vote whenever possible and if possible, vote for Negroes.

The New England Anti-slavery Society was founded by Garrison and other whites.

By this year the American Colonization Society had sent 1,420 Negroes to Africa.

In the debates in the Virginia legislature of 1831 to 1832, Thomas Dew said with pride that "Virginia is in fact a Negro-raising state for other states" and that raising slaves was "one of their greatest sources of profit."

A slave rebellion broke out under the leadership of Nat Turner, a literate Virginia slave whose chief disciples were Henry Porter, Hark Travis, Nelson Williams and Samuel Francis. A group of 20 to 30 slaves massacred some 50 whites in Southampton County, Virginia. Approximately 3,000 armed men responded to the uprising and a wholesale slaughter of Negroes ensued. Turner was captured and hanged on November 11, 1831, in Jerusalem, Virginia.

The Confession of Nat Turner, edited by Thomas R. Gray, was published in Baltimore. Its confessional and autobiographical nature made it a prototype for an important genre in American Negro literature.

From Nat Turner's Rebellion to the outbreak of the Civil War, the slave was set upon by stringent enforcement of slave codes, further reduction in educational opportunities, and almost complete suspension of manumission. This period also saw the decline of the "repatriation" movement sponsored by the American Colonization Society.

U.S. Attorney General John Berrien found the South Carolina Negro Seamen Act of 1822 to be a constitutional exercise of a state's police power to "regulate persons of color within its own limits." The next Attorney General Roger Taney also upheld the act in the face of British protest and affirmed the legal inferiority of all Negroes in the United States. Anticipating his Dred Scott decision of 25 years later as Chief Justice of the U.S. Supreme Court, he claimed that Negroes had no constitutional rights because the framers of the Constitution did not regard them as citizens.

A mob descended on a Negro area in Providence, R.I. In the encounter that followed, a white sailor was killed by a shot fired by a Negro defending himself against the mob. Violence erupted again the following day; the militia was called in but repulsed by stones thrown by the white mob. On the fourth day of violence, two companies of militia were called in and finally stopped the mob by firing into the crowd, killing four rioters and wounding 14. 18 houses were destroyed. This riot was precipitated by the reaction of whites against employment of Negro workers.

Ohio law prevented Negroes from serving on juries.

In the Ohio case of POLLY GRAY v. OHIO, the State Supreme Court ruled that a person having more white blood than Negro blood was white, and thus not subject to "black laws." The case involved eligibility of a Negro as a witness in the trial of a quadroon. This decision was upheld in 1834 in WILLIAMS v. DIRECTORS OF SCHOOL DISTRICT #6.

North Carolina law required all Negro traders and peddlers to be licensed.

South Carolina law forbade manufacture or sale of liquor by Negroes.

Indiana law required Negroes entering the state to give bond, provided for hiring out and possible expulsion of Negroes who failed to comply, also provided a penalty for harboring Negroes who had not given bond and guaranteed the right of a slave owner to carry his slaves through Indiana.

Mississippi law forbade free Negroes to remain in the state. Mississippi law also forbade any slave or free Negro from preaching the gospel except to Negroes in his own neighborhood with written permission of his master and with six respectable white slave owners present. Penalty was 39 lashes.

A New Haven, Connecticut, town meeting voted by about 700 to 4 to exclude a proposed Negro college from the city. The proposed college, for instructing Negroes in agriculture, mechanical arts, science, etc., was to be under the leadership of Simon Jocelyn and Arthur Tappan.

A Negro grammar school was established by the city of Boston in the North End. However, it was discontinued in 1835 because of low attendance caused by the movement of Negroes from North End to the western part of the city.

James Walker Hood (1831-1918) was a Bishop of the African Methodist Episcopal Zion Church. Hood was granted in 1856 a license to preach. In 1860, he was ordained Deacon in Boston and sailed for Halifax, Nova Scotia. He returned to the United States in 1863 when he became a member of the Reconstruction Constitutional Convention. Hood was ordained a Bishop in 1872. His published works were: *The Negro in the Christian Pulpit* (1884), *One Hundred Years of the Methodist Episcopal Zion Church* (1895), *The Plan of the Apocalypse* (1900).

For a little over a year, a Negro newspaper, *The African Sentinel and Journal of Liberty*, was published in Albany, N. Y. by John E. Stewart.

Negro women in Philadelphia founded the Female Literary Society. This society had 20 members in 1832. The members wrote literary pieces which the group criticized.

Slavery was prohibited in the Bolivian Constitution of that year.

1832

Negroes in Philadelphia owned $350,000 worth of taxable property.

A group of Philadelphia Negroes met to protest legislative efforts to curtail liberties of Negroes. They declared that Negroes formed 8% of the population of the city but only 4% of its paupers. They also claimed that 400 to 500 Negroes were mechanics despite the prejudices and difficulties they encountered in learning trades.

In Philadelphia the Second Convention of People of Color met in Benezet Hall on June 4 and the next day in the First African Presbyterian Church. They resolved to establish a society or agent to purchase land in Canada for Negroes "who may be, by oppressive enactments, obliged to flee from these

United States," and to raise money to aid the project. Eight states were represented at this convention by 30 delegates. The convention opposed national aid to the American Colonization Society and urged the abolition of slavery in Washington, D. C.

There were American Colonization Society chapters in every state except Rhode Island and South Carolina.

When the New England Anti-slavery Society was founded in Boston, about one-quarter of the first 72 members were Negroes.

The address by Judge William Gaston to the graduating class of the University of North Carolina referred to slavery as "the worst evil that affects the southern part of our Confederacy" and urged its "extirpation."

By this year slave prices, due to the increase in demand for slaves in the Southwestern states, improved methods of agriculture, and the employment of slaves for work in factories, had increased sharply. A rise of 25% in prices over the previous three years reflected the increased value the South placed on slave labor. This increase in value was one of the reasons for a new atmosphere of antagonism against any anti-slavery opinion voiced in either the North or the South.

The average price of a prime field hand 18 to 25 years old was about $500.

Two hundred Negroes emigrated from New York to Trinidad.

Thomas Dew, as editor of a pro-slavery paper, used historical, theological, and anthropological arguments in defense of slavery. These views were readily accepted in the deep South. Dew denied the possibility or advisability of solving the slavery problem by colonization. He supplied many former anti-slaverites, such as Thomas Ritchie, James Paulding, Joseph Gales and Edmund Ruffin, with rationalization for reaffirming slavery.

Alabama law set a fine of $250 to $500 for teaching any free Negro or slave to read, write or spell and set punishment by flogging for any free Negro who associated with slaves without written permission from the owners or overseer of the slaves. It prohibited assembling of more than five male slaves at any place off the plantation to which they belonged except in places of public worship in the presence of white persons. No slave or free Negro could "preach, exhort, or harangue" any slave or free Negro except in the presence of five "respectable slave holders," unless the person preaching was licensed by a Christian body of the neighborhood and the listeners were members of that body.

Virginia law labeled all meetings of free Negroes for teaching, reading, or writing as "unlawful assembly" and authorized magistrates to break up such meetings and inflict up to 20 lashes on offenders. The same law provided fines of $10 to $100 for a white person teaching slaves. The law was strictly enforced whereas the 1819 law forbidding teaching of slaves and free Negroes had not been.

Prudence Crandall admitted a Negro girl, Sarah Harris, to her school in Canterbury, Connecticut. The townspeople protested and white students were withdrawn. Miss Crandall admitted more Negroes. The Connecticut legislature passed a law forbidding a school for Negroes who were not residents of the state without written permission of town selectmen. Miss Crandall was imprisoned and ostracized. The school was vandalized and demolished.

When Charles B. Ray, a Negro, entered Wesleyan University in Middletown, Conn., the students protested until he agreed to leave. Ray went to New York where he opened a boot and shoe store.

The New York African Free School had 862 pupils.

Negroes in Pittsburgh, Pennsylvania, founded the Pittsburgh African Education Society.

Negroes formed a Sunday School in Washington, D.C., in the Smothers School-House, after Negro children were expelled from Sabbath schools and white churches.

William Paul Quinn began his work as a circuit preacher and missionary of the AME Church in Western Pennsylvania, Ohio, Indiana and Illinois. By 1844 he had established 47 churches with a membership of two thousand.

Providence Negroes organized the Providence Temperance Society. At one time this society had approximately 200 members.

Joseph Hayne Rainey (1832-1887), Negro Congressman from South Carolina, was a barber at the outbreak of the

Civil War. In 1862, Confederate authorities drafted him to work on the fortifications of Charleston. He escaped and went to the West Indies. In 1867, after returning to the U.S., he became a member of the executive committee of the newly formed Republican Party of South Carolina. The following year he was elected a delegate from Georgetown to the State Constitutional Convention. He was elected to the State Senate. In 1870, Rainey was elected to the U.S. House of Representatives. He took the place of B. F. Whittemore, whose credentials the House had refused to accept. He continued to serve until 1879, when he was replaced by a Democrat.

John Chavis published a sermon in North Carolina called *The Extent of the Atonement*, which sold widely. Chavis was a Negro who had studied privately with President Witherspoon at the College of New Jersey, later Princeton University, and had become a minister and teacher of both whites and Negroes in North Carolina.

The establishment of literary societies by Negroes in Philadelphia continued. One was the Library Company, another was the Banneker Society.

Boston Negro women organized the Afric-American Female Intelligence Society. In that year the society was addressed by Maria Steward, "probably the first Negro woman lecturer and writer."

1833

The American Anti-slavery Society was formed in Philadelphia by Negroes and whites. Among the Negroes who helped organize it were Robert Purvis, a wealthy young man who lived in a suburb of Philadelphia; James McCrummell, a Philadelphia dentist; and James G. Barbadoes, a Boston reformer. There were three Negroes on the first executive committee. They were: Samuel E. Cornish, minister and editor; Theodore S. Wright, a minister in New York; Peter S. Williams, an Episcopal priest.

John B. Vashon, a Negro veteran of the War of 1812, organized the "first Anti-slavery Society west of the mountains" in Pittsburgh. He also promoted the foundation of an educational institution and was its first president.

In the North Carolina case of STATE v. EDMUND, Judge Daniel upheld the right of a free Negro to own slaves when he stated: "By the laws of this State, a free man of color may own land and hold lands and personal property including slaves."

Solomon Humphries, a free Negro, operated a successful grocery store in Macon, Georgia. He had about $20,000 worth of property and several slaves.

An English visitor to New York City reported that most Negroes were Whigs and anti-Jackson.

Letters on Slavery by James D. Paxton, a Virginia Presbyterian minister, were published. The letters were intended to prove the "moral evil of slavery" and "the duty of Christians" to free the slaves.

Virginia law established a colonization board to be supported by a poll tax on free Negroes. The board's function was to deport Negroes to Liberia.

James Madison, long an advocate of the emigration of free Negroes, became president of the American Colonization Society.

Mormons were driven out of Independence, Mo., because the local inhabitants thought that the Mormons were trying to free the slaves.

The Charleston, S. C., *Courier* called slavery a blessing and necessary for agriculture.

An attack on Negroes in Detroit was set off by the rescue of Thornton Blackburn and his wife from arrest as fugitive slaves.

A Savannah, Ga., ordinance provided fines up to $100 or a whipping of up to 39 lashes for a slave or free Negro who taught a slave or free Negro to read or write, or who kept a school for that purpose.

A penalty of $100 was provided by Georgia for employing a Negro, slave or free, to set type or to perform any labor in a printing office that required a knowledge of reading or writing.

Delaware law imposed a tax of $5 for every slave sold out of the state, and every slave brought into the state. The money provided for the education of white children. No provision was made for the education of Negro children.

Connecticut law forbade the establishment of a school for

Negroes not inhabitants of Connecticut, and forbade boarding any Negro for instruction who was not an inhabitant of the town where the school was located without written consent of a majority of the magistrates and selectmen of the town. This law was repealed in 1838.

Oberlin College, which admitted both white and Negro students, was founded. When Professor Asa Mahan of Lane Seminary was offered the presidency of Oberlin in 1835, he accepted on condition that Negroes be accepted on equal terms with others. By the outbreak of the Civil War, Negroes made up one-third of the student body at Oberlin.

The Alabama Legislature authorized the mayor and aldermen of Mobile, Alabama, to grant licenses to persons to instruct the children of "free colored Creoles." The children instructed had to have a certificate from the mayor and aldermen. The reason for this exception from the general Alabama Law of 1832 forbidding instruction of Negroes was the treaty of 1803 with France in which the rights of citizenship had been guaranteed to Creoles.

James Enoch Ambush, a Negro, established a school for Negroes in the basement of the Israel Bethel Church on Capitol Hill. He later, in 1843, established a school in Washington known as the Wesleyan Seminary.

Benjamin M. McCoy, a Negro, opened a school for Negroes on L Street in Washington, D. C. He left in 1836 to run the free public Colored School in Lancaster County, Pa., but returned to Washington in 1837 and re-opened his school in the basement of Asbury Church, remaining there for twelve years.

Fanny Hampton, a Negro, opened a school for Negroes in the same year on the corner of K and 19th Street.

Mr. Talbot, a white man, opened a school for Negroes in a private house in the rear of Franklin Row, Washington, D. C.

New York Negroes organized the Phoenix Society, a literary society. The group started ward societies whose functions included registering all Negroes in the ward, urging them to join the society and to attend school, maintaining a circulating library in the ward and procuring employment for those with skills. The society conducted an evening school for adults and also a high school for Negroes.

The Presbyterian Synod of South Carolina and Georgia stated that at this time in the South there were "not twelve men exclusively devoted to the religious instruction of the Negroes," and there were only five Negro churches in the South and not enough room for Negroes in the white churches. They also stated that no Bibles were available for Negroes.

Publication began of *O Homem de Cor*, the first newspaper devoted to Brazilian Negroes. As its motto it published a quotation from the Imperial Constitution on the masthead: "Every citizen may be admitted to civil, political and military public offices, with no qualifications except those of his talents and virtues." The periodical lasted five issues and was in the forefront of the abolition movement. Its importance lies in that it was the first Latin American periodical devoted exclusively to Negroes, and its publisher was a Negro.

The British Act of August 1833 gave the slave holders in the West Indies compensation of £20,000,000 for the abolition of slavery. All children younger than six years, or all new-born were freed. All slaves became free but house slaves had to work for their old masters for five years and the plantation slaves were to work for seven years before freedom. At this time there were 800,000 slaves in the British West Indies. On the Isle of Antigua the Negroes were set free immediately.

1834

In mid-summer a group of whites estimated between 400 and 500 entered the Flying Horse, an amusement area in the Negro quarter of Philadelphia, and attempted to drive the Negroes out. In the ensuing street fight, the whites were driven off. The following night a regrouped mob went through the Negro quarter destroying homes and personal property and beating Negroes. On the third night of rioting the mob was dispersed by the mayor and sheriff, supported by a posse. One Negro, Stephen James, was killed; 31 houses and two churches were destroyed. The town meeting of September 15 condemned the riots and voted reimbursements for the damage done but also condemned the defense of fugitive slaves by Negroes and the noise in the Negro churches. The cause of

the riots was generally laid to the hiring of Negro workers
and the unemployment of whites. It was recommended that
Negroes take care to behave "inoffensively" and not to be
"obtrusive" in passing along the streets or in assembling
together. The Philadelphia riot was followed by riots in
Columbia, Pa., Trenton, N.J., Rochester, N.Y., Southwark,
Lancaster and Bloomfield, N.J.

After a white mob in Columbia, Pa., destroyed homes in
the Negro section, a meeting of white workingmen blamed
the riot on abolitionist attempts to amalgamate the races.
They agreed on a boycott of merchants who hired Negroes
to do white labor. Later a group of white leaders met with
Negro property owners to urge them to sell their property at
"a fair valuation" to local whites. Mob violence continued
meanwhile. A wealthy Negro coal and lumber dealer was
prompted by this to sell his stock at a loss and to close his
business.

A Palmyra, New York, citizens meeting in October resolved that owners of houses and tenements occupied by
Negroes of poor character be requested to use all rightful
means to remove these tenants and not to rent thereafter to
any person of color.

The *Liberator* reported a petition of a group of New Haven
citizens complaining that the movement of Negroes into previously white areas made real estate values fall by 20 to 50%.

In Utica, New York, a mob drove delegates to an anti-
slavery meeting out of town.

Bishop Onderdonk of the New York Diocese of the Protestant Episcopal Church strongly urged Rev. Peter Williams,
a Negro, of St. Philips Episcopal Church in New York to
resign from the American Anti-slavery Society so that the
Church might avoid controversial issues and maintain itself
"on the Christian side of meekness, order and self-sacrifice to
common good, and the peace of the community." Williams
complied.

From this year on Negro preachers were gradually outlawed in many Southern states and slaves were required to
attend the church of their masters.

The New York City Zoological Institute in a pamphlet
describing its animals stated that "people of color are not

permitted to enter except when in attendance upon children and families."

The New Jersey Constitution confined suffrage to whites.

South Carolina law forbade teaching a slave to read or write, aiding him to read or write, or keeping a school for teaching slaves or free Negroes. Penalty was a fine up to $100 and imprisonment up to six months for whites, up to $50 fine and up to 50 lashes for free Negroes and up to 50 lashes for slaves. The informer was declared a competent witness and given one-half of the fine. This same law restricted the employment of Negroes as clerks and salesmen.

A group of Connecticut citizens petitioned the legislature for entry restrictions against Negroes to prevent a great influx of cheap Negro labor that would drive out the "sons of Connecticut."

Among 396 slaves, owned by Franklin and Armfield, shipped to New Orleans in this year and the next, there were only two full families, 20 husbandless mothers with 33 children among them ranging from two weeks to twelve years.

A Convention of People of Color met in New York. It set aside July 4th as a day of prayer and addresses on the condition of the Negro.

"Les Artisans," an organization of free colored mechanics, was incorporated in New Orleans. Victor Sejour, later a Negro poet and dramatist, was a member.

William Lloyd Garrison reported that three-quarters of the subscribers to the *Liberator* were Negroes.

Theodore Weld reported that approximately 75% of 3,000 Negroes in Cincinnati had "worked out their own freedom."

The Tennessee Constitution in 1834 declared free Negroes exempt from military duty in peace time and from paying the poll tax.

Robert Purvis and his wife, Negroes of Philadelphia, received passports stating that they were citizens of the United States.

An academy for Negroes opened at Canaan, N.H., with 28 white and 14 Negro students.

The New York African Free School was transferred from the Manumission Society to the New York Public School

Society. At that time the New York African Free School property was appraised at $12,130.22. The registration was almost 1,400 pupils, although average attendance was about half that number. After the transfer the Negro schools declined apparently because of the 1834 riots and because the Public School Society was less well known among Negroes than the Manumission Society. Also, the Public School Society had discontinued some practices of the school and dismissed some teachers.

John B. Vashon, a Negro, was elected president of a temperance society and of a Moral Reform Society in Pittsburgh.

Henry Blair of Maryland, a Negro, patented a corn harvester.

William Wells Brown, a Negro, escaped to Ohio and began steam boating on Lake Erie.

Rufus Lewis Perry (1834-1895), a Negro Baptist clergyman, missionary, educator and journalist, was born a slave in Smith County, Tenn. His parents, Lewis and Mary Perry, were slaves of Archibald Overton. Lewis Perry was a Baptist preacher and an able mechanic and carpenter. He was allowed to work in Nashville where Rufus attended school until his father ran away to Canada. The family was forced to return to the plantation. In 1852 Rufus Perry was sold to a slave dealer who intended to take him to Mississippi. Rufus escaped and went to Canada. He became a teacher and was ordained a minister in 1861. Perry served as editor of the *Sunbeam* and of the *People's Journal*. He was co-editor of the *American Baptist* from 1869 until 1871. From 1872 to 1895 he was joint editor of *The National Monitor*. In 1887 he was awarded a Ph.D. from the State University at Louisville, Ky. In 1893 he published a book entitled *The Cushite; or the Descendants of Ham as seen by Ancient Historians.*

Alonzo J. Ransier (1834-1882), Negro Congressman, was born of free parents in Charleston, S.C. Before the Civil War, he worked as a shipping clerk. In 1865 he served as Registrar of Elections, in 1866 attended the first Republican Convention in South Carolina, and then went to Washington, D.C., to lobby for federal protection of Negroes. A presidential elector and chairman of the State Executive Committee in 1868, he was chosen Lt. Governor of South Carolina in 1870. Ransier was elected to the House of Representatives in 1873, where he worked for civil rights protection, national tariff, a 6-year presidential term and funds to improve Charleston Harbor. He returned to Charleston in 1875 and worked as a day-laborer for the city.

Henry McNeal Turner (1834-1915), Bishop of the AME Church and an editor and author, was born near Abbeville, S.C. He worked in cotton fields after his father's death and was apprenticed to a blacksmith. Turner learned to read at 15, and was later employed by a law firm where he learned to write. In 1853, after joining the Methodist Episcopal Church, he was licensed to preach. He became a successful revivalist among Negroes and was ordained a deacon in 1860 and an elder in 1862. Installed as pastor of the Israel Church in Washington, he was appointed by President Lincoln in 1863 army chaplain attached to the First Regiment of Colored Troops. President Johnson appointed him chaplain in the regular army. He resigned in order to build up the AME Church in Georgia. Turner was one of the founders of the Republican Party of Georgia and was elected delegate to the Georgia Constitutional Convention of 1867. In 1869 he was appointed Postmaster at Macon, Ga., by President Grant. He relinquished this post because of the opposition of whites. Serving as a customs inspector and government detective, he then in 1876 became manager of the African Methodist Episcopal Book Concern in Philadelphia. From 1880 through 1892 Turner served as Bishop of his Church for Georgia. For the next twelve years he was chancellor of Morris Brown College in Atlanta, Ga. Turner traveled widely and visited South and West Africa where he introduced African Methodism. He became an advocate for the return of Negroes to Africa. He also founded several periodicals: in 1889 *The Southern Christian Recorder* and in 1892 the *Voice of the Missions*. He published in 1885 *The Genius and Method of Methodist Policy*.

Slavery was outlawed in Jamaica.

1835

The American Anti-slavery Society raised money for distribution of anti-slavery tracts in the South. By mid-summer 25,000 copies of *Slave's Friend* and 50,000 copies each of *Human Rights, Anti-Slavery Record* and *The Emancipator* had been printed and many sent to the South. The result of these publications was panic and terror in the South.

To curb the activities of the abolitionists, President Jackson sent a message to Congress which contained the following passage: "I must also invite your attention to the painful excitement produced in the South, by attempts to circulate through the mails, inflammatory appeals, addresses to the passions of the slaves, in prints and in various sorts of publications, calculated to stimulate them in insurrection, and produce all the horrors of a servile war. There is, doubtless, no respectable portion of our countrymen who can be so far misled as to feel any other sentiment than that of indignant regret, at conduct so destructive of the harmony and peace of the country, and so repugnant to the principles of our national compact, and to the dictate of humanity and religion." Jackson further suggests in this message to Congress to pass a law that "will prohibit, under severe penalties, the circulation in the southern States, through the mails, of incendiary publications, intended to instigate the slaves to insurrection."

A mob in Georgetown tried to lynch Reuben Crandall who was in a Washington jail charged with circulating abolitionist newspapers. When they failed they attacked homes and churches of free Negroes.

Amos Dresser, a Negro member of the Ohio Abolition Society, was arrested in Nashville, Tennessee, and accused of circulating insurrectionary pamphlets among the slaves. A Committee of Vigilance of 62 citizens tried him, found him guilty, beat him, and forced him to leave the city.

In the House of Delegates in Virginia, Representative Wise declared that "attacking the institution of slavery means attacking the safety and welfare of our country."

Georgia law forbade employment of slaves or free Negroes in druggists' stores and required that poisonous drugs be kept under lock and key.

An anti-Negro riot in Philadelphia was set off by the attempt of a "half-witted Negro" to murder a white man. As a year before, the police did little to curb the violence.

A Negro, named McIntosh, was burned to death in St. Louis for killing an officer who was trying to arrest him. For denouncing this lynching Elijah Lovejoy had his printing office destroyed.

The shop of a Negro barber was mobbed in Pittsburgh. An attempt was made to drive Negroes from Pittsburgh.

White mechanics in Washington, D.C., demolished the restaurant of Benjamin Snow, a Negro who was accused of making derogatory remarks about the wives of the mechanics. Snow escaped and fled to Canada.

A riot growing out of a dispute at the Navy Yard in Washington, D.C., developed into ransacking of homes of prominent Negroes, supposedly looking for anti-slavery papers. Most Negro school houses were torn or burned down. John F. Cook, principal of the Smothers School, was forced to flee. He established a school in Columbia, Pa., and did not return to Washington until the fall of 1836.

The Michigan Constitution limited franchise to whites.

The provision of the 1776 North Carolina Constitution giving all adult freemen with the required property elective franchise, without regard to color, was repealed by a vote of 66 to 61. North Carolina was the last Southern state to deny Negroes the right to vote.

In North Carolina, schools for free Negroes taught by whites became illegal, and Negroes had to be taught in private homes by Negroes.

Noyes Academy in Canaan, N.H., which admitted Negro and white students was moved by oxen to nearby swamps after its removal had been voted by a town meeting.

The city authorities suppressed schools for free Negro children conducted by clergymen in Charleston, South Carolina. Daniel Payne, a Negro born of free parents in Charleston, South Carolina, was forced by state law to close the school he had operated there for the past six years. He went to New York and then entered the Lutheran Seminary in Gettysburg, Pa.

At the annual meeting of the American Anti-slavery Society in May, Negro and white choirs sang on the same platform. Some abolitionists objected bitterly, claiming that this helped to provoke anti-Negro riots in New York that July.

William Ellery Channing published *Slavery* as a reply to

Southern apologists of slavery. Channing attacked the institution of slavery on the grounds that it was irrational and immoral, and a denial of democracy. The Southern planter's concept of a Golden Age of Greece resting on slavery Channing considered an absurdity.

David Ruggles became secretary of the New York Vigilance Committee, to raise funds to help slaves escaping to freedom.

A committee of the Ohio Anti-slavery Convention assumed that a survey of two districts of Cincinnati was a representative sample of the approximately 2,500 Negroes in the city and thus concluded that the following estimates were valid:

1. 476 slaves purchased their freedom for a total of $215,-522.04, averaging $452.77 each.
2. 346 children were still in slavery.
3. A number were still working out their freedom while their free papers were retained as security.

The American Moral Reform Society, composed largely of Philadelphia Negroes, replaced the Convention movement. This society urged abandonment of separate Negro conventions, integration into white society wherever possible, and adherence to principles of brotherly love and non-resistance. Samuel Cornish, editor of the *Colored American* in New York, opposed this movement.

A school for Negro children was established in the Baptist Church on Western Row in Cincinnati. The teachers' salaries were paid partly by a white educational society and partly by contributions from Negroes. The teachers and the school encountered great opposition in the city leading occasionally to the closing of the school.

The Mulberry Street building of the African Free School in New York City became the Colored Grammar School No. 1, with an attendance of 317 pupils and with A. Libolt as principal. There were six primary schools for Negroes in various parts of the city, with combined attendance of 925. The next year John Peterson, a Negro, replaced Libolt as principal of Colored Grammar School No. 1.

The Smith School House was built for the education of Negro children in Boston with money left by Abiel Smith.

The city of Boston contributed $200 a year to the school and the parents of the students paid 12½ cents a week.

Nelson Wells, a Negro, established the Wells School in Maryland for the instruction of free Negro children. Wells left $7,000 to the school on his death.

The Charter of Cleveland, Ohio, stated that schools were to be open to all white children. However, Negro children were regularly admitted along with whites.

Baltimore had ten Negro congregations. Slaves and free Negroes were members. Baltimore also had 35 Negro benevolent societies.

Benjamin Tucker Tanner (1835-1923), bishop of the African Methodist Episcopal Church, was born in Pittsburgh, Pa., and attended Avery College in Allegheny City, Pa., from 1852 to 1857. In 1856, he became a licensed preacher of the AME Church and in 1857 he entered Western Theological Seminary. Tanner became in 1868 editor of the *Christian Recorder* and in 1888, the editor of the *AME Church Review*.

1836

Congress introduced the "gag rule" that no anti-slavery petition should be read, printed, committed or in any way acted upon by the House, but be laid upon the table without debate or discussion. This was generally considered a direct violation of the Constitution. In 1845, the "gag rule" was at last, especially through the intervention of John Quincy Adams, defeated.

By this year the cooperation between Southern and Northern Whigs had been weakened by the difference in their attitude toward slavery. Northern Whigs were generally hostile to slavery, while the Whig Party in the South included the owners of from ⅔ to ¾ of all the slaves in the South. The *Richmond Whig,* in September 1835, had advocated cessation of trade with the North until abolitionist activity was ended.

The New York's Women's Anti-slavery Society barred Negroes from membership. A similar society in Fall River, Massachusetts, did admit Negroes to membership despite protests from some members.

Lewis Tappan proposed that a Negro minister deliver an

address before the American Anti-slavery Society. The other Abolitionist leaders objected that the time had not yet come to mix with Negroes in public.

North Carolina law required $1,000 bond before manumission of a slave, to insure his good behavior and his departure from the state within 90 days.

A free Negro, George Jones, was arrested in New York City on a fabricated charge of assault and battery. He went with his captors on his employer's assurance that he would be protected. Less than 2 hours after his capture, he was brought before the city recorder, proved to be a slave on the word of the kidnapers, and then shipped to the South.

In the case of FOGG v. HOBBS in Pennsylvania, it was decided that free Negroes were not freemen in the language of the state Constitution, and thus could not vote.

James G. Birney began publication of *The Philanthropist* in Cincinnati. A few weeks later a mob destroyed his press. The mob then turned to the destruction of the Negro section of Cincinnati.

Isaiah D. De Grasse, a Negro, sought admission to the General Theological Seminary of the Protestant Episcopal Church of New York. He was told by Bishop Benjamin T. Onderdonk of the New York Diocese that he might attend classes, but could not live in the dormitory or be a formal member of the school. De Grasse refused to accept the arrangement and left.

The Methodist Episcopal Church, which had opposed slavery in 1780, in this year disclaimed "any right, wish, or intention to interfere in the civil and political relation between master and slave, as it existed in the slave-holding states of the Union."

Henry Boyd, a Negro, built a factory at the corner of 8th Street and Broadway in Cincinnati for the manufacture of bedsteads. When Boyd had arrived in Ohio in 1826, he had been unable because of prejudice to get work as a cabinetmaker. He had, however, had a successful business as a builder for a number of years, for a while in partnership with a white man. His furniture manufacturing required at one time 4 buildings and 20 to 50 workmen, Negroes and whites. He invented a machine to produce rails for beds, for which

he obtained a patent in the name of a white man. His buildings were frequently damaged or destroyed by fire, and he
eventually had to abandon his furniture business when he
lacked insurance to pay for the damage of the last fire in
1859.

Rev. Peter Williams, a New York Negro, received a U.S.
passport stating that he was a U.S. citizen.

By this year the AME Church had 86 churches, 4 conferences, 2 bishops, 27 ministers, 7,594 members, and $125,000
worth of property. The AME Church conference of this year
set up a quarterly magazine under the direction of George
Hogarth of Brooklyn, N.Y.

The first Negro Baptist Church in Baltimore was established.
The founders were M. C. Clayton and Noah Davis.

Negroes organized the Providence Baptist Association in
Ohio. This was an association of Negro Baptist churches, the
first such in the U.S.

Dr. John H. Fleet opened a school for Negroes in a school-
house on New York Avenue in Washington, D.C. He was a
Negro who had been educated in schools with white children,
such as the Georgetown Lancasterian School. He studied
medicine in Washington in the office of Dr. Thomas Henderson, and attended lectures at the Medical College. His school
continued until 1843 when it was burned.

Rev. J. W. Lewis, a Negro, established the New England
Union Academy in Providence, R.I., offering Negroes instruction in history, botany, bookkeeping, and natural philosophy. Tuition was $3 a quarter.

A Society for the Promotion of Education Among Colored
Children was organized in New York. It established two
schools for Negroes, one on Thomas Street and one on Center
Street.

Colored Grammar School No. 2 opened in New York City
in a new building with 210 pupils and R. F. Wake, a Negro,
as principal.

Philadelphia Negroes founded the Rush Library Company
and Debating Society.

Jefferson F. Long (1836-1900), Negro Congressman, was
born a slave near Knoxville, Ga. He moved to Macon, and

after working for a merchant tailor, opened a tailoring shop
of his own. From 1865 through 1869 he became influential
in the Republican Party. Elected to Congress in 1869, he
strenuously advocated enforcement of the 15th Amendment,
and universal suffrage in Washington, D.C. Serving one
term, he retired to Macon, but remained active in the state
Republican Party.

Suspiros Poeticos was published in Paris. It included a
poem, "A Saudade," which marked the first appearance of the
slave as a figure in Brazilian literature. The poet Domingos
Magalhaes' portrayal of the oppressed Negro, longing for
freedom and a return to his homeland from the New World
exile, became a stereotype of the Brazilian romantic movement. Magalhaes, a white man, was a crusading abolitionist
journalist, as well as a poet.

1837

The Weekly Advocate, a New York newspaper, was
founded. The editor was Rev. Samuel E. Cornish, the publisher, Philip A. Bell, and the general manager, Charles B.
Ray.

The *Colored American* denounced segregated schools as
providing little advantage because they "so shackled the intellect of colored youth." It also deplored separate churches and
all separate institutions for Negroes as contributors to the
persecution and neglect of Negroes.

Elijah Lovejoy, was murdered in Alton, Ill., for defending
a newsman's right to oppose slavery. Lovejoy advocated in
his *Observer* immediate abolition. Mobs destroyed three of
his presses, and while guarding another new press, he was
killed in November.

New York City Negroes owned $1,400,000 worth of tax-
able real estate, and had $600,000 deposited in savings banks.

James McCune Smith, a Negro, established a medical practice in New York after receiving his M.D. from the University
of Glasgow. He later gained a reputation for calculating
mortality rates for insurance companies. He was the author
of several scientific papers, and a man of wide interests and
reputation.

Madame Bernard Couvent, a free Negro woman in New
Orleans who owned several slaves, left her property on

Grands Hommes and Union Streets for establishing a free
school for Negro orphans. This school was eventually built
in 1848.

A Negro, John Horse, shared command with Alligator
Sam Jones and Wild Cat in the Seminole Indian defeat of
American troops at the Battle of Okeechobee in December.

In May, the Anti-slavery Women of America met in convention in New York with Sarah Douglass, a Negro, on the
Central Committee.

There were 18,768 Negroes in Philadelphia. 250 had paid
$79,612 for their freedom. The real and personal property
owned by Negroes there was almost $1,500,000. They owned
taxable property of $359,626.

Philadelphia Negroes had 16 churches with over 4,000
communicants.

The Institute for Colored Youth was established with
$10,000 left by Richard Humphreys. The school was run by
a Society of Friends, and taught mechanical and agricultural
arts and trade. In 1839 a farm was purchased in Bristol
in Philadelphia County where boys could be taught farming,
shoemaking, etc. It continued until 1846. The school was
revived in Philadelphia in 1852 with Charles L. Reason as
teacher, with branches for boys and girls.

The Pennsylvania Supreme Court ruled in July that Negroes could not legally vote, citing a 1795 court decision
barring Negro suffrage. There was no record of the 1795
case, but the Chief Justice asserted that the memory of a
good friend, a Philadelphia lawyer, was sufficient record.

Judge John Fox of Bucks County, Pa., ruled in favor of
Democratic candidates for county office who claimed that
they had been defeated by the margin of Negro votes. Fox
ruled that Negroes did not have the right to vote.

Of 737 Negroes committed for trial in Philadelphia in the
first six months of the year, only 123 were actually brought
to trial.

235 out of 1,673 inmates of the Philadelphia County Alms-
house were Negroes. This came to 14% of the paupers,
compared with 7.4% of the population that was Negro.

Indiana law provided that only white inhabitants in each
township should make up the local school corporation.

The price of a "prime field hand" 18 to 25 years old was $1,300 just before the panic of 1837.

From this year through 1848, Northern and Western states refused to comply with requests from Southern officials to return fugitive slaves.

Negroes of Cincinnati formed the School Fund Institute of Ohio to provide for the education of Negroes.

Pinckney Benton Stewart Pinchback, also known as Percy Bysshe Shelley Pinchback (1837-1921), the son of a white planter and Negro slave mother, was born free because his mother was freed. As a boy he was sent to Ohio. In New Orleans, in 1862, he created the Corps d'Afrique, composed of Negro troops for the Union Army, and received a commission from the federal government. He resigned in September because of racial difficulties, but subsequently he was authorized to raise a company of Negro cavalry. After the War, in 1867 Pinchback organized a local Republican Club. He was elected in 1868 to the Louisiana Constitutional Convention and then the State Senate. In 1871, elected president pro tem of the State Senate, he became Lt. Governor when the incumbent died. Between Dec. 9, 1872, and Jan. 13, 1873, he served as governor of Louisiana while Governor Warmoth was subject to impeachment proceedings. P. B. S. Pinchback was elected in January 1873 to the U.S. Senate. The Senate refused to seat him (probably because he had a white wife). He fought unsuccessfully for three years to be seated. In later years he was appointed surveyor of customs in New Orleans, and to some other honorary posts.

James T. Rapier (1837-1882), Negro Congressman and labor leader, was born of free parents in Florence, Ala. His father, a wealthy planter, provided a tutor for Rapier and later sent him to Montreal College in Canada, the University of Glasgow in Scotland, and Franklin College in Tennessee. As a successful cotton planter, Rapier became involved in reform of the Alabama State Constitution and the founding of the state Republican Party, serving as its Vice President. Interested in organizing urban and rural workers, he helped establish and chaired the first state Negro labor convention. He edited and published the *Montgomery Sentinel* to present his views on Negro solidarity and was elected to the House of Representatives in 1872. Although the power of the Ku Klux Klan and the Democratic Party ended his political career after one term, he later served as U.S. revenue officer in Alabama.

Rev. Hosea Easton's *A Treatise on the Intellectual Character and Political Condition of the Colored People of the U.S.* (published in Boston), was a sociological history of Negro oppression by a Negro.

George Moses Horton's *The Hope of Liberty* was reprinted in Philadelphia under the title *Poems of a Slave*.

Olaudah Equiano or Gustavus Vassa, an autobiography of a Negro, was published in Boston.

Negroes in Canada were given the vote.

British Guiana abolished slavery.

1838

A "formal organization" of workers of the Underground Railroad was set up in Philadelphia under the presidency of Robert Purvis, a wealthy Negro of Philadelphia.

Connecticut provided for trial by jury for Negroes who appealed their seizure as fugitives.

Frederick Douglass escaped from slavery in Maryland.

Charles Remond became a professional abolitionist. At first a follower of Garrison and an advocate of non-violence, he later favored slave revolts. He was Vice-President of the New England Anti-slavery Society, and President of a county unit of that Society. Remond was the first Negro lecturer employed by an anti-slavery society. Falling more and more under the shadow of Frederick Douglass, Remond evidenced a growing resentment towards him.

By this year in Philadelphia, there were 100 Negro "benefit societies" with 7,448 members. The initiation fees were between $2.50 and $5, and monthly dues were $.50. They provided sick benefits at $1.50 to $5 a month, paid funeral expenses and aid for widows. They were also social clubs.

In this year in Philadelphia, there were nine free schools for Negroes, with 1,116 pupils enrolled, and average attendance of 713; three partly-free schools with enrollment of 226, and average attendance of 125; three pay schools with white teachers, where enrollment was 102 and average attendance was 89; ten pay schools with Negro teachers, with an enrollment of 288 pupils, and an average attendance of 260. This made a total of 25 schools for Negroes, with 1,732 pupils enrolled, and an average attendance of 1,187, out of a total school-age Negro population of 3,025.

The Abolition Society of Philadelphia reported that 997 out of 17,500 Negroes in Philadelphia County had learned trades, but only 350 actually worked at their trades at this time.

Of 16 Negro churches in Philadelphia, there were: one Episcopal with 100 members and $36,000 worth of property; one Lutheran with 10 members and $120 worth of property; eight Methodist, with 2,860 members and $50,800 worth of property; two Presbyterian with 325 members and $20,000 worth of property. Total membership was 3,995, and total property value was $114,000.

The new Pennsylvania Constitution, with the vote clearly restricted to white men, was overwhelmingly approved by the electorate in October, despite protests by Philadelphia Negroes that it amounted to taxation without representation.

A mob in Philadelphia burned a shelter for Negro orphans, stoned a Negro church and attempted to burn another Negro church. Soon after the Philadelphia incidents, violence spread to other cities.

By this year Jim Crow was an accepted synonym for Negro.

A railroad corporation bought 140 slaves for $159,000 to work on the construction of a railroad between Jackson and Brandon, Miss.

Negroes of Fredericksburg, Va., asked the State Legislature for permission to send their children out of the state to school. They were refused.

Virginia law forbade the return to the state of Negroes who had gone North to school.

Ohio law denied Negroes the right of education at public expense.

North Carolina law declared void all marriages between whites and Negroes, or people of color, to the third generation.

North Carolina law relieved master workmen of the obligation to teach free Negro apprentices to read and write. Many continued to do so, however.

The *Colored American* reported that the arrival of destitute Irishmen was forcing Negroes out of their places of business and labor, especially on the wharves and in domestic service. However, some want-ads specified Negroes, not Irishmen.

Edward A. Jones, a Negro, was attacked by students in the College of New Jersey (now Princeton) when he returned to the Theological Seminary for his 10th reunion.

Kentucky law forbade slaves to travel.

The First Bethel Baptist Church was organized in Jacksonville, Fla., with four whites and two Negroes as charter members. Later the whites and Negroes separated.

12 Negro Baptist churches in Illinois joined together in the Wood River Baptist Association.

The AME Zion Church in Boston was founded with Rev. Jehial C. Beman as pastor.

Massachusetts Negroes demanded an end to segregation on trains, steamboats and stagecoaches. Although no law was passed, the threat of legislative action in the 1840's gradually prompted railroad directors to abandon segregation in Massachusetts.

New Bedford, Mass., allowed Negroes and whites to attend public schools together.

The city of Providence voted to support two schools for Negroes.

A periodical called *The National Reformer* was begun by William Whipper and other Negroes. This was the publication of the Moral Reformers.

The Mirror of Liberty, a quarterly magazine, was edited by David Ruggles, a Negro.

1839

James G. Birney, an abolitionist, organized the Liberty Party and ran for the presidency as its candidate in 1840 and 1844. In addition to being the first abolitionist political organization, the Liberty Party favored government action to find markets for western wheat. The Liberty Party felt that the U.S. Government only heeded the commercial needs of the South. At the London General Anti-slavery Convention in 1840, Birney urged England to buy western wheat and use India as a source of cotton. Birney received 62,300 votes in the 1840 election, mostly from New England. The votes Birney took away from Clay in the election of 1844 allowed Polk to win the presidential election. The Party received support from leading Negro abolitionists, including Henry Highland Garnet and Samuel R. Ward.

Samuel R. Ward, a fugitive slave, became a professional antislavery agent in 1839 for the American Anti-slavery Society. He had been educated in New York, and became a Presbyterian minister there. He pastored a white church in South Butler, N.Y. Ward was one of the first Negroes to join the Liberty Party. He later fled to England and Jamaica, where he died in poverty.

The *Colored American* criticized the abolitionists for devoting too much time to slavery in the South, and overlooking the "soul-crushing bondage of the Northern states."

In July, a group of Africans led by Cinque, revolted, killed the captain and seized their Spanish slave ship off the coast of Cuba. They sailed the ship, the *L'Amistad*, to Montauk, L.I. When tried before the Supreme Court, John Quincy Adams defended them and won their freedom. The 54 Africans gained much public attention and learned to read and write. With the help of Lewis Tappan, public appearances were arranged to raise enough money to pay the Africans' passage home. Cinque gave several public lectures in his native Mendi which were then translated. They received religious instruction and when one of the group was asked if he would again kill the captain of the slave ship, he replied that he now would rather pray for him. Cinque, asked if he would not pray for the captain, answered, "Yes, I would pray for him, and kill him too." In 1841, accompanied by five missionaries, they returned to their native country.

Negro real estate holdings in Providence, R.I., were valued at $50,000. Over ⅔ of the Negroes in Providence lived in houses which they themselves owned.

Cincinnati Negroes formed the Iron Chest Company, a real estate company which constructed three brick buildings and rented them to white men.

In response to Negro petitions for repeal of anti-immigration laws, the Ohio legislature declared that Negro residents had no constitutional right to petition the legislature for any purpose. The requirement of Negroes in Ohio to post bond for good behavior was repealed in 1849. This was the only case of a state repealing such a law before the Civil War.

Ohio passed a strict fugitive slave law.

There were riots in several New York cities against employment of Negro workers.

The U.S. State Department rejected the application of a Philadelphia Negro for a passport on the grounds that the Pennsylvania Constitution limited suffrage to white males, and thus did not recognize Negroes as citizens.

The African Baptist Church in Mobile, Ala., was formed when Negroes and whites of the First Baptist Church split. The Negro church was admitted that year to the Bethel Association.

The first Negro Baptist church in Washington, D.C., was organized by Sampson White.

Daniel Payne was ordained by the Franckean Synod of the Lutheran Church, and became a pastor of a Presbyterian Church in East Troy, N.Y. He later joined the AME Church, and became a bishop of that Church in 1852. He was president of Wilberforce University in Ohio during and after the Civil War.

Robert Smalls (1839-1915), Negro Congressman, was born in Beaufort, S.C., son of Robert and Lydia Smalls, slaves of the McKee family. Smalls was allowed to acquire a limited education. He moved with his master to Charleston, where he became a waiter. Confederate authorities in 1861 pressed him into the service of the Confederate Navy. He became a member of the crew of the *Planter*. In 1862, in the absence of white officers, Smalls navigated the *Planter* into the line of the blockading Federal squadron outside Charleston harbor. The Federal forces, upon receiving the *Planter,* made Smalls a pilot in the U.S. Navy, commissioned him a captain, and then promoted him to commander. At a meeting of Negroes and northerners in 1864 at Port Royal, he was elected to the National Union Convention. Smalls became a delegate in 1868 to the State Constitutional Convention, and served in the State

House of Representatives. He then served as a State Senator
between 1870 and 1874. In 1875 he was elected to Congress
and served until 1887. While his Congressional career was
not particularly notable, he did make some important speeches
that attacked the election tactics of the South Carolina Democrats, and supported a bill to provide equal accommodations
for the races on interstate conveyances. From 1865 to 1877,
Smalls served in the State Militia, rising to the rank of Major
General. Convicted of accepting a bribe in 1877, he was
pardoned by Gov. W. D. Simpson. In 1895, as one of six
Negro members of the State Constitutional Convention, he
made an attempt to prevent the practical disenfranchisement
of his race. The last 20 years of his life he spent in Beaufort
as collector of the port.

Canadian Negroes were admitted to jury service.

Joaquim Machado de Assis (1839-1908) was a mulatto
born in Recife whose novels deal with the upper-class Carioca
society which was almost totally white. Machado de Assis is
generally considered the greatest Brazilian novelist, and one
of the great novelists of modern times. Although he sympathized with the Negro's plight, Machado did nothing to
help him, probably because he was accepted into white
society, and even married a Portuguese aristocrat. In 1881,
he published *Memorias Posthumas de Braz Cubas;* an ancil-
lary theme in this novel is the pernicious effects of slavery
on both slave and master. In 1878 he published *Yaya Garcia.*
In this the faithful slave, Raymundo, is the only fully drawn
Negro character in any one of Machado's works.

Tobias Barreto (1839-1889) was a successful jurist, lawyer
and linguist, as well as a poet in Brazil. Only one of his
poems. *A Escraxidao,* deals with slavery. Barreto did his best
to hide his Negro heritage so that his acceptance into white
upper-class society would be easier.

1840

U.S. Census: Negro population in the U.S. was 2,873,648,
or 16.1% of the total U.S. population, of whom 386,293 were
free. Of Northern free Negroes 93% lived in states where
they were legally or practically excluded from voting. Only
Massachusetts, New Hampshire, Vermont, and Maine permitted Negroes to vote on an equal basis with whites.

There were 2,427 Negroes in Boston, representing 2.5% of the total population of the city.

The free Negro population in North Carolina was 22,732, or 3.01% of the total state population. Slaves numbered 245,-817, or 32.6% of the total population.

Ohio had 17,342 Negroes, of whom 2,255 lived in Cincinnati. The latter owned $209,000 worth of real estate and $19,-000 worth of church property. A real estate company known as the Iron Chest built homes for Negroes. One freedman whose total property was worth $12,000 to $15,000 owned seven houses in Cincinnati and 400 acres of land in Indiana. Cincinnati Negroes had four Sabbath schools with a regular attendance of 310; one Baptist and two Methodist churches with a total membership of 800, a Total Abstinence Temperance Society with 450 members, and a Sabbath School or Youth Society with 180 members. One-fourth of the city's Negro population belonged to temperance organizations, compared with less than a tenth of the whites.

Pennsylvania had 47,854 free Negroes, and 27% of the Negroes in Philadelphia were servants.

In this year 160 Negroes emigrated from Philadelphia to Trinidad.

The U.S. census for the year 1840 for the first time enumerated the "insane and idiots" in the population. It revealed that the incidence of such mentally disturbed persons was 11 times higher among free Negroes than among slaves. In the South the ratio was one insane or idiotic among 1,558 Negroes, while in the North the ratio was one among 144.5 Negroes. Southerners, such as Calhoun, and some Northern defenders of slavery, seized upon these statistics as proof of the benefits of slavery and the evils of freedom for Negroes. However, Dr. Edward Jarvis, a Massachusetts doctor and specialist in mental disorders and a founder of the American Statistical Association, investigated the census statistics, and reported in January 1844 that many Northern towns listed more insane Negroes than their total Negro population, and some towns which listed insane Negroes had no Negroes at all in their population. Petitions by the American Statistical Association and by a group of New York Negroes to Congress resulted in no change in the census report.

A Negro, Henry Highland Garnet, delivered a speech attacking slavery at the American Anti-slavery Convention. When William Lloyd Garrison and his followers seized control of this organization, the New York abolitionists led by Lewis Tappan (a white) formed the American and Foreign Anti-slavery Society. Five Negroes served on its first executive committee: Samuel E. Cornish, Christopher Rush, George Whipple, Charles B. Ray, and James W. C. Pennington. This society formed the nucleus of the newly-established Liberty Party, which had James G. Birney as its first Presidential candidate.

Pope Gregory XVI in his Bull against slave trade cites Bull of Pius II in 1462 to prove an anti-slavery attitude of the Church. He claims that Paul III, in 1537, Urban VIII, in 1639, Benedict XIV, in 1741 and Pius VII opposed the slave trade. But in fact these Bulls were not against slavery in general, clearly not against the African slave trade. What these Papal edicts were concerned with was the enforcement of the old, already in the Middle ages accepted rule, that between Christian nations prisoners of war or other captives should not be reduced to slavery.

The British Government paid an indemnity for slaves freed when American ships were forced by the weather into English colonial harbors. It had refused the claim of a ship so distressed in 1835, declaring that it could take no responsibility for fugitives, since slavery had been abolished in the British colonies.

A New York law provided trial by jury for alleged fugitive slaves.

Vermont instituted trial by jury to defend fugitive slaves. The law was repealed in 1843 but renewed in 1850.

Near Cincinnati, Ohio, a Mr. Van Zandt was fined $12,000 (his entire property) for carrying nine fugitives from Kentucky in his farm wagon.

Massachusetts repealed a law forbidding intermarriage between whites and Negroes, mulattoes or Indians.

Indiana forbade marriage between white persons and persons with one-eighth or more Negro blood. There were fines of $1,000 to $5,000 and prison terms of 10 to 20 years for violators, $500 for clerks who issued marriage licenses to such couples, $1,000 to $10,000 for ministers who married such couples. In 1841, the penalties were repealed, although the prohibition remained. In 1842, the penalties were re-enacted and remained in effect until 1852.

Tennessee law provided that all children between the ages of 6 and 21 had the privilege of attending public schools. Although no law forbade the education of Negroes, in practice public schools were attended exclusively by whites.

The *National Anti-Slavery Standard,* a Negro newspaper, carried on a dispute with the *Colored American.* The former opposed "all exclusive action on the part of the colored people except where the clearest necessity demands it," claiming that separate institutions merely perpetuated public prejudices.

Friends in Delaware formed the African School Association in Wilmington. The association established a school for girls and another for boys.

William C. Nell, a Boston Negro, headed a list of signers of the petition to the Massachusetts Legislature asking that public schools be opened to Negroes.

A similar petition submitted to the Boston School Committee by a group of whites and Negroes was refused.

The Elyria, Ohio, *Advertiser* reported that residents of Troy, Ohio, destroyed a school for Negro children established by a white man.

In Cincinnati, three tuition schools for Negroes were being operated, two with 65 pupils each and one with 47 pupils. The pupils paid $3 per quarter. In addition, a school sponsored by the (white) Ladies Anti-slavery Society provided instruction for 54 pupils.

Daniel Payne opened a school in Philadelphia for Negroes.

In Washington, D.C., Alexander Cornish established a school for Negroes in his home. He had an average of 40 pupils. Margaret Hill also opened a school for Negroes in Georgetown, D. C.

James W. C. Pennington became pastor of the African Congregational Church in Hartford, Conn., and later served as president of the Hartford Central Association of Congregational Ministers, in which he was the only non-white member. He was five times elected to the General Convention for the Improvement of Free People of Color.

John Wesley Gaines (1840-1912), clergyman and leader in

the establishment of the African Methodist Episcopal Church
in the South, was born a slave on the plantation of Gabriel
Toombs. He was licensed to preach in 1865, and then helped
organize churches for the AME Church. Gaines was the
founder, treasurer and president of the board of trustees of
Morris Brown College in Atlanta, Ga., which opened in 1885.
He was made a bishop in the AME church in 1888, and in
1890 his *African Methodism in the South* was published. In
1897, his book *The Negro and the White Man* was published.

John A. Hyman (1840-1891), Negro Congressman, was
born a slave near Warrenton, N.C. Sold and taken to Alabama, he managed to educate himself. In 1868 he attended
the North Carolina Constitutional Convention, served for six
years in the state legislature, and in 1875 was elected to
Congress for one term. He lived in Washington, D.C., until
his death, and worked at a minor post in the revenue service.

James Milton Turner (1840-1915), Negro leader and Minister to Liberia, was born a slave in St. Louis County, Virginia, on the plantation of Charles A. Loring. His father,
John Turner (also known as John Colburn), was removed
from Virginia by Benjamin Tillman after the 1831 slave insurrection led by Nat Turner. Taught veterinary medicine by
Benjamin Tillman, Turner's father purchased his freedom, and
in 1843 purchased the freedom of his wife and their son,
James Milton Turner. At 14, Turner's parents sent him to
Oberlin College. In the Civil War he served as a Northern
officer's servant. After the war, Turner directed his attention
to Negro public education and, in April 1866, he was appointed to the Kansas City School Board. He was authorized
to conduct a school for Negroes during the winter; no earlier
Negro public school in Missouri is recorded. He was reappointed in June 1868, and later became interested in the
Negro Institute in Jefferson City, Mo. He gave and collected
money and served as trustee for what is now Lincoln University. During Reconstruction, he became a figure in Republican politics, and on March 1, 1871, became minister resident
and consul general to Liberia. He held this office until 1878.
In 1886, he presented to President Cleveland the claim of the
Negro members of the Cherokee Nation. He secured $75,000
of the Congressional funds allotted to the Cherokee Nation
for the Negro tribesmen. In Ardmore, Okla., in 1915, Turner
was killed in an explosion. His body was transported back to

St. Louis, Mo., where a funeral conducted by Negro Masons was the largest ever held for a Negro in the city of St. Louis.

The first Negro newspaper in Philadelphia appeared, the *Demosthenian Shield*.

Samuel E. Cornish and Theodore S. Wright published *The Colonization Scheme Considered in Its Rejection by the Colored People*, in Newark, N.J.

Frank Johnson of Philadelphia, a Negro, organized an orchestra. He specialized in martial music, and played in England, before Queen Victoria.

1841

134 slaves on the *Creole*, en route from Richmond to New Orleans by sea, seized control of the ship (after killing one officer) and headed for Nassau. They were led by Madison Washington, a slave. Their status was finally settled in 1853 by arbitration between the U.S. and Britain. The British government was to pay $110,000 in compensation for having allowed the slaves to go free.

In June, an Englishman in Cincinnati harbored a runaway slave and resisted his master's attempt to reclaim him. In August, two Negroes killed a German farmer near Cincinnati, and a white woman was supposedly insulted by two Negro men. On Aug. 29, a street fight between whites and Negroes in Cincinnati turned into a violent anti-Negro riot. For five days Negroes were shot and their homes burned. The State Militia was called in, and city authorities persuaded 300 Negro men to go to jail for their own security. Complying on the understanding that their families would be protected, the Negro men after their release discovered that their wives and children had been attacked by the mob. A few white men were arrested for this attack but none were punished.

In Atlanta, Ga., there were separate Bibles for Negro and white witnesses in court.

Boston authorities required Negroes mourning the death of President William Henry Harrison to march at the end of the funeral procession.

According to a New York law, out-of-state slave owners could not keep their slaves in the state for more than nine months.

J. W. Loguen, a former slave who became a bishop of the African Methodist Church (1869), settled in Syracuse, N. Y., where he was involved with the Underground Railroad in sheltering fugitive slaves.

The New York Legislature stated that any school district could establish separate schools for whites and Negroes.

South Carolina law forbade Negro and white cotton-mill hands from looking out of the same window.

Blanche K. Bruce (1841-1898), U. S. Senator, was born in Farmville, Prince Edward County, Va. A quadroon or octoroon, he was taken to Missouri several years before the Civil War, and at Brunswick learned the printer's trade. In 1861, Bruce escaped and in Hannibal, Mo., organized a school. After the War, he took a two-year course at Oberlin College. He then went to Mississippi, and in 1869 became sergeant-at-arms of the State Senate. He held many local positions in Mississippi at different times, serving as county assessor, tax collector, sheriff, superintendent of schools, and member of the Levee Board. He became a wealthy planter and a prominent member of the Republican Party. He was elected Senator from Mississippi in 1874. Bruce was the only Negro during Reconstruction to serve a regular term in the U.S. Senate. Bruce later settled in Washington and became Register of the Treasury under President Garfield. In 1889, President Harrison appointed him recorder of deeds in Washington, D. C., and in 1895 he was again recalled to be Register of the Treasury.

In Brooklyn, N.Y., *The African Methodist Episcopal Church Magazine* was edited by George Hogarth.

James W. C. Pennington, a Negro, published a *Textbook on the Origin and History of the Colored People.*

Although the author of *Sketches of the Higher Classes of Colored Society in Philadelphia* was anonymous, he stated in the text that he was a Negro. Thus, it was the first sociological study of book length on the Northern urban Negro by a Negro.

Charles L. Reason, a Negro and professor at Central College in New York, wrote an anti-slavery tribute, *Freedom,* cataloging incidents in the world's long struggle for liberty.

In Cuba, Negroes represented 58.5% of the population. Of these, 152,838 were free, and 436,495 enslaved.

1842

The Dorr Rebellion in Rhode Island against the conservative forces controlling the state, led to the new constitution which extended suffrage to the Negroes.

When Edward Prigg had Margaret Morgan, an escaped slave, seized and returned to her mistress, he was arrested and convicted of kidnaping. In defense, his counsel claimed the 1826 Pennsylvania "personal liberty" statute under which he was convicted was unconstitutional and in conflict with the Fugitive Law of 1793. The majority Supreme Court opinion in PRIGG v. PENNSYLVANIA by Justice Story upheld Prigg's conviction and stated that the Fugitive Act had to be enforced by federal officials and that states could not be made to act. Subsequently other states passed "personal liberty" laws.

William Wells Brown, a former slave and a steamboat operator on Lake Erie, conveyed 69 fugitive slaves across Lake Erie to Canada.

George Latimer was seized in Boston as a fugitive, and held so that his claimer, James B. Grey of Norfolk, Va., could have time to gather evidence. The people of Boston raised such an outcry against Latimer's imprisonment that it was agreed he would be released for $400, which was promptly raised. William Lloyd Garrison's magazine published Frederick Douglass' letter on this case. It was Douglass' first appearance in print.

The U.S. Senate, at the instigation of Sen. John C. Calhoun, voted to exclude Negroes from the Army and Navy except as cooks, stewards and servants; the House did not vote on this bill.

The *Register,* a Raleigh, N.C., newspaper, reported that Allen Jones, a free Negro blacksmith, was dragged from his home and whipped by some whites of Raleigh for having described being tarred and feathered by a Raleigh group to the Anti-slavery Convention in New York. A town meeting including many prominent citizens met to protest and condemn this outrage as a violation of the law.

Maryland law made it a felony for a free Negro to "call for, demand, or receive" abolition newspapers, etc.

Violence erupted between Irish and Negro coal miners in Pennsylvania.

When Negroes of Philadelphia paraded to celebrate abolition of the slavery in the West Indies, whites attempted to break up the parade. The battle ended in the wounding and killing of several, and the destruction of the New African Hall and the Negro Presbyterian Church.

The Episcopal Convention of the Pennsylvania Diocese reaffirmed a 1795 vote to exclude representatives from Negro churches.

Alexander Crummell (a Negro born in New York in 1819) was ordained an Episcopal minister and later had a parish in New York.

The Institute for Colored Youth was incorporated in Philadelphia.

The Philomathean Institute of N. Y., and the Philadelphia Library Company and Debating Society applied for admission to the International Order of Odd Fellows. When they were refused because of their race, Peter Ogden, a Negro, acquired a charter for the first Negro American lodge, Philomathean No. 646 of New York.

Robert C. De Large (1842-1874), Negro Congressman, was born a slave in Aiken, S.C. With some education, he became a successful farmer in South Carolina during Reconstruction. Elected to the State Legislature, he was then chosen for the House of Representatives in 1871. De Large returned to South Carolina as a Congressman investigating irregularities in his election. The House Commission on Elections declared his seat vacant in 1873. He died in 1874, having served one year as a Charleston city magistrate.

Robert B. Elliot (1842-1884), Negro Congressman, was the son of West Indian parents living in Boston, Mass. He was educated abroad in Jamaica, High Holburn Academy in London, and Eton. Upon returning to the U.S., he became editor of the *Charleston Leader,* a delegate to the South Carolina Constitutional Convention in 1868, and a member of the state's lower house. He was elected a U. S. Representative in 1871. He then served two terms, and retired to New Orleans and practiced law.

Lucius Henry Hosley (1842-1920), a bishop of the Colored

Methodist Episcopal Church, was born of an African slave,
Louisa, and James Holsey, a slave master. In 1868 he was
licensed to preach. He helped to found Paine College in
Augusta, Ga., Lane College in Jackson, Tenn., Holsey
Industrial Institute in Cordele, Ga., and the Helen B. Cobb
Institute for Girls in Banesville, Ga. Holsey compiled a *Hymn
Book of the Colored Methodist Episcopal Church in America*
and published it in 1891. In 1894 he published a *Manual of
the Discipline of the Colored Methodist Episcopal Church in
America.*

Josiah T. Walls (1842-1905), Negro Congressman, was
born of free parents in Winchester, Va. He moved to Florida
and had become a successful farmer by 1860. He was drafted
into the Confederate Army, was captured, and by 1865 had
become a sergeant-major in the Union Army. A member of
the Florida State Legislature, he was elected to Congress from
1871 to 1877, and advocated support for the Cuban Revolution. Walls was almost ruined as a planter by severe weather
conditions, and accepted the superintendence of a farm at
Tallahassee.

The National Watchman, a newspaper edited by William
G. Allen, a Negro, began publication in New York, in Troy.
Henry Highland Garnet was associated with Allen in this
enterprise. This newspaper was published until 1847.

William Wells Brown published a narrative of his life as a
slave. Lunsford Lane published a similar narrative in this
year.

Minstrelsy had become a distinctive form of American
entertainment. Dan Emmett, with four other white actors,
formed a company to perform Negro minstrelsy. Edwin Christy became a star of minstrelsy in this period. Earlier companies
included the Virginia Minstrels, Congo Melodists, Ethiopian
Serenaders and Georgia Minstrels. All of the earlier companies were made up of whites in black-face.

Uruguay freed her slaves.

1843

The United States and Great Britain agreed to patrol the
West Coast of Africa in order to intercept ships engaged in
the slave trade. Between 1843 and 1852, with only sailing

vessels to pursue the slavers, the United States Navy captured 19 slave ships. Six of the captains were convicted.

The Liberty Party National Convention included Negro delegates, speakers and officials. Henry Highland Garnet of New York was a member of the executive nominating committee. Charles B. Ray was elected a convention secretary, and Samuel R. Ward led the convention in prayer and also addressed the convention. This was the first time Negroes had actively participated in the leadership of a national political party in the U. S.

The Liberty Party was endorsed by a Negro convention in Buffalo, N.Y., which also denounced the American Colonization Society, and heard Garnet issue a militant call to slaves to rise up against their oppressors.

The Massachusetts Legislature, in response to petitions arising out of the Latimer case, ignored the Federal Fugitive Law of 1793, and passed a law forbidding state officials from aiding the recapture of fugitive slaves or from using state jails for their imprisonment. The penalty for such action was either fine or imprisonment.

A similar Vermont "personal liberty" law forbade state officials from aiding the recapture of fugitive slaves and carried penalties of up to $1,000 fines and up to five years imprisonment.

On Feb. 24, the Massachusetts Legislature repealed a 1786 law against interracial marriages.

In response to the desires of local citizens, a special Mississippi law was passed to enable Henry Lee, a free Negro barber, to live in Vicksburg with his family. He was required, however, to practice barbering and no other trade. The same law gave county boards of police the power to make similar exceptions.

North Carolina law forbade taxes on free Negroes for support of common schools, which they could not attend. This was apparently merely a clarification of what had been the normal policy for some time.

U.S. Attorney General Hugh Legare declared that Negroes were neither aliens nor citizens, but were somewhere in between. He said that Negroes could apply for benefits under the land preemption act.

A Maryland law forbade the formation of secret societies of Negroes; another authorized justices to search any free Negro suspected of having abolition papers, etc., "using as little violence to the feelings of such free Negro or mulatto as is compatible."

James W. C. Pennington, pastor of the African Congregational Church in Hartford, Conn., represented Connecticut at the World Anti-slavery Convention in London. The same year he represented the American Peace Convention at the meeting of the World Peace Society in London.

A former N. Y. slave named Isabella, changed her name to Sojourner Truth, and began to travel about the U.S. preaching and lecturing.

Richard Henry Boyd (1843-1922), a Negro clergyman, was the son of Indiana Dixon, a slave of a planter in Mississippi. Named Dick Gray by his master, he changed his name to Richard Henry Boyd in 1864. He learned to read in 1865, and in 1870 was ordained a Baptist minister. In 1872, Boyd organized the first Negro Baptist Association in Texas, and in 1897 formed the National Baptist Publishing Board, which issued the first series of Negro Baptist literature ever published. Boyd published *Pastor's Guide; the Church Directory* and *Jubilee and Plantation Songs.*

The Mystery, a Negro newspaper in Pittsburgh, began publication.

Negroes in New Orleans began publishing *L'Album Littéraire, Journal des Jeunes Gens, Amateurs de la Littérature,* a monthly review in French. It included poems, stories, fables and articles. It later became a fortnightly.

Teixeira E. Sousa (1812-1881) published in 1843 the first Brazilian novel, *Filha do Pescador.* Sousa's masterpiece, the epic *A Independencia do Brasil,* dealt with the nation on the eve of its break with Portugal. Sousa emphasized the multiracial nature of the populace and showed his desire that the races mix so that the true Brazilian, a mulatto, would ultimately emerge. In 1852, he published "Maria ou a Menina Rouhada" in Paul Brito's magazine, *Marmota Fluminense.* "Maria" was the first novel in Brazilian literature in which Negroes were the leading characters. It dealt with Afro-Brazilian customs, religion and sorcery.

1844

In New York, James G. Birney, the Liberty Party candidate, so weakened Clay that Polk carried the state and won the presidential election.

Rev. Moses Dickson of Cincinnati and 11 other Negroes formed an Order of 12 of the Knights and Daughters of Tabor to rescue Negro slaves and to overthrow the institution of slavery by military means if necessary.

In Cincinnati a high school for Negroes was established by Rev. Hiram Gilmore.

In Connecticut, state officials were forbidden from arresting fugitive slaves; however, they were not to impede recapture of such slaves by federal officials.

Jonathan Walker (apparently a white man) was imprisoned, sentenced to stand in the pillory, and branded on the hand with the letters SS for "slave stealer." He had been overtaken and captured sailing from Pensacola for the Bahamas with seven fugitive slaves.

L. W. Paine, a white machinist from Rhode Island working in Georgia, was imprisoned for six years for persuading slaves to escape.

The Committee of Free Colored Citizens sent a petition to the U.S. Senate protesting the anti-Negro remarks of Secretary of State Calhoun to the British Ambassador to the U.S., and making a statement of facts about the social conditions of Negroes in the Northern states. Dr. James McCune Smith wrote and signed the petition.

The Methodist Church of the U. S. split on the issue of whether or not a bishop could hold slaves. The Southern members organized the Southern Methodist Episcopal Church.

The new Constitution of New Jersey confined suffrage to whites.

North Carolina law, on pain of a fine of $10, forbade free Negroes to sell alcoholic beverages, except those which they had made themselves.

Richard Theodore Greener (1844-1922), an educator and lawyer, was born in Philadelphia. He moved to Boston in 1849, and became in 1870 the first Negro to receive a degree from Harvard College. Greener taught school and served as principal of Summer High School. Briefly, he served in the office of the U. S. Attorney for the District of Columbia, and in 1873 became associate editor of the *New National Era*. Until 1877, he held the Chair of Mental and Moral Philosophy and Logic at the University of South Carolina, when the school was closed to Negroes. He had been admitted to the Bar in South Carolina in 1876, and then became instructor in the Law Department of Howard University in 1877, and dean in 1879. He is known for his controversy with Frederick Douglass.

Elijah McCoy (1844-1928), Negro inventor, was born in Canada, moved to Michigan and began to work in 1872 as an inventor. He was granted over 72 patents in his lifetime, most of which related to lubricating appliances for engines. He was a pioneer in the art of steadily supplying oil to machinery from a cup so as to render it unnecessary to stop a machine to oil it. Many of his inventions were long in use on the locomotives of the Canadian and Northwestern Railroads and on the steamships of the Great Lakes.

Charles E. Nash (1844-1913), Negro Congressman, was born in Opelousas, La. A bricklayer, he joined the Chasseurs d'Afrique Regiment of the Union Army, and rose to sergeant-major. Appointed U. S. Customs Inspector for Louisiana, he was elected to the House of Representatives in 1874. After serving one term, he became the town postmaster and died in New Orleans.

James E. O'Hara (1844-1905), Negro Congressman, was born of free parents in New York City. Having studied law at Howard University, he was admitted to the Bar in 1873. He had already served a term in the North Carolina State Legislature, and in 1875 was a delegate to the North Carolina Constitutional Convention. Elected to Congress in 1882 and 1884, he worked for civil rights legislation, equal access and accommodations. After failing to gain a third term, he practiced law in New Bern, N. C.

John Henry Smyth (1844-1908), a Negro lawyer, diplomat and educator, was born in Richmond, Va., of a slave father, Sully Smyth. Until 1857, he attended a Quaker school and at 14 was admitted to the Pennsylvania Academy of Fine Arts. He attended the Institute for Colored Youth, and graduated in 1862. Smyth taught in Philadelphia public schools until 1865, when he went to England with the intention of studying under Ira Aldridge, the Negro actor. The latter died, and Smyth was unable to carry out his plan. Thus, in 1869 he returned to the U. S. and entered Howard University Law School. Graduated in 1872, he became cashier of the Wilmington, N.C. branch of the Freedmen's Savings and Trust Company of Washington. In 1874 Smyth began to practice law, and the following year became a delegate to the State Constitutional Convention. On May 23, 1878, he was appointed minister resident and consul general of Liberia, a position he held until 1885, when he became editor of the *Reformer,* in Richmond, Va. Smyth secured the establishment of the Virginia Manual Labor School at Hanover, which opened in 1899.

Placido, a Negro, and one of Cuba's great poets, took part in the revolt of 1844. He was later executed for his participation in this revolt.

1845

The "gag rule," which since 1836 had prevented anti-slavery petitions from being heard in the House of Representatives, was rescinded, largely through the work of John Quincy Adams, of Massachusetts, and Joshua Giddings of Ohio.

New England Negroes, including Henry Weeden, William C. Nell, Judith Smith, Mary L. Armstead and Thomas Cummings, formed a Freedom Association to assist fugitive slaves.

By 1845, Negroes could attend schools with whites in Salem, New Bedford, Nantucket, Worcester and Lowell, Mass.

An orphanage for Negro children was established in Cincinnati by Salmon Chase and other whites and Negroes.

Georgia passed a law against contracts with Negro (slave or free) mechanics.

John Tucker, "one of the Negro pioneers" in Indianapolis, was attacked and killed on a downtown street by a band of whites, shouting: "Kill the damned nigger." Two men were arrested; one of them was convicted of manslaughter, and sentenced to three years at hard labor. The actual murderer, however, escaped.

The Lyceum in New Bedford, Mass., excluded Negroes from membership and allowed them to sit only in gallery seats. As they had previously had the same privileges as whites, Ralph Waldo Emerson, Charles Sumner, Theodore Parker and many local abolitionists threatened to boycott the Lyceum, and subsequently the abolitionists organized a rival Lyceum.

The first Negro lawyer, Macon B. Allen, was admitted to the Bar in Worcester, Mass. He had practiced law in Maine for the two preceding years.

William Henry Lane, a Negro minstrel dancer, received top billing with a white minstrel company; his stage name was "Juba."

Minstrelsy for the next half century was the most popular American entertainment form. The previous year, E. P. Christy had worked out the minstrel formula which companies followed for the rest of the century. As late as 1919, three large minstrel companies were touring the U.S. Performances often included jubilee singers, plantation songs, camp meeting songs, field-hollers and work songs, all rich in the African musical techniques and rhythms that contributed to jazz. Minstrelsy also provided a training ground, especially in the 1890's, for Negro jazz musicians. For example: Jack Laine led a minstrel band in New Orleans in 1895; in 1896, W. C. Handy joined Mahara's Minstrels and became its leader in 1897; Ma Rainey performed with Rainey's Rabbit Foot Minstrels, and Jelly Roll Morton with the McCabe and Young Minstrels in 1910.

Edmonia Lewis (1845-1890), a sculptress, and the first Negro woman to study in Europe and distinguish herself in art, was born of Negro-Indian parents, near Albany, N.Y. She attended Oberlin College, and in 1865 was introduced to William Lloyd Garrison. She was given commissions to do busts of prominent people. In 1870, the Story Family of Boston sent her to Italy to study, where she remained most of her life. She, like Bannister, had a successful showing at the Philadelphia Centennial Exposition in 1876. Among her better marble statues are the *Death of Cleopatra, The Marriage of Hiawatha, The Madonna with Infant* and *Forever Free.* Her portrait busts done in Roman classical style include

Lincoln, Longfellow, John Brown, Charles Sumner and William Story.

Frederick Douglass' narrative of his experiences was published.

Les Cenelles, the first anthology of Negro verse in America, was published. It contained 82 poems, the work of 17 New Orleans poets, and was 215 pages long. Reviewed in *La Chronique* on Jan. 30, 1848, it was the idea of Armand Lanusse, a free Negro born in New Orleans in 1812, who contributed 16 poems to it.

In Cuba, the law for the repression of the slave trade to Cuba was passed.

1846

David Wilmot, a Representative from Pennsylvania, proposed the exclusion of slavery from the territory acquired from Mexico in the Mexican War, not because of "morbid sympathy for the slave," but for the "cause and rights of white freemen." The Wilmot Proviso was defeated in the Senate.

The New England Working Man's Association, organized the previous year, passed a resolution at its convention in Lynn, Mass., expressing concern for Negroes' as well as for their own rights.

A New Jersey law abolished slavery. However, non-residents travelling in the state could bring in and take out a "usual number" of household slaves.

An abolitionist, Gerrit Smith, attempted to encourage independent farming and voting among Negroes, and offered to distribute 140,000 acres of his own land in upstate New York to 3,000 Negroes, in parcels of 40 to 60 acres. The project failed because much of the land was poor, and many Negroes did not have the capital needed to start a farm. In 1848, fewer than 30 families were settled on the land.

A Constitutional amendment to grant equal voting rights to New York Negroes was defeated by popular vote.

When he arrived in Boston, Captain Hannum of the brig, *Ottoman,* found a runaway slave on board his ship. He set sail to return the runaway slave to captivity, was followed by a steamer sent out of Boston to rescue the runaway, but eluded the rescue boat. A protest committee was appointed in Boston.

Rev. Moses Dickson of Cincinnati and 11 other Negroes met in St. Louis and formed a secret and militant organization, the Knights of Liberty. They agreed to disperse for ten years to form secret societies to emancipate the Negro. In 1856 there were said to be 47,240 Knights of Liberty. The organization then disappeared from view, and emerged in 1871 as the Temple and Tabernacle of the Knights and Daughters of Tabor, in Independence, Mo.

A petition by a group of whites and Negroes, led by George Putnam, a Negro, to the Boston School Committee for the opening of public schools to Negroes, was refused.

Of the prisoners in Eastern Penitentiary in Pennsylvania, between 1829 and 1846, 14% of the whites were pardoned, and 2% of the Negroes. In the same period, the average sentence for whites was 2 years, 8 months, 2 days, and for Negroes 3 years, 3 months and 14 days.

A Kentucky law provided a penalty of imprisonment for enticing slaves to run away or inciting them to rebellion. Another Kentucky law forbade free Negroes from manufacturing or selling liquor.

Virginia's Governor Smith proposed to the state legislature that a law be passed whereby each county might have the right to vote upon the question of removing free Negroes from the county. At that time there were approximately 47,000 free Negroes living in Virginia.

The Abyssinian Baptist Church of New York had 424 members, and was headed by Rev. Sampson White.

Norbert Rillieux, a Creole in Louisiana, patented a vacuum cup which "revolutionized sugar refining methods in that day."

Jeremiah Haralson (1846-1916?), Negro Congressman, was born of slave parents in Muscogee County, Ga. Moving to Alabama after emancipation, he was elected to the House of Representatives in 1874. Accused of fraud and close friendship with Jefferson Davis, he served only two terms. He moved to Colorado and was killed in a hunting accident.

A paper, "The Influence of Climate on Longevity, with

Special Reference to Life Insurance," by Dr. James McCune Smith, a New York Negro, was published.

Gonçalves Crespo (1846-1883) was educated at the University of Coimbra. He is considered by Aubrey Bell, a leading historian of Portuguese literature, as the finest poet of the Parnassian school and one of the major poets in the Portuguese language. Of his poems, *A Sesta, Na Roca,* and *Cancao* deal nostalgically with plantation Negroes, their earthiness, durability and beautiful women.

1847

Frederick Douglass was elected president of the New England Anti-slavery Society.

Frederick Douglass and Martin Delany started the *North Star,* an abolitionist newspaper in Rochester, N. Y., on Dec. 3. The paper became the rallying point for the Negro abolitionists.

William Alexander Leidsdorff, son of a Danish father and mulatto mother from the Danish West Indies, launched the first steamboat in San Francisco Bay. He was a prosperous business man, and well-known in the San Francisco government. He was a member of the City Council, school committee, etc., and was appointed vice-consul to Mexico under Commodore Stockton's military rule of California in the Mexican War.

20,240 Negroes lived in Philadelphia. Of these approximately 57% were natives of the state.

Of the 11,000 Negroes in central Philadelphia, approximately 4,000 were domestic servants. The rest were mostly laborers, artisans, coachmen, expressmen, and barbers. They were paying over $6,000 in taxes, and owned real estate valued at $400,000. Approximately 8% of them, over 300, were freeholders. In Philadelphia, in this year, out of 4,466 Negro children: 1,888 were enrolled in schools, 504 were at work or apprentices, and 2,074 were at home and unaccounted for.

Pennsylvania passed a "personal liberty" law forbidding state officials from aiding in the enforcement of the 1793 Federal Fugitive Law, and prohibited the use of state jails in fugitive slave cases. Persons claiming Negroes were subject to fine and imprisonment if they attempted violence, and slaveholders were denied the right to transport their slaves through the state.

A petition from the Kentucky Legislature asking for a more stringent fugitive slave law resulted in the Act of 1850.

Whigs of both the Northern and Southern wings opposed the annexation of Mexican territory in a party platform. The Southern Whigs, however, denied that Congress had any power to restrict the right of slaveholding in the territories. The Southern Whigs succeeded in having the party's presidential nomination go to Zachary Taylor, a Southerner and a slaveholder, rather than Henry Clay who stood for compromise on the slavery question.

Louisiana established a common school system for "the education of white youth."

Missouri law forbade the instruction of Negroes or mulattoes in reading or writing.

The Prince Hall Lodge of Masons in Massachusetts, the First Independent African Grand Lodge in Pennsylvania, and the Hiram Grand Lodge in Pennsylvania formed a National Grand Lodge of Negroes.

The Independent Order of Good Samaritans and Daughters of Samaria was organized by Negroes and whites to promote temperance. In separate district grand lodges, at first, Negroes could vote only on matters which concerned Negroes. As their membership increased, the whites dropped out, and the Negroes eventually gained control of the Order. In 1877, a Negro was elected Grand Sire.

Robert Morris of Boston, and George B. Vashon, a graduate of Oberlin, were admitted to the Bar. Both were Negroes. Vashon also taught classics at New York Central College.

John R. Lynch (1847-1939), Negro Congressman, was born of slave parents in Concordia Parish, La. In Mississippi, after attending night school, he served in 1869 as a justice of the peace in Adams County, and later was elected to the State Legislature, subsequently becoming Speaker of the House. Active in the state Republican Party, he was a member of the House of Representatives from 1873 to 1877 and again from 1881 to 1883. A delegate to the Republican National Convention, he presided over the Presidential convention in 1884. Appointed fourth auditor of the Treasury in 1889 and U.S. Paymaster in 1898, he retired in 1911 to private practice as a lawyer. Lynch published two books, *The Facts of Reconstruction* and *Some Historical Errors of James Ford Rhodes.*

Isaiah Thornton Montgomery (1847-1923), founder of Mount Bayou, Miss., was born a slave on the Hurricane Plantation, owned by Joseph E. Davis, brother of Jefferson Davis. At the age of 9, he worked in his owner's office. After the Civil War, the plantation of the Davis brothers was turned over to Isaiah's father, Benjamin Montgomery, for $300,000 in bonds, and the plantation was operated by Montgomery until a court decision returned the land to Davis' heirs 13 years later. Montgomery founded Mount Bayou on 30,000 acres of land in 1887 in the Mississippi Yazoo delta. Eventually, this principally agricultural community grew to 3,000 persons and was self-sufficient, forming its own bank and farmers' cooperative. The influence of Mount Bayou also affected surrounding communities with the formation of the Mount Bayou National Farm Loan Association, which insured Federal loans and sustained the community over various seasons of agricultural depression. Montgomery, along with Booker T. Washington, was a founder of the National Negro Business League. He was the only Negro at the Mississippi Constitutional Convention in 1890. Along with President Theodore Roosevelt, he spoke at ceremonies dedicating the Lincoln Memorial at Hodgensburg, Ky.

The AME Church began publication of *The Christian Herald,* a weekly magazine. Its name was changed to *The Christian Recorder* in 1852.

1848

Present at the organizational convention of the Free Soil Party in Buffalo, N.Y., were Negroes such as Samuel R. Ward, Henry Highland Garnet, Charles L. Reason, Henry Bibb and Frederick Douglass. Martin Van Buren, chosen as the Presidential candidate, ran on a platform advocating the exclusion of slavery from the new Mexican lands.

In September, support for the new party was voted by a colored convention in Cleveland, Ohio.

The Democratic nominee, Lewis Cass, had recently suggested "squatter sovereignty" to decide whether or not new Mexican lands would have slavery. The Democratic and the Free Soil Parties lost to the Whig candidate, Zachary Taylor.

The Citizen's Union of Pennsylvania was organized by Negroes to work for first-class citizenship. In 1848, Philadelphia Negroes owned $531,809 worth of real estate, exclusive of church property.

Of male Philadelphia Negroes, 3,358 were 21 years or over. There were 1,581 laborers; 557 waiters, cooks, etc.; 286 mechanics; 276 coachmen, carters, etc.; 240 sailors; 166 shopkeepers, traders, etc.; 156 barbers; 96 in miscellaneous occupations. Of 4,249 Negro women, 21 years or over, 1,970 were washerwomen, 486 seamstresses, 786 day workers, 213 in trades, 290 housewives, 156 servants, 173 cooks, 103 ragpickers. These figures exclude 3,716 live-in servants in white families. Of 4,798 Negroes in Philadelphia aged 5 to 20, 1,940 were schoolchildren, 1,200 were unaccounted for, 484 were at home, 33 were helpless, 274 were working at home, 354 were servants, 12 were sweeps, 18 were porters and 230 were apprentices.

In Charleston, S.C., the figures for workers in certain occupations were: building trades, 213 slaves, 41 free Negroes; clothing trades, 103 slaves, 329 free Negroes; food trades, 105 slaves, 74 free Negroes; furniture trades, 12 slaves, 1 free Negro; nurses and sextons, 3 slaves, 14 free Negroes; transportation trades, 87 slaves, 20 free Negroes; bookbinders, 3 slaves, 0 free Negroes; printers, 5 slaves, 0 free Negroes; millwrights, 0 slaves, 5 free Negroes; navigation, and sailors, 101 slaves, 7 free Negroes; unclassified mechanics, 147 slaves, 9 free Negroes; miscellaneous occupations and servants, 6,576 slaves, 95 free Negroes; superannuated or disabled, 92 slaves, 5 free Negroes. In Charleston slaves and not free Negroes were sailors and plasterers. Boatmen and most of the city's carpenters and coopers were slaves. Free Negroes and not slaves were tavern keepers, hotel keepers, milliners and storekeepers.

Martin Donato, a free Negro of St. Landry, La., died leaving a Negro wife and children, 4,500 arpents of land, 89 slaves and personal property worth $46,000.

A Rhode Island law forbade state officials from enforcing the 1793 Federal Fugitive Law.

Kentucky demanded that Ohio's Governor Bell extradite 15 persons on the charge of aiding a fugitive to escape. Bell refused, stating that Ohio law did not construe men as property.

Virginia law provided the death penalty for advising or conspiring with a slave to rebel. Postmasters were required under penalty to give notice of the arrival of insurrectionary books, etc., which would then be burned.

Captain Drayton and another officer of the schooner Pearl, were sentenced to 20 years imprisonment for trying to rescue 75 fugitive slaves who had escaped from Washington, D.C. Drayton was pardoned by President Fillmore in 1852.

The clause of the Illinois Constitution of 1848 that barred further immigration of Negroes to the state, was ratified 2 to 1 by popular vote. This provision was rarely invoked, however, although it remained law until 1865.

Attendance in school for Negroes in New York City was 1,375.

The president of Harvard, Edward Everett, announced that a Negro applicant would be judged only by his qualifying examinations, and "if the white students choose to withdraw all the income of the College will be devoted to his education."

A manual labor school for Negroes, later known as Union Literary Institute, was established near Newport, Ind.

Florida law established common schools and gave all taxpayers the right to vote at district meetings, but only white children could attend the schools.

Lewis Temple, a Negro, invented the toggle harpoon which became increasingly important to the whaling industry of New England.

Christopher Harrison Payne (1848-1925), a Negro Baptist clergyman, lawyer and U. S. official, was born in Red Sulphur Springs, Monroe County, Va. His mother was the daughter and had been the slave of James Ellison who taught her to read and write; his father, Thomas Payne, was a cattle drover. Between 1861 and 1864, Payne was a body servant in the

Confederate Army. After the war, he attended night school in Charleston, W. Va., and in 1868 passed the examination for a teacher's certificate. Converted to the Baptist faith in 1875, he was ordained in 1877. In 1880 he became pastor of the Moore Street Baptist Church in Richmond, Va. He was appointed missionary for the eastern division of Virginia in 1883, and on April 1, 1884, was installed as pastor of the 1st Baptist Church of Montgomery, W. Va. Payne founded the *West Virginia Enterprise* "for the purpose of disseminating correct information about the achievements of the colored people," and later started *The Pioneer* at Montgomery, W. Va. The weekly, *Mountain Eagle,* was also founded by Payne. Active in the Republican Party, he was rewarded with the position of Deputy Collector of Internal Revenue at Charleston, W. Va. Between 1889 and 1893, he studied law, and was admitted to practice in W. Va. in 1896. He was the first Negro elected to the state legislature. He served as U.S. internal revenue agent in 1898 and 1899, and in 1903, was made U. S. consul at St. Thomas in the Danish West Indies. He remained at the post until the U.S. purchased these islands in 1917. He continued to reside in the islands and served as prosecuting attorney and police judge.

The Past and Present Condition and the Destiny of the Colored Race was published in Troy, N.Y., by Henry Highland Garnet, the Negro abolitionist.

1849

U. S. Secretary of State, John M. Clayton, stated that passports were not issued to Negroes, and that they were granted U. S. protection abroad only when they were in the service of U. S. diplomats.

Citizens of Color in Connecticut met in New Haven with Rev. Beman as president and S. M. Africanus of Hartford as secretary, to protest their disenfranchisement by Connecticut law, and to seek ways of securing the right to vote.

The Ohio legislature repealed some of the "black laws" including the requirement that Negroes post bond in order to enter the state. They also repealed the ban on Negro testimony in court. The Ohio Legislature also passed a law establishing publicly-supported schools for Negro children.

Philadelphia had for Negroes one grammar school with

463 pupils, and two primary schools with 339 pupils. They also had one infant school with 70 pupils, run by the Pennsylvania Abolition Society. Twenty Negro private schools with an enrollment of 300 pupils were also in Philadelphia. The total number of pupils in the Negro schools was about 1,300.

New York Central College in McGrawville, N.Y., was founded by the American Baptist Free Mission Society. It admitted both sexes and both races, and appointed a Negro to the faculty, William G. Allen. When Allen announced his engagement to a white student he was forced to flee the anger of the townspeople. By 1858, the college was bankrupt and closed finally in 1861.

Avery College for Negroes in Allegheny City, Pa., was established with a $300,000 bequest of Rev. Charles Avery. Both Negroes and whites served on the faculty.

When the Negroes of Cincinnati took advantage of a new state law (allowing the school tax on Negro property to be used for the education of Negroes), by electing trustees, organizing a school system and employing teachers, the city officials refused to turn over the money to the Negro trustees on the grounds that they were not voters, and thus could not be officeholders. The trustees contested the matter in the courts and eventually won.

A Negro, Benjamin F. Roberts, sued the city of Boston on behalf of his 5-year-old daughter, Sarah. He asked for damages because the city refused to allow her in white public schools. The case was argued by Charles Sumner and Robert Morris, a Negro lawyer, with no success. The Supreme Court of Massachusetts rejected the appeal and and established in its decision the precedent for the controversial "separate and equal" doctrine in U.S. law.

A Negro school abolition organization was set up in Boston by Jonas Clark and 227 others. They tried to have the courts declare separate schools unconstitutional, and to prevent the use of the Negro Smith School. Finally, they started an opposition school for Negroes and whites taught by Rev. Daniel Foster, a Negro preacher.

7.4% of Negroes of Philadelphia County owned property.

William Whipper and Stephen Smith, Negroes of Columbia, Pa., had a business operation which included stock of several thousand bushels of coal and 2,250,000 feet of lumber, 22 railway cars on the Baltimore to Philadelphia route, $9,000 of stock in the Columbia Bridge, $18,000 of stock in the Columbia Bank. Smith also owned 58 houses in Philadelphia, and some in Lancaster and Columbia.

A white gang, known as the "Killers of Moyamensing," led an armed raid on the Negroes of Philadelphia. The militia was called out, three whites and one Negro were killed, and 25 persons were hospitalized.

The Maryland Legislature repealed an 1832 law forbidding the bringing of slaves into the state.

Virginia law stated that the right of citizenship in the state was confined to free white persons.

Wisconsin law disenfranchised Negroes.

Harriet Tubman escaped from slavery in Maryland, and subsequently returned to the South 19 times, rescuing over 300 slaves.

Martin R. Delany, a Pittsburgh Negro, was admitted to Harvard Medical School.

John V. DeGrasse of New York and Thomas J. White of Brooklyn, both Negroes, were allowed to study medicine at Bowdoin College.

Charles L. Reason, a Negro, became professor of belles-lettres and French at Central College, McGrawville, N.Y., which admitted both white and Negro students.

The first Negro gold miner in California was Waller Jackson, who sailed around Cape Horn, from Boston, and mined at Downieville, Calif. Several hundred other Negro miners came to California during the gold rush.

Archibald Henry Grimké (1849-1930), a Negro lawyer, author and publicist, was the son of Henry Grimké, of South Carolina, and Nancy Weston, a family slave. Grimké attended Lincoln University, receiving his B.A. in 1870, an M.A. in 1872, and an LL.B. from Harvard Law School in 1874. Between 1883 and 1885 he was editor of the *Hub* in Boston. At this time he wrote a series of articles for the *Boston Herald,* the *Boston Traveler* and the *Atlantic Monthly.* An active member of the American Negro Academy, he served as president from 1903 to 1916. He was American consul to Santo Domingo in 1894. Grimké was an active biographer, and published a life of William Lloyd Garrison, in 1891, and *The Life of Charles Sumner, the Scholar in Politics* in 1892. His other works were *Right on the Scaffold, or The Martyrs of 1822* (1901); *The Ballotless Victim of One-Party Governments* (1913); "The Sex Question and Race Segregation" in *Papers of the American Negro Academy, 1915* (1916); *The Ultimate Criminal* (1915); and *The Shame of America, or, The Negro's Case against the Republic* (1924). In 1919, the Spingarn Medal from the N.A.A.C.P. was awarded to Grimké.

Thomas Ezekiel Miller (1849-1937) Negro Congressman, was born of free parents in Ferebeeville, S. C., and attended public schools and Lincoln University. Miller was admitted to the Bar in 1875, in South Carolina. He practiced law in Beaufort and became active as a politician. A State Senator in 1880, he was elected for one term to the House of Representatives in 1889, and to the South Carolina Constitutional Convention in 1895. He served as president of the State Colored College in Orangeburg.

James W. C. Pennington's *The Fugitive Blacksmith: His Early Life* was published in London.

1850

U.S. Census: Negro population in the U.S. was 3,638,808, or 15.7% of the total U.S. population. 434,495, or 11.9%, were free. More than one-half of these free Negroes lived in slave states. Of the 3,204,313 slaves, it is estimated that approximately 400,000 lived in cities and towns, while 2,800,000 lived on farms or plantations, 1,800,000 of them on cotton plantations. The slave population in selected states was: Alabama, 342,844; Arkansas, 47,100; Washington, D. C., 3,687; Delaware, 2,290; Florida, 39,310; Georgia, 381,682; Kentucky, 210,981; Louisiana, 244,809; Maryland, 90,368; Mississippi, 309,878; Missouri, 87,422; New Jersey, 236; North Carolina, 288,548; South Carolina, 384,984; Tennessee, 239,459; Texas, 58,161; Virginia, 472,528; Utah Territory, 26.

Mulattoes made up 11.2% of the total Negro population in the U.S., and 25% of Northern Negroes. 159,000 mulattoes were free.

The white population of the South was 6,184,477, of which

76% were yeoman farmers owning no slaves; of the 347,525 slaveholders, only 11 owned 500 or more, 254 owned 200 or more, and approximately 8,000 owned 50 or more. Thus 7% of whites owned 75% of the slaves.

A prime field-hand sold for approximately $1,600.

The main products of slave labor in the U.S. were: cotton valued at $98,603,720; tobacco, $13,982,686; cane sugar, $12,378,850; hemp, $5,000,000; rice, $4,000,000; molasses, $2,540,179—a total of $136,505,435. The numbers of slaves used in each type of agriculture was proportionate to the amount produced.

School attendance and adult illiteracy among Negroes in 16 cities were the following:

	Total free Negro population	Free Negroes in School	Illiterate Free Negroes
Boston, Mass.	2,038	1,439	205
Providence, R.I.	1,499	292	55
New Haven, Conn.	989	360	167
Brooklyn, N.Y.	2,424	507	788
New York City	13,815	1,418	1,667
Philadelphia, Pa.	10,736	2,176	3,498
Cincinnati, Ohio	3,237	291	620
Louisville, Ky.	1,538	141	567
Baltimore, Md.	25,442	1,453	9,318
Washington, D.C.	8,158	420	2,674
Richmond, Va.	2,369	none	1,594
Petersburg, Va.	2,616	none	1,155
Charleston, S.C.	3,441	68	45
Savannah, Ga.	686	none	185
Mobile, Ala.	715	53	12
New Orleans, La.	9,905	1,008	2,279

Approximately the same percentage of white children and Negro children attended school in New York City.

The census showed 100,591 whites and 217 free Negroes in school in North Carolina, and of the 12,048 free Negro adults 5,191 or 43% were literate.

Fugitive slaves amounted to 1,011 or .0315% of the total slave population.

Capt. Thomas B. Sullivan estimated that one-half of American seamen, or about 75,000, were Negroes.

Approximately 960 Negroes had come to California, either as slaves or as freemen.

Ohio had 25,279 Negroes, 3,237 of them living in Cincinnati.

Michigan had 2,500 Negroes.

In Virginia, almost one-fifth of free Negroes, and only about one-tenth of the whites lived in towns.

The free Negro population of North Carolina was 27,463 or 3.16% of the total population of North Carolina. 73% of the families in North Carolina owned no slaves, and more than one-half of the slave owners had less than 10 slaves.

Free Negroes in Pennsylvania numbered 53,626 out of a total state population of 2,311,786.

The 1850 Compromise over issues causing sectional conflict in the U.S. provided that: (1) California would enter the U.S. as a free state; (2) other land gained from Mexico would be organized into territories with no provision one way or the other on slavery; (3) Texas would receive money in exchange for ceding land to the New Mexico Territory; (4) a more stringent fugitive slave law would be enacted; (5) the slave trade in the District of Columbia would be abolished.

The Federal Fugitive Slave Law allowed any claimants of a runaway slave to take possession of the Negro upon establishing proof of ownership before a federal commissioner. No safeguards, such as jury trial or judicial hearing for the captive, were included. The Act provided fines of $1,000 and imprisonment for six months of citizens or officials who failed to aid in the capture of fugitives. Within 36 hours of the passage of the Fugitive Slave Law, 40 Massachusetts Negroes departed for Canada, and the Negro population of Columbia, Pa., dropped from 943 to 437.

By this year the Whig Party was breaking up. The anti-Jackson issues that had united Southerners and Northerners in 1834 had died, and the Compromise of 1850 highlighted their differences on slavery. Northern Whigs disapproved of the Fugitive Slave Law, to which one Southern Whig replied, "Take secession, nullification and hail disunion as a blessing, rather than yield the Fugitive Slave Law." However, the majority of Southern Whigs were willing to accept slavery limitations as a price for preserving the Union. Thus, early in 1850 at the Nashville Convention, a nonpartisan gathering of Southern politicians, the Whigs defended admission of

California to the Union; in contrast, the Southern Democrats opposed admission because slavery was outlawed there. Within the next two years, most Southern Whigs had transferred their allegiance to the Democratic Party, since the Northern Whigs were so strongly anti-slavery.

The first recorded enforcement of the Fugitive Slave Law of 1850 was in September against James Hamlet, a free Negro in New York who was arrested as a fugitive slave belonging to Mary Brown of Baltimore. Money was raised for him, and he was bought from slavery in October.

A constitutional amendment to grant equal voting rights to New York Negroes was defeated by popular vote.

Citizens of Lehigh County, Pa., asked that all Negroes be expelled from the state.

Virginia law placed an annual per capita tax of $1 on free Negroes.

A Vermont law called on state's attorneys to defend fugitive slaves.

The Ohio Colored Convention reported the formation of the Colored American League to assist runaway slaves, improve the condition of Negroes and encourage Negro communities to establish military companies.

David Clay, an Ohio Negro, advertised his manufactured plows which could be made any size and plow a depth of 8 to 20 inches.

Returning to the South for the first time since her escape, Harriet Tubman went to Baltimore and led her sister and two children to freedom.

New York Negroes formed the American League of Colored Laborers to promote a union of skilled workers, to encourage the practical education of Negroes and to assist Negroes in establishing businesses. Its president was Samuel R. Ward.

A Negro Masonic Lodge was organized in Louisville, Ky., despite white opposition.

Pleasures and Other Miscellaneous Poems by Daniel Payne, a Negro and a bishop of the AME Church, was published.

The Queiróz Law closed Brazil's principal sources of slaves.

1851

Frederick Douglass split from William Lloyd Garrison on the tactics and strategy of the abolitionist movement. In an address before the Annual Convention of the American Antislavery Society, he supported political action and opposed the dissolution of the Union, as a move that would place slaves at the complete mercy of the South. Declaring that the Constitution implied the eventual extinction of slavery, Douglass predicted that slavery would end in violence.

A Mr. Miller was killed in Maryland on his way back to Nottingham, Pa., with a free Negro girl who was kidnapped from his house and taken to Baltimore.

A slave catcher named Gorsuch was killed by free Negroes in Christiana, Pa., when he and his assistants refused to leave the home of William Parker, a free Negro.

A new Virginia constitution provided that slaves henceforth emancipated would be made slaves again if they remained in the state more than 12 months.

A Virginia law imposed upon county sheriffs or sergeants the duty of summoning a special court to hear evidence concerning an escaped slave if the county or corporation court was not in session, thus facilitating the recovery of fugitives.

Thomas M. Sims was arrested in Boston as an escaped slave of Mr. Potter of Virginia. Sims was sent to Virginia on the *U.S. Acorn*, despite the protests of Boston abolitionists such as Wendell Phillips and Theodore Parker.

California law denied Negroes the right to testify in court against a white man.

The Indiana Constitution of 1851 barred further admission of Negroes to the state. Violators, however, were seldom prosecuted. This constitution also denied the vote to Negroes and mulattoes, and excluded them from the militia.

Negro abolitionists in Boston rescued a fugitive slave named Shadrach from a courtroom in February. In October, a fugitive slave named Jerry was rescued in the same way in Syracuse, N.Y.

Detroit Negroes, of whom there were approximately 1,000, owned about $30,000 worth of property.

Knight and Bell, Negro plasterers in Cincinnati, received a

contract for plastering the public buildings of Hamilton County.

The Industrial Congress, "a short-lived, national organization of reformers and workingmen," admitted Negro delegates to its convention.

The *New York Tribune* reported a clash between Negro and white workers at the Hazel River Works in Culpepper County, Va. One Negro was killed.

The Mechanics Association of Portsmouth, Va., protested the teaching of trades to slaves because slave carpenters, coopers, etc., degraded the white mechanics by their competition.

New York Negroes formed a committee to welcome the Hungarian revolutionary, Kossuth. George T. Downing, a young Negro labor leader, was chosen to make the address of welcome.

Myrtilla Miner, a young white woman of New York, went to Washington to establish an academy for Negro girls. Her school eventually became a college bearing her name.

Alberry Whitman (1851-1902), Negro poet, was born into slavery. Educated at Wilberforce, he came under the influence of Bishop Payne. He was widely read and cultivated, and had a superb memory. His first volume, *Leelah Misled,* published in 1873, had no verse dealing with the race problem. His 20-volume *Not a Man and Yet a Man,* published in 1877, was a long, melodramatic story about a mulatto slave who rescued his master's daughter during an Indian massacre. He fell in love with her, and then underwent all sorts of tribulations until he ended up in Canada—a free man. Another long narrative poem, *The Rape of Florida*, published in 1884, done in Spenserian stanzas, concerned the white man's oppression of the Seminoles. Its significance was that Whitman saw the Indian in a position analogous to that of his own people. In Whitman's subsequent long poems, *The Octoroon,* in 1901, and *The Southland's Charm and Freedom's Magnitude*, published in 1902, he showed his preference for mulattoes, claiming that pure blacks do not exist, and championed acceptance of mulattoes into white society. His few dialect poems (e.g., *Tobe's Dream*) were the best done by a Negro before Dunbar.

Lectures on American Slavery by Frederick Douglass was published.

The *Colored Man's Journal*, a Negro newspaper, began publication in New York.

The *Liberty Party Paper* merged with Douglass' *North Star*.

The Colored American Institute for the Promotion of the Mechanic Arts and Sciences exhibited work of Negro mechanics in Philadelphia in April. There were: portraits by Videll of New York and Wilson of Philadelphia; marine paintings by Bowser; exhibits by Dutere; and exhibits of artificial teeth by Dr. Rock. Also shown at this convention was an invention by Roberts for replacing derailed cars on tracks. *The Pennsylvanian* called it the "first exhibition of its kind in the U.S."

Elizabeth Taylor Greenfield, a Negro raised by a Quaker woman, sang for the Buffalo Musical Association, and was immediately compared to Jenny Lind and the other great sopranos of the era. She had a range of 3¼ octaves, and gave concerts in the U.S. and Europe.

Colombia abolished slavery.

1852

Harriet Beecher Stowe's book *Uncle Tom's Cabin,* portraying the plight of the slave in highly emotional language, was published. In its first year, over 300,000 copies were sold.

Martin R. Delany, a Negro physician, called for the establishment of a Negro "Promised Land" in Central or South America, because of his lack of hope for improvement of the Negro's position in the U.S.

Negroes applied for jobs at businesses owned by members of the executive committee of the American and Foreign Anti-slavery Society. Some were rejected, and the rest were given menial jobs.

A petition from the free Negroes of San Francisco for removal of the prohibition against Negro testimony against white men in court was refused by the state assembly.

Delaware law provided for taxation of all property, Negro and white, for support of schools for white children.

A bill was introduced in the Georgia Legislature to permit the education of slaves as a means of increasing their value.

It failed by 2 or 3 votes in the Senate, although it passed the lower house.

Another Georgia law placed a per capita tax of $5 a year on free Negroes.

Kentucky law forbade immigration of free Negroes into the state on pain of imprisonment.

There were 3,500 Negroes in Cincinnati. 200 of them were property owners who paid real estate taxes. Their total property was valued at $500,000. 450 Negro children attended school, including 50 in high school. There were six Negro churches.

Evening schools for Negroes were opened in New York City, one for males and one for females, with a combined attendance of 379 pupils.

William Still, a Negro, became chairman of the Acting Vigilance Committee of Philadelphia, which harbored runaway slaves and helped them escape to Canada.

Sojourner Truth, a former New York slave, attended the Second National Women's Suffrage Convention in Akron, Ohio, and delivered her famous "A'n't I a woman?" speech.

Dr. James McCune Smith, a Negro, was nominated to serve on a 5-man committee to draft a constitution for the "Statistic Institute," of which he became a leading member.

Simon Gray, a Negro slave, was the captain of a lumber company flatboat on the Mississippi River. He traveled freely as a company agent and lived and vacationed apart with his family.

Jan E. Matzeliger (1852-1889), Negro inventor, was born in Dutch Guiana, came to the U.S. as a young man and served as a cobbler's apprentice, first in Philadelphia and then in Lynn, Mass. Although he died at 37, he made a profound contribution to the leather industry with his "sole machine." This machine was the first appliance of its kind, capable of performing all the steps required to hold a shoe on its last, grip and pull the leather down around the heel, guide and drive the nails into place, and then discharge the complete shoe from the machine. The patent was bought by the United Shoe Machinery Co. of Boston, which made millions on the basis of Matzeliger's invention. The company soon expanded to include 40 subsidiaries and employed tens of thousands of people in its plants.

George H. White (1852-1918), Negro Congressman, was born in Rosedale, N. C., and was educated at Howard University. He taught in North Carolina and pursued legal studies. Admitted to the Bar in 1879, he gained a reputation as a brilliant lawyer. A State Congressman in 1880, State Senator in 1884, and State Solicitor in 1886, he was elected to the House of Representatives in 1897 and re-elected in 1899. He spoke for equal constitutional rights for Negroes.

William C. Nell's *Services of Colored Americans in the Wars of 1775 and 1812* was published. This was issued in a revised form in 1855, as *The Colored Patriots of the American Revolution with Sketches of Several Distinguished Colored Persons to which is Added a Brief Survey of the Condition and Prospects of Colored Americans.*

Three Years in Europe, a description of his travels by William Wells Brown, a former slave, was published.

Martin R. Delany, a Negro, published *The Condition, Elevation, Emigration and Destiny of the Colored People of the U.S., Politically Considered* in Philadelphia.

The *Alienated American,* a Negro publication, began in Cleveland with W. H. H. Day as editor.

1853

Professor Dew of William and Mary College in Virginia, Chancellor Harper of the South Carolina Supreme Court, Senator Hammond of South Carolina and Gilmore Simms jointly published a book entitled *Pro-Slavery Argument.* In this book, slavery was defended from several points of view; the most significant was the defense by Senator Hammond. He reasoned that the white Northern factory worker was a wage slave, and the industrial society was completely callous to him; in contrast, in the South the slave lived under the paternalistic slave-holder. The appearance of *Uncle Tom's Cabin* the previous year gave impetus to publications defending slavery.

A *New York Herald* editorial urged the U.S. Government to make emigration of free Negroes to Liberia more attractive. The newspaper felt that the Negro's "racial inferiority" made him a burden on the U.S.

783 Negroes were transported to Liberia in the course of this year.

Virginia law levied a poll tax on free male Negroes between 21 and 55 years. The money was to be used to raise a fund for removal of free Negroes to Africa.

Illinois law forbade entry of Negroes and mulattoes into the state.

Another Illinois law provided that Negroes could be advertised and sold at public auction if they did not produce certified proof of freedom and post bond guaranteeing good behavior.

A planned slave revolt in New Orleans involving 2,500 slaves was averted when a free Negro informed.

Negroes, led by William C. Nell, petitioned for admission to the Massachusetts militia.

In the case of FOREMANS V. TAMM in Pennsylvania, Tamm, a Negro who had settled on a piece of land and gained title by pre-emption, sought redress when Foremans, a white man, evicted him. The case was decided in favor of Tamm on the grounds that, though Negroes were politically without rights in this state, they had civil rights, including acquisition and pre-emption of land.

The Society of Progressive Friends was organized in Pennsylvania to oppose slavery more aggressively than conservative Quakers had wished to do.

Pennsylvania Negroes petitioned the State Legislature to secure protection for them when they travelled in slave states.

Striking Irishmen on the Erie Railroad were replaced with armed Negroes.

Alexander Crummell, an American Negro Episcopal priest, took a degree from Queens College, Cambridge University in England. He then went to Liberia.

The Episcopal Convention of the N.Y. Diocese voted to admit representatives from St. Phillip's Episcopal Church (Negro) after a 7-year battle led by John Jay, grandson of the first Chief Justice.

Robert Purvis of Philadelphia, a Negro, refused to pay a school tax because his children were excluded from the public school.

Indiana law stated that Negroes should not be taxed for school purposes.

The Board of Education of the City and County of New York took over the white and Negro schools of the Public School Society. A Normal School for Negro teachers was established. Attendance in Negro schools was 2,047.

Ohio law transferred control of Negro public schools to managers of the white school system.

Anne Douglass, a white woman from South Carolina, was imprisoned in Norfolk, Va., for violating a state law against instruction of Negroes.

On July 6, delegates from several states founded the National Council of Colored People in Rochester, N.Y., to encourage the mechanical training of Negroes.

A Negro YMCA was organized in Washington, D.C., by Anthony Bower, a Negro.

By this year all Southern cities had Negro bands and military parades were usually accompanied by a Negro brass band. These bands were composed of free Negroes and house slaves who played European march music in imitation of white concert bands. When the former field slaves were allowed to join these bands after the Civil War, they contributed African influences to them.

George Washington Murray (1853-1926), Negro Congressman, was born of slave parents in Rembert, S.C., and received an education and attended South Carolina University for two years. A teacher by profession, in 1888 he was Republican Party chairman for Sumter County, S.C. Appointed customs inspector for Charleston Harbor by President Harrison in 1893, in 1895 he was elected to Congress. He advocated better educational opportunities for Negroes. Murray left politics after an unsuccessful attempt to lead a Negro faction away from the Republican Party.

Clotel, or the President's Daughter, by William Wells Brown, was published in London. The novel was basically an abolitionist polemic concerning an illegitimate daughter of Thomas Jefferson, who tried to escape from slavery and was ironically killed in the Potomac within sight of her father's house. Much of the book was given over to a detailed description of the "peculiar institution" which the author knew so well. When *Clotel* was published in 1867 in the U.S. in

Boston, the story was altered: Jefferson was replaced by an anonymous Senator.

Solomon Northrup's *12 Years a Slave* was published.

By this year Portugal had received £2,850,965 in bribes from the British Government to stop the slave trade.

1854

The Kansas-Nebraska Act, proposed by Stephen Douglas of Illinois to encourage rapid settlement in the Mid-West, was passed. The Act repealed the Missouri Compromise's prohibition of slavery north of the 36° 30′ line in territories when it allowed "squatter or popular sovereignty" in Kansas and Nebraska on the slavery issue.

The Republican Party was created to oppose the Kansas-Nebraska Act's opening of the West to slavery.

In Peoria, Ill., Abraham Lincoln made his first public statement in opposition to the extension of slavery in the new territories: "Slavery is founded in the selfishness of man's nature—opposition to it, in his love of justice. These principles are an eternal antagonism, and when brought into collision so fiercely, as slavery extension brings them, shocks, and throes, and convulsions must ceaselessly follow."

In April of 1854, anti-slavery forces organized the New England Emigration Aid Society to settle "free-soilers" in Kansas.

Connecticut law provided punishment by fine and imprisonment for falsely and maliciously representing a free person to be a slave, and for maliciously seizing a free person with intent to enslave.

Rhode Island law forbade state officials from enforcing the 1850 Federal Fugitive Slave Law.

Vermont law provided penalties of fine and imprisonment for attempting to kidnap a free person to remove him from the state as a slave.

Anthony Burns, an escaped slave, was captured in Boston and sent back to the South despite an attempt by Boston citizens to rescue him. An escort of 2,000 U.S. soldiers accompanied Burns through the Boston streets. Burns was later freed, attended college and became a pastor of the Zion Baptist Church in Canada.

In August, delegates from 11 states met in Cleveland at the National Emigration Convention of the Colored People. Most of the delegates were from Ohio and Pennsylvania. They advocated establishment of a Negro colony on the grounds of Negro racial pride as well as from a desire to escape oppression.

The Ohio State Senate expelled a Negro editor from his seat in the reporters' section on the grounds that laws of nature required strict separation of the races.

The *New Bern Atlantic* of North Carolina, complained of the "notorious fact" that day schools were being operated for the benefit of free Negroes in the town.

A white woman in Norfolk, Va., was found to be conducting a school for Negroes in defiance of the state law.

The first school for Negro children in San Francisco was started in the basement of the St. Cyprian AME Church, with 23 pupils.

Ashmun Institute, later Lincoln University, was founded by Presbyterians.

Martin R. Delany, the Negro graduate of the Harvard Medical School, distinguished himself for his work in a cholera epidemic in Pittsburgh.

Dr. John V. DeGrasse, a Negro, was admitted to the Massachusetts Medical Society.

John M. Langston, a Negro and a graduate of Oberlin College and School of Theology, was admitted to the Bar in Ohio, after the examination committee found that he had more white than Negro blood.

James Bland (1854-1911), popular songwriter, was born of free parents in Flushing, N. Y. His father, Allen M. Bland, was a college graduate and an examiner in the U.S. Patent Office. Educated at Howard University, Bland wrote over 600 popular songs, among them *Carry Me Back to Ole Virginny, Oh, Dem Golden Slippers, In the Evening by the Moonlight.*

Francis Ellen Harper's *Poems on Miscellaneous Subjects* was published. She was a Negro.

Venezuela abolished slavery.

Jose Do Patrocino (1854-1905) of Brazil, son of a priest and a Negro vegetable peddler, was very sympathetic toward slaves from early childhood. He spent his later life as an abolitionist. In 1877, he published *Motta Coquiero*. The story concerns the murder of a plantation owner as retaliation for a murder he did not commit. Its importance lies in the careful examination of racial tensions and conflicts on a plantation in Brazil among whites, Negroes and mulattoes.

1855

The first convention of California Negroes was held in the Colored Methodist Church of Sacramento in November. 49 delegates attended, and the chairman was William H. Yates of San Francisco. They protested against the exclusion of Negroes as witnesses in court against white persons, and claimed that the approximately 6,000 Negroes in the state had capital of about 3 million dollars.

New York Negroes formed a Legal Rights Association and employed Chester A. Arthur and others to defend them after they deliberately violated segregation rules on public transportation in New York City. They won a case in that year in which damages were awarded to a Negro woman who was expelled from a segregated railroad car.

Rev. James W. C. Pennington of New York refused to leave the 6th Avenue horsecar in New York when he was requested to do so. He was thrown off, sued the company and won the case.

New York Negroes established the State Suffrage Association to work for amendment of the constitution to give Negroes equal voting rights.

There were 3,000 Negro children between four and 17 years of age in New York City, of whom 913 attended public schools, 240 attended a Negro orphan asylum school, and 125 attended private schools. This compares with the 159,000 white children between the ages of four and 17, of whom 43,858 attended public schools, 2,826 attended public corporate schools, and 17,560 attended private schools. The average attendance was about the same for both groups. The proportion of Negroes to whites in public schools was about 1 to 40. The money spent by the Board of Education on school building and sites for Negroes and for whites was about $1,000 for Negroes to $1,600,000 for whites.

The New York Liberty Party nominated Frederick Douglass for New York Secretary of State, the first time a Negro had been nominated for a state office. Douglass and Dr. James McCune Smith, along with Lewis Tappan and Gerrit Smith, called a convention of Radical Political Abolitionists at Syracuse, N.Y. James McCune Smith presided over the convention. The next year the Political Abolition Party nominated Gerrit Smith for President of the U.S. and Samuel McFarland for Vice-President.

87% of gainfully employed Negroes in New York City worked in menial or unskilled jobs.

When N. Y. longshoremen struck to protest wage cuts and attacks on their union, Negroes served as strikebreakers. At Morgan's London Line docks the Irish longshoremen fled when it was discovered that a Negro was armed. Within a few months the old workers came back, replacing most of the Negroes.

Per capita ownership of property of Ohio Negroes compared favorably with that of Ohio whites. Negroes in Cincinnati owned $800,000 worth of property, and in the whole state they owned $5,000,000 worth of property.

Philadelphia Negroes owned $2,655,693 in real and personal property. They paid $9,766.42 in taxes that year. 19,000 Negroes owned real property valued at $800,000. Negroes had incorporated 108 mutual benefit societies with 9,762 members, and had deposited $28,366 in Philadelphia banks.

Maine, Massachusetts and Michigan passed "personal liberty" laws forbidding state officials from aiding in the enforcement of the Fugitive Slave Laws of 1793 and 1850.

Captain Fountain brought 21 fugitive slaves from Norfolk, Va., to Philadelphia, concealed in a cargo of grain on his ship.

In a memorial, North Carolina citizens asked the state legislature to authorize the education of Negroes, to allow Negroes to marry, and to forbid separation of Negro families.

The General Assembly of North Carolina had since 1791 passed 37 acts of emancipation freeing altogether 98 Negroes.

Brigham Young declared that one drop of Negro blood prevented a man from entering the Mormon priesthood, thus making a distinction between white and Negro male members of the faith.

On April 28, segregation in Massachusetts schools was

abolished by law. The following September, Boston schools were integrated with no incident.

Cincinnati Negroes formed the "Attucks Guards," a military company.

My Bondage and My Freedom by Frederick Douglass was published.

The *Herald of Freedom*, a Negro publication, began in Ohio with Peter H. Clark as editor.

The *Mirror of the Times*, a Negro newspaper in San Francisco, began publication.

1856

The Republican Party was formally organized, including members of the Whig and Democratic parties committed to a free-soil policy in the West. The South interpreted this policy as abolitionist.

In Kansas, pro-slavery groups tried to discourage settlement by "free-soil" advocates. Their attack on the town of Lawrence was avenged by John Brown at the massacre of Pottawatomie Creek.

Senator Sumner of Massachusetts was beaten to insensibility in the Senate by Representative Brooks of South Carolina after he severely criticized slavery and legislators who favored it.

Proceedings of the State Convention of Colored Citizens of the State of Illinois reported the formation by Negroes of the Repeal Association to work for revocation of the state "black laws."

Negroes in the New England states had $2,000,000 invested in business, not including agriculture, according to a report of the National Convention of Colored Americans in Philadelphia. Negroes in Ohio, Illinois and Michigan had $1,500,000 invested, and in New York and Pennsylvania Negroes had $3,000,000 invested. New York City Negroes had $600,000 deposited in savings banks.

A fair price for a healthy 30-year-old Negro woman with a child was between $700 and $800. She was worth one-sixth to one-quarter more than a non-breeding woman.

Mining companies sometimes owned slaves, but in general hired them from their owners for $120 to $200 a year.

U.S. Attorney General Caleb Cushing declared Negroes did not have the right to apply for benefits under the land pre-emption act of 1841.

An Indiana Negro was convicted for the violation of the state's Negro exclusion law for bringing a Negro woman into the state in order to marry her. The conviction was upheld in the State Supreme Court.

A New York jury refused to convict a railroad company for expelling a Negro minister from a railroad car, on the grounds that common carriers were not required to carry persons when it would adversely affect their interests.

The Maroons in Bladen and Robeson counties, North Carolina, terrorized the countryside.

Negroes were given by Virginia law the right to enslave themselves, by petition to the legislature, to a master of their choosing. The master would pay the court one-half the valuation of the slave.

Virginia law forbade the selling of poisonous drugs to free Negroes or slaves.

Margaret Garner, a Kentucky slave, tried to kill her children to keep them from being recaptured in Ohio and sent back to slavery. She succeeded in killing one. On the way back to Kentucky she unsuccessfully tried to drown herself and another child in the river.

Galilean Fishermen, a secret organization, was founded by Negroes in Baltimore.

Ohio Negroes were again given control over their schools.

Supported by Methodists, Wilberforce University in Ohio was established for Negroes. Four Negroes, Alfred J. Anderson, Rev. Louis Woodson, Ishmael Keith and Bishop Payne, and 20 white men were on the original board of trustees.

Berea College in Kentucky was founded. It followed a policy of integration until 1907 when the U.S. Supreme Court upheld a Kentucky law of 1904 requiring segregation of the races.

Timothy Thomas Fortune (1856-1928), Negro newspaperman, editor and writer, was born in Marianna, Fla. During Reconstruction his father became a state legislator. It was probably through his father that Fortune met a white congressman, William J. Purman, who secured Fortune a position as customs inspector in Delaware. During his term as inspector he attended Howard University. Upon graduation in 1881, he went to New York and a year later became editor of the New York *Globe*, a Negro weekly. In 1884 Fortune moved to the New York *Freeman*. In this year he published *Land, Labor and Politics in the South*. In 1885 Fortune published *The Negro in Politics*. Fortune was an advocate of full equality for the Negro. In 1887 he formed the Afro-American League which worked for full rights for Negroes, including voting rights, an anti-lynching bill and the equitable distribution of school funds. By 1890 the Afro-American League had representatives in 21 states. During the 1890's, Fortune became a follower of Booker T. Washington. He edited the *New York Age*, a pro-Washington paper and did ghost writing and publicity for Mrs. Washington. He maintained tight control of the Afro-American League, turning aside the efforts of Monroe Trotter and George Forbes to re-establish its early egalitarian militancy. Although Fortune helped Booker T. Washington write his autobiography, Washington was put off by the vehemence of Fortune's attacks on Trotter and Forbes, and by Fortune's alcoholism. In 1914 Fortune established the Washington *Sun*. Until a short time before his death in 1928 he directed the publication of *Negro World*, house organ of the Universal Negro Improvement Association.

Granville T. Woods (1856-1910), Negro inventor, developed an egg incubator, a system of telegraphing from moving trains, and improvement in electric railways and the phonograph. General Electric and Bell Telephone bought many of his inventions, and he marketed others through his own company.

Elymas Rogers, a Negro Presbyterian minister, wrote a satire in verse, *The Repeal of the Missouri Compromise Considered*. The author feared liberal Massachusetts would be forced to obey the Fugitive Slave Law. The poem is filled with references to incidents such as the Brooks-Sumner scandal dealing with the slavery question.

William J. Grayson's poem (consisting of over 1,600 lines), published this year, was perhaps the best expression by a Southerner of the Greek Ideal. This was the concept held widely in the South that slavery allowed for the development of a humane and cultivated society (i.e., the Golden Age of Greece).

1857

In DRED SCOTT V. SANFORD, the abolitionists supported the suit before the U.S. Supreme Court. Having lived with his master on free soil, Scott sued for his freedom on the basis of residence. The decision written by Chief Justice Roger B. Taney declared that Negroes were not citizens and that Congress had no power to exclude slavery from the territories, thus making the Missouri Compromise unconstitutional.

The Commissioner of the U.S. General Land Office announced that since Negroes were not citizens they could not qualify for public land grants in the West.

A convention of Negroes in Philadelphia was called largely to denounce the Dred Scott decision.

New York City Negroes paid taxes on real estate worth $1,400,000. The value of their churches in the city was $250,000; they had $1,121,000 deposited in savings banks, and personal property worth $710,000.

A free Negro in St. Paul's Parish, South Carolina, was said to have 200 slaves, a white wife and a white son-in-law.

A New Hampshire law declared that African descent, previous servitude or color of skin was not a disqualification from becoming a full citizen of the state, and that Negroes shared equal suffrage with whites. Any slave brought into the state by his master was given his freedom, and holding another person as a slave was made a felony punishable by hard labor from one to five years.

Maine law declared all slaves brought by their masters into the state free.

Ohio passed a "personal liberty" law (repealed a year later) forbidding the use of state jails in fugitive slave cases.

At the Knoxville Southern Commercial Convention, Edward Bryan of South Carolina presented a motion to annul Article 8 of the Webster Ashburton Treaty of 1843 in which the United States and Great Britain had agreed to maintain ships off the African coast to suppress the slave trade. The motion was approved 66 to 26, with delegates from Maryland, North Carolina and Tennessee dissenting.

Tennessee passed a law which facilitated the re-enslavement of free Negroes.

The clause in the Oregon Constitution which forbade further admission of Negroes to the state was ratified by an 8 to 1 majority of the popular vote.

Wisconsin Negroes petitioned the State Legislature for the right of franchise.

Mifflin Gibbs and John Lester, Negro proprietors of a store in San Francisco, protested in an open letter that the tax collector had come to their store and carted off $20 or $30 worth of goods because they had refused to pay a California poll tax on the grounds that they were not allowed to vote and thus owed no poll tax.

The New York Society for the Promotion of Education Among Colored Children appealed to a commission appointed by the governor to investigate the city's schools for an improvement of Negro education. Charles B. Ray was president of this society, and Philip A. White was secretary; both were Negroes.

Henry Plummer Cheatham (1857-1935), Negro Congressman, was born in Henderson, N.C. He studied law after receiving a B.A. and M.A. from Shaw University. Register of deeds in Vance County from 1884 to 1888 and principal of the Plymouth State Normal School in 1888, he was elected twice to the House of Representatives as a Republican. President McKinley appointed Cheatham recorder of deeds in Washington, D. C. From 1901 until his death, he worked for and supervised a Negro orphanage in North Carolina.

Hinton R. Helper's book, *The Impending Crisis*, was published. Helper, a North Carolina white man, argued that slavery had caused much of the disparity between the economic growth of the North and the South. Almost a million copies of the book were sold.

Franklin Webb, the author of *The Garies and their Friends*, was a member of the free Negro population of Philadelphia. Consequently his concern in this novel, published in London, was not the slavery question but discrimination. The novel dealt with the caste system which prevented Negroes from advancing themselves materially. It also dealt with mixed marriages and job discrimination.

1858

In June, in his acceptance speech for the nomination for Senator from Illinois, Abraham Lincoln stated: "A house divided against itself cannot stand. I believe this government cannot endure permanently half *slave* and half *free*. I do not expect the Union to be *dissolved*. I do not expect the house to *fall*, but I *do* expect it will cease to be divided."

Lincoln, in his summer debates with Stephen Douglas, forced Douglas to alienate many of his Southern supporters with his "Freeport heresy," advocating popular sovereignty in spite of the Supreme Court's decision in the Dred Scott case.

In these debates, Lincoln, in October, clearly stated that the Republican party was committed to the abolition of slavery: "We think it is a moral, a social and a political wrong. . . . On the other hand . . . there is a sentiment which treats it as not being wrong. That is the Democratic sentiment of this day."

In September, in his debates with Stephen Douglas, Lincoln had denied a desire to create a political and social equality between Negroes and whites and opposed intermarriage, enfranchisement and Negro political officials. He had also said that "there is a physical difference between the . . . races which I believe will forever forbid the two races living together on terms of . . . equality."

A prime laborer sold for $800.

At the Montgomery Convention of 1858, the Georgia delegate Kimbree's resolution to support the opening of the slave trade was tabled 71 to 3. Roger Pryor, editor of the *Richmond South*, expressed the attitude of the delegates when he called it "an unworthy issue, . . . repugnant to the instincts of Southern chivalry." Although favoring secession if a Republican was elected, Pryor was opposed to secession to "kidnap cannibals from Africa." Similar resolutions were defeated by the legislatures of Alabama, Arkansas, Louisiana, Mississippi, South Carolina and Texas.

Congress's English bill, enacted in May, broke a deadlock over the acceptance or rejection of the Lecompton Constitution submitted by pro-slavery forces preparatory to Kansas' admission as a state. The bill provided for resubmission of the constitution to a popular vote. It was rejected, and Kansas could not become a state until January, 1861.

U.S. Attorney General Jeremiah S. Black ruled that a slave could not be granted a patent, on the grounds that a slave was not a citizen and could not enter into an agreement with the government. Neither could a slave assign his invention to his owner. For this reason Jefferson Davis was unable to patent a boat propeller invented by his slave, Benjamin Montgomery.

John Brown rescued 11 slaves in Missouri, taking them to Kansas and eventually to Canada.

At Chatham, Canada, in May, John Brown held an anti-slavery convention which 34 Negroes attended.

A Vermont law, similar to New Hampshire's legislation of 1857, declared that African descent was no disqualification from citizenship of the state. It freed any slave who entered the state, with or without permission of his master, and made holding another person as a slave punishable by one to fifteen years in prison, and fines up to $2,000.

Wisconsin and Kansas passed "personal liberty" laws.

Ohio repealed its 1857 "personal liberty" law.

37 citizens of Oberlin and Wellington, Ohio, were indicted for rescuing John Rice who had been captured as a runaway slave by two kidnappers. Some of the defendants were imprisoned pending trial, but the sentences finally imposed were light.

Texas passed a law to facilitate the re-enslavement of free Negroes.

A free Negro could not acquire a slave except "by descent" according to Virginia law.

The Virginia case of BAILY et al. v. POINDEXTER declared void a will allowing slaves to choose between emancipation and being sold at auction, on the grounds that slaves had no legal capacity to choose.

A California law (repealed the next year) forbade immigration of additional Negroes or mulattoes into the state.

Maryland law forbade free Negroes and slaves from having or using boats on the Potomac River.

In Philadelphia, when streetcars were introduced, the company allowed Negroes to ride only on the front platform.

Dr. John S. Rock made a speech in Boston in March, expressing his pride in his race. Rock was an abolitionist, a doctor, and the first Negro lawyer admitted to practice before the U.S. Supreme Court.

Two Negro doctors graduated from Berkshire Medical School.

A free school for Negroes was opened in Washington, D. C., by the St. Vincent de Paul Society, an association of Negro Catholics, under the direction of Father Walter.

Booker Taliaferro Washington (1858?-1915), Negro leader and educator, was born a slave on a plantation in Franklin County, Virginia. After the Civil War he went to West Virginia and worked in coal mines, attending school at night. In 1872, Washington enrolled in Hampton Institute in Virginia, travelling 500 miles, mostly by walking. He worked his way through school as a janitor and graduated in 1875. He taught for a brief period in Malden, West Virginia, and then went to Wayland Seminary in Washington, D.C. After his stay at Wayland, he became an instructor at Hampton Institute. In 1881, Washington was chosen to organize a school for Negroes at Tuskegee, Alabama, on an annual budget of $2,000. He rapidly developed Tuskegee, emphasizing industrial training; in its first two decades 40 buildings were erected, almost exclusively by the students themselves. An extremely powerful and effective public speaker, Washington lectured throughout the United States and Europe. His emphasis on Negro quiescence in the struggle for political and social rights met a receptive audience in America, and Booker T. Washington became the principal spokesman for the Negro in America. He summarized his position on the Negro's place in America in his famous opening speech at the Cotton States Exposition, held in Atlanta, Georgia, in 1895. In this address, he advised the Negro to "cast down your bucket where you are," saying in effect that the Negro should accommodate to the conditions of the South. His position was that the white Southerner was, in reality, the Negro's friend, and that if Negroes applied themselves in economic pursuits, conditions in the South would improve. Although Washington found himself at odds with more militant Negroes such as W.E.B. Du Bois, his position was so agreeable to whites, North and South, and his prestige as educator and national figure so extensive in Negro eyes, that

Washington assumed and held the mantle of the national leader of Negroes in America. Washington's aim was one of economic self-reliance, and in 1900 he organized the National Negro Business League. In 1901, Washington published his autobiography, *Up From Slavery*. He also wrote: *The Future of the American Negro* A1899), *Character Building* (1902), *Working With the Hands* (1904), *Tuskegee and Its People* (1905), *Putting the Most into Life* (1906), *Life of Frederick Douglass* (1907), *The Negro in Business* (1907), *The Story of the Negro* (1909), *My Larger Education* (1911), and *The Man Farthest Down; a Record of Observation and Study in Europe* (1912).

Daniel Hale Williams (1858-1931), Negro doctor, was born in Hollidaysburg, Pa. Williams moved to Janesville, Wis., was educated at Hare's Classical Academy and received a degree in medicine from Northwestern University in 1883. Williams later became an anatomy lecturer at Northwestern and served for 4 years on the Illinois Board of Health. Having begun practice in 1883 in Chicago, Williams was concerned that hospitals discriminated against Negroes as interns and nurses. Through his efforts, Provident Hospital in 1891 was established, where Negroes could receive training in hospital work. Williams, in 1893, conducted the first open-heart surgery under the most primitive conditions.

The Escape, a drama by William Wells Brown, a Negro, was published in Boston.

1859

On October 16, John Brown raided the Federal Arsenal at Harpers Ferry, Va., to seize arms with which to free the slaves. Negroes in Brown's band included Lewis Sheridan Leary, Dangerfield Newby, John Anthony Copeland, Shields Green and Osborn Perry Anderson. Apprehended by Col. Robert E. Lee, Osborn Perry Anderson escaped, Leary and Newby were killed, and Copeland, Green and John Brown were hanged.

At the Vicksburg Southern Commercial Convention, a resolution demanding the re-institution of the slave trade was adopted. Tennessee and Florida opposed the resolution. The delegations from South Carolina and Texas split their vote.

Karl Marx quotes in "Das Kapital" a report by the New York *Daily Tribune* of December 20, 1859 about a Grand

Union demonstration held in New York under the slogan "Justice for the South." The main speaker was Charles O'Conor, head of the New York Bar Association, who said amid "thunderous applause": "Now, gentlemen, to that condition of bondage the Negro is assigned by nature. . . . He has strength, and has the power to labor; but the hand which created him denied to him either the intellect to govern, or willingness to work. Both were denied to him. And that nature which deprived him of the will to labor, gave him a master to coerce that will, and to make him a useful and valuable servant . . . useful for himself and for the master who governs him. . . . I maintain that it is not injustice to leave the Negro in the condition in which nature placed him, to leave him in a state of bondage, and the master to govern him . . . nor is it depriving him of any of his rights to compel him to labor in return, and afford to that master just compensation for the labor and talent employed in governing him and rendering him useful to himself and to the society around him." In addition, O'Conor said: "It is the duty of the white man to treat him kindly and it is the interest of the white man to treat him kindly. It is not pretended that the master has a right to slay his slave. Why, we have not a right here in the North to be guilty of cruelty and inhumanity to our horses!" (This Grand Union demonstration was supported by three former U.S. Presidents and the Mayor of New York.)

In Vicksburg, Miss., those favoring the reopening of the slave trade organized the African Supply Association with J. D. B. DeBow as president.

A shipload of slaves from the *Clothilde* was landed at Mobile Bay, Alabama.

Between 1859 and 1862, of the 170 slave expeditions to Africa, 74 emanated from New York.

Georgia law forbade manumission by will or deed or other means after the death of the owner.

Louisiana passed a law facilitating the re-enslavement of free Negroes.

North Carolina forbade the sale of alcoholic beverages to a free Negro except on written statement by a physician or magistrate that it was necessary for medicinal purposes.

Ohio law denied the right to vote to anyone with "a distinct and visible admixture of African blood." Before this, men nearer white than black had been considered white by Ohio law.

1,031 Negroes were in public school in Philadelphia; 331 were in private schools. In addition, there were four evening schools, 19 Negro Sunday schools with 1,667 pupils, and four Sunday schools run as missions of white churches with 215 pupils.

In the Ohio case of VAN CAMP V. BOARD OF EDUCATION OF LOGAN, OHIO, Chief Justice Peck upheld separate schools for Negroes, deciding that children who were ⅜ African and ⅝ white, and who were colored in appearance and generally regarded as colored, could not attend white schools. The previous color line had been one-half.

Baltimore free Negroes paid school taxes of $500, but their children were excluded from the tax-supported schools.

A Rhode Island bill to abolish segregation in schools failed by two votes.

Arkansas law required free Negroes and mulattoes either to leave the state by the end of the year, or to choose masters "who must give bond not to allow such Negroes to act as free."

A slaveholders' convention in Baltimore refused to recommend the expulsion of free Negroes from Maryland, despite the protests of many that free Negroes were injuring the business of white mechanics by monopolizing hotel labor and encroaching on barbering, coach business, etc. The majority felt that free Negro labor was essential to business in the state.

352 free Negroes in Charleston, South Carolina, paid taxes on $778,423 worth of real estate. 108 free Negroes owned 277 slaves and paid $12,342.02 in taxes on them.

A mulatto in Philadelphia sued a streetcar company after being ejected from the car. He was given a nominal award so that the case could be appealed. Two years later, the District Court of Philadelphia ruled that a railroad company might lawfully refuse to allow Negroes in its cars.

A mulatto woman in Cincinnati who was thrown out of a streetcar by the conductor, brought an action for assault and battery, and won.

Samuel T. Wilcox, a Negro who had a grocery business in

Cincinnati, had $59,000 worth of property. He did up to $140,000 worth of business a year in the 1850's.

California again allowed Negroes and mulattoes to immigrate.

1,700 Negroes in Philadelphia were engaged in various trades and occupations.

Taxed real estate owned by Negroes in New York City was $1,400,000. In addition, Negroes in Brooklyn owned approximately 1 to 1½ million dollars worth of property.

The report of the governors of the Almshouses in New York City revealed that there were 67,998 whites and 2,006 Negroes in these public institutions. The total of white prison inmates in New York was 43,115 and 1,136 Negroes.

George Bentley, a Negro minister in Giles County, Tenn. debated a white minister on the principles of Baptism, and emerged the victor. He preached to whites and Negroes.

Roderick Badger, a free Negro, practiced dentistry in Atlanta, Ga.

George Wylie Clinton (1859-1921), Negro bishop was born in Cedar Creek Township, Lancaster County, S. C. He was one of the first to become a student at the University of South Carolina from 1874 to 1877 when it opened to Negroes. In 1877, Negroes had to leave as a result of legislation restricting the use of the university to whites. Clinton taught school for 12 years during which time he read law in the office of Allison and Connors, in Lancaster County. He was licensed as a local preacher of the AMEZ Church in 1879. Clinton edited the *Afro-American Spokesman*. He helped start the *Quarterly Review* of the AMEZ Church, and was editor of *The Star of Zion*. Consecrated a bishop in 1896, he participated in the Southern Sociological Congress, in the work of the Interracial Commission of the South, and in that of the Federal Council of the Churches of Christ in America.

Henry Ossawa Tanner (1859-1937) an American painter, was the son of a Negro clergyman. He entered the Pennsylvania Academy of Fine Arts and studied under Eakins and William Chase. He went to Atlanta where he worked as an illustrator, photogravure and art instructor at Clark University. The patronage of Bishop and Mrs. Hartzell was instrumental in encouraging Tanner's belief in his own abilities. They sent him to Paris to study. He studied at Julien Academy for five years. His range of subject matter was enormous —plantation Negro studies, European peasant studies, landscapes, animal pictures and Biblical paintings. In 1896 his *Daniel in the Lion's Den* received honorable mention at the Paris Salon. The *Resurrection of Lazarus* was purchased in 1897 by the Luxembourg Gallery, and in 1900 Tanner received the Lippincott Prize and Silver Medal at the Paris Exposition. He also received awards at the Buffalo Exposition, St. Louis Exposition, and a Gold Medal at San Francisco. Tanner also received the French Legion of Honor. Stylistically, Tanner was of the academician realistic art of his mentors Eakins, Laurens, and Constant; although he used Negroes as subject matter, he worked strictly within the European conventions of his day.

The *Afro-American Magazine*, a literary magazine put out by Negroes, began publication.

The *Anglo-African*, a Negro magazine in New York, began publication.

"Blake, or the Huts of America" by Martin R. Delany was originally published in The *Anglo-African* of January-July, 1859. Unfortunately it survived only in fragments. The narrative was a great departure from the *Uncle Tom's Cabin* formula of abolitionist novels. Delany focused on slavery as an exploitive labor system. His hero tried to organize the slaves for a general insurrection throughout the South, and preached class solidarity. Delany was probably quite attuned to contemporary Socialist thought and possibly knew of Marx.

1860

U.S. Census: Negro population in the U.S. was 4,441,830 or 14.1% of the total U.S. population. 488,070 or 11% were free, 3,953,760 were slaves.

In 1860, Negroes represented less than 1% of the total population of the following states: Maine, New Hampshire, Vermont, Massachusetts, Indiana, Illinois, Michigan, Wisconsin, Minnesota, Iowa, Nebraska, Kansas, Colorado, New Mexico, Utah, Nevada, Washington, and Oregon. States in which Negroes were less than 5% of the total population were: Rhode Island, Connecticut, New York, New Jersey, Pennsylvania, Ohio, and California. The percentage of Negroes of the total population of the following states was: Missouri 10%, Delaware 19.3%, Maryland 24.9%, Washington, D. C. 19.1%, Virginia 34.4%, North Carolina 36.4%, South Carolina 58.6%, Georgia 44.1%, Florida 44.6%, Kentucky 20.4%, Tennessee 25.5%, Alabama 45.4%, Mississippi 55.3%, Arkansas 25.6%, Louisiana 49.5%, and Texas 30.3%.

90% of the Negroes were born in the U.S., and 13% were visibly of part-white descent.

The number of free Negroes by state was: Maine 1,327, New Hampshire 494, Massachusetts 9,602, Rhode Island 3,952, Connecticut 8,627, Vermont 709, New York 49,005, New Jersey 25,318, Pennsylvania 56,949, Delaware 19,829, Maryland 83,942, Virginia 58,042, North Carolina 30,463, South Carolina 9,914, Minnesota 259, Iowa 1,069, Kansas 189, Georgia 3,500, Alabama 2,690, Mississippi 773, Louisiana 18,647, Tennessee 7,300, Kentucky 10,684, Ohio 36,673, Indiana 11,428, Illinois 7,628, Missouri 3,572, Michigan 6,799, Arkansas 144, Florida 932, Washington, D. C. 11,131, Oregon 128, California 4,086, Texas 355.

Mulattoes made up 13.2% of the total Negro population in the U.S.

44% of the Negroes lived in the South, and they comprised 37% of the population of the South.

16% of the Negro population lived in urban areas.

Southern free Negroes tended to live in urban areas and held property with an estimated value of $25,000,000. 10,689 free Negroes lived in New Orleans and were teachers, jewelers, architects and lithographers. They owned over $15,000,-000 worth of property. Free Negroes in Maryland paid taxes on over $1,000,000 worth of real property. Twelve individuals owned property valued at over $5,000 each.

Maryland law prohibited manumission of Negro slaves, and provided for authorization of free Negroes to renounce their freedom and become slaves.

Of 2,929 Negro males over 14 years in Massachusetts, for whom occupation was checked, 2,398 or 78.4%, had some occupation. Of 484 Negro males in Ward 6 of Boston (ward of highest Negro concentration), 440 or 90.9% had distinct occupations, compared with 90.6% of total population.

Boston had approximately 2,000 free Negroes. They were found in almost 100 different occupations, including paper-hanging, photography, engraving, tailoring, quarrying, etc.

They practiced such professions as law, teaching, dentistry and the ministry.

Two Negroes were named as jurymen in Worcester, Mass. This was the first instance of Negro jurors in the state.

The total value of real property owned by free Negroes in North Carolina was $480,986. The total value of personal property owned by free Negroes in North Carolina was $564,657, for a total $1,045,643 or a Negro per capita wealth of $34. The per capita wealth of Negro property owners was $287. There were 1,048 free Negro farmers in North Carolina. About 50% of them owned some land. David Reynolds of Halifax County, for example, owned $3,000 worth of land. Thomas Blacknall of Franklin County had $6,000 worth of land, and owned three slaves. In North Carolina, $100 worth of land was "adequate for farming purposes" at that time. In North Carolina, there were eight free Negro slave owners with a total of 25 slaves. In 1830 there had been 191 free Negro slave owners, with a total of 620 slaves.

Of the 3,287 free Negroes in Charleston, S. C., 371 were taxpayers. They had approximately $1,000,000 worth of real estate and 389 slaves.

22,185 free Negroes lived in Philadelphia. 12,500 free Negroes lived in New York City.

Virginia law provided for sale into "absolute slavery" of free Negroes convicted of offenses "punishable by confinement in the penitentiary."

Only 2,000,000 out of 7,000,000 white Southerners owned slaves, and 7% of the total population in the South owned nearly 3,000,000 of the 3,953,760 slaves.

Prime field hands were selling for $1,000 in Virginia and $1,500 in New Orleans.

The total value of Southern manufactures in 1860 was $238,000,000.

The U.S. produced five million bales of cotton, as compared to three million in 1852 and 1½ million bales in 1822.

32,629 Negroes in the U.S. were in school in this year. The percentage of free Negroes who were literate was: Delaware 26.4%, Washington, D.C. 41.3%, North Carolina 46.6%, Tennessee 46.9%, Maryland 48.9%, Virginia 54.2%, Kentucky 56.2%, Missouri 59%, Texas 61.9%, Alabama 63.8%,

Georgia 65.8%, Arkansas 68%, South Carolina 68.5%, Mississippi, 71.8%, Louisiana 71.9%.

Barney Ford, a runaway slave, arrived in Colorado. He built the Inter-Ocean Hotel in Denver, was a successful businessman, active in politics of the territory.

By this year there were some 500 Negroes who travelled from Canada to the South to rescue slaves.

Sylvester Gray, a free Negro, petitioned Congress for the return of his land which he had settled in Wisconsin in 1856, in accordance with the pre-emption act of 1841, and on which he had spent $223. He had received a letter from the Commissioner of the General Land Office revoking his claim on the grounds that he was not a citizen according to the Dred Scott decision.

Five states: Massachusetts, Maine, New Hampshire, Vermont and Rhode Island granted Negroes equal suffrage rights by this year. These states contained 6% of the total Northern Negro population.

By this year 28 Negroes had received degrees from recognized colleges in the U.S.

In a prenomination speech in New York, Abraham Lincoln explained the Republican policy towards slavery ". . . As an evil not to be extended, but to be tolerated and protected only because of and so far as its actual presence among us makes that toleration and protection necessary."

The 1860 Republican Party platform opposed the extension of slavery into the Western territories, calling it "revolutionary" and "subversive of the peace and harmony in the country."

The Democratic platform supported the Dred Scott decision, and opposed the "personal liberty" laws passed to subvert the Federal Fugitive Slave Law of 1850.

The radical abolitionists, including Frederick Douglass and Gerrit Smith, refused to support Lincoln for President, believing instead that they should vote only for those favoring complete abolition. Douglass wrote in the *Liberator*: "I care nothing about that anti-slavery which wants to make the territories free, while it is unwilling to extend to me, as a man, in the free states, all the rights of a man."

A N.Y. Republican reported that of the 32,000 N.Y.

Republicans who voted for Lincoln, only 1,600 endorsed the state Negro suffrage amendment.

In his message to Congress on Dec. 4, President Buchanan advocated Constitutional amendments upholding the principles of the fugitive slave acts.

Karl Marx thought that the hanging of John Brown would start the American movement of slaves which he considered to be "the greatest event in the world" of the time. "The signal, once given, will make the thing by and by serious— what will then happen to Manchester?" By transferring the headquarters of his "International" from Europe to America, Marx hoped, Communists would be able to activate a Negro movement.

1861

In February, Jefferson Davis became the President of the Confederate States of America, organized in Montgomery, Ala. In his Inaugural Address, he endorsed slavery "as necessary to self-preservation."

The Confederate Constitution of March 11, counted slaves as 3/5 of a person for the purpose of representation and taxation, forbade an external slave trade, advocated the protection of the institution of slavery and the "right of property in Negro slaves."

On March 21, the Vice President of the Confederacy, Alexander Stephens, claimed that the new Government "rests upon the great truth that the Negro is not equal to the white man, that slavery, subordination to the superior race, is a natural and normal condition . . . our new Government, is the first in the history of the world, based upon this great physical, philosophical, and moral truth."

The average price in gold of a 20-year-old male slave in the Confederacy during the Civil War fell from a high of $1,050 in 1861 to $100 in 1865.

Frederick Douglass' editorial in *Douglass' Monthly,* May 1861, called for a harsher war and said: "Let the slaves and free colored people be called into service, and formed into a liberating army, to march into the South and raise the banner of emancipation among the slaves."

After the fall of Fort Sumter, many Negroes volunteered for the army, but were refused.

On July 22, the Senate resolved that "this war is not waged . . . for any purpose . . . of overthrowing or interfering with the rights or established institutions of . . . southern States."

In New York, Negroes formed a military drill club, but the police disbanded it, and the governor of New York refused the services of 3 regiments of Negroes.

In October, the War Dept. refused the offer of a Michigan Negro, Dr. G. P. Miller, to organize "5,000 to 10,000 freemen to take any position that may be assigned to us." Offers from other Negroes were also refused.

After the defeat at the first Battle of Bull Run in July, Lincoln instructed that 50,000 slaves for volunteer labor be organized for the Quartermaster Dept. of the Army. Sensitive to the feelings of the border states, he opposed statements on slavery and the arming of Negroes. The Army subsequently used non-enlisted Negroes in the Quartermaster, Commissary, Medical and Engineer Services. Negroes served in the Union Army as pioneers, scouts, laborers, hostelers, teamsters, wagoners, carpenters, masons, laundresses, hospital attendants, fortification, highway and railroad builders, longshoremen and blacksmiths. They also served as servants and orderlies to officers from 1861 to the end of the War.

The Union officer, Maj. Gen. John A. Dix, would not allow fugitives within his lines. However, James H. Lane, an abolitionist Senator from Kansas, and then Brigadier General in the Union Army, encouraged slaves to flee to his state and fight with Union troops.

In Virginia, Brig. Gen. Benjamin F. Butler was the first Union officer to declare that Negro slaves who fell into Union hands were "contraband of war," since Confederates used them in building defenses. Butler utilized the escaped slaves for construction, etc. Butler's decision became Union policy.

There was no consistent Federal policy about captured or fugitive slaves. On August 6, Congress passed the Confiscation Act, declaring that any property used with the owner's consent to aid in insurrection became the lawful subject of prize and capture. If that property was slaves, they were to be freed. Taking advantage of this Act, General Fremont proclaimed from his headquarters in Missouri that slaves from all owners who take up arms against the Union shall be "de-

clared free men." But President Lincoln requested a modifica-
tion of Fremont's extension of the Act toward an emancipation of slaves. This the general declined to do and he was
therefore removed from the army. One of his successors, Maj.
Gen. Henry W. Halleck, ejected fugitive slaves from camps
under his command.

In October, Thomas A. Schott, the acting Secretary of War,
directed Brig. Gen. Thomas W. Sherman, commanding the
expedition to the southern coast, to avail himself "of the
services of any persons, whether fugitives from labor or not,
who may offer them to the National Government." These
were to be employed "in such services . . . as you may deem
most beneficial to the service; this however not being a
general arming of them for military services." General Sherman never acted on this authorization.

An island, Hilton Head, S. C., became the center for fugitives. They were put to work growing cotton for the Treasury
Department.

Secretary of the Navy Gideon Wells, on Sept. 25, authorized the enlistment of Negroes into the Union Navy, under
the same forms and regulations as applied to other enlistments. The Negroes, however, could achieve no higher rank
than "boys" at a compensation of $10 per month and one
ration a day. In the campaign, however, against the Hatteras
Forts, fugitive slaves served as gun crews on Union boats.

With Gen. Butler's permission, the American Missionary
Association opened a school for freedmen in Tennessee.
Shortly thereafter, the AMA established schools on planta-
tions, and in Hampton, Norfolk, Portsmouth and Newport
News.

The Confederacy used Negroes as teamsters, hospital attendants, railroad bridge and road repairmen, and in arms
factories, in the iron mines and for building and repairing
defenses. The Government at first hired slaves from their
masters, but when owners appeared reluctant to part with
their Negroes, slaves were impressed.

Individual Confederate states were recruiting free Negroes.
Tennessee authorized the use in military services of all free
males of color between the ages of 15 and 50. This conscription was often done without prior notice. Negro women
were impressed for camp and hospital service.

North Carolina made it illegal for free Negroes to acquire slaves.

William C. Nell, appointed a post-office clerk in Boston, became the first Negro to hold a civilian job under the Federal Government.

The Negro population of Upper Canada was 11,223. Only 190 Negroes were in Lower Canada.

Cuba's population was 43.2% Negro, of whom 232,493 were free and 370,553 were enslaved.

1862

Lincoln's proposal for the emancipation of Washington, D.C. Negroes became law in April. Compensation of not more than $300 was awarded for each slave and $100,000 was provided for the emigration of freedmen to Haiti or Liberia.

In April, Congress passed Roscoe Conkling's resolution that the U.S. would cooperate with any state adopting a plan of gradual emancipation and compensation.

In May, the House of Representatives failed to pass a law to confiscate and free all slaves belonging to rebels.

President Lincoln, in his public reply to an editorial by Horace Greeley as to the purpose of the war, said, "My paramount object in this struggle is to save the Union, and not either to save or to destroy slavery. If I could save the Union without freeing any slaves I would do it; if I could save it by freeing all the slaves I would do it; and if I could do it by freeing some and leaving others alone, I would also do that."

Acting on Lincoln's suggestion in his Annual Message, Congress appropriated $500,000 for the colonization of slaves of rebellious masters, and authorized the exchange of diplomatic representatives with Haiti and Liberia.

In August, Lincoln held a meeting with prominent Negroes, and urged them to support colonization.

President Lincoln signed a bill abolishing slavery in the territories in June. In July a measure became law, setting free all slaves of masters disloyal to the U.S. Lincoln's draft of a general emancipation proclamation was opposed by most of his Cabinet.

In September, Lincoln issued a preliminary proclamation, that on January 1, 1863, all slaves in states where people were in rebellion were to be free.

The Radicals in Congress pressed for a change in the official government policy towards the use of Negro troops.

In March, military commanders were forbidden to return fugitive slaves.

Congress authorized the President to employ "persons of African descent" and to use them in any way necessary in the Confiscation Act of July 16. More specifically, on July 17, in the Militia Act, Congress authorized the President to employ Negro troops. If a volunteer were a slave, his family was to be set free. His pay was set at $7 ($3 less than that of a white private).

On August 6, President Lincoln refused the offer of two Negro regiments from Indiana and told them "that he was not prepared to go the length of enlisting Negroes as soldiers. He would employ all colored men as laborers, but would not promise to make soldiers of them."

Although the new Secretary of War, Edwin M. Stanton, gave no support to Maj. Gen. David Hunter's First South Carolina Volunteers, he authorized Brigadier General Butler to plan for five companies of Negroes, gave Gen. O. M. Mitchell the right to use them as guards and scouts in Alabama and on Aug. 25 appointed Gen. Rufus Saxton to recruit up to 5,000 Negroes at the same pay as whites (equal pay was never honored).

By the end of 1862, the following Negro regiments had been organized: 1st, 2nd and 3rd Regiments of Louisiana Native Guards. General Saxton's re-organized 1st South Carolina Volunteers (already commended for bravery in coastal raids), and the unofficial 1st Kansas Colored Volunteers.

Despite the Confiscation Act, Union generals in the field made their own policy about fugitives. In West Tennessee, General Grant appointed John Eaton to take charge of fugitives. He and General Butler of Louisiana leased abandoned plantations to whites, and hired out the ex-slaves. They did not ensure that ex-slaves were paid.

Lincoln nullified General Hunter's proclamation of emancipation for Georgia, Florida and South Carolina.

In December, General Saxton, commanding the Department of the South, issued a general plan for dealing with fugitives. Abandoned lands were to be used for the benefit of ex-slaves. Two acres were to be allotted for each working member of a family. Tools were to be furnished by the Government. Corn and potatoes were to be planted for personal use. Cotton was to be planted for Government use. Since only a small amount of land was available, the superintendents appointed were not always interested in the project, and finally the government sold much of the seized land.

Other generals used fugitives as guides, scouts and even spies. They did heavy labor or served as cooks and teamsters, but were rarely armed.

The defenses of the city of Corinth, Mississippi, built in preparation for the battle of October 1862, were the work of Negroes, organized into squads of 25 each and commanded by army personnel.

Negro pickets successfully protected contraband camps from Confederate attacks on St. Simon Island off the coast of Georgia, and again on St. Helena Island, S.C.

The National Freedmen's Relief Association was formed in New York. The Contraband Relief Association was founded shortly afterwards in Cincinnati (later changing its name to the Western Freedmen's Aid Commission). The Friends Association for the Relief of Colored Freedmen was founded in Philadelphia. The Northwestern Freedmen's Aid Commission was founded in Chicago. In 1865 all of these organizations united as the American Freedmen's Aid Commission.

White workers in the North resisted the Negro as a laborer because the Negro was often used as a strikebreaker, and whites feared competition would depress wages. In a minor riot in New York, Negro women and children employed in a tobacco factory were mobbed. In New Jersey agitation resulted when Negroes were employed on the Camden and Amboy Railroad.

In the South, the labor shortage was so acute that most states authorized impressment of Negroes.

To stop Negroes from running away, the Southern states strengthened patrol laws by cancelling exemptions from patrol, requiring them to be made more often, imposing fines and/or prison for failure to patrol. Several states moved their

Negroes to the interior, away from the Union lines. North Carolina moved more than 2,000 slaves.

Captured Negroes were hanged or made to work in irons. The Confederate War Department outlawed Union generals who armed Negroes. If captured, these generals were to be executed.

The Morrill Land Grant College Act was passed, providing federal funds for state universities. Generally, the funds were used only for white schools, but Hampton Institute received ⅓ of the Virginia grant, Chaflin College and Alcorn in Mississippi also received funds.

Mary Jane Patterson graduated from Oberlin College. She was the first Negro female college graduate in the U.S.

Gradual abolition of slavery in Paraguay was completed.

1863

The Emancipation Proclamation was announced on Jan. 1. President Lincoln freed all slaves except those in states or parts of states that were not in rebellion. Exceptions to the Proclamation included 13 parishes of Louisiana, West Virginia, 7 counties of eastern Virginia, which included Norfolk and Portsmouth, or a total of 800,000 Negroes were excluded. The Emancipation Proclamation included a statement that Negro volunteers to garrison or man vessels would be accepted.

In February, after much debate, Thaddeus Stevens' bill calling for 150,000 Negro soldiers, or 150 regiments, was passed in the House, 83 to 54. The Senate did not act on the bill, considering it unnecessary in light of the 1862 Militia Act.

During the early months of 1863, Col. E. A. Wild, Brig. Gen. Daniel Ullmann, Governor Andrew of Massachusetts, the governor of Rhode Island, and Gen. Nathaniel P. Banks were authorized to recruit Negro troops by the War Department.

In May, the War Department's General Order No. 143 fully organized and centralized control of Negro troops as the United States Colored Troops (USCT). From this point on, Negroes were mustered into the army directly.

The Bureau for Colored Troops was established to administer USCT affairs under Maj. Charles W. Foster.

By July, 30 Negro regiments had been federalized, and the President and government were officially committed to their use.

Most Negroes served in the infantry, some in the cavalry, and engineer units, and in batteries of light and heavy artillery. They participated in 449 engagements of which 39 were major battles. The USCT were used increasingly up to 1865. Only four combat regiments of Negroes were never federalized and therefore never formed part of the U.S. Colored Troops. These four regiments were the 29th Regiment of Connecticut Volunteer Infantry, the 5th Regiment of Massachusetts Cavalry, and the 54th and 55th Regiments of Massachusetts Volunteer Infantry. On March 25 Brig. Gen. Lorenzo Thomas, as a representative of the War Department, began traveling through the Mississippi Valley to recruit officers and men for the USCT, and to investigate the arrangements for existing troops and contraband camps. Generals Halleck and Grant gave their support, and Frederick Douglass wrote articles calling for volunteers. War Department General Order No. 144 established a careful system of examining boards to choose officers for Negro regiments. The boards were uniformly severe and almost 40% of the applicants were rejected during the war. In general, the officers of the USCT were better than their counterparts in the regular army. The War Department discouraged Negroes from becoming officers, and only 75 to 100 were appointed, three-quarters of them in General Butler's Department of Louisiana.

The highest ranking Negro officer, Lt. Col. Alexander T. Augusta, was appointed "surgeon of the U.S. Colored Troops" in 1863. Later Dr. Augusta was transferred from his unit when his two white assistant surgeons complained to the President about serving under a Negro officer.

A battery of light artillery from Kansas was unique in that all three of its officers were Negroes.

Maj. George L. Stearn appointed by Governor Andrew of Massachusetts, became second only to Thomas as a leading Negro recruiter. In contrast to Thomas, Major Stearn opposed impressment, offered enlistment bounties and established schools for his Negro troops.

General Ullman remarked of his Negro troops in June: "They are far more in earnest than we. I have talked with hundreds of them. They understand their position full as well as we do. They know the deep stake they have in the issue . . . that, if we are unsuccessful they will be remanded to a worse slavery than before. They also have a settled conviction that if they are taken, they will be tortured and hung. These impressions will make them daring and desperate fighters."

Throughout the war, Departmental and divisional commanders varied in their use of Negro troops. In the trans-Mississippi West, they generally served in combat, for example at Cabin Creek, Indiana Territory and Baxter Springs. In the Departments of Tennessee and of the South, they did fatigue detail, had little time for drill, and were often treated unfairly. Along the Atlantic Coast, both situations existed.

At the Battle of Port Hudson, in May, Captain André Cailloux, a well-to-do free Negro of New Orleans, led his men in battle. With a shattered left arm, he encouraged his troops for the final attack. He died running ahead of them, crying "Follow me," in French and then in English.

Sgt. William H. Carney, of Company C, 54th Massachusetts Colored Infantry, was awarded the Congressional Medal of Honor for his bravery in the Battle of Fort Wagner, S. C. When the standard bearer was killed, he picked up the regimental colors and led the attack to the fort. He was badly wounded on two occasions during the fighting.

Robert Blake, serving on the *U.S.S. Marblehead,* was awarded the Navy Medal of Honor for his part in routing the enemy off Legaréville in the Stono River.

In July, in the last stages of the Battle of Vicksburg, eight Negroes manning the siege works were killed by a Confederate mine.

In October, at the contraband camp at Pine Bluff, Arkansas, a group of untrained Negroes repulsed a Confederate attack on the camp. Five were killed and 12 wounded. The captain of the camp reported that they deserved "the applause of their country and gratitude of the soldiers."

On July 18, despite poor rations, a forced march the day before and extensive fatigue detail, the 54th Massachusetts Colored Infantry led the ill-planned assault on Morris Island, S. C. The Island was taken, but the unit suffered about 42% casualties.

Despite successive official orders and investigations, some Negro or assigned troops were unfairly treated by their officers or division commanders.

In September, the Commissioner for the Organization of Colored Troops reported to the Secretary of War that "the colored men here are treated like brutes; any officer who wants them, I am told, impresses on his own authority; and it is seldom that they are paid . . . one was shot."

The 65th U.S. Colored Infantry recruited in Missouri, was sent in December to Benton Barracks, without any hats or shoes, thinly clad, without proper feeding provisions. 100 soldiers died in the first two months.

Brig. Gen. Q. A. Gillmore, in command of the Department of the South, reported that Negro troops, detailed for fatigue duty, had been employed in one instance at least to prepare camps and perform menial duty for white troops.

The commanding officer of the 14th U.S. Colored Infantry wrote, "it behooves the friends of this movement [the use of Negroes as soldiers] to secure a favorable decision from the great tribunal, public opinion. This cannot be done by making laborers out of these troops; . . . [it is] degrading to single out colored troops for fatigue duty while white soldiers stand by."

From this time on, Negroes were also enlisted as soldiers in white regiments, serving as wagoners, teamsters and under-cooks.

The conditions in Federal refugee camps were generally atrocious with a mortality rate of approximately 25%.

James Seddon, Confederate Secretary of War, advised Lt. Gen. E. Kirby Smith that white officers of Negro troops, when captured, "had best be dealt with red-handed in the field, or immediately thereafter."

All Negro prisoners captured in Jackson, Louisiana, were shot. Stories also existed of hangings, enslavements and forced labor on chain gangs.

With an acute labor shortage, the Confederate government passed a General Impressment Law. Planters often refused to cooperate, however, fearing loss of their slaves to the government.

Kentucky slave owners voiced opposition to the recruitment of Negroes, fearing the loss of their slaves to the Army.

The New York draft riots occurred in this year. The New York Democratic Party, which controlled the City Council, was strongly opposed to the Civil War. Boss Tweed was a major anti-war spokesman. The Democratic Governor of New York, Horatio Seymour, denounced the Conscription Act passed by Congress early in 1863 as unconstitutional. Under the act, conscription began in July. The act permitted a man to buy his way out of the draft by paying $300; thus it discriminated against poor Irish immigrants. The atmosphere was such that the Irish draftees felt they were being called upon to fight a war to free Negroes, who would then flood the city to take their jobs. On July 13, riots broke out in New York City. Any Negroes found by rioters were beaten, often to death. The Negro orphan asylum was burned to the ground. The riots lasted through July 16, and cost at least 1,200 lives and some $2 million in property damage. Along with Negro homes, town houses and brownstones of the wealthy were also sacked and burned.

In its state Constitution, West Virginia provided for separate schools for Negroes.

The New England Freedmen's Aid Society established schools in South Carolina (in towns and on plantations). 5,000 Negroes attended these schools in 1863. General Banks established a public education system in the Department of the Gulf. By the end of 1864 there were 95 schools, 162 teachers, 9,571 day students and 2,000 evening students.

As an experiment in colonization, 500 Negroes were sent to Cow Island, Haiti. The experiment failed miserably, and President Lincoln had to send a ship to bring them home.

Charles "Buddy" Bolden (1863-1931), Negro jazz musician, was born in New Orleans. He grew up amid the brass band craze, playing cornet. In 1897 he organized the first real jazz band, and for 7 years he was considered "king" of jazz in New Orleans. Horns were the favorite instruments of New Orleans Negroes because they were easily carried in parades and because they were cheap. Bolden's first band consisted of cornet, trombone, clarinet, guitar, string bass and drums. He and most of his men could not read music. One of the famous instrumentalists who played in this band was Bunk Johnson.

1864

Despite the hatred of Negroes shown in the July, 1863 Draft Riots, New York City cheered at the parade of its Negro regiment, the 20th USCT.

In July, a Federal law enabled Northern states to recruit in occupied areas of the South.

In December, the 25th Corps was organized as an all-Negro regiment. The regiments usually did fatigue duty in the encampment around Richmond, Virginia.

In the February election held in the Louisiana Territory under Union control, and authorized by President Lincoln, Negroes were denied the right to vote. The Louisiana Constitutional Convention, elected only by white suffrage in Union-held areas, met in April. The delegates abolished slavery by a vote of 72 to 13, but appealed to Congress for compensation. After the intervention of the governor and the Union commanding general, the Convention did not categorically exclude Negroes from voting. The Louisiana State Legislature, elected from Union-held territory, which met in October, 1864, refused to grant suffrage to Negroes, forbade intermarriage, but abolished slavery.

Despite the efforts of the War Department, reports of ill-treatment, equipment of the poorest kind, inadequate medical personnel, and excessive fatigue duty continued to be made by the generals commanding Negro regiments.

In the North there were Negro physicians, but only eight were appointed surgeons in the Army, and six were attached to hospitals in Washington, D.C., while the other two remained with Negro regiments for only a very short time.

Sgt. William Walker, a Negro of the 3rd South Carolina Volunteers, was shot by order of a court martial for having led the men of his company to stack arms and to refuse to serve until the agreement under which they had enlisted, equal pay, was met. At least three other Negro soldiers died for similar protests, and over a score in the 14th Rhode Island Heavy Artillery were jailed.

Lt. Col. Augusta, a Negro surgeon for the USCT, found it necessary to tell Sen. Henry Wilson that the army paymaster at Baltimore had "refused to pay him more than $7 per month," the pay of a Negro enlisted man after clothing deduction, and that this payment had been rejected. A letter from the Senator to the Secretary of War on April 10, 1864, resulted in an order two days later to the Paymaster General to compensate the surgeon according to his rank.

In mid-June, Congress in its Army Appropriations Bill authorized the same enlistment bounty for Negroes and whites. Equal pay was made retroactive to Jan. 1, 1864, for "all persons of color who were free on the 19th day of April, 1861."

In order to receive their equal pay, many Negroes with officers' approval, lied about their status in 1861. Massachusetts' Governor Andrew had the State Legislature pay the difference in wages.

In July, the Federal government entitled the families of Negroes who had been killed in the war to pensions. No provision had been made previous to this bill.

Between May 1864 and April 1865, most Negro troops were used in the campaign against the Army of Northern Virginia. At the Battle of Chaffin's Farm in September, 14 of the 37 Congressional Medal of Honor winners were Negroes.

At Petersburg, Va., in June, the Negro division under Gen. W. F. Smith attacked the fort and made a mile-wide gap in the Confederate defenses.

Negro regiments also battled with Confederate forces in Mississippi and Alabama. In December, at Wolf River Bridge, Tenn., the 2nd Regiment of West Tennessee Infantry of African Descent, was formally commended by its commander.

Joachim Pease, a Negro seaman on the *U.S.S. Kearsarge,* was awarded the Navy Medal of Honor.

John Lawson and James Mifflin, Negro loaders on the *Hartford* and *Brooklyn,* respectively, won Congressional Medals of Honor for their part in the Battle of Mobile Bay.

The following Negroes were awarded the Congressional Medal of Honor for valor at the Battle of New Market Heights; Pvt. William H. Barnes, 38th USCT; 1st Sgt. Powhatan Beaty, 5th USCT; 1st Sgt. James H. Bronson, 5th USCT; Sgt. Maj. Christian A. Fleetwood, 4th USCT; Pvt. James Gardiner, Company I, USCT; Sgt. James Harris, 38th USCT; Sgt. Alfred B. Hilton, 4th USCT; Sgt. Major Milton

M. Holland, 5th USCT; Cpl. Miles James, 5th USCT; 1st Sgt. Alexander Kelly, 6th USCT; 1st Sgt. Robert Pinn, 5th USCT; 1st Sgt. Edward Radcliff, 38th USCT; and Pvt. Charles Veal, 4th USCT.

Sgt. Maj. Thomas Hawkins, 6th USCT, was awarded the Medal of Honor for rescuing the regimental colors from the enemy at the Battle of Deep Bottom, Va.

Sgt. Decatur Dorsey, 39th USCT, took the colors and led the men in his unit against the Confederates at the Battle of Petersburg, Va., on July 30.

President Lincoln's conservative stand on Reconstruction caused radical abolitionists such as Frederick Douglass to endorse John C. Fremont's candidacy for the Presidency.

At the Republican Convention in June, which took place in Baltimore, the plank supporting the abolition of slavery was written into the party platform.

In the Presidential election, over ⅔ of the seats in both Houses were won by Union-Republicans.

Karl Marx wrote to President Lincoln from London and assured him of the solidarity of the European workers in the battle to abolish slavery in America. According to the minutes of the International Worker's Association, Lincoln answered "in a more than formal way."

The Wade-Davis Bill, of June 1864, was in opposition to President Lincoln's policies. This bill held that the Confederate States were out of the Union, that they occupied the status of territories, and that it was the business of Congress to provide conditions for readmission. Among the provisions in the Wade-Davis Bill for readmission into the Union was the abolition of slavery. However, this bill did not include a guarantee of Negro suffrage. President Lincoln, unwilling to commit himself to a specific Reconstruction plan, and believing that Congress did not have the constitutional power to abolish slavery, utilized the pocket veto.

An anti-slavery state constitution was drawn up and accepted by an all-white electorate in Arkansas.

In May, Negroes at Port Royal, S. C., participated in a meeting which elected delegates to the Republican National Convention. Robert Smalls and three other Negroes were among the delegates, but were denied seats.

In October, the National Negro Convention in Syracuse, N.Y., called for Negro suffrage. Among the delegates were: Frederick Douglass and George L. Ruffin. Ruffin was to become the first Negro to sit on the bench of Massachusetts.

In December, a bill forbidding discrimination in the hiring of mail carriers was passed by the House and Senate.

At Davis Bend, Miss., 25 miles south of Vicksburg, Federal officials seized six plantations and settled Negroes on the land. By the end of the year, 75 Negroes were settled. They raised crops which gave them profits up to $1,000 each after repaying credit advanced by the government. In 1865, 1,800 Negroes finished the year with a total cash balance of $159,200.

Jefferson Davis opposed a resolution suggesting the use of slaves as soldiers. However, this resolution was passed at a meeting of Confederate governors.

Because of the great labor shortage in the South, the Confederate government voted to impress 20,000 slaves. Slave owners in many cases still refused to cooperate.

The status of captured Negro soldiers stalemated prisoner exchange negotiations until the last months of the war. It became obvious that the South considered them as recaptured property, whether former slaves or not. The war was over before any Negroes were released.

In April, Confederate General Buford promised to execute all Negro soldiers captured; if the Federal forces surrendered, he would return them to their masters. Confederate General Hood threatened to execute the officers and men of the Negro regiments if their commander did not capitulate.

Throughout the year Confederate officers reported the execution of captured Negro soldiers. Near Lewisburg, Tenn., two white officers were murdered and another officer wounded and left for dead. These officers were commanders of Negro troops.

The worst example of Confederate slaying of Negro troops was at Fort Pillow, Tenn., on April 12. A Confederate cavalry force under Maj. Gen. Nathan B. Forrest, captured the Fort garrisoned by Negro soldiers. Wholesale slaughter followed, and every sort of atrocity took place. Approximately 300 soldiers, many of them wounded, plus women and children, were killed.

By this year the American Missionary Association had 3,000 Negroes at school, with 52 teachers. At least 5 of the teachers were Negroes. These schools were in Virginia. In North Carolina another 3,000 students and 66 teachers worked in the American Missionary Association schools.

The African Negro Methodist Episcopal Church founded Western University in Kansas.

George Washington Carver (1864-1943), Negro scientist, was kidnapped at the age of 2 and separated from his mother. Carver worked his way through high school, and after numerous rejections, was finally accepted by Simpson College in Indianola, Iowa, as its first Negro student. Carver continued his studies at Iowa Agricultural College at Ames, Iowa. In 1894 he took his B.A. and in 1896 his M.A., whereupon he joined the faculty as its first Negro member. In 1896 Carver went to Tuskegee Institute at Booker T. Washington's request. Washington's concern was with the Southern agricultural economy, and how the poor Negro farmer could sustain himself. Carver's research was primarily in such staple Southern foods as sweet potatoes and peanuts. In the course of his life Carver developed some 300 products from the peanut, such as dyes, plastics, soap, ink and many others now in common use. Carver also developed new products from sweet potatoes, wood shavings and cotton stalks. His life was not without honor if it was without financial benefits. Carver was continually exploited by Southern commercial firms who made millions off his discoveries. In his own life he had an almost saint-like quality, beloved by everyone who ever met him. In 1917 he was made a Fellow of the Royal Society of Arts in London, and in 1923 he received the Spingarn Medal. In 1939 he was awarded the Theodore Roosevelt Medal for Distinguished Research in Agricultural Chemistry. In 1940 the International Federation of Architects, Engineers, Chemists and Technicians gave him a citation. He received several honorary degrees from various universities. The farm near Diamond Grove, Mo., where he was born is now maintained as a national monument by the U.S. Government.

The U.S. recognized Haitian sovereignty. General Fabre Geffrard of Haiti introduced his plan to bring "industrious men of African descent from the U.S."

B. RECONSTRUCTION

History knows restitution. Societies have at times, moved by conscience or guilt, offered compensation to aggrieved peoples. The American Negro did not receive any restitution after Emancipation. He profited for a time from the aftereffects of the Civil War, from the conflicts between South and North, mostly in regard to political rights. For a time during Reconstruction he was represented more widely in legislative bodies than at any time up to the present.

1865

One in every 20 Negroes could read and write. By 1900 one in every 2 Negroes could read and write.

An estimated 100,000 of 120,000 artisans in the South were Negroes, but by 1890, the skilled Negro worker had been eliminated as competition for Southern whites.

The Chesapeake Marine Railroad and Dry Dock Co. was founded in Baltimore. It was Negro-owned, and employed over 300 Negro mechanics who were discriminated against in the shipyards. It had 12 years of profit.

In Cincinnati, Negroes owned a half a million dollars in taxable property. In New York, Negroes had invested $755,-000 in Negro businesses. In Brooklyn, not part of New York City at this time, Negroes invested $76,000 in Negro businesses. Negroes owned unencumbered property in New York valued at $733,000; in Brooklyn at $276,000; and in Williamsburg at $151,000. According to the June 1865 census, there were 16,509 freedmen in Memphis, Tenn., of which only 220 were indigent. For the past three years, 1863-1865, they had been maintained by Negro benevolent societies, who contributed $5,000 for the support of the Negro poor.

On Jan. 31, the House passed the 13th Amendment. The Senate had already done so. This amendment abolishing slavery then went to the states for ratification.

After much debate a bill passed in both Houses declaring wives and children of Negro soldiers in the Federal service to be free.

A bill was introduced in the Confederacy permitting the

voluntary enlistment of slaves in the Confederate Army with freedom guaranteed at the end of hostilities. This bill was buried in committee. However, Gen. Robert E. Lee was calling for Negro soldiers. In Virginia a resolution was passed allowing the Army to enlist slaves if agreeable settlement was made with the slave's master. After Virginia passed this resolution, the House and Senate of the Confederacy allowed the Army to enlist Negroes. This resolution stipulated that no change was to be made in slave-master relationships and that Negroes were to receive the same pay and rations as white troops.

On March 13, Jefferson Davis signed a bill allowing the Confederate States to fill their military quota by using Negroes, but the number of slaves recruited was not to exceed 25% of the able-bodied male slave population between 18 and 45. This measure came too late to help the Confederacy, and only on the eastern seaboard could any number of Negroes be recruited.

By this year an estimated 40,000 Negroes were living in Canada. The census of 1861 had counted approximately 11,000. The increase was probably due to fugitive slaves and contrabands leaving the U.S. during the Civil War.

During the war, 178,895 Negroes had been inducted into the Union Army, representing 9% to 10% of the total forces. Approximately 3,000 were killed in battle; more than 26,000 died from disease; 14,887 deserted, representing 7% of the total desertions. Between November, 1864, and April, 1865, approximately 49,000 Negroes enlisted, and 4,244 joined from Confederate states. On July 15, 1865, the 123,156 Negroes serving in the Union Army were assigned as follows: 120 infantry regiments, total 98,938; 12 heavy artillery regiments, total 15,662; 10 batteries of light artillery, total 1,311, and 7 cavalry regiments, total 7,245.

Aaron Anderson, a landsman on the *U.S.S. Wyandanch,* won the Navy Medal of Honor for bravery at Mattox Creek on March 17.

In Lincoln's funeral procession, the Irish Immigrant Organization refused to march with Negroes. New York's Council refused to allow Negroes to march. It was only because of the intervention of the police commissioner, that a place in the procession was assigned to Negroes. Police protection was necessary to insure the safety of the Negro marchers.

Four companies of the 54th USCT became the first Negroes to participate in an inaugural parade.

President Johnson followed the ideas on Reconstruction outlined in the Wade-Davis Bill, but he followed Lincoln in insisting that Reconstruction was the function of the president. Arkansas, Louisiana, Tennessee and Virginia already had governments loyal to the U.S. Johnson recognized them as legal. Between May and July, Johnson appointed governors in North Carolina, Mississippi, Georgia, Texas, Alabama, South Carolina, and Florida. By the end of 1865 the governors had called State Conventions elected by whites only, which nullified secession, abolished slavery, and repudiated debts.

In May President Johnson's Amnesty Proclamation to all who took the oath of allegiance was issued. The exceptions to the Amnesty Proclamation were: (1) Civil and diplomatic officers of the Confederacy; (2) Confederates who left U.S. judicial posts; (3) officers above the rank of colonel in the Army, or lieutenant in the Navy; (4) Confederates who left Congress; (5) Confederates who left the armed services of the U.S.; (6) Confederates who mistreated war prisoners; (7) Confederates who fled the U.S.; (8) Confederates who attended West Point or the Naval Academy; (9) Confederates who were governors of Confederate states; (10) Northerners who fought for the South; (11) persons whose taxable property value was over $20,000. By mid-1866, because of President Johnson's liberal view on amnesty, very few rebels remained unpardoned.

1,800 Negroes were settled on confiscated plantations in Davis Bend, Miss. By the end of the year, they had a cash balance of $159,200. Despite the wishes of Stevens and Sumner, land confiscation and redistribution to Negroes was never authorized by Congress, and no real land reform was carried out. When President Johnson pardoned the owners of plantations in Davis Bend, the land was returned to them.

General Sherman issued Special Field Order No. 15, by which the South Carolina and Georgia Sea Islands, south of Charleston, and the abandoned lands along the rivers for a distance of 30 miles inland were to be used for the settlement

of Negroes on plots not more than 40 acres. Gen. Rufus
Saxton was appointed Inspector of the settlements. In January,
1866 President Johnson removed Saxton and most of the land
was returned to its original owners.

In December 1865, Thaddeus Stevens submitted a plan to
the Republican caucus which (1) claimed Reconstruction as
the business of Congress; (2) regarded the President's steps
as provisional; (3) postponed consideration of admission of
members from Southern states; (4) suggested a joint committee of 15 be appointed to study conditions of the Confederate states. A resolution creating the joint committee
passed the House 129 to 35, with 18 not voting, and passed
the Senate in February of 1866.

Congress had, in fact, followed an independent policy since
January 1865, by forbidding Virginia, North Carolina, South
Carolina, Georgia, Florida, Alabama, Mississippi, Louisiana,
Texas, Arkansas and Tennessee representation in the Elec-
toral College.

The first three drafts of the Reconstruction Bill, introduced
in the House on Jan. 16, Feb. 21, and Feb. 22, all confined
suffrage to white males, although one draft admitted Negro
soldiers to the vote.

The Freedmen's Bureau was established as part of the War
Department. The Commissioner of the Bureau was to be appointed by the President, with the consent of the Senate. The
Commissioner had the authority to "control all subjects relating to refugees and freedmen." He could set aside abandoned
tracts of land up to 40 acres to be leased to freedmen at a
low rent, giving them the right to buy the land at the end
of three years. Union army officers would be used as assistant
commissioners, and the Secretary of War could issue provisions, clothing and fuel to the freedmen and refugees. The
Bureau established schools, hired teachers, made provisions
for transportation, issued food and clothing and with an expenditure of over $2,000,000 treated 450,000 medical cases.
The death rate of freedmen was reduced from a high of 38%
in 1865, to 2.03% in 1869.

The Arkansas State Legislature adopted the 13th Amendment by unanimous vote.

The 13th Amendment was passed in the Alabama Legislature by a vote of 75 to 15, with the following amendment:

"Be it further resolved, that this amendment to the Constitution of the U.S. is adopted by the Legislature of Alabama,
with the understanding that it does not confer upon Congress
the power to legislate upon the political status of freedmen in
his state."

The Confederate States elected Congressmen to the 39th
Congress. Among the Congressmen elected by the solely
white electorate were Alexander Stephens, the former Vice-
President of the Confederacy, and four former Confederate
generals, 5 colonels, 6 Cabinet officers and 58 Congressmen.

The U.S. Senate in the Trumbull Resolution recognized as
legitimate the Louisiana government that had been set up by
a Constitutional Convention. Louisiana held legislative elections in the Union controlled territory. Only whites voted.
The advocates of Negro suffrage, led by Wade and Charles
Sumner convinced the Senate to reverse itself and withdraw
recognition.

The Black Codes were regulations written into the State
Constitutions that regulated Negro life. Generally they made
Negroes subject to virtual slavery if convicted of vagrancy.
Children separated from their parents could be made slaves.
Negroes could come into court as witnesses only in cases in
which Negroes were involved. Access to land was limited,
and the right to bear arms was forbidden. Negro employment
was limited to contract labor. Some of these Codes were
repealed under Northern pressure.

The South Carolina Constitution of that year provided
that: no Negro could enter the state unless, within 20 days
after arrival, he had put up a bond of $1,000, to ensure his
good behavior. A Negro had to have a special license for any
job except as a farmer or servant. The license included an
annual tax of from $10 to $100. Negroes were forbidden to
manufacture or sell liquor. Work licenses were granted by a
judge, revocable on complaint, and in case of revocation, the
penalty was a fine double the amount paid for the license,
half of which went to the informer.

South Carolina created special courts for Negroes. The
local magistrate "shall be especially charged with the supervision of persons of color in his neighborhood, their protection, and the prevention of their misconduct."

The Mississippi Constitution required every Negro to submit evidence annually from the mayor or member of the police board proving that he had a lawful home and employment.

The property provision of the Mississippi Black Codes said that Negroes were forbidden to rent or lease land, except in incorporated towns or cities, in which places the corporate authorities controlled the land.

In a Louisiana Black Code, all agricultural workers were required to make contracts with employers during the first ten days of each January; workers could not leave their employers until the contract expired; refusal to work would be punished by forced labor on public works. The Negro was required to work 10 hours a day in summer and 9 hours a day in winter.

The rules for contracting Negro servants to white masters in a South Carolina Black Code were: masters were allowed to work servants under 18 "moderately." Over 18, servants could be whipped on judicial authority. Wages and time period had to be specified in writing. Sunday and night work were forbidden. Unauthorized attacks and inadequate food were not allowed. The wages were fixed by a judge. Failure to make contracts was made a misdemeanor, punishable by fine. Farm labor was required from sunrise to sunset, with intervals for meals. Visitors were not allowed without the master's consent. Enticing away another's servants was punishable by fine. To sell farm products without written consent of the master was forbidden. The contract had to be in writing, witnessed by whites and certified by a judge. Any white man could arrest a Negro he saw commit a misdemeanor.

Mississippi and Florida enacted laws segregating public transportation.

Texas passed a law requiring every train to have special cars for freedmen, but it did not say Negroes could not ride in other cars.

The *Klu Klux Klan* was formed in Tennessee.

Wisconsin rejected a proposal to let Negroes vote. Minnesota and Connecticut also voted against Negro suffrage.

A Negro convention held in Raleigh, N.C., adopted resolutions for the repeal of discriminatory laws, for proper wages, protection and education.

A Negro convention in Charleston, S.C., protested the results of the state constitutional convention.

On May 4, Joseph Smith 3d, son of the Mormon prophet Joseph Smith, had a revelation that Negroes were truly equal and not banned from the priesthood. This was accepted into the doctrine of the Reorganized Church of the Latter Day Saints, which now has many Negro members, but not the regular Mormon Church centered in Salt Lake City, Utah.

There were 250,000 members of the Methodist Episcopal Church, South.

The American Missionary Association founded Atlanta University at Atlanta, Ga.

The American Baptist Home Mission helped found Virginia Union University, and Shaw University in Raleigh, N. C.

Adam Clayton Powell Sr. (1865-1953), was born in Franklin County, Va. He worked his way through Rendville Academy in West Virginia by working in the neighboring coal mines. He graduated in 1885. Three years later Powell entered the Wayland Seminary in Washington, D. C. In 1892 he received his first church, the Ebenezer Baptist Church in Philadelphia. A year later he accepted the post of minister at the Immanuel Baptist Church in New Haven, a position he held until 1908. While in New Haven, Powell gained a reputation as a lecturer and writer, publishing in 1895 a *Souvenir of the Immanuel Baptist Church*, and lectured all over the East Coast and in California. Powell also tried to organize the New Haven Negroes to become a political force, but factionalism and jealousy of Powell destroyed the effort. In November, 1908, Powell became pastor of the Abyssinian Baptist Church in New York City. One of his first political acts was to lead a campaign to force the city to rid the area in which the church was then located (40th Street on the West Side) of the prostitutes who infested the locale. In 1910, Powell joined the newly formed NAACP and was appointed to its Finance Committee. He remained active in community work, trying to convince white merchants in Negro areas to hire Negro help, and trying to have a Harlem Community Center built. By 1920, Powell was a figure of national prominence. His sermons were often published in pamphlet form, and he made over $1,200 from the sale of *Watch Your Step* and *The Valley of Dry Bones*. In 1932 Powell was nominated as a

Presidential elector-at-large by the Republican Party of New York state. In 1937, Powell retired to be succeeded by his son, Adam Clayton Powell Jr.

George Moses Horton published *Naked Genius,* a volume of poetry.

Charles Hicks, a Negro, organized the Georgia Minstrels. In 1882 they became part of Callender's Consolidated Spectacular Colored Minstrels.

Massillon Coicou (1865-1908), Negro poet, was born in Port au Prince, and educated at Frères de l'Instruction Chrétienne and Lycée Pétion. Like so many prominent Latin American literary figures, Coicou was also a politician. He was in the Cabinet of President Thiresias S. Sam, and served as Minister to Paris. He founded the literary intellectual magazine *L'Oeuvre* and wrote two collections of poetry, *Les Poésies Nationales* (1891), a work full of enthusiasm for his native land and his revolutionary idealism, and *Impression et Passion* (1902), a more thoughtful, meditative collection. In 1904, *Dessalines Liberté,* the best of Coicou's dramatic works, appeared; its theme is Haitian independence. Premiered in Paris, it has become a classic of the Haitian theater. Coicou spent his last years as a popular, outspoken professor of philosophy at the most prominent lycée in Port au Prince. Evidently either too outspoken or too popular, he was executed by a firing squad in 1908.

1866

Cotton sold at 30¢ a pound. The crop was only 1,900,000 bales in comparison to over 5,000,000 in 1861.

Freedmen in Florida had secured homesteads covering 160,000 acres of land.

The National Labor Union, organized at Baltimore, proclaimed that Negroes must be unionized so that they could not be used as scabs.

Military banks that would safeguard Negro deposits were established in New Orleans, Norfolk, Va., and Beaufort, S. C. The Beaufort bank received deposits of $200,000.

On July 4, President Johnson issued another proclamation of general amnesty.

On August 20, President Johnson officially declared the Civil War to be ended.

Prominent Negroes met with President Johnson to ask him to grant and guarantee Negro suffrage.

President Johnson sent Carl Schurz on a tour of the South. His report displeased Johnson because it showed the failure of Johnson's Reconstruction plan. It was, however, very influential in supporting the Radical position that the Negro needed Federal assistance.

During the 39th Congressional session, 140 different proposals to change the Constitution were made, including 45 on apportionment and 31 on civil and political rights.

The Conservative Republicans of the 39th Congress advocated two Constitutional amendments: (1) Negroes to be guaranteed equal civil (not political) rights; (2) states without Negro suffrage to suffer reduced representation in Congress and in the Electoral College. The Radical Republicans led by Thaddeus Stevens and Charles Sumner, advocated: (1) disenfranchisement of Southern whites; (2) creation of a new South based on universal Negro suffrage.

Congress declared that no Representatives or Senators from any Southern state would be seated until both Houses of Congress declared a state entitled to such representation.

Tennessee's Representatives and Senators were readmitted to Congress.

The Civil Rights Act was passed by both Houses of Congress, March 14, 1866. This Act conferred citizenship on Negroes ("all persons born in the U.S. and not subject to any foreign powers, excluding Indians not taxed.") It gave citizens "of every race and color" equal rights to make contracts, sue, testify in court, purchase, hold and dispose of property, and to enjoy "full and equal benefit of all laws." It made all citizens subject to "like punishment, pains and penalties." It made violations of the act punishable by fine and/or imprisonment. It gave jurisdiction to the U.S. District Courts and gave power of arrest to U.S. marshals and attorneys. President Johnson vetoed the Civil Rights Act. It was passed over his veto on April 6 and April 9. This act was designed to nullify the Black Codes.

A bill was introduced in Congress to give Negro males the right to vote in the District of Columbia. This bill was passed in December by both Houses of Congress. A referendum tak٫n in December, among white voters of Washington, D. C., on the question of Negro suffrage, showed 6,591 against and 35 for.

The Joint Committee of 15 (composed of Radical and Conservative Republicans) issued its 800-page report. 100,000 copies of this report were distributed. The majority conclusions were: (1) Constitutional amendments were required to protect Negroes, including proposals for the 14th Amendment; (2) ultimate control of Reconstruction was within Congress's jurisdiction.

The 14th Amendment: (1) incorporated the substance of the Civil Rights Act of 1866 into its first section; (2) prohibited the states from enacting laws which abridged the privileges or immunities of U.S. citizens, from depriving persons of life, liberty or property without due process, from denying any person the equal jurisdiction of its laws; (3) enabled Congress to reduce a state's Congressional representation when a state denied an adult male the right to vote for any reason other than crime or rebellion; (4) declared anyone who held Federal or state office and had joined the Confederacy, ineligible for public office until pardoned by two thirds of Congress. The 14th Amendment was passed by the House on May 10, 128 to 37, 19 not voting, and by the Senate June 8, 33 to 11, 5 not voting. (This amendment was not ratified until 1868) President Johnson denounced the 14th Amendment and urged the Southern states not to ratify it. Among the Southern states, Tennessee was the only state that accepted the 14th Amendment.

The original Freedmen's Bureau Bill was amended in February. It extended the Bureau's life. The provisions of the amended Freedmen's Bureau set annual salaries of Bureau officials at $500 to $1,200 and validated titles granted in pursuance of General Sherman's orders of Jan. 1865. It also instructed land to be procured and schools and asylums to be erected. It made it the duty of the President to extend military protection where civil rights were denied. Depriving another of his lawful rights was to be punishable by $1,000 fine and/or one year in prison. The Bureau's power to supervise labor contracts was increased, and it was authorized to establish special courts if justice was unobtainable in regular courts. Johnson vetoed the Freedmen's Bureau Bill, claiming that Congress could not legislate for the states that were unrepresented. Congress did not override the veto. Six Republicans in the Senate deserted their party, and the vote was 30 to 18.

In May, the House passed 96 to 32, a bill on the Freedmen's Bureau to replace the one President Johnson had vetoed. The new Freedmen's Bureau Bill contained the following provisions: (1) the Bureau's life was limited to two years; (2) land held under General Sherman's field orders was to be restored to the original owners; (4) property was to be appropriated for educational purposes; (5) military protection of civil rights was guaranteed. President Johnson, in June vetoed this bill, but it was passed over his veto on the same day.

The Federal Government through the Freedmen's Bureau and other agencies issued almost 4,000,000 rations to an average of 21,700 people per month (14,000 whites and 7,000 Negroes).

As a part of his opposition to Congress, President Johnson attempted to form a new party. The National Union Convention was held in August in Philadelphia, with representatives from both North and South, but mostly Democrats. Its Declaration of Principles stated that: Congress had no right to deny Congressional representation to any state; each state had the right to decide voting qualifications; the Constitution could not be amended unless all states were represented in Congress. They also endorsed Andrew Johnson, denied a desire to restore slavery, and proclaimed the invalidity of the rebel debt.

In September in Philadelphia, a convention of Southern Loyalists and Northern Republicans met. The delegates included Horace Greeley, John Jacob Astor, Carl Schurz, Frederick Douglass, and Thomas Benton. Douglass was elected from Rochester, N. Y.; although his election was considered a great "honor," he was asked by a committee not to attend because of the furor his presence might cause. "Gentlemen," he replied, "with all respect, you might as well ask me to put a loaded pistol to my head and blow my brains out, as to ask me to keep out of this convention, to which I have been duly elected." The convention adopted a declaration calling for suffrage for all men.

Massachusetts became the first Northern state to elect

Negroes to its Legislature. They were Edward G. Walker and Charles L. Mitchell.

New Mexico repealed a law forbidding intermarriage.

The Republican Party of Alabama was organized by William R. Smith and C. C. Sheets. These were two white men from the north Alabama hill country.

A Negro convention in Mobile, Ala., called on Congress to guarantee their freedom.

Nebraska's Constitution of 1866 gave suffrage only to whites.

The Tennessee Legislature confined suffrage to whites.

In a riot in Memphis, Tenn., 46 Negroes and two white liberals were killed; about 75 were wounded. 90 homes, 12 schools and four Negro churches were burned.

In a New Orleans riot, 35 Negroes were killed and more than 100 wounded.

Two Negro cavalry units, the 9th and 10th, comprised of Negro Civil War veterans, were organized.

The Methodist Episcopal Church founded the Centenary Biblical Institute in Baltimore. This Institute later became Morgan State College. They also founded Rust College at Holly Springs, Miss.

The American Missionary Association founded: Trinity at Athens, Ala., Gregory at Wilmington, N.C., and Fisk at Nashville, Tenn.

Henry Thacker Burleigh (1866-1949), Negro concert baritone and composer was born in Erie, Pa. Burleigh began singing in local choirs and won a scholarship to study with Dvorak at the National Conservatory of Music in New York. He later taught at the conservatory, and was the soloist from 1894 to 1946 at St. George's Church in New York, and also at Temple Emanu-el for more than 20 years. In his many concert tours, he sang his own compositions and made famous his arrangements of such Negro spirituals as *Deep River* and *Were You There?*

Matthew Alexander Henson (1866-1955) Negro explorer, was born in Charles County, Md. Orphaned at an early age, he shipped out as a cabin boy. The captain of the vessel, recognizing his abilities, encouraged him to read and study.

While working at a naval supply shop in New York City, Henson met Robert Peary, a naval engineer. Henson and Peary developed a close friendship, and Henson became Peary's right-hand man on geographical expeditions to Central America and Greenland for the U.S. Navy. In 1888 Peary and Henson went to Baffin Bay. Henson, because of his knowledge of Eskimo language and his experience as a navigator, was an invaluable aid to Peary. Between the 7 Arctic expeditions that Peary and Henson made over the next quarter of a century, Peary lectured widely while Henson became consultant to the American Museum of Natural History in New York on Arctic geography. Henson was internationally acknowledged as one of the leading authorities on the Arctic. On their 1908-1909 expedition he was the first man to set foot on the North Pole and planted the U.S. flag atop the world. On April 6, 1954, Henson received the last of his many decorations on the occasion of the 45th anniversary of the discovery of the North Pole. The presentation was made by President Eisenhower.

1867

The National Labor Union at its second annual conference in Chicago, formed a committee on Negro labor.

President Johnson issued another amnesty proclamation which left only a few hundred rebels unpardoned.

In March, just before the session ended, the 39th Congress passed the Tenure of Office Act, in which the President was required to obtain the consent of the Senate to remove officials from office. Violation was made a misdemeanor, and thus constituted grounds for impeachment. Also a misdemeanor and grounds for impeachment was violation of a section inserted in the Army Appropriation Act. This law forbade the President from issuing orders to the Army except through the General of the Army.

To insure an almost continuous session of the Legislature, the 39th Congress passed an act convening the 40th Congress immediately. In this way, the Radicals kept the House of Representatives and the Senate in session, ready to vote for President Johnson's impeachment should he violate the Tenure of Office Act or a special section of the Army Appropriations Act.

The First Reconstruction Act in effect abolished Southern state governments which had been operating for 1½ years and returned the South to military rule. This Act said that: (1) new state conventions were to be held; (2) all males were eligible to vote (except certain Confederates); (3) all Constitutions were to guarantee the Negro the right to vote; (4) state Constitutions were to be submitted to the electorate for approval, and only then could the governor and legislature be elected; (5) Congress had to approve the final state structure, and only after Congressional approval would military governors be removed, Southern Congressmen seated, and states accepted back into the Union. (6) new State Legislature had to ratify the 14th Amendment. This First Reconstruction Act was passed by Congress, vetoed by President Johnson, repassed by Congress and became law on March 2.

The 40th Congress passed two supplementary Reconstruction Acts. The Act of March 23 divided the South into five military districts and gave the district commanders powers to "protect all persons in their rights of person and property, to suppress insurrection, disorder and violence, and to punish . . . all disturbers of the public peace." They could remove civil office-holders, make arrests, try civilians in military courts, and use Federal troops to preserve order. It gave commanders the responsibility of enrolling qualified voters and excluding from the voting lists those barred by the 14th Amendment. It authorized commanders to hold elections for delegates to state constitutional conventions. President Johnson, in appointing commanders for the military districts, removed General Sheridan and appointed General Thomas, a Virginia Democrat, in his place. General Hancock, a loyal Johnsonian, was appointed for the District of Louisiana and Texas. He also removed General Sickles in the Carolinas and replaced him with General Canby.

In the second supplementary Act of Reconstruction Congress provided that the district commanders were subject to the General of the Army, and not the President. This bill was vetoed by President Johnson, and repassed by the 40th Congress over the President's veto.

Of the 65,000 troops in Federal service, only 25,000 were stationed in the South.

Threatened with Congressional reorganization, the Supreme

Court played a passive role in Reconstruction. In MISSISSIPPI v. JOHNSON, and GEORGIA v. STANTON, the Court was asked to enjoin the President and the Secretary of War from enforcing the Reconstruction Acts on the grounds that they were unconstitutional. The Court evaded the issue, however, deciding in both cases that it had no power to enjoin an executive officer "in the performance of his official duties."

Three times Charles Sumner tried and failed to amend the Reconstruction Acts to include provisions that the Freedmen's Bureau provide homes and schools for Negroes.

The Freedmen's Bureau issued some 3½ million rations, somewhat down from 1866. By 1867, 46 hospitals with 5,292 beds had been set up by the Bureau.

After voter registration was carried out under the provisions of the Reconstruction Act and its supplements, Negroes constituted a majority of electors, although a minority in population in South Carolina, Georgia, Florida, Alabama, Mississippi and Louisiana. In Virginia, Arkansas, Texas and North Carolina, whites still constituted a larger part of the registered voters, but in these four states sizable numbers of whites in mountain sections voted Republican. There was a Republican preponderance in all State Constitutional Conventions except Virginia.

The Union League began to organize clubs in the South.

At the first Republican Party convention ever held in Mississippi, ⅓ of the members were ex-slaves.

In July the Republican Party of South Carolina was organized at Columbia. A state committee was formed which included J. H. Rainey, a Negro.

Voter registration listed in South Carolina, 78,982 Negroes and 46,346 whites. Ten counties had a majority of white voters, 21 counties had a majority of Negro voters. Mississippi voter registration listed: 60,167 Negroes and 46,636 whites. Negro voters were in a majority in 33 out of the 61 counties. Extensive Negro majorities existed in the following counties: Adams, Bolivar, Claiborne, Hinds, Issaquena, Lowndes. Noxubee, Warren, Washington, Yazoo and Tunica. Negro U.S. Senator Revels came from Adams County, as did Representative Lynch; Negro Senator Bruce lived in Bolivar.

General Canby, the military district commander for North

and South Carolina, reported that for the first 18 months, ending June 30, there were 197 murders and 548 cases of aggravated assault.

Membership lists differed as to the number of Negroes and Carpetbaggers represented at the state Constitutional Conventions. What appears to be a representative listing of the state delegates follows: Alabama, white 83 and Negro 17; Arkansas, white 68 and Negro 7; Florida, white 29 and Negro 17; Georgia, white 133 and Negro 33; Louisiana, white 52 and Negro 40; Mississippi, white 68 and Negro 17; North Carolina, white 107 and Negro 13; South Carolina, white 34 and Negro 63; Texas, white 81 and Negro 9; Virginia, white 80 and Negro 25.

In general the state Constitutional Conventions (1) provided for universal manhood suffrage; (2) granted equal rights to Negroes; (3) set up a system of public education; (4) organized the judiciary on a popular basis; (5) instituted democratic reforms in government machinery.

Iowa and Dakota admitted Negroes to the ballot.

Ohio voted against Negro suffrage by 50,629 votes.

State Baptist organizations were created in Virginia and Alabama. The Consolidated American Baptist Convention was created and lasted until 1880, when it was replaced by the National Baptist Convention.

Howard University was chartered by the Federal Government and established in Washington, D. C.

The American Missionary Association founded the following schools: Emerson at Mobile, Ala., Storrs at Atlanta, Ga., Beach at Savannah, Ga., and Talladega in Alabama.

The Presbyterians added Biddle University to Lincoln University, which was founded in 1854.

Morehouse College was founded as the Augusta Institute in Augusta, Ga. It was supported by the American Baptist Home Mission Society.

Sarah Breedlove Walker (1867-1919), a pioneer Negro business woman, known throughout her later life as Mme. C. J. Walker was born in Delta, La., in abject poverty. Orphaned at 6, she married at 14 and at 20 was left a widow with a small daughter. She then moved to St. Louis, worked as a laundress and attended school at night. In 1905 Mme. Walker hit on a formula for a preparation for "improving the appearance of the hair of the Negro." She travelled for two years to promote the preparation. Her mail-order business grew, and in 1910 she founded laboratories for the manufacture of various cosmetics.

1868

At the 3rd Annual Conference of the National Labor Union in New York City, the subject of Negro labor was not brought up, although at the 1867 Conference a special committee on Negro labor had resolved to consider the problem at this meeting.

President Johnson vetoed the bill giving suffrage to District of Columbia Negroes. It was passed over his veto by Congress.

On Feb. 24, the House voted to institute impeachment proceedings against President Johnson. Throughout 1867, a House Committee had gathered evidence about Johnson's political and private life. On March 13, 7 Republican Senators voted with the Democrats against impeachment. The final vote was 35 to 19, 1 short of the necessary two-thirds majority.

Congress passed a law denying the Supreme Court jurisdiction in cases involving the writ of *habeas corpus*. This prevented the Court from ruling on certain cases concerning the constitutionality of the Reconstruction Acts, e.g., EX PARTE MCCARDLE. In this case McCardle, a Mississippi editor who had been tried before a military commission for criticizing Reconstruction, challenged the jurisdiction of the military commission and asked for a writ of *habeas corpus*. The Supreme Court refused to hear the case because of the March 27th law.

In June the report of the Congressional Committee on Lawlessness and Violence was issued. The Committee reported that 373 freedmen between 1866 and 1868 had been killed by whites, that 10 whites had been killed by freedmen.

11 amendments were introduced into Congress before the 15th Amendment was finally decided upon.

In December, the 15th Amendment was enacted by Congress to safeguard Negroes against a future white supremacy, by guaranteeing that their right to vote could not be "denied or abridged by the U.S. or any State."

The Republicans did not include in their Presidential platform a demand for free Negro suffrage in Northern states, since several Northern states had recently rejected the idea. Instead, their platform read: "The guarantee by Congress of equal suffrage to all loyal men in the South was demanded by every consideration of public safety, of gratitude and of justice, and must be maintained; while the question of suffrage in all the loyal states properly belongs to the people of those states." The Democrats' platform called the 13th and 14th Amendments "unconstitutional, revolutionary and void."

The Freedmen's Bureau issued 2½ million rations.

Alabama was readmitted in March. The Alabama state government had been organized by the Union League Republican Organization, with John C. Keffer as its leader.

An Alabama statute made it unlawful to unite in one school Negro and white children.

Arkansas' Representatives and Senators were readmitted to Congress.

Florida was readmitted to the Union. Because of Florida's Ku Klux Klan violence, Governor Reed asked for Federal troops. This request was not acted upon. The KKK was particularly violent in Florida. There were 235 murders from 1868 to 1871.

Whites gained partial control of the Georgian government and ejected all Negro members of the Legislature on the basis that the right to hold office had not been specifically bestowed upon newly enfranchised freedmen. Congress declared that Georgia did not have a republican form of government, denied their Congressional Representatives seats, and placed the state under military rule again. Georgia was readmitted after ratification of the 15th Amendment.

Louisiana's Representatives and Senators were readmitted to Congress. Prior to the November 1868 election in Louisiana, 2,000 persons were killed or wounded. In the parish of St. Landry, the Klan killed or wounded over 200 Republicans, hunting and chasing them for two days through fields and swamps. A pile of 25 dead Republicans was found half-buried in the woods. A "Negro hunt" took place in Bossier Parish. 120 corpses were found in the woods or taken out of the Red River. 297 persons were slain in the parishes adjacent to New Orleans during the month before the election.

At the Mississippi Constitutional Convention, 17 of the 97 delegates were Negroes.

North Carolina was readmitted to the Union.

48 delegates to South Carolina's Constitutional Convention were white, and 76 Negro. Of the 48 whites, 15 came from the North. From 1868 through 1887, South Carolina sent 6 Negroes to the U.S. Congress. They were: A. J. De Large, Robert Elliot, Robert C. Cain, Robert B. Rainey, R. H. Ransier, and J. H. Smalls. The South Carolina Constitution was adopted by a vote of 60,000 to 2,800. South Carolina was readmitted to the Union. The South Carolina Legislature met in July: in the Senate there were 21 whites, 6 of whom were Democrats, and 10 Negroes; in the House there were 46 whites, 14 of whom were Democrats, and 78 Negroes. Francis Cardozo, a Negro, was appointed secretary of state of South Carolina, and served until 1872. From 1872 through 1876, he was the state treasurer. South Carolina repealed a law forbidding intermarriage. This law was reenacted in 1879.

Minnesota, Maine, New Hampshire, Vermont, Massachusetts, Rhode Island and Nevada permitted Negroes to vote. Negro suffrage was defeated in Missouri and Michigan.

The American Missionary Association founded Hampton Normal and Agricultural Institute, in Hampton, Va. At this institution Booker T. Washington was educated. The association also founded Knox at Athens, Ga., and Burwell at Selma, Ala.

William Edward Burghardt Du Bois (1868-1963) was born in Great Barrington, Mass. He received a B.A. from Fisk University in 1888. In 1895 he was the first Negro to be awarded a Ph.D. from Harvard University. His dissertation, *The Suppression of the African Slave Trade to the U.S.A., 1638-1870*, was published as the first volume of the Harvard Historical Studies in 1896. In the last decade of the 19th and the first decade of the 20th century, Du Bois gained a reputation as a prominent Negro scholar and civil rights activist. Du Bois was an eloquent defender of full rights for Negroes through the Niagara Movement, which he founded in 1905, and which enlisted prominent Negroes, and through *The Horizon*, a magazine he edited from 1907 until it folded in 1910. In addition to his demands for full equality, Du Bois was known for his opposition to Booker T. Washington and for his exposition of the theory of "the talented tenth." Briefly, Du Bois' idea was that those Negroes who had gained success had the responsibility to lead the struggle to liberate all Negroes. In 1910, Du Bois joined the newly formed NAACP, and became the editor of its official publication, the *Crisis*, a position he held until 1934. Du Bois' career in the NAACP was a stormy one due to his militancy. In 1919, he formed a Pan-African Conference that lasted until 1929. It never became an important force, and the NAACP only half-heartedly supported it. In 1926, he visited Russia for 2 months and began to speak of socialism as a prerequisite for Negro liberation. In 1934, however, Du Bois came out for Negro autonomy, "non discriminatory segregation," as he called it. This, plus his apologetics for Japanese imperialism (Du Bois admired Japan for being a powerful colored nation) alienated the leadership of the NAACP, and in 1934 he was forced to resign. From 1934 to 1944, Du Bois taught at Atlanta University. During this period he produced his major opus, *Black Reconstruction in America*, and an autobiography, *Dusk of Dawn*, 1940. In 1944, he was fired from Atlanta University, but Walter White brought him back into the NAACP as head of its Department of Special Research. Du Bois was still too militant for the NAACP, and in 1948 he was dismissed. By this time, however, Du Bois had become active in the world peace movement, attending international peace conferences and forming, in 1950, the Peace Information Service, which worked to ban nuclear weapons. Also in 1950, Du Bois ran for the U.S. Senate from New York on the American Labor Party ticket. In 1951, Du Bois was indicted by a Federal grand jury for failing to register the Peace Information Center as the American agent of a foreign principal. Du Bois was finally acquitted. By 1952, Du Bois rejected all forms of Negro rights movements in favor of a world socialist movement, and 5 years later joined the Communist Party. He maintained a typical independence, condemning the Communist plan for an autonomous Negro state.

In 1960, Du Bois moved to Ghana, where he died on Aug. 28, 1963.

Sissieretta Jones (1868-1933), Negro opera singer, was born Matilda S. Joyner in Portsmouth, Va. Receiving her musical training at the Academy of Music in Providence, R. I., and the New England Conservatory, she was the first Negro singer to appear at Wallach's Theater in Boston. Throughout her life she made concert tours in the U.S., South America, the West Indies and Europe, where she became known as "Black Patti," after the Italian soprano, Adelina Patti. In 1892 she sang at the White House, and subsequently organized Black Patti's Troubadours, that appeared in the U.S. for 19 years.

William Wells Brown published his history, *The Negro in the American Rebellion.* Previously a novelist, Brown has been called the first creative prose writer of importance among Negroes.

The famous slave narrative *Behind the Scenes by Elizabeth Keckley, Formerly A Slave, but More Recently A Modiste and Friend to Mrs. Abraham Lincoln; or Thirty Years A Slave and Forty Years in the White House,* was published.

In Cuba, Carlos Manuel de Cespedes, granted his slaves freedom. He also advocated and agitated for a revolution against Spain.

1869

At the 4th annual conference of the National Labor Union in Philadelphia there were 142 representatives of whom 9 were Negroes. It was decided that Negroes should form their own unions, which would send delegates to future conferences. Generally, organized labor ignored the Negro, or accepted him only in Negro unions. An example of this practice was the case of Lewis H. Douglass, the son of Frederick Douglass, who worked in the Government Printing Office, but was not allowed to join the printers' union.

The Colored National Labor Union was organized in Washington, D. C. Isaac Myers was elected president. It recommended cooperatives, loan associations and the purchase of land. The theory behind the land purchase was that more landowners would mean fewer laborers and thus higher wages.

The 41st Congress had two Negro representatives: J. H. Rainey from South Carolina and J. F. Long, from Georgia. In the Senate the only Negro was H. R. Revels of Mississippi.

The pre-emancipation status of the Negroes who served as Congressmen in this Reconstruction Era were: Slaves: Lynch, Smalls, DeLarge, Murray, Haralson, Turner, Nash, Long, Bruce, Hyman, White, Cheatham, Rainey. Born free: Miller, Walls, Ransier, Elliot, Cain, Revels, Rapier, O'Hara, Langston.

James Garfield introduced a resolution in the House to reduce representation of Southern states as a penalty for denying Negroes the vote, in accordance with Section 2 of the 14th Amendment. No action was taken.

In TEXAS v. WHITE, the Supreme Court ruled that the Southern ordinances of secession had been null and void, and that the Southern states had never ceased to be in the Union. Although this rejected the basis of the Reconstruction Acts (that the states had left the Union, and thus the Union had the right to set standards for readmission), the Court declined to consider the constitutionality of the Reconstruction Acts, fearing Congressional reorganization.

The Freedmen's Bureau, according to a report by the commissioner, Gen. Oliver Howard, had spent $13,579,816 on freedmen.

In Mississippi, J. R. Lynch, a Negro, was nominated for secretary of state on the Republican Party ticket. Lynch was a well-educated Methodist preacher who had come to Mississippi from Indiana. H. R. Revels was nominated as Republican candidate for the State Senate. He was an African Methodist Episcopal pastor in Natchez. Revels was elected.

In Mississippi, 716 officers and men comprised the total complement of Federal troops stationed in Mississippi. In Texas, 4,612 Federal troops were stationed, primarily to serve as protection against Indians.

The South Carolina Legislature had ten Negro and 21 white Senators, 78 Negro and 46 white Representatives.

Tennessee's Democratic Party regained control of the state from the Republicans.

2 Negro Infantry Regiments were formed, the 24th and

the 25th. With the Negro cavalry units formed in 1865, Negro troops now totalled 12,500 men.

Indiana authorized the establishment of separate schools for Negroes.

Straight University in New Orleans received its charter. The law school was granted the right to qualify any of its graduates for immediate admission to the Louisiana bar.

The American Missionary Association founded Le Moyne College in Memphis, Tenn. and Tougaloo University in Mississippi.

Scenes in the Life of Harriet Tubman, as told by Sarah Bradford, was published.

Francis Ellen Harper published her epic poem, *Moses, a Story of the Nile*. Her *Poems on Miscellaneous Subjects*, published in 1854, had sold 10,000 copies in five years.

1870

U.S. Census: There were 4,880,009 Negroes in the U.S., who represented 12.7% of the total U.S. population.

12% of the Negroes were mulattoes, or 584,049. The number of mulattoes was lowest in the South. 125 mulattoes per 1,000 Negroes, as compared to 255 for the North and 553 for the West.

The percentage of Negroes born in the South but living in the North and West was 3.3%. The percentage of Negroes born in the North and West and living in the South was 4.9%.

Chicago had 3,696 Negroes. The Negro population of Chicago doubled each decade until 1900.

Negro literacy was 18.6%. In 1880, it had risen to 30%, and by 1890 to 42.9%.

The percentage of total population that attended school in Southern states was: white, 13.5%, Negro, 3.07%.

Between 1870 and 1901, 22 Negroes served in Congress; 2 Senators and 20 Representatives.

The Mississippi State Senate was convened in January, Negro State Senator H. R. Revels opened the session with a prayer. About ¼ of the State legislators were Negroes, and they demanded one of the three U.S. Senate vacancies. The three vacancies consisted of a short unexpired term; a normal term; the full term to follow the unexpired term. J. R. Lynch, the Negro secretary of state was considered for the short term, but it was decided not to create a vacancy in an important elective office that would necessitate a new election, H. R. Revels, State Senator from Adams County, was nominated by a Negro conference, then the party caucus, and on Jan. 20, 1870 was elected to the U.S. Senate to fill the unexpired term. Revels presented his credentials for his seat in the U.S. Senate on Feb. 23. This caused a three-day debate with two objections: (1) Revels' election had been certified by General Ames, the military governor, and his right as an army officer to certify elections was questioned; (2) some claimed Revels was ineligible because, as a Negro he had not been a citizen for 9 years. On Feb. 25 he was accepted by a vote of 48 to 8. Revels was assigned to the Committee on Education and Labor. He made several reports to the Senate for the Committee, and introduced three minor bills. None were passed. Among Revels' important votes in the Senate were: (1) the readmission of Texas under Carpetbag government; (2) the enforcement of the 15th Amendment; (3) a change in the naturalization laws by striking out the word "white"; (4) the abolition of franking privilege; (5) a Federal election law with penalties; (6) Federal aid for steamship service to Mexico; (7) eligibility of General Ames to become governor. He voted against making public the proceedings of the Committee on Southern Outrages.

In South Carolina, Robert B. Elliot was nominated to run for the House of Representatives in Columbia's 3rd district. Elliot was elected by a margin of 7,000 votes. Robert C. De Large and J. H. Rainey, both Negroes, were also elected to Congress, representing South Carolina.

In the Enforcement Acts of May 31, 1870, and Feb. 28, 1871, the use of force or intimidation to prevent citizens from voting was made punishable by a fine or imprisonment. The President was authorized to use the military to enforce the 15th Amendment. Congressional elections were placed under Federal supervision.

Sen. Charles Sumner introduced a bill providing equal rights in transportation, hotels, theaters, schools, churches, cemeteries and juries. This bill was not passed until 1875, and in its final version the school desegregation provision had been deleted.

In the Freedmen's Bureau schools, there were 3,300 teachers and 149,581 pupils.

The Liberal Republican Party originated in Missouri, where a coalition of Democrats and dissatisfied Republicans won control of the state and restored full political and civil rights to the ex-Confederates.

The composition of State Legislatures in the South was as follows: Alabama, whites 73 and Negroes 27; Arkansas, whites 71 and Negroes 9; Georgia, whites 149 and Negroes 26; Mississippi, whites 77 and Negroes 30; North Carolina, whites 101 and Negroes 1; South Carolina, whites 49 and Negroes 75; Texas, whites 82 and Negroes 8; Virginia, whites 116 and Negroes 21.

In October, Governor Reed of Florida asked for Federal troops to cope with Klan violence. This request was not granted.

Georgia's and Mississippi's Representatives and Senators were readmitted to Congress.

The Democratic Party in North Carolina regained control of the state from the Republicans. 12,000 fewer Republicans voted than in the previous elections, largely because of Klan intimidation. In Caswell County in northern North Carolina, a strongly Republican area, the Klan whipped or beat 21 men, whites and Negroes, and killed two, one white, between April and May. In Alamance County, N. C., in February, the Negro Republican leader, Wyatt Outlaw, was hanged. The Klan violence was widespread in these two Republican counties. Thirteen known murders committed by the Klan caused Governor Holden to declare that these counties were in a state of insurrection and to send in the militia. Upon gaining control of the State Legislature, the Democrats impeached Governor Holden.

Tennessee enacted a poll tax. It was suspended in 1871 and repealed in 1873 due to pressure from poor whites.

Texas' Representatives and Senators were readmitted to Congress.

Virginia was readmitted to the Union.

Between 1870 and 1890, 11 Negro members of the 9th U.S. Cavalry, one Negro member of the 10th U.S. Cavalry and two Negro members of the 24th Infantry Regiment, were awarded Congressional Medals of Honor for their bravery in the Indian Wars.

There were a half million members of the Negro Baptist Church, compared with 150,000 in 1850.

The Colored (later Christian) Methodist Episcopal Church permitted the Southern churches to form their own conference—the Methodist Episcopal Church, South. The first general conference of the Methodist Episcopal Church, South, was held in Jackson, Tenn. Henry Miles and Richard Vanderhorse were elected bishops.

The African Methodist Episcopal Zion Church had 200,000 members, compared to 26,746 in 1860.

The Methodist Episcopal Church founded Clark College in Atlanta, Ga.

The American Baptist Home Mission helped found Benedict College in South Carolina.

Robert Sengstacke Abbot (1870-1940), Negro newspaper publisher, was born on St. Simon's Island, Ga., spent his childhood in Savannah and went to school at the Beach Institute (then Claflin Institute) in Orangeburg, S.C., and finally Hampton Institute in Virginia, from which he was graduated as a master in the trade of printing. Abbot served an apprenticeship at the *Savannah News* between 1890 and 1896. In 1896 he went to Chicago where race would not be as much of a barrier to jobs in the newspaper field, but was refused full membership in the International Typographical Union and was denied full-time employment. Between 1898 and 1903, he attended Kent College, was graduated with a law degree and practiced for a short period in both Chicago and Gary, Ind. In 1905, Abbot initiated a newspaper, the *Chicago Defender;* the first issue appeared on May 5. This newspaper was the first large-city Negro paper to serve the needs of the growing communities of Southern Negro immigrants. Abbot's newspaper was not limited to Negro news. The *Defender* was a crusading newspaper. Upon the death of Abbot, his nephew, John Sengstacke, became the paper's director. The *Defender's* daily circulation is now somewhere around 40,000. During his lifetime, Abbot received many honors. He was appointed a member of the Illinois Race Relations Commission by Governor Lowden in 1919 and received honorary degrees from several colleges. In 1941, the Robert S. Abbot Memorial Award was set up by the *Chicago Defender*. It is given annually to a person who has made a distinguished contribution to improve race relations. A Robert S. Abbot scholarship has been instituted at Lincoln University in Missouri, and is given annually to a journalism student.

Will Marion Cook (1870-1947), Negro composer, was born of educated parents, both graduates of Oberlin, in Detroit, Mich. He studied violin and after 3 years at Oberlin College went to the Berlin Conservatory of Music to study under the great German violinist Joachim. Ill health forced him to return to the U.S. in 1898. Cook wrote music for several of the best musicals during the first two decades of the 20th century. Also a serious composer, he studied orchestration under Dvorak in 1899-1900. He adopted, refined and wrote music from the tradition of Negro folk songs for large orchestras with great success, long before William Dawson or Gershwin. Four of his most successful works were the art songs, *Rain Song, Swing Along, Wid De Moon,* and the adaptation to orchestra of a Negro sermon, *Exhortation.*

Several Negroes were denied entry to the Supreme Lodge of the Knights of Pythias in New York. Negroes who could pass for whites joined the Knights of Pythias, learned the ritual, and finally in 1880 founded the Colored Knights of Pythias, and organized a lodge in Vicksburg, Miss. By 1905, there were 1,628 lodges with 70,000 members.

1871

The second meeting of the Colored National Labor Union took place on Jan. 9. Congress was petitioned for a national system of educational and technical training.

The Freedmen's Savings and Trust Company, a Negro-owned bank, had 34 branches, and deposits of $20 million. This bank failed in 1874.

The following Negroes were elected to the 42nd Congress,

as Representatives: J. T. Walls of Florida, R. S. Turner of Alabama, J. H. Rainey, Robert C. DeLarge and Robert B. Elliot of South Carolina.

James Garfield again proposed a resolution in the House to reduce the representation of Southern states as a penalty for denying Negroes the vote, in accordance with Section 2 of the 14th Amendment. Again this resolution was not adopted.

The Report of the Congressional Investigating Committee on the KKK was published in 1871. This committee had studied 9 counties in South Carolina for a six-month period. Their findings were: the Klan lynched and murdered 35 men and whipped 262 men and women; shot, mutilated, or burned the property of 101 people, and committed two sexual offenses. For the same period, Negroes killed four men, beat one man, committed 16 other outrages and committed no sexual offenses. The committee also reported they had found that the Klan had murdered 74 men in Georgia and 109 in Alabama between 1868 and 1871.

The 3rd Enforcement Act, also known as the Ku Klux Klan Act, permitted the President to suspend *habeas corpus*. This Act expired in 1872 and was not renewed. This Act imposed heavy penalties on persons "who shall conspire together, or go in disguise . . . for the purpose . . . of depriving any person or any class of persons of the equal protection of the laws, or of equal privileges or immunities under the laws."

In the U.S. v. SOUDERS, the Supreme Court held that the Enforcement Acts applied only to Congressional elections. The Court also ruled in U.S. v. HALL that all the rights guaranteed by the first eight amendments were the "privileges and immunities" mentioned in the 14th Amendment. This decision was overruled by the MAXWELL v. Dow case of 1899.

Governor Reed of Florida again asked for Federal troops to cope with Klan violence. This was his third request since 1868, and again was denied. Jonathan Gibbs, the Florida secretary of state, a Negro, reported before a Congressional Committee that 153 Negroes had-been murdered in Jackson County, Fla., alone.

The Georgia Democratic Party regained control of the state from the Republicans.

In the Mississippi Legislature, 38 out of 115 members were Negroes. In Mississippi, 640 persons were indicted under the Enforcement Acts, however none were convicted. A race riot broke out in Meridian, Miss.

In Kemper County, Miss., between 1869 and 1871, 35 Negroes were known to have been killed by the Klan, and Negro whippings were an almost nightly occurrence.

According to the records of A. W. Cummings, President of Spartanburg Female College in Spartanburg County, S. C., from Oct. 1870 to July 1871 there were 227 known victims of Klan aggressions.

Virginia reapportioned its election districts, to minimize the Negro vote.

Rev. Moses Dickson, of Independence, Mo., founded the International Order of 12 of the Knights and Daughters of Tabor, a national secret society. Its object was to spread Christian religion and education, acquire real estate and avoid intemperance. 200,000 members were claimed by 1900.

New Orleans Negro secret societies and fraternal organizations were represented by their 13 bands at funeral ceremonies for President Garfield. A particular function of these bands was to play at funeral processions.

Howard University established a law school.

Oscar De Priest (1871-1951), first Negro Congressman from a Northern state, was born in Florence, Ala. De Priest moved to Kansas in 1877 with his parents, Alexander R. and Mary De Priest. He ran away from home and became a painter and master decorator in Chicago. Wealthy from his stock market and real estate investments, he was twice elected Cook County Commissioner, in 1904 and 1906. In 1915, he became the city's first Negro alderman and was elected U.S. Congressman from 1929 to 1934. His affiliation with the Republican Party in the post-Depression years ultimately contributed to his defeat in the 1934 election.

Isaac Hathaway (1871-?), Negro sculptor and ceramist, was born in Lexington, Ky. He studied art at the New England Conservatory and ceramics at Pittsburgh Normal College. He headed the ceramics department of Alabama State Teachers College. He is famous for his portrait busts of Douglass, Dunbar and Washington. Hathaway designed the

Federal memorial coins of Washington and George Washington Carver.

James Weldon Johnson (1871-1938), Negro poet, teacher, diplomat, NAACP executive secretary, was born in Jacksonville, Fla. He was educated at Atlanta and Columbia Universities. He wrote lyrics for songs until 1917, when his first book of poetry was published, *Fifty Years and Other Poems*. Although Johnson owed much to Dunbar, he was not a dialect poet. This book, one of the most important in Afro-American literature, was a first expression of race pride. It also contained many beautiful lyrics which had no reference to race. Johnson constantly protested against "southern justice" and the inferior status granted to the Negro. He is the first Negro poet who takes pride in his blackness without apology. Johnson's poems, *Lift Every Voice and Sing*, was set to music by his brother, J. R. Johnson, and came to have the status of a Negro national anthem. Between 1916 and 1930, Johnson was an active and influential member of the NAACP as a field secretary, and then the executive secretary. During this period he conducted an extensive study of Negro culture. The 1920's was the era of the Harlem Renaissance, and Johnson, like Alain Locke and Langston Hughes, devoted much of his time to non-creative editorial work. In 1920 he published *Self Determining Haiti* based on personal observations and a good background in Latin-American affairs. Among the works he edited were, in 1922 *The Book of American Negro Poetry*, the first anthology of Negro verse ever published; 1925, *The Book of American Negro Spirituals*, the first anthology collected by a Negro of his own oral literary tradition; 1926, *Second Book of American Negro Spirituals*. Through these three books he made the reading public, both Negro and white, aware for the first time, of the vast scope and rich mine of Negro literature. In 1927, Johnson's *God's Trombones: "Seven Negro Sermons in Verse"* was published. Although Johnson claimed this work to be a preacher's sermons he reconstructed from memory, they must be considered original creative work of his own. The rhythms of these poems are cadenced with long beat measures, giving them a striking chant-like quality. They were made for oratorio or concert hall adaption. Johnson never wrote another collection of poetry. His subsequent work was non-fictional and autobiographical. Among his other activities, he served as a school principal and a lawyer, also as U.S. consul at Venezuela and Nicaragua.

The Fisk Jubilee Singers went on a tour of Europe and America, thus bringing Negro spiritual music to new and larger audiences.

In Brazil, the Rio Branco Law was issued. This law stipulated that children of slaves should be free.

Brazilian abolitionists forced through a law which made owners free a slave who could pay his market value.

1872

The Negro-owned Freedmen's Savings and Trust Company had 70,000 depositors.

The Democratic Party endorsed Horace Greeley, the Presidential candidate of the Liberal Republicans. They also accepted the platform of the Liberal Republicans, which included adherence to the 13th, 14th, and 15th Amendments.

Congress passed a sweeping Amnesty Act, which pardoned almost all of those made ineligible for office under the 14th Amendment. Thus, the officials of the Confederacy could re-enter politics.

The Freedmen's Bureau ceased to exist. Negroes could no longer rely on that agency for sustenance in an emergency. With the extinction of the Freedmen's Bureau, Negroes, often tenants of native whites, ceased political activity when threatened with expulsion from the land.

Alabama's law forbidding intermarriage was voided by a state court. The court reversed itself in 1877.

Georgia instituted school segregation.

The North Carolina Legislature passed a law granting pardon and amnesty for any crimes committed on behalf of any white secret organization.

In March, under provision of the Enforcement Acts, *habeas corpus* was suspended and Federal troops moved into South Carolina. 500 Klansmen were arrested, but only 55 were eventually convicted.

Charlotte E. Ray became the first Negro woman graduate of any law school in the U.S. She attended Howard University.

Paul Laurence Dunbar (1872-1906), Negro poet, was born in Dayton, Ohio. His father had been a slave on a Kentucky plantation who had escaped to Canada before the Civil War. He returned to fight in the 55th Massachusetts Infantry. After the war, Dunbar's father worked in Dayton as a plasterer. The young Dunbar was educated in the schools of Dayton, and served as president of the Literary Society. He published *Oak and Ivory* in 1893. In 1894, Dunbar was employed by Frederick Douglass in the Haiti Building at the World's Columbian Exposition in Chicago. Dunbar's second book of poems, *Majors and Minors,* was printed in 1895. It received a full-page review in *Harper's Weekly.* In 1896, Dodd & Mead Co. published *Lyrics of a Lowly Life. The Uncalled* was written in England in 1898. Dunbar was the first American poet to investigate the Negro subculture and to handle its folk-life with any degree of fullness or comprehension. His dialect poetry reflected the "plantation school" influence. The "plantation school" was a group of white southern Ku Klux Klan writers who through novels like *Red Rock* and *The Clansman* perpetuated the myth of the antebellum South. Dunbar's Negroes are all happily resigned "Uncle Toms," moaning about the ante-bellum days when they did not have the burden of freedom to cope with. However, Dunbar's poetry went far beyond the "plantation school" in its feeling and quality. Dunbar, not from the deep South, knew about the area only from his mother, an ex-slave. He managed to idealize such rural experiences as spelling bees, church services, cotton picking, etc. Many of his best poems, are about children, e.g., *Candle-lighting Time,* and *Little Brown Baby.* Dunbar's *Complete Poems* were published in 1913. His novels were: *The Uncalled,* 1896; *The Love of Landry,* 1900; *The Fanatics,* 1901; *The Sport of Gods,* 1902. He also wrote a one-act musical sketch, *Uncle Eph's Christmas,* in 1900.

U. S. Grant and the Colored People by Frederick Douglass was published.

The population of Brazil consisted of 38.2% whites, 19.7% Negroes, and 42.2% mestizos.

1873

The Freedman's Bank of Charleston, S.C., had $350,000 in deposits and 5,500 depositors.

The following seven Negroes were elected to the 43rd Congress: Robert B. Elliot, R. H. Cain, A. J. Ransier, J. H. Rainey, of South Carolina; James T. Rapier of Alabama; J. T. Walls of Florida, and John R. Lynch of Mississippi.

The U.S. Supreme Court in its Slaughter-House cases, although not dealing directly with Negroes, ruled that the 14th Amendment's privileges and immunities referred only to the inherent characteristics of U.S. citizenship. The minority opinion felt that the amendment applied to privileges and immunities which citizens enjoyed as citizens of states, agreeing with Congress that Negroes needed protection from hostile state laws.

The Colfax Massacre took place in Colfax, Grant Parish, La., 350 miles northwest of New Orleans. The village had between 75 and 100 inhabitants, mostly Negroes. The parish population was approximately 500, divided equally between white and Negro. In the Louisiana elections of 1872, fraud was claimed by both Democrats and Republicans. Both parties claimed that they had won the Governorship, and both gubernatorial candidates, McEnery, the Fusion Democrat claimant, and Kellog, the Republican claimant, commissioned a judge and sheriff for Grant Parish. On March 23, Kellog's appointees arrived in Colfax and took possession of the courthouse. They were guarded by armed Negroes. Tension grew, and several shooting incidents occurred at the end of March and beginning of April. Christopher Nash, as Democratic sheriff of Grant County, formed a posse of white inhabitants of the county at Summerfield Springs, 4 miles north of Colfax, and sent out a call for help to the neighboring parishes. About 100 white volunteers answered his call. On April 13, the armed whites entered the town. They battled the Negroes all day, and finally were victorious. That night they slaughtered most of the Negroes they had captured. The next day U.S. troops were sent in. However, they never caught any of the leaders of the white band.

The Branch Normal School was founded at Pine Bluff, Ark. It later became the Arkansas Agricultural, Mechanical and Normal College.

William C. Handy (1873-1957), Negro composer, was born in Florence, Ala. His father was a minister. At school Handy came under the influence of a musician and refused to follow the ministry as his parents desired. Instead, he bought a cornet and began to study music. In his late teens, Handy left for Birmingham, Ala., where he taught school and worked in the ironworks. The Depression of 1893 put him out of work and in desperation he organized a group of musicians and traveled to the Columbian Exposition at Chicago. Handy returned South after the exposition, and became a bandleader with a successful minstrel group, Mohara's Colored Minstrels. He moved to Memphis and wrote the campaign songs for mayor Edward Crump in 1909. *The Mayor Crump Blues* were transformed into his first national success, *The Memphis Blues.* Over the next 20 years Handy's music became popular. His *Evolution of the Blues* was performed in 1924 by Vincent Lopez at the Metropolitan Opera House in New York City. In 1926, Handy had his own music publishing house, and in 1928 Handy's concert illustrating the development of Negro music marked the pinnacle of his success. In 1914 Handy wrote *The St. Louis Woman,* later better known as *The St. Louis Blues,* that is perhaps the most famous of all his tunes.

William A. Harper (1873-1910) A Chicago-born Negro, was a student of Henry Ossawa Tanner, whom he met in Paris. He was educated at the Chicago Art Institute. Harper was an extremely talented landscapist. His *Avenue of Poplars, Last Gleam, The Hillside,* and *The Grey Dawn* indicated a promising future. However, his early death in 1910 prevented his full development.

J. Rosamund Johnson (1873-1954), Negro composer, was born in Jacksonville, Fla., son of a Baptist minister. Like his brother, James Weldon, he received a good education, and attended the New England Conservatory of Music. In 1900 Johnson began collaborating with Robert Cole. In 1902, *The Red Moon,* one of the early Cole-Johnson successes, was published. Among the early popular songs of Cole and Johnson were *Under the Bamboo Tree, Congo Love Song, Nobody's Looking but the Owl and the Moon,* and *My Castle on the Nile.* After Cole's death, Johnson collaborated with his brother on *God's Trombones.* He also taught at the New York Conservatory of Music, and in the 1930's acted in *Porgy and Bess, Mamba's Daughters* and *Cabin in the Sky.*

Francis Ellen Harper published *Sketches of Southern Life.*

Alberry Whitman's volume of verse, *Leelah Misled,* was published.

Puerto Rico abolished slavery.

1874

By this year Georgia Negroes owned more than 350,000 acres of land.

Frederick Douglass was elected president of the Freedmen's Saving and Trust Company. The bank failed in this year. The Charleston branch owed over $250,000 to 5,296 depositors, and the Beaufort, S.C. branch owed to 1,200 depositors some $77,000.

Blanche K. Bruce, from Mississippi, a Negro, was chosen by the Republican party caucus to run for the Senate (he received 52 of 80 votes). He was elected on Feb. 3 against very weak opposition. Three Democratic State Senators voted for him.

Governor Ames, a Republican, dismissed ex-U.S. Senator H. R. Revels from his position as president of Alcorn College.

The Democratic Party regained control of Alabama, Arkansas, and Texas.

Virginia again reapportioned its election districts, further minimizing the Negro vote. It also abolished the New England township system, thus taking control of local government out of Negro hands.

William Wells Brown published *The Rising Son.*

Justin Holland, a Negro, published his *Comprehensive Method for the Guitar,* long a standard work.

1875

B. K. Bruce of Mississippi served in the U. S. Senate from 1875-1881. He was the only Negro during Reconstruction to serve a regular term in the Senate.

The following seven Negroes were elected to the 44th Congress as Representatives: J. R. Lynch, Mississippi; J. T. Walls, Florida; Jeremiah Haralson, Alabama; John A. Hyman, North Carolina; Charles E. Nash, Louisiana; J. H. Rainey and Robert Smalls, South Carolina.

The Civil Rights Act (originally proposed in 1870 by Charles Sumner) guaranteed Negroes against social disabilities initiated by states or municipalities. This act guaranteed equal rights in conveyances, theaters, inns, and juries. It went beyond the rights granted by Congress in the Reconstruction Amendments.

James Garfield re-introduced his resolution in the House for reducing representation of Southern states as a penalty for denying suffrage to Negroes, in accordance with Section 2 of the 14th Amendment. Again no action was taken.

There were 16 Negroes and 17 whites in the South Carolina Senate; 61 Negroes and 63 whites in the House.

Ex-U.S. Senator H. R. Revels left the Republican Party and joined the Democrats. In a letter to President Grant, he claimed that the Republicans had become corrupt and dishonest.

The United Presbyterians founded Knoxville College at Knoxville, Tenn.

Maj. Charles Redman Douglass, Frederick Douglass' youngest son, was appointed consul to Santo Domingo by President Grant.

Mary McLeod Bethune (1875-1955), Negro educator, was born in Mayesville, S.C. She attended Scotia Seminary in North Carolina and the Moody Bible Institute in Chicago. Refused as a missionary by the Presbyterian Board of Missions, she devoted her efforts to Negro education. In 1904 she established the Daytona Normal and Industrial Institute for Negro Girls, later merged with the Cookman Institute as Bethune-Cookman College. She served as Presidential adviser from 1930 to 1944. She helped Franklin D. Roosevelt organize the National Youth Administration and was Director of the Division of Negro Affairs between 1936 and 1944. In 1935, she received the Spingarn Award.

Carter Goodwin Woodson (1875-1950), a Negro historian, was born in New Canton, Va., the son of a tenant farmer who was an ex-slave. Woodson was too poor to afford an education and spent most of his youth working in Virginia coal mines, attending school 4 months of the year. He entered Douglass High School at 20 and was graduated with honors at 22. He then attended Berea College and was graduated with honors. In 1901, Woodson was sent to the Philippines as a school supervisor. In 1907 he received his B.A. from the University of Chicago and in 1908 his M.A. He did graduate work at the Sorbonne and received his doctorate from Harvard in 1912. Woodson's primary interest was Afro-American history. He was the first American to champion Afro-American studies. In 1915, primarily through Woodson's efforts, the Association for the Study of Negro Life and History was established. He became its director and editor of its scholarly quarterly, *The Journal of Negro History*. In 1922 Woodson published *The Negro in our History,* the first textbook of its kind. In 1926 he established Negro History Week and was awarded the NAACP Spingarn Medal. He was Dean of Liberal Arts at both Howard and West Virginia State College.

The Fisk Jubilee Singers raised enough money to construct the first important building at Fisk University.

The jockey who rode Aristides, winner of the first Kentucky Derby, was Oliver Lewis, a Negro.

1876

During the Congressional session of this year, B. K. Bruce, the Negro Senator from Mississippi, introduced a bill on racial affairs which was reported out of committee adversely. He also presented two petitions, neither of which received any consideration. Bruce, in an executive session of the Senate, denounced President Grant and the Republican Party for not caring about the Southern Negro, and then refused to go to the White House in response to a summons from Grant. On March 3, Senator Bruce made his first speech. He upheld the validity of P. B. S. Pinchbacks's election. Pinchback was a Negro Senator from Louisiana. He was not admitted. In his second major speech Bruce spoke in favor of a resolution to investigate the Mississippi elections of 1875 in which the Republican Party had dropped from a majority. Bruce charged fraud and intimidation. His resolution was passed.

In Mississippi, the Democratic Party regained control of the state from the Republicans.

A letter from E. M. Albretta, a Negro Republican canvasser in Horn Lakes, Miss., dated June 29, 1876, was sent to George W. Boutwell, U.S. Senator: "The Democrats told the colored voters, if they went to the polls on election day they would be killed. They intended to carry this election with powder and shot, and that they would kill every Republican speaker in the country if it did not go Democratic. . . . The chairman of our county committee . . . was shot in the last canvass."

Between 1876 and 1894, 52 Negroes served in the lower house of the North Carolina Legislature.

The Supreme Court in U. S. v. CRUIKSHANK decided that "the right of suffrage is not a necessary attribute of national citizenship; but that exemption from discrimination in the exercise of that right on account of race, etc., is. The right to vote in the States comes from the States; but the right of exemption from prohibitive discrimination comes from the U. S. . . . The 14th Amendment prohibits a state from denying to any person within its jurisdiction the equal protection of the laws, but this provision does not, any more than the one that preceded it, . . . add anything to the rights which one citizen has under the Constitution against another. . . . The power of the national government is limited to the enforcement of the rights guaranteed."

In the U. S. v. REESE, the Court decided that "the 15th Amendment to the Constitution does not confer the right of suffrage. The power of Congress to legislate at all upon the subject of voting at state elections rests upon this Amendment and can be exercised by providing a punishment only when the wrongful refusal to receive the vote of a qualified elector at such election is because of his race, color or previous condition of servitude." The Court thus ruled that Sections 3 and 4 of the Enforcement Act of May 31, 1870, were unconstitutional, as this act had authorized Congressional action against discrimination in voting in general, without mentioning the type of election or the conditions of the 15th Amendment: race, color or previous condition of servitude.

Rutherford B. Hayes' election to the U.S. presidency was contested by Tilden, the Democratic candidate. Two sets of Electors presented themselves from Louisiana, South Carolina, and Florida.

An Alabama law stated that Negro and white prisoners were not to be confined in the same "apartments."

A letter from D. Alleber, parish of West Feliciana, Tax Collector's Office, St. Francisville, La., dated May 18, 1876, was sent to Senator O. P. Morton, Washington, D. C.: "Sir: The telegraph has no doubt informed you of the wholesale slaughter of Negroes on the line of Louisiana and Mississippi.

We have ascertained that 38 Negroes were shot and hung. The lives of the few white Republicans now left are in imminent danger."

In order to further minimize the Negro vote, Virginia reapportioned election districts for a third time.

Property owned by the African Methodist Episcopal Church had increased seven-fold in value since 1856, and its membership had increased from 75,000 in 1866 to 200,000 in 1876.

In August, ex-U.S. Sen. H. R. Revels was reappointed president of Alcorn College by the Democratic governor of Mississippi.

Rev. Washington Brown established the Grand Foundation of True Reformers by consolidating local, existing groups of True Reformers. The Grand Foundation of True Reformers was a Negro secret society. Rev. Brown's attempt to create a mutual benefit organization on a national scale failed.

Edward Bouchet received a Ph.D. in physics from Yale University. He is believed to be the first American Negro to receive a doctorate.

Edward M. Bannister won a medal at the Philadelphia Centennial Exposition for his landscape *Under the Oaks.*

Bert Williams (1876-1922), Negro vaudeville star, was born Egbert Austin in the Bahamas, moved to California with his family and studied civil engineering. He abandoned this career, however, and in 1895 formed an immediately successful vaudeville team with George Walker. Between 1895 and 1909, they starred in and produced shows in the U.S. and England. They were famous for their characterizations with Walker the dandy, and Williams in black-face, using Negro dialect. After Walker's death in 1909, Williams sang and toured for 10 years with the Ziegfeld Follies. During this period, Williams was something of an anomaly. The only Negro in an almost all-white field, he escaped the anti-Negro sentiment of these years.

1877

In conferences at the Wormley Hotel in Washington, D.C., on Feb. 26 and 27, Rutherford B. Hayes promised Southern delegates that he would remove Federal troops from the

South, and leave the states alone in return for support from Democratic Southern Congressmen when the House voted for President. Upon Hayes' election, he removed Federal troops from South Carolina and Louisiana. In the first five months of Hayes' Administration one-third of his Southern appointees were Democrats.

R. H. Cain, J. H. Rainey, and Robert Smalls of South Carolina, all Negroes, were elected to the House of Representatives.

B. K. Bruce, the Negro Senator from Mississippi, was appointed chairman of a select committee on Mississippi River levees. When the chairman of the Manufacturers Committee resigned, he, being the senior member, served as acting chairman until a successor was appointed. Bruce presented a petition asking Federal aid for emigrants to Liberia. He voted against reducing the Army.

In HALL v. DE CUIR, the U.S. Supreme Court ruled that a state could not prohibit segregation on a "common carrier" because of the burden such laws placed on interstate commerce.

In GREEN v. STATE OF ALABAMA, the State Court upheld the law against intermarriage.

In South Carolina, Florida, and Louisiana, the Democratic Party regained control of the state.

In Georgia, school segregation was made an article of the State Constitution.

There were 571,506 Negro children in school.

Henry O. Flipper became the first Negro graduate of West Point.

Meta Vaux Warrick Fuller (1877-?), Negro sculptress, was born in Philadelphia. She graduated with honors from the Pennsylvania School of Industrial Art. In 1899, she went to Paris to study for three years at Colarossi's Academy. Her sculptures, *The Medusa* and *Christ in Agony*, done at school, attracted considerable attention. In 1903, *The Wretched*, a sculpture exhibited at the Paris Salon, made her famous in art circles and especially brought her the esteem of Auguste Rodin. She soon fell under Rodin's influence, as can be seen in her subsequent *Secret Sorrow, Oedipus, Death on the Wing, The Man Who Laughed, John the Baptist, Three Gray Women* and a group sculpture of the Fates. In 1907 Meta Warrick received a commission to do a series of commemorative figures illustrating the history of the Negro for the Jamestown Tercentennial Exposition. Her style became less symbolic and more realistic. Her subsequent work during the 1920's and '30's dealt mostly with Negro subjects and was commissioned by Negro and liberal organizations.

May Howard Jackson (1877-1930), sculptress, was born in Philadelphia. Graduated from the Pennsylvania Academy of Fine Arts in 1899, she married Sherman Jackson and moved to Washington, D.C., where she maintained a studio for the duration of her life. Partly because she never studied in Paris, she never tried to imitate academic continental styles. Her work was very much in the mainstream of her white American contemporaries. Negro themes dominated all her work, from the busts of Paul Laurence Dunbar and W. E. B. Du Bois to *The Mulatto Mother and Her Child* and *Head of a Child.*

Alberry Whitman's poem, *Not a Man and Yet a Man,* was published.

Isaac Murphy, a Negro jockey, won the St. Leger Stakes at Churchill Downs.

Negroes represented 32.2% of Cuba's population.

C. "SEPARATE BUT EQUAL"

1. The Darkest Period

After Reconstruction, practically all political rights given the American Negro resulting from the conflict between South and North, were retracted. A gradual levelling took place. Before the Civil War the question was how to free the Negroes in the South from the violence of the slaveholders. Following Reconstruction the question became how to free the Negroes from the violence of all the whites, in the South and in the North. Some of the worst conditions facing Negroes now prevailed over the entire nation rather than just the Southern region. In fact, this was the darkest period in the history of the Negro in America.

Economically, the tremendously growing industry used in this period the Negro as a strikebreaker and as a supply for the army of unemployed reserve, and brought him in steady conflict with the masses of hard-working new immigrants.

1878

The Democrats, a majority in the 46th Congress, attached riders to appropriation bills which left the Army without funds and took away the President's power to use Federal troops to insure fair elections. Although Hayes approved these changes, he vetoed eight subsequent bills that attacked other provisions of the Enforcement Acts.

Federal troops were removed from Louisiana and South Carolina. Their Republican governors were ousted and Negroes disenfranchised.

Between 1876 and 1878, South Carolina had 4 Negro and 14 white Senators, 58 Negro and 64 white Representatives in its state legislature.

In the 1878 Congressional elections, only 62 of the 294 Southern counties with a Negro majority went Republican, compared to 125 in 1876.

In Abbeville County, S. C., with twice as many Negroes as white, only 3 Republican ballots were cast in the entire
282

county, as compared to 1,500 votes in 1874. Fairfield County, with a 3-to-1 Negro-white ratio, had not one Republican vote in 1878, although in 1874 the Republican Party received two-thirds of the votes.

Virginia again reapportioned its election districts to minimize the Negro vote.

A bill introduced by Horace Page of California, empowering Congress to reduce the representation of any state that abridged the suffrage, was tabled in the House Judiciary Committee.

On December 2, 1878, the U.S. Attorney-General's report revealed that Southern Democrats had stuffed ballot boxes and committed political murders in South Carolina, Louisiana, Texas, and Virginia. On the same day that the Attorney-General's report was issued, Rutherford B. Hayes in his annual message to Congress specifically and generally accused the South of abrogating the rights of Negroes. A Senate committee was appointed to investigate the Southern elections. It found fraud, murder, and intimidation in South Carolina, Louisiana, and Mississippi. The committee found that, in Louisiana alone, 40 political murders had been committed. The committee called for a renewal of Federal protection for Negroes.

Two pension bills introduced by B. K. Bruce were passed by the Senate. Bruce reported a bill for the improvement of the Mississippi River and the development of the channel and levee system. The Senate passed the bill, but the session ended before the House had considered it. He also presented petitions on prohibition and the refund of the cotton tax, and spoke for integration in the Army, but with no result.

William Stanley Braithwaite (1878-1912) was born in Boston, Mass., and is considered the most cosmopolitan Negro literary figure until Johnson. Braithwaite was greatly influenced by the English poets such as Swinburne and Ernest Dowson. *Lyrics of Life and Love in* 1904 was Braithwaite's first collection and provided a striking contrast to the dialect poetry of other Negro poets. In 1908, his *House of Falling Leaves,* a second volume of poetry, elaborated his mystical aestheticism and tended toward obscurantism. He was one of the first critics to hail James Weldon Johnson's early work as the first real Negro poetry. Braithwaite never wrote a poem or an essay which would lead the reader to believe he was Negro. He also wrote prose: (1920) *Our Essayists and Critics of Today,* critiques of prominent U.S. and British essayists and literary critics; (1919), *Story of the Great War,* a popular history of World War I; (1959), *Bewitched Personage,* a biographical study of the Brontë family, Braithwaite's greatest achievement is as an anthologist of verse. He edited an annual series from 1913 to 1929 called *Anthology of Magazine Verse.* All the poems were culled from popular and little magazines of the day, and he included many of Edgar Lee Masters' "Spoon River" poems, Vachel Lindsays' "Chants" and much of Sandburg's free verse long before they were published in book form. His other anthologies include volumes devoted to *Elizabethan Verse,* 1906; *Georgian Verse,* 1908; *Restoration Verse,* 1909; *Massachusetts Poets,* 1931; *Anthology of Magazine Verse of 1958,* his last work.

Charles Sidney Gilpin (1878-1930), Negro actor, was born in Richmond, Va. His father was a Negro and his mother white. After attending St. Francis School for Catholic Children, he went to work for the *Richmond Planet.* In 1903, Gilpin was with the Canadian Jubilee Singers of Hamilton, Ontario, and with Williams and Walker's Abyssinia Company and Gus Hill's Smart Set between 1905 and 1906. A member of the Pekin Stock Company in Chicago in 1907, he then toured with the Pan-American Octette and joined Old Man's Boy Company. In 1916, he settled in New York City and became manager of the Lafayette Theater Company in Harlem, a Negro dramatic stock company in the city. He first appeared in a Broadway cast as William Custis, the Negro clergyman in the American production of John Drinkwater's *Abraham Lincoln,* which opened Dec. 15, 1919. Playing Brutus Jones in Eugene O'Neill's *Emperor Jones,* he opened at the Provincetown Playhouse on MacDougall Street, Nov. 1, 1920, and moved uptown with the play to the Princess Theater Jan. 29, 1921. He was one of 10 to receive the Drama League Award in 1921. Gilpin received the Spingarn Medal from the NAACP in the same year.

Jack Johnson (1878-1946), a Negro heavyweight boxing champion, was born in Galveston, Tex. Johnson learned to fight by working out with professional boxers as he hoboed around the U.S. From 1899 to 1908, he fought 100 bouts and lost only 3. On Dec. 28, 1908, Johnson won the heavyweight boxing championship from Tommy Burns. He lost the title to Jesse Willard in 1915.

Bill "Bojangles" Robinson (1878-1949), Negro dancer, vaudevillian, and movie star, was born in Washington, D.C., and raised by his grandmother, a former slave. He first appeared in vaudeville in 1896 on the Keith circuit. In 1927 he starred in Broadway's *Blackbirds*. He later worked in the movies. His best-known films were *Harlem is Heaven,* 1932; with Shirley Temple, *The Little Colonel, The Littlest Rebel,* and *Rebecca of Sunnybrook Farm.*

James Monroe Trotter, a Negro, published *Music and Some Highly Musical People,* a collection of biographical sketches of Negro composers and musicians who specialized in non-Negro classical music.

1879

In May, Gen. James Chalmers of Mississippi and a group of Southern whites "closed" the Mississippi River by threatening to sink all boats carrying Negroes. They frightened ship owners into stranding 1,500 Negroes along the banks of the river. Gen. Thomas Conway, of New Jersey, described the situation in a letter to President Hayes: "Every river landing is blockaded by white enemies of the colored exodus; some of whom are mounted and armed, as if we were at war. . . ." Under threats of Federal intervention, the shipping companies resumed service.

A resolution was introduced by Senator Windom of Minnesota to study the practicability of encouraging Southern Negro migration to other parts of the U.S. This first suggestion of assistance to Negroes since the abolition of the Freedmen's Bureau died in the Senate.

40,000 Southern Negroes fled to the Midwest to escape the political and economic conditions of the South.

North Carolina Negroes began a migration to Indiana. Amid conflicting testimony before a Senate committee, some Republicans indicated that the migration had been stimulated by Indiana Republicans who wanted, through Negro immigration, to develop a Republican majority in the state.

The Colored Farmer's Alliance was founded as the brother organization of the all-white Farmer's Alliance, forerunner of the Populist Movement. Almost 1,250,000 Negroes joined.

House Democrats attached a rider to the Army Appropriation Bill forbidding the use of Federal troops at elections.
President Hayes vetoed it on April 29.

The Readjusters, a dissenting Southern Democratic group,
gained prominence in Virginia. They captured 56 of the 100
seats in the Virginia House of Delegates, and 24 of the 40
seats in the Virginia Senate. Led by William Mahone, they
advocated repudiation of the state debt and openly appealed
to Negroes.

South Carolina re-enacted a law forbidding intermarriage.

The following Negroes served in the 45th Congress: Representatives R. H. Cain, J. H. Rainey and Robert Smalls of
South Carolina; as well as Sen. B. K. Bruce of Mississippi.

In February, Vice President Wheeler was absent, and for
some time B. K. Bruce presided over the Senate. He voted
against a bill to restrict Chinese immigration. Bruce was
appointed chairman of a Select Committee on the Freedmen's Bank, which had failed in 1874.

The African Methodist Episcopal Zion Church founded
Livingston College in North Carolina.

William Geary "Bunk" Johnson (1879-1949), Negro jazz
musician, was born in New Orleans. He studied with Wallace
Cutchey, and in 1896 was second cornetist in the Buddy
Bolden Band. From 1911 through 1914 he played with the
Eagle Band in New Orleans. After that he toured with
minstrel shows and played in county fairs until he retired
from music in 1931. He was "rediscovered" in 1938, and
as late as 1945 Johnson was playing in New York and
Boston with Sidney Bechet.

Isaac Murphy, the Negro jockey, won the Travers Stakes
at Saratoga. He won 35 of the 75 races he entered in 1879.

1880

U.S. Census: There were 6,580,793 Negroes in the U.S.
representing 13.1% of the population.

The Negro literacy rate was 30% compared to 18.6% in
1870.

The percentages of total population attending school in the
Southern states was: white, 18.3%, up from 13.5% in 1870;
Negro, 13.07%, up from 3.07% in 1870.

Of all Negroes in the U.S. 75% lived in the former Confederate States: Virginia, 41.8%; North Carolina, 37.9%; South Carolina, 60.7%; Georgia 47%; Florida, 47%; Tennessee, 26.2%; Alabama, 47.5%; Mississippi, 57.5%; Arkansas, 26.3%; Louisiana, 51.5%; Texas, 24.7%.

Central Georgia, north Florida, western Mississippi, south central Alabama, east central Louisiana, eastern North Carolina and southeastern Virginia formed the major black belt. The Negro percentages of total populations of the counties in these districts were:

State	County	% Negro
Virginia	Amelia	70.7
"	Prince Edward	67.6
North Carolina	Edgecombe	69.6
" "	Craven	66.2
" "	Halifax	69.8
South Carolina	Aiken	54.0
" "	Charleston	69.9
" "	Georgetown	82.3
" "	Beaufort	91.9
" "	Sumter	73.1
Georgia	Burke	77.5
"	Lee	83.5
Alabama	Dallas	82.6
"	Greene	82.8
"	Lowndes	81.9
Florida	Alachua	60.8
Mississippi	Bolivar	85.6
"	Washington	86.2
"	Adams	78.8
"	Tunica	91.7
"	Sharkey	77.6
"	Coahoma	82.2
Louisiana	Tensas	91.1
"	East Carroll	91.4
"	Madison	90.9

In Virginia, of the total oystermen, a very profitable occupation at this time, about half were Negroes.

The percentage of Negroes born in the South living in the North and West was 3.2%. The percentage of Negroes born in the North and West but living in the South was 5%.

The net intercensal migration for Negro males, age 15 to 34, for the decade 1870 to 1880 was: Alabama, —20.9%; Georgia, —4.6%; Mississippi, 4%; Illinois, 37.1%; Michigan, 12.5%; New York, 23.9%. These figures meant that in Alabama, for example, between 1870 and 1880, 21 men, age 15 to 34, left the state for every 100 Negroes in the state. The lack of a minus sign means the reverse. Thus, 24 Negro males, age 15 to 34, entered New York State for every 100 Negroes in the state.

There were approximately 7,400 Negroes in Chicago, compared to 3,696 in 1870.

Negro immigration to Kansas and Indiana ended in this year. The migrating Negroes found the North cold, much of the land infertile, and that there were already more Negroes than could be employed.

In STRAUDER v. WEST VIRGINIA, the U.S. Supreme Court made its only interpretation favorable to Negroes until 1900. The Court held that the laws excluding Negroes from juries violated the equal protection clause in the 14th Amendment.

Senator Bruce of Mississippi was very active in the Senate in this year. He introduced 21 bills, none of which became law. The majority of these were of a private nature, but some dealt with the Geneva Award for the Alabama claims, aid to education, railroad construction and reimbursement of depositors in the Freedmen's Bank. He spoke on behalf of admitting duty-free clothing sent from England to destitute Negroes in Kansas. He also supported a more enlightened Indian policy, urging the division of land among Indians. On May 4, he presided over the Senate. In the second session of 1880, he introduced a bill to have the Freedmen's Bank property bought by the government. It passed in the Senate, but was never considered by the House.

Senator Bruce reversed his opinion of Grant and supported him at the Republican National Convention. At the Convention, Senator Bruce was called to the chair to preside temporarily. At one point several delegates were asking for recognition. Bruce recognized James Garfield, who made such a good impression on the Convention that he was nominated for President. Bruce himself received 8 votes for Vice President.

James Garfield won the Presidential election by a plurality

of less than 10,000 votes out of a total of 9,000,000 votes cast. Garfield campaigned on a "bloody shirt" platform, promising protection to the Southern Negro.

Populists always had trouble beating Democrats in elections because the Democrats used the Negro vote, gaining it by force, intimidation and bribery. For example, in the 1880 Georgia gubernatorial election, the Democratic incumbent, Colquitt, was re-elected although he received a minority of the white vote. He was, however, able to collect the great majority of the Negro vote.

By this year the Democrats gained three-quarters of the seats in the Mississippi Legislature. The Legislature failed to re-elect Senator B. K. Bruce, giving him only 4 votes.

Mississippi re-enacted a law "omitted" in 1871 forbidding intermarriage.

Florida's 1868 Constitutional proviso that literacy tests for voting be instituted after 1880 was ignored, due to pressure from poor whites.

Concurrent with the founding of the National Baptist Convention at Montgomery, Ala., two smaller groups were established, the Foreign Mission Baptist Convention of the U.S.A. and the American National Baptist Convention.

The African Methodist Episcopal Church had 40,000 members.

William Wells Brown published *My Southern Home*.

A Brazilian anti-slavery society was established.

In Cuba, slavery was abolished by royal decree and the patronato system was instituted by which slaves could remain under the protection of their ex-masters for a period of years. In the period from 1880 to 1884, 60,550 slaves were emancipated in Cuba.

By this year European penetration of Black Africa had begun. Much African art was rescued from missionaries, to be included in ethnological museums in London and Paris. Anthropology was a new burgeoning science at this time, which accounts for the establishment of ethnological museums. Most African art was, during the late 19th century, considered esthetically "immature" and often was used as exhibits in the racist case for imperialism. Germany, in the late 1890's began to expand into Africa, and amassed great collections of African art at Berlin, Hamburg, Bremen, Leipzig, Frankfurt, Munich, and several smaller cities. The German collections were amassed by scholars and anthropologists who took African art seriously.

1881

In his Inaugural Address President Garfield claimed that only education could solve the Southern Negro problem. He had not, however, in correspondence or in conference with prominent educators worked out a plan before his assassination.

In his first message to Congress, President Arthur implied that, until Negroes became literate, they might justifiably be disenfranchised.

President Arthur recognized that the Republican Party needed Southern support to ward off the Democratic challenge, and supported the Virginia Readjusters. In this year the Republicans of Virginia endorsed the whole Readjuster ticket. Henceforth, only a skeleton Republican Party existed in Virginia.

Representatives Robert Smalls of South Carolina and John R. Lynch of Mississippi were the only two Negroes elected to the 47th Congress.

Ex-Senator B. K. Bruce of Mississippi was offered the post of either minister to Brazil or third assistant to the Postmaster General. He refused both, but was then appointed and confirmed Register of the Treasury and took office in May.

Rhode Island repealed a law forbidding intermarriage.

Tennessee enacted the first Jim Crow law segregating railroad coaches. This law directed railroad companies to provide for Negroes separate first-class cars on portions of trains equivalent to the first-class cars for whites, instead of relegating them to second-class accommodations, as had been the custom.

Tuskegee Institute, with a $2,000 appropriation from the Alabama Legislature, opened in a single building with 30 students, and a faculty of one, Booker T. Washington. The institute provided secondary education as well as teacher training. George Washington Carver joined the faculty in 1896 as director for agricultural research.

The African Negro Methodist Episcopal Church founded Allen University in Columbia, S.C.

Lewis Latimer, a Negro, patented the first incandescent electric lamp with carbon filament. Latimer also made drawings for the first telephone for Alexander Graham Bell, and was the chief draftsman for General Electric and Westinghouse. He also wrote the first textbook on the lighting system used by the Edison company.

Jack Haverly's Callender Minstrels, a Negro company, made its first European tour with great success. The Callender Minstrels were the most famous and successful of all minstrel companies.

1882

In Georgia, the Populists, led by Tom Watson, campaigned for the Negro vote, advocating free education for Negroes and the abolition of the convict lease system. The Negro vote was instrumental in electing Watson to the lower house of the Georgia Legislature.

U.S. Attorney-General Brewster attempted to safeguard free elections. In Charleston, S.C., he had a group of influential men arrested, but could not secure convictions. Brewster then ordered the U.S. Marshal in Charleston to arrest immediately anyone who interfered with free elections. This too was ineffectual. Discouraged, Brewster after the summer of that year virtually ignored the pleas of wronged Negroes. Brewster promised to investigate, but never did, the case of Daniel Payne, senior bishop of the African Methodist Episcopal Church. Payne was expelled from a Florida train because he refused to ride in a second-class car when he had purchased a first-class ticket.

A special election law passed in South Carolina created a separate ballot and ballot box for each office. It authorized election managers to speak to voters only when requested to read titles, and said that ballots in the wrong boxes would not be counted.

In PACE v. ALABAMA, the U.S. Supreme Court ruled that an Alabama statute providing severer punishment for interracial fornication than fornication with the same race did not violate the equal protection clause of the 14th Amendment.

Sections of the Enforcement Act of April 20, 1871, penalizing individuals who conspired to impede provisions of the 14th and 15th Amendments, were declared unconstitutional. The Supreme Court ruled in U.S. v. HARRIS that these amendments applied to states and not to individuals.

48 Negroes were lynched in this year.

The Colored Methodist Church founded Lane College in Jackson, Tenn.

Benjamin Brawley (1882-1939), Negro writer, was born in Columbia, S.C. He was a clergyman, a widely read and erudite man, who wrote a few poems similar to those of the late Victorians. His greatest effort was *Seven Sleepers of Epheuses,* which was technically very successful. Brawley had a considerable reputation as an historian of the Negro people. He pioneered the field with such works as *A Short History of the American Negro,* 1913; *The Negro in Literature and Art in the U.S.,* 1918; *A Social History of the American Negro,* 1921. He also wrote the first biography of Paul Laurence Dunbar, published in 1936.

Father Divine (1882-1965), also known as Major M. J. Divine, was born George Baker, near Savannah, Ga. An itinerant garden worker and sometime preacher, in 1907 he moved to Baltimore where he became a "God in Sonship" with Father Jehovah. By 1919, when he moved to Sayville, L.I., he had proclaimed himself God and had started his Peace Mission movement. From the beginning, the movement was nondenominational and interracial, and the theme of the movement was universal peace. In 1931, Father Divine and some 80 of his followers were arrested on a disorderly conduct charge, stemming from a noisy singing session. He was sentenced to a prison term, but 4 days later the sentencing judge dropped dead of a heart attack. Father Divine was purported to have said, "I hated to do it." The subsequent publicity he received swelled the ranks of his movement. Father Divine moved into Harlem, using the funds from his followers to support missions that provided cheap meals and rooms for Negroes who were hard hit by the Depression. Father Divine's life had always been somewhat out of the ordinary. In 1949 he appeared at the Federal Trust Company in Newark with $500,000 in cash. A judge once called him a "methodical home-breaker" and his trips with female followers gained notoriety. In 1941, he moved into a Philadelphia mansion, Woodmont, the gift of a wealthy white disciple, John De Voute. The 32-room mansion sits on 73 acres. Father Divine lived there until his death in September, 1965. He suffered from arteriosclerosis and had remained out of the public eye since 1963. At his death, 25% of his movement was composed of white men. The movement's properties, none of which was in Father Divine's name, were estimated as worth $10 million. The mission ran a great many businesses, including hotels, beauty parlors and moving firms, scattered throughout the U.S. and in Austria, Australia, Sweden, West Germany, Switzerland, and England.

The third edition of Frederick Douglass' *Life and Times of Frederick Douglass,* was published.

1883

In the Civil Rights cases of 1883, the Republican-dominated U.S. Supreme Court declared the Civil Rights Act of 1875 unconstitutional. It ruled that the Act's guarantees of equal rights went beyond the powers granted to Congress in the Reconstruction Amendments. Justice Bradley, speaking for the majority, declared that Congress could not properly "cover the whole domain of rights appertaining to life, liberty, and property, defining them and providing for their vindication."

Angered at President Arthur's refusal to help the Negroes in any way, the National Convention of Colored People, meeting in Louisville in September, refused to endorse Arthur's Administration. There were suggestions that Negroes form a separate party.

The Virginia Readjusters were crushed by the regular ("Bourbon") Democrats in the 1883 state elections. A race riot that erupted in Danville, Va., on the Saturday prior to the elections contributed to the defeat.

Once again Virginia reapportioned to minimize the Negro vote, and amended city charters to reduce Negro representation on city councils.

In this year 52 Negroes were lynched.

Negroes James E. O'Hara of North Carolina and Robert Smalls of South Carolina were elected to the 48th Congress.

Maine and Michigan repealed laws forbidding intermarriage.

William A. Hinton (1883-1959), Negro doctor, scientist, professor, was born in Chicago, educated at Harvard Medical School, served as a voluntary assistant in pathology at Massachusetts General Hospital, and then practiced for 8 years at the Boston Dispensary and the Massachusetts Department of Health Laboratories. From 1916 to 1952, he directed the Boston Dispensary Laboratory. Hinton became a world-renowned authority on venereal disease. He developed the Hinton Test, and the Davies-Hinton Test for the detection of syphilis. In 1949, after serving as an assistant lecturer in preventive medicine and hygiene, he became the first Negro professor at Harvard University Medical School.

Ernest Everett Just (1883-1941), Negro biologist, was born in Charleston, S.C., and educated in public schools for Negroes in Orangeburg, S.C. He worked his way to New York in 1900, and applied to and was accepted at Kimball Academy, from which he was graduated in 1903. From there he went to Dartmouth and was graduated *magna cum laude* in 1907. In 1908 he became a member of the faculty at Howard University, where he remained for the rest of his life. Just wrote many important treatises on chromosome makeup in animals and cellular theory that gave him a considerable international academic reputation. He published papers on experiments with protoplasm, showing how living cells take up and hold water, which helped in the determination of the structural relations of water to the colloids of the cell and to electrolytes. In 1915, Just was awarded the first Spingarn Medal.

Arthur W. Mitchell (1883-   ), first Democratic Negro Congressman, was born in Alabama and educated at Tuskegee Institute and the universities of Columbia and Harvard. Serving in Congress for Illinois from 1934 to 1942, he was also a successful landowner and lawyer in Washington, D.C. In Congress and in the court, he worked for civil rights. Successfully arguing his own case before the Supreme Court in 1941, he gained the decision against Jim Crow railroad regulations. He retired to his estate in Virginia in 1942.

George Washington Williams published his *History of the Negro Race in America.*

1884

Between 1876 and 1884, Negro voting had dropped by one-third in Louisiana, by one-fourth in Mississippi, and by one-half in South Carolina.

In this year 50 Negroes were lynched.

In Alabama it became unlawful for Negro and white convicts to be chained together or to be confined in the same cell.

Senator Blair introduced a bill for Federal Aid to Education. It passed in the Senate, but was defeated in the House.

Ex-Senator B. K. Bruce was put in charge of the Negro exhibit at the World's Cotton Exposition, held in New Orleans, November, 1884 to May, 1885. Bruce received favorable press notices for this display of Negro achievements.

The Southern Methodist Episcopal Church founded Paine College in Augusta, Ga.

William Scott (1884-1964), Negro artist, studied in Indianapolis, Chicago, and Paris, and exhibited at the Paris Salon, 1912-1913. He showed Tanner's influence in his landscape, *Rainy Night at Etaples.* Upon his return to the U.S., Scott received a series of commissions for murals for the City Hospital in Indianapolis, the Illinois State House, Fort Wayne Court House, and later several Negro colleges and YMCA's. During the 1930's, after spending some time in the West Indies on a Rosenwald Grant, Scott devoted his talents to sketches of West Indian natives and to colorful tropical landscapes.

The African Methodist Episcopal *Review* was founded.

Alberry Whitman's narrative poem *The Rape of Florida,* was published.

Moses Grandy, an ex-slave, published an account of his experiences.

Gussie Davis, a Negro, wrote *When Nellie Was Raking the Hay,* a popular musical piece of the time.

Trainer William Bird and Jockey Isaac Murphy (both Negroes), won the Kentucky Derby with Buchanan.

The Toledo baseball team, champions of the Northwestern League, had a Negro catcher, Moses Fleetwood Walker.

Brazil's slave population stood at 3,000,000.

1885

Elected to the 49th Congress as Representatives were the Negroes Robert Smalls of South Carolina and James E. O'Hara of North Carolina.

In this year 74 Negroes were lynched.

Ex-U.S. Sen. B. K. Bruce retired from his position as register of the Treasury, to which he had been appointed in 1881. Bruce became a popular lecturer.

Between 1885 and 1889, only 2 Negroes in the U.S. received doctorates, compared to 347 whites.

The African Negro Methodist Episcopal Church founded Morris Brown University in Atlanta, Ga.

Huddie "Leadbelly Ledbetter" (1885-1949), Negro folk-singer, was born in Louisiana and raised in Texas. The son of a former slave, he was self-educated. In his wanderings as an itinerant musician in the South he met Blind Lemon Jefferson, a Texas street singer and guitarist, who taught many of his songs to Ledbetter. In 1918, Ledbetter was convicted of murder and served 7 years. In 1930 he was again sentenced for attempted homicide and served 4 years. He was then paroled in the custody of folklorist John Lomax, who took him North to sing in concerts and make recordings. Among his best known songs are *Good Night, Irene; Rock Island Line* and *On Top of Old Smoky*. In 1949 Ledbetter had a successful tour in France. He is primarily responsible for the worldwide interest in American folk music.

Ferdinand "Jelly Roll" Morton (1885-1941), Negro jazz musician, was born in Gulfport, La. His grandfather had been a member of the Louisiana Constitutional Convention of 1868. His father was a small businessman. However, Morton was a manual laborer in a barrel factory. When he began his musical career in 1902 in Storyville, New Orleans' red-light district, he was considered to have disgraced his Creole family in New Orleans. Morton's great contribution to jazz was as a composer. His songs: *King Porter Stomp, Wolverine Blues, Millenburg Joys, Georgia Swing, Kansas City Stomps and Wild Man Blues.* Between 1926 and 1930, recording for Victor label with his Red Hot Peppers, established Morton as the first great jazz composer.

Joe "King" Oliver (1885-1938), Negro jazz musician, and one of the early giants of jazz, was born on a Louisiana plantation and grew up in New Orleans. In 1923 his Creole Jazz Band, which included Louis Armstrong as second clarinetist, made the first series of recordings by a Negro jazz band. His influence was inestimable, but by 1928 when he moved to New York his popularity and success had begun to decline, and in his final years Oliver worked in a poolroom in Savannah, Ga.

George Washington Williams published *The Negro in the American Rebellion.*

In New Orleans, Negroes still performed in Congo Square. Slaves had since 1817 been allowed to do voodoo dances, using African drums, gourds, etc. By this year, however, the triangle, jew's harp and other European musical elements had been incorporated into the performances. This blending of West African and European musical traditions would ultimately be called jazz. These dances helped preserve the African musical heritage in New Orleans. The Calinda and the Bamboula, both based on African dances, were frequently performed. Originally the beat was provided by bones stuck on the head of a cask, the chanting of women and metal pieces on the ankles of men.

The Saraiva-Cotegipe Law of Brazil declared all slaves free at the age of 60.

1886

There were 60,000 Negro members of the Knights of Labor; total membership was 700,000.

Senator Blair, for the second time, introduced a bill for Federal Aid to Education which passed in the Senate, but was again defeated in the House.

In this year 74 Negroes were lynched.

William L. Dawson (1886-   ), Negro Congressman, was born in Albany, Ga. Educated at Fisk University, at Kent College, and the Law School of Northwestern University, Dawson began to practice law in Illinois. Active in Republican state politics, he became a city alderman in 1935. He changed parties under Franklin D. Roosevelt, and rose in the Democratic organization, becoming the first Negro to serve as vice chairman of the National Committee. Elected to the House of Representatives in 1943, he became chairman of the Committee on Government Operations.

Georgia Douglas Johnson (1886-1966), Negro poetess, was born in Atlanta, Ga.; educated at Atlanta University and Oberlin Conservatory. While teaching in Alabama and working for the Government in Washington, D.C., she published *The Heart of Woman,* 1918; *Bronze,* 1922, and *Autumn Love Cycle,* 1928.

Alain Leroy Locke (1886-1954), Negro literary critic, was born in Philadelphia, attended Harvard and became a Rhodes Scholar at Oxford. Locke is best known as a critic and popularizer of the writers of the Harlem Renaissance. His anthology of their writings, *The New Negro,* appeared in 1925 and *The Negro in American Culture* was completed by Margaret Butcher two years after his death in 1956. For several years Locke served as chairman of the philosophy department at Howard University.

Walter Adolphe Roberts (1886-   ), Negro writer, was born in Kingston, Jamaica. From 1902 to 1918, he was a reporter, first in Jamaica and then in the U.S. From 1914 through 1918, he was foreign correspondent in France for the *Brooklyn Eagle.* Between 1918 and 1921, he edited *Amslee's Magazine,* and later Hearst's *International Magazine.* His works include: *Pierrot Wounded and Other Poems,* drawn from his wartime experiences, published in 1919; *Pan and Peacocks,* a second collection of poems, 1928; *Sir Henry Morgan, Buccaneer and Governor,* a biography, 1933; *Semmes of the Alabama,* a biography of the Confederate naval officer, published in 1938; *Six Great Jamaicans,* a collection of biographical sketches, 1952; *Havana, Portrait of a City,* a travelog and social history, 1953; *Jamaica, Portrait of an Island,* 1955. In 1956 Roberts became editor of the Pioneer Press in Kingston, Jamaica.

George W. Chadwick's *Second Symphony* was published. It was the first symphonic work using Negro folksongs.

In Cuba the patronato system was terminated, and the patrocenados came under the protection of the state.

1887

Negro membership in the Knights of Labor increased by 30,000 in one year, bringing the total Negro membership to 90,000 out of the total membership of a half million.

Ohio repealed a law forbidding intermarriage.

Florida enacted a railroad car segregation law, modeled after Tennessee's 1881 law. An additional provision specified that no white man was allowed to insult or annoy a Negro in his (the Negro's) car. All the Southern states followed Florida's example.

In this year 70 Negroes were lynched.

Charles Chesnutt's short story "The Goophered Grapevine" was published in the *Atlantic Monthly*. This was the first time a Negro work of fiction reached a large white audience.

Gussie Davis, a Negro, wrote *The Lighthouse by the Sea*.

In Chicago, Frank Peters founded a semi-professional and probably the first Negro baseball team, the Union Giants.

Marcus Garvey (1887-1940), Negro nationalist and reformer, was born in Jamaica of a large family. In 1901 he was apprenticed to a printer, and later was a print shop foreman in Kingston, Jamaica. It was there he became aware of the poor conditions under which Negroes lived, and participated in the first, unsuccessful strike by the printers' union. While working at the Government Printing Office he organized the National Club and began publishing *Our Own*. Leaving his job, he started the newspaper, *The Watchman,* a financial failure. After attempting to earn money in Central and South America, he returned to Jamaica in 1911, and founded the Universal Negro Improvement Association. The organization was unsuccessful until Garvey came to the U.S. In 1917 in New York City, he founded a newspaper, *The Negro World,* gained supporters for his "Back to Africa" movement, and was later able to establish over 30 branches of the UNIA in the U.S. His Negro steamship company, Black Star Line, consisting of three ships making a triangular voyage between New York, the West Indies and Africa, was his first commercial venture. Although $500,000 was subscribed, the line failed and Garvey was arrested and tried for fraud. Convicted, he served 2½ years. The African Communities League and the Negro Factories Corporation, two other business attempts, also failed. His plans for African colonization of Germany's former colonies were ignored by the League of Nations, and Liberia, afraid Garvey wished a personal African empire, withdrew its support. His sentence was commuted in 1927, and President Coolidge had him deported to Jamaica. A world tour in 1928 failed to raise enough money to pay exorbitant debts in New York incurred by his staff, and even the funds of the Jamaica branch of the UNIA were taken from him in adverse court decisions in the U.S. He then worked to improve the legal status and living conditions of Jamaicans, and ultimately won a seat on a local council. He died in near-obscurity in Kensington, England.

Negroes represented 32.4% of Cuba's population.

1888

By dropping the issue of race and campaigning for a protective tariff, Benjamin Harrison, the Republican Presidential nominee, received more Southern votes than any other candidate since the end of Reconstruction.

Henry Cabot Lodge proposed a new Force Act, to protect the Southern Negro. This proposal was rejected by Congress.

Senator Blair of New Hampshire introduced his third bill for Federal aid to education. It was passed in the Senate but again defeated in the House.

Mississippi authorized the railroads to designate separate waiting rooms for Negroes and whites.

In this year 69 Negroes were lynched.

Two Negro banks were founded, the Savings Bank of the Grand Fountain United Order of True Reformers in Richmond, Va., and the Capital Savings Bank in Washington, D. C.

Fenton Johnson (1888-1958), Negro poet, was born in Chicago and educated at the University of Chicago. His poetical works include *A Little Dreaming*, 1914; *Visions of the Dusk*, 1916; *Songs of the Soil* and *WPA Poems*. His prose work is represented by *Tales of Darkest America*, published in 1920.

Sargent Johnson (1888-   ), Negro sculptor, was born in Boston, but lived and worked in San Francisco and has exhibited annually in San Francisco Art Association exhibitions since 1925. He also exhibited annually with the Harmon Foundation from 1928 through 1935. Most of his sculptures are busts noted for their character portrayal. The subject matter of almost all his sculpture is American Negroes. His other work includes drawings, in which the dominant stylistic influence is African and Aztec art.

Horace Pippin (1888-1946), Negro painter, was born in Westchester, Pa. Partially paralyzed as a soldier in World War I, he began painting in 1920. His war scenes, domestic still lifes and landscapes, all done in a primitive, vivid style, have been praised by art critics and bought by major collections in the U.S., such as the Whitney Museum and the Barnes Foundation. Among his most famous paintings are *Cabin in the Cotton,* 1944; *Buffalo Hunt* and *John Brown Goes to His Hanging.*

Pike Barnes, Negro jockey, won the Futurity (the first held) at Sheepshead.

In Brazil 600,000 slaves were freed by Princess-Regent Isabel's declaration.

1889

The following Negroes were elected to the 51st Congress: H. P. Cheatham of North Carolina, Thomas E. Miller of South Carolina, and J. M. Langston of Virginia.

Benjamin Harrison in his message to Congress was the first President since Grant to claim that the Federal Government had to protect the free exercise of the ballot.

President Harrison appointed ex-Senator B. K. Bruce Recorder of Deeds for the District of Columbia, a position Bruce held until 1893, when he again retired.

Sen. M. C. Butler of South Carolina introduced a bill to provide for migration of Negroes from Southern states. This bill failed to come to a vote.

Negroes in North Carolina burned President Harrison and his Cabinet in effigy. A committee was formed to go to Congress to protest the abandonment of the Negro by the Republican Party.

The Southern Democrats sought to extinguish the Populist movement, holding over the white farmer the threat of Negro competition. For example, Henry Grady, a Georgia Democrat, made this statement to a Farmer's Alliance meeting: "There is no room for divided hearts in the South . . . the only hope and assurance of the South [is] the clear and unmistakable domination of the white race."

Texas enacted a railroad segregation law.

In this year 92 Negroes were lynched.

Hampton Institute created the People's Building and Loan Association. In 20 years, 1889 to 1909, it lent $375,000 to Negroes in the Hampton area, helping them acquire 375 houses and lots.

The Virginia Organization of True Reformers, a Negro secret society, established a bank.

A Negro bank, the Mutual Trust Company, in Chattanooga, Tenn., was established.

Asa Philip Randolph (1889-   ), Negro union leader, was born in Crescent City, Fla. Educated at the City College of New York, he later edited *The Messenger,* and wrote articles for *Opportunity* magazine. In 1925 he founded the Brotherhood of Sleeping Car Porters and led it to prominence as the strongest of the Negro labor unions. In 1935 he was a member of Mayor LaGuardia's New York City Commission on Race. He was active in the protests which led to the Executive Order ending discrimination in defense industries during World War II. After the war he effectively lobbied for a permanent Fair Employment Practices Committee. In 1947 Randolph and Grand Reynolds organized the League of Non-Violent Civil Disobedience Against Military Segregation. He led a delegation of Negro leaders in conferring with President Truman in March 1948 and told him that Negroes would refuse to register for the draft if it meant serving in a Jim Crow army. He later told the Senate Armed Services Committee that he would personally aid draft resisters, which he did. In 1957 he became a vice-president of the AFL-CIO and later a member of the executive council. At the 1959 AFL-CIO convention he charged organized labor with discrimination, provoking the anger of Pres. George Meany and censure by the AFL-CIO executive committee. In this same year he met with more than 75 Negro union leaders and chaired the National Steering Committee of the Negro American Labor Council (NA-

LC). He directed the organization until 1963. He was a leader of the 1963 March on Washington. In March of 1964 Randolph and Bayard Rustin led a march by 3,000 on Albany, N.Y. to demand equal civil rights and social reforms from Governor Rockefeller and the New York Legislature.

Two Negroes played on the varsity football team at Amherst College, William Tecumseh Sherman Jackson and William Henry Lewis. Lewis later played for Harvard.

Pike Barnes, a Negro jockey, won the Champagne Stakes.

1890

U.S. Census: There were 7,488,676 Negroes in the U.S., representing 11.9% of the population.

An estimated 92.5% of the Negroes were born in the South. This compared to 93.3% in 1880, and 93.4% in 1870.

Of the total number of Negroes 15.2% were mulattoes, as compared to 12% in 1870. The percentage of mulattoes was lowest in the South, where there were 159 mulattoes per 1,000 Negroes, compared to 390 per 1,000 in the West and 644 per 1,000 in the North.

The Negro death rate was 32.4% compared to 20.2% for whites.

The net intercensal migration for Negro males, age 15 to 34, for the decade 1880 to 1890 was: Alabama, —8.8%; Georgia, 2.9%; Mississippi, —4.1%; Illinois, 28.7%; New York, 32.1% Thus, for every 100 Negroes in Alabama, 9 males, age 15 to 34, left Alabama between 1880 and 1890, and for every 100 Negroes in New York, 32 male Negroes, age 15 to 34, entered New York between 1880 and 1890. Other figures show that 241,855 Negroes who had been born in the South were living in the North and West, while 23,268 Negroes born in the North and West were living in the South.

There were approximately 14,800 Negroes in Chicago, compared to 7,400 in 1880.

The Negro population of New York City stood at 23,000.

Of the Southern Negro population 18.7% attended school, compared to 13.07% in 1880 and 3.07 % in 1870.

The Negro literacy rate rose to 42.9%, compared to 30%

in 1880. Geographically, illiteracy among Negroes was distributed as follows: North Atlantic states, 21.2%; South Atlantic states, 60.1%; North Central states, 32.2%; South Central states, 61.2%; West, 23.2%.

Negroes owned 120,738 farms, and approximately 19% owned their own homes.

In Virginia, Negroes owned, free and unencumbered, 28,-621 homes, compared to 82,516 homes that were rented by Negroes. By 1900, 34,234 homes were owned by Negroes, and rentals dropped to 75,895.

Of the Negro population 57% was engaged in agriculture, fishing and mining, compared to 47% of the native white population and 26% of the foreign-born white population. Of the Negro population 31% was engaged in domestic and personal service, as opposed to 12% of the native white and 27% of the foreign-born white; 6% of the Negroes were engaged in manufacturing, compared to 19% of the native white population and 31% of the foreign-born whites. In trade and transportation, the percentage of Negroes was 5%, while 16% of the native white and 14% of the foreign-born white were so employed. Only 1% of Negroes were in the professions, in contrast to 6% of the native white and 2% of the foreign-born white.

In the Black Belt counties of southern Virginia, Negro laborers were so numerous that wages averaged only $10 per month.

Negro membership in labor unions was as follows: barbers union, 200 Negroes; brick and clayworkers, 50 Negroes; longshoremen, 1,500 Negroes; painters, decorators, and paperhangers, 33 Negroes; tobacco workers, 1,500 Negroes. By 1900, 32,069 Negroes had been unionized.

Negro teachers and professors totaled 15,100. This figure had risen to 21,267 by 1900.

Susie Elizabeth Frazier became the first Negro woman appointed to teach in the New York City public schools.

There were 909 Negro physicians. This figure rose to 1,734 in 1900. Negro dentists numbered 120, and rose to 212 by 1900.

There were 134 Negro journalists and 431 Negro lawyers by this year.

12,159 Negroes were clergymen.

By this year 90,000 Negroes were Catholics, although there were fewer than 30 Negro priests.

In December, U.S. Senator Dolph of Oregon introduced a resolution to investigate elections and to ensure that the 14th and 15th Amendments were not being violated. This resoluion was buried in committee.

In June, Representative Henry Cabot Lodge introduced a bill for the Federal supervision of national elections. It authorized the appointment of Federal supervisors representing both parties if a specified number of voters petitioned for it. These supervisors would have the power to pass on the qualifications of voters and place in the ballot boxes ballots that had been wrongfully refused by local officials. The bill passed in the House by a vote of 155 to 149. Senator Hoar of Massachusetts introduced a similar bill in the Senate that was laid aside on a technicality.

Although Senator Blair's bill for Federal aid to education was defeated in the Senate, the Morill Act was amended to assure equal land-grant funds for Negro education where a segregated system existed.

In the period between 1890 and 1910, of a total of 528 cases before the Supreme Court involving the 14th Amendment, only 19 dealt with Negro rights.

In the U.S. Supreme Court's decision IN RE GREEN, states were given complete jurisdiction over the election of Presidential electors, as they were state officials. Thus the Court made possible the disenfranchisement of Negroes in Presidential elections.

In LOUISVILLE, NEW ORLEANS, AND TEXAS RAILROAD V. MISSISSIPPI, the Court ruled that a state could constitutionally require segregation on carriers.

The AFL in a convention resolution voiced disapproval of unions that denied membership on the basis of race.

In this year 85 Negroes were lynched.

There were 16 Negro members of the Louisiana General Assembly.

In August, the Mississippi Constitutional Convention met to rewrite the 1868 Reconstruction Constitution. Of the 133 delegates, only one was a Negro, Isaiah Montgomery. At this time, Negroes represented 56.9% of the population of Mississippi. On Oct. 22, the convention decided that it was unnecessary to submit the Constitution to the electorate. On Nov. 1 it was approved. A suffrage amendment in this Constitution imposed a poll tax of $2 on voters, barred voters convicted of bribery, burglary, theft, arson, perjury, murder, or bigamy. It also barred people who could not read, understand or interpret any section of the State Constitution.

Ben Tillman was elected Governor of South Carolina through the support of poor whites. Although known as a demagogic Negro hater, Tillman received the endorsement of the National Colored Farmer's Alliance.

The Alabama Penny Savings and Loan Company was founded by Negroes in Birmingham, Ala.

Claude McKay (1890-1948), Negro poet and novelist, was born in Jamaica. McKay came to the U.S. in 1913, having already published two books of poetry, *Songs of Jamaica* in 1911 and *Constab Ballads*. He studied at Tuskegee and Kansas State before moving to New York City and devoting himself to poetry. He was an associate editor of the *Liberator* and a major figure in the Harlem Renaissance. His poetical works include *Harlem Shadows,* 1922; *Selected Poems,* 1953; and *Songs in New Hampshire,* 1920. His prose works include the novels, *Home to Harlem,* 1927; *Banjo,* 1929; *Banana Bottom,* 1933, and his autobiography, *A Long Way From Home,* 1937.

George Dixon, a Negro, won the world bantamweight boxing championship. He held the title from 1890 to 1892. In 1892 Dixon refused to fight in the New Orleans Olympia Club unless it set aside 700 seats for Negroes. For the first time in the club's history, Negro spectators were allowed in.

Pike Barnes, a Negro jockey, won the Belmont and Alabama Stakes, and Isaac Murphy, another Negro jockey, won the Kentucky Derby.

1891

There were 196 industrial employers in the South who used 7,395 Negroes, largely as menials.

In Virginia's 16 major cities and towns, Negroes owned $3,207,069 worth of land. This represented over a third of the total value of land owned.

Rep. H. P. Cheatham of North Carolina was the only Negro elected to the 52nd Congress.

At the Nationalist Populist Convention in Cincinnati, Southern white representatives attempted to segregate the delegates of the National Colored Farmer's Alliance, which had a membership of 1,300,000 members. The attempt was overwhelmingly defeated.

An alliance of Southern Democrats and Silver Republicans was able to prevent Representative Lodge's bill on the supervision of Federal elections from being brought up for consideration.

President Harrison, in his third message to Congress on Dec. 9, proposed a non-partisan commission to examine the workings of elections, since Lodge's Federal elections bill had died. The commission was never appointed.

There were 112 Negroes lynched.

Alabama instituted railroad segregation.

Georgia became the first state to segregate streetcars.

Governor Tillman of South Carolina failed to obtain State Senate approval of a railroad segregation bill. However, he succeeded in having a law passed which placed a prohibitive tax on labor agents who were enticing Negro farm laborers to migrate, and convinced the state Democratic executive committee to prescribe that a Negro would be allowed to vote only if 10 white men would vouch for his loyalty.

Virginia again reapportioned its election districts to minimize the Negro vote.

Dr. Daniel Hale Williams, a Negro, incorporated Provident Hospital, the first training hospital for Negro doctors and nurses in Chicago.

Edwin Richard Dudley (1891-   ), Ambassador to Liberia, was born in South Boston, Va. Having received a law degree from St. John's Law School, he worked on the legal staff of the NAACP and as Assistant Attorney General for New York State. President Truman made him Ambassador to Liberia in 1948. He has served as Borough President of Manhattan in New York City and on the State Supreme Court.

James P. Johnson (1891-1955), Negro jazz pianist, was

born in New Brunswick, N.J. He studied music as a child
and made his professional debut in 1904. In the 1920's he
recorded player piano rolls, toured with road shows and
appeared in films. In the 1930's he spent more time composing. His *Symphony Harlem* was written in 1932. In 1949
he wrote the music for the show *Sugar Hill*. One of Johnson's
most important disciples was Fats Waller, whom he met in
1919. Duke Ellington was also greatly influenced by Johnson.

Archibald Motley (1891-   ), Negro painter, was born in
New Orleans. He won the Chicago Art Institute's Francis
Logan Medal for character study in 1925, for his *A Mulatress.*
In 1929, his portraits, *My Grandmother,* and *Old Snuff
Dipper,* won the Harmon Gold Medal, and he was awarded
a Guggenheim Fellowship for 2 years' study in Paris. Motley's
best works, technically, among them his portrait study, *The
Young Martiniquan* were done at this time. After he returned
from Paris his work became more surrealistic, emphasizing
the squalor and bizarre aspects of ghetto life. His style, once
restrained, was now highly imaginative, a combination of
Dutch realism and American humor. In 1933, 6 canvasses and
his WPA projects received wide acclaim. A series of murals
on the life of Frederick Douglass at Howard University and
murals for the State St. Library in Chicago were among them.

Charles Wesley (1891-   ), Negro historian and educator,
was born in Louisville, Ky., and educated at Fisk, Howard,
Yale and other major universities. He received numerous
academic awards, including a Guggenheim Fellowship for
1930-31. Professor and dean at Howard University, he became president of Central State (Wilberforce) College in
1942. Among his major works are *Negro Labor in the U.S.
1850-1925. A Study in American Economic History,* published in 1927; *Richard Allen, Apostle of Freedom,* 1935; *The
Collapse of the Confederacy,* 1938; *The Negro in America,*
1940.

In Boston, the *Creole Show* was the first Negro production
to feature singing females.

The Onward Brass Band, a Negro group from New
Orleans, traveled to New York and won wide attention and
first place in a band contest.

The first Negro-white boxing match of significance between

James J. Corbett and Peter Jackson, a Negro who was champion of Australia, ended as a 61-round draw.

Isaac Murphy again won the Kentucky Derby.

1892

There were 160 lynchings of Negroes. Since 1882, over 1,400 Negroes had been killed in this manner.

President Harrison presented a bill to Congress to prevent the lynching of foreign nationals.

The Democratic platform of 1892 denounced Representative Lodge's Federal elections bill.

The Republican Party platform said: "We denounce the continued inhuman outrages [lynchings] perpetuated upon American citizens for political reasons in certain Southern States of the Union."

In February at the Populist Convention in St. Louis, William E. Warwick of the Virginia National Colored Farmer's Alliance served as assistant to the secretary. Ignatius Donnely, a white politician, declared: "I tell you, my friends, what we propose to do; we propose to wipe the Mason-Dixon's line out of our geographies; we propose to wipe the color line off all our politics."

The Southern whites divided into Populist and Democratic parties, both attempting to gain the Negro vote, at first by friendship and finally by bribery, intimidation, and fraud.

The Populists (especially in Georgia) sought to effect an alliance of the poor Negro and the poor white. As Tom Watson, the gubernatorial candidate, explained; "Now the People's Party says to these two men, you are kept apart that you may be separately fleeced of your earnings. You are made to hate each other because upon that hatred is rested the keystone of the arch of financial despotism which enslaves you both. You are deceived and blinded that you may not see how this race antagonism perpetuates a monetary system which beggars you both."

When H. S. Doyle, a Negro preacher who had been campaigning for Watson, was threatened with lynching; on Watson's call, 2,000 armed white farmers guarded him for two nights.

Generally, only in Georgia was there a substantial Populist

appeal to the Negro. In Texas, however, 2 Negroes were appointed to the state executive committee at the first state convention. This became a standard procedure at other conventions, and in Arkansas the state platform included a resolution suggested by I. Glopsy, a Negro: "That it is the object of the Peoples' Party to elevate the downtrodden sons and daughters of industry in all matters before the people, irrespective of race and color."

White Populist red-necks drove some Negroes out of the party by their violence and rowdiness. In Washington, Ga., John Heard, a white Populist, shot at some Negroes who attended a Democratic meeting. Similar incidents led Negro political leaders in Douglas County, Greene County, and Athens, Ga., to refuse endorsement to the Populists.

To forestall Populist victories, the Democratic Party appealed for Negro votes. For example, in an Alabama election campaign, Democrats tried to attract Negro votes by calling attention to the legislative measures that had benefited Negroes, such as aid to Negro education. Democrats also sponsored picnics and barbecues for Negroes.

In Georgia, the Democratic Party organized a Negro Democratic Club, the Northern Club (named after the Democratic gubernatorial candidate).

When friendship proved unsuccessful, the Democrats used other tactics. A circular issued by a Wilkes County Democratic chairman suggested the use of economic power to intimidate voters: "This danger [of Populist victory] however can be overcome by the absolute control which you yet exercise over your property. It is absolutely necessary that you should bring to bear the power which your situation gives over tenants, laborers and croppers."

The *Clarion Ledger,* a Jackson, Miss., newspaper, tried to scare the white voters in this manner: "A division of the white vote means the balance of power in the hands of the Negro, and this means the devil's own time wherever it exists."

In Georgia, white Democrats murdered 15 Negroes during this election campaign.

When all else failed, Democrats stuffed the ballot boxes. For example, the total vote in Augusta, Ga., was double the number of registered voters.

The Virginia Organization of True Reformers, a Negro secret society, began publishing a newspaper, *The Reformer.* By 1900, it had a weekly circulation of 8,000.

A Voice from the South, by the Negro educator Anna Julia Cooper was published.

Sissieretta Jones, a Negro singer, was invited to perform at the White House.

In New York City, a Negro athletic club, the Calumet Wheelmen, was formed.

William Henry Lewis, a Negro who had played for Amherst and Harvard, was named All-American by Walter Camp.

George Dixon, a Negro, became the world's feather-weight boxing champion. He held the title from 1892 to 1900.

1893

The AFL, at its 13th national convention, unanimously adopted a resolution affirming unity of labor regardless of race.

Rep. George W. Murray of South Carolina was the only Negro elected to the 53rd Congress.

Arkansas made separate railroad waiting stations compulsory.

There were 117 lynchings of Negroes.

Ex-Mississippi Senator B. K. Bruce was made a trustee of the public schools of Washington, D.C. He served until 1898.

The American National Educational Baptist Convention was created.

Thomy Lafon, a free Negro tycoon of New Orleans, worth ½ million dollars at his death, had "contributed so much to the development of the city that the State Legislature ordered a bust of Lafon to be carved and set up in some public institution in New Orleans."

William "Big Bill" Broonzy (1893-1957), Negro country blues singer, was born in Scott, Miss. His mother was a former slave from whom he learned many Negro songs. Working as farmhand, janitor and preacher, while composing and singing the blues, in the course of his life he wrote over 300 songs. Broonzy went to Chicago in 1920, where he was a redcap. He made his first recordings for Paramount Records in 1926. He played guitar, accompanying Clarence La Font and Bumble Bee Slim. In the late 1930's he was singing blues on Perfect and Vocalion Records, and in 1938 he sang in Carnegie Hall.

Paul Laurence Dunbar published his first collection of poetry, *Oak and Ivy*.

Gussie Davis wrote *The Fatal Wedding*.

Wiliam Henry Lewis, the Negro football player at Harvard, was named by Walter Camp to the All-American team for the second time.

Willie Sims, a Negro jockey, won the Belmont Stakes.

1894

At its 14th convention, the AFL again unanimously adopted a resolution affirming the unity of labor regardless of race.

Like other railroad unions, Eugene V. Debs' American Railway Union excluded Negroes from membership. The Brotherhood of Boilermakers and Iron Shipbuilders, the International Brotherhood of Electrical Workers and the International Association of Machinists followed the same policy.

The Populists gained control of the North Carolina Legislature with the support of the remnants of the old Republican organization and dismantled the Democratic election machinery.

In February, Congress repealed the provision of the Enforcement Act of May 31, 1870, dealing with the right to vote, and made no appropriations for special Federal marshals and election supervisors.

Virginia enacted new election codes in which: (1) registration certificates had to be secured far in advance of an election; (2) a change in residence, or changes in precinct boundaries required obtaining a new certificate; (3) candidates' names would be arranged on ballots by office, not by party as was previously the case; (4) time in the polling booth was limited to 2½ minutes.

During the elections of 1894, Negroes were openly bribed.

In the Charlotte, Va., *Dispatch,* a Negro Democrat reported that Negro votes "can be cornered at half-price."

In the Nov. 16th issue, the *Louisiana Populist* commented on recent elections: "All the hill parishes where the white people are in the majority, the Populists polled big majorities, but in the river parishes, where the Negroes were in the majority, the Democrats succeeded in maintaining white supremacy with the Negro votes."

In the election of 1894 in Texas, of 14 counties with Negro populations of more than 50%, 7 voted Democratic, 4 voted Republican and 3 voted Populist.

In this year 135 Negroes were lynched.

Harvard University awarded its first Ph.D. to a Negro, W. E. B. Du Bois. Du Bois was the only Negro to receive a doctorate between 1890 and 1894, compared to 876 whites.

E. Franklin Frazier (1894-1962), Negro historian and sociologist was born in Baltimore. Educated at Howard University and the University of Chicago, he taught in the sociology department of Howard and occasionally at Columbia University. A Guggenheim Fellow in 1940-41, president of the American Sociological Society in 1948, and expert on race for UNESCO, he is best known for his book, *Black Bourgeoisie.* His other works include: *The Negro Family in Chicago* (1932); *The Negro Family in the United States* (1948 rev. ed.); *The Negro in the United States* (1957 rev. ed); *Race and Culture Contacts in the Modern World* (1957); *The Negro Church in America* (1961).

Bessie Smith (1894?-1937), Negro blues singer, was born in poverty in Chattanooga, Tenn. She was discovered by Ma Rainey at the age of 13. Bessie Smith toured with the Rabbit Foot Minstrels, and gradually achieved recognition on the Negro vaudeville circuit. She began recording in 1923 with *Down Hearted Blues.* Her accompanist on many of her later recordings was James P. Johnson. Her career declined during the Depression, partly because people were not buying records, partly because of personal problems. In 1937, she died in Mississippi after an automobile accident. She had not been permitted to enter the nearest hospital because it was for whites only. Today Bessie Smith is generally recognized as one of jazz's greatest talents, and many consider her the greatest of the blues singers.

Jesse Ernest Wilkins (1894-1959), Assistant Secretary of Labor, was born in Farmington, Mo., educated at the University of Illinois and Chicago School of Law. In 1953 President Eisenhower chose him as first vice president of the Committee on Government Contracts, and in 1954 Assistant Secretary of Labor.

Appointed, by Walter Stowers and William H. Anderson, was published in Detroit. This was the first Negro novel to reflect the racism that came with Jim Crow, and the "black peril phobia" of the 1890's. It treated peonage, convict-labor, lynching, disenfranchisement and segregation as aspects of systematic repression.

Willie Sims, the Negro jockey, won the Belmont Stakes for the second year in a row.

1895

By 1895, Negro school enrollment had increased 59% from 1876. The equivalent figure for whites was 106%.

Booker T. Washington, in his Atlanta Compromise speech of Sept. 18, renounced equality for the time being, urged the acceptance of a subordinate position for Southern Negroes in politics, and advocated education for the practical end of gaining a livelihood. In fact, this speech accepted social and political inequality in exchange for economic and educational help.

In 1895 the Populist-controlled North Carolina Legislature passed a new election law in which each party was represented on all registration boards and heavy penalties were prescribed for vote-buying and selling. Many Negro officials and 300 Negro magistrates were appointed. The State Legislature also passed a county government bill which took the power of appointing local officials from the Legislature and gave it to the residents of each county. Thus, the Democrats retained control of local government, but Negro counties could now elect Negro officials.

In Georgia, despite strong Populist sympathy, the Democrats were able to control the Negro vote. They often paid the taxes of Negroes so that they would vote Democratic. In Augusta's 4th Ward, heavily Negro, the vote was 9 for the Populist, Watson, and 989 for his Democratic opponent.

Florida enacted a law requiring segregated education in private schools as well as in public schools (a law segregating public education had been passed earlier). The law imposed penalties on teachers, administrators, and patrons of integrated schools.

In 1895 South Carolina revised the Reconstruction Constitution of 1868. The new Constitution effectively disenfranchised most Negroes. It required payment of all taxes, educational tests or property worth $300, a poll tax of $1 and two years residence.

When the National Machinists' Union refused to remove a racial exclusion clause from its constitution, the AFL organized a new union, the International Machinists' Association. The National Machinists Union then dropped its exclusion clause, but retained a secret pledge whereby members brought only whites up for membership.

In Washington County, Mississippi, 7,000 Negroes and 1,500 whites were declared competent for jury duty, but only whites were picked. This exclusion was contested before the Supreme Court in GIBSON v. MISSISSIPPI. The Court effectively excluded Negroes from juries by ruling that there was no proof of exclusion on the grounds of race or color in this case.

In this year 112 Negroes were lynched.

George W. Murray, a South Carolina Negro, was re-elected to the 54th Congress.

The Negro National Medical Association was founded.

In Atlanta, Ga., the National Baptist Convention, the Foreign Mission Baptist Convention of the U.S.A., the American National Baptist Convention, and the American National Educational Baptist Convention were combined in the formation of the National Baptist Convention of the U.S.A.

Florence Mills (1895-1927), Negro singer, dancer and comedienne, was born in Washington, D.C. She made her stage debut at the age of 6 with her sister in a singing act. Later, and until 1919, she led a cabaret act with Ada "Bricktop" Smith, Cora Greene and Mattie Hight. They played such places as Chicago's Old Panama Cafe. She subsequently joined a group known as the "Tennessee Ten," but achieved her first significant stage success in the musical comedy revue of 1922, *Shuffle Along*. She also had a long run with *Plantation*, on Broadway. She later toured with her company in *Dixie to Broadway*. In 1926 she was regarded as one of the most popular performers on the European continent. Florence Mills had wide success with the revue *Blackbirds*, in London, despite an attempt by the British Artists' Federation to bar her from the English stage. She gave credit for her dancing skill to Bill "Bojangles" Robinson, who taught her how to dance on the roof of a rooming house while she was performing at the Panama Cafe. At her funeral in 1927 it was estimated that 3,000 attended the funeral and 150,000 people lined the streets in order to watch the procession. Among the celebrities who attended were James Weldon Johnson, Johnny Dunn, Jack Benny, and Ethel Waters.

William Grant Still (1895-   ), Negro composer, was born in Woodville, Miss. Educated at Wilberforce University, the Oberlin Conservatory of Music, and the New England Conservatory, he began as an arranger for jazz orchestras. Still's original compositions were first played in 1926. Since then, his songs, symphonic poems, opera and symphonies have been performed by major orchestras in the U.S. and Europe. He conducted a program of his own works in 1936 at the Hollywood Bowl. He also wrote successful musicals, including *From Dixie to Broadway* in which Florence Mills starred.

Paul Laurence Dunbar's *Majors and Minors* was published. It received a favorable, full-page review in *Harper's Weekly* in its issue of June 27, 1897, by William Dean Howells.

1896

Homer Plessy, a New Orleans Negro, attempted to ride in a white railroad car, and was arrested and convicted. Testing the Louisiana law of 1890 segregating railroad carriages, Plessy appealed to the Supreme Court. Justice Brown, writing the majority opinion in PLESSY V. FERGUSON, called the creation of "separate but equal" accommodations a "reasonable" use of state police power. In addition, he denied that the 14th Amendment had "been intended to abolish distinction based on color, or to enforce social as distinguished from political . . . equality, or a co-mingling of the two races upon terms unsatisfactory to either." Justice John Marshall Harlan dissented. Justice Harlan wrote: "The judgment this day rendered will, in time, prove to be quite as pernicious as the decision made by this tribunal in the Dred Scott case. The thin disguise of equal accommodations . . . will not mislead anyone nor atone for the wrong this day done."

South Carolina adopted the "white primary"; only whites could vote in the Democratic primary.

The Republican Party platform said: "We proclaim our unqualified condemnation of the uncivilized and preposterous practice well-known as lynching, and the killing of human beings suspected or charged with crimes without due process of law."

In the 1896 Presidential election, William Jennings Bryan ran on both the Democratic and Populist tickets. Southern whites were divided, however, between Populists and Democrats. Both sought the Negro vote. For a while, the Populists upheld the cause of the Negro. The Populist platform of Georgia contained a plank denouncing "lynch law." In Louisiana, Negroes held the balance of power between the Populist-Republican Fusion and the Democrats. This led to much violence. On the day of the state election, the militia was sent into St. Landry Parish after Republicans and Populists seized the town of Washington and forced the Democratic election official to register the Negroes. Two Negroes were murdered and many beaten by white Democrats.

The Democrats were victorious in Louisiana, and between 1896 and 1904 adopted literacy, property, and poll tax requirements to disenfranchise Negroes. These restrictions and the "grandfather clause" of 1898 reduced the number of registered Negro voters from 130,334 in 1896 to 1,342 in 1904.

The North Carolina elections were also marked by violence. In Franklington, state troops were called out to prevent a race riot. A riot did occur in Pearson County. Nevertheless, the North Carolina Populists won a substantial victory in the election.

This year 77 Negroes were lynched.

The Boilermakers and Shipbuilders Union was admitted to the AFL. Its members were pledged to propose only white men for membership.

Richard L. Davis, an Ohio Negro, was elected to the national executive board of the United Mine Workers. Davis, along with other Negro miners, had been a local union official since the United Mine Workers was organized in 1890.

The National Association of Colored Women was founded in the summer of this year in Washington, D.C. By 1901, it had chapters organized in 26 states. A nurses' training school was set up in New Orleans, and hygiene teams were sent to four states to aid the Negroes there. Land was purchased in Memphis for an old folks' home, and in Tennessee and Louisiana the Legislatures were petitioned for repeal of Jim Crow laws. Plans to establish Mothers' Congresses, to teach Negro mothers how to care for their children, were implemented.

A Negro bank, the Nickel Savings Bank of Richmond, Va., was founded.

George Washington Carver became the director of agricultural research at Tuskegee Institute.

Malvin Gray Johnson (1896-1934), Negro artist, was born, in Greensboro, N.C. He attended the National Academy in New York City and won the Otto Kahn special prize at the Harmon Show in 1928 for *Swing Low Sweet Chariot,* a depiction of plantation slaves' fantasies. During his life, Johnson experimented with many forms. His early work showed great impressionist influence. Then he evolved toward cubism; his last and most mature work utilized African pictorial elements. The subject matter in these last works was plantation life in the contemporary South. The two most significant series of canvasses were *Virginia Landscapes,* of which "Red Road" and "Convict Labor" were most outstanding. A second series was a gallery of Negro portraits done in water color. Johnson was probably the most talented Negro painter until his untimely death.

W. E. B. DuBois published *Suppression of the African Slave Trade,* the first title in the Harvard Historical Studies, and inaugurated the Atlanta University Studies. These studies, held between 1896 and 1914, dealt with a different phase of Negro life each year, and represented "the first real sociological research in the South."

Hearts of Gold by J. McHenry Jones, was published in Wheeling, W.Va. This work continued the trend started by Walter Stowers' and William H. Anderson's novel, *Appointed.*

It focused the new reign of terror on poor whites who feared the Negroes for economic reasons.

Paul Laurence Dunbar published a collection of poems, *Lyrics of a Lowly Life,* which won national attention.

Gussie Davis wrote *In the Baggage Coach Ahead.*

From this year through 1917, ragtime was popular in the U.S., spread by itinerant pianists from the South and Midwest at midways and fairs. Ragtime represented a blending of West African rhythm and European musical form, with emphasis on the European. It originated in the Midwest, and not in New Orleans. Whites as well as Negroes were performers. Ragtime developed about the same time as jazz emerged in New Orleans. The styles were largely separate, and did not merge for some 20 years. Scott Joplin, a Negro with classical training, was the greatest composer of ragtime. Attempts were made to incorporate ragtime into the European tradition. James P. Johnson composed choral works, concertos and symphonies in ragtime. However, they were rhythmically too complex for most performers, and the public was not ready for them. Orchestral ragtime survived in a simplified form but with complicated rhythms as Dixieland.

The first known example of the spasm band was in New Orleans, where Emile "Stale Bread" Lacoume, "Cajun," "Whiskey," "Warm Gravy," and "Slew Foot Pete" played improvised music on homemade instruments on street corners.

Willie Simms, the Negro jockey, won the Kentucky Derby.

1897

There were 123 Negroes lynched.

By the end of 1897, 7,372 cases were tried under the Enforcement Acts, 5,172 in the South and 2,200 in the North. Only 1,432 of these cases resulted in conviction.

Arkansas adopted the "white primary."

G. H. White of North Carolina, a Negro, was elected to the 55th Congress.

President McKinley reappointed ex-Senator B. K. Bruce as Register of the Treasury. Bruce held the post until March, 1898, when he died.

The American Negro Academy was founded by Alexander Crumwell. Its purposes were the promotion of literature, science, art, the fostering of higher education, and the defense of the Negro. Its officers were S. G. Atkins, principal of the Slater Normal School in Winston-Salem; L. B. Moore, dean at Howard University; W. H. Crogman, president of Clark University, Atlanta, Ga.

Andrew J. Beard, a Negro, received $50,000 for his invention of the "Jenny Coupler," an automatic device for coupling railroad cars.

Elijah Muhammed (1897-   ) was born Elijah Poole in Sandersville, Ga., the son of a Baptist preacher who had been a slave. In 1923, with his wife and 2 children, he moved to Detroit. He held several menial jobs, but the depression of 1929 left him without work. Around 1930, he met Fard Muhammed, also known as Wali Fard, who had founded the Black Nation of Islam. Fard converted Elijah Poole who changed his name to Elijah Muhammed. Muhammed became Fard's trusted lieutenant and in 1932 was entrusted with establishing and running a temple in Chicago. Two years later Muhammed returned to Detroit to become Fard's Minister of Islam and heir apparent. In June, 1934, Fard disappeared. Several of Fard's followers, jealous of Muhammed's quick rise and afraid of his more militant attitude, accused him of doing away with Fard and drove him out of the movement. Elijah Muhammed returned to Chicago and organized his own movement, the Black Muslims. He deified Fard as Allah and claimed quasi-divinity for himself for having known Allah. In 1942, Muhammed was arrested for sedition. He had been openly sympathetic to Japan (as a colored nation) and had urged Negroes not to serve in the war. He was convicted and served three years in jail. Elijah Muhammed has never been well received by the bulk of the civil rights community, but the Muslims have been recognized as a potentially powerful political group in the Negro community. As of 1960, the organization had more than 100,000 members, real estate worth $500,000, 50 temples, numerous storefront missions, and 2 universities of Islam in Detroit and Chicago. The university in Detroit is accredited through the 9th grade.

Sidney Bechet (1897-1959), Negro jazz musician, was born in New Orleans. He began playing the clarinet at 6. As a teen-ager he played with Freddie Keppard's band and the Eagle Band, and in 1916 he joined King Oliver's Olympia

Band in New Orleans. In 1919, Bechet played with Will Marion Cooke's Southern Syncopated Orchestra in New York. When he returned to New York in 1921 after a European tour, he began playing soprano sax along with the clarinet. He again toured Europe and Russia in the mid-1920's, and in 1928 joined Noble Sissle's band in Paris, playing with it until 1938, both in Europe and the U.S. During the 1940's he played with Eddie Condon, principally in New York, and then began to spend most of his time in Europe, living in Paris where he died.

James Edwin Campbell, a Negro, wrote *Echoes from the Cabin and Elsewhere,* a collection of dialect poetry employing Gullah speech of the South Carolina coast. The poetry was replete with superstitions and folklore of the Gullah people.

Daniel Webster Davis published a collection of dialect poems, *Weh Down Souf.* Though technically good, it depicted the Negro as a simple-minded, happy-go-lucky character.

Storyville, the official red-light district of New Orleans, was opened. The playing of jazz became a full-time profession instead of a mere avocation for solo pianists such as Jelly Roll Morton.

Willie Simms, the Negro jockey, won the Brighton Handicap.

1898

In the Spanish-American War, in Teddy Roosevelt's charge up San Juan Hill the 9th and 10th Negro Cavalry participated. At the Battle of El Caney, the 25th Negro Infantry took part and captured a Spanish fort.

The following Negroes of the 10th U.S. Cavalry received the Congressional Medal of Honor for bravery at Tayabacoa, Cuba: Pvt. Dennis Bell, Pvt. Fitz Lee, Pvt. William H. Thompkins, Pvt. George Wanton. For rescuing a fellow soldier while under fire in Santiago, Cuba, Sgt.-Maj. Edward L. Baker, 10th U.S. Cavalry, also received the medal.

Daniel Atkins, a ship's cook, and Robert Penn, a fireman First Class, were awarded the Navy Medal of Honor for bravery during the Spanish-American War.

A Congressional Amnesty Act removed the last disabilities on ex-Confederates.

In WILLIAMS V. MISSISSIPPI, the U.S. Supreme Court ruled that a poll tax did not violate the 14th Amendment.

There were 101 lynchings of Negroes.

Throughout the South in this year, segregation laws were strengthened and expanded, particularly as regards public transportation.

Georgia adopted the "white primary."

Louisiana, in order to protect its poor whites from the stringent voting requirements of 1896, added a "grandfather clause" to its State Constitution. Under this clause, if a man's father or grandfather had voted on Jan. 1, 1867, his name would be added to the permanent registration list, regardless of his ability to comply with the other voting requirements. By 1900, there were only 5,320 Negroes registered in Louisiana, compared to 130,344 Negro voters in 1896.

In North Carolina, as a result of Populist-Republican victories in 1894 and 1896 and the County Government Bill, there were 300 Negro magistrates and a total of 1,000 Negro officeholders. In the election of this year, however, white supremacy became the major issue. There were riots in Wilmington, N.C., and after the victory of the Democratic white supremacy advocates, 400 whites led by an ex-Congressman invaded the Negro district and injured, burned, killed, and chased Negroes out of town.

A South Carolina law established segregation for first-class railroad coaches. In 1900 a law extended segregation to all classes.

In Lake City, S.C., the appointment of a Negro postmaster touched off a white riot. The postmaster and his family were murdered and his house burned.

Illinois coal companies, in Pana and Verden, used Southern Negroes as strikebreakers. The violence occasioned by the strikes and its ultimate failure caused hostility among white and Negro members of the United Mine Workers.

On March 17, former Senator B. K. Bruce died as a result of diabetes. His funeral services at the Metropolitan African Methodist Episcopal Church in Washington, D.C., attracted a large crowd of both races. Congressmen acted as honorary pallbearers, and a tribute by Senator Allison was read.

S. W. Rutherford, a Negro, started the National Benefit

Insurance Company, and C. C. Spaulding began the North Carolina Mutual Benefit Insurance Company.

There were three Negro magazines, three daily papers, 11 school papers and 136 weekly papers. Two of the three magazines were quarterly Methodist reviews. Of the weeklies, 13 of the 70 were published by religious organizations, secret and fraternal societies.

The Virginia Organization of True Reformers, a secret Negro benevolent society, established a home for the aged outside Richmond, Va.

Fletcher 'Henderson (1898-1952), Negro jazz musician, was born in Cuthbert, Ga. He attended Atlanta University, where he majored in chemistry and mathematics. Henderson, in 1920, left Georgia for New York to do graduate work in chemistry. In 1922 he took a job as a song demonstrator for a New York music publisher, Black Swan, to pay his expenses. He soon became a full-time pianist at the publisher's recording studio. In 1924 he took his 9-piece band to Roseland in New York City, where he made famous his call-and-response arrangements with improvised soloists. His tenor saxophonist, Coleman Hawkins, made the saxophone a jazz instrument. Henderson's band frequently played at the Savoy Ballroom and the Apollo in Harlem after the Roseland's closing hour of one o'clock. His was the first big band to become famous playing jazz. In the 1920's he also made many records accompanying Bessie Smith. In the 1930's Henderson arranged for the Benny Goodman band. Some of his most important arrangements for Goodman were *Sometimes I'm Happy, King Porter Stomp* and *Down South Camp Meeting*. While continuing to lead his own band, he also played piano in the Goodman orchestra. Perhaps his greatest contribution to jazz music was as a pioneer in writing arrangements for large swing bands.

Paul Robeson (1898-   ), Negro actor and concert singer, was born in Princeton, N.J. His father, a fugitive slave, worked his way through Lincoln University and became a Presbyterian minister. Robeson attended Rutgers University, where he won many academic and athletic honors, including Phi Beta Kappa and selection for the All-American football team. Robeson paid for his education at Columbia Law School by playing professional football, but became interested in acting, and since 1924 he has been acclaimed both in Europe and the U.S. as an actor and concert singer. His major theatrical roles include Eugene O'Neill's *All God's Chillun Got Wings, The Emperor Jones, The Hairy Ape;* the musicals, *Show Boat* and *Porgy and Bess,* and Shakespeare's *Othello.* He also appeared in the movie version of *The Emperor Jones, King Solomon's Mines* and the *Song of Freedom.*

Paul Laurence Dunbar published a collection of his magazine articles, *Folks from Dixie,* and his novel, *The Uncalled,* in New York City. The novel is a spiritual autobiography of a boy who rejects the ministry for which he was groomed by his family. The hero and all the characters are white. *The Uncalled* is important in that it remains his only good novel, and the first to be widely read by whites.

Clorindy, the Origin of the Cakewalk, with lyrics and book by Paul Laurence Dunbar and music by Will Marion Cook, was produced at the Casino Theater in New York City and created an immediate sensation. It more than any other work bridged the gap between minstrel show and musical. Cook and Dunbar conceived it as an operetta. The theme of the story was music, specifically the origin of the dance known as the cakewalk in New Orleans in the 1880's. The idea was primarily Cook's.

A Trip to Coontown, by Robert Cole and William Johnson, was the first musical comedy by Negroes for Negroes. Cole also wrote in 1900 the highly successful *A Shoo Fly Regiment,* a musical about Negroes in thĕ U.S. forces in the Spanish-American War. Several of its songs became hits: *Louisiana Lize, I Must Have Been a-Dreaming, No One Can Fill Her Place, Katydid, The Maiden with Dreamy Eyes, The Cricket and the Frog.*

Willie Simms, the Negro jockey, won the Kentucky Derby and the Brighton Handicap.

1899

Between 1899 and 1937, approximately 150,000 Negro aliens were legally admitted to the U.S.

The Negro Representative, G. H. White, of North Carolina, was re-elected to the 56th Congress.

At the Sixth Atlanta Conference for the Study of Negro

Problems it was announced that between 1870 and 1899, Negroes had paid more than $15 million in tuition and fees to private institutions, more than $45 million in indirect taxes, and a total of $25 million in direct school taxes.

In CUMMING V. RICHMOND COUNTY the Supreme Court held improper a request from Negroes in Augusta, Ga., to end public support for two white high schools after the only Negro high school had been closed.

In MAXWELL V. DOW, the Supreme Court overturned the 1871 decision in U.S. V. HALL, ruling that the "privileges and immunities" of the 14th Amendment were not to be included as provisions of the Bill of Rights.

This year 85 Negroes were lynched.

Trainmen called for the exclusion of Negroes from their profession.

John Mitchell, president of the United Mine Workers, testified before the Federal Industrial Commission that Negroes were encouraged to join the United Mine Workers, and objected to them only when used as strikebreakers.

North Carolina enacted legislation to segregate railroads.

Between the years 1895 and 1899, three Negroes received doctorates, compared to 1,244 whites.

Aaron Douglas (1899-), Negro artist, was born in Topeka, Kan., and educated at the University of Nebraska. He left a teacher's position at Kansas City High School to study under Winolo Reiss in New York City. He did many illustrations for books dealing with Negro subject matter, and became interested in the styles of African art and successfully managed to synthesize African designs with modern abstractions. He ranks with the Mexican, Miguel Covarrubias, as an outstanding exponent of Negro types and design motifs. His work includes several illustrations for books by Harlemites of the 1920's, murals on Afro-American themes in Harlem's Club Ebony, Chicago's Hotel Sherman, Fisk University Library and at the 135th Street Harlem Branch Library. During the early 1930's, he studied easel painting under De Waroquier and Despiau in Paris on a Barnes Foundation grant. In 1933, he had a still-life and portrait exhibit at Cas Delbos Gallery in Paris.

Edward Kennedy "Duke" Ellington (1899-   ), Negro, jazz musician, was born in Washington, D.C. At the age of 7, Ellington began to study piano. He attended Armstrong High School in Washington, where he studied music. He also studied with Henry Grant. While in high school, he organized a band, the Washingtonians. In 1923, Fats Waller persuaded Ellington to come to New York. Ellington's Washingtonians worked in Harlem and at the Kentucky Club downtown. They began to record as Duke Ellington's Kentucky Club Orchestra. From 1927 through 1932, the Ellington band played at the Cotton Club, from which they made frequent radio broadcasts. Ellington's first record hit in popular music was *Mood Indigo* in 1930 (the original title was "Dreamy Blues"). In 1933, the band made its first European tour. It was at that time enlarged to include 6 brasses and 4 reeds. Other Ellington hits of this period were *Solitude*, 1933; *Sophisticated Lady*, 1933; *In a Sentimental Mood*, 1935; *Daybreak Express, Blue Ramble, Blue Harlem*, etc. Ellington estimates that he has composed some 1,500 songs. He became so well known in the late 1920's and early 1930's in New York that he was one of the few Negro jazz musicians steadily employed during the Depression. In 1943 he played at Carnegie Hall his own composition *Black, Brown and Beige*, a 50-minute serious work telling the story of the Negro people in America. It helped to shift jazz from dance to concert music. Ellington has established a world-wide reputation, and is generally considered one of the most important musical minds and talents of this century.

Clifton R. Wharton (1899-) diplomat and Ambassador to Norway, was born in Baltimore. Educated in the law at Boston University, he joined the Foreign Service in 1925. He served in a variety of posts in Africa and Europe, and was the first Negro to head an American embassy in Europe, as Minister to Rumania in 1958 and Ambassador to Norway from 1961 to 1964.

Houghton-Mifflin published two collections of Charles Chesnutt's short stories *The Conjure Woman* and *The Wife of His Youth, and Other Stories of the Color Line*. These and Dunbar's *The Uncalled* were the first works of prose fiction written by Negroes to reach a mass white audience.

Imperium in Imperio by Sutton Griggs was published in

Cincinnati. The author was a Baptist preacher and lecturer on the race question. This novel was the first black nationalist, anti-white, and even anti-mulatto expression in fiction. The story involved a young "black power" advocate who formed a revolutionary secret society which was anti-white and anti-mulatto. The ultimate aim of the society was to seize Texas and create a separate Negro republic. Grigg's subsequent novels were toned down in their militancy and sought Negro accommodations with the old plantation owners for protection from the poor whites.

Sons of Ham, by Bert Williams and George Walker, was produced at the Grand Opera House, New York City. It initiated a 10-year collaboration which lasted until Walker's death. Williams and Walker were the first successful American musical team, and set a trend in musical writing that was continued by Rodgers and Hart, Rodgers and Hammerstein, Lerner and Lowe, etc. In 1906 Williams and Walker starred in *Abyssinia* by Alex Rogers, Jesse Shippe and Will Marion Cook. In 1907 the same authors produced *Bandana Land.*

Negroes represented 32% of Cuba's population.

1900

U.S. Census: Of the total U.S. population 8,833,994 were Negroes, representing 11.6% of the population. 89.7% of the Negroes lived in the South and represented one-third of the total Southern population.

Between 1900 and 1930, the native Negro population increased 33.9%; native white population 68.4%; foreign-born white population, 30.6%; foreign Negro population 232%.

The life expectancy of Negroes averaged approximately 34 years, as opposed to the white life expectancy of approximately 48 years.

In the years following 1900, the South declined as an area of Negro immigrant residence. In 1900, three Southern divisions, South Atlantic, East South Central, and West South Central, contained 37.2% of the foreign-born Negro population. By 1910, this percentage dropped to 22.5%, despite mass immigration during the decade, and by 1930 only 14.7% of foreign-born Negroes lived in the South.

Net intercensal migration for Negro males ages 15-34 for

the decade 1890-1900, in selected states was: Alabama, —12.5%; Georgia, —7.6%; Mississippi, —2.6%; Illinois, 53.9%; Michigan, 10.5%; New York, 55.2%. Thus, from 1890 to 1900, for every 100 Negroes in Alabama, 12 Negro men aged 15-34, left Alabama. During this period, for every 100 Negroes in New York, 55 Negro men aged 15-34, entered New York.

The percentage of Negroes living in urban metropolitan areas was in the total U.S. 26.6%; in the North, 61.1%; in the West, 66.7% and in the South, 22.1%.

Cities having a Negro population of more than 10,000 were: Washington, D.C., 86,702; Baltimore, 79,258; New Orleans, 77,714; Philadelphia, 62,613; New York, 60,666; Memphis, 49,910; Louisville, 39,139; Atlanta, 35,727; St. Louis, 35,516; Richmond, 32,230; Charleston, 31,522; Chicago, 30,150; Nashville, 30,044: Some other cities had populations ranging from 10,000 to 30,000.

In the following cities, Negroes outnumbered whites: Charleston, S.C.; Savannah, Ga.; Jacksonville, Fla.; Montgomery, Ala.; Shreveport and Baton Rouge, La.; and Vicksburg, Miss.

54.5% of Negroes lived in central city areas, and represented 6.5% of the total central city residents. In the North, 2.5% of such residents were Negroes. In the West, 1.3% and in the South, 29.6%.

The percentages of Negroes and whites engaged in gainful occupations, 45.2% for Negroes, and 37.3% for whites, reflected that more Negro than white women worked.

In the preceding decade there were over 50 strikes of white workers against Negro labor. The white workers demanded discharge of Negro employees and an end to the hiring of Negroes.

The AFL, at its annual convention adopted a policy of Negro locals where the existing situation warranted it.

The Tobacco Workers International Union gave up an attempt to forbid racial discrimination, and began to organize separate Negro locals.

There were 91,019 dues-paying members in the United Mine Workers, and approximately 20,000 were Negroes.

32,069 Negroes were members of labor unions.

The total value of farm property owned by Negroes was $499,943,734.

The average acreage of farms operated by Negroes in the U.S. was 51.2 acres, as opposed to 160.3 for whites. The average value of farms operated by Negroes was $670, as opposed to $4,003 for whites.

The Negro professional class included: 21,267 teachers and professors; 15,528 preachers; 1,734 doctors; 212 dentists; 310 journalists; 728 lawyers; over 2,000 actors and showmen; 236 artists, sculptors and art teachers; one Negro Congressman, G. W. White of North Carolina; 3,915 musicians and music teachers; 247 photographers; 52 architects, designers, draftsmen and inventors.

Approximately 24% of U.S. Negroes owned their own homes.

There were 4 Negro banks in the U.S.

Some 64 Negro drugstores had been established, each with a capital of at least $1,000.

Charles P. Graves, president of Gold Leaf Consolidated Company of Montana and Illinois, a mining company, reported his property at a value of $1,000,000. He was the first Negro millionaire.

Booker T. Washington called a group of Negro businessmen together in Boston, and organized the National Negro Business League. 400 delegates from 34 states elected Washington the first president.

44.5% of Negroes were illiterate. Geographically, the breakdown was: North Atlantic, 13.8%; South Atlantic, 47.1%; North Central, 21.7%; South Central, 48.8%; Western 13.1%.

By this year, more than 2,000 Negroes had college degrees. Between 1900 and 1910, 4 doctorates were awarded to Negroes, two each from Negro and from integrated colleges.

There were 21,267 Negro teachers, and 1,500,000 Negro school children. Four states had Negro state colleges, Virginia, Arkansas, Georgia, and Delaware.

The 6th Atlanta Conference for the Study of Negro Problems stated that "American Negroes have in a generation, (1870 to 1899), paid directly $40,000,000 in hard-earned cash for educating their children," and found the results "gratifying."

Approximately 100,000 Negroes were Catholics in the U.S. with about 50 Negro priests.

W. E. B. Du Bois attended the meeting of the African and New World Intellectuals in London. The conference's "Address to the Nations of the World," written by Du Bois, contained Du Bois' first recorded use of the dictum "The problem of the 20th century is the problem of the color line." Du Bois also attended the first Pan-African Congress in London, and was elected vice-president. The Congress was intended to be a permanent organization protesting imperialism and working for self-government of colonized people. Du Bois, along with Monroe Trotter and other militant Negroes, also supported the Democratic Party, primarily because of its anti-imperialist stand and what they felt was a sympathetic attitude towards the Philippines.

On Jan. 20, G. H. White, the Negro Representative from North Carolina, introduced the first bill to make lynching of an American a federal crime. The bill died in committee, and 105 Negroes were lynched in 1900.

In New Orleans, white mobs assaulted Negroes, burned and robbed their homes and stores for three days.

By this year the number of registered Negro voters in Louisiana had dropped to 5,320.

North Carolina adopted a "grandfather clause." This amendment to its State Constitution granted descendants of people who were registered voters before Jan. 1, 1867, exemption from other registration qualifications.

A South Carolina law extended segregation to second-class railroad coaches; first-class cars were already segregated.

Virginia adopted segregation on steamships and railroads.

As Negro migration to the North continued, white hostility grew. Crowds of white hoodlums frequently attacked Negroes in Northern cities. On several occasions white citizens dragged Negroes off the street cars of Philadelphia with cries of "lynch him, kill him."

The national secret society, International Order of Twelve of the Knights and Daughters of Tabor, founded in 1871, claimed 200,000 members in 1900.

Booker T. Washington dispatched a team of Tuskegee graduates to Togoland in West Africa, at the request of the German government to teach the Africans there how to grow cotton. The project extended over a 6-year period.

At the Ecumenical Missionary Conference in New York, Rev. S. Morris, a Negro Baptist, called for the use of Negro missionaries because white missionaries hampered the work of "the gospel" by importing their prejudices.

Augusta Savage (1900-1962), Negro sculptress, studied at Cooper Institute. She was greatly influenced by African sculpture and techniques. In 1928 she was denied entrance to the Fontainbleau School for Talented American Artists because of her race. A Rosenwald Fund grant, however, enabled her to study in France for 2 years. During the 1930's she organized an art studio workshop in Harlem, which later became affiliated with the WPA. Through the workshop, and some of her own sculptures, most notably *African Savage,* and *The Tom-Tom,* she has exerted considerable influence upon young Negro artists.

Ethel Waters (1900-   ), Negro singer and actress, born in Chester, Pa., was the first woman to sing W. C. Handy's *St. Louis Blues.* Since 1927, she has appeared in numerous Broadway revues, musicals and dramas, including *Blackbirds, As Thousands Cheer, At Home Abroad, Cabin in the Sky, Member of the Wedding.* She also appeared in the movies *Cabin in the Sky, Manhattan* and *Pinky.* She created the character of "Beulah" in both the radio and TV series.

Louis Armstrong (1900-   ), Negro jazz musician, was born in New Orleans. He was a regular "second liner" of the New Orleans marching bands. A fan of the cornetist Bunk Johnson, he played tamborine, bugle and finally cornet in the Waif's Band. Armstrong first played cornet professionally in a trio in a saloon at age 15, and in 1918 he joined Kid Ory's band. Then, until 1921, he appeared in Fate Marable's band on excursion boats on the Mississippi River, where he perfected his style. In the mid-1920s he moved to Chicago and began to play the trumpet. Moving to New York, he appeared briefly with Fletcher Henderson. His own recording groups in the 1920's were the Hot Five and Hot Seven. It was with these groups that he produced his finest work. In 1929, with Luis Russell's orchestra, he made his first important big-band records. In 1932, Armstrong made his first overseas tour and played at the London Palladium. He then toured Europe, staying there until 1935 when he took over Luis Russell's band, which he led as his own until 1946. It was during this period that he began to use novelty songs as well as jazz, and began to sing as well as play. In 1944 he took part in the first jazz concert in the Metropolitan Opera House in New York City. Also in this year he organized a sextet for the film *New Orleans.* He took his sextet to Europe in 1949 and 1952, and to Japan in 1954. Armstrong remains one of America's and Europe's most popular musicians and entertainers. A direct descendant of the cornetists Buddy Bolden and King Oliver, and the predecessor of the great jazz trumpeters Eldridge, Gillespie and Davis, he was the first of the great modern jazz soloists.

Hale A. Woodruff (1900-   ), Negro artist, was born in Cairo, Ill. He studied at the Herron Institute in Indianapolis and was sent by local citizens to Paris to continue his studies. On his return from Paris, he became an instructor at Atlanta University. Woodruff was primarily an academic landscapist, specializing in Georgia scenes. He did WPA murals for Howard Junior High School and the Atlanta School of Social Work. Included in the latter were two panels of Negro neighborhoods, entitled *Shantytown* and *Mud Hill Row.* The *Atlanta Constitution* claimed, "The young Negro artist is one of the modern masters. This exhibition is really one of the finest that will be shown anywhere."

Negroes published 3 daily newspapers in Norfolk, Va., Kansas City, Mo., and Washington, D.C. They also published 150 weekly newspapers.

The Reformer, the weekly paper of the Virginia Organization of True Reformers (a secret Negro benevolent society), established in 1892, had a circulation of 8,000.

Booker T. Washington's *Up from Slavery* was published.

In his novel, *The House Behind the Cedars,* Charles Chesnutt introduced the mulatto as a tragic figure, neither black nor white. The mulatto was later to preoccupy many writers and was to become a stereotype.

In this year Paul Laurence Dunbar published a collection of his magazine articles, *The Strength of Gideon* and a novel, *The Love of Landry.*

James Weldon Johnson composed the song, *Lift Every Voice and Sing,* which became a sort of national anthem for Negroes in the U.S.

An establishment called The Marshall became important in the artistic life of New York. It was a hotel run by a Negro, which had become a center of fashionable life new to Negroes. For nearly ten years, beginning in 1900, the Marshall was headquarters for actors, musicians, composers, writers and the better-paid vaudevillians.

Marshall W. "Major" Taylor, a Negro, was the sprint champion of the U.S. in bicycle racing.

1901

W. E. B. Du Bois stated that there were many Negro intellectuals who refuted Booker T. Washington as a popular leader, refusing to accept his position that the Negro was to give up social equality for the time being.

George Forbes and Monroe Trotter began publishing *The Guardian,* which demanded full equality for Negroes, and opposed the ideas of Booker T. Washington.

President Roosevelt invited Booker T. Washington to the White House for an interview and dinner, outraging Southerners and pleasing many Negroes.

Alabama adopted a "grandfather clause."

Florida and Tennessee Democrats adopted "white primaries."

North Carolina and Virginia instituted Jim Crow laws for streetcars.

Richmond Barthé (1901-   ), Negro artist, born in New Orleans of mixed Creole stock was discovered by Lyle Saxon and a Catholic priest, both of whom provided the funds for his formal art study at the Chicago Art Institute. In 1928, Barthé practically abandoned painting for sculpture. During the early years he concentrated primarily on bust portraiture. In 1929 Barthé received a Rosenwald Grant to pursue his studies in New York City. Between 1933 and 1936, the Whitney Museum purchased three of Barthé's works, *Blackberry Woman, Comedian,* and *African Dancer.* He had had six one-man shows in New York City by 1936. His work ranged from portrait busts such as *Mask, Black Boy, Filipino*

Head, The Blackberry Woman, and *West Indian Girl,* to African portraits. Barthé is the only Negro sculptor in the National Academy of Arts and Letters.

Sterling Brown (1901-   ), Negro writer and educator, was born in Washington, D.C. He attended Williams College and Harvard University. He has taught at Virginia Seminary, Fisk, Lincoln, Vassar, Minnesota and the New School. Most recently, he was professor of English at Howard University. During the Depression he served as editor for Negro affairs on the Federal Writers Project, and was a staff member of the Carnegie-Myrdal study of the Negro. His works include *Southern Road,* a book of narrative and lyrical poems published in 1932, much of which is in dialect; two studies of the Negro, in 1928, *The Negro in American Fiction* and *Negro Poetry and Drama.* In 1941 he edited *Negro Caravan,* an anthology of Negro writers.

Roy Wilkins (1901-   ), executive director of the NAACP, was born in St. Louis, Mo. His mother having died when he was quite young, Wilkins was raised by an aunt in St. Paul, Minn. He attended the University of Minnesota where he majored in sociology. While a college student, he edited a Negro weekly, *The St. Paul Appeal,* and became secretary of the local NAACP chapter. Upon graduation in 1923, he accepted a job as managing editor of the Negro weekly, *The Call,* in Kansas City, Mo. Again he served the local NAACP as a secretary. A vigorous editorial campaign waged in the early 1930's against the re-election of a segregationist Senator brought him to the attention of the national NAACP. In 1931 he joined the National Secretariat of the NAACP as assistant executive secretary. In 1932, by disguising himself as an itinerant laborer, he investigated the treatment of Negroes on Mississippi flood-control projects for the NAACP. His report led to a Senate investigation and an upgrading of working conditions. From 1934 to 1949, Wilkins succeeded W. E. B. Du Bois as editor of the *Crisis,* the official magazine of the NAACP. During World War II Wilkins served as a consultant to the War Department on the training and placement of Negroes, and he was a consultant to the American delegation to the UN Conference in San Francisco in 1945. In 1949 Wilkins became acting executive secretary of the NAACP, when Walter White took a leave of absence. Concurrently he was chairman of the National Emergency Civil Rights Mobilization, which sent 4,000 people to Washington in January, 1950. When Walter White returned to the NAACP in June, 1950, Wilkins became administrator of internal affairs, a position he held until White died in 1955, whereupon Wilkins was made executive secretary. In 1965 Wilkins became executive director. Roy Wilkins was one of the major sponsors of the Aug. 28, 1963, march on Washington. Since 1964 a gap has emerged between moderate civil rights leaders, personified by Wilkins, and more militant Negroes. The gap widened in July, 1966, at the annual NAACP Convention, when Wilkins characterized the concept of "black power" as "a reverse Hitler, a reverse Ku Klux Klan." Dissatisfaction with Wilkins has now spread to the NAACP itself. At its July, 1968 convention, a group of "Young Turks" walked out in protest against the moderation of the NAACP.

The Marrow of Tradition, Charles Chesnutt's novel, was published. It was based on actual events which occurred in Wilmington, N.C. during the 1898 elections, when Negro voters were driven from the polls. The moral dilemma presented here was central to the Negro community at the time. Should the Negro (as represented by the protagonist Dr. Miller) retaliate against the white man with violence, or should he suppress his desire for revenge and try to win the whites over with Christian love and understanding. The protagonist chose the latter.

Paul Laurence Dunbar published a novel, *The Fanatics.*

Alberry Whitman's poem, *The Octoroon,* was published.

Joe Walcott, a Negro welterweight, became the world's champion. He held this title through 1904.

Joe Gans, a Negro, became the world's lightweight champion. He held this title through 1908.

In Canada, the Negro population stood at 17,437. However, Jamaicans and Haitians were not counted in the census classification as Negro.

1902

John D. Rockefeller pledged $1,000,000 to an agency that was being created to promote education without discrimination as to race sex or creed. His gift led to the formation of the General Education Board in 1903.

The International Longshoremen's Association had 20,000 members, of whom 6,000 were Negroes.

Wages for farm workers in South Carolina were $10.79 per month, in New York $26.13 per month.

85 Negroes were lynched in this year.

Louisiana instituted a Jim Crow street-car law.

Alabama and Mississippi Democrats adopted "white primaries."

Virginia adopted a "grandfather clause" amendment for its State Constitution.

Gertrude "Ma" Rainey began singing the blues. She was born in Columbus, Ga., in 1886. Her parents were Negro show people. At 15 she married Will Rainey and began performing with his troupe, the Rabbit Foot Minstrels. Louis Armstrong, Buster Bailey, Charles Green and Fletcher Henderson were among her accompanists at various times. Ma Rainey retired in 1933 and died in 1939.

Marian Anderson (1902-   ), Negro concert and opera singer, was born in Philadelphia. She studied with Giuseppe Boghetti, and was given a European scholarship by the National Association of Negro Musicians. She has sung with many orchestras, including the Philadelphia Symphony and the New York Philharmonic. She made her Town Hall debut in 1935, sang first with the Metropolitan Opera in 1955, made a world-wide concert tour for the State Department in 1957, and in 1958 served on the U.S. United Nations delegation.

Langston Hughes (1902-1967), Negro poet, was born in Joplin, Mo., and educated at Columbia and Lincoln universities. He was a recipient of Guggenheim and Rosenwald Fellowships, and poet-in-residence at the University of Chicago from 1949 to 1950. His early poems appeared exclusively in the *Crisis* and expressed pride in his blackness. Between 1931 and 1940, his poems angrily protested white injustice. From 1940 to his death, he wrote again of the Negro, de-emphasizing his relation to the white world. Hughes' works include *Weary Blues* and *Fire,* published in 1926; *Fine Clothes to the Jew,* 1927; *Not Without Laughter,* which won the Harmon Award for Literature in 1930; *Ways of White Folks,* 1934; *The Big Sea,* 1940; *Shakespeare in Harlem,*

1942; *Fields of Wonder,* 1947; *Simple Speaks His Mind,* 1950; *Montage on a Dream Deferred,* 1951; *Laughing to Keep from Crying* and *First Book of Negroes,* 1952; *Simple Takes a Wife,* 1953; *Famous American Negroes,* 1954; *Sweet Flypaper of Life,* 1955; *I Wonder as I Wander,* 1956; *Tambourines to Glory,* 1958; *Selected Poems,* 1959; *African Treasury,* 1960; *Ask Your Mama,* 1961; *Fight for Freedom,* 1962; *Five Plays,* 1963, and *Simple's Uncle Sam,* 1965.

James Melvin "Jimmie" Lunceford (1902-1947), Negro jazz musician, was born in Seaside, Ore. He studied music with Paul Whiteman's father, Wilberforce J. Whiteman Jr., and was graduated from Fisk University. Lunceford also studied at the City College of New York. In the mid 1920's he played reeds with the bands of Elmer Snowden and Wilber Sweatman. He began leading his own band in Memphis in 1927. In Buffalo, from 1930 to 1933, he became nationally known. His band was among the most successful Negro bands of the 1930's. His swing arrangements were by Sy Oliver, his trumpet player, and Edwin Wilcox, his pianist.

William H. Johnson (1902-   ), Negro artist, was born in Florence, S.C. He studied under Charles Hawthorne and George Luks at the New York National Academy of Design. He won both Cannon and Hall Garten prizes given by the Academy. Sent to France in 1926 by the Academy, he fell under the influence of Cézanne, Rouault and Soutine. In 1930, upon returning from Europe, he won the Harmon Medal for a series of French and Danish landscape scenes, and still-lifes. He returned to Florence, S.C., and did a series of regional landscapes and portraits of Negro residents. His Southern pictures are noted for their atmospheric effects and the keen eye for satire and realism.

James Lesesne Wells (1902-   ), Negro artist, was born in Georgia. The son of a minister, educated at Lincoln University, Columbia University and the National Academy of Design, he taught an adult education program at the Harlem Art Workshop, sponsored by the Harlem Public Library. Greatly influenced by African design motifs, he distinguished himself in media such as wood blocks, etching and lithography, emphasizing design over human representation. He had one-man shows at the Weyhe Galleries, the Delphic Studios and the Brooklyn Museum. His lithographs include a series on African design motifs, views of industrial towns, illustrations of the Bible and sketches of CCC camp activities. Wells also had a successful career as an oil painter. His *Flight into Egypt* won the Harmon Gold Medal in 1931. Several of his oils were purchased by the Phillips Memorial Gallery in Washington, D.C.

Paul Laurence Dunbar published *The Sport of the Gods.* It reiterated the "old plantation school" thesis that the rural Negro became demoralized in the urban North.

Alberry Whitman's poem, *The Southland's Charm and Freedom's Magnitude* was published.

In Dahomey, with lyrics and book by Paul Laurence Dunbar and music by Will Marion Cook, was the most successful, artistically and financially, of all Negro musicals. It opened to enthusiastic notices on Sept. 2, 1902, at the Globe Theater in Boston. The play ran for 3 years, and like all Negro musicals included dancing, full orchestration and lavish, spectacular scenery. In 1907 a command performance of *In Dahomey* was given for Edward VII in London.

The French film *Off to Bloomingdale Asylum,* a slapstick comedy used Negroes for the first time in a movie. The director, George Melies, described the film as follows: "An omnibus drawn by an extraordinary mechanical horse carries four Negroes. The horse kicks and upsets the Negroes, who falling, are changed into white clowns. They begin slapping each other's faces and by blows become black again. Kicking each other, they become white once more. Suddenly they are merged into one gigantic Negro. When he refuses to pay his carfare, the conductor sets fire to the bus, and the Negro bursts into a thousand pieces."

An immigration that lasted from this year through 1919 brought over 90,000 immigrants to Cuba from Haiti and Jamaica.

1903

From this year through 1909, John D. Rockefeller gave some $53,000,000 to the General Education Board in four large gifts, and empowered its trustees to dispose of the principle whenever they saw fit. The Board seemed especially interested in providing means for the preparation of teachers for Negro schools in the South.

William English Walling, Lillian Wald, Jane Addams and others founded the National Women's Trade Union League.

Fannie Garrison Villard opposed the reaction to Negroes in the North and objected to what she saw as a regression in abolitionist sentiment.

President Theodore Roosevelt appointed William D. Crum, a Negro, to be the collector of the port of Charleston, S.C.

An Arkansas Federal Court decision in U.S. v. MORRIS declared a law which discriminated against Negroes in housing unconstitutional.

Arkansas, South Carolina and Tennessee instituted Jim Crow streetcar laws.

Kentucky and Texas Democrats adopted the "white primary."

The U.S. acquired the Canal Zone, in Panama, which included many Negroes living in the area. Many more Negroes were brought from the Caribbean Islands to work on the Panama Canal.

A Negro real estate operator started developing Harlem for Negroes.

Countee Cullen (1903-1946), Negro poet, was born in New York City. The son of a minister, he was educated in New York City, earning a B.A. from New York University and Phi Beta Kappa in 1925, and an M.A. from Harvard in 1926. His poetry began to appear in the NAACP house organ, the *Crisis,* when Cullen was only 15. In 1923 his verse was published in white magazines and in 1928 he received a Guggenheim Fellowship. When Cullen began to write, he was influenced by Tennyson, Millay, Housman, Robinson and Keats. He was essentially a lyrical and emotional poet. *Color* was Cullen's first and best collection, published in 1925. Technically, Cullen's skill was not matched by any Negro poet. Much of his poetry dealt with Harlem Negro life, but Cullen never tried to exploit Negro themes. Included are many sonnets of protest and some poems like "The Shroud of Color" and "Heritage," about the poet's search for his identity and African roots, themes common to all writers of the Harlem Renaissance. "The Black Christ," published in 1929, was a long narrative poem about a lynching. Like most of his later poetry, it was devoid of the imagination and directness of his early lyrics.

Du Bois' collected short works were published under the title *Souls of Black Folk.* The book contained attacks against Booker T. Washington's ideas of work and money, his lack of emphasis on dignity and manhood, and his failure to oppose discrimination.

Paul Laurence Dunbar published a collection of prose entitled *Lyrics of Love and Laughter,* and a book of verse, *In Old Plantation Days.*

The Negro poet, Joseph S. Cotter, Sr., of Louisville, Ky., published the drama, *Caleb, the Degenerate.* It was concerned with the racial theories of Booker T. Washington.

Harry T. Burleigh, a Negro composer, wrote *Jean,* a popular hit on a distinctly white subject.

1904

Andrew Carnegie financed a meeting of Negro leaders, called for by Booker T. Washington. At the meeting the Committee of 12 for the Advancement of the Interests of the Negro Race was formed. Washington pledged his support for "absolute civil, political and public equality" which allowed Du Bois to join in good faith, but Du Bois soon withdrew, feeling that Washington was dictatorial in his control of the organization. The Committee of 12 failed to convince the Pullman Company to reject Jim Crow. It spent money discreetly to defeat disenfranchisement in Maryland by hiring lobbyists, etc. It also published a number of pamphlets on Negro self-help and economic achievement.

Negroes in Augusta, Atlanta, Columbia, New Orleans, Mobile and Houston had been boycotting street-cars to protest Jim Crow legislation. In this year Houston Negroes organized their own, short-lived, transportation network.

Kentucky passed a law establishing segregation in all schools in the state, public and private. Berea, an integrated college, challenged the law, but in BEREA COLLEGE V. THE COMMONWEALTH OF KENTUCKY, the Court of Appeals upheld the law.

A Negro shot and killed a white officer in Springfield, Ohio. A mob gathered and broke into the jail where the Negro was being held, murdered him, hung him to a telegraph pole and

riddled his body with bullets. Whites then began to destroy
the Negro section of town, beating and burning Negroes and
Negro-owned property. As a result of this riot, many Negroes
left Springfield, Ohio, and never returned.

In Statesboro, Ga., two Negroes were accused of murdering
a white farmer, his wife and three children. After two weeks
of "safekeeping" in Savannah, Ga., the Negroes were brought
back to Statesboro, for trial. They were convicted and sentenced to be hanged. Meanwhile, white citizens had worked
themselves into a frenzy of race hatred. Two Negro women
had been whipped for allegedly crowding two white girls off
the sidewalk. When the sentence was passed on the Negroes,
a mob forced its way into the jail, overpowering a company
of Savannah militia whose rifles were not loaded. The Negroes
were then dragged out of the courtroom and burned alive.
This was the signal for wholesale terrorism. One Negro was
whipped for riding his bicycle on the sidewalk, and another
"on general principles." The Negro mother of a 3-day old
infant was beaten and kicked, and her husband was killed.
Houses were wrecked, terrified Negroes left the county. Law
enforcement agencies never made an attempt to punish either
the mob or the mob leaders.

By this year the Negro had been disenfranchised in nearly
every Southern state. According to the Populist leader, Tom
Watson, he could still vote in Georgia because "they do not
dare to disenfranchise him, because the men who control the
Democratic machine in Georgia know that a majority of the
whites are against them. They need the Negro to beat us
with."

Mississippi and Maryland instituted Jim Crow streetcar
laws.

South Carolina segregated its ferries.

Charlotte Hawkins Brown began the Palmer Memorial
Institute in North Carolina. Its president, she also became a
prominent leader of the National Association of Colored
Women.

Ralph Bunche (1904-   ) was born in a Detroit slum. Both
his parents died when he was eleven, and he was raised by his
grandmother, an ex-slave. An athletic scholarship gave him
the means to attend the University of California, from which
he received his B.A. in 1927. He received his masters and his

Ph.D. from Harvard in 1928 and 1934, respectively. The years up to the outbreak of World War II were spent in post-graduate work at Northwestern University, the London School of Economics, and the University of Capetown, in teaching, primarily at Howard University, and in research. Bunche did extensive traveling in his researches on colonial administration and race relations. In 1941, he entered government service, first with the Joint Chiefs of Staff and then from 1942 to 1944 with the OSS. In July, 1945 Bunche became the first Negro to serve as a division head in the Department of State. This career was short-lived, however, for in 1946 Ralph Bunche was named director of the Trusteeship Division of the United Nations. He held this position until 1948, when he was made principal director. In 1955 he was appointed an Under Secretary of the UN, and in 1958 he was promoted again to Under Secretary of Special Political Affairs, the post he currently holds. Bunche has carried out a number of special missions for the UN. In 1948-49, he served as UN moderator on Palestine. For his efforts in bringing peace to that area, he was awarded the Nobel Peace Prize in 1950. In 1960, Bunche served as a special UN representative to the Congo, and in 1963 he was with the UN Mission to Yemen. Bunche was awarded in 1963 the Presidential Medal of Freedom.

William "Count" Basie (1904-   ), Negro band leader, was born in Red Bank, N.J. As a youth he was influenced by Harlem pianists James P. Johnson and Fats Waller. He spent his formative musical years in Kansas City, and it was there that he joined Bennie Moten's band. Upon Moten's death, he founded his own band. Basie's style laid the foundation for later developments such as bop and cool jazz. From Kansas City, Basie took his band to Chicago and then to New York in 1936. In 1937, Basie's band made its first recordings for Decca. Basie, along with Duke Ellington, has been the great mover of the big jazz band.

Charles Richard Drew (1904-1950), a Negro physician and founder of the Blood Bank, was born in Washington, D.C. He received a preliminary education at Dunbar High School, and graduated in 1906 from Amherst with highest honors. Drew attended McGill University Medical School in Mon-treal, where he won first prize in physiological anatomy, two fellowships in medicine and honors in athletics. He received his M.D. and Master of Surgery degrees in 1933. In 1935 he became an instructor of pathology at Howard University; he received a Rockefeller Fellowship in 1938 and used it for postgraduate work at Columbia Medical School, receiving a Doctor of Medical Science Degree in 1940. In 1941 Drew's report on the Blood Plasma Project in Britain guided the subsequent development on this project in the U.S. and Britain. That same year the American Red Cross set up blood banks, coordinated under his chairmanship. After the war Drew left his post at the Blood Bank project to become chairman of surgery at Howard Medical School. Up until his death in an auto accident, Drew wrote articles on hematology for medical journals. He was internationally recognized as one of the world's leading hematologists.

Booker T. Washington published "Cruelty in the Congo Country," in *Outlook,* expressing the hope that once the Congo was "reformed," Negro Americans could assume a constructive role in its development.

The Heart of Happy Hollow, a collection of prose, was published by Paul Laurence Dunbar.

William Stanley Braithwaite's poems, *Lyrics of Life and Love* were published.

James Madison Bell's collected poetical works were published.

Coleman Hawkins (1904-   ), Negro jazz musician, was born in St. Joseph, Mo. He began playing piano at age 5. In 1923 he made his first records with Fletcher Henderson, with whom he played for a decade. He was the first jazz musician to attain fame as a tenor saxophonist. In 1939 his recording of *Body and Soul* made him famous.

Thomas "Fats" Waller (1904-1943), Negro jazz musician, was born in New York City, where his father was a minister of the Abyssinian Baptist Church in Harlem. He received a sound classical music training as a boy, and by the age of 15 accompanied such blues singers as Bessie Smith. He was the first jazz musician to use the organ successfully as a jazz instrument. In the 1920's he played at theaters, night clubs and Harlem rent parties. In 1932 Waller toured Europe and won wide recognition. He also composed popular song hits, among the most successful of which are *Ain't Misbehavin'* and *Honeysuckle Rose.*

George C. Poag, of Milwaukee, Wisc., became the first American Negro Olympian. He was a hurdler who placed third in both the 200 meter and 400 meter races at the 1904 Olympics in St. Louis. Joseph Stadler, a Negro from Cleveland, Ohio, also competed in these games but did not place.

John B. Taylor, a Negro of the University of Pennsylvania, was intercollegiate champion in the 440-yard dash.

Between 1904 and 1906, Joe Walcott held the welterweight boxing title for the second time.

1905

W. E. B. Du Bois called a conference of Negro leaders in Niagara Falls, Canada. Their Declaration of Principles said: "We believe that Negroes should protest emphatically and continually against the curtailment of their political rights. We believe in manhood suffrage; we believe that no man is so good, intelligent or wealthy as to be entrusted wholly with the welfare of his neighbor." The group went on to demand equal economic opportunity, equal education, a fair administration of justice, and an end to segregation. For three years this group, incorporated as the "Niagara Movement," met and renewed their protests against injustice. By 1908 this group had won the respect and support of large numbers of Negroes, including the Equal Suffrage League, and the National Association of Colored Women's Clubs.

The Committee for Improving Industrial Conditions of Negroes in New York City, and the National League for Protection of Colored Women were formed in New York. These groups aimed at equality in economic and social spheres. The League for the Protection of Colored Women was founded by Mrs. William Baldwin Jr. and Frances Kellor. It had branches in New York, Philadelphia, Baltimore, and Norfolk, Va. It was biracial, with a Negro field secretary. The organization grew out of an investigation of the practices of New York employment agencies toward Negro girls newly arrived from the South and looking for work. The organization counseled, helped find housing and jobs for these new arrivals.

The Industrial Workers of the World (IWW) constitution provided that "no working man or woman shall be excluded from membership in unions because of creed or color."

Voice of the Negro, a respected Negro magazine, began to criticize Booker T. Washington's philosophy.

By this year Booker T. Washington's control of the Afro-American Council had weakened, and it gave up its support of a restrictive franchise.

Booker T. Washington served as vice-president of the Congo Reform Association. Robert E. Park was recording secretary, and G. Stanley Hall was president. Park was a sociologist and Hall was an educator.

28 Negro banks had been organized in the years from 1899 through 1905.

Ernest W. Lyon, American Minister to Liberia, a Negro, helped create the New York Liberian Steamship Line, in his continuing efforts to establish closer commercial relations between the U.S. and Liberia.

Through the influence of Booker T. Washington, Charles W. Anderson, a Negro politician, was appointed collector of internal revenue for the Wall Street district of New York City.

Anna T. Jeanes, daughter of a wealthy Philadelphia Quaker, gave $200,000 to the General Education Fund to help improve rural Negro schools in the South.

Florida instituted a Jim Crow streetcar law.

Georgia became the first state to segregate its public parks.

Frank Marshal Davis (1905-   ), Negro poet, was born in Arkansas City, Kan. He was graduated from Kansas State College with a degree in journalism. In 1931, Davis founded the *Atlanta Daily World* in Georgia, and remained editor until 1934 when he became feature editor of the *Associated Negro Press* in Chicago. In 1937, he was a Rosenwald Fellow in Poetry, and lecturer in Jazz history at the Lincoln School in Chicago. Three collections of his poetry have been published: *Black Man's Verse,* 1935; *I am the American Negro,* 1937; *47th Street,* 1948. Davis has mastered many poetic forms, and was one of the first to write poem ballads with jazz rhythm ("Four Glimpses of Night"). Some of his poetry is imitative ("Robert Whitmore" is an ironic epitaph in the manner of Edgar Masters), but most of it is very personal and honest.

Robert N. C. Nix (1905-   ), Negro Congressman, was

born in Orangeburg, S.C. He moved with his family to New York where he received his early education. A graduate of the University of Pennsylvania Law School, he worked as an advocate for Federal and state departments. In 1958 Nix was elected to Congress to fill the unexpired term of a Congressman from Philadelphia. He has been a consistent advocate for civil rights.

On May 5, the first issue of the weekly, *The Chicago Defender,* appeared.

George Edmund Haynes, a Negro graduate student at Columbia University, made an extensive study of social and economic conditions among Negroes in New York City, and published it in his book, *The Negro at Work in New York City.*

Charles Chesnutt published his final novel, *The Colonel's Dream.*

Paul Laurence Dunbar's *Lyrics of Sunshine and Shadow* was published.

Earl "Fatha" Hines (1905-   ), Negro jazz pianist, who developed the trumpet style of piano playing, was born in Duquesne, Pa. He studied piano while at Schenley High School in Pittsburgh, and worked at the local clubs. In 1927 he played with Louis Armstrong. Throughout the 1920's and 1930's, Hines often led his own band, and in the 1940's his orchestra included many of the early bop musicians—Gillespie, Parker, etc.

Ernest Hogan, a Negro vaudevillian and song writer, starred in *Rufus Rastus,* a musical for which he wrote the lyrics and collaborated on the music. In 1907, he starred in *Oyster Man.*

The first modern jazz band was heard on a New York stage, and probably any stage. Organized at The Marshall, it was known as the Memphis Students, a singing, playing, dancing orchestra which made use of banjos, mandolins, guitars, saxophones, drums, plus a violin and several brass instruments, and a double bass. Among the 20 performers were Ernest Hogan, comedian, Abbie Mitchell, soprano, and Ida Forsyne, dancer. The band became a hit; one of its innovations was the introduction of a dancing conductor, Will Dixon.

The earliest known American film with a Negro cast was a derogatory one-reeler, *The Wooing and Wedding of a Coon*.

The film *Fights of a Nation* was made with a little bit of insult for everyone. A Mexican was characterized as a treacherous greaser, a Jew as a briber, a Spaniard was a foppish lover, an Irishman as a quarrelsome drunkard, and a Negro as a razor-wielder with natural rhythm.

The Smart Set, a Negro athletic club, was started in Brooklyn, N.Y.

Bob Marshall, a Negro, was selected for the All-American football team. Marshall starred at the University of Minnesota.

1906

Another race riot erupted in Springfield, Ohio.

In Greensburg, Ind., when a Negro half-wit was convicted for criminally assaulting his employer, a white mob did not succeed in taking him from the authorities, but they did destroy property, beat Negroes and drive some from the city.

In August, in Brownsville, Texas, a Negro soldier of the 1st Battalion of the 25th Infantry, USCT, had an altercation with a white Brownsville merchant. For this Brownsville was put off limits for the Battalion. In protest, a dozen or more Negro soldiers entered the town, shooting wildly in the streets, killing one white man, wounding two others including the chief of police. Three companies finally became involved in the riot, and only the firm stand of the commander at Fort Brown kept the incident more or less under control. In November, on the basis of an inspector's report, claiming that Negroes had murdered and maimed citizens, and the refusal of the men involved to testify, President Roosevelt dishonorably discharged the three companies and disqualified them from future military or civil service. John Milholland, of the Constitution League, and Senators Tillman, S.C. and Foraker, Ohio spoke for the Negro soldiers. In December Senator Foraker insisted that a full and fair trial should have preceded such drastic punishment.

The biggest of the Southern race riots between 1900 and 1910 occurred in Atlanta, Ga. during the week of Sept. 24th. Days before the riot there was talk of disenfranchising Negroes. The press urged a revival of the Klan, and offered

rewards for a "lynching bee." On Saturday, Sept. 22, a newspaper reported four assaults on white women by Negroes.
Sunday was quiet, but on Monday rioting erupted in Brownsville, an Atlanta suburb. Negroes had heard that rioting had
begun in Atlanta, and that Negroes were being slaughtered.
They sought asylum in Negro institutions, Clark University
and Gammon Theological Seminary. Others collected arms for
defense. Law officers began arresting Negroes for the possession of arms, one officer shot into a crowd of Negroes. The
fire was returned, killing one officer and wounding another.
Whites then set out upon a general destruction of Negro life
and property. Four Negroes, all substantial citizens, were
killed, and many were injured. J. W. E. Bowen, president of
Gammon, was beaten over the head with a rifle butt by a
police officer. The houses of Negroes were looted and burned.
For several days the city was paralyzed, factories closed, all
transportation stopped. Numerous Negroes sold their property
and left. White citizens confessed shame and condemned the
rioters. A group of responsible Negro and white citizens came
together and organized the Atlanta Civic League to work for
improvement of social conditions and to prevent other riots.
No action, however, was brought against the rioters. As a
result of the Atlanta Riot, the Afro-American Council became more militant and less amenable to Booker T. Washington's direction. At the October convention they vigorously
condemned ballot restrictions, Jim Crow and mob violence.

The Niagara Meeting at Harpers Ferry published a manifesto written by W. E. B. Du Bois, protesting white actions
toward Negroes: "Stripped of verbose subterfuge, and in its
naked nastiness, the new American creed says: fear to let
black men even try to rise lest they become equals of the
white. And this in the land that professes to follow Jesus
Christ. The blasphemy of such a course is only matched by its
cowardice."

In Macon, Ga., several hundred Negroes met at a state
convention under the leadership of William Jefferson White,
and formed an Equal Rights Association, rejecting Booker T.
Washington's philosophy.

William H. Baldwin, president of the Long Island Railroad,
encouraged a group of Negroes and whites to investigate the
employment problems of the Negro. As the Committee for

Improving the Industrial Conditions of Negroes, they tried to find jobs without racial prejudice from employers or unions.

R. T. Sims, a Negro, became a national organizer for the IWW. He served the IWW until 1919, when he attempted to set up a Negro union organization.

By this year there were small Negro YMCA's in Washington, Philadelphia, New York and Baltimore.

To protest and fight against Jim Crow streetcar rules, Negroes in Austin, Nashville and Savannah, organized their own transportation companies. These companies were all short-lived.

A Montgomery, Ala., city ordinance went beyond the state Jim Crow law and insisted on separate streetcars for Negroes and whites.

Louisiana Democrats adopted the "white primary."

Josephine Baker (1906-   ), Negro entertainer, was born in St. Louis, Mo. At the age of 15 she ran away from home as Bessie Smith's maid. While traveling with the famous Negro blues singer, she quickly established herself as a singer in her own right. After several minor parts in Broadway shows, in 1925 she went to Paris as a member of the "Revue Nègre." A sensational success, she later starred at the Folies Bergère. During World War II, she sang to raise funds for war relief, and was a nurse with the Free French Forces. She retired in 1956, and lives in France.

Cabell "Cab" Calloway, (1907-   ), Negro musician and performer, was born in Rochester, N.Y., and raised in Baltimore. In 1928 he went to Chicago where he led the Alabamians, and in 1929 took this band to New York. His record of *Minnie the Moocher*, made in 1931, established Calloway as a novelty singer. He has also appeared in such movies as *Singing Kid, Stormy Weather* and *Sensations of 1945*. In 1952 he took the role of Sportin' Life in *Porgy and Bess*. Calloway has remained active both as a musical performer and in the theater.

Jay Saunders Redding (1906-   ), Negro writer, was born in Wilmington, Del., into a closely knit, religious, middle-class family. Both Redding's parents were Howard University graduates, and insisted that all their children attend college. Redding was on the staff of the *Brown Literary Quarterly* at

Brown University. His first story, "Delaware Coon," was published in Eugene Jola's avant garde *Transition* magazine in 1928. For the next 10 years Redding taught and attended graduate school at Brown and Columbia universities. In 1939, *To Make a Poet Black,* his first book, was published. In 1950, *They Came in Chains.* a general study of the Negro in the U.S., and *A Stranger Alone,* a biographical novel, were published. In 1952, *On Being a Negro in America,* a personal study of the effects of American racism on a Negro appeared. While working for the State Department in India, he wrote *An American in India,* a detailed analysis of India's people and government. In 1958, *The Lonesome Road,* his second novel, was published. Since 1943, he has been on the faculty of Hampton Institute as a professor of English.

J. Mord Allen, a Negro boilermaker and poet, had his collection of humorous dialect verse, *Rhymes, Tales and Rhymed,* published.

Bob Marshall, the University of Minnesota football star, was again selected for the All-American team.

1907

In CHILES V. C & O RAILROAD, the Supreme Court held that a railroad might enforce rules requiring interstate Negro passengers to occupy separate facilities, regardless of the statutes of any particular states the railroad passed through.

Oklahoma adopted Jim Crow streetcar and railroad laws, and only whites were allowed to vote in the Democratic primaries.

Under pressure from Legislators on Jan. 15, President Roosevelt revoked the civil disability of the Brownsville, Texas, soldiers. After several months of study, the majority of the Senate Committee upheld the President's contention as to the guilt of the accused soldiers. A stinging minority report, however, was written by Senator Foraker (Ohio), denouncing the findings of the majority.

The Niagara Movement met in Boston, supported by the New England Suffrage League, and the Equal Rights League of Georgia.

William Lloyd Garrison, II, wrote that there had never been an affirmative majority for the abolition of slavery in the North except for the brief period when the Emancipation

Proclamation was signed, and that Northerners had simply been more subtle in their opposition to Negroes.

The National Business League, a Negro organization, had 320 branches.

Because of the contributions of philanthropists, and the cooperation of the Southern Boards of Education, farm demonstration agents had helped to improve rural conditions.

Anna T. Jeanes gave an additional million dollars to the General Education Board for rural Negro schools in the South.

Augustus F. Hawkins (1907-   ), Negro Congressman, was born in Shreveport, La., and raised in California. A graduate of the University of Southern California, he was elected to the State Assembly in 1934. Before his election to the House of Representatives in 1962, he worked for civil rights, health, welfare, housing and labor legislation.

Robert Weaver (1907-   ), the first Negro Cabinet member, was born in Washington, D.C. He abandoned a career as an electrician because of union discrimination. He received a Ph.D. in economics from Harvard University, and became an aide to the Secretary of the Interior in 1933. In 1934, Weaver became an adviser to the PWA Housing Division, and in 1938 a Special Assistant to the Administrator of the U.S. Housing Authority. During World War II, he directed the Negro Employment and Training Branch of the Labor Division of the War Production Board and of the Negro Manpower Commission. From 1944 to 1955, Weaver worked as a visiting lecturer, was professor of economics at the New School for Social Research in New York City, and directed the fellowship programs of the John Hay Whitney Foundation and the Julius Rosenwald Fund. In 1955, he became Rent Commissioner of New York. He headed the Federal Housing and Home Finance Agency in 1961, and in 1966 was named to the Cabinet at the first director of the Department of Housing and Urban Development. Weaver has written four books: *Negro Labor: a National Problem,* 1946; *The Negro Ghetto,* 1948; *The Urban Complex,* 1964; *Dilemmas in Urban Development,* 1965.

John B. Taylor, of the University of Pennsylvania, was intercollegiate champion in the 440-yard dash for the second time.

Cuba's Negro population was 274,272, or 13.4% of the total population.

1908

On Aug. 14 and 15, a riot in Springfield, Ill., became so violent that the governor called in 4,200 militia men. The riot started when the wife of a streecar conductor claimed she had been raped by a Negro, George Richardson, who had been working in the neighborhood. Before a special grand jury the woman admitted that she had been beaten by a white man whose identity she refused to disclose, and that Richardson had no connection with the incident. But feelings were high against Richardson, and officials took him and another Negro accused of murder to a nearby town. A mob wrecked the automobile of the owner of a restaurant whose car had been used to move the Negroes, and began to surge through the town. City officials made several unsuccessful attempts to disperse the mob, and then the governor called out the militia. More than 2,000 Negroes left the city, and hundreds fled to the militia camps as the mob began to destroy Negro homes. It burned a barber shop, lynched the barber and dragged his body through the streets. The next night, Aug. 15, an 84-year-old Negro who had been married to a white woman for more than 30 years, was lynched. Order was restored only after the militia patrolled the streets. A total of 2 Negroes were lynched, 6 killed, and over 70 Negroes and whites wounded. 100 arrests were made, with 50 indictments. The alleged leaders of the riot escaped punishment, and the community engaged in a political and economic boycott to drive out the remaining Negro residents.

Oswald Garrison Villard spoke out editorially in his newspaper, *The New York Evening Post,* against the Springfield race riots. William English Walling, a white reformer and writer, in an article, "Race War in the North" which appeared in the liberal periodical, *The Independent,* condemned the Springfield riot and those who contributed to it by inflaming race hatred and not opposing it. Walling urged Negroes first to seek protection from proper authorities when attacked, and then to defend themselves and resist to the extent that rioters would think twice before coming again. The article called for a group of citizens to stop the spread of racism that dominated the Springfield riots and threatened the entire

North, and eventually political democracy itself. Led by Walling's close friend, Charles Edward Russell, the Liberal Club in New York City responded enthusiastically to Walling's proposals to establish a bi-racial organization for this purpose. Oswald Garrison Villard wanted to name the organization "The Committee for the Advancement of the Human Race."

The Niagara Movement had its last meeting in Oberlin, Ohio.

The Anna T. Jeanes Fund inaugurated the Jeanes Teacher Program, to improve the quality of instruction in Negro rural schools.

At Howard University the first Negro sorority, Alpha Kappa Alpha, was organized.

Because of Theodore Roosevelt's actions in the Browns-ville, Tex., incident, and encouraged by the big city Democratic machines in the North, a large number of Negroes gave their support to the Democratic Party. Booker T. Washington and his circle became exceptional in their support for the Republicans.

The U.S. Supreme Court upheld the Kentucky Court of Appeals' decision in BEREA V. THE COMMONWEALTH, that seggregation of all schools was constitutional. The opinion reflected the Court's attitude that segregation was a matter best left to the states.

Georgia added a "grandfather clause" amendment to its State Constitution. Like the Alabama clause of 1901, however, the amendment enfranchised descendants of veterans.

Ida B. Wells Barnett, an anti-lynching and civil rights crusader, became the first president of the Negro Fellowship League.

Thurgood Marshall (1908-   ), Negro Justice of the Supreme Court, was born in Baltimore, Md. He received his B.A. from Lincoln University and his law degree from Howard University in 1933, graduating first in his class. From 1936 through 1961, he served the NAACP as special counsel and as director of its Legal Defense and Education Fund. Marshall argued the famous cases that led to the 1954 Supreme Court school desegregation rulings. In 1961, President Kennedy appointed Marshall to a U.S. Circuit Court judgeship. In 1965, he was made U.S. Solicitor General, and

1967 he became the first Negro Justice of the U.S. Supreme Court.

Frederick O'Neal (1908-   ); Negro actor, born in Brook-ville, Miss., was first active in local productions of the Urban League. After working in St. Louis to found a Negro acting group, the Ira Aldridge Players, he acted in its productions until 1937, when he went to New York. Organizer and direc-tor of the New York American Negro Theater, he also starred in the play *Anna Lucasta* and other Broadway productions. He won the Drama Critics Award for best supporting actor in 1945, appeared in several movies and has acted on television.

Adam Clayton Powell Jr. (1908-   ), Negro Congressman, the son of a famous Negro minister, was born in New Haven, Conn. He received a B.A. from Colgate in 1930, an M.A. from Columbia in 1932, and his D.D. (honorary) from Shaw University in 1935. Powell was a major civil rights activist in Depression Harlem. In 1930 he organized a campaign for Negro jobs and was successful in integrating the staff of Harlem Hospital. He persuaded many Harlem businesses to hire Negroes, and campaigned against the city bus lines that refused to hire Negroes. He also directed a relief center that dispensed food, fuel and clothing to needy Negroes. In 1939, as chairman of the Coordinating Committee on Employment, he led a demonstration campaign that succeeded in forcing the World's Fair to hire Negroes. Meanwhile, Powell had succeeded his father as pastor of the Abyssinian Baptist Church in 1937, a post he holds today. In 1941, Powell was elected to the New York City Council, and in 1945 to the House of Representatives. In the House, Powell quickly be-came noted as a civil rights leader. He personally desegre-gated many Congressional facilities, Washington restaurants and theaters. He was the first to propose legislation to the effect that Federal funds should not be given to any project in which there was discrimination. He was the first man to introduce legislation to desegregate the armed forces, and he established the right of Negro journalists to sit in the House and Senate press galleries. Made chairman of the House Com-mittee on Education and Labor in 1960, the Powell Commit-tee helped pass 48 pieces of social welfare legislation, earning him a letter of gratitude from President Johnson. In 1967, however, Powell's House colleagues raised charges of corruption and financial mismanagement against him. In January he was stripped of his chairmanship and barred from the House, pending an investigation. On March 1, 1967, Powell was denied a seat in the House by a vote of 307 to 116, despite the committee's recommendation that he only be censured, fined and placed at the bottom of the seniority list. On April 11 a special election was held to fill Powell's seat. Powell, who was not campaigning and was on the Island of Bimini and who could not even come to New York City because of a court judgment against him in a defamation case, received 74% of the Harlem vote cast.

Josh White, (1908-   ), Negro folksinger and composer, was born in Greenville, S.C. He began his career as the Singing Christian, a gospel singer. After a brief career as Pinewood Tom, he decided to use his real name. He has given concerts all over the world, made numerous records, appeared on Broadway, and starred in the CBS TV series *Back Where I Came From.*

Richard Wright (1908-1960) was born in Natchez, Miss., on a plantation. When his father deserted the family, his mother took care of them until Wright was in his early 20's. He then moved to Chicago, did manual jobs and joined the Communist Party. In 1937, the "Ethics of Living Jim Crow" was published in a WPA anthology, *American Stuff.* It was an autobiographical series of sketches in which the author described how the Negro learned to play his role in the Southern Jim Crow system. *Uncle Tom's Children,* published in 1938, as a collection of four novellas, was Wright's first book. All the stories dealt with race friction in the South, and the book was hailed by Alain Locke as the "strongest note yet struck by one of our writers in the staccato protest realism of the rising school of proletarian fiction." The four novellas are a tetraptych of protest against Southern lynch law and the Negroes' plight. Wright was dissatisfied at the sympathetic reception and the emphasis on the author's compassion shown by *Uncle Tom's* reviewers. *Native Son,* Wright's most probing work into the plight of the lower-class urban Negro was published in 1940. Like Dreiser in *An American Tragedy,* Wright focused on a murderer and expanded to an indictment of the capitalist system which created him. Bigger Thomas had much less freedom of choice than Dreiser's protagonist, and was almost totally conditioned by his environment. *Native Son* was Wright's greatest achievement, and perhaps the best novel written by a Negro up to that time. Its influence upon subsequent Negro novelists was immeasurable. In the context of American fiction, Wright belongs with the school of Chicago naturalists which began at the turn of the century with Dreiser and Frank Norris. Wright also wrote *The Outsider* in 1953; *Black Power,* 1954; *The Colored Curtain,* 1956; *The Long Dream,* 1958, and *Lawd Today,* 1963.

The House of Falling Leaves, a second collection of verse by William Stanley Braithwaite, was published.

Freddie Keppard, of African and French ancestry, and the Original Creoles, a Negro band, played jazz in New Orleans. Keppard took his Original Creole Band to Chicago and New York in 1913, to Los Angeles in 1914, and to Coney Island in 1915. In 1917 he had a recording offer from Victor Phonograph Co., but he turned it down because he was afraid other bands would steal his "stuff." The honor of being the first jazz band to record thus went to the all-white Original Dixieland Jass Band.

John B. Taylor of the University of Pennsylvania was intercollegiate champion in the 440-yard dash for the third time. He led the American Olympic team at the London Olympics, and won first place in the 1600 meter relay.

Jack Johnson knocked out Tommy Burns for the heavyweight championship of the world.

2. The Genesis of the NAACP

Significant for the political history of 20th century America is that the labor movement, and this includes especially the Socialists and the Communists, avoided in reality to identify with the struggle of the Negro for equality—in obvious contrast to the genesis of the Republican party which developed out of the Abolitionist movements of the 1820's and 1830's.

Only certain individuals among the Liberals and Socialists, not as political groups, activated the Negro defence by creating the NAACP. In this period, the most important Negro personality was Dr. W. E. B. Du Bois; in 1903, he made the famous statement: "The problem of the 20th century is the color line."

1909

In response to the Springfield, Ill. riots which occurred a year before, William Walling, a wealthy Southerner and Socialist settlement worker, author of the article, *Race War in the North;* Mary White Ovington, a Socialist humanitarian who had worked among New York City Negroes, and Dr. Henry Moskowitz, a social worker, met and decided to launch a campaign to help the Negro. Oswald Garrison Villard joined the group and on Feb. 12 wrote their call for a conference: "We call upon all believers in democracy to join in a national conference for the discussion of present evils, the voicing of protests and the renewal of the struggle for civil and political liberty." The group was expanded and made biracial when Lillian Wald, Florence Kelly (founders of the National Women's Trade Union League), Bishop Alexander Walter of the AMEZ Episcopal Methodist Church, and William Henry Brooks of St. Marks Methodist Episcopal Church were invited to join. Between May 31 and June 1, the National Negro Conference met in New York City. Members of the Niagara Movement attended. However, Monroe Trotter, suspicious of the aims of the whites, refused an invitation. In addition to the original group, some other participants in the conference were Jane Addams, William Dean Howells, Livingston Farrand, John Dewey, John Milholland, W. E. B. Du Bois, and Oswald Garrison Villard. The members decided to incorporate as a National Committee for the Advancement of the Negro Race. Before final incorporation, the name was changed to the National Association for the Advancement of Colored People (NAACP). They demanded equal civil, political, and educational rights, an end to segre-

357

gation, the right to work, the right to protection from violence and intimidation, and criticized the nonenforcement of the 14th and 15th Amendments. A permanent committee of 40 was established to administer the affairs of the organization.

Senator Foraker of Ohio succeeded in forcing through a bill which established a court of inquiry to pass on the cases of the discharged Brownsville, Tex., soldiers. It provided that all the discharged soldiers who were qualified for re-enlistment were to be deemed eligible. Any such soldier was to receive the "pay, allowances and other rights and benefits that he would have been entitled to receive according to his rank from said date of discharge, as if he had been honorably discharged . . . and had re-enlisted immediately."

Moorfield Storey stated that the Negro's condition would be improved only if the South were broken up and the 15th Amendment enforced. He felt that the rights of the Negro would have to be protected by public opinion in other parts of the country.

Only once in its history has the Supreme Court invoked its contempt power. In this year it cited the sheriff of Chatanooga, Tenn., for having allowed a lynch mob to hang a Negro who had been granted a stay of execution pending an appeal. But there is no record of any punishment.

The U.S. Supreme Court upheld the murder conviction of Marcellus Thomas, of Harris County, Texas, but stated that "it may be that the jury commissioners did not give the Negro race full *pro rata* with the white race in the selection of the . . . jurors of this case."

Mobile, Ala., instituted curfew laws applying only to Negroes.

Pres. Charles W. Eliot of Harvard denounced any mixture of racial stocks, and supported the South's demand for complete separation of the races.

Thomas Wentworth Higgins, a former abolitionist, stated it was a mistake to give suffrage to Negroes as a class; that no white community would permit supremacy of colored races.

Matthew Henson, a Negro, went with Admiral Peary's expedition to the North Pole and placed the U.S. flag at the Pole.

Nann Helen Burroughs, educator and later an active member of the National Association of Colored Women and the NAACP, became the first president of the National Training School for Women and Girls.

Lester Young (1909-1959), Negro tenor saxophonist, was perhaps the single most important transitional figure in the development of bop, the significant jazz form of the 1940's and 1950's. Young played several instruments, especially tenor saxophone, with his family on the carnival circuit in the Midwest. He appeared with Fletcher Henderson's band, with Andy Kirk in Kansas City, and from 1936 through 1940 with Count Basie.

Booker T. Washington's *Story of the Negro* was published.

Sigmund Lubin began production on two separate series of short comedy films featuring Negroes named Sambo and Rastus. They had all-Negro casts, and bore such titles as *Rastus in Zululand* and *Rastus Got His Turkey*. This series depicted Negroes as obedient, childlike characters, who were always in and out of ridiculous situations. They were Lubin's greatest financial successes.

Jean Brierre (1909-   ), Negro poet, was born in Jérémie, Haiti. After finishing school in Haiti, he went to the Sorbonne and Columbia for his university education. During the 1940's he held two prominent positions in Haiti, as secretary-general of the Union of Haitian writers and Artists, and as Director of Cultural Affairs in the Department of Foreign Affairs. His books of verse include: *Le Petit Soldat,* 1933; *L'Adieu à la Marseillaise,* a free verse drama in tableau form on the life of Toussaint l'Ouverture, 1939; *Nous Garderons le Dieu*, poems written in memory of a fellow Haitian poet, Jacques Romain, 1945. In 1947, *Black Soul,* a long epic poem was published. He also edited *Province,* an anthology of Haitian verse in three volumes.

1910

U.S. Census: There were 9,827,763 Negroes in the U.S., 10.7% of the population. Of the Negroes 20% were classified as of "mixed blood."

The life expectancy for Negro males was 34 years; for Negro females, 38 years.

89% of the Negro population of the U.S. lived in the South.

25% of the Negroes lived in cities, 60.4% of these in the central city. Washington, D.C., had the largest number of Negroes, with 94,000 residents. New York City's 92,000 Negroes represented 1.9% of the population. Negroes accounted for 52.8% of the Charleston, S.C., population. The Negro population in Chicago jumped 148% from 44,000 to 109,000 in the years between 1910 and 1920. The increase of whites in Chicago for the same period was only 21%.

Of the Negro population 50.4% worked in farm occupations; 49.6% were engaged in nonagricultural activities.

Negroes owned 218,972 farms, up from 120,738 in 1890. The average size of Negro farms was less than 10 acres.

There were 350,000 Negro factory workers.

Only 2.5% of employed Southern Negroes and 3% of employed Northern Negroes were in the professions, including many ministers and teachers without high school or college educations.

Between 1910 and 1920, 11 Negroes served in the diplomatic and consular corps, including a Minister to Haiti and the Ambassador to Liberia.

The Capital Savings Bank of Washington, D.C., the first Negro bank owned by the Grand Fountain of the United Order of True Reformers, failed. This led to the dissolution of the Grand Fountain Society in 1911.

By 1910, in most of the Southern states, at least twice as much was spent per pupil on whites as on Negroes.

By this year there were 100 colleges for Negroes, most of which admitted women.

As a result of Abraham Flexner's critical study of medical education in the U.S., 3 Negro medical schools were discontinued. Flexner's criticism was that these schools did not have the staffs or the resources to provide proper medical education.

There were 35,000 Negro American churches with 3½ million members.

In May, despite factional disputes, a refusal of support from Booker T. Washington, lack of funds, and resignations, the formal organization of the NAACP was completed, primarily through the efforts of Oswald Garrison Villard. Moorfield

Storey of Boston was elected president, William English Walling chairman of the executive committee, Francis Blascoer national secretary, Oswald Garrison Villard assistant treasurer, and W. E. B. Du Bois, the only Negro officer, director of publicity and research, and editor of *Crisis*. A national committee of 100 and an executive committee of 30 from its members were planned. The presence of W. E. B. Du Bois on the staff branded the organization as radical from the beginning. Many feared that it would be an irresponsible organization that would draw its main inspiration from the Niagara Movement. It was denounced by many white philanthropists, and even some Negroes thought it unwise. In November, Joel Spingarn was elected to the executive committee. His brother Arthur, a lawyer, joined the New York branch when it was organized in January, 1911. The first local branch of the NAACP was established at Chicago. By 1912, nine branches had been established. The number of branches doubled in the years 1913 and 1914. Oswald Garrison Villard helped cover the expenses of the fledgling organization with rental fees from the New York Evening Post building. Voluntary contributions and membership fees were the principal sources of income. The NAACP's first program advocated the widening of industrial opportunities for Negroes, sought greater police protection for Negroes in the South, and crusaded against lynching and lawlessness. It planned to hire lawyers to contest prejudicial laws. Between 1910 and 1914, the NAACP publicized lynchings stories.

Rev. John Haynes Holmes and Rabbi Stephen Wise drew attention to lynchings in the South by constant sermons and public speeches.

Residential segregation ordinances appeared in a number of Southern and border states. In Baltimore, the NAACP had the first of these residential restrictions declared unconstitutional. However, the city enacted two others, the last of which was considered in the Louisville, Ky., segregation case of BUCHANAN v. WARLEY, in 1917.

In his efforts to help Pink Franklin, a Southern Negro sharecropper, who had been convicted of murder, Oswald Garrison Villard became convinced of the need for a legal redress committee for the NAACP. One of the NAACP's first legal cases involved the arrest of an Asbury Park, N.J., Negro for murder. The Negro had been given the third degree. There was no evidence against him, and an NAACP lawyer secured his release. A similar case occurred later in Lakewood, N.J., and the NAACP lawyer again secured release.

In November, the first edition of the *Crisis* appeared; 1,000 copies were printed. By 1918, circulation had increased to 100,000.

W. E. B. Du Bois, in an article in the *Crisis,* held that a person should have the right to choose his spouse regardless of race, but for the present, widespread intermarriage would be a social calamity.

The NAACP sent Du Bois to the International Congress of Races in London, partly to represent the NAACP, and partly to counteract Booker T. Washington, who was touring England giving lectures. It had been reported in the U.S. that Washington was telling English audiences that Negroes in America were making strides toward full citizenship. In his speeches before the Congress in London, Du Bois made it clear that Negroes were suffering under grave legal and civil disabilities, and that only by a fierce struggle would they overcome them. Du Bois circulated a statement in London criticizing and contradicting Washington. He accused Washington of misrepresenting the truth of his dependency on certain powerful interests for philanthropy.

Booker T. Washington's secretary, Emmett S. Scott, went to Liberia as Washington's choice for a Negro member of the 3-man commission appointed by the President of the U.S. to make recommendations concerning the financial plight of the country and threats to its sovereignty. Washington felt that Liberia was a testing ground for the Negro's ability to handle his own affairs. He believed that the country's history proved his point that political power without a firm economic base and a body of skilled artisans was detrimental to group welfare. He urged the American Government to aid Liberia, and at one time felt so strongly about the matter that he considered accepting a post as Liberian chargé d'affaires in the U.S.

The Farmers Improvement Society of Texas was founded. Inspired in part by the trend toward self-help and racial solidarity, and in part by the white agrarian organizations then at their peak, the society first improved the homes of village and rural Negroes in the Oakland, Tex., area, and then branched out into improving farming methods, paying illness and death benefits, and providing cooperative buying and selling. The movement spread all through Texas and into Oklahoma and Arkansas. It had 21,000 members, a cooperative business of $50,000 per year, and subsidiary institutions such as an agricultural college and a bank.

Julius Rosenwald, in his initial contribution to the YMCA movement among Negroes, gave $25,000 toward the erection of the Wabash Ave. building in Chicago. In succeeding years his gifts for 13 buildings amounted to $325,000.

In this year over one-third of Boston Negroes voted for the Boston Democratic gubernatorial candidate.

Oklahoma added a "grandfather clause" amendment to its State Constitution.

Bayard Rustin, (1910–   ), Negro leader, joined the Young Communist League (YCL) in 1936. Sent by the YCL to New York as an organizer, Rustin attended CCNY. In 1941, he left YCL to join the Fellowship of Reconciliation. In 1942 he went to California to help protect the property of Japanese-Americans who had been interned. In 1943, he was imprisoned for 2½ years for refusing to serve in the Army. Upon his release he became chairman of the Free India Committee, and was jailed several times for sitting in at the British Embassy. In 1948, in recognition of his efforts, the Congress Party of India invited Rustin to India, where he stayed for 6 months. Meanwhile, in 1947, he had helped organize the first Freedom Ride in North Carolina. Arrested and put on a chain gang, his subsequent exposé of chain-gang life led to its abolition in North Carolina. He also directed A. Philip Randolph's Committee Against Discrimination in the Armed Forces which saw President Truman desegregate the Army in 1948. He served as Race Relations Secretary for the Fellowship of Reconciliation and helped to organize the Congress of Racial Equality. During the Montgomery Boycott in 1955–56, Martin Luther King asked Rustin to help with organization. Rustin drew up the initial plans for the Southern Christian Leadership Conference, and served King as a special assistant for 7 years. Rustin also continued his pacifist activities, serving as executive secretary of the War Resister's League (1953–64), organizing the first London Ban-the-Bomb

March in 1959, and in 1960 protesting French atomic explosions. He was chief organizer of the 1963 March on Washington, director of the first New York City school boycott on Feb. 3, 1964, and since 1964, executive director of the A. Philip Randolph Institute.

James Morris Webb's *The Black Man, the Father of Civilization* was published.

With the decline of Negro minstrelsy and the accompanying revival of "black peril" hysteria, the Negro could perform only in Harlem. During the decade 1910–1920, Ed Hunter's Crescent Theater on 135th Street and the Lafayette were the leading Negro theaters in Harlem. They featured all-Negro musicals, Negro versions of Broadway hits and revivals of standard classics from the European theater.

Art Tatum (1910-   ), Negro jazz musician, was born in Toledo, Ohio. As a child he studied violin and piano. He began playing professionally on radio station WSPD in Toledo. In 1932 he came to New York as a pianist for Adelaide Hall. Tatum's piano technique and harmonic variations distinguish his playing. In 1943 he formed with Tiny Grimes on guitar and Slam Stewart on bass what was to become one of the great jazz trios.

"Mother" Seames, a legendary figure in Negro tennis, had her own tennis courts in Chicago where she taught the game to Negroes.

The Louisville Cubs, an all-Negro team, was considered the best Southern baseball team.

Jack Johnson defeated James Jeffries for the heavyweight boxing championship of the world.

The film of the Jack Johnson–Jim Jeffries heavyweight championship bout created an interstate edict against fight films, and may have convinced film producers to keep Negroes out of movies.

1911

The National Urban League was founded. It combined: the Committee on Urban Conditions Among Negroes, founded in 1910 by George Haynes and Mrs. William Baldwin Jr.; The National League for the Protection of Colored Women, organized by Mrs. Baldwin and Frances A. Kellor

in 1905; and the Committee on Industrial Conditions of
Negroes in New York, founded in 1906 by John Scottron,
Fred Moore, Eugene Roberts, William Bulkley, Abraham Lef-
kowitz and William Schieffelin. George Edmund Haynes
and Eugene K. Jones served as the first executive officers of
the Urban League. It received support from Julius Rosenwald, Mrs. William H. Baldwin, Booker T. Washington, Kelly
Miller, Roger N. Baldwin, Robert R. Moton, and L. Hollings-
worth Wood. The Urban League tried to open new opportunities for Negroes in industry and to assist newly arrived
Negroes in their problems of adjustment in urban centers.
Branches were opened in many large cities to meet migrants,
direct them to jobs and lodgings, and to offer information on
how to live in the city. The league developed a program for
training young men and women for social work, established
fellowships to support students at the School of Philanthropy
in New York, and established part fellowships to make possible in-service training at the league's national office in preparation for field work. In the 1920's and 1930's, the league
sponsored publicity to convince businessmen to hire Negroes.

Booker T. Washington was severely beaten in New York
City for allegedly approaching a white woman. This incident
caused both radical and conservative Negro leaders to rush
to the defense of Washington, and for a while, because of this
incident, tension was reduced between these groups.

W. E. B. Du Bois joined the Socialist Party.

In BAILEY V. ALABAMA, the Supreme Court declared peonage unconstitutional.

The John F. Slater Fund, administered largely by J. L. M.
Curry, began its support of county training schools, and within
a decade more than 100 such institutions had been assisted.

Jane Edna Hunter organized the Working Girls' Home
Association (Phillis Wheatley Association) in Cleveland to
assist Negro women in finding employment.

The Phelps-Stokes Fund was established by the will of
Caroline Phelps-Stokes for the "education of Negroes, both
in Africa and the U.S., and of North American Indians and
of needy and deserving white students." Its most notable work
was done in Africa and Afro-American education. The
Phelps-Stokes Fund established the Booker T. Washington In-

stitute in Liberia in 1929. The fund brought several Africans to the U.S. each year to study. In 1942, the fund sponsored a conference to discuss the implications of the Atlantic Charter to Africa, and published the report of that conference as *The Atlantic Charter and Africa from an American Standpoint.* In 1958, the fund sponsored the research and publication of bibliography of the Negro in Africa and America, by Monroe Work. One of the fund's major projects was the sponsoring of an encyclopedia of the Negro, under the directorship of W. E. B. Du Bois in the late 1930's. In 1946, after 35 years of activity, only four members of the 18-man board of trustees were Negroes.

A story of a Negro lynching appeared in the papers on an average of every 6 days in 1911.

A racist supremacy controversy raged over the scheduling of the Jack Johnson and Bombardier Wells heavyweight championship fight in London. This fight was to prove the racial superiority issue once and for all. A protest, headed by Rev. F. B. Meyer, honorary secretary of the National Free Church Council, succeeded in having the fight called off because of the tensions generated.

Franz Boas, professor of anthropology at Columbia University, in his most influential work, *The Mind of Primitive Man,* authoritatively denied inherent superiority of any race.

Mahalia Jackson (1911–   ), Negro singer, was born in New Orleans. Her father was a minister, and she became acquainted with gospel songs at an early age. She began recording in 1934, and achieved national prominence in 1945 with *Move On Up a Little Higher.* Since 1950, she has given numerous concerts, made many well-known record albums, and is considered one of the world's greatest gospel singers.

The Negro Society for Historical Research began.

W. E. B. Du Bois published *The Quest of the Silver Fleece* in Chicago. In this novel, Du Bois correlated the cotton industry with structural racism. This was the first Negro work to expostulate the economic causes of the caste system. It was inspired by the muckracking classics of Sinclair, and especially Frank Norris' studies of the Midwestern wheat and railroad monopolies.

Claude McKay published his first book, *Songs of Jamaica.*

Sigmund Lubin produced *For Massa's Sake,* which told of a slave who sold himself to free his kind master of debt. The The Uncle Tom stereotype was quite popular in early films.

In Jamaica, Marcus Garvey began the Universal Negro Improvement Association. Its avowed purposes were: (1) to promote unity among all Negroes regardless of nationality; (2) to improve their living conditions; (3) to found independent Negro states and communities in Africa; (4) to found Negro businesses and commercial enterprises.

David Roy Eldridge (1911-   ), Negro jazz trumpeter, was born in Pittsburgh, Pa. As a child he learned to play drums and trumpet. He appeared with Horace Henderson in 1926. Later he played with Speed Webb, Jack Whyte, Elmer Snowden and other bands. In 1933 he organized his own band, besides playing with Teddy Hill's and Fletcher Henderson's bands. In the 1940's he played with Gene Krupa, Artie Shaw and the Benny Goodman Sextet. Eldridge is ranked as one of the most influential and important jazz instrumentalists.

1912

A housing segregation law was passed in Louisville, Ky. The law provided that city blocks with a majority of Negroes were designated as black blocks, and those with a majority of whites as white blocks. Negroes were not allowed to move into white blocks, and vice versa. Baltimore, Richmond, and Atlanta followed Louisville's lead, and Negro ghettos sanctioned by law, became well established in many parts of the country.

There were three Presidential candidates: Woodrow Wilson, a Democrat, born in the South, would make only the vaguest concessions to Negroes. William Howard Taft had thoroughly alienated Negroes. Theodore Roosevelt, while appealing to Negro voters in the North, had refused to seat Negro delegates from the South at the Progressive Party Convention. Roosevelt had also allowed Southern whites to exclude the NAACP's platform amendment calling for the repeal of unfair discriminatory laws and the complete enfranchisement of Negroes. W. E. B. Du Bois withdrew from the Progressive Party to support Woodrow Wilson. Du Bois' rationalization for supporting Wilson was that while Wilson was a Virginian, and was long president of a college which did not admit Negro students, Wilson was a cultivated scholar and therefore Du Bois felt that Wilson would treat the Negro and his interests with farsighted fairness. He wrote: "Wilson will not be our friend, but he will not belong to the gang of which Tillman, Vardaman, Hoke Smith and Blease are the brilliant expositors. He will not advance the cause of an oligarchy in the South. He will not seek further means of Jim Crow insult, he will not dismiss black men who'esale from office, and he will remember that the Negro . . . has a right to be heard and considered, and if he becomes President, by the grace of the black man's vote, his Democratic successors may be more willing to pay the black man's price of decent travel, free labor, votes and education." Wilson also gained the support of the NAACP, the National Independent League and the Colored National Democratic League.

In his first formal statements on Negroes, Wilson said that he wished to see "justice done to the colored people in every matter; and not mere grudging justice, but justice with liberality and cordial good feeling." Wilson further stated: "I want to assure them [the Negroes] that should I become President of the U.S., they may count on me for absolute fair dealing, for everything by which I could assist in advancing the interests of their race in the U.S."

Upon winning the Presidential election, Wilson's first Congress sent to the Administration the greatest flood of bills proposing discriminatory legislation against Negroes that had ever been introduced into an American Congress. Bills advocated segregation on public carriers in Washington, D.C.; the exclusion of Negroes from Army and Navy commissions; separate accommodations for Negro and white federal employees, and the exclusion of all Negro immigration.

Only the following unions in the AFL had a significant number of Negro members by this year: United Mine Workers, 40,000; Teamsters, 6,000; Cigar Makers, 5,000; Hotel and Restaurant Employees, 2,500; Carpenters, 2,500; Painters, 250.

The Southern District of the Forest and Lumber Workers Union of the IWW met in Convention in Louisiana. About half the 35,000 members were Negro, but there were no Negroes at the convention. Bill Haywood, who was attending, asked why, and was told that integrated assemblies were contrary to Louisiana law. "If it's against the law, the law should be broken," Haywood responded, and the convention was integrated.

The NAACP had 11 branches with a total of 1,100 members. At the first meeting of the formally incorporated NAACP in January, Oswald Garrison Villard was chosen chairman of the board of directors.

In New York, the NAACP desegregated New York theaters, and in New Jersey Palisades Amusement Park.

J. W. E. Bowen, in 1912, asked for Negro bishops in the Methodist Church "because the true elevation of a race to a higher level would have to come from within."

The International Conference on the Negro met at Tuskegee.

Julius Rosenwald, was appointed to the Board of trustees of Tuskegee Institute.

Carl Van Vechten, a white music critic, novelist, photographer and art patron, was one of the most important figures in Mabel Dodge's literary and intellectual salon. He was the first to establish a link between the Harlem Renaissance and the Greenwich Village artistic movements. Van Vechten had convinced the rather unwilling Mabel Dodge to permit Negroes to attend one of her famous artists soirées.

Willard Motley (1912-1965), Negro author, was born of a middle-class family in Chicago. After high school, he spent the 1930's as a transcontinental drifter and odd-jobs man. At the age of 29, he began writing what was to become his first and most successful novel, *Knock on Any Door*, published in 1947 after six years of writing and revising. Motley wrote in the tradition of the Chicago naturalists, which included Norris, Dreiser, Anderson, Farrell, Algren, Wright. Motley, a tireless perfectionist, produced only three more novels: *We Fished All Night*, 1951; *Let No Man Write My Epitaph,* 1962; *Let Noon Be Fair,* 1966. None of Motley's novels deals with race or Negro life as a main theme.

James Weldon Johnson published the *The Autobiography of an ex-Colored Man.* This was the first novel by a Negro to become a permanent part of American literature. It was free of the melodrama that had marked most of the previous Negro novels. Despite the title, it was not autobiographical.

The narrative consisted of a series of episodes in which the hero runs the gamut of Negro experiences in America. Although the race question appears, it never becomes a major theme. It is perhaps the first Negro novel to deal with the Negro in his own environment and not in relation to whites. Johnson's novel helped point the way to the "new Negro movement of the Harlem Renaissance."

Claude McKay published *Constab Ballads.*

Howard B. Drew, a Negro sprinter for UCLA, held the AAU championship in the 100-yard dash. Theodore Cable was inter-collegiate champion in the hammer throw.

1913

A cotton depression was felt throughout the South in this year.

Most of the segregation legislation introduced in the first Wilson Congress the previous year failed to pass, but Wilson, by executive order, segregated most of the Negro Federal employees so far as eating and rest-room facilities were concerned.

Oswald Garrison Villard asked President Wilson to appoint a National Race Commission to study the status of Negroes. Wilson refused. In addition, Wilson appointed white men to posts traditionally given to Negroes, i.e., Ambassador to Haiti and to Santo Domingo.

The executive board of the NAACP advised all branches and groups seeking affiliation with the national organization to include white members to meet the requirements of the association.

Booker T. Washington continued to use his influence to try to discredit the NAACP and to halt fund raising. The radical element responded with personal attacks against Washington. The radicals and conservatives would not be reconciled until his death in 1915.

The National Alliance of Postal Workers, a Negro group of mail clerks, was organized.

Approximately 100 old-age homes and orphanages had been established through Negro charity.

The National Negro Retail Merchant's Association was organized.

The Julius Rosenwald Fund was founded by Julius Rosenwald, president of Sears Roebuck, and lasted until 1948. It spent over $5 million on Negro colleges, provided a wide assortment of scholarships and fellowships for Negroes, and supported many special projects. The fund was not set up specifically for Negro education, however, and it spent a total of some $22.5 million on school grants. Included among its special projects was a program set up in the 1920's to give financial assistance to Negro medical students and a contribution which enabled the United Negro College Fund to be created in 1944. The sculptors Richmond Barthé and Augusta Savage, the painter Charles White, historian John Hope Franklin, choreographer Katherine Dunham and composer William Grant Still were recipients of Rosenwald Fellowships.

Virginia Democrats adopted the "white primary."

Girls of the Alpha Kappa Alpha split away and formed the Delta Sigma Theta sorority. Julia Quander, president of Alpha Kappa Alpha, incorporated and established national chapters for both colleges and alumnae. Thus, AKA and DST became a national movement of Negro collegiate women spreading across 40 states and into Africa and Haiti.

Robert Hayden (1913–   ), Negro poet, was born in Detroit and educated at Wayne State and the University of Michigan. In 1946 he joined the faculty of Fisk University, and in 1940 published *Heartshape in the Dust,* his first collection of poems. He gained an immediate success. In 1947 Hayden received a Rosenwald Fellowship, and in the following year *The Lion and the Archer,* his second volume of poems, was published. *A Ballad of Remembrance*, published in 1962, is Hayden's most recent collection. Hayden's poems are introspective with vivid imagery. He is one of the most widely translated of American Negro poets.

Lionel Hampton (1913-   ), Negro jazz musician, was born in Louisville, Ky., and raised in Chicago where he played drums in the *Chicago Defender* Boys' Band. In 1928 he moved to California and played in the Paul Howard Orchestra. It was there that he began to play the vibraharp. In 1930 he made his first recorded solo on vibraharp, *Memories of You*, with Louis Armstrong. He organized his own band in Los Angeles, and later played on records with Benny Goodman, Gene Krupa and Teddy Wilson. He formally joined the Goodman band in 1936 and stayed until 1940, when he again organized his own orchestra. In 1942 his record of *Flyin' Home* was a great hit, and established him in the big-band field. Hampton was perhaps the first jazz musician to feature the vibraharp or vibraphone.

Certain novels by Negro authors of this decade—Oscar Micheaux's *The Conquest,* 1913, and his *Forged Note,* 1915; Henry Downing's *The American Cavalryman,* 1917; Mary Etta Spencer's *The Resentment,* 1920—ignored the existence of the color line, maintaining that there was no barrier that hard work and diligence could not overcome. These writers accepted the American success story, and their protagonists were Negroes playing white roles. The heroes were modeled on white heroes: the Western pioneer, the empire builder in *The American Cavalryman* and the hog king in *The Resentment.* This trend, right after Johnson's *Autobiography of an Ex-Colored Man,* resolved the ambiguity which had plagued the Negro novel to this point. Subsequent writers would either accept the irrefutable fact of their blackness, the peculiar heritage and all that it implied, or they would ignore it.

From this year through 1939, William Stanley Braithwaite edited the *Anthology of Magazine Verse,* including works by Negro and white poets.

James Weldon Johnson published his poem, *Fifty Years,* commemorating the anniversary of the Emancipation Proclamation.

Howard B. Drew was again AAU champion in the 100-yard dash, and Theodore Cable again won the intercollegiate championship in the hammer throw.

Aime Cesaire (1913–   ), Negro author, was born in Martinique and educated at Lycée Louis le Grand, Paris, where with a fellow student Leopold Senghor he founded the literary movement known as "Negritude." He continued his education at the Sorbonne, and has remained in France as Martinique's representative to the French parliament for the last two decades. He published, in 1939, a prose work rejecting French culture for Martinique, *Cahier d'un Retour au Pays Natal. Les Armes Miraculeuses,* his 1946 first collection of poems, deals with that of tropical beauty of his island. His next collections of verse, *Soleil Cou Coupé* and *Ferrements* were published in 1948 and 1959 respectively. His first play, *La Tragedie du Roi Christophe,* about Henri Christophe, dictator of Haiti, appeared in 1963.

1914

The NAACP reached a membership of over 6,000, with 50 branches. Circulation of the *Crisis,* its house organ, was 31,540.

A dispute developed between Oswald Garrison Villard and W. E. B. Du Bois over Du Bois' handling of the *Crisis.* In January, Villard resigned as chairman of the executive board and became chairman of the finance committee and treasurer. Joel Spingarn succeeded Villard as chairman.

By this year, Monroe Trotter had left the NAACP and attacked both Washington and Du Bois.

Two of Booker T. Washington's most loyal supporters, S. John Williams of Chicago and John Q. Adams of St. Paul, were officers in their local NAACP branches.

According to the National Negro Business League, there were 40,000 Negro businesses in the U.S. At the league's convention, Boley, an all-Negro town in Oklahoma, pointed to its self-government and its Negro officials, its $150,000 high school, its cement sidewalks and attractive residences, its Masonic Temple, its electric light plant and waterworks, and its 82 business concerns, including a bank, 3 cotton gins and a telephone system, as indicative of what Negro self-help and racial cooperation could accomplish.

A delegation headed by Monroe Trotter obtained an audience with the President to protest segregation. The conference ended when Wilson ordered Trotter out of his office for what he deemed insulting language.

Kenneth B. Clark (1914-   ), Negro psychologist, was born in the Panama Canal Zone. He received his Ph.D. from Columbia University in 1940, and has since become one of the foremost social psychologists in the nation. He prepared much of the research used in the famous school desegregation cases argued before the Supreme Court. His books include: *Desegregation, An Appraisal of the Evidence; Prejudice and Your Child* and *Dark Ghetto.* In 1961 he received the Spingarn Award.

Romare Bearden (1914–   ), Negro artist, was born in Charlotte, N.C. He studied under George Grosz at the Art Students League in New York City, and has used various styles including social realism and abstraction; in the 1960's he became known for his photo montages. *Street Corner, He is Arisen* and *The Burial* are among his most famous works.

Owen Dodson (1914–   ), Negro author, was born in Brooklyn, N.Y., and educated at Bates College and Yale University. Two of his plays were produced at Yale, *Divine Comedy* and *Garden of Time* (1939). He taught drama at Spelman College in Atlanta, and was on the faculty of Howard University. His group, the Howard Players, has toured Norway, Denmark, Sweden and Germany. His plays have also been performed off-Broadway. In 1946, *Powerful Long Ladder,* a book of poems, was published, and in 1951 his first novel, *Boy at the Window.* In 1962, *The Summer Fire*, a short story, won a Paris Review Prize. In 1964, *A Bent House,* his second novel, and *Cages,* his second book of poems, were finished on a Guggenheim Fellowship.

Ralph Ellison (1914–   ), Negro author, was born in Oklahoma City, Okla., and attended Tuskegee Institute from 1933 through 1936. He began writing in 1939, and worked on WPA projects. He edited *The Negro Quarterly* in 1942. Since 1952, Ellison has held teaching and writer-in-residence positions at Bard, Rutgers, University of Chicago and Yale. *Invisible Man,* published in 1952, is perhaps the most ambitious novel ever attempted by a Negro writer. Although the background of the novel is a Negro one, Ellison was primarily concerned with the spiritual condition of modern urbanized man. The novel won the 1953 National Book Award. In the *New World Journal* poll of 100 U.S. writers, *Invisible Man* was selected as the most important American novel since World War II. In 1964, *Shadow and Act,* a miscellaneous collection of short articles and essays was published.

The Lafayette Stock Company was formed in Harlem for the promotion of the Negro theater.

Oscar Michaeux founded Oscar Michaeux Pictures with studios in New York City, and produced *The Wages of Sin* and *The Broken Violin,* both of which featured all-Negro casts. Michaeux was the first Negro film producer, and his was the first all-Negro company. His films were designed for a Negro audience and were shown primarily in ghettos and Southern shanty towns.

Darktown Jubilee, the first movie to star a Negro, Bert Williams, an extremely talented vaudevillian, was met with hisses, catcalls, boycotts, and caused a race riot in Brooklyn, N.Y. Williams never again performed in a film.

The fourth movie version of *Uncle Tom's Cabin* was directed by William Daley for World Pictures. It featured Sam Lucas in the title role. Lucas was the first Negro actor to play Uncle Tom, and several of the minor characters were also played by real Negroes. This set the trend to use Negroes rather than whites with burnt cork to play Negroes in motion pictures.

Coon Town Suffragettes, a Sigmund Lubin film, satirized the current feminist movement by giving it a shantytown setting with Negro washer women trying to keep their fun-loving husbands out of saloons.

Howard B. Drew broke the world's record in the 100-yard dash and the 220-yard dash.

1915

Farm labor wages fell to 75¢ a day, or less. Boll weevils devastated the cotton crop. There were major floods during the summer. As a result, Negroes migrated North in great numbers.

In June, in GUINN v. U.S., the Supreme Court pronounced in violation of the 15th Amendment and thus unconstitutional the suffrage provisions of the Oklahoma and Maryland Constitutions. The NAACP had challenged Oklahoma's "grandfather clause." Morfield Storey argued the case for the NAACP.

The NAACP unsuccessfully tried to prevent the showing of D. W. Griffith's *Birth of a Nation.* The film was based on the violently anti-Negro book by Thomas Dixon *The Klansman.* It told a distorted story of Negro emancipation, enfranchisement and debauchery of innocent women. The association also tried to counteract its influence by making their own film, *Lincoln's Dream,* but the project never materialized. However, 3 years later, the NAACP convinced several states to ban Griffith's film arguing that it fostered race hatred at a time of national crisis.

The NAACP employed 2 legislative agents to keep track of all anti-Negro bills introduced in Congress. In the first 3 months of the year, 6 Jim Crow bills for Washington, D.C., had been introduced, and an anti-intermarriage bill for the capital had been passed by the House. The NAACP, by canvassing and distributing literature, contributed to the House defeat of an immigration bill forbidding even literate Negroes to enter the country.

U.S. Negroes protested President Wilson's order for the occupation of Haiti by the U.S. Marines.

Since 1900 1,100 Negroes had been lynched.

By this year almost all the Southern states provided for "white primaries."

North Carolina Democrats adopted a "white primary."

A faction of the Louisiana State Republican Convention refused admission of Negroes to the convention in the Grunewald Hotel in New Orleans.

The trend of Southern legislation was exemplified by a South Carolina labor code which prohibited textile factory owners from allowing laborers of both races to work in the same room, to use the same entrances, stairs, pay windows, lavatories, drinking cups, or water buckets.

For the first time in any state, Oklahoma law required separate phone booths.

Booker T. Washington died.

Oscar DePriest was elected alderman in the densely populated Negro section of Chicago, the South Side.

The Railwaymen's International Benevolent and Industrial Association was established.

The National Baptist Convention of the U.S.A. was incorporated.

Between 1915 and 1919, 8 Negroes received doctorates, 4 from Negro institutions and 4 from integrated universities.

William H. Hinton became an instructor in the Harvard Medical School.

John Hope Franklin (1915-   ), Negro historian, was

born in Rentiesville, Okla., and was educated at Fisk and
Harvard University where he received a Ph.D. in 1941. He
has taught at North Carolina State, Howard and Brooklyn
College, and the University of Chicago. His books include:
Free Negro in North Carolina, a study of the social status of
the Negro in N.C. in pre-Civil War times, 1943; *From Slavery
to Freedom*, 1947; *Militant South*, 1956; *Reconstruction After
the Civil War*, 1961; *The Emancipation Proclamation*, 1963.
Franklin is one of the leading Reconstruction revisionist historians who followed Du Bois' example in *Black Reconstruction* of re-evaluating the social position and political performance of the post-Civil War Southern Negro.

W. E. B. Du Bois' book, *The Negro*, was published. It dealt
with Negro history from ancient Egypt to the present. Du Bois,
writing from the Marxist point of view that both white
workers and the Negro race were exploited by white capital,
predicted the unification of the exploited classes against white
capital.

The Karamu Theater in Cleveland, Ohio, was founded by
Russell and Rowena Jellifes as part of a private philanthropic
social welfare center. The Jellifes were upper-class whites.
Karamu is a Swahili word meaning "center of enjoyment" or
"center of community." The theater was a recreation center
for ghetto dwellers, white and Negro. The Jellifes encouraged drama and theater, especially among the Negroes. The
great Negro actor, Charles Gilpin, founded a stock company,
Gilpin Players, which produced and wrote plays especially for
the Karamu house. During the 1930's the theater premiered
almost all of Langston Hughes' plays. The Jellifes retired in
1963, leaving the Karamu a generous endowment to continue
its productions. Although not exclusively a Negro theater, the
Karamu, which also houses a superb collection of African art,
remains the best and most dynamic Negro theater in the U.S.

Scott Joplin, a Negro, composed a ragtime opera,
Treemonisha.

Jess Willard, a white prize-fighter, defeated the Negro
champion, Jack Johnson, for the heavyweight boxing title. It
was rumored that Johnson threw the fight to relieve the racial
tensions built up by his reign as champion and to escape
punishment for a charge that he had violated the Mann Act.

1916

An official investigation by the Department of Labor set the total migration of Negroes from the South over a period of 18 months at 350,000. Among the causes listed were general dissatisfaction with conditions, the boll weevil, floods, the crop system, low wages, poor housing, poor schools, unfairness in court proceedings, and lynchings.

The seriousness of the Negro migration to the North was demonstrated in Jacksonville, Fla., where an ordinance was passed requiring migration agents to pay a fee of $1,000.

The Urban League held its Conference on Migration. It issued recommendations for employers and migrants to help ease urban problems.

Jesse Washington, a Negro, was publicly burned in Waco, Tex., before a cheering mob of thousands of men, women, and children.

In South Carolina, a well-to-do Negro farmer, Anthony Crawford, was mobbed and killed for impudence in refusing to agree to a price for his cotton seed.

The Anti-lynching Committee of the NAACP was established. It served as an investigating agency, information-disseminating bureau, etc.

In January, Oswald Garrison Villard resigned from the board of the NAACP due to his continuing conflict with W. E. B. Du Bois over the militant articles in the *Crisis.*

With Booker T. Washington's death, W. E. B. Du Bois planned and Joel Spingarn as president of the NAACP sponsored a meeting for reconciliation between the various factions of the Negro movement. The Amenia Conference at Spingarn's home included representatives of all points of view from Emmet Scott to Monroe Trotter. The meeting was generally successful; the delegates agreed on the fundamental issues: equal education, enfranchisement, end to lawlessness, and the protection of civil liberties.

James Weldon Johnson was appointed field secretary and organizer for the NAACP in the South. Until this time the NAACP had been an entirely Northern organization.

The NAACP succeeded in forcing Congress to hold hearings on anti-intermarriage and Jim Crow bills for Washington,

D.C. Southern Congressmen refused to attend the hearings, and the bill introduced to ban the practices failed to pass. The NAACP also attempted to insert strong Negro rights planks into the Republican and Democratic platforms. W. E. B. Du Bois, disillusioned with Wilson, supported the Republican candidate, Hughes, although he had given no support to Negroes. Oswald Garrison Villard, however, continued to support President Wilson.

There were altogether 67 Negro public-schools with fewer than 20,000 students.

In March, Charles Young commanded a squadron of the 10th Cavalry on General Pershing's punitive expedition to Mexico against Francisco Villa. Promoted to colonel, Young was the highest-ranking Negro officer at the time of World War I. Despite his opposition, he was retired from active service at the opening of hostilities. He died in 1922 after organizing the Liberian Army for the U.S., and was buried in Arlington National Cemetery.

John Oliver Killens (1916-   ), Negro writer, was born in Brooklyn, N.Y., and was educated at Howard University, Terrell Law School, Columbia and New York University. During World War II he served for 26 months in the amphibious forces in the South Pacific. In 1950 he founded the Harlem Writers' Workshop. In 1954, *Youngblood,* an autobiographical novel was published. In 1959 *Odds Against Tomorrow,* his original screenplay, was made into a movie with Harry Belafonte, Robert Ryan and Ed Begley; it was released by United Artists. Since then, Killens has written three books: *And Then We Heard the Thunder,* a novel, 1963; a nonfiction account of the civil rights movement, *The Black Man's Burden,* 1965; *Sippi,* a novel, 1967 .

Frank Yerby (1916-   ), Negro novelist, was born in Augusta, Ga., and was educated at Haines Institute and Fisk University. He taught at Florida A&M and Southern University in Baton Rouge. *Health Card,* his first published short story, won an O. Henry Award in 1944. In 1946, *The Foxes of Harrow,* Yerby's first historical novel, was published. The novel was a best seller, and the pattern for his subsequent novels was set. Since 1946, Yerby has produced one novel per year from an almost fixed formula: *The Vixens,* 1947; *The*

Golden Hawk, 1948; *Pride's Castle,* 1949; etc. He is without doubt the best-selling Negro novelist.

The Association for the Study of Negro Life and History was founded by Carter G. Woodson, who became editor of its publication, *The Journal of Negro History.*

The collected poems of George Marion McClelland, *The Path of Dreams,* was published.

Frederick Douglass Pollard, a Negro, was named to the college All-American team.

In August, the U.S. purchased the Danish West Indies for $25,000,000. When the Danish Foreign Minister asked for guarantees of kind treatment of the inhabitants, the American Minister replied that the people of the U.S. were "so well acquainted with the true character of the Negroes that they could make them more content than the Europeans."

1917

Moorfield Storey argued the case for the NAACP in BUCHANAN V. WARLEY before the U.S. Supreme Court. The Court held a Louisville, Ky., city ordinance requiring Negroes and whites to live on separate blocks unconstitutional, as it "destroyed the right of the individual to acquire, enjoy and dispose of his property," in violation of the due process clause of the 14th Amendment. The NAACP thus won a victory against segregated housing ordinances begun in 1910.

Negroes in New York elected a Negro, E. A. Johnson, to the State Assembly.

The NAACP voted that its nominating committee be composed of whites and Negroes.

Marcus Garvey came to New York and founded a newspaper, the *Negro World.* On a speaking tour of the U.S. he gained tremendous support for his Negro nationalist organization, the Universal Negro Improvement Association (UNIA).

Samuel Gompers' unsympathetic attitude toward Negroes resulted in the failure of the Resolutions Committee to act on anti-discrimination resolutions at the National Convention of the AFL in 1917, 1921 and 1924. William Green, the next president, continued this policy.

Between this year and 1928, A. Philip Randolph and

Chandler Owen edited the Negro radical *Messenger* magazine in New York City, and advocated better employment opportunities for Negroes through cooperation with organized labor.

This year 38 Negroes were lynched.

Anywhere from 40 to 100 Negroes were killed in a July race riot in East St. Louis, Ill. The NAACP defended 10 Negroes for murder in the aftermath of the riot, and raised funds to give assistance to Negroes left destitute as a result of the riot. The Anti-lynching Committee, created in 1915, was reorganized as the Anti-lynching and Mob Violence Fund.

Opposition in Chicago's white residential districts to Negro purchases of property resulted in the bombing of the S. P. Motley home on Maryland Avenue. The front of the building was blown off, and $1,000 worth of damage was done. The police found no clues and made no arrests.

In response to the East St. Louis riot, New York Negroes organized a silent protest parade, and 10,000 marched through the city on July 28. When the Parade Committee merged with the NAACP, many formerly uninvolved Negroes were brought into the association. Secret fraternal organizations began to contribute to the association in reaction to the riot.

In October, Negro soldiers of the 15th New York Infantry in Spartanburg, S.C., were refused service and beaten. To prevent another Brownsville, Tex., riot, the regiment was sent to Europe.

On Aug. 23, in Houston, Tex., a battalion of the 24th Infantry USCT fought with white residents; 17 whites and 2 Negroes were killed. The NAACP engaged a defense attorney for the soldiers and campaigned for clemency. President Wilson commuted 10 death sentences to life imprisonment. NAACP efforts led 4 years later to the release of some and a reduction in life sentences for others. Its efforts continued until 1938 when President Roosevelt released the last prisoner.

Joel Spingarn, acting as an individual, convinced the War Department to establish an officers' training camp for Negroes. Sections of the NAACP bitterly opposed this as segregation, but the association in the end put itself on record as in favor of separate camps, since there was no chance of having Negroes trained as officers in regular training camps.

In May, the Central Committee of Negro College Men was

established at Howard University. In an effort to answer Gen. Leonard Wood's challenge to secure 200 Negroes of college rank for the establishment of a Negro officers school, the committee collected 1,500 volunteer college men.

Southern protests over the training of Northern Negroes in the South forced a conference of high government officials. It was found logistically impossible to accede to the Southern demands, although a brief attempt was made.

On Oct. 15, 639 Negroes were commissioned in the U.S. Army: 106 captains, 329 first lieutenants and 204 second lieutenants. In the same month Secretary of War Newton D. Baker appointed Emmet J. Scott as special assistant to the Secretary of War to serve as "confidential adviser in matters affecting the interests of 10 million Negroes of the U.S., and the part they are to play in the present war."

After President Wilson declared war on Germany, recruiting stations generally refused to accept Negroes. At the time approximately 10,000 Negroes were in the regular Army (9th and 10th Cavalry, 24th and 25th Infantry, USCT) and 10,000 in the National Guards of Connecticut, Illinois, Maryland, Massachusetts, New York, Ohio, Tennessee, and Washington, D.C.

The Selective Service Act provided for enlistment of all able-bodied men from 21 to 31, and on July 5, registration day, more than 700,000 Negroes registered.

The Immigration Act of this year established a literacy test that excluded all aliens over 16 years of age who were physically able to read but could not read English or some other language or dialect. The tests subsequently showed that Negro immigrants were more literate than the Negro population they joined in the U.S.

Gwendolyn Brooks (1917-   ), Negro poet, was born in Topeka, Kan., but grew up and was educated in Chicago, Ill. In 1931, her first poetry was published in the *American Childhood* magazine. In 1945, her first book of poems, *A Street in Bronzeville,* was well received, and she was selected as one of the 10 outstanding women of the year by *Mademoiselle* magazine. This book also won her two Guggenheim Fellowships for creative writing. Her second book of poems, *Annie Allen,* published in 1949, won the Pulitzer Prize. Her poetry is lyrical and emotional in style. She published, in 1953, *Maud Martha,* an autobiographical novel. Two additional collections of verse are *Bronzeville Boys and Girls* (1956) and *The Bean Eaters* (1960).

Regina Goff (1917-   ), Negro educator, was born in St. Louis, and was educated at Northwestern and Columbia Universities. After receiving her doctorate in child development, she supervised and taught child development programs for the Florida State school system and at Morgan State College in Maryland. Appointed Assistant Commissioner in the Office of Education of the Department of Health, Education and Welfare, she has directed the Federal educational programs for underprivileged and handicapped children, such as Operation Head Start.

Ossie Davis (1917-   ), Negro actor and playwright, was born in Cogdell, Ga. Davis, who is the husband of actress Ruby Dee, is considered one of the most prominent actors of today. He has appeared on Broadway in *Job, Wisteria Trees, A Raisin in the Sun* and *Purlie Victorious,* which he also authored. He has acted in many movies and on TV.

Dizzy Gillespie (1917-   ), Negro jazz musician, was born John Birks Gillespie in Cheraw, S.C. The son of a bricklayer who was a part-time musician, young Gillespie studied trombone, trumpet and music theory on scholarship at Laurinburg Institute, an industrial training school in North Carolina. In 1935 he moved to Philadelphia and worked with Teddy Hill's band and later with Cab Calloway. In the early 1940's, Gillespie came under the influence of Charlie Parker in Earl Hines' band, and was one of the group that formulated bop at Minton's Playhouse. Gillespie, one of the great innovators of bop, is noted for his technical facility. He has toured Europe with his own group, particularly Scandinavia, and is considered one of the main influences on European jazz.

Lena Horne (1917-   ), Negro entertainer, was born in Brooklyn, N.Y., and began her career at the age of 16 at the Cotton Club as a singer and dancer. She had a lead role in *Blackbirds* of 1939, and sang with Charlie Barnett's band. Since 1942, she has become a success as a nightclub entertainer, movie star (*Panama Hattie,* 1942; *Cabin in the Sky,* 1943; *Stormy Weather,* 1943; *Meet Me in Las Vegas,* 1956), recording artist and Broadway actress (*Jamaica,* 1957).

Jacob Lawrence (1917-   ), Negro painter, was born in Atlantic City, N.J. His numerous works in oils chronicle Negro history and life in the Northern ghettos in a somewhat primitive, realistic style, similar to that of the Mexican artists of the 1930's. His works are owned by the Metropolitan Museum of Art, the Whitney and the Museum of Modern Art. He is most famous for his historical panels, *The Life of Toussaint l'Ouverture, The Life of Harriet Tubman,* etc., painted between 1937 and 1942.

Claude McKay's poem, *The Harlem Dancer,* first appeared in *The Seven Arts* magazine under the pen name of Eli Edwards. This poem eventually led to the Harlem Renaissance of the 1920's.

James Weldon Johnson's *50 Years and Other Poems* was published.

James Weldon Johnson's *The Harlem Chronicler* termed 1917 the most important date in the history of the Negro in the American theater.

Three one-act plays (*The Rider of Dreams, Simon the Cyrenian* and *Granny Maumee*) by the white poet Ridgely Torrence were presented on Broadway with an all-Negro cast. The use of Negro life as material for serious theater and of Negro actors and performers in nonmusical theater was acceptable hereafter. The show was very successful and marked "the first time anywhere in the U.S. for Negro actors in the dramatic theater to command the serious attention of the critics and the general press and public."

Harry T. Burleigh, a Negro, wrote *Little Mother of Mine,* which was popularized by a white tenor, Enrico Caruso.

Paul Robeson was named to the All-American collegiate football team as an end by Walter Camp.

Negroes organized a tristate (New York, New Jersey, Pennsylvania) tennis association. One of the earliest champions was Lucy Slowe, later dean of women at Howard University.

Storyville, the official red-light district of New Orleans, was closed. Although musicians had been going North before the closing of Storyville, its shutdown accelerated the movement of jazz and jazz musicians, in particular to Chicago.

The Original Dixieland Jass Band made its debut in New

York. It consisted of five white performers who had learned jazz from New Orleans Negroes, especially Joe Oliver. This date is frequently given as the beginning of the Jazz Age.

In January, the treaty for the purchase of the Danish West Indies was ratified. The Marines occupied the islands, and the military government existed until 1931.

1918

By the end of World War I, there were 50,000 Negroes in service battalions (stevedores, butchers, laborers, etc.), representing a significant part of the American labor force in France. Some 10,000 Negroes served in the U.S. Navy. Their enlistments, however, were restricted to messmen. By the end of the war, 367,000 Negroes had been drafted, representing 11% of the American Expeditionary Forces.

More than half of these Negro troops were assigned to the 92nd and 93rd Combat Divisions. The 92nd Division, approximately 12,000 men, although subject to German propaganda about fighting for a nation in which they were second-class citizens, held the sector (St. Dié) to which they were assigned. The whole 367th Infantry Battalion of the 92nd Division was awarded the Croix de Guerre, and 43 enlisted men and 14 Negro officers of the 92nd received the Distinguished Service Cross. The 369th U.S. Infantry (15th New York Regiment) in Champagne, defended 20% of all territory held by the U.S. troops in May. In July, at Minnaucourt, it bore the brunt of the German offensive. The 369th also was the first unit of the Allied armies to reach the Rhine. It never lost a man through capture, or a trench or foot of ground, and won the Croix de Guerre for action at Maison-en-Champagne. Two of its Negro soldiers, Henry Johnson and Needham Roberts, after repelling a German raiding party were the first Negroes ever to win the Croix de Guerre. Johnson was from New York and became the most famous World War I Negro soldier.

The 370th U.S. Infantry fought in the Argonne Forest in July and August. In September it was put into the 59th French Division and pursued the Germans into Belgium; 21 of its men received the Distinguished Service Cross and 68 the Croix de Guerre. The men of the unit were the first U.S. troops to enter the fortress of Laon, held by the Germans for

4 years. The 371st Infantry Regiment attached to the 157th French Division fought in the front lines in the Avoncourt and Verrieres subsectors from April to June. At Monthois in September it captured railroad cars and a munitions depot, various other supplies and men. Of its officers, 3 won the French Legion of Honor; 34 officers and 89 enlisted men won the Croix de Guerre, and 14 officers and 12 men won the Distinguished Service Cross. The 372nd U.S. Infantry, USCT, composed of Negro National Guardsmen from Washington, D.C., Ohio, Massachusetts and Maryland, was also attached to the French 157th Division. For its gallantry in the final campaign (the September offensive), Vice Admiral Moreau decorated the regimental colors with the Croix de Guerre and Palm. On Oct. 1, General Goybet of France commended the 371st and 372nd Infantry Divisions, USCT: "Your troops have been admirable in their attack. You must be proud of your officers and men, and I consider it an honor to have them under my command. The bravery and dash of your regiments won the admiration of the Moroccan Division, who are themselves versed in warfare. Thanks to you. During these hard days, the division was at all times in advance of all other divisions of the Army Corps. I am sending you all my thanks. . . . I call on your wounded. Their morale is higher than my praise."

A Division of Negro Economics was created in the Department of Labor, headed by George E. Haynes. Haynes set up local and state committees to help reduce Negro-white friction; they held conferences in 12 states.

Emmet Scott of the War Department called a conference of 31 leading Negro newspapermen. They supported the war, denounced mob violence and called for the use of Negro Red Cross nurses, the appointment of Negro war correspondents, and the return of Col. Charles Young to active duty. The last two demands were granted. Young was sent to train troops in Illinois 5 days before the armistice.

Negroes purchased $250,000,000 worth of bonds and stamps for the war effort.

One of the few Negro journals not to support the war wholeheartedly was the *Messenger*, published in New York by A. Philip Randolph and Chandler Owen. For an article, "Pro-Germanism Amongst the Negroes," they were sentenced to jail for 1 to 2½ years, and the *Messenger* was denied second-class mailing privileges.

The AFL invited Robert Moton, head of Tuskegee Institute, Emmet Scott of the War Department, Eugene K. Jones of the National Urban League, and Fred Moore of the *New York Age,* a Negro newspaper, to discuss the "unionization of Negroes." Little came of this meeting, as most unions still refused to accept Negroes.

There were 58 Negroes lynched in this year.

A race riot in Chester, Pa., resulted in 5 deaths, and in Philadelphia a riot resulted in 4 dead and 60 injured.

An anti-lynching bill drawn up by Joel Spingarn and George Hornblower was introduced in the House of Representatives on June 6 by Warren Gard of Ohio. The bill aimed at protecting potential draftees, so the end of the war made it obsolete.

The NAACP had 88,500 members, and 300 branches, half of whom were in the South.

A new civil rights law passed in the state of New York extended the equal accommodations privileges of earlier acts to include every conceivable type of public business, skating rinks, billiard parlors, bowling alleys, ice-cream parlors, etc.

John H. Johnson (1918-   ), Negro publisher, was born in Arkansas. Johnson is one of the most successful businessmen in the U.S. today. He is the publisher of *Ebony, Jet, Negro Digest* and *Tan*, which have a combined circulation of well over 2 million. A graduate of Northwestern and Chicago Universities, Johnson began his publishing career in 1942, when he started the *Negro Digest* with $500 he had borrowed. By 1943 it had a circulation of 50,000. He is a member of the National Advisory Council, Office of Economic Opportunity.

1919

Between June and December 76 Negroes were lynched and there were 25 race riots. This was called "Red Summer."

In April four Negroes and two white policemen died in a race riot in Millen, Ga. Seven lodges and five churches belonging to Negroes were burned, and a Negro prisoner was lynched.

In May residents of Chicago's predominantly white Kenwood and Hyde Park districts met to oppose the Negro "invasion" of the area. In June a bomb destroyed a house which S. P. Motley planned to buy in that area.

In Washington, D.C., on July 19, because of an alleged assault upon a white woman, the chief of police called for a general questioning and search of all Negroes found on the streets after dark. Following this order soldiers and sailors went throughout the southwest district shooting at people on the streets and unlawfully entering their homes. Several persons were critically hurt. The police were unable to prevent a repetition of violence on Sunday night when five Negroes were attacked and beaten by white marines and soldiers. Mobs roamed the streets until early Monday morning. At this point Negroes began to organize to protect themselves. Guns were secured and patrols drove up and down Washington streets. United States Provost Guard was called in to restore order.

The Chicago race riot began on July 27. An imaginary line in the water separated a generally recognized white beach from a generally recognized Negro beach. When four Negroes attempted to enter the water from the white side they were driven away by whites. They returned with more Negroes and the whites began to throw stones. Eugene Williams, a 17-year-old Negro, entered the water on the Negro side and drifted across the "line," supported by a railroad tie. After the crowd began to throw stones Williams released the tie suddenly and drowned. Negro witnesses alleged that a white man named Stauber had thrown the stone that killed him and demanded that policemen arrest Stauber. The police refused and instead arrested a Negro on a white man's complaint. Negroes then attacked the arresting officer. Reports and rumors circulated rapidly and new crowds began to gather. Five white men were injured in clashes near the beach. After dark, Negroes in white districts suffered severely. Between 9 P.M. and 3 A.M., some 27 Negroes were beaten, 7 stabbed and 4 shot. On Monday Negroes returning from work were attacked by whites. Trolleys were pulled from their wires, and Negro passengers were dragged to the street and beaten, stabbed or shot. Four Negro men and one white were killed and 30 Negroes beaten. Rumors and terror again spread rapidly throughout Chicago. A rumor that white occupants in

a building at 35th Street and Wabash Avenue had shot a
Negro caused Negroes to gather about the building. The
white tenants sought police protection, and 100 policemen
responded. In a clash with the mob the police killed four
Negroes, injured many more. The following day, Tuesday,
July 29, Negroes traveling through white areas were again
attacked. Negroes living in white sections were driven from
their homes, and their houses were looted, wrecked and
burned. By Wednesday night Mayor Thompson yielded to
pressure and asked the help of the three regiments of militia
which had been waiting in nearby armories during the most
severe rioting. They immediately took up positions throughout
the south side. A heavy rain Wednesday night and Thursday
kept many people in their homes and by Friday the rioting
had abated. Total casualties in the Chicago riot were fixed at
38 deaths (15 whites and 23 Negroes) and some 537 injured.
A coroner's jury found that Eugene Williams, the Negro boy,
had drowned from fear of the stone throwing, which kept
him from swimming to shore.

In Georgia, on Sept. 1, Negro schools and churches were
burned.

In Knoxville, Tenn., two persons died and four were
critically injured in rioting. The disorder followed a mob
attack on a jailed Negro man. Although quickly dispersed,
mobs continued to form and Negroes barricaded themselves
at one street corner in an attempt to defend themselves. A call
went out to the 4th Tennessee Infantry who exchanged fire
with the barricaded Negroes. Six persons were killed and 20
injured.

Rioting erupted on Sept. 28 in Omaha, Neb. The incidents
were largely attributed to an inflammatory article in local
newspapers. During the outbreak of violence the courthouse
was set on fire, and a Negro prisoner who was attempting to
escape the fire was seized and hanged. The mob was estimated at several thousands. Two thousand troops were called
in to maintain order and check rioting, but still another man
was shot and widespread damage was done to local businesses.
There was looting of sporting goods stores and other businesses. By Oct. 1 the Army had control of the town.

The mob violence against Negroes and the second-class

citizenship of Negroes was attacked by the NAACP at its July convention, the National Equal Rights League at its September convention, by the National Race Conference and the National Baptist Convention in October.

In May the NAACP held a national Anti-Lynching Conference in New York. Many prominent Negro and white politicians and business leaders attended. Charles Evans Hughes was the principal speaker. Three resolutions were passed: (1) lynching should be made a Federal crime, (2) the NAACP should organize local committees to work for state legislation, (3) the Anti-lynching Committee should carry on a systematic fund-raising and publicity campaign. The NAACP also financed and sponsored a Pan-African Conference in Paris, at which nine African countries were represented by 12 delegates, the West Indies by 21 and the United States by 16. NAACP members included W. E. B. Du Bois and Joel Spingarn.

A town ordinance of Sommerville, Tex., forbade the circulation of Negro newspapers and stated that "every darkey must read a paper edited by a Confederate veteran."

The Attorney General of Texas attempted to close down the NAACP in the state by claiming it was not chartered to do business in Texas. John Shillady, secretary of the NAACP, went to Texas in August to defend the NAACP as a civic and educational organization. Shillady was beaten unconscious in the streets of Austin.

In October Negro farmers in Elaine, Arkansas, attempted to organize the Progressive Farmers and Household Union to protest the low prices paid for cotton by white planters. Anti-Negro riots broke out and over 200 Negroes were killed, 79 Negroes were indicted and brought to trial on charges of murder and insurrection. The NAACP conducted an investigation and took on the defense of the accused. Over $50,000 was raised by the N.A.A.C.P. before the case was closed in 1925. Twelve Negroes were sentenced to death, but only six convictions were upheld by the Arkansas Supreme Court. By 1921 the NAACP had secured dismissal of the six cases in which death sentences had not been upheld by the Court. In 1923 the United States Supreme Court reversed the convictions of the six sentenced to death. The Court also ordered the Federal District Court to ascertain whether a fair trial had been granted. Governor McRae in 1923 commuted the sentences to short prison terms. By January, 1925, the last of the 67 Negroes serving terms had been released.

The Commission on Interracial Cooperation was organized by William Alexander.

Two Negroes, T. J. Pree and R. T. Sims, a former IWW organizer, attempted to set up an independent Negro labor movement. They formed the National Brotherhood Workers of America. Initial support came from the Negro shipyard and dock workers at Newport News, Norfolk and Portsmouth, Va. A. Philip Randolph became a member of the board of directors. The AFL fought the National Brotherhood and in 1921 the brotherhood was dissolved.

In August at Pennsylvania Station in New York City, red caps (porters) joined the AFL. They had organized the Brotherhood of Railway Station Attendants.

The American Federation of Labor voted in its Atlantic City meeting to abolish discrimination in union membership. Samuel Gompers said in addressing the meeting, "The action of the convention removes every class and race distinction from the movement. It should mark an era in the struggle of the Negro for equality rights, as well as advance in the history of the political and economic liberty in America."

Over 2,500 male Negro immigrants were brought from the Caribbean by the Federal Government to work as construction laborers in South Carolina. Negro laborers were also imported from the Bahamas to work on truck farms on the east coast of Florida and for private contractors on Government construction work in Charleston, S.C.

For the next 10 years Negroes immigrated from the French colonies of Martinique and Guadeloupe to the United States. Most settled in New York City. The U.S. Department of Labor had ceased the issuance of permits for the importation of laborers from the British colonies in January.

The U.S. Government opened a town exclusively for Negroes at Truxton, Va., near the naval station at Portsmouth, where most of its inhabitants were employed.

An anti-mob bill was passed by the Tennessee Legislature to provide a measure against lynching. A force of 600 men was to be available upon call of the Governor to maintain order in the cases of threatened outbreaks of violence.

At the request of a committee of Negro businessmen and professionals, Governor Hobby agreed to recommend an anti-lynching bill to the Texas Legislature. Governor Bickard of North Carolina, Governor Manning of South Carolina and Governor Henderson of Alabama, also favored legal action to punish lynchers.

The Philadelphia Yearly Meeting of Friends took an official stand against lynching, at its 225th annual session. A committee was established to seek the end of this "national crime."

The General Assembly of the Presbyterian Church unanimously placed itself on record against lynching.

The United Irish Societies, comprising some 50,000 Irish-Americans in a meeting in Philadelphia, unanimously voted that all oppressed people, whether white, yellow or black, should be free and accorded equal rights.

The Republican County Committee of New York moved to have Congress enforce the 15th Amendment.

A mass meeting was held in New York to establish a committee of 100 which would seek to influence the 66th Congress to enforce the 15th Amendment. The committee was to have representatives from all Negro organizations in New York State.

The International League of Darker People was formed at the New York estate of Mrs. C. J. Walker. The league was committed to organizing all Negro delegates to the Paris Peace Conference; included in this group were Mary Howard Jackson, the Negro sculptress from Washington, D.C.; Rev. Julius Austin of Pittsburgh and Adam Clayton Powell Sr. of New York.

The U.S. Army Chief of Staff ruled that "in the matter of colored officers being commissioned in the army, there is to be no exclusion on account of color."

At the request of President Wilson, Robert Moton, head of Tuskegee Institute, visited American Negro troops in Alsace-Lorraine and elsewhere. He reported their condition satisfactory.

General Pershing awarded the Distinguished Service Cross
for acts of extraordinary heroism to 12 Negro members of the
370th Infantry (Illinois) and 8 Distinguished Service Crosses
to Negro members of the 371st Infantry (South Carolina).

The Legislature of South Carolina voted $100,000 for a
memorial for Negro soldiers and an equal amount for a white
soldiers' monument.

The Jewish Welfare Board of Camp Mills established a
school for the instruction of demobilized Negro troops in
English, bookkeeping, arithmetic and carpentry.

West Virginia admitted Negroes to juries as a result of the
case of the STATE V. YOUNG. In an appeal to the State Supreme Court it was contended that Young, who had been
sentenced to life imprisonment, had been denied equal protection of the law since he had been convicted by an all-white
jury. The court reversed a lower court decision and directed
Negroes to sit on the new jury.

In a speech to the Urban League Conference held in
Detroit, Mich., George E. Haynes, director of Negro economics of the U.S. Department of Labor, stated that "in ship
building during the war, 24,637 Negro workers were employed. The number has been reduced since the war to
14,075. 20% of these men were in skilled occupations. Since
the war Negro workmen in skilled occupations have shown a
decrease of only 20.7%, while unskilled occupations show
[a decrease of] about 48%."

Under the auspices of the War Work Council of the YWCA
young Negro women were admitted to train as YWCA
workers.

Charles H. Roberts, a Republican, became the first Negro
elected to sit on the Aldermanic Board of New York City.

Nat "King" Cole (1919-1965), Negro entertainer, was born
in Montgomery, Ala., as Nat Coles. His father, a minister,
took the family to Chicago where Cole learned to play the
piano and organ. In night school he formed several combos,
and in 1936 appeared in the road company of *Shuffle Along*.
In 1937 he formed the King Cole Trio. His first recording,
in 1943, *Straighten Up and Fly Right,* an original composition, was an immediate success. Until his death he was one of
the most popular singers in America. Among his most famous

songs are *Paper Moon, The Christmas Song, Nature Boy, Mona Lisa, Pretend* and *Somewhere Along the Way.*

Charles White (1919-   ), Negro artist, was born in Chicago, and studied at Chicago's Art Institute, the Art Students League of New York and the Taller de la Grafica in Mexico City. Most of White's works is in three media: murals, woodcuts and lithographs. His murals show a strong Orozco influence. The main theme of his work is the strength and endurance of the Negro people. His Negroes are proud and dignified, much like Orozco's peasants. White's panel *The Contribution of the Negro to American Democracy* at the Hampton Institute is one of his best and most representative works. It depicts Negro abolitionists, educators, soldiers and working people in a strikingly rhythmic, solid design.

Charles Christian (1919-1942), Negro jazz guitarist, was born in Dallas and raised in Oklahoma City. He studied guitar with his father and played bass in Alphonso Trent's orchestra. In 1939 he joined Benny Goodman's band. It was with Goodman that he became the first jazz man to feature single-string solos on electric guitar. Christian was the pre-eminent jazz guitarist of his day, and his influence remains powerful in the jazz field today.

Jack Roosevelt Robinson (1919-   ), Negro athlete and political leader, was born in Cairo, Ga., and raised in Pasadena, Calif. Robinson was educated at UCLA where he starred in football, track and baseball. During World War II, he served as a second lieutenant in the U.S. Army. In 1945, while he was playing for the Kansas City Monarchs, a Negro baseball team, Branch Rickey signed him to a contract for the Brooklyn Dodgers, and assigned him to the Montreal Royals, a farm club of the Dodgers. On April 10, 1947, Rickey announced that Robinson would play for the parent club. He thus became the first Negro ballplayer in the major leagues. Robinson distinguished himself as a professional athlete and won the Most Valuable Player award of the National League in 1949. At his retirement in 1956, segregation on the playing field had been broken in professional sports. Robinson has pursued a successful business career and has been influential in Republican politics.

American Negro musicians were in demand in Paris, where jazz and ragtime were very popular. A representative of the

Casino de Paris arrived in New York to organize a Negro orchestra of 50 men.

A circuit of Negro theaters was formed with Lester A. Walton general manager.

The Lafayette Theater in Harlem opened under the management of E. C. Brown, a Negro.

Daniel Gregory Mason, a white composer, published *String Quartet on Negro themes,* Opus 9. White musicians were beginning to explore Negro music and traditions.

Richard Lonsdale Brown, a Negro artist, first gained distinction for his exhibition at Ovington Art Galleries. He anticipated the sharp Oriental sketch-line inset details on high-keyed, geometrically flat backgrounds, which 15 or 20 years later were the high mode of American modernists.

William N. Cunningham, a Negro track star at the University of Pennsylvania, was refused admission to a meet with the Naval Academy at Annapolis because the Academy's runners refused to compete with a Negro.

Fritz Pollard became the first professional Negro football player. From 1919 to 1933 Negroes participated in professional football. In the period from 1933 to 1946 they were excluded.

The Negro population of Cuba was 323,117, or 11.1%.

1920

U.S. Census: The Negro population in the United States was 10,463,131, or 9.9%. Of these, 15.9% were classified as of mixed blood.

The life expectancy of Negro males was 45.5 years, compared to 54.4 years for white males. The life expectancy of female Negroes was 45.2 years compared to 55.6 years for whites.

The crude birth rate for Negroes was 31.3 per thousand, 15% higher than for whites.

Of northern Negroes 8% were illiterate, but 60% of Negro children living in the North attended school. In the South 85% of all Negro pupils were enrolled for the first four grades, and 26.3% of Southern Negroes were illiterate. This compared to 5.2% of Southern whites who were illiterate.

Of the total Negro population 6.5% lived in the Northeast section of the United States. The percentage in the North Central states was 7.6%, in the South 85.2% and in the Western states 0.8%.

Migration of Negroes from the South to the North and West for the decade 1910 to 1920 was given by the Census Bureau as 330,000.

In the period from 1910 to 1920 the total Negro population of New York, Chicago, Philadelphia and Detroit had increased by nearly three-quarters of a million.

Foreign-born Negro females had a higher naturalization rate than foreign-born Negro males. This was not true of any other racial group.

46.6% of Negroes were employed in farm occupations. The value of Negro farm property exceeded $2¼ billion.

In August, Marcus Garvey opened the national convention of the Universal Negro Improvement Association (UNIA) at Liberty Hall in Harlem. During a month-long meeting speakers were heard on the condition of Negroes throughout the world. At the conclusion of the meeting 3,000 delegates unanimously passed a bill of rights for Negroes, and declared Aug. 31 a national holiday for Negroes. The Black Star Steamship Corporation was also established to transport interested Negroes to Africa.

The AFL national convention voted for resolutions supporting the unionization of Negroes and opposing discrimination. The Brotherhood of Railroad Clerks was asked to delete the phrase "only white" from its membership qualifications. Proposals for regular cooperation between white and Negro labor leaders were defeated.

By this year NAACP leadership, except for the national board, had become largely Negro. In 1920, James Weldon Johnson became the first Negro secretary. The NAACP began a long struggle for the liberation of Haiti. James Weldon Johnson was sent there by the NAACP to investigate. His report showed that 3,000 Haitians had been killed by U.S. Marines, torture had been practiced, and rigid censorship imposed, Haitian freedom, he concluded, had been destroyed by the U.S.

W. E. B. Du Bois editorialized in *Crisis* that a race war

might be inevitable. At the time, there was widespread feeling among whites that the Negro movement was "Bolshevist." The joint committee investigating seditious activity for the New York State Legislature claimed that the NAACP's official publication, *Crisis*, contributed to "revolutionary radicalism." Two bills introduced into Congress, the Sterling Bill and the Graham Bill, denied postal privileges to printed matter which appealed to racial prejudice with the intention of bringing about rioting and violence. These laws were viewed as threats by the editors of *Crisis*, since Southerners interpreted lynching protests as such an incitement. The NAACP raised a vigorous and successful protest against passage of these bills.

A revived Ku Klux Klan had 100,000 members in 27 states.

There were 61 lynchings of Negroes in this year.

The Supreme Court of Arkansas handed down a decision reversing the cases of 6 of the Negroes who twice had been condemned to death for alleged participation in the riots in Elaine.

The Republican National Committee in Chicago passed a ruling which defeated the "lily whitism" of the Southern delegates to the National Convention. The committee also said that Negroes must be admitted to state and district conventions.

Annie Simms Banks of Winchester, became the first Negro woman to be a fully accredited delegate to a state political convention.

Walker G. Alexander of Orange, N.J., was elected the first Negro representative to the New Jersey House of Assembly.

Justice Ebert, an IWW official, stated, "The IWW organizes the Mexican miner, the Spanish fireman, the Negro worker, in fact all races. . . . As long as they are wage workers . . . the IWW welcomes . . . every one of them."

The Brotherhood of Dining Car Employees was organized on a national basis.

Because existing life insurance companies wrote policies for Negroes only under exceptional circumstances, the supreme Life and Casualty Co. was formed to provide them with insurance coverage. Headquarters were in Columbus, Ohio.

The NAACP awarded its Spingarn Medal to W. E. B. Du Bois for his "founding and calling together of the First Pan-African Congress."

James Farmer (1920-   ), founder of CORE, was born in Marshall, Tex. At first interested in medicine and then in the ministry, he was graduated from Wiley College, and in 1941 received his Bachelor of Divinity degree. Refusing ordination for a segregated congregation, he became involved in national antidiscrimination and pacifist organizations. In 1942, he established the Congress of Racial Equality (CORE), and served as its first director. Utilizing Ghandi's tactics of nonviolence and passive resistance, CORE worked to end discrimination in public facilities through the sit-in, standing line and Freedom Ride. He was a major leader of the 1963 March on Washington. Farmer, as a popular writer, lecturer and radio commentator, has donated his fees to CORE. He resigned as national director of CORE in 1966.

John Lewis (1920-   ), Negro jazz pianist and composer, was born in La Grange, Ill., and raised in Albuquerque, N.M. He began studying piano at the age of 7. Lewis attended the University of New Mexico, majoring in anthropology and music. After receiving his discharge from the Army, he joined Dizzy Gillespie's band as arranger and pianist. In 1947 his *Toccata for Trumpet and Orchestra* was played at Carnegie Hall by the Gillespie Band. Lewis began his long association with the Modern Jazz Quartet in 1952. He has also served as music director of the Monterey Jazz Festival.

Charlie Parker (1920-1955), Negro musician, was born in Kansas City. He began playing the saxophone as a child, and by 15 was playing professionally. In 1939 he moved to New York City, and in 1941 made his first recording with Jay McShann. Parker has said that he began playing bop, the jazz development so intimately connected with his name, soon after he came to New York by experimenting with a standard band number, *Cherokee*. Known as "Yardbird" and the "Bird," Parker was the dominant jazz figure of the 1940's and 1950's.

William Warfield (1920-   ), Negro baritone, was born in Arkansas, the son of a Baptist minister. A graduate of the

Eastman School of Music, he appeared in *Set My People Free* and *Showboat* on Broadway; he played Porgy in the 1952 European production of *Porgy and Bess*. Recognized as a leading baritone, Warfield has been on concert tour for the State Department as a soloist with the Philadelphia Symphony Orchestra in 1955, 1956, 1958 and 1966. Warfield starred with the New York City Opera Company in 1961 and 1964, and in 1967 was the soloist with Pablo Casals at the Pacem in Terris II Convocation in Geneva, Switzerland.

In this year, an important cultural movement among Negroes, generally designated as the Harlem Renaissance, began. It lasted from 1920 to 1930. Between 1890 and 1920 over 2 million Negroes had migrated North. During the 1920's a Negro intelligentsia developed in many Northern ghettoes. Societies for Negro advancement such the NAACP and the Urban League, with their house organs, *Crisis* and *Opportunity,* fostered the new cultural revival. Literary societies, such as the Writers' Guild in New York City, Black Opals in Philadelphia, the Saturday Evening Quill Club in Boston and the Ink Slinger in Los Angeles, propagated the race pride and cultural self-awareness which inevitably resulted from the inbred ghetto environment. At the same time an international "Negro" cult in the arts began. Starting with the discovery of African art by the Cubist painters in Paris, prior to World War I, there was an increasing interest in Negro and Black African culture. By the early 1920's this Negro cult had reached major proportions in Paris. Writers such as Apollinaire, Cocteau, etc., were using Negro themes and anthologizing African poetry. Jazz had already captured the field of American popular music, and it was being used and transformed in the avant garde compositions of Milhaud, Poulenc and Honegger. In the United States the distinct quality of Negro culture became evident in white literature. Between 1915 and 1930 a flourishing interest in the Negro was exemplified by such works as O'Neill's *Emperor Jones,* Anderson's *Dark Laughter.* Such white writers as Paul Green, Vachel Lindsay and Dubose Heyward adapted Negro styles or masks in writing their works.

W. E. B. Du Bois published a volume of poems and essays entitled *Dark Water.*

Fenton Johnson's collection of short stories, *Tales of*

Darkest America, was published. Johnson, a Negro, had previously written three collections of verse, published in 1914, 1915 and 1916.

The success of the writers of the Harlem Renaissance killed the Harlem theater movement in this decade. Broadway bought out the Harlem Renaissance with such musicals as *Shuffle Along, Goat Alley,* 1921; *Strut, Miss Lizzie,* 1922; *The Plantation Review,* 1922; *How Come,* 1923; *Chip Woman's Fortune,* 1923; *Chocolate Dandies,* 1924; *From Dixie to Broadway,* 1924; *Topsy and Eva,* 1924. The popularity of movies also led to the closing of several theaters.

Emperor Jones, Eugene O'Neill's first hit, opened at the Provincetown Theater in Greenwich Village, starring a Negro, Charles Gilpin, in the title role. Gilpin was acclaimed one of the ten best actors of the year.

Ten Nights in a Barroom, made by Colored Players Film Corp. of Philadelphia, starred Charles Gilpin, a Negro actor, and was one of the most successful of the Negro films of the 1920's.

The first authentic blues record, *Crazy Blues,* was made by Mamie Smith, a Negro singer.

Elizabeth Prophet, a Negro sculptress, was a native of Providence, R.I. In the 1920's she exhibited in the Paris Salon and in New York City art galleries. Her finest work, *Congo Head,* became part of the Whitney Museum's permanent collection.

The 135th Street branch of the New York Public Library began special exhibits of Negro painters. A Librarian, Ernestine Rose, and an artist, Winfred Russell, organized the shows.

The National Negro Baseball League was organized.

The Haitian author and educator, Louis Morpeau, compiled the *Anthologie Haitienne des Poètes Contemporains, 1904-20.* An important collection, it included some of Morpeau's poems and brought Haitian poetry to the attention of French writers.

1921

Between this year and 1924 a substantial number of Southern Negroes migrated to the North and West. They moved because of agricultural disorganization, loss of new and old jobs to whites, and the discontent Negro soldiers felt on returning to Southern conditions.

Only one of the 63 lynchings in this year took place in a Northern state.

In Tulsa, Okla., riots broke out after it was rumored that a Negro had attacked a white orphan girl. Of the 31 persons killed, 21 were Negroes, and damage was estimated to exceed $1½ million. Property damage was largely the result of a fire which destroyed a 10-block area in the Negro section and left 3,000 Negroes homeless. State troopers were called in on the morning of June 1, augmenting local units of guards called out the night before. Troops were removed during the week of June 11. Though 75 rioters were arrested, many were released; 30 whites were arrested for looting. A grand jury convened to investigate the riots found the police chief and several minor officials guilty of dereliction of duty on the night of the riot. During the presentation of the investigation an attempt was made to shift the blame to Negroes, but the jury declared that most Negroes were not implicated.

On Oct. 11, the Rules Committee of the House of Representatives began to hear testimony on the need for an investigation of the new Ku Klux Klan.

The House Judiciary Committee reported favorably an anti-lynching bill introduced by Congressman Dyer of Missouri. The bill resulted from the NAACP's Anti-Lynching Conference held in New York in 1919. It made lynching a Federal crime. President Harding addressed an audience in Birmingham on race problems. He stated that although he did not support social equality, he advocated economic and political equality for the Negro. He supported the familiar attitude of the time, that the Negro should emphasize a race pride based on race improvement. The Negro, the President continued, "should seek to be 'the best possible black man, and not the best possible imitation of a white man.' Racial amalgamation there cannot be."

James H. Hubert, executive secretary of the New York Urban League, accused the Metropolitan Life Insurance Co. of discrimination against Negroes in employment practices.

Negroes founded the National Insurance Association.

A Negro newspaper, *New York Age*, reported that about

80% of the businesses on 135th Street between Lenox and Seventh Avenues in Harlem were owned by Negroes. "In this block there are 84 places of business," the newspaper reported, "16 of which are white and 58 are colored." These businesses included a tobacconist, restaurant, electricians and photographers among others.

Wesley Redding was appointed the first Negro detective sergeant of the New York City police.

A Commission on Negro churches and Race Relations was established by the Federal Council of the Churches of Christ in America. The commission was to use the churches to bring about better relations between the races.

Charles Gilpin, the Negro actor, was awarded the Spingarn Medal for his performance in the title role of Eugene O'Neill's *Emperor Jones.*

Erroll Garner (1921-   ), Negro jazz pianist, was born in Pittsburgh, Pa. He never learned to read music, although his father was a pianist. In 1937 he began playing with local bands. At 23 he came to New York and played in clubs, particularly on 52nd St. His single-note right-hand playing accompanied by a guitarlike strumming of chords with his left hand set a distinctive jazz style.

James P. Johnson, a Negro, made the first jazz piano solo recording *Carolina Shout* for Okeh Records.

A Negro film company, Colored Feature Photo Plays, Inc., was organized. Its aim was to produce "high class photo plays featuring colored actors and actresses."

1922

In January, Marcus Garvey was arrested and charged with the use of the mails to defraud through the selling of stock and membership in false and fraudulent organizations, and also for selling passages to Africa on a mythical vessel. Garvey was indicted by a Federal grand jury on Feb. 16. In August, Garvey's written resignation was rejected when the Third Annual Meeting of UNIA re-elected him supreme head. In October, Marcus Garvey was the principal speaker at the North Carolina Negro state fair. He explained that there was nothing radical about his proposal to found the United States of Africa. "The black man gets his cue from the white man," he said, "and the white man is somebody because

he has some [material] things. The white man has machinery
and he has the government. He counts. . . . " Garvey stated
that the white man was not made superior by God, but
made himself superior. The Negro, according to Garvey, had
to do the same. He said there was no reason to dislike the
white man because of his hatred. "He despises . . .[Negroes]
because . . . [he is] after something that belongs to him."

An independent Harlem group established its own slate
of candidates for the 21st Congressional District, to be
nominated in a September primary. Heading the list was
William H. Ferris, who was connected with Garvey's UNIA.

The U.S. House of Representatives passed the Dyer Anti-
Lynching Bill that provided that "any state or municipal
officer charged with the duty of protecting the life of any
person, who may be put to death by a mob, and who fails
to make all reasonable efforts to prevent the killing, . . .
shall be punished by imprisonment, for not exceeding five
years, or by a fine of $5,000 or less or by both. . . . Any
person who participates in a mob murder, is declared to be
guilty of a felony." The bill further provided a sum of
$10,000 to be paid to the victim's family by the county
where the person was put to death.

Republican Senators voted to abandon the Dyer Anti-
Lynching Bill. This action took place after a lengthy filibuster associated with the Liberian Loan Bill, used as a
delaying tactic by Southern Senators against the Dyer Bill.

The Fordney Bill passed by the House of Representatives
authorized a $5 million loan by the United States to Liberia.
Although approved by President Harding and Secretary of
State Hughes, in an extra session of the 67th Congress the
bill was effectively defeated by being returned to the Senate
Finance Committee.

The Lincoln Memorial was dedicated in Washington, D.C.,
after 20 years of planning. Speakers included President Harding, former President Taft and Robert Moton, president of
Tuskegee Institute in Alabama. Moton praised Lincoln for
preserving the Union, but also underscored the contribution
of the Negro, emphasizing a continuous loyalty to the country. According to a report submitted by James Weldon Johnson, segregation was practiced at the dedication ceremony.

Washrooms, restaurants and public buildings were closed to Negroes. Negro ticket holders to the ceremonies also found a special section roped off for them behind the white section.

There were 51 Negro lynchings: 30 of them were lynched after being held by the police.

On May 6 three Negroes were burned at the stake in the public square of Kirvin, Tex., while 500 whites looked on. All three had been in the custody of the police.

A petition presented to Harvard stated that the university discriminated against Negroes. A letter sent from President Lowell of Harvard to two Negro students expressed administration policy: "If Harvard were faced by the alternative of either admitting Negroes to the freshman halls where white students are compelled to go or of excluding Negroes altogether, it might be compelled like other colleges, to adopt the other alternative."

Two Negro women became the first Negro women to receive law degrees in the State of New York. The degrees were awarded by New York University.

Negro women from Africa, Haiti, the West Indies, Ceylon and the United States met in Washington, D.C., to establish an International Council of the Women of the Dark Races. The first annual meeting was to be held in 1923 in Sweden.

In this year the NAACP advocated the liberation of Haiti from American domination.

A grant of $25,000 was made by the Carnegie Corporation and an equal amount by the Rockefeller Memorial to sustain the publication of *The Journal of Negro History* and to increase the research done in Negro history, especially about the free Negro prior to 1861 and during Reconstruction.

The Harlem Tuberculosis and Health Committee, a branch of the New York Tuberculosis and Health Association, was founded to combat the disease among New York Negroes. The largest number of reported cases were Negroes. The campaign was largely unsuccessful, for between 1929 and 1933, the ratio of Negroes rose to four for every one case among whites. The ratio had previously been between 2 and 3 to 1.

McDonough Memorial Hospital was begun. This was to be

the first hospital in New York State to be wholly operated by Negroes.

Charles C. Diggs (1922-   ), Negro Congressman, was born in Detroit, Mich. Educated at the University of Michigan and Fisk, he was drafted into the Army Air Force in 1942. Discharged as a second lieutenant, he returned to Detroit and became involved in the family business, the largest funeral home in Michigan. He was elected to the State Senate in 1951, and in 1954 to the House of Representatives. Active on behalf of Southern Negroes in particular and for civil rights in general, he has worked for voter registration, antidiscrimination in the armed forces and Federally financed programs.

Floyd McKissick (1922-   ), national director of CORE, was born in Asheville, N.C. A graduate of the University of N.C. Law School, he served in Europe as a sergeant in the U.S. Army during World War II. As a lawyer in Durham, N.C., he successfully defended his daughter's suit for admission to an all-white public school. In January, 1966, he succeeded James Farmer as national director of CORE.

The Harmon Foundation was founded to promote greater opportunities for Negroes in the fine arts. In 1928 the foundation began an annual exhibition of Negro art. Eventually the Harmon Gallery in New York City was opened for the permanent display of Negro art. Through the years the foundation has built up an impressive permanent collection. The foundation presents awards to leading Negro artists and writers. Countee Cullen was the first recipient of its gold medal for literature in 1927. In 1930 Langston Hughes received the same prize. Winners in the fine arts include Laura Wheeler Waring, a painter, in 1927.

Claude McKay's book of poetry, *Harlem Shadows*, was published. It exalted Negro life and lampooned Negroes who tried to pass as white.

A Negro, Leslie Pinckney Hill, wrote *Wings of Oppression,* a collection of verse.

One Exciting Night, directed by D. W. Griffith, introduced the stereotype of the Negro as a foolish and superstitious coward into the cinema. Porter Strong, who played the Negro, was white.

Charles Mingus (1922-   ), Negro musician and composer, was born in Nogales, Ariz. Mingus studied trombone, cello and bass in Los Angeles with Britt Woodman and Red Callendar. From 1941 through 1943, he played with Louis Armstrong. His first recording was made in 1947, a bop album on Decca Records. It included his own work, *Mingus Fingers.* Mingus has played with Red Norvo, Billy Taylor, Charlie Parker, Duke Ellington and Art Tatum. In recent years he has spent more and more time composing. Mingus is one of the more influential musical figures in the development of modern jazz.

1923

James Weldon Johnson stated in the *New York Age* that there were many reasons other than low wages for Negroes to leave the South, and that until there was fairer treatment, Northern migration of Negroes would continue.

Some Southern states strictly enforced laws regulating contract labor for the Northern market. South Carolina arrested a labor agent for "secretly enticing Negro laborers" and fined him $500. In Virginia a man hiring for a cement factory in New Jersey was fined $1,000 for soliciting labor without a city license.

In this year, 29 Negroes were lynched.

From 1923 to 1927 Harlem's death rate was 42% higher than that of the entire city. Twice as many Harlem mothers died in childbirth as did mothers in other districts. Infant mortality was 111 per thousand live births. Deaths from tuberculosis, pneumonia, heart disease, cancer and stillbirths were 2½ to 3 times the city rate.

On June 21, Marcus Garvey, president general of the UNIA, was convicted of using the mails to defraud and sentenced to 5 years in prison, fined $1,000 and required to pay court costs. Garvey was allowed a 4-month period to appeal. In an interview at the New York City "Tombs," Garvey said, "Most of my troubles are the result of the efforts of my opponents of the colored race. There are light-colored Negroes who think that the Negro can always develop in this country. They also resent the fact that I, a black Negro, am a leader." In an earlier statement to the judge he had said, "I regard America as the greatest national friend of the Negro . . . .

[but] I feel the dawn for the Negro race will come and my children and people will appreciate my sacrifice. I am satisfied to serve any sentence the court may impose." In his trial Garvey had acted as his own attorney.

Riots erupted in Rosewood, Fla., after an alleged attack on a white woman by three Negroes; four Negroes and two whites were killed and many wounded. Six buildings in the Negro community were burned and when all the Negro inhabitants had fled, another mob formed and 12 remaining structures were burned.

The Abyssinian Baptist Church opened its new Harlem building on 138th Street. The structure cost $300,000. The minister was Rev. Adam Clayton Powell Sr., who had served the congregation since 1908.

The Julius Rosenwald Fund that had been founded in part to help create better rural schools for Negroes reported that to date 1,700 schools and 49 teachers' homes had been built in Southern states, at a total cost of $6.2 million. Negroes had contributed 25.6% and whites 5.6%, public funds accounted for 49%, and Julius Rosenwald of Chicago for 19.3%.

President A. Lawrence Lowell's ruling that Negro freshmen at Harvard University could not reside in the freshman dormitories was rescinded by the Harvard Corporation. It stated "that in the administration of rules for admission Harvard College maintains its traditional policy of freedom from discrimination on grounds of race and religion." The Harvard Corporation further stated "that men of the white and colored races shall not be compelled to live and eat together, nor shall any man be excluded by reason of his color."

Col. Charles Young who had held the highest rank gained by a Negro in the U.S. Army in World War I died in this year. Speakers at the funeral in the Great Hall of City College of New York included Theodore Roosevelt, W. E. B. Du Bois and F. W. Seaden of the United States Military Academy. The hall was filled with members of military fraternities and Negro civic organizations.

Watt Terry, a New York City realtor, was described by the National Negro Business League as the largest individual Negro real estate owner in the country. His holdings, estimated to exceed $1,000,000, consisted of between 45 and 50 parcels of real estate in New York City and in Brockton, Mass.

Garrett A. Morgan, a Negro, who had invented the gas mask, developed an automatic traffic light.

Cane, a novel by Jean Toomer was published. Toomer was a cultivated Negro of Creole origin, educated in the U.S. and France. Although the novel was poorly received at the time, it is now considered one of the best works of the Harlem Renaissance.

Wes Montgomery (1923-1968), Negro jazz guitarist, was born in Indianapolis. He taught himself to play guitar and appeared with Lionel Hampton beginning in 1948. In the 1950's he played in and around Indianapolis. His first recordings were made with his brother, Buddy, on vibes. In 1959 he went to San Francisco to play with Mastersounds, his brother's group, and later came to New York. Although self-taught, Montgomery is ranked along with Charlie Christian as the greatest of the jazz guitarists. In 1967 he was a top-selling jazz recording artist. Three of his best selling albums were *A Day in the Life, Going Out of My Head*, and *Movin' Wes*.

"King" Oliver's Band was the first Negro jazz orchestra to record on a major record label.

Jelly Roll Morton recorded with the New Orleans Rhythm Kings. This was probably the first time a Negro musician recorded with a white band.

Rev. J. W. H. Eason, who until 1922 had been Marcus Garvey's closest associate, was assassinated. After Garvey had ousted him from the UNIA, Eason had founded an opposition group, the Universal Negro Alliance, and had bitterly denounced Garvey. He had planned to appear as a witness against Garvey in Federal court.

Although the Senate twice refused to pass an anti-lynching bill introduced by Representative Dyer in 1922 and again in 1923, the NAACP succeeded in convincing President Coolidge to condemn lynching in his annual message to Congress.

Sen. Joseph S. Frelinghuysen, a Republican of New Jersey, introduced a joint resolution providing for the appointment of a Federal Commission on Lynching, authorized to make investigations to provide information for Congress in order to draw up legislation to prevent lynching.

After considerable debate the Pennsylvania House of Representatives passed the Stevens Anti-lynching Bill. It was almost a replica of the Dyer bill, introduced and subsequently dropped in the Senate.

The Governor of New Jersey signed into law a bill to suppress mob violence and lynching. It placed responsibility on the local authorities to maintain peace and to protect citizens from mob violence.

In October of 1919 in Elaine, Arkansas, a group of Negro farmers who were attempting to unionize were fired upon. A riot resulted, 12 Negroes were sentenced to death and 67 to long prison terms in a trial which had involved the whipping of witnesses and the presence of a mob in the courtroom. As the case of MOORE V. DEMPSEY the NAACP appealed to the Supreme Court for a writ of *habeas corpus*. The Court ruled in favor of the NAACP, declaring that due process was violated if a trial was disorderly, or dominated by a mob. This decision was affirmed by the Supreme Court in similar cases in 1934, 1940, 1942, 1948, 1949, 1954 and 1957.

A judge of the county court of Hennepin County, Minnesota, declared that all boxing and prize fighting was illegal until the Minnesota State Athletic Commission revoked its rule prohibiting bouts between Negro and white boxers. The ruling was made upon petition of the Equal Rights League, which maintained that Rule 33 of the Minnesota Athletic Commission was a violation of the 14th Amendment.

Jackie "Moms" Mabley, the Negro comedienne, had her first success at Connie's Inn in New York City.

1924

The meeting of the Negro Sanhedrin or All-Race Sanhedrin Conference opened in Chicago with Kelly Miller of Howard University at its head. Of 61 organizations of Negroes, more than 50 attended. Discussions considered all aspects of Negro life in the U.S. The Mayor of Chicago, William E. Dever, gave the main address, emphasizing the inevitability of the Negro achieving his rights and "wiping out all lines of inequality that are based upon the color of one's skin." The Sanhedrin, in contrast to Du Bois' Pan-African Congress and

Garvey's Universal Negro Improvement Association, attempted to make possible a single voice for all Negroes to avoid duplications of functions and to focus attention on the situation of the Negro in the U.S.

At the 25th anniversary meeting of the Negro Business League, Robert Moton, its president, stated in his address that during the 25 years of its existence, small and large Negro businesses had increased from 20,000 to 65,000. In the same period, Moton stated, from $300,000,000 to $1.7 billion was accumulated in realty holdings by Negroes.

The National Negro Finance Corporation was established as an auxiliary of the National Negro Business League. Capitalized at $1,000,000, its purpose was to enable Negro businessmen to expand their enterprises as well as to offer a stock fund investment opportunity for Negroes.

The National Negro Bankers Association was founded.

The Democratic National Convention in New York City was attended by 13 national Negro political leaders. One issue at the 1924 convention was whether a strong stand should be made against the KKK. Advocates of such a stand were Northern whites such as McAdoo and Smith. It was opposed by the Southern leadership, headed by Senator Harrison of Mississippi. *The Chicago Defender,* Negro newspaper, reported that there was no segregation of delegates at the convention. The paper reported that segregation did exist at the Republican Convention.

A New York State civil rights law was invoked against Walter Hampden Inc. for discriminating against Negroes at the National Theater in New York City.

Representative Emanuel Celler, Democrat of New York, introduced a bill to authorize the formation of a commission on the racial question. He proposed three whites from the North, three whites from the South and three Negroes be appointed by President Coolidge. In response to the Celler Bill, *The Chicago Defender* said, "Despite the fact that this idea was endorsed by the President, we think such a commission is a useless instrument. It does not meet the issue at all. We have been commissioned to death. . . . We have too many studies and reports already. . . . What we need is a party organization and leadership which will give us our own representatives in Congress and in the Senate to look after our own interests. . . . Let the members of Congress see to it that the election laws are properly obeyed in the South and that the franchise is given to all citizens, regardless of color.

The Ku Klux Klan had approximately 4-½ million members.

There were 16 Negroes lynched in this year.

A mass meeting of Negroes and Virgin Islanders was held in New York City to demand that Congress grant a permanent form of civil government to the Virgin Islands, insure the rights of all citizens on the Islands and remove the legislative barriers to trade and commerce which existed between the Islands and the United States.

The Immigration Act of this year excluded Negroes of African descent from entry into the United States.

George Eastman of the Kodak Co., Rochester, N.Y., gave Tuskegee and Hampden Institutes $1 million each.

A list compiled by the American Federation of Negro students named the following as the greatest American Negroes: George Washington Carver, James Weldon Johnson, Henry O. Tanner, W. E. B. Du Bois, Paul Laurence Dunbar, Col. Charles Young, Booker T. Washington, Madame C. J. Walker and Robert S. Abbott.

James Baldwin (1924-   ), Negro author, was born in Harlem, N.Y. He was trained for the ministry and planned to succeed his father as a preacher. After six years of frustration and two writing fellowships, Baldwin went to Paris. He spent 9 years there and completed his first novel in 1951, *Go Tell It on the Mountain*. This novel concerns a ghetto adolescent who becomes a store-front preacher. It gives a masterful description of the role religion plays in Negro American life, pointing out that all Negro children are its victims, and that in the end the church offers no salvation from the brutal facts of the ghetto. In 1954, *The Amen Corner*, a play dealing with store-front preachers, was produced at Howard University; commercial exposure came a decade later. Baldwin's second novel, *Giovanni's Room*, appeared in 1956. In 1957, *Notes of a Native Son*, a collection of essays, established Baldwin as a major contemporary American voice. He is quite possibly one of the best essayists in American letters today. His other works include: *Nobody Knows My Name*, 1961, a second book of essays; *Another Country*, 1962, Baldwin's third and most ambitious novel; *The Fire Next Time*, a long essay about racial tensions in America, 1963; *Blues for Mr. Charlie*, a play about racial violence in the South, produced on Broadway in 1964; *Going to See the Man*, 1966 a collection of short stories; *Tell Me How Long the Train's Been Gone*, 1968, a novel. Baldwin's gifts as a writer are best revealed in his essays rather than fiction or drama. He has also written virtually 1,000 poems, none of which have been published because he feels that they are too personal.

John T. Biggers (1924-   ), Negro artist, was born in Gastonia, N.C. Educated at the Hampton Institute, and later at Penn State University, he came under the guidance of Walter Lowenfeld, chairman of the department of art education. Biggers is primarily a muralist, and greatly influenced by José Orozco and Charles White. His paintings depict the conditions and hopes of the contemporary Southern Negro. One of his most important works is the series of murals at the Houston Negro YMCA, *The Contribution of American Women to American Life and Education*. In the late 1950's Biggers visited Ghana and Nigeria. This experience resulted in a book, *Ananse, the Web of Life in Africa*, which concentrated primarily on the life of the people in the towns and villages he had visited.

Sidney Poitier (1924-   ), Negro actor, was born in Miami, Fla. Brought up in the Bahamas, he returned to the U.S. in 1939. After four years in the Army during World War II, he was accepted by the American Negro Theater. In 1950 he made his first movie, and has since become the most prominent Negro movie star in America. In 1964 he won the Academy Award for best actor in the film *Lilies of the Field*. He also starred in Lorraine Hansberry's play, *Raisin in the Sun*, produced on Broadway in 1959. His films include: *Cry the Beloved Country*, 1952; *Blackboard Jungle*, 1956; *Edge of the City*, 1957; *The Defiant Ones*, 1957; *Something of Value*, 1957; *Porgy and Bess*, 1959; *Patch of Blue*, 1966; *Guess Who's Coming to Dinner*, 1967; *For Love of Ivy*, 1968.

John A. Williams (1924-   ), Negro author, was born

in Hinds County, Miss., and raised in Syracuse, N.Y. Williams worked at several jobs and seemed to have had experiences as varied as Willard Motley's. In 1961, *Night Song*, a novel, was published. Williams became the center of controversy in 1962 when the American Academy of Arts and Letters awarded him a $3,500 grant for study in Rome. The American Academy jury unanimously elected Williams, but the Rome Academy nullified the decision. In 1963, *Sissie*, a novel portraying successive generations of a Negro family, was published. *This Is My Country Too,* a record of travels through the U.S., originally written on commission from *Holiday* magazine, appeared in 1965. In the same year he wrote *Journey to Nigeria*, a documentary produced for National Educational Television. The program was filmed in 1964, though not released until after *This Is My Country, Too,* which is, in a sense, a sequel to it. Both book and TV program make up a fascinating record of an American Negro's odyssey toward self-discovery. They are unique in American literature. In 1967, *The Man Who Cried I Am*, Williams' third novel, was published.

William White, a Negro, published *The Fire In the Flint,* the only novel of the 1920's to concern itself with Negro-white relations in the South during the height of the KKK revival.

Sidney Woodward, a noted Negro concert tenor, died. Woodward was born in Georgia and moved to Boston. He later went to Germany to study voice at the Dresden Conservatory. He gave concerts in major European countries, including a performance for the King and Queen of England.

Roland W. Hayes, a Negro tenor, was awarded the Spingarn Medal.

The National Ethiopian Art Theater School opened under the general direction of Anne Wolter. The movement was sponsored by the Harlem Community Theater Organization. Its curriculum included all aspects of theater training. It had classes in stagecraft, acting and dance.

Marie Blair, a white actress, was chosen to play opposite Paul Robeson in the Eugene O'Neill play *All God's Chillun Got Wings*. A considerable stir was aroused in the white press.

Noble Sissle and Eubie Blake, both Negroes, wrote several popular musicals in the 1920's. After *Shuffle Along* came *Chocolate Dandies*, in 1924. This musical revue introduced Josephine Baker as a dancer. Sissle and Blake split up in the late 1920's, each touring the country with his own independent orchestra. Blake made something of a comeback in the movie *Harlem Is Heaven* (1932), an independent Lincoln Pictures Production which co-featured Bill "Bojangles" Robinson.

Louis Armstrong left Chicago to go to New York to play with Fletcher Henderson at the Roseland Ballroom on Broadway. Henderson's arrangements were used in the second half of the 1930's by large swing bands. especially Benny Goodman.

1925

The Chicago Defender, on the occasion of its 20th anniversary, demanded "that all workmen's organizations open their doors to all workmen, without regard to color."

During the life of the IWW (1905-1925) about 100,000 membership cards were issued to Negroes. The most important IWW work among Negroes was in the Louisiana and Texas lumber industry and among the Negro longshoremen of Philadelphia, Baltimore and of Norfolk, Va.

The Urban League founded the Trade Union Committee for Organizing Negroes. It hoped through the committee to encourage union membership and discourage use of Negroes as strikebreakers. The committee was disbanded in 1927 with few achievements.

In July a feature article in the *New York World* reported that a movement was under way in the AFL to organize Negro workers. A committee was formed by Frank R. Crosswaith, a Socialist Party candidate for the office of New York secretary of state.

At the fifth mass meeting of the Brotherhood of Sleeping Car Porters, held in the Abyssinian Baptist Church in New York City, Hugh Frayne, AFL organizer in New York State, pledged its support of Negro efforts to achieve the same rights and privileges as white workers.

Lovett Fort-Whiteman, a former member of the American

Communist Party, organized the American Negro Labor
Congress. In October delegates from many states came to the
Congress in Chicago. The primary aim of the ANLC was
"to serve as an effective medium of contact between workers
of all races, and a fighting weapon for their complete emancipation."

The NAACP asked President Coolidge to remove American
troops from Haiti. The memorandum to the President contained the allegation that the Haitian Constitution had been
violated by the occupation by American troops.

Through the efforts of the NAACP fourteen men sentenced
to 21 years at the Arkansas State Farm prison for taking part
in the Elaine, Ark., race riots of 1919 were freed by Governor McRae after having served five years. Previous attempts
to seek pardons had been refused by the Governor.

The Supreme Court of the State of Michigan barred color
discrimination in the sale of property. The suit involved
two white real estate dealers of Muskegon, Mich., Porter
and Wyman. The former sued Wilbratt and Auxilie Barrett
(whites) for selling property to a Negro, Wilson Robinson,
in violation of a restrictive agreement concerning the resale
of the property.

George W. Holt, a St. Louis Negro, was restrained from
living in his own house or renting to another Negro by a
circuit judge.

Dr. Ossian Sweet, a Negro, moved into a white neighborhood in Detroit. In September, an angry white mob surrounded and stoned the house. Shots were fired, and one
white man was killed. Dr. Sweet and ten friends who were
visiting that day were arrested. The NAACP secured the
services of Clarence Darrow to defend the men. The first
jury called could not reach a verdict. In the second trial,
Sweet's son, Henry was acquitted, and the charges against
the other 10 were dropped.

A Detroit mob stoned the residence of Dr. Alex L. Turner,
a Negro, and drove him from his newly purchased home in a
white neighborhood.

In the fall of 1925, Detroit's Mayor, John W. Smith,
appointed an interracial commission to formulate "a program

for bettering relations beween the races." Reinhold Niebuhr was chairman. The commission's report was published in the spring of 1926. Discussing Negroes moving into white neighborhoods as the immediate cause of the 1925 racial riots in Detroit, the report stated that fear of property value depreciation had caused the friction. The commission found, however, that individual home ownership for Negroes should be encouraged, and that banks should make it easier for Negroes to acquire loans for this and for business purposes. The report also suggested that banks should employ more Negroes. It advocated city or private support for improved and new housing in Negro districts, and insisted on the immediate need to eradicate the unsanitary conditions in Negro areas, especially where there was no sewage disposal. On the subject of crime, the commission found that the high Negro crime rate resulted from the difficulties Southern Negroes had adjusting to urban conditions. The rate would drop as assimiliation progressed. Evidence of police brutality was cited, and the report suggested that police officers serving in Negro areas be screened for racial prejudice and that more Negro officers be employed. The commission felt that Negroes were not receiving equal consideration in the courts and did not have adequate legal counsel. Remedial classes for Southern migrants' children and the hiring of more Negro teachers were advocated. In the sections on health, recreation and welfare, the commission asked for increased hospital facilities, particularly for unwed mothers and those with venereal diseases; more Negro nurses and doctors were needed, summer camps and day nurseries should be established for Negro children. The juvenile court was urged to reconsider its policy of not hiring Negro social workers, and the Department of Welfare to employ more Negroes, particularly as caseworkers.

The Supreme Court of Kansas ruled that a restaurant keeper was not bound by the same requirements as the owners of inns, hotels and boarding houses in statutes against discrimination. In this case, KANSAS v. BROWN, a Negro had sued a restaurant owner for refusing to serve him.

More than 2,000 delegates at the convention of the International Council of Women in Washington, D.C., walked out when segregation was attempted. The President of the

National Federal of Colored Women's Clubs, Hallie Q. Brown, led the demonstration.

Students at Fisk University staged a protest against Fayette Avery McKenzie's presidency. President McKenzie then demanded that a petition supporting his administration be signed. On their refusal to sign, he insisted that the students leave the campus and pressed charges of disorderly conduct against five of the leaders. Their arrest solidified both sides in the struggle between alumni and student groups and McKenzie. Over 400 students left the campus in protest. They contended that McKenzie favored his white business friends, and was administering the university in an autocratic fashion after having dissolved the student government association. They alleged that he had barred newspapers critical of him from the school library. Several months later McKenzie resigned.

Howard University students rioted and staged a strike in opposition to a compulsory military program and the so-called "twenty cut" faculty ruling whereby a student who did not attend classes might subsequently be suspended. In all, a total of 17 grievances was drawn up and supported by 1,200 striking students. An alumni committee was formed to negotiate with the faculty. Some Student Council members asserted that the university was placing military training above academic studies. The student council demanded that "all students on strike be reinstated without penalty; that compulsory education in all branches be reduced to two years; that control of all social activities of students be given over to the council; that students be given representation on the academic council." When the junior college of Howard University was disbanded some of the leading faculty members were dismissed. They included Kelly Miller, Alain Locke and Alonzo Brown, all of whom had sympathized with the student strike.

Sen. William B. McKinley introduced the Dyer Anti-Lynching Bill into the Senate in a strengthened form. The bill provided that any officer who failed to make a reasonable effort to protect a prisoner from mob violence would be guilty of a felony and, upon conviction, punished by imprisonment, not exceeding five years, or a fine of $5,000, or both. Anyone conspiring with the official would also be liable to a felony conviction.

In the past 10 years 7 states had passed laws designed to suppress lynching. This brought the number of states with anti-lynching legislation to 13.

According to a report issued by Tuskegee Institute 16 persons were killed as a result of mob violence. This figure included lynchings and burnings at the stake.

President Coolidge in his message to Congress in December, stated, "Our country has no more loyal citizens [than the Negroes]. . . . They need reassurance that the requirements of the government and society, to deal out to them evenhanded justice will be met. . . . It is fundamental of our institutions that they seek to guarantee to all our inhabitants the right to live their own lives under the protection of the public law. This does not include any license to injure others materially, physically, morally, to incite revolution, or to violate the established customs which have long had the sanction of enlightened society. But it does mean the full right to liberty and equality before the law without distinction of race or creed. . . . An enlarged freedom can only be secured by the application of the golden rule."

Marcus Garvey lost his appeal for a new trial. The U.S. Circuit Court ruled that he must pay his $1,000 fine and serve 5 years in a Federal prison.

A Negro, Clifford Wharton, a graduate of the Boston University Law School, gained admission to the American Government's new school of diplomacy. White students at the foreign service school refused to attend classes with Wharton, and so the school graduated him without requiring his attendance at classes. Wharton was then appointed an attaché to Liberia.

Elbert R. "Doc" Robertson, a Negro inventor, died after years of litigation with railroad companies over patent rights on his inventions. In Nashville, Tenn., he had invented the chilled groove wheel, used by all railroads. Although it was patented, he maintained that it had been stolen by a white man who sold it to the Chicago Railway Co. In a lengthy legal battle the U.S. Supreme Court decided in his favor and awarded him $13,000,000 in royalties. In addition to the chilled grove wheel, Robertson invented the third rail used by elevated railroads in various cities, and a mold in which concrete pillars were made for building foundations.

Frederick Douglass' nomination for the Hall of Fame at Columbia University was approved by Gov. Al Smith.

James Weldon Johnson was awarded the Spingarn Medal.

Sammy Davis, Jr. (1925-   ), Negro entertainer, was born in New York City. As a little boy he appeared in vaudeville with his father in the Will Mastin Trio. The trio was active throughout the 1930's, and in 1946 became a successful nightclub act. Throughout his career, Davis has been known for his exceptional versatility as an entertainer. His movie appearances include *Rufus for President*, 1931; *Porgy and Bess*, 1959; *Oceans 11*. A recording star, he had been a successful Broadway actor in two plays, *Mr. Wonderful*, and *Golden Boy*; a television star, and a successful author—*Yes I Can*, an autobiography, was published in 1966.

Malcolm X (1925-1965), founder of the Organization of Afro-American Unity, was born Malcolm Little, in Omaha, Neb. After his father's death, having completed the 8th grade, he left school and came to New York. He worked as a waiter at Small's Paradise in Harlem. In 1946, at the age of 21, he was sentenced to a 10-year prison term for burglary. While in prison, Malcolm X became a convert to the Black Muslim sect. After his release he spoke publicly to white and Negro groups in colleges on the evils of whites and the need for Negro revenge. When in 1963 he said the death of President Kennedy was yet another result of white evil and violence, he was suspended from the Black Muslim movement. He then traveled to the Middle East, seriously studied the Moslem faith and returned to the U.S. to found a new nationalist group, the Organization of Afro-American Unity. He was shot to death by a group of Negroes in 1965 in New York, and buried as Al Hajj Malik al-Shabazz, the name he had taken in 1964.

Countee Cullen, a Negro, had his first and best collection of poetry, *Color* published.

The New Negro edited by Alain Locke was published. An anthology of verse, fiction and nonfiction, by Harlem writers, it defined and aimed the Harlem Renaissance movement.

Appearances by Garland Anderson a full-length drama by a Negro was produced on Broadway. It dealt with a nonracial theme, ran for 23 performances, and was subsequently revived on Broadway and in London.

Harlem by Wallace Thurman, opened at the 42nd Street Apollo and ran 93 performances.

The Florian Slappey series of movies was produced and written by Octavius Roy Cohen, primarily for the Negro market. These were shorts, as were all Negro movies, which enjoyed a large popularity throughout the 1920's. Cohen's comedies were full of the most vulgar blackface humor.

The Boston Athletic Club refused admission to a Boston University football player, on the ground that he was a Negro. Boston University and several other athletic clubs joined in a protest.

As a result of the efforts of former alderman, George W. Harris, and many civic organizations, Negro physicians were admitted to practice at Harlem Hospital in New York City.

Manhattan's population density was 223 people per acre; in the Negro districts it was 336.

Émile Roumer, a native of Jérémie, Haiti, published his first collection of poetry, *Poèmes d'Haiti et de France*. Roumer, educated in France and England, was one of the founders of The *Revue Indigène*.

1926

A survey issued by the Office of Race Activity for the Congregational Church Extension Boards reported that of 12 million Negroes in the U.S. only 5 million attended a church. According to the report, the church was steadily losing its influence in city life, where Negroes were adapting to urban life and to the complex industrial society. Exclusive of the South, statistics concerning the religious affiliation of Negroes in the 7 largest Northern cities—New York, Chicago, Washington, Detroit, Cleveland, Boston, Buffalo—showed that nearly two-thirds of the entire Negro population had no religious affiliation. The report stated: "The church, it is asserted, fails to meet the problems of the laborer in his struggle against the oppression of low wages and unfair working conditions. It fails to meet the problems of the small family head in his battle against rent gouging and wretched housing conditions. In dealing with fundamental social issues, the church too often finds its own hands tied by economic complications."

The census of religious bodies listed the number of churches among Negroes, and congregations with which foreign-born Negroes usually affiliated: African Orthodox Church, 13; African Orthodox Church of New York, 3; Christian Church, 1,044; Lutheran congregations (United Lutherans) 3,650; Wesleyan Methodist, 619; Moravians, 127; Episcopals (Protestant and Reformed), 7,368; Roman Catholic, 16,940; Seventh Day Adventist, 1,981.

The Negro newspaper *The Chicago Defender* added additional planks to its platform for America: "(1) the opening up of all trades and trade unions to blacks as well as whites;" (2) the appointment of a Negro to the President's Cabinet; (3) Negroes to be in police departments over the entire U.S.; (4) Negroes to be admitted as engineers and firemen on all American railroads, steamships and government controlled industries; (5) government schools to be opened to all American citizens, in preference to foreigners; (6) Negro motormen and conductors to be placed on street railways throughout the U.S.

According to Bulletin No. 7 of the Industrial Relations Department of the National Urban League, there was a growing sentiment within the ranks of organized labor to include Negro workers. Mentioned was the attempt to organize 2,500 tobacco workers in Philadelphia. In Hot Springs, Ark., the report noted, there had been some change in attitudes in union sentiment among bricklayers, plumbers and electricians. In New York City, a Harlem theater was being picketed because of the use of nonunion operators in other houses owned by the same chain. In Chicago, limited concessions were made to Negro electricians by the Electrical Workers Union.

In Chicago, 100 Negro women workers struck against the Moras Stuffed Date factory, because of wage cuts. Their grievance committee consulted with John Fitzpatrick of the AFL and Lovett Fort-Whiteman of the American Negro Labor Congress on methods of organization. The strikers were supported by the International Workers Aid, which gathered funds to provide food for those unable to obtain it. Several pickets were arrested by the Chicago police.

A report of the Department of Labor showed 136,065 Negroes were employed by railroads lines in the U.S., of whom 95,713 were classified as laborers. The largest category, Pullman and train porters, totaled 20,224.

A vice president and organizer of Chicago's Afro-American Flat Janitors Union, Edward Dunn, was murdered by regular white union members who declared Dunn's union illegal.

A report of the Commission on Slavery was read and presented to the Council of the League of Nations. The commission's report stated: "It has been notorious for years that the cotton crop of the Southern states is raised and harvested by a system of enforced labor in which members of the [Negro] race are held in virtual slavery."

President Coolidge, in his message to Congress said in part, "The social well-being of our country requires our constant efforts for the amelioration of race prejudice and the extension to all elements of equal opportunity and equal protection under the laws, which are guaranteed by the Constitution. The federal government especially is charged with this obligation in behalf of the Colored people of the nation. Not only their remarkable progress, their devotion and their loyalty, but our duty to ourselves under our claim that we are enlightened people requires us to use all our power to protect them from the crime of lynching. Although violence of this kind has very much decreased, while any of it remains we cannot justify neglecting to make every effort to eradicate it by law."

Delegates to the Interdenominational Students Conference in Evanston, Ill. (it had a membership of about 1,000 university students from all over the world) found that not all in attendance could be served in the theaters and restaurants. Agitated discussion brought forth the proposal to boycott all restaurants which discriminated. Several hundred students then marched across town and ate lunch in Negro restaurants. As a result of these incidents, discussions continued throughout the conference on the question of the race problem in the U.S.

In this year 23 Negroes were lynched.

Victor L. Berger, Socialist Representative of Wisconsin, again introduced anti-lynching legislation similar to bills introduced by William McKinley in the Senate and L. C. Dyer in the House.

The anti-lynching bill introduced in the Senate by William McKinley failed to be reported out of committee.

Judge H. C. Cage of New Orleans ruled a city ordinance providing for Jim Crow residential sections not in accordance with justice and fairness and refused to order it obeyed.

Judge James P. Drew of Pittsburgh refused to honor extradition papers demanding the return of Sandy Huser, a Negro, to North Carolina to stand trial for violation of the 18th Amendment. Drew declared that he knew Huser could not obtain a fair trial in the South because Negroes were not allowed to serve on juries. Huser was freed.

In Georgetown, Del., Harry Butler, a Negro, charged with attacking a 12-year-old white girl, was convicted and sentenced to death in 8 minutes. The defendant had been held secretly prior to the trial, and at the end of the trial 500 persons were permitted, after being searched for guns, to enter the courtroom. The state militia held off the remainder of the mob of approximately 2,000 whites.

In Aiken, S.C., a mob terrorized the town for hours as a result of a not-guilty verdict in the second trial of 2 Negro men and a woman for the murder of a sheriff in April. The men were lynched. The mob also attempted to seize the judge who had rendered the decision. It was later reported by a special investigator of the NAACP that the KKK had been closely involved in organizing the attacks and that a prominent lawyer and several public officials were deeply implicated. The investigation which followed the lynchings proved fruitless; the grand jury returned a verdict that they found insufficient evidence and thus could not return an indictment against the known lynchers.

White mobs burned churches and attacked Negro families during riots in Carteret, N.J. As a result of the riots, all Negroes left the town. The rioting followed the indictment of Robert Ducrest, a Negro, for the murder of John Carroll, a white boxer.

Congress started a move for segregated bathing beaches in

Washington, D.C. On May 1, a bill was passed in the Senate establishing such beaches. On May 8, President Coolidge signed the bill into law. The NAACP organized to fight the bill as unconstitutional.

A bill was introduced into the Senate by an Arkansas Democrat, Thaddeus H. Caraway, to prohibit intermarriage between races in the District of Columbia. Any child of such a marriage would be considered illegitimate. Any minister or any person who had violated the provisions of this bill would be guilty of a felony and subject to a fine not exceeding $1,000.

Rev. W. T. Johnson appeared before the State Legislature of Virginia to make an appeal for the defeat of House Bill No. 30, the Massenburg Bill, which required segregation in public halls, theaters, motion picture houses and all places of public entertainment and assemblage. Among those in favor of the bill was Col. W. S. Copeland, publisher of the Newport News *Daily Press*, who said that graduates of Hampton Institute, a Negro college, were carrying "notions of social equality" throughout the state. Another man, as reported by *The Chicago Defender*, said "that radical agitators without the state, aided by their white allies, were attempting to break down the color line, which was the salvation of both races." The Massenburg Bill was passed.

The Supreme Court case of CORRIGAN AND CURTIS V. BUCKLEY arose when Mrs. I. R. Corrigan, a white, violated a covenant she had signed with 27 owners of contiguous property which forbade that their property "shall ever be used or occupied or sold, conveyed, leased, rented or given to Negroes." When Mrs. I.R. Corrigan agreed to sell her Washington, D.C., home to Mrs. Helen Curtis, a Negro, M. Buckley, a neighbor, obtained a court order forbidding the sale. The NAACP appealed to the Supreme Court, but the case was dismissed. The Court thus upheld the decision of the Washington, D.C., Court of Appeals that such an agreement did not restrain the alienation of property, but only its use.

The home of Dr. Charles Garvin, a Negro of Cleveland, Ohio, was bombed. Dr. Garvin had been recently appointed assistant surgeon at the hospital of Western Reserve. When Dr. Garvin purchased his home in the summer of 1925, a group of whites tried to keep Garvin from occupying his house.

Mrs. Indiana Little, a well-known Negro social worker of Birmingham, Ala., and a group of Negro women were beaten by registration officials because they attempted to register and vote. Upon entering the court house, they were assaulted by L. K. Bowen, a white man. Arrested by deputy sheriff Henry Hill, they were jailed until a bond of $300 could be posted. Bowen was alleged to have said, "Don't you niggers know yet that voting is a white man's business?"

Roland Hayes, a leading Negro tenor, refused to go on stage at the Lyric Theater in Baltimore for a recital until segregation practices had ended. He threatened to cancel the engagement, until he was assured that Negro audiences would be afforded seating privileges.

The Louisiana Legislature passed a bill which made it "unlawful for any person to go on premises of plantations in the night, and move or assist in the moving of any laborer or tenant without the consent of the owner or proprietor." Maximum penalty was a fine of $1,000 and 6 months imprisonment. This law was in addition to legislation which prohibited Northern labor representatives from operating in the state. This latter law, for the most part, was unenforceable, and industry in the state, especially the sugar cane industry, suffered from insufficient labor.

Following the devastation of a hurricane which swept through major parts of Florida, and most especially Miami, Negroes were forced into reclamation activities by armed Marines. One woman was shot for protesting against her son being forced to work.

Negro citizens of Daytona Beach, Fla., were ordered to carry signed passes if they wished to stay in the city after dark.

At the suggestion of the New York Urban League, John D. Rockefeller purchased an entire block containing 60 city lots, bounded by 7th and 8th Aves. between 149 and 150 Streets in New York City. This constituted the fourth step in Rockefeller's plans for providing low-rent housing for Negroes.

James Stanley Durkee announced his resignation as president of Howard University, following a series of student uprisings. Groups of alumni had worked openly to oust the president.

Bishop Gregg, a leader of the AME Church and past president of Wilberforce University, was elected the first Negro head of Howard University. When Bishop Gregg declined the appointment, Mordecai Johnson, pastor of the First Baptist Church in Charlestown, W. Va., was chosen president. Johnson was born in Paris, Tenn., in 1890. He was graduated from Morehouse College in 1911, and taught English there for one year. He received a B.A. from the University of Chicago. A divinity student at Rochester (N.Y.) Theological Seminary from 1913 to 1916, he received his Bachelor of Theology from Rochester. Johnson received a Master of Theology from Harvard University in 1923.

Carter G. Woodson, a leading Negro historian, was awarded the Spingarn Medal for his work in collecting and publishing records of the Negro in America.

William Saunders Scarborough, a Negro scholar and educator and ex-president of Wilberforce University, died at the age of 74. For 43 years, he was connected with Wilberforce in various departments, and was its president from 1908 to 1920. Scarborough was born in Macon, Ga., in 1852. In 1877 he was elected the head of the Classical Department of Wilberforce University. He published many books relating to classical Greece. He was also active in the Ohio Republican Party.

Bessie Coleman, a Negro flyer, was killed when her plane crashed at Jacksonville, Fla. She had performed stunt flying all over the country for large audiences; the First World War had stimulated her interest in flying, and she studied with various clubs in Europe. Her abilities attracted international attention, particularly from the German airplane inventor, Fokker.

Negro History Week was introduced by Carter G. Woodson of the Association for the Study of Negro Life and History in Washington, D.C.

With a grant of $10,000 from the Carnegie Corp., the New York Public Library purchased his private collection of history and literature of Negroes from Arthur A. Schomberg. Schomberg had long been a patron of the 135 Street branch library, of which Ernestine Rose was the librarian.

She had much success in organizing neighborhood center libraries, and it was Ernestine Rose who called together Negro scholars and leaders to plan a library collection for the Negro community. The branch library received a new designation as the Division of Negro Literature and History. Schomberg was born in Puerto Rico in 1874, came to New York in 1891, and worked for many years as a bank messenger for the Bankers Trust Co. He resigned this job in 1932 to become the curator of the collection.

Earl Hyman (1926-   ), Negro actor, was born in North Carolina. An established performer in the American theater, an actor on Broadway and at the American Shakespeare Festival, Hyman after a trip to Scandinavia learned Norwegian by studying translations of Shakespeare. In 1963, the director of the Den National Scene Theater in Bergen, Norway, asked him to play Othello. He returned in 1965 to do Emperor Jones, and has been highly honored by Norwegian artists.

Miles Davis (1926-   ), Negro jazz musician, was born in Alton, Ill., and grew up in East St. Louis, Mo. The son of a well-to-do dentist, he began playing the trumpet at the age of 13. In 1945, he came to New York to study at Julliard. There he played informally with Parker, Coleman Hawkins and Benny Carter. Cool jazz is often dated from the Davis recordings of 1949 and 1950.

Langston Hughes' article on "The Negro Artist and the Racial Mountain" was published in the *Nation* magazine. Attacking assimilation, Hughes urged the Negro artist to make full use of distinctive material at his disposal. The Negro should write from his experience and utilize the material of his subculture, and not imitate whites. This article, more than any other statement, summed up the mood of the young Negro artists of the 1920's.

Nigger Heaven by Carl van Vechten, a white, was published. Van Vechten glamorized lower-class Negro life in Harlem as all fast cabarets, easy violence and love affairs. He made the Negro a symbol of sexual freedom and moral honesty in an era of false values. More than any other work, *Nigger Heaven* opened up Harlem nightlife to white tourists. It also was the most controversial novel among Negro intellectuals of the 1920's. Like Du Bois, many thought it an affront to the Negro race, while others such as James Weldon Johnson praised it.

A Negro magazine, *Fire*, was started by Thurman, Zora Neale Hurston, Aaron Douglas, John P. Davis and Bruce Nugent. Like the *Messenger*, *Broom*, *Transition*, *Harlem* and the house organs of the NAACP and the Urban League, the magazine encouraged and published Negro writers.

Frank Withers, Negro orchestra leader and jazz musician, gave a very successful concert in Moscow. He had previously played in fashionable Paris Cafés.

Theodore "Tiger" Flowers won the world's middleweight boxing title. Flowers was the first American Negro world champion since Jack Johnson. Later in the year, Flowers lost the title to Mickey Walker.

1927

Dean Kelly Miller of Howard University in an address to Kappa Alpha Psi fraternities, said, "The white race has furnished leaders for us. No man of one group can ever furnish leaders to people of another group, unless he is willing to become naturalized into the group he seeks to lead." Miller also expressed the belief that it would be well if all philanthropy were stopped and Negroes supported and maintained their own institutions. In referring to the Negro college man, he said, "The young American Negro is practically asleep."

Clarence Darrow told students of Tuskegee Institute that "cash money" was the key to real power. He reviewed the history of relations between Negroes and whites, a record which he said every white man ought to be ashamed of. The present generation of Negroes in America, according to Darrow, could not hope for a full measure of the constitutional rights that were theirs, but it was their duty to work and fight for these rights for their children.

The NAACP conducted a long legal fight against the Texas law that only whites could vote in the Democratic primary. The NAACP test case was initiated by Dr. L. A. Nixon of El Paso against the judge and associate judge of elections, C. C. Herndon and Charles Porras, who had issued a certificate "confirming that they had declined to permit him

to vote." The NAACP argued that the Texas law was a
violation of the 15th Amendment and also of United States
Statute 2004. The Texas law read in parts: "In no event shall
a Negro vote in a Democratic primary election held in the
state of Texas, and should a Negro vote in a Democratic
primary election such ballot shall be void." In contrast, the
Chicago Defender reported that Mexicans and Chinese could
and did legally cast their ballots. The case reached the Supreme
Court as NIXON V. HERNDON. Justice Holmes wrote the
majority decision in favor of Nixon, calling the Texas law
an obvious infringement of the 14th Amendment. In his
decision Justice Holmes stated that "That amendment [the
Fourteenth] while it applies to all, was passed as we know,
with a special intent to protect the Blacks from discrimination
against them. That amendment not only gave citizenship and
the privileges of citizenship to persons of color, but it denied
to any state the power to withhold from them the equal
protection of the laws. . . . States may do a good deal of
classifying that it is difficult to believe rational, but there are
limits, and it is too clear for extended argument that color
cannot be made the basis of a statutory classification affecting
the rights set up in this case." Texas then repealed the law
but enacted a resolution allowing local Democratic committees
to determine who was qualified to vote in primaries.

The U.S. Supreme Court ruled unconstitutional codes of
the State of Louisiana and the city of New Orleans by which
Negroes were prohibited from living in white residential
communities unless the whites had given their permission in
writing. THE NEW ORLEANS SEGREGATION CASE, as it was
known, was originally tried in the courts of New Orleans
when Benjamin Harmon, a white, tried to convert an apartment house into a building for Negroes. The lower court had
enjoined the plaintiffs from using the house for this purpose.
In arguing the case before the Supreme Court, NAACP
lawyers invoked the Louisville decision of 1917, BUCHANAN V.
WARLEY, which had involved a local ordinance prohibiting
Negroes from living in neighborhoods where whites pre-
dominated.

Negro property holders in Dallas, Tex., obtained an injunction to restrain the city from enforcing its municipal segregation ordinance. The ordinance supported private covenants

between property holders which restricted the sale of property to Negroes.

A Greyhound bus driver, Glen Branoski, a white, was fined $50 and costs, and spent 20 days in jail as a result of his committing assault and battery against a Negro woman traveler. He had attempted to impose an arbitrary Jim Crow seating policy on the Indianapolis to Cincinnati run.

The Supreme Court of Colorado outlawed discrimination in the activities and social functions of the state's public schools in the case of JONES, ROSS AND JENKINS V. THE SCHOOL BOARD OF DENVER.

The Illinois House of Representatives passed a bill which prohibited the state from granting recognition to any institution of learning that refused admittance to applicants on account of race, color or creed.

Citizens of Toms River, N.J., demanded that Edgar M. Fink, the supervising principal of the public schools, be dismissed because he discriminated against pupils. The demand was upheld by the Supreme Court of New Jersey which ordered school authorities not to discriminate on the basis of color.

In LUM V. THE STATE OF MISSISSIPPI the U.S. Supreme Court upheld a lower court decision, and ruled that Mississippi state school segregation laws were constitutional. In presenting this opinion, the Court maintained its earlier separate but equal educational facilities ruling.

Although the Negro schools of Little Rock, Ark., were overcrowded, the Board of Education announced that a vacant school would be used for its new administrative headquarters.

In Georgia a revised anti-miscegenation law required the acquisition of a color profile of every citizen by the State Health Department's Vital Statistics Bureau. When any person sought a marriage license, clerks were required to consult the person's statistics before issuing the marriage license.

The Pennsylvania Federation of Labor adopted a resolution urging that all races be admitted to international unions. The resolution in part read, "whereas, many of our unions exclude Negroes from membership . . . such exclusion is contrary to the very fundamental democracy and brotherhood upon which the labor movement is built. . . . if we bar the Negro from our unions he will work as a non-union man."

The 47th national convention of the AFL refused to move for acceptance of Negro workers by all member unions. The convention affirmed the separate union policy.

A. Philip Randolph led his union, the Brotherhood of Sleeping Car Porters, in a protest for wage increases and an end to "professional begging," receiving tips for a living. The Pullman Co. refused to arbitrate on the grounds that there was no dispute as its company union fulfilled the needs of the porters. Before the Railroad Mediation Board established to handle the dispute Randolph replied that company unions were useless. He maintained that the committees which purported to examine grievances were dominated by the representatives of the company district superintendent. If a hearing of a grievance could be held, he explained, the length of time for a disposition might be as long as a year. In the gathering of evidence in a grievance the company alone had the right to question a passenger in a complaint. In addition the porter could have no one to represent him, and was subject to dismissal without protection of rights. Randolph asserted that when fellow porters were asked to sit on a hearing, they were paid by the company to render a favorable decision. This was accompanied by a "stool pigeon" system. Finally, he claimed that the porter instructors and welfare workers were not selected because of specialized knowledge, but on the basis of questionable personnel records which compelled them to carry out practically any order of the superintendent. Later in the year the Interstate Commerce Commission refused the Pullman Co.'s request to dismiss the petition from Randolph's union to investigate company rates, wages and working conditions.

The Negro Labor Conference and representatives of the NAACP and the National Urban League met to support the Brotherhood of Sleeping Car Porters. The meeting endorsed the Brotherhood's activities and opposed scab labor and government by injunction.

In Kansas City, Mo., Pullman porters were asked to sign a petition for more wages, but were not permitted to read it. The petition was, in fact, a resolution against the Brotherhood of Sleeping Car Porters. It pledged cooperation with the Pullman Co. and called for the continuance of harmonious relation between the Kansas City porters and "our District Superintendent." It stated, "The Kansas City district [porters] realize that the propaganda the Brotherhood of Sleeping Car Porters is putting out is harmful, both nationally as well as locally, and that we shall neither morally nor financially support an organization of that kind."

Blanket charges were preferred against Bennie Smith, an agent for the Brotherhood of Sleeping Car Porters in Jacksonville, Fla. Smith had come to Jacksonville to organize a porters' local. When the Pullman Co. officials learned of Smith's activities, they told the police of "the evils" of such an organization, and in particular that Smith was teaching social equality. Arrested twice, Smith was finally freed through the efforts of his attorney.

In the soft-coal fields of Pennsylvania and West Virginia the United Mine Workers lost control of the mines when the companies brought large quantities of Negro laborers from the South. In an effort to gain sympathy for a general strike call in April against nonunion Negro labor, Philip Murray, the international vice president of the UMW, wrote in a letter to the Pittsburgh Council of Churches: "Those men, imported from the cotton fields of the South, are a menace to the peace of the community. White men and women and Negro men and women mix and mingle together. There are cases where white men live with Negro women, and Negro men live with white women."

The local Urban League in Chicago initiated a boycott of white-owned stores in Negro neighborhoods that would not hire Negroes as clerks or sales people. During the Depression this kind of boycott took place in most of the major cities.

Leaders of civil rights organizations including the NAACP, the Lincoln-Douglass Conference, the National Equal Rights League, the National Race Congress and many church groups visited President Coolidge, denouncing segregation, lynching and disenfranchisement. Delegations also visited Congress. These visits were the first by the Lincoln-Douglass Conference, which from 1927 on annually petitioned Congress

at the opening of each session. President Coolidge again
denounced lynching.

The Dyer Anti-Lynching Bill was introduced for the third
time by Rep. Leonidas C. Dyer, Republican of Missouri.

In this year, 16 Negroes were lynched.

When a Negro was accused of attacking a white girl in
Coffeeville, Kan., whites told the Negro community that they
intended to lynch the man and to march on the Negro
section. Equipped with army rifles, tear-gas bombs, pistols,
bayonets and axes, the Negroes left their section in company
formation, dug small trenches at the entrance of the Negro
section and stopped the white mob of 150, from seizing the
suspect. Fighting broke out and continued for two days until
three units of the National Guard arrived. Ten white men
were killed and 13 men and women were wounded.

A white mob in Little Rock, Ark., took John Carter, an
18-year-old Negro convicted of slaying an 11-year-old white
girl, from the city jail, burned him and dragged his body
through the streets of the town. As a result of this violence
thousands of Negroes left town.

A Negro representative from St. Louis County, John Davis,
introduced an anti-lynching bill in the Missouri Legislature.

Harley V. Speelman, Register of the Treasury, was dismissed by President Coolidge for segregating employees in his
department.

Demands of equal rights made to the Mayor of Memphis,
Tenn., by a Negro political organization, the West Tennessee
Civic and Political League, were explicitly refused by the
Mayor. He said, "There is no use in mincing words about
the matter, and my answer to the demands of this Negro
political league, is a direct positive statement that there will
be no Negro policemen, no Negro firemen, no removal of
the restrictions now governing the admission of Negroes to
the white parks of the city."

The Mississippi overflowed from Arkansas to the Gulf of
Mexico, leaving thousands of whites and Negroes homeless
and destitute. The white refugees were well housed and well
fed. The Negro refugees, most of them poor tenant farmers,
lived under concentration camp-like conditions. Herbert

Hoover was in charge of the flood relief. Walter White was sent by the NAACP to investigate. His reports led to public protest and eventually some conditions were improved.

The House of Representatives passed the Senate's bill which conferred citizenship upon the inhabitants of the Virgin Islands, the vast majority of whom were Negro. The population of the Islands was about 23,000. Some 3,500 Virgin Islanders were living in New York City.

The Pan-African Congress held its fourth annual meeting in New York City. Distinguished Negroes from all over the world attended, and W. E. B. Du Bois presided.

The Julius Rosenwald Fund contributed $25,000 toward the development of a $500,000 endowment for the medical school of Howard University.

Marcus Garvey was released on Dec. 1 from Atlanta prison; he had been eligible for parole since Oct. 7, 1926. Six months before a petition of 200,000 signatures had been sent to President Coolidge, who ordered his release. He was deported to Jamaica, British West Indies, immediately upon release.

Anthony Overton, a Negro banker, was awarded the Spingarn Medal for this year. Overton was the president of the Victory Life Insurance Co. and of the Douglass National Bank of Chicago.

Hubert H. Harrison, Negro lecturer and author, died in New York. For the 10 years preceding his death, Harrison was one of the most picturesque figures in Harlem. Hundreds of persons had gathered around his soap box to hear him call for the Negro people to seek economic freedom. Because of his eloquence, Marcus Garvey had appointed Harrison as commissioner of education for the Universal Negro Improvement Association, and for a time editor of the *Negro World*. Harrison had come to New York from St. Croix in the Virgin Islands when he was 17. In 1910 he had become an instructor in English and economics at the Harlem School of Social Science. He had also been a special lecturer at New York University, uptown branch. Besides contributing to major newspapers, he contributed to *New Republic* and was assistant editor under Piet Vlag of *Masses*. He also attempted several publications of his own, one being *The New Negro*.

Harry Belafonte Jr. (1927-   ), Negro entertainer, was born in New York City. As a boy he lived in the West Indies, but primarily grew up in New York. After serving in the Navy during World War II, he began an acting career, but quickly concentrated on singing. After 1950, in his appearances and recordings, he popularized folk-singing. He has also acted in two Broadway plays, *John Murray Anderson's Almanac* (1953), and *Three for Tonight* (1955), and in numerous movies and on TV.

Leontyne Price (1927-   ), Negro opera singer, was born in Laurel, Miss., and educated at Central State College in Ohio. She also studied at Julliard, and made her professional debut in the revival of Virgil Thompson's *Four Saints in Three Acts*. A successful concert artist, in 1954 she sang for the NBC Opera Company in *Tosca*. After numerous other appearances, she sang *Il Trovatore* with the Metropolitan Opera in 1961. A member of the permanent company, she opened the 1966 season in Samuel Barber's opera *Anthony and Cleopatra*.

Aaron Douglas, the prominent Negro painter, illustrated James Weldon Johnson *God's Trombones: 7 Negro Sermons in Verse*. His more recent works include murals for Fiske University, Bennett College and the New York Public Library.

Laura Wheeler Waring, a Negro portrait painter and illustrator, received the Harmon Award for fine art.

Under the auspices of Alain Locke, an exhibition of nearly 1,000 articles of native African crafts was held in New York City. The collection was owned by a Belgian, Blondaiu.

The Negro actor Frederick O'Neal started the Ira Aldridge Players in St. Louis, Mo.

The Rochester Symphony Orchestra performed *Darker America,* a symphonic poem by the Negro composer, William G. Still.

Universal International Pictures produced the sixth and last version of *Uncle Tom's Cabin,* with a Negro actor, James B. Lowe, as Uncle Tom. Charles Gilpin, who had made a reputation as Emperor Jones on Broadway, was first chosen for the role but quit after arguing continually with the director, Harry Pollard, over the characterization of Uncle Tom. Gilpin believed it to be a slur on his race. The version with Lowe did depict Uncle Tom as a man of more dignity than the previous films.

The Harlem Globetrotters, a performing Negro basketball team, was organized by Abe Saperstein.

Luc Grimard, a Negro from Cap Haitien, Haiti, published his first two collections of verse in Paris, *Sur Ma Flute de Bambous* and *Ritournelles*.

1928

A statistical and epidemiological report released based on the 1920 population figures showed that the life expectancy for white males was 54.1 years, while for Negro males, it was 40.5 years. For white females, life expectancy was 56.4 years, as opposed to 42.3 years for Negro females. Diseases which figured in Negro mortality were tuberculosis, with a rate of 202 per hundred thousand in the Southern states; pneumonia with a rate of 145.9 per hundred thousand. TB was found to be excessively high for Negroes between the ages of 25 and 30.

In the United States there was one hospital bed for 139 whites, and one bed per 1,941 Negroes.

In unskilled labor Negroes represented 60% of all tobacco workers; 24% of the chemical workers; 21% of all building workers, 39% of saw mill hands. In semi-skilled work Negroes represented 29% of the glass workers, 42% of all fish packers; 32% of the longshoremen.

In January, A. Philip Randolph and a delegation of the Brotherhood of Sleeping Car Porters reported to President Coolidge the goals of the Brotherhood: a wage scale that would permit the abolition of the tipping system, better working conditions and regular hours. In March the Interstate Commerce Commission dismissed the Brotherhood's petition to consider wage practices in relationship to the tipping system, for want of jurisdiction (the grounds on which Pullman Co. lawyers had argued). Immediately preparations for a national strike in all Pullman cars were announced in Kansas City by Ashley L. Totten, an assistant general organizer. The strike was to create a crisis such that an emergency board under the Federal Railway Labor Act would have to be convened to consider the porters' dispute with the Pullman Co. Of 7,000 members of the Brotherhood, 6,000 supported the strike. On June 15 the United States Mediation Board refused to consider the impending strike an emergency situation, and thus would not create an emergency board. On the advice of the president of the AFL, William Green, the strike was postponed. He said in a telegram to Randolph, "I am of the opinion that it would be unwise to engage in a strike now. Economic conditions are unfavorable to the success of such undertaking because of a lack of understanding. Public opinion has not been crystallized in support of your demands. For obvious reasons a strike at this time would play into the hands of the Pullman Company." In part, Green's stand was a response to the rumor that Pullman had nearly 5,000 Filipinos ready to take the places of members of the Brotherhood. In August, Randolph stated that the Pullman Co. was trying to force porters and maids into signing "yellow dog" contracts at so-called "good will" meetings, where they were asked whether or not they intended to remain loyal to the company and were told they must have nothing to do with the Brotherhood. In October, Randolph announced that the Brotherhood would not vote in the forthcoming elections for the employee representation plan (the Pullman Co. union). In November, Pullman asserted that 98% of the porters had voted for this employee representation plan. Randolph appeared before the United States Mediation Board and accused the company of irregularities in the voting. For example, although porters were supposed to place ballots in the ballot boxes themselves, in many instances porter instructors and welfare workers had taken the ballots from the porters in their homes and on their trains.

A subcommittee of the Senate Interstate Commerce Commission reported widespread dissatisfaction among Negroes in the Pittsburgh and Central Pennsylvania coal region. The report represented observations made by the striking miners and the strikebreakers. Before the start of the strike, a mine superintendent estimated that only 10% of the workers were Negroes. After the strike began, he told the subcommittee that 60% of those who continued to work were Negroes. In another area the number of Negro strikebreakers was approximately 30%. The barrack camps were described as filthy, poorly ventilated and crowded.

The National Interracial Conference attended by 200 dele-

gates from 16 national, civic and social welfare organizations
was held in Washington, D.C. The results of research designed
"to construct a reasonably faithful picture of Negro life and
the status of race relations in the United States" were heard.
One of the primary issues facing the conference was trade
union exclusion of Negro workers. A report declared, "real
industrial status tests will come within the next 10 years,
when we will begin to be qualified for advancement out of
the unskilled and semi-skilled class to the skilled and directive
types of work." Two factors favoring the Negro worker,
according to Professor Carpenter, a principal speaker at the
conference, were the restriction of immigration and the
"relative ineffectiveness of class and color prejudice in large-
scale mechanistic industry." Two factors of uncertainty were
the growth of prejudice in the North and the "the difficulty
which the worker appears to be experiencing in making himself at home in the trade union movement."

A. William Jones, a Negro, addressed the Sixth Comintern
World Congress in Moscow. He said that those who were not
classified as white must be given more active work in the
American Communist Party to take advantage of the "enormous revolutionary possibilities opened up by work among
the masses." He bitterly criticized American Communists for
paying insufficient attention to the Negro problem, and stated
that race prejudice existed inside the American Communist
Party.

The Paul Laurence Dunbar Apartments were opened in
Harlem. This housing project, capitalized by John D. Rockefeller, was considered by many to be a major housing reform.
Opportunity, the magazine of the National Urban League,
hailed it as representing a "new philanthropy." The occupants,
however, had a median wage of about $149 a month, which
was nearly $40 a month higher than the average Harlem
family's income. Rockefeller sold the Dunbar apartments in
1937, because in the Depression many of the tenants could
not meet the rent.

The Dunbar National Bank, organized by John D. Rockefeller Jr. and associates, opened in Harlem.

A committee of prominent people in New York City
worked to interest the proprietors of large department stores
along 125th Street in Harlem to employ Negro men and

women as sales people. The Urban League and the Fellowship of Reconciliation gave strong support to this effort.

Harlemites, formerly residents of the West Indies, formed
the West Indies Committee of New York to advance the civic
and political, social and economic interests of their group.
Committees on social welfare, naturalization, business development and charitable aid were formed. C. A. Petioni served
as president.

A joint meeting of West Indians and American Negroes
took place under the auspices of the Citizens Welfare Council
of Harlem to encourage relationship between the two sectors
of the Harlem community.

Secretary of Commerce Herbert Hoover on April 5 ordered
the abolition of segregation in his department.

In five Southern states a total of 10 Negroes were lynched.

Victor L. Berger, a white Socialist of Wisconsin, introduced into the House of Representatives a bill outlawing the
Ku Klux Klan. The law called for a maximum punishment
of 10 years in jail and a $5,000 fine. Berger also introduced
an anti-lynching bill.

The attempt of a policeman to arrest a Negro in Harlem
led to a riot in which more than 2,500 people fought with
some 150 policemen. The disorder was stopped by reinforcements of police and firemen who turned their hoses on the
milling crowds.

In Gary, Ind., Alberta Cheeks, a Negro high school
student, lost a suit to allow her to attend the local white high
school.

Prophet Noble Drew Ali's Moorish Temple of America,
founded in Chicago in 1913, had 17 subordinate temples in
15 states.

Home to Harlem was published by Claude McKay. It
concerned a Negro soldier who deserted in World War I and
returned to Harlem. McKay glamorized the street life of the
Harlem poor.

W. E. B. Du Bois published *Dark Princess,* a novel dealing
with the race problem on an international scale. The hero
works with an East Indian princess to form an organization,
the "Great Council of Darker Peoples," which included

Chinese, Japanese and all people of color. The novel also had a black nationalist West Indian, who operates a terrorist organization to assassinate white racists and Klansmen. The prime significance of this novel is neither plot nor characterisation but the issues involved. Du Bois' main interest was in promoting the idea of unity among colored peoples of the world, investigating their compatibility with each other, and discovering what role the American Negro would play in such an alliance.

Meek Mose by Frank Wilson, who at that time had the title role in *Porgy,* opened at the Princess Theater on Broadway and ran 32 performances. It was subsequently revived by the Federal Theater in the 1930's.

J. E. Clare McFarlane, a native of Jamaica, edited the first anthology of Jamaican poetry, *Voices from Summer Land.*

1929

Only 98 Negroes were listed in *Who's Who in America.*

In a detailed and comprehensive study of mental disease among Negroes in New York State, conducted by Dr. Benjamin Maltzburg in this year and completed in 1931, it was found that the Negro rate of first admissions to state hospitals was 151 per hundred thousand, compared to 74 for whites. However, of persons born in the state, whites had a rate of 45 as compared to 40 for Negroes. Among persons born out of New York State, the rate was 186 for Negroes, 151 for whites. This indicates that the discrepancy between Negroes and whites in the overall figures, and a major reason for mental disease among Negroes, was the migration from the South and the conditions which caused the migration.

President Hoover in his inaugural address stated that he would be President of all the people. On law and order he said, "The most malign of all dangers today is disregard and disobedience of law. . . . Our whole system of self-government will crumble if officials elect what laws they will enforce or citizens elect what laws they will support. . . . If citizens do not like a law their duty as honest men and women is to discourage its violation; their right is openly to work for its repeal." Herbert Hoover did not appoint any Southerners to his Cabinet.

President Hoover appointed a fact-finding commission to study the problem of law enforcement in the United States. No Negroes were included on the commission and one member, George Wickersham, had been president of the National Bar Association when it refused membership to Negroes.

To help insure Federal funds for Negro education in the South, the NAACP pressed President Hoover to appoint Negroes to the National Advisory Committee on Education. Hoover appointed Mordecai Brown, president of Howard University; Robert Moton, president of Tuskegee, and John Davis, president of West Virginia State College.

Before Oscar De Priest, the Negro Republican Representative from Chicago's 1st District, was sworn in on April 15, he was accused of election fraud and had difficulty in obtaining office space. The charges of fraud were unsupported and Rep. Fiorello H. LaGuardia offered the office next to his to De Priest. De Priest was the first Negro Congressman since 1901 and the first to be elected to Congress from a Northern state.

Mrs. Oscar De Priest's attendance at the official White House Congressional tea became a national cause célèbre; the Florida House of Representatives adopted a resolution condemning "certain social policies of the Administration in entertaining Negroes in the White House on a parity with white ladies." Senator Blease of South Carolina introduced a resolution to the effect that President and Mrs. Hoover should "remember that the house in which they are temporarily residing is the 'White House,' and that Virginia, Texas, Florida, Tennessee and North Carolina contributed to their becoming its custodians."

On June 21, largely through the efforts of Congressman De Priest, the Washington Auditorium was opened to Negro organizations.

On Aug. 30, Representative De Priest addressed a Harlem rally of 2,500 at the Abyssinian Baptist Church: "You will never be able to get what you want politically unless you elect leaders who will fight for your interest. . . . White people, as a rule, elect Negroes that they can control. Negroes will never get a square deal unless you elect your own leaders. . . . Don't complain about racial discrimination. Change it by practical politics. Remember that no one can really lead you but one who has been Jim Crowed as you have." Lieutenant Colonel Fillmore of the 365th N.Y. Infantry, a Negro candidate for district leader, said at this meeting that "90% of the population of the district is made up of Negroes. We feel that the time has come when we must have our leader, one of our own race, and that the emoluments of office belong to us. This is a fight to determine whether the 10% white population shall control the district in which more than 300,000 Negroes live."

Rep. Fiorello H. LaGuardia of New York, a candidate for Mayor of the City of New York, delivered a speech against some Jim Crow judges in New York City. He criticized the practice of appointing Southern judges to Federal benches in New York and, as an example, referred to Judge John E. Martineau of Arkansas, who discharged a jury for having found a Negro not guilty. The jury was berated and abused by him in the courtroom.

The United Colored Socialists of America was established in Harlem, as a propaganda organization for socialism. Directed by Negro socialists, its purpose was "the unification and education of that large mass of intelligently discontented Negroes who recognize the fact that both Republican and Democratic parties stand actively alike as two peas in a single pod on the pressing problems of the Race."

New York Socialists chose a Negro, Frank R. Crosswaith, as their candidate to fill the unexpired term of the late Royal M. Weller, Democrat of the 21st Congressional District, which included Harlem. Crosswaith, formerly an organizer for A. Philip Randolph's union, had been elected in June to the national executive committee of the Conference for Progressive Labor Action, and was committed to the creation of an American Labor Party.

Marching to the tune of "John Brown's Body," and jazz tunes, 300 tenants and scores of children marched in the streets of Harlem to protest the expiration of rent control laws. The parade of marchers was led by the Harlem Tenant's League, the Council of Working Class Women, the American Negro Labor Congress, and groups from the Communist Party.

An effort by Rep. George H. Tinkham of Massachusetts

and Sen. A. H. Vandenberg of Michigan to amend the Congressional reapportionment bill, to reduce the representation
of states which denied the vote to Negroes, was defeated by
Southern Congressmen.

The Brotherhood of Sleeping Car Porters held its annual
labor conference in Chicago. Members were told that "in
order to fit in the scheme of organized industry today,
[members] must mobilize their economic power to compete
with that of the employing class." Addresses were made concerning crime, juvenile delinquency, housing and health
conditions of workers.

The AFL granted temporary admission to the Brotherhood
of Sleeping Car Porters. Members of the Brotherhood
attended and spoke at the AFL convention in October.

William Green, president of the American Federation of
Labor, inaugurated a series of speeches in New York and
Chicago designed to underscore the support of the AFL for
the Brotherhood of Sleeping Car Porters. Green's speeches
were to help recruit 10,000 members for the Brotherhood by
Sept. 1. He said the AFL would resist any attempt by the
Pullman Co. to impose a company union on the porters.

The International Ladies Garment Workers Union
announced that it would organize the 4,000 Negro workers in
dress shops in New York City.

The integrated National Textile Workers Union struck
against the textile mills in Gastonia, N.C. The strikers claimed
that they were attacked by the police chief and a detachment
of deputized civilians. The police chief and three deputies
were killed, and 71 workers were beaten and thrown in jail.
The International Labor Defense of New York City undertook the defense of 15 union members charged with murder.

Some 1,200 delegates attended Marcus Garvey's UNIA
Sixth Annual Convention. Delegates came from the United
States, the West Indies, Europe and Africa. Some attempt
was made to reorganize the Black Star Shipping Line.

Marcus Garvey, while jailed in Kingston, Jamaica, for
contempt of court, was elected to the Kingston Council and
St. Andrew Corporation.

In Chicago the NAACP started a campaign against bus
companies that practiced segregation.

The Urban League organized a "Jobs for Negroes" movement to boycott merchants whose customers were Negroes
but who did not hire Negroes. Boycotts took place in St.
Louis, Pittsburgh, Chicago, Cleveland and other Midwestern
cities. The campaign had limited success.

The Liberty Life Insurance Co. of Illinois, the Supreme
Life & Casualty Co. of Columbus, Ohio, and the Northeastern
Life Insurance Co. of Newark, N.J., merged to form the
Supreme Liberty Life Insurance Co. with homes offices in
the Liberty Life Building, Chicago. This amalgamation of
Negro life insurance companies had estimated assets of $1.5
million.

Albon Holsey of the National Negro Business League
formed the Colored Merchants Association. Its aim was to
establish Negro cooperative stores to help combat the effects
of the Depression. None of the stores lasted more than
two years.

By November, according to the National Urban League
column in *The Chicago Defender,* unemployment had affected
Negro workers all over the nation.

From 1929 through the next decade cotton production
dropped from 43 million acres to 23 million. In this period
three out of four Negro farmers received at least 40% of
their income from cotton. Negroes produced approximately
one-third of the Southern cotton crop.

In this year, seven Negroes were lynched.

In Princess Anne, Md., a fight between a white man and a
Negro over the right of Negroes to congregate in white
business communities on Saturday night resulted in a riot;
300 Negroes were driven from town.

In Lincoln, Neb., a mob of whites drove 200 Negroes
from town after a white policeman was shot. Governor
Weaver ordered that those persons driven out must be permitted to return, and that if any further difficulties ensued,
martial law would be instituted.

A Negro, Claude D. Green, manager of a local Chicago
club, was shot to death by six members of the Moorish
Temple of America, a cult organized in 1913, which had
formerly used his club for meetings. At the time of his

death, Green was allied with a faction opposed to Timothy Drew, known as prophet Noble Drew Ali, founder of the cult. The prophet was accused of the crime; he died five month later. It was commonly believed that the ordeal of his trial, together with the treatment he received at the hands of the police, were directly responsible for his death.

Following Drew's death, a gun battle broke out between Chicago policemen and members of the Moorish Temple of America. One member of the society and one police officer were killed when the Chicago police came to a building occupied by the Moorish Society in search of Charles Kirkman, reported to have been kidnapped the day before by four imported gunmen.

In its struggle for Haitian liberation the NAACP drew up a series of charges of incompetence against American administration. United States troops were not withdrawn from Haiti until 1934.

Students took possession of campus buildings to protest the suspension of Dean S. L. Hargrove of Langston University in Langston, Okla. When the president of the University failed to make a definitive charge against the students, police refused to help quell the disturbance. The protest was called off when the state board of regents visited the institution and agreed to a number of the student demands.

Two Negro schools, New Orleans University and Straight College, merged to form Dillard University, under the control of the American Missionary Society and the Methodist Episcopal Church. A hospital and medical college were to be added to this new university.

John Conyers Jr. (1929-   ), Negro Congressman, was born in Detroit, Mich. Educated as a lawyer at Wayne State University, he became active in Detroit as a union lawyer and a referee for the Michigan Workmen's Compensation Department. In 1963, he was a Presidential appointee to the National Lawyers' Committee for Civil Rights Under Law. With the aid of local unions, he won the Democratic primary in 1964 and was elected to the House of Representatives. He was a co-sponsor of the Administration's Medicare program.

Martin Luther King Jr. (1929-1968), Negro leader, was born in Atlanta, Ga., and was educated at Morehouse College

and Crozier Theological Seminary. He was ordained a minister in 1947, and attended Boston University where he received
his Ph.D. In 1954, he became minister of the Montgomery
(Ala.) Dexter Avenue Baptist Church. King headed the
Montgomery bus boycott of 1956; he was jailed and his
house was bombed. Out of the boycott came the Southern
Christian Leadership Conference (SCLC), of which he was
the head. In 1959, King moved to Atlanta to be co-pastor
with his father of the Ebenezer Baptist Church. In 1960,
when the sit-in movement began, the SCLC was quick to
support it, and aided in the formation of the Student Non-
Violent Coordinating Committee (SNCC). King himself
joined the Atlanta sit-ins in the fall of 1960; when he was
arrested and jailed without opportunity to post bail, Presidential candidate John F. Kennedy intervened and had King
freed. In the 1960's King led various campaigns: sit-ins,
protest marches, demonstrations. In December, 1961, he led
the movement in Albany, Ga. In April 1963, King led the
demonstrations in Birmingham, Ala., which resulted in the
jailing of 3,300 Negroes. The summer of 1963 saw the
March on Washington, and in 1964 King led a campaign in
St. Augustine, Fla. Early in 1965 he led a voter registration
drive in Selma, Ala., that occasioned the Selma-Montgomery
march. In 1966 King went North to protest housing discrimination in Chicago and its suburb of Cicero. During the last
two years of his life, he was a leader of the anti-Vietnam war
movement. On April 15, 1967, he spoke to a New York
peace parade and rally of 200,000 persons. In February, 1968,
he participated in a Washington, D.C., demonstration of
Clergy and Laymen Concerned About Vietnam. In March,
1968, King went to Memphis to help the city's striking
garbage men. He was also in the midst of planning a Poor
People's March on Washington. On April 4, 1968, in
Memphis, Tenn., he was assassinated. King received the
Nobel Peace Prize, on Dec. 10, 1964.

Claude McKay published *Banjo,* in which the hero is like
the protagonist of *Home to Harlem.*

Richard B. Harrison, drama instructor at North Carolina
A. & T., was chosen to play De Lawd in Marc Connelly's *The
Green Pastures.*

There were 3 successful film companies specializing in

Negro films: Micheaux Pictures Co. of New York, an all-Negro concern; Colored Players Film Corp. of Philadelphia, a white group, and Liberty Photoplays Inc., of Boston, a mixed company.

The first Negro talkies were produced in this year. *Hearts of Dixie,* a Fox production, billed Stepin Fetchit as the star and stereotyped him as the shuffling Negro clown. It was made to exploit the new gimmick of sound, and the producers were primarily interested in the singing and dancing sequences. Clarence Muse and Mildred Washington also appeared in this first all-Negro movie made by a major studio. *Melancholy Dame,* a short talkie comedy for Negroes, was directed by Octavius Roy Cohen. It was a sucessful dialect comedy, starring Evelyn Preer, Eddie Thompson and Spencer Williams, all Negroes.

Hallelujah, was directed by King Vidor, with an all-Negro cast headed by Daniel Haynes, Nina Mae McKinney, Victoria Spivey, William Fountain, Harry Gray, Fannie Belle de Knight. Vidor was a talented director, and although his depiction of cotton field shanty life has been called sentimental and melodramatic, it marks the first time in films that Negroes were treated with dignity.

The Movietone Follies of 1929 had a separate segment using Negro dancers. In all subsequent musical revue movies, such as Warner Bros.' *Thank Your Lucky Stars* and Paramount's *Star Spangled Rhythm,* Negroes performed in separate sequences.

Kansas City and the Southwest became the focal point of jazz. Andy Cook and his Clouds of Joy, with Mary Lou Williams at the piano, were the leading performers.

A Negro, Panama Al Brown, was bantamweight boxing champion.

1930

U.S. Census: There were 11,891,100 Negroes in the U.S., representing 9.7% of the total population. The percentage of Negroes in the Northeast was 9.6%; in the North Central states, 10.6%; in the South, 78.7%, and in Western states, 1%.

In the North and West 88% of all Negroes lived in urban areas; 32% of the Negroes in the South lived in urban areas.

Negro illiteracy was 16.3%. Of the Negro illiterates 93.6% lived in the South. Per capita expenditure per white school child was $44.31 in areas where segregation was legally mandatory; for Negro students it was $12.57.

The Depression hit the Southern Negroes in agriculture the hardest. Two-thirds of Southern Negroes were sharecroppers or wage laborers. In 1930 1,112,510 Negroes were employed as agricultural laborers. By 1940 this figure had dropped to 780,312. Of the Negroes 13.1% were owners or managers, in contrast to 42.4% of the whites in Southern agriculture.

Between 1930 and 1940 the total Negro rural farm population decreased 4.5%.

Approximately 22 major unions officially discriminated against Negroes. This figure was reduced to 13 by 1943, to 9 by 1949, and 2 by 1963.

R. L. Mays, a Chicago Negro, was president of the Railway Men's International Benevolent Industrial Association and executive officer of the Interstate Order of Locomotive Firemen, Yard and Train Service Employees and Railway Mechanics. He organized a convention of Negro railroad workers to combat "the tendency to eliminate from railway service our men now employed as skilled shop workers, trainmen, and locomotive firemen and yard switchmen," by organizing existing Negro workmen's associations. Mays asked those in control of American industry to recognize character instead of color and to give jobs to Negroes. The convention met in Detroit, Mich.

Only 1% of the employees in the Southern oil and gas production field were Negroes, and only 10% of the employees in automobile-created jobs were Negroes. Southern Negroes were principally employed as teamsters, drivers, maintenance and construction men on city and state projects and as menials in the wholesale and retail trade in banking, brokerage houses and insurance. In the South whites were in the majority as workers in hotels, restaurants and boarding houses. In the U.S. Negroes employed as launderers and laundresses numbered 329,163 in 1930; by 1940 the figure had been reduced to 47,734. In 1930 some 107,739 Negroes were employed as iron and steel laborers; by 1940 Negro employment in that industry was down to 40,818. In this period there was one substantial increase in Negro occupations: Negro teamsters numbered 19,566 in 1930; by 1940 there were 137,121 Negro teamsters.

A small percentage of Negroes displaced from jobs in the South moved westward. The Negro population in the Western states between 1930 and 1940 increased by 2.1%. Migration to Northern cities of Southern Negroes was relatively low as the general unemployment of unskilled workers was such that whites were now hired for traditionally Negro jobs.

Of the 116,000 Negroes in professional jobs, over two-thirds were teachers or ministers.

The total number of Negro policemen in the United States was 1,297; only 7% of whom were employed in the Deep South. There were no Negro policemen in Mississippi, South Carolina, Louisiana, Georgia, Alabama, Arkansas and Virginia.

The 2,946 Negro undertakers represented one-tenth of all United States undertakers.

The number of Negro contractors fell to 2,400, or 1.6% of the total number of contractors in the United States.

There were 944 Negro banking and brokerage entrepreneurs and officials, clerks and accountants and 9,325 insurance executives, managers, etc. The first figure was less than 1 for every 600 white workers in such positions, and the second represented about 2% of the national total of such workers.

Four Negro banks failed in Chicago.

Seventy Negro building and loan associations had assets of $6,600,000. These assets represented less than 1% of the total for all building and loan associations. The number of associations fell to 30 by 1938, and assets to $3,600,000.

The foreign-born Negro population of the United States was 98,620, or 0.99% of the total Negro population. Of all Negro immigrants in the United States, 73% were born in the West Indies. 91,677 foreign-born Negroes, or 93%, resided in urban areas. Of these, 65% lived in New York City.

Between 1930 and 1939, there were 1,666 executions under civil authority in the U.S. Of these, 827 were white and 816 Negro. In the two major crime categories, of a total 1,514 executed for murder, 804 were white and 687 Negro; of the total of 125 executions for rape, 10 were white and 115 Negro.

In Detroit, 19.5% of the Negroes voted Democratic. The percentage increased to 36.7% in 1932, 63.5% in 1936, and reached 69.3% in 1940.

John H. Parker, once an opponent of Negro suffrage, was nominated to the Supreme Court by President Hoover. The NAACP protested and through a strong nation-wide campaign influenced the Senate to vote against his confirmation. The NAACP then waged a campaign against those Senators who had voted for Judge Parker, and was credited with the defeat of 11 of them when they ran for re-election.

In this year 20 Negroes were lynched.

The American Communist Party organized the League of Struggle for Negro Rights (LSNR). Langston Hughes was elected president. The league united several Negro groups in a sweeping program to eliminate wrongs against the Negro, and envisioned the eventual establishment of a Negro republic in America. However, the NAACP and the National Urban League, and the majority of Negroes steered clear of the LSNR. It therefore accomplished little.

In the summer, in the Negro section of Detroit, a mysterious person known variously as Farad Mohammed, F. Mohammed Ali, Prof. Ford, Wally Farad, and W. D. Fard, began to peddle to Negroes silks and other articles purported to be from Africa. He preached about the "home country" of the Negroes and about their "true religion" of Islam. He preached against the white race and against Christianity, and gained many converts, who hired a hall which they called the Temple of Islam. These people were the initiators of the movement later called the Black Muslim. Fard's origins, racial and national, are not known. Many thought him to be an Arab. In his teaching, Fard used the writings of Joseph F. "Judge" Rutherford, leader of Jehovah's Witnesses; Van Loon's *Story of Mankind*, Breasted's *The Conquest of Civilization,* the Koran, the Bible, etc. Fard wrote two manuals for his followers: *The Secret Ritual of the Nation of Islam*, which is taught orally; and *Teaching for the Lost-Found Nation of Islam in a Mathematical Way*. He founded a University of Islam, actually an elementary and secondary school. He created the Muslim Girls Training Class for teaching home economics and proper behavior as wife and mother. Fard founded the Fruit of Islam, a military protection group. He appointed ministers of Islam and assistant ministers. In 1934, Fard disappeared and was succeeded by Elijah Muhammed, born Elijah Poole in Georgia, one of Fard's earliest lieutenants. Muhammed moved the Muslim headquarters to Chicago. He became the Prophet, and Fard was identified with Allah. Black Muslims believe that "their leader," the Hon. Elijah Muhammed, is the messenger of Allah, directly commissioned by Allah himself, who came in person under the name of Fard to awaken Negroes to their superiority over whites. The religion explains that all men were originally black with two sides to their natures, the white half represented the weaknesses and evils of man, the black half, the strengths and virtues. A scientist had separated the two halves. Whites had been given 6,070 years to rule and then the blacks would reign. The Negro hegemony will begin in 1984. Most Black Muslims in Detroit from 1930 to 1934 were recent immigrants from the rural South and were "functionally illiterate."

Blind Lemon Jefferson, one of the great Negro country blues singers, was found frozen to death in a Chicago snowstorm.

Lorraine Hansberry (1930-1965), Negro playwright, was born in a comfortable, middle-class family in Chicago, and was educated at the University of Wisconsin and Roosevelt University. She first appeared in print in Robeson's *Freedom*, a monthly newspaper, during the early 1950's. In 1959, *A Raisin in the Sun*, her first play, was produced on Broadway. *A Raisin in the Sun* is more important as a cultural event than as a work of drama. It was among the first full-length Negro plays to be taken seriously by a white audience. Although Miss Hansberry cited Sean O'Casey as the greatest influence on her drama, she does not approach him in quality of language, plot or vitality. The play is essentially similar to conventional "soap opera." The success of *A Raisin in the Sun* catapulted her to a fame somewhat out of proportion to her actual achievement. She was expected to be a spokesman for the Negro poor, when in fact she merely articulated the aspirations of the Negro bourgeoisie. She was very militant about integration but very anti-black nationalist or separatist. In 1964, *The Sign in Sidney Brustein's Window,* her second play, closed a critical and financial failure on the night of her funeral. A third play, *Les Blancs,* is to be produced posthumously on Broadway in the '68-69 season.

The Depression changed the emphasis in Negro writing from the race problem to class oppression. During the 1930's left-wing and Communist periodicals such as *The New Masses* and *The Nation* were among the few to accept Negro manuscripts and give the white audience Negro views.

Ornette Coleman (1930-   ), Negro jazz musician, was born in Fort Worth, Tex. He is largely a self-taught musician, although in 1959 he attended the School of Jazz at Lenox, Mass. Coleman first played with Peewee Cranton's Rhythm and Blues Band in New Orleans. From 1952 to 1954 he had his own band in Fort Worth, Tex. He then moved to Los Angeles and made his first recording in Hollywood on alto saxophone. In 1959 he formed his own quartet. Coleman, a composer as well as a saxophonist, violinist and trumpeter, has toured Europe and influenced European jazz. Though infrequently heard, and with only a few LP's, Coleman is one of the new giants of modern music, and is hailed as the first true innovator since bop.

Edward S. Silvera, a Negro, contributed verse to the collection *Four Lincoln Poets.* His poems are free verse lyrics, similar in style to those of Emily Dickinson.

This decade saw a revival in attempts to create a local Harlem theater. In the early 1930's, Rose McClendon and Dick Campbell organized a Negro People's Theater at the Lafayette as a stock company. The Harlem Players presented Negro versions of *Sailor Beware* and *Front Page.* Two other companies, Harlem Experimental Players and the Harlem Suitcase Theater, were also organized.

Una M. Marson, a Negro from Jamaica, had a first collection of poetry, *Tropic Reveries,* published. Subsequent collections appeared in 1931, 1937 and 1945.

1931

On March 25, on a freight train traveling from Chattanooga to Memphis were several boys, white and Negro, and
two white girls, all hitching rides on the freight. Near Stevenson, Ala., a fight broke out among the whites and Negroes,
and five whites were thrown from the train. These boys
aroused the townspeople of Stevenson by telling them that
Negro boys were riding the trains with two white girls. The
station master telegraphed ahead and, when the train pulled
into Paint Rock, Ala., an angry posse was waiting. The Negro
boys fled, but nine were captured: Andy Wright, Roy White,
Haywood Patterson, Eugene Williams, Clarence Norris,
Charley Weems, Ozzie Powell, Willie Roberson and Olen
Montgomery. They became the Scottsboro Boys. Although
they were captured at random, all nine were charged with
the rape of the two white girls, Victoria Price and Nancy
Bates. Eugene Williams was only 13 years old; Willy Roberson was practically crippled with a severe case of venereal
disease; Olen Montgomery was almost completely blind. The
testimony of the two white girls who claimed they had been
raped was sufficient evidence for the Southern jury. By April
9, 1931, eight were condemned to death, and Roy White was
given a life sentence. At this point the International Labor
Defense, a Communist Party organ, entered the case. At the
same time the NAACP, which had not been previously
involved, wanted to take over the defense of the Scottsboro
Boys. A vicious propaganda campaign against the NAACP
by the ILD convinced the boys' parents to let the ILD handle
the defense. With the entry of the ILD into the case, it
became a cause célèbre. The ILD sent "Mother" Wright to
Europe; she led demonstrations in 28 countries. A world-wide
protest was coordinated by the ILD. American embassies and
consulates were picketed and stoned all over Europe and
Latin America. Mass demonstrations were held in major
American cities. Telegrams and letters poured in on the
United States President, the Governor of Alabama and the
presiding judge. It has been estimated that some $1,000,000
was raised by the Communist Party, although it has been
charged that not all the money went to the boys' defense. The
ILD hired one of the most prominent lawyers in the country,

Samuel Liebowitz of New York. On Nov. 7, 1932, the United
States Supreme Court ordered a new trial. Then began a
long, complicated legal battle. The most dramatic event of
1933 was Nancy Bates' withdrawal of her testimony. It had
become clear that both girls' reputations were questionable.
When they had been examined by Paint Rock doctors after
the train had been stopped, the examinations had revealed
only dead spermatozoa, signifying, not the rape they claimed,
but intercourse that had taken place previously. Lester Carter,
a white companion, claimed that the girls had had relations
with hoboes in Chattanooga, with whom they had stayed the
night before the train ride. Furthermore, although Victoria
Price testified that she had been cut and was bleeding from
various wounds that occurred during the rape, the doctors
who examined her found no such cuts and no blood. In
spite of this and of the fact that Nancy Bates withdrew her
testimony on April 17, 1933, the jury rendered a verdict of
guilty. The death sentence was mandatory. Judge Horton, the
presiding judge, was so outraged that he wrote a brief condemning the verdict and granted the defense request for a
new trial. The third trial was held in November, 1933; again
the verdict was guilty. Liebowitz carried the fight to the
United States Supreme Court, and on April 1, 1935, the
convictions were reversed. The court stated that a fair trial
was denied the Scottsboro Boys because Negroes were excluded
from the jury. New warrants were sworn out by Victoria
Price, and in November a grand jury returned new indictments for rape. It was now apparent that although the ILD
had been able to save the boys, it could not free them. In
December, 1935 the Scottsboro Defense Committee was
formed. It was a coalition of the ILD, the NAACP, the
American Civil Liberties Union, the League for Industrial
Democracy and the Episcopal Federation for Social Service.
The National Urban League was an unofficial member. C. I.
Watts, of Huntsville, Ala., and Allan Chalmers were added
to the defense team. Watts was an important addition, for he
was a local man. Liebowitz, a New Yorker and a Jew, had
met with much hostility from the jury. From this time on, the
NAACP assumed most of the burden of legal costs. In addition, several prominent attorneys such as Clarence Darrow
aided the defense committee. By 1937, realizing the hopelessness of the attempt to execute the nine boys, the prosecution

offered 7-year sentences if the boys would plead guilty. The deal was refused. The prosecution then offered to free four and to prosecute five for assault. The committee agreed, and Roberson, Montgomery, White and Williams were freed. The prosecution, however, now discredited itself by saying it was all a mistake and the boys were innocent, after maintaining for 6½ years their guilt. The defense committee helped those freed with jobs and education. Meanwhile the prosecution went back on its word concerning the penalties of the five remaining boys. Norris was condemned to death. Andy Wright was sentenced to 95 years in prison, Weems and Patterson to 75, and Powell to 20. The defense committee then negotiated with Governor Graves. He promised to pardon the boys in November, 1938, but he too went back on his word. In 1939, the Defense Committee directed its efforts to the parole board, in an attempt to free them. The work went very slowly. On Nov. 18, 1943, Weems and Norris (whose death sentences had been commuted to life imprisonment) were freed. Not until 1948 was Powell released. In 1948 Patterson escaped from Kilby prison. Allan Chalmers, who for some years had been the principal lawyer, aided him by refusing to divulge his whereabouts. In 1950, Patterson was arrested by the FBI in Detroit. The NAACP pressured Michigan Gov. G. Mennen Williams not to extradict Patterson and the Governor agreed. At last Patterson was freed. His book, *Scottsboro Boy*, was published in that year by the Civil Rights Congress, a Communist organization. The book detailed the horrible prison conditions that prevailed in the South. Finally, on June 9, 1950, Andy Wright, the last of the Scottsboro Boys, was freed.

Roy Wilkins became assistant secretary of the NAACP.

W. E. B. Du Bois emphatically rejected Communism in an article entitled "The Negro and Communism" in the NAACP journal, *Crisis*. However, Du Bois did become a Communist at the age of 93.

The Sharecroppers Union was organized in Tallapoosa, Ala., to aid Negro tenants and sharecroppers. Direction of the movement came from the Communist Party headquarters in Birmingham, Ala. Attempts of law enforcement officials and white vigilantes to stamp out the organization drove it underground. It continued to operate in Tallapoosa and Chambers

Counties. By 1933 it claimed 3,000 members, including a few white sharecroppers. In 1934, it undertook its first strike in Tallapoosa County. In some areas the striking cotton pickers involved in the strike were successful and received the 70¢ per hundredweight the union demanded. The union was dissolved in 1936, and its members were advised to join other organizations.

The urban Negro was much harder hit by unemployment than the white worker. In January, 1931, in 19 major cities with substantial Negro population, at least 25% of all male and female Negro workers were unemployed. In Detroit 60% of male Negro workers and 75% of the female Negro workers were unemployed.

Twelve Negroes were lynched in this year.

The Commission on Interracial Cooperation organized the Association of Southern Women for the Prevention of Lynching.

Slaves Today, a Story of Liberia, by George Schuyler, was published. Schuyler deals with the descendants of the original founders of Liberia and their exploitation of the native Africans. The irony, Schuyler points out, is that the old antebellum South still persists in Liberia, only now the sons of freed slaves have assumed the role of plantation masters. Schuyler also published *Black No More,* an original satirical fantasy about the race problem in the U.S. It ridicules virtually the whole spectrum of American society, from the KKK to the NAACP, the Southern aristocrats to the New York City liberals.

Gorilla Jones, the Negro middleweight, became champion of his division.

Young Jack Thompson, a Negro welterweight, became champion of his division.

The Negro population of Cuba was 437,769, or 11% of the total population.

1932

No mention of Negroes was made in the platforms of the Democratic, Farmer-Labor, Prohibition or Socialist Labor parties.

The Republican Party platform stated: "For 70 years the

Republican Party has been the friend of the American Negro. Vindication of the rights of the Negro citizen to enjoy the full benefits of life, liberty and the pursuit of happiness is traditional in the Republican Party, and our party stands pledged to maintain equal opportunity and rights for Negro citizens. We do not propose to depart from that tradition nor to alter the spirit or letter of that pledge."

The Socialist Party platform called for "the enforcement of Constitutional guarantees of economic, political and legal equality for the Negro." It also called for "the enactment and enforcement of drastic anti-lynching laws."

The Communist Party platform read: "The Communist Party is the political party of the oppressed masses of the people—the industrial workers, the persecuted Negroes, the toiling farmers. The Communist Party enters this election campaign explicitly to rally the toilers of the city and country, Negro and white, in a united struggle for jobs and bread, for the fight against imperialist war. . . . The Negro people, always hounded, persecuted, disfranchised, and discriminated against in capitalist America, are, during this period of crisis, oppressed as never before. They are the first to be fired when layoffs take place. They are discriminated against when charity rations are handed out to the unemployed. They are cheated and robbed by the Southern white landlords and evicted from their lands and homes when their miserable income does not enable them to pay rent. When they protest against this unbearable oppression and persecution they are singled out for police attacks in the North and for lynch victims in the South. Over 150 Negroes have been barbarously lynched at the instigation of the white ruling class . . ." In this platform the Negro reform leaders were attacked as "shamelessly aiding the white master class in these vicious attacks." James W. Ford, a Negro, was the Vice Presidential candidate on the Communist ticket.

In the Presidential election, Franklin D. Roosevelt did not receive very much of the Negro vote. To a certain extent the Negro still identified with the Republican Party. Also Roosevelt's running mate, John Nance Garner was a Texan. In Chicago, for example, Roosevelt received only 23% of the Negro vote. Another factor in the low Negro vote for Roosevelt may have been that James W. Ford, a Negro, was the Vice Presidential candidate of the Communist Party. However, Roosevelt soon became extremely popular, due to the ties which he and Mrs. Roosevelt established with prominent Negroes. Roosevelt also employed Negro advisers in numbers much greater than previous Administrations. The "Black Cabinet" included: Robert Vann, assistant to the Attorney General; William Hastie, Assistant Solicitor, in the Department of the Interior; Eugene Kinckle Jones, adviser on Negro Affairs in the Department of Commerce; Lawrence Oxley, in the Division of Negro Labor in the Department of Labor; Mary McLeod Bethune, director of the Division of Negro Affairs of the National Youth Administration; Edgar Brown, adviser on Negro Affairs in the Civilian Conservation Corps; Frank Horne, in several capacities with Federal housing programs, and William Trent as a race relations adviser in the Department of the Interior and in the Public Works Agency.

The NAACP published 10,000 copies of a leaflet, *Mississippi River Slavery—1932;* it was the result of an investigation made by Roy Wilkins and George Schuyler into conditions on Federal flood-control projects. Wilkins and Schuyler carried out their investigations by working on some projects. In 1933 Senate investigations began and resulted in the government setting minimum standards for conditions and for wages for all workers.

The peace movement of Ethiopia was organized in Chicago and petitioned President Roosevelt to use relief funds to settle Negroes in Africa.

In this year six Negroes were lynched.

White employees of the Illinois Central Railroad fought Negro workers to keep them out of railroad jobs. Ten Negro trainmen were killed.

Communist attempts at infiltration of the Black Muslim movement proved unsuccessful.

There were 117 Negro institutions of higher learning; of these 36 were public. All but seven of the private colleges and universities had a church affiliation. Before 1937 only five offered graduate-level education.

Between 1913 and 1932, the Rosenwald Fund had aided

in the construction of more than 5,000 Negro school buildings in 15 Southern states. Negroes contributed 17% of the money disbursed by the Fund.

Howard University began publication of the *Journal of Negro Education.*

Not Only War by Victor Daly was published. The novel concerns the racial tensions over white women in France, and is a vitriolic attack on the racism in the Army during World War I.

The Conjure-Man Dies, the first Negro detective novel, was published by Rudolph Fisher.

Infants of the Spring by Wallace Thurman was published. It was one of the last novels of the Harlem Renaissance.

Ray Charles (1932-   ), Negro blues singer, pianist, organist and saxophonist, was born in Georgia. Blind since childhood, he received his musical training at the School for the Blind in St. Augustine, Fla. At 15, he began to perform locally, and at 17 organized a trio. From his first recording in 1957, with his instrumental combinations of popular, gospel and modern jazz, Charles has been one of America's most popular musical performers.

Eddie Tolan, an American Negro, won gold medals at the Los Angeles Summer Olympics for the 100-and 200-meter dash, setting a new world's record for the 100-meter. Edward Gordon, another Negro athlete, won the running broad jump.

Kid Chocolate, a Negro prize fighter, won the featherweight boxing championship. He held his title through 1934.

From this year the trend of Negro immigration has been away from the United States, reaching its peak in 1933, when the total number of Negroes admitted to the United States was 84, while departures amounted to 1,058. Almost all Negro immigration to the United States came from the Crown Colonies and the dependencies of Great Britain and France in the West Indies.

3. From the New Deal to Brown v.
Board of Education

The impact of the New Deal, of the new Labor Union movement (CIO) and of the democratization processes during and after the Second World War upon the American Negro was at best peripheral. Whatever he achieved was much less than the economical, social and educational possibilities afforded.

An interesting and positive factor was the influx of Negroes from the West Indies during the 20's and 30's and of Puerto Ricans since the war—somewhat similar to the great immigrations and their meaning for the American melting pot.

1933

According to the October report of the Federal Emergency Relief Administration, percentages of Negroes and whites on relief, were: United States total: Negroes 17.8%, whites 9.5%; urban Negroes 26.7%, whites 9.6%; rural Negroes 10.9%, whites 9.6%; urban Northern Negroes 25.4%, whites 9.8%; urban Southern Negroes 26.5%, whites 13.6%; rural Southern Negroes 3%, whites 3.8%.

The Good Neighbor League, founded in this year by Solomon Lightfoot (Elder) Michaux, Negro gospel leader, fed 250,000 indigent persons at its Happy News Café in Washington, D.C. In 1932 Michaux had supported the Presidential candidacy of Franklin D. Roosevelt instead of the Republican Herbert Hoover. He later used the league as part of the Roosevelt political machine and organized the vote among Negroes.

Angelo Herndon, a 19-year-old Negro from Cincinnati, who said he had come to the South with the message of Communism, led a hunger march to petition county commissioners for relief due to Negroes. He was arrested and convicted of attempting to incite insurrection. The state based its case on Herndon's possession of literature distributed by the U.S. Communist Party. Some of the literature advocated self-determination for Black Belt Negroes. Herndon's attorney, Benjamin J. Davis Jr., said, "The only offense Herndon committed was that he asked for bread for children—his only crime is his color." Herndon was sentenced to 20 years on a chain gang.

460

Between 1933 and 1934, Federal studies indicated that
one-third of Southern land, and more than one-half of the
land in Virginia, Georgia, Tennessee, Texas, Oklahoma and
Kentucky, was eroded to some extent. Cotton prices fell to
half the pre-1914 level. Foreign countries bought cotton from
their dominions, because of the Agricultural Adjustment
Administration (AAA) curtailment of production and destruction of surplus. The world price was also influenced by the
introduction of synthetic materials, especially rayon.

The AAA program was directly responsible for a decline
in the number of Negro sharecroppers and tenants in the
South. Its policies inadvertently forced out the poorest farmers, of whom many more were Negro than white. Due to the
reduction of crop acreage, many Negro tenant farmers and
sharecroppers lost their livelihood. In addition, under the
AAA, benefit checks for curtailment of production were
made out to landlords, who often failed to pass them on to
their Negro tenants. AAA cash benefits made mechanization
possible and white landowners mechanized production to eliminate tenants and thus to increase their own percentage of
profits. For example, a 1939 study showed that with mechanization a reduction from 40 to 24 families was possible in the
Mississippi Delta area. Jobs created by mechanization went
to white labor.

Although vast numbers of Southern Negroes voted in
AAA crop referendums, large landowners were overrepre-
sented on local AAA administration committees. Negroes
were rarely allowed to vote for these committees, even if
established in primarily Negro areas. All benefit and acreage
decisions were made by these local committees, without adequate, if any, Negro voice. Complaints were heard by white
boards.

Southern lien laws made it difficult for Negro share tenants
and sharecroppers to borrow from government agencies and
credit cooperatives such as the Federal Land Bank, the Farm
Credit Administration and the Federal Farm Mortgage Corporation, because the Negroes had nothing to offer as security.
Even owners and cash tenants who had some resources had
less valuable land than whites to offer as security, and thus
had to apply for smaller loans.

Competition between poor Negroes and whites and local

government racial attitudes impeded cooperation and development of agricultural unions to combat the ill effects of Federal
legislation. Interracial organizations were concentrated in the
Southwest; not until 1940 did they appear in the South. The
Socialist Party organized with other groups the Southern
Tenant Farmers Union. It was composed of small farmers,
sharecroppers and laborers, both Negro and white, in Tennessee, Arkansas, and later Texas and Oklahoma. About half
Negro, it held interracial meetings in violation of state and
county laws, and thus encountered frequent violence. Membership probably never exceeded 30,000. There was little
conflict between whites and Negroes within the organization.
However, the Southern Tenants Farmers Union accomplished
relatively little in its efforts to acquire Federal benefits and
to fight displacements resulting from AAA policies.

Low-cost housing during the Depression was built largely
with funds supplied by the United States Housing Authority,
later the Federal Public Housing Authority. About one-third
of the units constructed were occupied by Negro families. In
the South separate projects were built for Negroes and
whites; some Northern projects were integrated and others
were not.

The Federal Housing Administration sponsored restrictive
covenants in building and rental programs.

The fact that the Home Owners Loan Corporation, the
Federal Home Loan Banks and the Federal Housing Administration followed conventional practices in granting loans
eliminated most Negroes.

The Tennessee Valley Authority hired Negroes as unskilled
laborers but did not admit them to training programs. Negroes
could not live in the Government communities of Norris and
Arthurdale.

The New Deal increased Negro educational facilities. The
Public Works Administration was especially successful in
school building projects in the North. Less than 10% of the
funds were used for Negro schools in the South.

The Works Projects Administration employed teachers in
adult education programs which taught 400,000 Negroes to
read and write. Student aid programs by the National Youth
Administration, the Agricultural Extension Service and the
Farm Security Administration also helped many Negroes.

53,000 Negroes, or 9.8% of the total employees, worked for the Federal government. The figure rose to 82,000 in 1938, or 9.9% of all Federal employees.

In August, Negroes in Atlanta, Ga., said "that in some cases competent and satisfactory Negro workers are beginning to be displaced by white men as a result of the higher wage scales provided by the NRA [National Industrial Recovery Act]."

Although the law creating the Civilian Conservation Corps (CCC) stated that "no person shall be excluded on account of race, color or creed," in fact, the CCC generally maintained a policy of strict segregation. Between 1933 and 1942, approximately 200,000 Negro boys worked in CCC camps. In New England and in the Western States, approximately 30,000 Negroes lived in integrated camps.

In New York a Negro minister, Rev. John Johnson, organized the Citizens League for Fair Play, which attempted to persuade white merchants to hire Negroes. Eventually several hundred jobs were opened to Negroes, but the bad feelings between white merchants and Negro residents continued, culminating in a riot in Harlem in 1935.

The NAACP lost its first attack on segregated education in the case of THOMAS HOCUTT V. THE UNIVERSITY OF NORTH CAROLINA, on a technicality.

The NAACP again challenged Texas' white-only primary. Dr. Nixon was again the plaintiff, as in 1924. Nixon was awarded damages by the United States District Court for having been denied the right to vote, but the law was not changed. The following year, however, Dr. Nixon was permitted to vote.

In this year 24 Negroes were lynched.

There were 38,000 Negroes attending colleges, 97% in colleges in the South.

Princess Malah, by John H. Hill, a Negro, was published. An "Uncle Tom" historical novel, it gives an exaggerated, bucolic view of the relations between Virginia aristocrats and their slaves. Hill made the poor whites the only real racists.

Banana Bottom, a poem by Claude McKay, expressed the fullest development of McKay's cultural dualism theme. The story, set in Jamaica, concerns the tensions and contrasts between a young Negro and a white missionary couple, who had brought her up.

Run Little Chillun by Hall Johnson was a successful Negro folk drama by a Negro. It ran 126 performances on Broadway.

The Emperor Jones directed by Dudley Murphy and independently produced by John Krimsky and Gifford Cochran, was to be the first of a series of film adaptations of Eugene O'Neill's plays. The film starred Paul Robeson. This movie employed an all-Negro cast and was faithful to the play. It had a considerable success among critics and audiences. In creating a Negro role of tragic grandeur, Robeson proved that Negroes need not be used only for light comedy or slapstick In the context of the history of the Negro in the cinema, this movie is a landmark in that it encouraged Negro movie companies to make serious films.

Benny Goodman began to use Negro musicians for recordings. He later broke the convention against Negroes and whites playing together in public when Teddy Wilson, a Negro, appeared with the Goodman band at the Hotel Congress in Chicago in 1936.

Tom Redcam, a Negro journalist in Jamaica, died. He wrote numerous popular ballads and songs which have become part of the island's folk culture.

Charles Ferdinand Pressoir, a Negro of Haitian descent and president of the Creole Academy, wrote a collection of poems, *Au Rhythme de Coumbites.*

1934

In a study of 30 cities (10 Northern, 7 border and 13 Southern), the proportion of Negro and white families on relief was shown to be: North—Negro, 52.2%, white, 13.3%; border—51.8%, 10.4% and South—33.7%, 11.4%. The study found that in three cities—Washington, D.C.; Norfolk, Va., and Charlotte, N.C.—between 70 and 80% of all households receiving relief were Negro.

Average annual income for Negro tenant and wage laborers in the South was $278; the average for whites was $452. Average annual income for Negro cash renters and share tenants was about $300; whites, $417.

The Federal Emergency Relief Administration inaugurated

a program to help the rural poor grow their own food. Between this year and 1941, $1,121,000,000 was allocated to this program, and $5.3 billion to the discriminatory AAA.

The National Recovery Administration (NRA) proved unsatisfactory to most Negroes. They were rarely represented at code hearings, and cost-of-living differentials were discriminatory. Under the steel, laundry and tobacco codes, among others, Negro workers received lower wages than whites.

The minimum wage regulations of the National Recovery Act contributed to the number of Negroes on relief. The NRA increased competition for jobs and thus encouraged discrimination. The Fair Labor Standards Act of 1938 setting minimum wages had a similar effect.

Clark Foreman of the Interior Department and E. K. Jones of the Commerce Department, both Negroes, set up interdepartmental committees to consider problems of Negroes under NRA and AAA. An NRA representative admitted that there was discrimination against Negroes in its operations. An AAA representative explained, "It may be said that the smaller the administrative unit, and the greater the degree of local control, the worse the conditions to which Negroes are subjected."

John P. Davis criticized the NRA for putting Negroes out of work and for raising prices.

Negro enrollment in the CCC was only 5.3% of the total enrollment, although Negroes represented 10% of the population. Enrollment was done by local officials, which allowed discrimination.

The NAACP began formulating of a plan for "systematic coordinated legal assault on discrimination in the schools."

A. Philip Randolph's resolution at the AFL National Convention to end union discrimination was rejected by the delegates. The AFL organization committee argued that no such discrimination existed, and supported the concept of separate unions for Negroes and whites. In 1935, after much debate the National Convention rejected a special investigation committee's suggestions to end discrimination.

The AFL and, in particular, the railroad brotherhoods discriminated against Negroes in the following ways: by constitutional, ritual and tacit agreement; through creation of segregated and auxiliary locals; by collusion with employers; by negotiating separate seniority and promotion agreements in contracts that kept Negroes in menial jobs; by controlling the craft licensing boards; by negotiating for Negroes without Negro representation or votes on the final contracts; by excluding Negroes from union hiring halls when the halls represented the only job source.

Probably not more than 2,500 of the 24,536 claimed membership of the American Communist Party were Negroes.

The popularity Roosevelt gained for the Democratic Party among Negroes was manifested in this year, when Arthur Mitchell, a Negro Democrat was elected to Congress from Chicago. He replaced Oscar De Priest, a Negro Republican who had been one of the most popular Negroes in the nation, by virtue of having been the only Negro in Congress.

The Louisiana Legislature repealed the poll tax. However, by 1936, only approximately 2,000 Negroes were registered.

An anti-lynching bill written by Senator Costigan of Colorado and Senator Wagner of New York was proposed. The NAACP sponsored the bill and placed large banners outside its New York office every day a man was lynched. The NAACP was unsuccessful in its attempt to have President Roosevelt endorse the bill and it did not pass.

Fifteen Negroes were lynched in this year.

The culmination of the NAACP's 14-year campaign for the liberation of Haiti occurred when President Roosevelt finally withdrew the United States troops.

W. E. B. Du Bois resigned as editor of the NAACP journal, *Crisis,* because his black nationalism conflicted with the NAACP policy of desegregation. He returned to the NAACP from 1944 to 1948. Roy Wilkins became editor of *Crisis.*

The Black Muslim leader, Fard, had about 8,000 adherents. Membership declined after his disappearance in this year. Elijah Muhammed moved his headquarters to Chicago. He was soon called "The prophet," and Fard was identified with Allah.

LeRoi Jones (1934-   ), Negro writer, was born in Newark, N.J., and was educated at Howard and Columbia

Universities. He has been a faculty member of the New School and Columbia. From 1960-65 Jones edited *Yugen*, a prominent Beat poetry magazine. Jones organized and ran the Black Arts Theater in Harlem, 1964-65, as part of HARYOU Act. In 1966 he moved to Newark, N.J., to run Spirit House, a Negro workshop in the arts. In 1967 he was arrested in connection with the Newark riots in July of that year; convicted in a very controversial trial the following March, he was sentenced to 2½ years. He later organized the United Brotherhood Party and became very active in local politics. Jones' works include: *Preface to a 20-Volume Suicide Note*, 1961, a collection of Jones' early poetry containing little about race; *The Moderns*, 1963, an anthology of contemporary short stories edited by Jones; *Blues People*, 1963, a long prose socio-historical study tracing the development of Negro blues music and how it reflects the Negro experience in the U.S.; *Dutchman*, 1964, his first commercially produced play. Jones followed this with several other one-acters, *The Slave, The Toilet, The Baptism*, all of which became increasingly vitriolic in their anti-white feelings. *The Dead Lecturer*, Jones' second collection of poems, was published in 1964. The poetry of this volume and subsequent ones reflect the development of Jones' increasingly anti-white anti-Semitic philosophy. *System of Dante's Hell* (1965), Jones' first novel; *Home* (1966), a collection of essays, and *Tales* (1967), a collection of short stories, are others of his writings. Jones was married to a Jewish girl and is the father of her child.

William Felton Russell (1934-   ), Negro basketball player and coach, was born in Monroe, La. Russell became in 1966 the first Negro coach of a professional sports team, the Boston Celtics of the National Basketball Association. An All-American at the University of San Francisco, Russell led the U.S. Olympic basketball team to the gold medal in 1956. Entering the NBA after the Olympics, Russell has five times been named Most Valuable Player, and the Boston Celtics with Russell as both player and now player-coach, have dominated the NBA.

A new Negro magazine, *Challenge*, edited by Dorothy West, began publication. Writers such as James Weldon Johnson and Langston Hughes contributed articles. The main

intent of the magazine was to revive the spirit of 1926, i.e., to
revive an interest in Africa and Afro-America. William
Attaway, Owen Dodson and Frank Yerby were also published
in *Challenge*. The editor was under constant attack for not
being politically radical and for being totally involved with
esthetic matters. Three years later the magazine was reorganized and retitled *New Challenge*.

The Ways of White Folks, an anthology of short stories
by Langston Hughes, dealt with race relations in rural Southern towns. Miscegenation was the common theme of approximately half the stories.

Jonah's Gourd Vine by Zora Neale Hurston was published.
The author utilized rural Negro folklore in a style modeled
upon preacher or Holy Roller rhetoric to achieve a very
original effect.

Legal Murder by Dennis Donague ran only 7 nights on
Broadway, but was the first of a protest-play cycle. It was
based on the Scottsboro case.

Negro Folk Symphony No. 1 by William L. Dawson, a
Negro composer, was performed by the Philadelphia Sym-
phony Orchestra at Carnegie Hall, under the direction of
Leopold Stokowski. Dawson was born in 1898 in Anniston,
Ala. He ran away to Tuskegee Institute, where Booker T.
Washington accepted him as a student. There he learned to
play many musical instruments. He attended Horner Institute
of Fine Arts in Kansas City and the American Conservatory
of Music in Chicago. Dawson became director of music at
Tuskegee Institute, remaining there until 1955.

1935

Median incomes of Negroes and whites in selected cities
were:

	Negroes	Whites	Negro Income lower by
New York City	$980	$1,930	49.2%
Chicago	726	1,687	56.9%
Columbus, Ohio	831	1,622	48.%7
Atlanta, Ga.	632	1,876	66.3%
Columbia, S.C.	576	1,876	69.3%
Mobile, Ala.	481	1,419	66.1%

The 3,500,000 Negro families receiving relief represented

21.5% of the total Negro population. Of the white population 12.8% were on relief.

Georgia, West Virginia, South Carolina, Florida, Kentucky, Tennessee, Alabama, Mississippi, Arkansas and Louisiana had higher white rural relief rates than Negroes. Southern relief administrators disbursed funds more easily to whites than Negroes. In addition, Southern Negroes on relief in rural areas received from $2 to $6 less per month than whites.

The average size of a Negro-operated farm in the South was 44 acres, compared to 131 acres for white-operated farms.

In the urban North approximately 50% of Negro families were on relief (3 to 4 times more than whites). In nine cities in the urban South 25% of Negro families and 11% of white families were on relief. More whites with an income below $500 were on relief than Negroes.

In urban areas Negro relief grants were smaller than white relief grants. The average for Negroes was $24.18, and for whites, $29.05.

Of relief cases who found employment, 8.8% of the Negroes received less in wages than they did on relief, while only 2.7% of the whites did.

The Social Security Act indirectly discriminated against Negroes by its exclusion of agricultural and domestic workers. Also, the sums received for old-age assistance were generally lower for Negroes than for whites.

Negro semi-skilled, skilled, clerical and professional workers had greater difficulty than white workers in gaining employment with the Work Projects Administration (WPA). This was demonstrated by percentages of skilled heads of families on relief in three representative states: Virginia: Negroes 25.7%, whites 43.3%; North Carolina: Negroes 19%, whites 42.9%; Mississippi: 11%, whites 35.4%. In these same states the percentages of skilled employed by WPA respectively were: Negroes: 9.3%, 9.4%, and 5.7%; whites, 27.2%, 28.8%, and 36.5%.

The Negro enrollment in the CCC was only 6.1% of the total enrollment, although Negroes constituted 10% of the population. There were 265 camps for Negro youths.

In its August issue, *Crisis* reported to Negroes "that the

powers that be in the Roosevelt Administration have nothing for them." In the October issue Walter White said, "The Attorney General continues his offensive against crime except crimes involving the privation of life and liberty to Negroes."

Senators Wagner of New York and Costigan of Colorado reintroduced an NAACP-drafted Federal anti-lynching bill. A filibuster killed this bill. Negroes were lynched at the rate of one every three weeks in this year.

The NAACP withdrew its support from Roosevelt when he refused to give his practical support to their anti-lynching bill, and because no civil rights legislation had been proposed in his term. The 26th annual convention of the NAACP met in St. Louis, and asked Harry L. Hopkins, Federal Emergency Relief administrator, to appoint a Negro as deputy administrator in every state with a large Negro population.

When the AFL convention refused to unionize unskilled labor, the CIO was organized. From the beginning race was relatively unimportant and the CIO created interracial unions in steel, automobile, rubber and packinghouse plants and factories. The generally integrated United Mine Workers was particularly instrumental in the maintenance of nondiscriminatory unionization.

The National Council of Negro Women was established in New York City. Mary McLeod Bethune served as its first president.

The National Association of Negro Business and Professional Women's Clubs was founded.

The International Council of Friends of Ethiopia was organized in New York with Willis N. Huggins, a Negro, as the executive secretary. Huggins pleaded Ethiopia's cause before the League of Nations.

Many Negroes left the Communist Party when it was revealed that Russia sold large quantities of oil, coal, tar and wheat to Mussolini, some of it directly to Africa, to be used against Ethiopia.

Ten Southern states spent an average $17.04 on each Negro pupil and $49.30 on each white student in elementary and secondary schools. Negro schools also had more pupils per teacher, less transportation, a shorter school term, and poorer facilities than the white schools.

Donald Murray attempted to integrate the University of Maryland Law School. The Maryland Court of Appeals ruled that the Maryland practice of providing scholarships for Negroes to attend out-of-state integrated law schools was an unequal practice and in violation of law and the Constitution. The decision was appealed and was upheld by the Supreme Court in 1936. Thurgood Marshall of the NAACP argued the case.

Despite the previous legal victories of the NAACP Negroes were still denied the ballot in the Texas Democratic primary. Supreme Court Justice Roberts upheld the Texas law which read: "Be it resolved that all white citizens of the state of Texas who are qualified to vote . . . shall be eligible to membership in the Democratic Party."

A Negro named Hollins had been convicted of rape in a trial in which he had no lawyer. After a second Oklahoma trial, the NAACP received a stay of execution and brought the case (HOLLINS V. OKLAHOMA) to the Supreme Court on the question of jury procedure. The Court ruled that the conviction of a Negro by a jury from which all Negroes were excluded was a violation of due process and void. A similar decision in NORRIS V. ALABAMA confirmed that exclusion of Negroes from juries was a violation of the 14th Amendment.

In this year 18 Negroes were lynched.

A riot in Harlem on March 19 was set off when a Negro boy was caught stealing a small knife from a 125th Street store. He escaped, but rumors spread that he had been beaten to death. Amid accusations of police brutality and merchant employment discrimination, Negroes smashed windows and looted. Three Negroes were killed, 200 store windows were smashed and over $200,000,000 in damage was done. An interracial committee on conditions in Harlem headed by E. Franklin Frazier, the Negro sociologist, reported that the riot was caused by "resentments against racial discrimination and poverty in the midst of plenty." Just prior to the riot Harlem businessmen who had been forced through a boycott to hire Negroes had secured an injunction on the basis of the Sherman Anti-Trust Act, and subsequently had fired the Negroes.

A. Philip Randolph was appointed a member of New York Mayor LaGuardia's Commission on Race.

A Negro chemist, Percy Julian, developed the drug Physostigmine for the treatment of glaucoma.

Ollie Miss, a novel about Negro sharecroppers, by the Negro novelist George Wylie Henderson was published. Emphasis is on farm activities, picnics, ball games, parties, etc., providing diversions from the everyday world. The book's importance is primarily sociological, as a portrait of the effect of the Depression on life in the Black Belt cotton fields.

Black Man's Verse by a Negro, Frank M. Davis, was published.

Mulatto, by Langston Hughes, culminated the protest-play cycle and was widely hailed by Brooks Atkinson and other New York critics. It was second only to *A Raisin in the Sun* as far as financial success by a Negro playwright. It ran 373 performances at the Vanderbilt Theater in New York City.

The Federal Theater, which existed from this year through 1940 as part of the WPA, became the most successful Harlem theater group. The Federal Theater Project in Harlem produced such works as J. Augustus Smith's *Turpentine* and W. E. B. Du Bois' *Haiti.* The project also performed such standards as Shaw and Shakespeare.

William G. Still's *Afro-American Symphony* was performed at the International Music Festival by the New York Philharmonic.

Todd Duncan, a Negro operatic singer, played the role of Porgy in George Gershwin's Negro folk opera, *Porgy and Bess.* John Bubbles, long-time Negro vaudeville star, appeared in the role of Sportin' Life.

John Henry Lewis, a Negro prize fighter, became light heavyweight boxing champion of the world. He held this title through 1939.

1936

The National Negro Congress (NNC) was founded by intellectuals at Howard University. They organized a coalition of religious, labor, fraternal and civic groups to work for a better economic situation for Negroes. The first meeting of the NNC took place in Chicago; 817 delegates representing states and organizations attended. A. Philip Randolph was elected president and John P. Davis, executive secretary. Local branches were established. The organization: (1) condemned any form of discrimination practiced against foreign-born Negroes in the United States; (2) opposed any attempt at deporting foreign-born Negroes or dropping them from relief; (3) sought to bring about a better relationship between foreign-born and native Negroes; (4) supported foreign-born Negroes in their struggle for economic and political freedom in their respective homes; (5) tried to bring about an international congress to establish better relations among Negroes throughout the world.

Members' of the Communist Party such as James W. Ford, helped to found the National Negro Congress, but Communist influence was not dominant at its inception in Chicago. At the first meeting, the executive secretary of the NNC, John P. Davis, suggested acceptance of much of the Communist program, especially in foreign affairs. In the following year the NNC showed a moderate labor-oriented stance. By the 1940 meeting in Washington, however, Communists were in complete control. The meeting passed several antiwar and anti-Roosevelt resolutions. Membership dwindled rapidly. A. Philip Randolph, president of the NNC, refused to stand for re-election because of Communist influence in the organization. Ralph Bunche also became disillusioned at the 1940 meeting.

The Communist Party set up the Negro People's Committee to Aid Spanish Democracy when the Spanish Civil War broke out. The committee had several branches, one headed by Lester P. Granger of the Urban League, until he determined that he had no control over the committee.

Of the 3,200 Americans who fought in the Spanish Civil War, between 60 and 80 were Negroes. There were about 10 Negroes in the first group of 550 Americans who formed the Abraham Lincoln Battalion. Most prominent was Oliver Law, a United States career Army man from Chicago. In April, 1937, Law was given command of the Lincoln Battalion, probably the first time an almost all-white American military unit was commanded by a Negro. Law was killed in action during an attack he led on Villanueva de la Canada, on July 13, 1937. Another Negro, Harry Heywood, served as assistant to George Aitken, the commissar of the 15th Brigade, which included the Lincoln and Washington battalions. Another Negro who served with distinction was Milton Herndon, the brother of Angelo Herndon, a well-known member of the U.S. Young Communist League. He headed a machine gun crew and was killed at Fuentes in the fall of 1937. Solaria Kee of Akron, Ohio, an American Negro nurse, also served with the American battalions in Spain.

The average income per family per year for Southern rural Negroes was $556, for whites, $1,535; for Southern urban Negroes, $635, for whites, $2,019; for Northern urban Negroes, $1,227, for whites, $2,616.

Of the urban Negro work force, 36% of the Negro males and 28% of the female were unemployed or in emergency work. For the white urban work force the figures were 21% and 19%.

An average dwelling unit for a Negro family had 3 rooms; for a white family, 5 to 6 rooms.

A survey of housing in four small Southern cities among non-relief families found that 60% of white dwellings had hot and cold water in kitchen and bathroom. Only 10% of the Negro dwellings had no indoor water supply, but more than 60% had no indoor water supply for the kitchen. More than 75% had no indoor water supply for the bathroom. Of the white dwellings 88% had a drain in the kitchen sink, but only 26% of the Negroes had drains.

The National Health Survey revealed that 73% of white families and only 9% of Negro families in cities of less than 10,000 had indoor flush toilets.

Mary McLeod Bethune was named director of the Negro Division of the National Youth Administration.

The WPA commissioned Richmond Barthé, Negro sculptor and artist to do a series of murals for the Harlem River Houses.

The platforms of the Democratic, Prohibition, Socialist Labor and Union parties made no mention of the Negro.

At the Democratic National Convention, "Cotton Ed" Smith, South Carolina Senator, and Mayor Burnet Maybank of Charleston walked out while a Negro minister was opening a session with a prayer. Smith said he would not support "any political organization that looks upon the Negro and caters to him as a political and social equal." Smith later walked out on a speech of Negro Congressman Mitchell of

Illinois. The South Carolina delegation officially protested the presence of Negroes.

The Republican Party platform said, "We favor equal opportunity for our colored citizens. We pledge our protection of their economic status and personal safety. We will do our best to further their employment in the gainful occupied life of America, particularly in private industry, agriculture, emergency agencies and the civil service. We condemn the present New Deal policies which would regiment and ultimately eliminate the colored citizen from the country's productive life, and make him solely a ward of the Federal Government."

Crisis condemned the Republican Party's pledge of "protection" of the Negro's economic status: "That is precisely what the Negroes do not want. His present economic status is the chief cause of his discontent."

Negroes did not like the Democratic platform any better than the Republican one, but they had some faith in Roosevelt's personal attitudes. Joel Spingarn, president of the NAACP, endorsed Roosevelt because "he has done more for the Negro than any Republican President since Lincoln." *Crisis,* the NAACP journal, said, "Even with their failures, they [the New Deal relief administrators, especially Harry Hopkins] have made great gains for the race in areas which heretofore have set their faces steadfastly against decent relief for Negroes."

The Communist Party platform read: "The Negro people suffer doubly. Most exploited of working people, they are also victims of jim crowism and lynching. They are denied the right to live as human beings." The party endorsed "abolition of poll taxes and other limitations of the right to vote." It demanded the release of political prisoners, among them Tom Mooney, Angelo Herndon and the Scottsboro boys. The party's platform continued: "We demand that the Negro people be guaranteed complete equality, equal rights to jobs, equal pay for equal work, the full right to organize, vote, serve on juries, and hold public office. Segregation and discrimination against Negroes must be declared a crime. Heavy penalties must be established against mob rule, floggers and kidnappers, with a death penalty for lynchers. We demand the enforcement of the 13th, 14th, and 15th Amendments to the

Constitution." James W. Ford was again Vice Presidential candidate on the Communist ticket.

The Socialist Party platform said that under Democratic rule, "lynching, race discrimination and the development of Fascist trends have continued unabated. Against these infringements of human rights the Democratic administration has kept an ominous silence."

In Chicago 49% of the Negro vote went to Roosevelt. In 1940 this vote increased to 52%.

Eight Negroes were lynched in this year.

In the 1934 case of BROWN, ELLINGTON, SHIELDS V. STATE OF MISSISSIPPI, three Negro farm laborers had been sentenced to death for murder. The only evidence was a confession by Ellington made under torture. When asked how severely he had whipped Ellington, the deputy sheriff stated, "Not too much for a Negro; not as much as I would have done if it were left to me." The convictions were upheld by the Mississippi Supreme Court, but the NAACP brought the case to the U.S. Supreme Court, where the conviction was reversed.

The NAACP represented Donald Murray in his attempt to be admitted to the University of Maryland Law School. The Supreme Court in PEARSON V. MURRAY ruled that Murray should be admitted. He was graduated in 1938.

William G. Still was the first Negro to lead a major symphony orchestra when he was guest conductor of the Los Angeles Symphony Orchestra in the Hollywood Bowl. Still was a composer of operas and symphonies and an arranger for Broadway shows, radio and motion pictures.

The Negro novelist, O'Wendell Shaw, published *Greater Need Below,* the first novel to deal with Negro college life. Shaw exposed the appalling education given Negroes at the tax-supported Negro colleges in the South. Their curricula were oriented to debase the Negro and their administrators were liaison men between Negro coeds and white businessmen in the community. Negro colleges and their Negro faculty and student bodies were humiliated by their white benefactors.

Black Thunder, by Arna Bontemps, is based on the slave insurrection of Gabriel Prosser (1800) and is notable for its accuracy and the objectivity with which it handles the slavery issue. A. B. Spingarn in *Crisis* called it "the best historical novel written by an American Negro."

Walk Together by Frank Wilson, a Negro playwright, ran 29 performances at the Lafayette in Harlem and inaugurated the Federal Theater Project in New York City.

Macbeth, the most highly acclaimed production of the entire Federal Theater Project in Harlem, included Canada Lee in the cast and was produced by John Houseman and Orson Welles.

Wilt Chamberlain (1936-   ), Negro basketball player, was born in Philadelphia and attended Kansas University. Twice voted All-American, he left college to play with the Harlem Globetrotters. In 1959 he signed with the Philadelphia Warriors of the NBA, and in his first season with the team broke the league scoring record. He has since dominated the field, playing with the San Francisco Warriors and the Philadelphia 76ers.

At the Berlin Olympics Jesse Owens, an American Negro, won gold medals in the 100- and 200-meter dash. In the 200-meter dash he set an Olympic record. Owens also set a world and Olympic record in the running broad jump, and a world record in the 400-meter relay with Ralph Metcalfe. Archie Williams, another American Negro athlete, won the 400-meter run, and John Woodruff the 800-meter.

1937

In contrast to only 18% of white males, 26% of all Negro males were unemployed. 33% of Negro females were unemployed, as against 24% of white females. Of the male non-white labor force in Northern states 39% was unemployed.

According to Erdmann D. Benyon in "The Voodoo Cult Among Negro Migrants in Detroit," in the *American Journal of Sociology,* there was in that year "no known case of unemployment" among the Black Muslims. He said they "no longer live in the slum section, but rent homes in some of the best economic areas in which Negroes have settled."

Large landowners could receive as much as $10,000 a year in AAA benefits. Statistics for 276 Southern plantations showed that owners' net income per plantation rose from $2,528 in 1934 to $3,590 in 1937; with the AAA now making direct payments to tenants on these plantations, the tenants' benefits increased from $11 a year in 1934 to $27 in 1937. This $27 represented 10% of the net cash income of the average tenant family. The AAA continued to give landlords reason for reducing the number of tenants and for replacing them with wage laborers so as to receive all of the acreage benefits. In spite of the Farm Security Administration (FSA), investigations by the director, William W. Alexander, and efforts to end discrimination in granting of loans, by and large the local administration of FSA funds remained in the hands of local farmers' committees on which Negroes were not represented. By 1942, the FSA program was cut back, partly because of antagonism toward its more enlightened racial policies.

In the South, only three-fifths of the Negroes 65 and over qualified for old-age insurance because of their former occupations. In both the North and South, Negroes covered often did not fully qualify because of restrictive stipulations. For example, if they had worked for the specific time but at a salary of $50 or less, they received lower benefits because of low previous income. However, under provisions of the amended Social Security Act for state matching-aid programs, the aged, the blind and children of broken homes fared better between 1937 and 1940. Discrimination in all categories continued to exist in some Southern states.

The white median period of enrollment in the CCC was 8 to 9 months; Negroes enrolled for 11 to 16 months.

By this year, the Housing Division of the Public Works Administration had built 21,319 units in 49 projects. Of these 14 projects were for Negroes only, 17 were integrated. Negroes occupied 7,507 units, about a third of the total. Rents, however, were high, shutting out the Negro who could not pay $24 month for three rooms.

The Supreme Court declared that the picketing of firms which refused to hire Negroes was a legal technique for securing redressment.

NAACP leaders such as Villard and White opposed Roosevelt's Supreme Court bill, fearing that it could eventually be used against Negroes.

Thurgood Marshall argued for equalization of public school

teachers' salaries before the Maryland Board ef Education. In Maryland, white teachers were paid almost twice as much as Negro teachers of the same grade. The NAACP took similar action in Kentucky and other states. In the Maryland case, Marshall argued on behalf of William Gibbs, a Negro teacher of Montgomery County, who was an acting principal at $612 per year. If he had been white, he would have received a salary of $1,475 per year. The board ordered salaries equalized throughout the county.

The NAACP successfully challenged the attempted exclusion of Negro Boy Scouts from the Scout Jamboree held in Washington, D.C.

The Harrison-Black-Fletcher Education Bill introduced in Congress failed to provide for equitable distribution of funds to Negroes. The NAACP began a major campaign against the bill in alliance with 24 other national organizations. The bill was amended somewhat, to the satisfaction of the NAACP; but although it passed the Senate, it was reported unfavorably in the House.

The NAACP, in its continuing fight for anti-lynching legislation, persuaded Rep. Joseph Gavagan of New York to introduce such a bill. It passed the House on April 15. The Senate version (Wagner-Van Nuys Anti-lynching Bill) was killed by filibuster.

James W. Ford, the Negro Communist, said, "We Communists desire to do everything possible in building and broadening the movement of the Negro people in cooperation with the NAACP, the National Congress, the Urban League, and other organizations." This "united front" attitude contrasted sharply with earlier Communist castigation of Negro organizations as reactionary.

In this year 8 Negroes were lynched.

The Pennsylvania Labor Relations Act denied state protection to unions which discriminated against Negroes.

Organized groups of red caps met in Chicago to form the International Brotherhood of Red Caps, later to become the United Transport Service Employees of America. Willard S. Townsend, a graduate of the Canadian Royal Academy of Science, and red cap union official, became its first president.

After affiliation with the CIO Townsend, still the union's president, became a vice president of the AFL-CIO.

The Negro Federal judge, William H. Hastie, was confirmed for the Federal Court in the Virgin Islands. In 1946, President Truman appointed Hastie Governor of the Virgin Islands.

William Melvin Kelley (1937–   ), Negro author, was born in New York City and was educated at Harvard University where he studied writing under Archibald MacLeish. His works include: *A Different Drum,* 1962, Kelley's first novel; *Dancers on the Shore,* 1964, a collection of 16 short stories; *A Drop of Patience,* 1965, a novel; and in 1967, *Dem,* a third novel.

Waters Edward Turpin published *These Low Grounds,* the first Negro attempt at a family chronicle novel. *These Low Grounds* deals with four generations of an Eastern Shore Maryland family, beginning prior to the Civil War and extending all the way to the Depression.

Their Eyes Were Watching God, by the Negro novelist Zora Neale Hurston, was her second and most successful novel. It deals, not with race as such, but with personal relations. Race prejudice appears as a subject intermittently.

River George, by the Negro novelist George W. Lee is principally concerned with sharecropping. A protest novel about organizing sharecroppers, it exposes the tenant-farm system as little more than a perpetuation of slavery.

Challenge, a magazine, was reorganized and published as *New Challenge.* Richard Wright replaced Dorothy West as the principal editor. The first issue contained an editorial manifesto, stating the magazine's intention to concentrate on social realism in fiction. Wright, in one article, even advocated a Stalinist party line on literature for young Negro writers.

I Am the American Negro, a collection of verse by Frank M. Davis, was published.

New Symphony in G Minor, by William G. Still, the Negro composer, was performed by the Philadelphia Symphony Orchestra.

Jack and David Goldberg founded a company called Negro Marches On, which made movies exclusively for Negroes.

Jack Goldberg had begun in 1925 putting on all-Negro theatrical revues. In 1937 he organized the first all-Negro newsreel company, which was still functioning in 1948. Throughout the late 1930's and the early 1940's, the Goldbergs continued to produce successful Negro films in Hollywood. Most of the stories were imitations of current Hollywood hits, but the Goldbergs' production were much more polished technically than those of other Negro companies.

Warner Bros. released the movie version of *The Green Pastures,* with an all-Negro cast.

On Easter Sunday, Eddie Anderson first appeared on the Jack Benny radio show. As Rochester, he became a regular member of Benny's group, appearing with him also in the subsequent TV series. Anderson's movies included *Star-Spangled Rhythm* and *Cabin in the Sky.*

Joe Louis, a Negro, defeated James A. Braddock to become the world's heavyweight boxing champion.

Henry Armstrong, the Negro prize fighter, became featherweight boxing champion.

A. J. Seymour, a Negro from British Guiana, published the first of five collections of his poetry, *Verse.*

1938

The Supreme Court heard the case of MISSOURY EX REL. GAINS VS. CANADA REGISTRAR OF THE UNIVERSITY ET. AL. Lloyd Gaines had been denied admission to the University of Missouri Law School and had appealed to the courts. The Supreme Court ruled that a state was required to allow Negro admission at the state university if equal educational facilities were not available. The practical effect of this decision was the creation of separate graduate schools for Negroes.

Thurgood Marshall was appointed by the NAACP as special counsel in charge of all its cases. He remained with the NAACP until 1961 when he became Federal Judge in the Circuit Court of Appeals.

Under the chairmanship of a Negro, Adam Clayton Powell Jr., the Greater New York Coordinating Committee for Employment prevailed upon the Uptown Chamber of Commerce to concede that its stores in Harlem should have at least one-third Negro employees and equal promotion opportunities.

While 9.8% of Federal employees were Negro, with few exceptions they held jobs as postal clerks, mailmen, unskilled laborers and janitors.

Negro participation in the administration of the WPA had been slight. In September, 1938, only 91 Negroes were employed at the Washington headquarters.

The Fair Labor Standard Act, by setting minimum wages, caused increased competition for jobs and thus encouraged discrimination against Negroes.

Crystal Bird Fauset, elected to the Pennsylvania House of Representatives, became the first Negro woman to be elected to a State Legislature.

In Birmingham, Ala., Negroes and whites were segregated in the state relief offices.

A *Fortune* magazine poll showed that 84.7% of the Negroes supported President Franklin D. Roosevelt.

In this year, 6 Negroes were lynched.

Oscar Robertson (1938-   ), Negro basketball player, was born in Charlotte, Tenn., and moved with his family to Indianapolis, Ind. He attended the University of Cincinnati and as a sophomore became the nation's leading scorer. A 3-time All-American, in 1960 he was signed by the Cincinnati Royals of the NBA. Robinson, known as the "Big O," is considered the greatest guard in the history of basketball, and his name has become synonymous with overall basketball skill. In 1964 he won the Most Valuable Player Award of the NBA.

Uncle Tom's Children by Richard Wright, a Negro, was published.

Two books by Sterling A. Brown, a Negro, were published. *The Negro in American Fiction* was a study of Negroes and Negro themes in American literature; *Negro Poetry and Drama* surveyed the Negro contributions in these areas.

In this year, the Goldberg movie company produced two films for Negroes: *Siren of the Tropics,* starring Josephine Baker, and *Mystery in Swing,* starring Monte Hawley, Marguerite Whittin and Bob Webb. The latter movie became one of their most successful films commercially.

Artie Shaw hired Billie Holiday, a Negro, to sing with his white band. One of the greatest of jazz singers, the daughter of an accomplished guitarist, she has been one of the great jazz influences, not only on other singers, but instrumentalists as well. She published an autobiography in 1956, three years before her death.

With a Carnegie Hall concert by the Negro musicians Meade Lux Lewis, Albert Ammous and Pete Johnson, boogie-woogie became an overnight craze, and began to be applied to almost all songs. Boogie-woogie developed from house-rent parties in the 1920's, especially in Chicago. The style originated with Negro pianists such as "Cat-Eye," "Jack the Bear" and "Tippling Tom."

Henry Armstrong, the Negro prize fighter, was both lightweight and welterweight boxing champion. Armstrong held the welterweight crown until 1940.

1939

The median income of white and non-white wage and salary workers, respectively, were: Male: white $1,112, non-white $460; female: white $676, non-white $246.

There were approximately 30,000 Negro retail stores and restaurants, employing 43,000 Negroes. Their total sales were approximately $71 million, or .02% of the national total. Between 1929 and 1939, sales had declined 28%, whereas the national total had declined only 13%.

There were 67 Negro insurance companies with incomes of $13 million.

There were 3,640 Negroes in the regular Army.

The Greater New York Coordinating Committee for Employment, led by Adam Clayton Powell Jr., demonstrated at the offices of the World's Fair in the Empire State Building, and succeeded in opening up several hundred jobs for Negroes.

More than one million Negroes had earned a living by being employed or given relief by the WPA. The WPA employed Negroes in many fields, including the professions and the fine arts. Negro artists, for example, were commissioned to paint murals in government buildings.

Although Negroes were generally represented proportionally on National Youth Administration programs, they were often underrepresented on the programs in Southern states.

Only 19.3% of the youths in NYA Out-of-school Work Projects were Negroes in the 17 Southern states and Washington, D.C., although they constituted 24.9% of the appropriate age group (15–24) in the population. The projects needed a local public service organization as a sponsor in the South, and these organizations were controlled by whites.

From 1936 to 1939, 12.5% of all rehabilitation loans granted by the Farm Security Administration were made to Negroes. Negro farmers constituted 12.6% of all farm operators. Although Negroes constituted 37% of the low-income farm families in the South, only 23% of the low-income loans were made to Negroes there.

The Negro who had received an FSA loan in the South had by 1939 repaid an average of 41%. The white, on the other hand, had repaid only 39%. The average annual net income of Negroes rose 62%, that of whites rose only 48%.

The case of LANE v. WILSON concerned an Oklahoma statute stipulating that those who had not registered within 12 days would never be allowed to register. Contested by I. W. Lane, a Negro, it was declared unconstitutional.

In July, the Ku Klux Klan in Greenville, S.C., issued a statement warning: "The Klan will ride again if Greenville Negroes continue to register and vote."

The Ku Klux Klan burned 25 crosses and paraded through the Negro section of Miami, Fla., the night before a municipal election carrying Negro effigies with signs saying "This Nigger Tried to Vote." Despite this, 1,000 of 1,500 registered Negroes voted the next day, led by Sam Solomon, a Negro businessman.

In this year two Negroes were lynched.

In April, Mississippi Senator Theodore C. Bilbo introduced a back-to-Africa bill in the Senate.

The New Jersey Supreme Court ruled in favor of an NAACP suit by declaring that the segregation of New Jersey beaches was illegal.

In 13 Southern states, only 99 of the 774 public libraries were open to Negroes.

The NAACP prepared nine cases for court action on the

right of Negro students to attend tax-supported universities in the states where they lived.

Joel Spingarn, president of the NAACP, died. He was succeeded by his brother Arthur.

Jane Matilda Bolin became the first Negro woman judge when she was appointed to the Court of Domestic Relations in New York City by Mayor Fiorello LaGuardia.

John Torres (1939–   ), Negro artist, studied at the Art Students League between 1959 and 1963 under Frank Reilly and John Hovannes. Torres showed remarkable gifts as a sculptor, mastering techniques in metal, wax (*Samari*), bronze, (*Horse Sketch*) and plaster, (*The Monument*). Torres' sculptures are never abstract, but do give the appearance of being recovered fragments from some ancient civilization. Since 1963 he has had successful one-man shows in New York City and has devoted much of his time to running an artists' workshop in the Henry Street Settlement in New York.

Drums at Dusk, Arna Bontemps' historical novel, deals with the Haitian Revolution and Toussaint l'Ouverture. With the exception of a few particulars at the beginning of the revolution, Bontemps is accurate in the depiction of the era and the conditions.

Oh Canaan by the Negro novelist Waters Edward Turpin was published. It deals with the great migration to Chicago, and covers the 20-year period from the race riot of 1919 to 1939. In this novel Turpin describes urban conditions of the Negro, the poor living conditions, the family disintegration and white hostility.

To Make a Poet Black, an anthology of essays and poems by a Negro Jay S. Redding was published.

Hale Woodruff, the Negro painter famous for his abstract modernist landscapes, was commissioned to do the Armistad murals showing scenes of the slave revolt for Talladega College. In the same year Woodruff became professor of art at Atlanta University, and in 1941 began sponsoring annual art shows there.

Secretary of the Interior Ickes arranged for Marian Anderson to give her Easter concert on the steps of the Lincoln Memorial when the Daughters of the American Revolution prevented her appearance at Constitution Hall, which they owned.

The Negro concert singer Dorothy Maynor, world famous through her concerts and appearances as a soloist in North and South America and Europe, made her debut in Town Hall in New York City.

Way Down South, a movie directed by Bernard Vorhaus and produced by Sol Lesser, starred Bobbie Breen, Clarence Muse, etc. An interracial Hollywood feature, its significance lies in the screenplay which was written by Langston Hughes and Clarence Muse, the lead Negro star.

Jed Buell produced and directed *Harlem on the Prairie,* the first all-Negro Western.

Jackie Robinson, a Negro, helped to lead UCLA's football team to an undefeated season. In the same year Robinson was a leading scorer in the Pacific Coast Conference in basketball.

1940

U.S. Census: There were 12,866,000 Negroes in the U.S., representing 9.8% of the population. Of the total, 84,000 were foreign-born, primarily West Indians.

Life expectancy of white males in the U.S. was 62.1 years, and for non-white males, 51.5 years; for white females, 66.6 years, and for non-white females, 54.9 years.

The infant mortality rate per 1,000 live births was 73.8 for Negroes and 43.2 for whites.

23.8% of Negroes lived in Northern and Western states. Net migration from the South since 1910 was 1,750,000, of whom 90% lived in urban areas. Only 37.3% of Southern Negroes lived in cities. The majority of Negroes still lived in Southern rural areas.

In the Southern cities, Atlanta and New Orleans, there were three and five areas, respectively, in which 90% of the residents were Negro. In Atlanta about half of the city had under 10% Negro residency. The Negro areas in Memphis and Birmingham were widely scattered and relatively integrated.

In the border cities of St. Louis, Baltimore and Washington, D.C., Negroes were virtually excluded from the major part of the city. Most lived in areas which were 75-90% Negro.

In the school year 1939–40, in 9 Southern states, per capita expenditure for public education for Negroes was $18.82; for whites, $58.69. In Mississippi, 5 times as much was spent per white child as per Negro child. In Louisiana, Alabama and Georgia, somewhat over 3 times as much was spent for white children as for Negro children.

Through the efforts of the NAACP in the case of ALSTON VS. SCHOOL BOARD OF THE CITY OF NORFOLK, a Federal Circuit Court of Appeals declared that, under the 14th Amendment, Negro teachers could not be denied pay equal to that of white teachers.

Percentages of distribution for male Negro employment in the South were: professional, technical, etc., 1.6%; managers, officials, proprietors, 0.9%; clerical workers, 1.2%; craftsmen and foremen, 3.6%; operators, 10.9%; service workers, 11.2%; non-farm laborers, 20.6%; total non-farm, 50%; farmers and farm workers, 50%. The percentages for Negro females in Southern states were: professional and technical, 4.4%; managers, officials, proprietors, 0.6%; clerical and sales, 0.9%; craftsmen and foremen, 0.1%; operatives, 5%; service workers, 58.%; service workers other than household, 8.9%; non-farm laborers, 0.9%; total non-farm, 79.6%; farm and farm workers, 20.4%.

Distribution of Negro workers among various types of occupations in the U.S. exclusive of the South was: professional and technical: male 3.1%, female 3.7%; managers, officials, proprietors: male 2.8%, female 1.1%; clerical and sales: male 5.6%, female 3%; craftsmen and foremen: male 7.7%, female 0.3%; operatives: male 19.6%, female 10.6%; service workers, private household: male 32.6%, female 64.6%; non-farm laborers: male 24.5%, female 0.8%; total non-farm: male 95.9%, female 99.8%; farm and farm workers: male 4.1%, female 0.2%.

The number of farm operators in the South by tenure and color was: Owners and managers, non-white, 174,000; white, 1,384,000. Tenants, non-white, 208,000; white, 700,000. Sharecroppers, non-white, 299,000; white, 242,000.

Of southern farmland, 8% was operated by Negroes, who represented 25% of the farm population.

Per capita average value of land and building in the South was $596. The national average was $1,116. The average acreage value was $23.89 for Negroes and $27.27 for whites. Negro-owned farms averaged 60.4 acres, which approximated the average 58.9 acres worked by a white sharecropper. The value of farm implements of Negro owners was $90; for whites, $322.

In Chicago, New York, Detroit and Philadelphia Negroes were virtually excluded from living in 80-95% of these Northern cities. Most lived in concentrated or contiguous areas which had over 90% Negro residency.

In HANSBERRY V. LEE, the Supreme Court overthrew an Illinois Supreme Court verdict by ruling that Hansberry was not bound by a restrictive covenant and could sell his house to a Negro if he desired. The NAACP handled part of this case.

A New York law forbade union discrimination and provided damages, fines and imprisonment for violation of the act. In 1945, in RAILWAY MAIL ASSOCIATION VS. CORSI, the Supreme Court declared the law constitutional.

In this year over 30% of U.S. longshoremen were Negroes. They made up 3.8% of automobile workers.

Only 5.4% of all workers in 20 major defense industries were Negro.

There were 3,939 Negro physicians and surgeons, an increase of only 740 since 1910. There were 1,175 Negro lawyers, an increase of 396 since 1910.

The National Negro Bankers Association had 14 members.

There were 210 Negro newspapers, mostly with local circulation, and 129 magazines. The *Pittsburgh Courier* had the largest circulation, 141,500 copies a week. *The Chicago Defender* was second with 83,500.

Negro publishers formed the National Newspaper Publishers Association.

Of Negro males 19.4% were unemployed compared to 12.4% whites; 35.9% of Negro females were unemployed, compared to 23.8% whites.

In New York, Chicago, Philadelphia, Detroit, Cleveland, Los Angeles, Pittsburgh, Cincinnati, Indianapolis (the Northern cities with the largest Negro populations), 45–56% of Negro males were employed, compared to 63–73% of whites. In the large cities of the upper and lower South, two-thirds of Negro males were employed, compared to three-quarters of white males.

From 1940 to 1949, the total executions under civil authorities in the U.S. was 1,284; of whom whites accounted for 490 and Negroes, 781. In the two major categories of murder and rape, the figures were respectively white, 458, Negro 595; and white, 19, Negro 179.

In the previous decade, approximately 300,000 Negro youths were employed in the CCC program. In 1940 30,000 Negroes were enrolled. The American Youth Commission stated that the CCC was not using a sufficient number of Negro supervisory and administrative personnel for Negro camps. Only two CCC companies were entirely staffed by Negroes.

Of those employed by the National Youth Administration, 13% were Negroes. This represented a fair proportion of the total Negro population, but the need for local sponsors for projects meant that Negroes were underrepresented in the South.

A low proportion of Negroes were in supervisory or administrative jobs in the WPA. In 14 Southern states, there were 11 Negro and 10,333 white supervisors.

The *Underwriting Manual* of the Federal Housing Administration advocated exclusion of Negroes and other minorities, and required adoption of racially restrictive covenants for new construction. These conditions were deleted in 1949; however, the FHA still refused to require builders to sell to Negroes.

The NAACP began a coordinated drive for desegregation of the Armed Forces. Walter White of the NAACP, T. Arnold Hill of the Urban League, A. Philip Randolph and other Negro leaders submitted a 7-point program to President Roosevelt. The NAACP also petitioned the Senators for Selective Service Reforms so that Negroes would be freely inducted. It also threatened lawsuits against local boards of edu-

cation that provided vocational defense training for whites
but not for Negroes.

Col. Benjamin O. Davis was appointed a brigadier general,
the first Negro general in American history.

Judge William H. Hastie, a Negro, was made civilian aide
to the Secretary of War.

Fewer than 5,000 of the 230,000 men in the Army were
Negroes.

There were 2 Negro combat officers, and 500 out of
100,000 Army Reserve officers were Negroes.

The Selective Service Act of September contained an
amendment introduced by Rep. Hamilton Fish of New York
providing that, in the selection and training of men under
the act, there should be no discrimination on account of
race or color.

In October, President Roosevelt announced that Negro
strength in the Army would be in proportion to the Negro
percentage of the total population; that Negro groups would
be organized in every major branch of the service, combatant
as well as noncombatant; that Negroes would have the opportunity to become officers and attend Officers Training Schools;
that Negroes would be trained as pilots, mechanics and technical aviation specialists. However, Negroes and whites
would not be mingled in the same regiments because that
would "produce situations destructive to morale and detrimental to the preparation for national defense."

This year four Negroes were lynched.

In Brownsville, Tex., seven prominent Negroes were run
out of town and Ebert Williams, an NAACP leader, was
murdered. These men had been leading a voting drive.

An Atlanta, Ga., ordinance segregated public parks except
for "so much of Grant Park as is occupied by the zoo."

Atlanta also passed a city ordinance requiring Jim Crow
taxis, with different colored signs to indicate the race they
served. It required that white drivers carry white passengers,
and Negro drivers carry Negro passengers.

A survey made by the Southern Regional Council indicated
that only about 2% of the Negroes of voting age in 12
Southern states qualified to vote under the state election laws.

Only 5% of Southern Negroes of voting age were registered
to vote. Of a population of 3,651,256 Negroes, 80,000 to
90,000 voted in the 1940 election in Alabama, Georgia,
Mississippi, Louisiana, Florida, Texas, South Carolina and
Arkansas.

The Democratic platform stated: "Our Negro citizens
have participated actively in the economic and social advances launched by this Administration, including fair labor
standards, social security benefits, . . . work relief prospects,
. . . decent housing, . . . We have aided more than half a
million Negro youths in vocational training, education and
employment." It further stated: "We shall continue to strive
for complete legislative safeguards against discrimination in
Government service and benefits, and in national defense
forces. We pledge to uphold due process and the equal protection of laws for every citizen regardless of race, creed or
color." This was the first time in the 20th century that the
Negro was mentioned by name in a Democratic National
platform.

The Republican Party platform said: "We pledge that our
American citizens of Negro descent shall be given a square
deal in the economic and political life of this nation. Discrimination must cease. To enjoy the full benefits of life, liberty
and pursuit of happiness, universal suffrage must be made
effective for the Negro citizen. Mob violence shocks the conscience of the nation and legislation to curb this evil should
be enacted."

In his book, *One World,* the defeated Republican Presidential candidate, Wendell Willkie, wrote in the chapter
"Our Imperialisms at Home" that American attitudes toward
Negroes were blatantly imperialist and impeded the war effort
by bringing America's sincerity into question with foreign
nations.

The Socialist Party platform favored Federal aid to education "on terms which eliminated discrimination against Negroes and other minority groups." It also declared: "We
renew our pledge for the maintenance and increase of civil
liberty for all groups regardless of race, color, or creed. We
support everywhere the fight against poll taxes, undemocratic
laws, and all limitations of suffrage. . . . Discrimination
against Negroes must be abolished."

The Communist Party platform read: "The Negro people, most exploited of the toilers, suffering from lynching and Jim Crowism, robbed of their constitutional rights, are being prepared to fight another war for 'democracy' in order to further enslave them." The Communist platform advocated the "Geyer Anti-Poll Tax Bill to give the vote to Negroes and white masses in the South," a guarantee for Negroes of "complete equality, equal rights to jobs, equal pay for equal work, the full right to organize, serve on juries and hold public offices," "death penalty for lynchers," and enforcement of the 13th, 14th and 15th Amendments. James W. Ford, a Negro, was vice presidential candidate on the Communist Party ticket for the third time.

When the Communists openly seized control of the National Negro Congress, most other groups and leaders left the organization.

The Negro Democratic vote in 1940 was estimated at 40% of the total Negro vote, compared to an estimate of 90% for the 1964 election. In the 1940 election, President Roosevelt lost much of the Negro vote he had built up since 1932. Negroes felt that the Administration had discriminated in some of the relief agencies and excluded Negroes from the preliminary defense preparations. The phrase "The Dirty Deal" became popular among Negroes at this time.

Richard Wright, a Negro, published his novel *Native Son.*

Heart Shape in the Dusk by the Negro poet Robert Hayden was published. His first collection of verse, it gained him immediate renown.

W. E. B. Du Bois founded his journal *Phylon* at Atlanta University.

The American Negro Theater was founded.

The Big White Fog by Theodore Ward was written for the Federal Project in Chicago but was produced at Lincoln Theater in Harlem. Brooks Atkinson thought it "the best serious play by Negro authorship about race problems."

Henwar Rodakiewicz directed *"One Tenth of Our Nation,"* a documentary about the inadequacies of Southern education for Negroes.

Jed Buell produced a Negro composite, *Mr. Washington Goes to Town,* of two of Frank Capra's successful films.

Hattie McDaniel, the Negro actress, received an Academy award as best supporting actress for her role in *Gone With the Wind*.

At Minton's Play House, on West 118th Street, Teddy Hill, Charlie Christian, Dizzy Gillespie, Dusty Young, Kenny Clarke, Thelonius Monk and Charlie Parker began playing bop. Their music was largely improvised, but used advanced harmonic and rhythmic ideas.

George Pace was bantamweight boxing champion in this year.

The percentages of Negro population in Central and South America were: Mexico, 0.4%; the Antilles, 39.3%; Guatemala, 0.1%; British Honduras, 25.6%; Honduras, 5.0%; El Salvador, 0.0001%; Nicaragua, 6.5%; Costa Rica, 4.1%; Panama, 13.1%; Colombia, 4.5%; Venezuela, 2.8%; English Guiana, 29.3%; Dutch Guiana, 9.6%; French Guiana, 0.3%; Ecuador, 2%; Peru, 0.4%; Bolivia, 0.3%; Brazil, 14%; Paraguay, 0.5%; Uruguay, 0.5%; Chile, 0.02%; Argentina, 0.04%. The average Negro population of Central and South America was 13.8% and 7.3%, respectively.

In Martinique, of a total population of 244,908, only 5,000 were white. This proportion was similar to Guadeloupe, while in French Guiana, whites outnumbered Negroes.

In July, a mass meeting of more than 500 West Indians living in New York adopted a Declaration of Rights and Self-Determination for the Caribbeans. The meeting was sponsored by the West Indies National Emergency Committee which protested against any transfer of West Indian Islands to the U.S. The committee was empowered to send a representative to the Pan-American Conference in Havana to present its declaration.

1941

The NAACP gave its approval and support to A. Philip Randolph's plan for a march of 100,000 Negroes on Washington, D.C. The NAACP gave both money and services of its staff to coordinate the march. The goal was to open jobs for Negroes, especially in defense plants, that were generally not hiring Negroes except as janitors. On June 25, President Roosevelt issued Executive Order 8802, forbidding employment discrimination in government and defense industries.

The march, set for July 1, was called off. This Presidential directive established the Fair Employment Practices Commission to implement it. The Communist Party had opposed A. Philip Randolph's march, believing that such a march would be against the interests of the American war effort.

Robert Weaver, a Negro, was appointed director of Integration of Negroes into the National Defense Program in the Office of Production Management.

When a Wright aviation plant hired two unskilled Negro workers, all its white workers went out on strike.

Dory Miller, a Negro messman on the U.S.S. *Arizona,* was awarded the Navy Cross for downing four enemy planes during the Japanese attack on Pearl Harbor. Continuing to serve as a messman, he was killed in action in the Pacific in 1943.

Immediately after the bombing of Pearl Harbor, the NAACP called on all Negroes to give wholehearted support to the war effort.

A study revealed five times as many Negroes draftees as whites were rejected. It also showed that 12.3% of the Negroes were rejected for lack of 4th grade reading ability, compared with 1.1% of whites.

The NAACP protested a War Department policy that white men needed a score of 15 on the Army Intelligence Test, while Negroes were required to score 39 to be admitted to the service.

By Nov. 30, there were 97,725 Negroes in the regular Army. During World War II, Negro anti-aircraft units fought in Burma, the Ryukyus, Normandy, Italy and North Africa. Negro engineer troops helped to build the Ledo Road in Burma, the Stilwell Road in China, and the Alcan Highway in Alaska and Canada. Negro transport units were found supplying all battle fronts.

In December, Gen. George C. Marshall wrote to Secretary of War Stimson: "The settlement of vexing racial problems cannot be permitted to complicate the tremendous task of the War Department, and thereby jeopardize discipline and morale."

The Department of War announced the formation of the

first Army Air Corps squadron for Negroes on Jan. 16, one day after a Howard University student, Yancey Williams, filed suit against the Secretary of War to force consideration of his application to be a flying cadet in the Army Air Corps.

Negroes in the Navy were allowed to serve only as mess attendants and stewards. However, several noncombatant Negroes demonstrated such heroism under fire that they were awarded the Navy Cross or the Bronze Star medal.

Negro soldiers training in the South were subjected to discriminatory treatment throughout the entire World War II period. In Alexandria, La., 28 Negroes were shot down by white civilians and officers; race riots broke out in the Mobile Naval Yard, Fort Bragg, (N.C.), Camp Davis and other Army camps.

In this year 4 Negroes were lynched.

More than 100 Negro officers were locked in the stockade at Freeman Field, Ind., for entering a white-only officers' club.

In the period of World War II (1941–45), 3 million Negro men registered for service. Of these, 701,678 served in the Army, 165,000 in the Navy, 5,000 in the Coast Guard, 17,000 in the Marines, and 4,000 Negro women served as WAVES and WACS. A half million Negro men and women served overseas, primarily in Europe and North Africa. The cumulative percentages of Negroes in the Armed Services were: Army: officers 0.7%, enlisted personnel, 10.3%. Navy: less than 0.5%, officers; 4.8%, enlisted personnel. Marines, no figures are available.

In the case of MITCHELL v. U.S., the Supreme Court held that the Interstate Commerce Act required Pullman companies to provide equal accommodations for Negroes. Congressman Arthur Mitchell, a Negro, had brought suit against the Pullman Company.

After a 4-week boycott of buses by New York City Negroes, local bus companies agreed to hire Negro drivers and mechanics.

A. Philip Randolph's anti-discrimination resolutions were repeatedly rejected by the AFL National Convention. The AFL leadership explained that it sympathized with the problem but could not interfere with the autonomy of its member unions.

The NAACP officially allied itself with industrial labor unions to advance Negro rights in the United Auto Worker strike against the Ford Motor Co.

The WPA employed 237,000 Negroes, who represented 16% of its total employees.

By this year, the U.S. Housing Authority had contracted for the construction of 176,000 dwelling units, 53,000 or 30.2% of which were for Negroes. The average income of USHA tenants was $832, which meant the exclusion of low-income Negroes.

Sen. Harry F. Byrd of Virginia proposed the abolition of the FSA in the interest of the war, but proposed the maintenance of the more discriminatory AAA benefits. In 1942 the FSA budget was curtailed.

Dr. Charles R. Drew, a Negro, became professor of surgery at Howard University after having set up and run the pioneer blood plasma bank at Presbyterian Hospital in New York, a model for systems later operated by the Red Cross. In 1940, Dr. Drew had gone to Europe to direct Britain's blood plasma project, and had served briefly as director of collection of blood plasma for the American armed services.

Blood on the Forge by the Negro writer William Attaway was published. The novel is a family chronicle, much superior to Turpin's *O Canaan.* Attaway focuses on the disintegration of the Negro's rural values and traditions under the pressure of the urban factory, the crowded tenement, and the restricted ghetto. According to Robert Bone, in his *Negro Novel in America,* the book is one of the best proletarian novels of the 1930's.

Negro Caravan, an anthology of Negro writing, was published by Sterling A. Brown.

The American Negro Theater, founded by Abram Hill and Frederick O'Neal (later president of Actors' Equity), produced plays by Abram Hill, Owen Dodson and other young Negro dramatists. Its most successful production was *Anna Lucasta,* an adaptation of a white play, and brought the company to Broadway, thus dissolving it in Harlem in 1944.

Canada Lee, successful amateur and professional Negro

boxer who had turned to acting as a career, appeared as Bigger Thomas in the stage version of *Native Son.* Lee's other most notable appearances include the movie *Cry the Beloved Country* (1952), *Lifeboat* (1944) and *Anna Lucasta,* which played on Broadway in 1944.

Dorothy Maynor, Marian Anderson and Paul Robeson, Negro singers, were among the 10 most highly paid concert artists in the U.S.

A Negro, Dean Dixon, at 26, conducted the New York Philharmonic Orchestra. He had already worked with the Symphony Orchestra he had founded in Harlem and with the NBC Summer Symphony.

Charles White, a Negro muralist, painted *Five Great American Negroes,* now owned by the Museum of Modern Art in New York City.

Chalky Wright, Negro prize fighter, was featherweight boxing champion.

1942

Of the housing units built under the U.S. Housing Authority, 33%, or 41,000 were for Negroes.

In Detroit, on Feb. 28, 1,200 persons armed with knives, clubs, rifles and shotguns gathered to prevent three Negro families from moving into the 200-unit Sojourner Truth settlement, designated by the U.S. Housing Authority as Negro housing. The *New York Times* reported that scores of Negroes and whites were injured as police tried three times to disperse the crowd with tear gas. Shots were fired. About 18 people were taken to hospitals, and 104 rioters were arrested. Mayor Jeffries ordered the moving halted. Occupancy of the homes by Negroes was postponed until April, when 12 families moved in with 800 state troopers standing guard.

Six Negroes were lynched in this year.

Roland Haynes, a pioneer Negro concert singer who in the 1920's had been one of the foremost singers in the U.S., was struck by a policeman and taken to the city jail of Rome, Ga., because he spoke up for his wife when she sat in one of the "white places" in a shoe store.

The local office of the Federal Employment Service in Portsmouth, Va., in its advertising for workers specified that Negroes could apply only for unskilled and domestic jobs.

Columbia, S.C., passed a ruling the effect of which was that a Negro had to be 87 years old to vote.

Detroit had the largest NAACP chapter in the country, 12,000 members.

The Congress of Racial Equality (CORE) was founded by James Farmer and a group of University of Chicago students. The organization soon achieved national prominence and participation.

By the end of the year, nearly half a million Negroes were in the Army but only 4.8% of the combat units were Negro whereas 20.7% of the service units were Negro.

Of the men who entered the Army between March, 1941, and December, 1942, 84% of the Negroes and 33% of the whites had test scores in the two lowest categories in the Army Classification Test, and 4% of the Negroes and 35% of the whites scored in the top two categories.

In March, Gen. Douglas MacArthur wired Gen. George C. Marshall that he would accept Negro troops and do everything he could to prevent friction and resentment on the part of Australians concerning them. Most other generals refused to accept Negro troops in combat areas. Several Negro combat units had to be broken up or retrained as service units because no assignment could be found for them.

Negroes in the Air Force numbered 77,592. They were organized in Air Base Security Battalions, a new type of unit designed to accommodate Negroes and assigned the task of protecting air bases from riots, parachute raids and aerial attacks. However, they were not provided for the most part with anti-aircraft weapons, and it soon became clear that they were superfluous in their present assignments and not wanted overseas. By 1943, many of these battalions were deactivated and the men retrained and assigned to service units.

A Negro Harvard medical school student, Bernard W. Robinson, became the first Negro to win a commission in the U.S. Navy when he became an ensign in the Naval Reserve.

Negroes were accepted for general service in the Navy, but only for service ashore. They were allowed to train for general ratings (as opposed to steward and mess service only), but only in segregated camps and schools.

The *Booker T. Washington,* the first U.S. merchant ship

with a Negro captain (Hugh Mulzac), was launched at Wilmington, Del.

Because Negro newspapers continually headlined stories of racial injustice in the Armed Forces, the Justice Department considered bringing charges of sedition against them. It also made it difficult for them to buy newsprint and paper. The NAACP called a conference of the editors of 24 Negro newspapers to set guidelines for criticism that would not lead to government suppression. The NAACP also secured the needed quotas of newsprint for these papers.

Elijah Muhammed was indicted in October for pro-Japanese sympathies. Black Muslims considered all non-whites black men.

Stokely Carmichael (1942-   ), Negro leader, was born in Trinidad and came to the U.S. in 1953. He was graduated from the Bronx High School of Science, and then Howard University where he was active in student affairs. One of the early civil rights workers in the movement of the early 1960's, Carmichael became a field worker for SNCC. He was arrested 27 times in Mississippi and Alabama. In 1966, he popularized the term Black Power and led part of the civil rights movement to a more militant attitude. In 1967, he relinquished leadership of SNCC to travel to Cuba and North Vietnam.

John H. Johnson, a Negro, began publication in Chicago of *Negro Digest*. He later added *Ebony*, a monthly picture magazine, and *Jet*, a weekly news magazine, to his publications.

Jay S. Redding, a Negro, published a report of his observations of the rural life of the Southern Negro, *No Day of Triumph*.

Margaret Walker, a Negro, won the Yale University Younger Poets Award for *My People*, a collection of poems.

Walter White, NAACP leader, conferred with leaders of the film industry about the undignified stereotyping of Negroes in films.

Thelonius Monk, who was to become one of the great innovators of modern jazz, began playing with Lucky Millinder's band.

Beau Jack, a Negro prize fighter, became lightweight boxing champion.

Roger Mais, a Jamaican Negro, published *Face and Other Stories,* a collection of short prose fiction.

Santo Domingo's population was 13% white, 19% Negro; the remainder mulatto. In Cuba, 27% of the total population of approximately 4 million was Negro. In Puerto Rico, Negroes represented 25.7% of the population.

1943

In the three years from 1940 to 1943, the Negro population of Los Angeles grew 30%, of Chicago 20%, of Detroit 19%, Norfolk, Va., 100%, and Charleston, S.C., 39%.

In Detroit, in the spring, 26,000 white workers struck the Packard Motor Plant in protest over the employment of Negroes. Walter White of the NAACP reported hearing one man scream to the assembly of strikers: "I'd rather see Hitler and Hirohito win the war then work beside a nigger on the assembly line." The riot began with a fistfight between a Negro and a white on the bridge leading from Belle Isle Park to the city. Rumors spread among both communities of various atrocities. White mobs attacked Negroes, dragging them from cars and entering Negro movie theaters. Negroes retaliated, smashing white-owned shops in Detroit's ghetto, Paradise Valley. In one day, 34 persons were killed. Of the Negroes killed, 17 were killed by the police. On the second day, at Walter White's request, President Roosevelt declared a Federal state of emergency and sent in 6,000 Federal troops and state troopers who established an uneasy peace. The NAACP set up relief headquarters, and Walter White remarked that the Negroes looked like the "bombed-out victims of Nazi terror in Europe." Thurgood Marshall reported on the looting and destruction of Negro property by the Detroit police, but no action was taken.

On May 25, a race riot began at a Mobile, Ala., shipyard when Negro workers were upgraded. Gov. Chauncey Sparks of Alabama ordered 7 companies of state guardsmen to be on the alert. Of the 8 men injured at the Atlanta Drydock & Shipbuilding Co., 7 were Negroes. The disturbance began when Negro welders were assigned to work on the same job with white welders. Police finally put down the riot, and the plant resumed operation after 7,000 Negroes were sent home from their jobs at the plant and throughout the city.

Membership was denied Negroes by 30 AFL unions in their constitutions, through understandings, or by creation of non-represented auxiliary unions. Among them were the airline pilots, railroad telegraphers, the glassworkers, granite cutters, plumbers and maintenance-of-way employees.

A race riot in Beaumont, Tex., on June 16, was precipitated by the rape of a young white mother. The riot lasted for about 15 hours. Ellis C. Brown, a 55-year-old white carpenter, and one other person were killed. Martial law was declared. At the height of the rioting crowds of white men surged into the Negro section, causing the closing of stores and cafes. Work at the Penn Shipyards was practically stopped.

Three Negroes were lynched in this year.

In August, in Harlem, a Negro woman, Margie Polite, argued with a white policeman. A Negro soldier objected to the way the policeman spoke to her, and to his saying that she would be arrested for disorderly conduct. The policeman allegedly was knocked down by the soldier and, fearing a further attack, shot him. The woman then ran down the street screaming that the soldier had been killed. He had in fact only been wounded. A riot ensued. It took, according to the *New York Times*, 8,000 State Guard troops, 1,500 civilian volunteers (mostly Negro), and 6,600 members of the city police, military police and civil patrol units to quell the riot. Five persons were killed and 400 injured. Hundreds of stores were wrecked and looted. Property damage was estimated as high as $5 million. About 500 people were arrested, all Negroes, 100 of them women. The dead were all Negroes, and all but approximately 40 policemen of the injured.

William H. Hastie, a Negro civilian aide to Secretary of War Stimson, resigned on Jan. 6 in protest over continued segregation of training facilities in the Air Force and the Army. A few weeks later the Air Force announced a program for the expansion of Negro pilot training with Negroes being accepted "throughout the entire technical training command as well as at the Air Force Officers Training School at Miami, Fla."

The 99th Pursuit Squadron, a Negro flying unit, flew its first combat mission in the Mediterranean theater.

The *USS Harmon,* named in honor of a Negro, was

launched. Leonard Roy Harmon had been killed in the Battle of Guadalcanal in 1942, and had received the Navy Cross for heroism.

The District Attorney of New York County announced to newspapers that terms such as "restricted" and "selected clientele" in advertisements were "generally understood and intended to mean that guests of Jewish faith or colored persons were not wanted by such hotels and resorts," and that he would prosecute newspapers which published such advertisement.

CORE staged its first sit-in demonstration in a restaurant in the Loop in Chicago.

William L. Dawson, a Chicago Negro and Democrat, became a member of the House of Representatives.

Benjamin J. Davis Jr., a Negro and a member of the National Committee of the Communist Party, was elected to the New York City Council. He was re-elected in 1945.

Charles S. Johnson began editing the *Monthly Summary of Events* and *Trends in Race Relations* (later called *Race Relations*) that developed out of a confidential assignment from President Roosevelt to write a monthly report on race relations.

He Who Would Die, the single collection of verse by H. Binga Dismond, a Negro, was published. Much of Dismond's social-protest poetry utilizes the Jim Crow theme. He also translated and re-adapted contemporary Haitian verse.

Paul Robeson played Othello at the Schubert Theater in New York for 296 performances, a record for Shakespeare on Broadway.

The movie *Cabin in the Sky* was released. A Negro, Katherine Dunham, choreographed the musical, which starred an all-Negro cast. Included in the cast were John Bubbles, Eddie Anderson, Ethel Waters, Duke Ellington, Louis Armstrong and many other prominent Negro artists.

20th Century-Fox released an all-Negro musical film *Stormy Weather,* starring Lena Horne, Bill Robinson, Cab Calloway, Dooley Wilson and many other Negro stars.

The Negro singer and actress, Lena Horne, played her first major screen role in *Panama Hattie.*

1944

Of the Negro troops overseas, 71% were in quartermaster, engineer or transport battalions. The first Negro unit to be sent into combat duty in Europe, the 92nd Division, was deluged with publicity. Less than two months after they arrived in Italy, one of their members, Capt. Charles F. Gandy of Washington, D.C., was mortally wounded in action on Mt. Cavala, for which he was awarded the Silver Star posthumously.

At Anzio Beach, Italy, the 387th Separate Engineer Battalion, composed of 500 Negroes, lost 4 officers and 11 men, and had 61 wounded even though it was not a combat unit. Three members received Silver Stars for gallantry.

The 99th Pursuit Squadron, the first Negro flying unit in the Air Force, flew its 500th combat mission. The squadron won a commendation from Air Force Commanding Gen. H. A. Arnold for its air combat performance over the Anzio-Nettuno beachhead. In June, the squadron became part of the 332nd Fighter Group under Col. Benjamin O. Davis Jr., a Negro. In March, 1945, this unit was given the Distinguished Unit Citation, the highest unit decoration, for a 1,600-mile, round-trip air attack on Berlin under Colonel Davis. By this time it had flown 1,578 combat missions. Officers and men received 95 Distinguished Flying Crosses, 1 Silver Star, 1 Legion of Merit, 14 Bronze Stars, 744 Air Medals and Clusters, and 8 Purple Hearts.

Approximately 500 Negroes were among the U.S. soldiers at Omaha Beach on D-Day. The 761st Tank Battalion, landing at Omaha Beach, Normandy, was the first Negro armored unit in combat in the war. General Patton of the 3rd Army, to which they were attached, said, "Men, you're the first Negro tankers ever to fight in the American Army. I would never have asked for you if you weren't good. I don't care what color you are, so long as you go up there and kill those Kraut sons-a-bitches." Beginning on Nov. 7, the 761st spent 183 days in action. Maj. Gen. M. S. Eddy said of it: "I consider the 761st Tank Battalion to have entered combat with such conspicuous courage and success as to warrant special commendation." Ten tanks from the battalion were chosen to be in the honor guard at the German surrender in Austria.

The 969th Negro Field Artillery Battalion fought at the Battle of the Bulge. Gen. Maxwell Taylor wrote to their commander in January, 1945: "The officers and men of the 101st Airborne Division wish to express to your command their appreciation of the gallant support rendered by the 969th Field Artillery Battalion in the recent defense of Bastogne, Belgium. . . . This division is proud to have shared the battlefield with your command. A recommendation for a unit citation of the 969th Field Artillery Battalion is being forwarded by this Headquarters."

When Secretary of War Stimson was questioned about the use of Negro combat units for labor, he wrote: "It so happens that a relatively large percentage of the Negroes inducted in the Army have fallen within lower educational qualifications, and many Negro units accordingly have been unable to master efficiently the techniques of modern weapons." Stimson further stated: "I do not believe that they [the Negro 93rd Squadron] can be turned into a really effective combat troop without all officers being white."

Negro women joined the WAVE for the first time.

The restriction of Negro Navy men to shore duty was abandoned. Thereafter, steps were taken to end segregation in training and mess and recreation facilities. Exclusion of Negroes from the Marine Corps and the Coast Guard was abandoned at about the same time.

The War Department announced the end of racial segregation in recreation and transportation facilities in all Army posts. The order was widely protested, and disobeyed in the South.

Negroes stationed on Guam were subject to discrimination, taunts and physical violence. On Christmas Eve the situation exploded when Negro soldiers on liberty were driven out of a white recreation area by gunfire. Shooting broke out on Christmas Day, and a Negro was killed and another wounded. Mass arrests of Negroes were made, but no whites were arrested. Of the Negroes 44 were sentenced to long prison terms, but the NAACP secured their release by appeals to the President and the War Department.

At Yerba Buena, 52 Negro sailors were charged with mutiny after racial trouble. The NAACP secured their return to duty.

The NAACP was so well regarded among Negro soldiers for its efforts on their behalf that they contributed liberally to it; $3,920 was contributed in August by a single unit in the Pacific. In October, the men of the 823rd Engineering Battalion gave $2,000.

Two Negroes were lynched in this year.

Gunnar Myrdal, in his book *American Dilemma*, wrote: "Segregation is now becoming so complete that the white Southerner practically never sees a Negro except as his servant and in other standardized and formalized caste situations."

The Virginia Legislature empowered the State Corporation Commission to require separate waiting rooms and other facilities in airports.

CIO leader Sidney Hillman believed that the basic interests of organized workers and Negroes were the same. He helped to integrate Negro workers into the political structure of the CIO, particularly in the Political Action Committee (PAC) which he headed. He also sought the participation of Negro leaders in the National Citizens PAC, which he set up in this year. Hillman said: "All that the Negro demands and is justly entitled to as an American citizen and as a worker are encompassed in the immediate and long-term objectives of the progressive movement. These objectives, the PAC has spelled out in its *Peoples Program for 1944*. Victory and peace, employment security, housing, health and education for all our people are among the PAC objectives." A statement sponsored by the NAACP "closely paralleled the CIO-PAC program."

In the case of JAMES V. MARINESHIP CORP., the Supreme Court decided that a person had the right to work in a closed shop without union membership when union membership had been denied to him on the grounds of race or color.

The Philadelphia Transportation Co. accepted a Fair Employment Practices Commission directive on the hiring and upgrading of Negroes as employees. On Aug. 1, the transport workers, not affiliated with the CIO, struck against the Philadelphia Transportation Co. over employment of Negro drivers. By noon, 4,500 operators had left their vehicles, and no subways, buses or other transportation ran. There were reports of widespread rioting in many areas of the city. Nine white persons were injured, one was beaten critically in a North Philadelphia borderline district. President Roosevelt ordered the Army to take over the Philadelphia Transit System, and gave his support to the FEPC directive.

From 1944 to 1948, Anna Arnold Hedgeman, a Negro, served as executive director of the National Council of the FEPC. From 1949 to 1953, she was assistant to the director of the Federal Security Agency.

In the case of SMITH V. ALLWRIGHT, the Supreme Court declared that "white primary" laws and rules that had excluded Negroes from taking part in Democratic primaries in the South were unconstitutional. The case involved a Texas law which said that "in no event shall a Negro be eligible to participate in a Democratic Party primary election held in the state of Texas." The Supreme Court said that the Texas primary was by law a part of "the machinery for choosing officials, state and national" and thus the white primary law violated the 15th Amendment.

The Democratic Party platform of this year read: "We believe that racial and religious minorities have the right to live, develop, and vote equally with all citizens and share the rights that are guaranteed by our Constitution. Congress shall exert its full constitutional power to protect these rights." Walter White, Negro leader, called this racial plank a mere "splinter." Negroes were upset by the lack of mention of the FEPC, anti-poll tax laws, anti-lynching legislation, or Armed Services discrimination, and also by the rejection of Henry Wallace as Vice Presidential candidate on the Democratic ticket. They associated Wallace's liberalism with their drive for equal rights. Several Negro newspapers, such as the *Pittsburgh Courier* and the New York *Amsterdam News,* supported Thomas E. Dewey, the Republican candidate.

The Republican Party platform stated: "We unreservedly condemn the injection into American life of appeals to racial and religious prejudice. We pledge an immediate Congressional inquiry to ascertain the extent to which mistreatment, segregation and discrimination against Negroes who are in our armed forces are impairing morale and efficiency, and the adoption of corrective legislation. We pledge the establishment by Federal legislation of a permanent Fair Employment Practice Commission. The payment of any poll tax should not be a condition of voting in Federal elections, and we favor immediate submission of a Constitutional amendment for its abolition." It also stated: "We favor legislation against lynching, and pledge our sincere efforts in behalf of its early enactment."

The Socialist Party platform said: "Democracy requires the application of the principle that each person is to be accorded social, political and economic equality, and judged solely on the basis of his own deeds, rather than by his race, religion, or national origin." It further stated: "We condemn anti-Semitism, Jim-Crowism and every form of race discrimination and segregation in the armed forces as well as civil life. We urge the passage of anti-lynching and anti-poll tax laws, and the prompt enactment of legislation to set up a permanent Federal Fair Employment Practice Committee. We affirm our historic opposition to any doctrine or practice of a master or favored race, not only in the realm of law, but in such labor unions—fortunately a minority—churches, political parties and other basic social organizations as today countenance it. One of the conditions that will help make permanent the end of racial prejudice is the maintenance of full employment." The party platform concluded: "An America disgraced by racial tensions which occasionally find expression in lynching and race riots cannot lead the way to a peace which depends upon world-wide reconciliation of races on the basis of equality of right."

The United Negro College Fund (UNCF) was chartered, with the aid of the Julius Rosenwald Fund and the General Education Board. William Trent Jr. was its first executive director. Its purpose was to provide financial support for Negro colleges. Currently the fund aids 32 private liberal arts colleges with cash grants. A major building fund-raising campaign was started in 1964. In 20 years the UNCF raised over $34 million for its participating colleges in non-capital funds (i.e., funds for purposes other than building). The UNCF also sponsors a scholarship program for African students in America and a fellowship program for Negro graduate students.

Frank Yerby, a Negro, won the O. Henry Award for his first published short story, *Health Card*. Like many of his early stories, it concerned Negro life in the South.

The Negro poet, Melvin B. Tolson, published his only collection of verse, *Rendezvous with America.*

Two Negroes, Hilda Simms and Frederick O'Neal, starred in the Broadway play *Anna Lucasta.*

Pearl Primus, an expert on Negro primitive dancing, made her first appearance on Broadway with her own dance troupe. Josh White was the balladeer.

At the age of 12, Philippa Schuyler, a Negro musical prodigy, performed *Manhattan Nocturne,* her own composition with the New York Philharmonic. She matured into a successful artist and also wrote several books.

The Negro actor Canada Lee narrated the first radio series on the race question, *New World A-Comin'.*

Bob Montgomery, the Negro prize fighter, won the lightweight boxing championship. He held this title through 1947.

Frank A. Collymore, a Negro and a native of Barbados, published two books of verse, *30 Poems* in 1944 and *Beneath the Casuarinas* in 1945.

1945

Col. Benjamin O. Davis Jr., a Negro, was named commander of Godman Field in Kentucky.

The 370th Negro Regiment of the U.S. Army was joined with a Japanese-American regiment and an American white regiment to make up a reconstructed 92nd Division. In April, this division fought in the Northern Appenines in Italy and moved successfully to Genoa. Though the Negro 92nd Division was plagued by difficulties and was later called by Gen. Mark Clark before a Southern audience in 1956 "the worst division I had," by July 10, 1945, its members had received 542 Bronze Stars, 82 Silver Stars, 12 Legion of Merit Awards, 2 Distinguished Service Crosses, and 1 Distinguished Service Medal.

There were 165,000 Negro enlisted men in the Navy and 53 officers. There were 17,000 Negroes in the Marine Corps. About 4,000 enlisted men and 4 officers in the Coast Guard were Negroes. By the end of the year, 95% of the Negroes in the Navy were still serving as messmen.

Phyllis Mae Dailey became the first Negro nurse in the Navy Nurse Corps.

In the early part of this year in Germany, shortages of troops caused the Army to use Negro platoons attached to white units to replace lost white soldiers. Col. John R. Ackor of the 99th Infantry Division reported: "The Negro platoons performed in an excellent manner at all times while in combat. These men were courageous fighters and never once did they fail to accomplish their assigned mission. They were particularly good in town fighting, and [were] often used as the assault platoon with good results. The platoon assigned to the 393rd Infantry is credited with killing approximately 100 Germans and capturing 500. During this action only 3 of their own men were killed, and 15 wounded."

Seven Negroes were lynched in this year.

The NAACP was invited to send a representative to the United Nations Conference in San Francisco. Walter White and W. E. B. Du Bois proposed the abolition of colonialism, and protested the action of the U.S., Britain and France in voting against the Chinese-Russian proposal that colonial independence be assured in the United Nations Charter.

The NAACP received $400,000 in contributions from all sources during World War II.

Congress killed the Fair Employment Practices Commission by refusing to vote funds for it.

The New York State Legislature passed the Ives-Quinn Bill which established the State Commission Against Discrimination. It was the first state to create such a commission. New Jersey followed soon after, and established a division against discrimination in the Department of Education. In 1946, Massachusetts created a Fair Employment Practices Commission. By 1965, 25 states had similar commissions.

Adam Clayton Powell Jr., a New York Negro and Democrat, became a member of the House of Representatives.

Judge Irwin C. Mollison, a Negro, was appointed to the U.S. Customs Court by President Truman.

Richard Wright's largely autobiographical *Black Boy* was published.

Chester Himes, a Negro, published his first novel, *If He Hollers Let Him Go*. Himes' subsequent works include *The Lonely Crusader* (1947), *Third Generation* (1954), *Cotton Comes to Harlem* (1965) and *Pinktoes* (1965).

Gwendolyn Brooks, a Negro, published *A Street in Bronze-ville,* her first book of poems.

Jack Goldberg produced and directed the film *We've Come a Long Way,* narrated by Elder Michaux. The documentary recorded the progress of the American Negro in the last 300 years.

Cecil Gant's recording of *I Wonder* was successful and marked the revival of record companies' interest in Negro blues music.

Ike Williams, Negro prize fighter, was NBA lightweight boxing champion.

Sandyland and Other Poems by H. A. Vaughan, a Negro, was published. Vaughan was born in Barbados and educated in England. He is also known for his *History of Barbados.*

1946

President Truman issued Executive Order 9808 creating the Presidential Committee on Civil Rights to study existing Federal protection of civil rights and ways to improve it. In 1947 the commission issued a report *To Secure These Rights,* recommending that the Civil Rights Section of the Justice Department be expanded to a full division, that Congress establish a permanent Fair Employment Practices Commission, and that Federal laws against lynching and for equal law enforcement and administration of justice be enacted.

There were about 200,000 Negroes on the Federal payroll in this year, compared to about 50,000 in 1933.

Of 22,672 second lieutenants in the Army, 818 were Negroes; of 5,220 colonels, 7 were Negroes; of 776 generals, 1 was a Negro.

The NAACP appointed a secretary of labor in its organization. It also named CIO president Philip Murray to the NAACP Board of Directors.

The case of MORGAN V. THE COMMONWEALTH OF VIRGINIA, dealt with the conviction in Virginia of Irene Morgan, a Negro, for refusing to move from the front to the rear of a Greyhound bus. The NAACP took the case to the Supreme Court where it was ruled that the law requiring segregation of Negroes on interstate buses was an unreasonable burden on interstate commerce and thus invalid.

In this year's elections, 30 Negroes won seats in legislatures of 10 states; 18 were Republicans and 12 were Democrats.

During this year, Negro voter registration increased from 5,000 to 25,000 in Atlanta, Ga.; from 1,200 to 20,000 in Savannah; from 2,500 to 15,000 in Jacksonville; from a few hundred to 7,100 in Augusta. In addition, over 350,000 new white voters were registered in Georgia. In the July Georgia Democratic primaries 100,000 Negroes voted. Within 3 days after the primaries, five Negroes were lynched in the state. One was Macio Snipes, a veteran, and the only Negro who voted in Taylor County, Ga. Snipes was dragged from his home and shot to death by 4 whites. A sign posted on a Negro church read: "The first nigger to vote will never vote again."

In this year six Negroes were lynched.

In February, in Atlanta, in an election for Congressman, the outcome of the vote was uncertain until the counting of the ballots of the last precinct, a predominantly Negro district. The man who had been running 100 votes behind won the election by 770 votes after the counting of this precinct's ballots. Soon after the county unit system was reintroduced in Georgia, enabling the small rural counties to outweigh populous Fulton County, where many Negroes lived. The candidate who won this special election in February was defeated in the July primary and the November general election.

The Boswell Amendment to the Alabama State Constitution provided for a literacy test as a means of restricting Negro voting. In DAVIS V. SCHNELL in 1949, a Federal District Court declared this provision unconstitutional.

A race riot in Athens, Ala., was touched off by a fistfight between two white war veterans and a Negro. The white mob that knocked down and trampled Negroes, injured between 50 and 100, was estimated at 2,000 at its peak. Ten white men were arrested, including the two whites involved in the fistfight. The Negro escaped. A local state guard company was mobilized and police from all over northern Alabama were called to restore order. In all, 16 persons were indicted in connection with this riot.

In Columbia, Tenn., on Feb. 26, Mrs. Gladys Stephenson, a Negro, and her son, a veteran, entered an appliance store to pick up a repaired radio. The white repairman started to hit Mrs. Stephenson when she protested the repair work was faulty. Her son defended her and knocked the repairman through a plate glass window. A white mob gathered and began beating mother and son, who were then thrown in jail. A lynch mob gathered in front of the jail. Assured that the Stephensons were still there, they raided the Negro section, firing into Negro houses from cars. Finally some Negroes fired back at a car that held white policemen, wounding four. State patrolmen were brought in and cordoned off the Negro area. On Feb. 28, policemen and guardsmen, armed with machine guns, entered the Negro section. Wholesale destruction, beating of Negroes and looting took place. Houses were invaded, and the Negro inhabitants were dragged into the streets and beaten while their houses were destroyed. Of about 70 Negroes arrested on no charge half were veterans. They were arraigned in a room filled with fully-armed soldiers, and the NAACP representative was denied permission to advise them. This riot had resulted in 2 killed and 16 wounded. On Feb. 28 two more Negroes were killed and a deputy sheriff and another Negro wounded in an outbreak of violence at the county jail. The NAACP sent an official protest to President Truman concerning the killing of the two Negroes. When 23 Negroes were charged with attempted first degree murder, the NAACP asked U.S. Attorney General Tom Clark to investigate. Oliver Harrington, publicity director for the NAACP, was threatened with grand jury action for having released information of the riots. Thurgood Marshall, in Columbia to try and defend the accused, was arrested on a false charge of drunken driving. In October, an all-white jury acquitted 23 of 25 Negroes on trial; 2 were convicted on a charge of attempted murder in the first degree. This was considered a victory for the defense. The *New York Times* reported: "The [state's] Attorney General and his two assistants appeared stunned by the verdict."

A riot in North Philadelphia on Sept. 29 lasted for about 10 minutes and involved over 100 Negroes and whites. They battled with clubs, bricks and milk bottles. As a result 11 persons, including 4 women, were arrested; 1 white man was killed, and a Negro was charged with homicide though no one had actually seen the Negro strike the white. The riot appears to have started when the man who was killed and his companions left a tap room and attempted to cause a nuisance at the home of Dr. Parish, a Negro. Residents of the house asked the men to leave, an argument ensued, and a fight broke out.

The American Nurses Association removed its barrier to Negro membership by allowing qualified nurses to join the association directly if their local societies refused to admit them.

Charles S. Johnson, a Negro, was a member of the U.S. National Commission at the first meeting of UNESCO in Paris.

The National Negro Congress petitioned the UN Economic and Social Council for aid in eliminating political, economic and social discrimination in the U.S.

William H. Hastie, a Negro, became Governor of the Virgin Islands.

The Foxes of Harrow, by a Negro, Frank Yerby, was published. A popular historical novel of the ante-bellum South, it became an immediate best-seller. This and his subsequent novels were directed toward a white audience, and scarcely, if at all, dealt with Negroes or Negro problems.

A first collection of verse, *Powerful Long Ladder,* by a Negro, Owen Dodson, was published. The verse consists of personal impressions of Negro life.

The Negro sculptor Richmond Barthé was commissioned to do a bust of Booker T. Washington for the New York University Hall of Fame.

Ruby Dee, wife of Ossie Davis, made her acting debut in the Broadway play *Jeb.* She has also appeared in *Raisin in the Sun* and *Purlie Victorious.* Her movie credits include: *The Jackie Robinson Story, Take a Giant Step, The Balcony,* and the film versions of *Raisin in the Sun* and *Purlie Victorious.*

Sarah Vaughan, a Negro jazz and blues singer who starred with the Earl Hines orchestra and Billy Eckstein's band, won the Downbeat Female Vocalist Award from 1946 to 1952.

Satchel Paige, the almost legendary Negro baseball pitcher, led his team to win the Negro World Series for the second time. He had pitched 64 straight scoreless innings and allowed only two runs in 93 innings during the 1946 season. Two years later he appeared in the major leagues.

From 1946 through 1951, Sugar Ray Robinson, a Negro, was the welterweight boxing champion.

1947

Median income of wage and salary workers was: white male, $2,357, and non-white, $1,279; female, white, $1,269, and non-white, $432.

The NAACP presented a 154-page "Statement on the Denial of Human Rights to Minorities in the Case of Citizens of Negro Descent in the U.S.A., and an Appeal to the United Nations for Redress." Among the scholars who worked on this were Du Bois, Milton Konvitz and Rayford Logan. It was presented on Oct. 23. No action was taken.

Henry Wallace said that the prevailing American attitudes toward Negroes, Jews and recent immigrants made the world laugh at American pretensions to democracy.

Between 1947 and 1962, 12 Negroes were lynched; 3 in 1949 and 3 in 1955.

A young South Carolina Negro who was being held in connection with the murder of a taxi driver was lynched. An all-white jury exonerated 28 men who had confessed to participation.

According to the Southern Regional Council, 12%, or about 600,000, of the Negroes of voting age in 12 Southern states qualified to vote. According to V. O. Key, less then 3% of the adult Negro population in Alabama, Louisiana and Mississippi was able to vote. Tennessee had the highest percentage (26%) of adult Negroes voting among Southern states.

Federal District Judge J. Waties upheld the right of Negroes to vote in South Carolina Democratic primaries. Thurgood Marshall argued the case.

Negro and white workers aided by the Political Action Committee of the CIO Tobacco Workers elected two members to the Winston-Salem (N.C.) city council, one of whom was a Negro clergyman, Rev. Kenneth R. Williams. He was the first Negro elected to a city or state office in the Deep South, except in all-Negro communities, in over a generation.

New York City had seven Negro judges.

The NAACP campaigned actively against the Taft-Hartley Bill.

In the case of the UNITED PUBLIC WORKERS v. MITCHELL, which involved the power of Congress to prohibit Federal employees from engaging in political activity, the Supreme Court opposed discrimination in the Federal Civil Service. It said: "Congress may not enact a regulation providing that no Republican, Jew or Negro should be appointed to Federal office, or that no Federal employee shall attend Mass or take any active part in missionary work."

CORE sent the first Freedom Ride group into the South in April.

Between 1947 and 1952, Jesse P. Guzman, the Negro educator and member of the Tuskegee faculty, edited *The Negro Yearbook*.

Ebony magazine was founded by a 27-year-old Negro, John H. Johnson of Chicago.

John Hope Franklin, a Negro historian, published *From Slavery to Freedom*.

Knock on Any Door by a Negro, Willard Motley, was published. The novel was a critical and financial success. It tells the story of an Italian slum boy who was more or less forced to become a criminal because of his environment.

Langston Hughes wrote the lyrics to Kurt Weill's score for *Street Scene,* called by some the first Broadway opera.

Our Lan', by Theodore Ward, a Negro, was produced on Broadway.

Afro-Cuban influence on jazz reached a peak when Dizzy Gillespie hired a Cuban Negro drummer Chano Pozo to play with his band in a Town Hall concert.

Jackie Robinson became the first Negro to play on a major league baseball team, the Brooklyn Dodgers.

The bantamweight boxing champion for 1947 was Harold Dade, a Negro.

1948

In June, A. Philip Randolph formed the League for Nonviolent Civil Disobedience Against Military Segregation. Randolph threatened to urge Negroes to resist induction by civil disobedience unless segregation and discrimination in the armed forces were banned.

In July, President Truman's Executive Order 9981 barred segregation in the Armed Forces and created the President's Committee on Equality of Treatment and Opportunity in the Armed Services, to end discrimination in military facilities and units.

1st Lt. Nancy C. Leftenant was the first Negro in the regular Army Nurse Corps.

President Truman created the Fair Practices Board in the Civil Rights Commission to deal with complaints of racial discrimination in Federal Government jobs. He also ordered the Justice Department to handle anti-discrimination suits brought by private individuals.

The Federal Government joined in a suit opposing enforcement of restrictive covenants in real estate in the case of SHELLEY V. KRAEMER. The Supreme Court decided that such covenants were unenforceable by state courts. In the case of HURD V. HODGE, the Supreme Court held restrictive covenants unenforceable in Federal courts. However, it was not held that these covenants were illegal *per se.*

In the case of PEREZ V. LIPPOLD, the California Supreme Court held that the California anti-miscegenation law violated the 14th Amendment because it unreasonably restricted the choice of one's mate.

In the 1947–48 school year, the average value of property, buildings and equipment for white school children in the Southern was over twice the value of facilities for Negro children. In the Deep South states of Alabama, Mississippi, South Carolina, Florida and Louisiana, the differential was between 3 and 4 to 1, in favor of white students.

By this year 30% of all the Negroes in school in the South were educated in buildings contracted under the Rosenwald Fund's aid program.

In the case of SIPUEL V. BOARD OF REGENTS, in which a Negro girl, Ada Lois Sipuel, sought admission to the University of Oklahoma Law School, the Supreme Court ruled that the state had to provide "equal protection" for Negroes at the same time it provided such protection for other citizens, and could not wait until such protection was demanded. Thus, since the state had not already provided the Negro law school, Miss Sipuel was entitled to immediate admission to the white law school. The Court, however, did not actually require admission. This step was first taken in SWEATT V. PAINTER in 1950. To meet the requirement of the Court, the University of Oklahoma set up a law school for Negroes. Ada Sipuel then refused to attend.

The University of Delaware announced that Negroes would be admitted to graduate courses not offered at Delaware State College for Negroes.

The University of Arkansas voluntarily admitted Negroes to its professional schools.

The League of New York Theaters and Actors Equity boycotted the National Theater in Washington because of its policy of racial discrimination. The theater was closed for 5 years, and reopened in 1952 under new management and a policy of nondiscrimination.

In the case of BROWN V. BASKIN, the Federal District Court invalidated the attempt of the South Carolina Democratic Party to bar Negroes by requiring party members to take an oath supporting segregation and opposing fair employment practices. The decision was affirmed by the 4th Circuit Court in 1949.

In November, the NAACP president, D. V. Carter, was beaten by whites for escorting Negroes to the polls in Montgomery, Ga. In Vidalia, Ga., Robert Mallard was warned not to vote. When he did, he was lynched by a band of hooded men. In Mississippi, Rev. William Bender, a teacher at Tougaloo College and president of a local branch of the NAACP, was kept from the polls by three white men with pistols.

The Democratic Party platform said: "The Democratic Party commits itself to continuing its efforts to eradicate all racial, religious and economic discrimination." It went on: "We again state our belief that racial and religious minorities must have the right to live, the right to work, the right to vote, the full and equal protection of the laws on a basis of equality with all citizens as guaranteed by the Constitution." The Democratic national convention in its 1948 platform called on Congress to support the President in guaranteeing "these basic and fundamental American principles: (1) The right of full and equal political participation; (2) the right

to equal opportunity of employment; (3) the right of security of person; (4) and the right of equal treatment in the
service and defense of our nation." As a result, 35 delegates
from Southern states walked out of the convention and supported Strom Thurmond of South Carolina as the Dixiecrat
or States' Rights Party candidate for President.

The States' Rights Party platform said: "We stand for
the segregation of the races, and racial integrity of each
race; the constitutional right to choose one's associates; to
accept private employment without governmental interference, and to earn one's living in any lawful way. We oppose
the elimination of segregation in employment by Federal
bureaucrats called for by the misnamed civil rights program.
We favor home rule, local self-government and a minimum
interference with individual rights. We oppose and condemn
the action of the Democratic convention in sponsoring a civil
rights program calling for the elimination of segregation,
social equality by Federal fiat, repudiation of private employment practices, voting and local law enforcement. We affirm
that the effective enforcement of such a program would be
utterly destructive of the social, economic and political life
of the Southern people."

The States' Rights or Dixiecrat Party received 38 electoral
votes, all from Southern states.

The Republican Party platform read: "Lynching or any
other form of mob violence anywhere is a disgrace to any
civilized state, and we favor the prompt enactment of legislation to end this infamy." It further stated: "right of equal
opportunity to work and of advance in life should never be
limited in any individual because of race, religion, color, or
country of origin. We favor the enactment and enforcement
of such Federal legislation as may be necessary to maintain
this right at all times in every part of this Republic. We favor
the abolition of the poll tax as a prerequisite of voting. We
are opposed to the idea of racial segregation in the armed
forces of the U.S."

The Progressive Party platform said: "The Progressive
Party condemns segregation and discrimination in its all forms
and in all places." The platform called for "a Presidential
proclamation ending segregation and all forms of discrimina-

tion in the Armed Services and Federal employment," "Federal anti-lynch, anti-discriminating, and fair employment practices legislation, and legislation abolishing segregation in interstate travel," and an anti-poll tax law, enactment of universal suffrage, and "full use of Federal enforcement powers to assure free exercise of the right to franchise," "a Civil Rights Act for the District of Columbia to eliminate racial segregation and discrimination in the nation's capital," "the ending of segregation and discrimination in the Panama Canal Zone, and all territories, possessions and trusteeships." The platform asked for the denial of Federal funds "to any state or local authority which withholds opportunities or benefits for reasons of race, creed, color, sex, or national origin."

The Communist Party platform declared: "The most shameful aspect of American life is the Jim Crowism, the terror and violence imposed upon the Negro people, especially in the South. Discrimination in employment, only slightly relaxed during the War, is once again widespread." The platform called for "a national FEPC law to be vigorously and fully enforced," the outlawing of the Ku Klux Klan and all "hate and terror organizations," the immediate end of "every form of segregation and discrimination in the Armed Forces, and the government services," and "Federal enforcement of the 13th, 14th and 15th Amendments."

The NAACP vigorously protested the U.N. settlement on the former Italian colonies, Cyrenaica and Somaliland. Cyrenaica was given to Britain and Somaliland to Italy. The NAACP proposed a plebiscite for national determination.

Ralph Bunche, a Negro, was made acting U.N. mediator in Palestine.

47th Street, a collection of verse by a Negro, Frank M. Davis, was published.

The Lion and the Archer contained Myron O'Higgins' first verse in book form. O'Higgins, a Negro from Chicago, was educated at Harvard.

The Resurrection and *Other Poems* by Jonathan Henderson Brooks (1904–1945) was published posthumously. In it Henderson, a Negro, showed his great mastery of form. The poems are very personal, full of symbolism and often mystical.

The Betrayal, a film produced by Oscar Micheaux, told of a Northern Negro farmer who married the woman he loved only after discovering that she was also a Negro.

The Goldbergs produced three films for the Negro market: Lena Horne in *Bronze Venus;* Pigmeat Markham in *House Rent Party*, and Mantan Moreland in *Mantan Messes Up.*

Charles Fonville, a Negro from Michigan, broke the world record for the 16-pound shotput with a throw of 58 feet.

At the London Olympics, the following American Negroes won Gold Medals: Harrison Dillard, 100-meter dash; Norwood Ewell, 200-meter dash; Willie Steele, running broad jump; Harrison Dillard, Norwood Ewell, Lorenzo Wright, 400-meter relay; Mal Whitfield, 1,600-meter relay; Alice Coachman, woman's high jump. American Negroes also won 1 silver medal and 3 bronze medals at the Olympics. Don Barksdale, an All-American basketball forward on the 1947 UCLA team, was a member of the U.S. Olympic basketball team.

Nearly one-half of all boxers listed in *Ring* Magazine were Negro.

Sandy Sadler, a Negro, was featherweight boxing champion.

1949

Federal law prohibited racial discrimination "with respect to any person or with respect to the position held by any person" in the Federal Civil Service.

New Jersey gave jurisdiction over public accommodations to an agency charged with ending discrimination in employment. The agency was to insure that "all persons shall have the opportunity to obtain . . . all the accommodations, advantages, facilities, and privileges of any place of public accommodation without discrimination because of race, creed, color, national origin or ancestry." New Jersey was the first state to do this. Later that year, Connecticut took similar action. In 1950, Massachusetts renamed its Fair Employment Practice Commission the Massachusetts Commission Against Discrimination. In 1952, New York and Rhode Island took similar action.

Connecticut extended jurisdiction of its Civil Rights Commission to cover public housing. It was the first state to provide an effective remedy against discrimination in public housing.

Six young Negro men, known as the Trenton Six, were convicted of the murder of an elderly white, second-hand store proprietor. The Civil Rights Congress, which had handled the case, then withdrew, and the NAACP filed a brief *amicus curiae* in the New Jersey Supreme Court. The Court reversed the convictions and ordered a new trial.

In the case of JOHNSON V. BOARD OF TRUSTEES, the University of Kentucky was ordered to open its graduate school to Negroes.

The Atlanta Negro Voters' League was founded to concentrate the Negro vote on candidates in local elections who were most favorable to Negroes.

WERD in Atlanta, the first Negro-owned radio station, went on the air.

Percentages of Negro officers and enlisted personnel for the Armed Forces were: Army: officers 1.7%, enlisted personnel 9.6%; Air Force: officers 0.06%, enlisted personnel 5.1%; Navy: officers less than 0.5%, enlisted personnel 4.5%; Marines: officers less than 0.5%, enlisted personnel 2.1%.

William A. Hinton, a Negro serologist, was made a professor at Harvard Medical School one year before his retirement. He had been an instructor there since 1915.

Congressman William L. Dawson became chairman of the House Expenditures Committee, the first Negro to head a standing committee of Congress.

William H. Hastie, a Negro, became judge of the 3rd U.S. Circuit Court of Appeal.

Wesley A. Brown became the first Negro graduate of the U.S. Naval Academy.

Juanita Hall, the Negro actress and singer, became nationally famous for her portrayal of "Bloody Mary" in the Broadway play *South Pacific*. She subsequently won a Tony, a Donaldson, a Box Office and the Bill Bojangles Award.

Four exceptional movies dealing with race relations were released for whites and Negro audiences in this year: *Lost*

Boundaries, Home of the Brave, Pinky and *Intruder in the Dust.*

Jackie Robinson received the National League's Most Valuable Player Award. He was also the National League batting champion, with an average of .342.

Joe Louis retired as world heavyweight boxing champion after holding the title for 11 years and 8 months, a record length of time.

Between this year and 1951, Ezzard Charles, a Negro, was heavyweight boxing champion.

1950

U.S. Census: There were 15,042,286 Negroes in the U.S., representing 10% of the population.

The life expectancy of whites males was 66.5 years; Negro males, 59.1 years; white females, 72.2 years; Negro females, 62.9 years.

The infant mortality rate per 1,000 live births was 44.5 for nonwhites and 26.8 for whites.

Of the Negro population 13.4% lived in the Northeast, 14.8% in the North Central states, 68% in the South, and 3.8% in the West.

In the intercensal migration of nonwhites between 1940 and 1950 483,000 went to the northeast, 632,000 to the North Central states, and 323,000 to the West. A total of 1,597,000 nonwhites moved from the South.

The following percentages of the total metropolitan populations were Negro: Baltimore, 19.8%; Boston, 2.2%; Chicago, 10.7%; Cincinnati, 10.5%; Cleveland, 10.4%; Detroit, 11.9%; Los Angeles, 5%; New York City, 8.1%; Philadelphia, 13.1%; Pittsburg, 6.2%; San Francisco-Oakland area, 6.6%; St. Louis, 12.8%; Washington, D.C., 23.1%.

60.6% of Negro families had incomes of less than $3,000; 28.4% of whites fell in this category.

Distribution of Negro workers among various types of occupations in the South was: Professional, technical, etc.: male, 2%; female, 6.3%. Managers, officials and proprietors: male, 1.4%; female, 1.3%. Clerical and sales: male, 2.4%;

female, 3.5%. Service workers, private household and other service workers: male, 11.2%; female, 63.6%. Non-farm laborers: male, 23.6%; female, 1.2%. Total non-farm: male, 65.6%; female 85.8%. Farmers and farm workers: male, 34.4%; female, 14.2%.

Distribution of Negro workers among various types of occupations in the U.S. exclusive of the South was: Professional, technical, etc.: male, 2.6%, female, 4.6%. Managers, officials, proprietors: male, 3%; female, 1.4%. Clerical and sales: male, 7.8%; female, 9%. Service workers, private household and other service workers: male, 21.4%; female, 56.7%. Non-farm laborers: male, 24.9%; female, 2.1%. Total non-farm: male, 97.9%; female 99.6%. Farmers and farm workers: male, 2.1%; female, 0.4%.

The number of employed Negro workers in selected professions per 10,000 Negroes in the population was: physicians and surgeons, 2.5%; dentists, 1%; lawyers and judges, 0.9%; college professors, 1.7%; teachers, 12.5%; musicians and music teachers, 3.7%; clergymen, 12.1%; social workers, 1.4%; pharmacists, 0.8%; female teachers, 45.1%.

Of the total Negro population, male and female, 25 years and over, 5.3% had no schooling; 22.2% had 1 to 4 years; 28.8% had 5 to 7 years, and 12.1% had 8 years; 14.5% had completed 1 to 3 years of high school, and 8.6% 4 years; 3% had completed 1 to 3 years of college, and 2.2% 4 years. The median school years completed was 7.2

Compared to 56.9% of whites, 34.9% of Negroes owned their own homes instead of renting.

In this year there were approximately 42,500 self-employed male Negro businessmen, by 1960, only 32,400. The number also fell for whites, but by a smaller percentage.

From 1950 to 1959 executions under civil authority in the U.S. totaled 717. Of these, 336 were whites and 376 Negroes. In the two major categories of murder, whites accounted for 316, and Negroes 280, and of rape, whites 13, Negroes 89.

In the summer a conference of lawyers associated with the NAACP was held in New York. It decided to mount a full-scale attack on educational segregation. Research was begun and a number of legal attacks initiated. In June, 1953, the Supreme Court ordered five school desegregation cases to be argued before it. This culminated in the famous BROWN V. BOARD OF EDUCATION decision on May 17, 1954.

In the case of SWEATT V. PAINTER, the Supreme Court ordered the admission of Herman Marion Sweatt, a Negro, to the previously all-white University of Texas Law School on the ground that the separate law school set up for Negroes was not equal and could not be made equal to the long-established and prestigious white law school.

In the case of SWANSON V. THE UNIVERSITY OF VIRGINIA, the University of Virginia Law School was ordered to admit its first Negro.

In the U.S. District Court case of WILSON V. THE LSU BOARD OF SUPERVISORS, Louisiana State University Law School was ordered to admit a Negro, Roy S. Wilson.

In the case of MCLAUREN V. OKLAHOMA, the Supreme Court ruled that the University of Oklahoma could not segregate McLauren, a Negro, who had gained admission to the graduate school, in the classroom, library or cafeteria. The Court said that such segregation violated the 14th Amendment because "such restrictions impair and inhibit his ability to study, engage in discussions and exchange views, with other students, and, in general, to learn his profession."

A State Court decision opened the University of Missouri to Negroes.

In the case of HENDERSON V. THE U.S., the Supreme Court ended dining-car segregation on railroads by requiring them to permit Negroes to occupy any empty seat in the diner instead of being confined to a partitioned section. This decision was based on the Interstate Commerce Act. The Justice Department joined the plaintiff in this case.

In the case of the CITY OF BIRMINGHAM V. MONK, a Federal Circuit Court of Appeals enjoined the enforcement of a Birmingham, Ala., residential segregation ordinance.

The national convention of the NAACP authorized an investigation of Communist infiltration. It was reported that Communists and left-wing groups had influenced or controlled the Richmond and San Francisco, Calif., Jamaica and other Long Island branches. The national office was authorized to seize the charters of Communist-controlled groups and to issue new charters to newly constituted non-Communist group.

The NAACP organized a National Emergency Civil Rights Mobilization (NECRM), a coalition of 60 groups. On Jan. 15, 4,000 delegates arrived in Washington, D.C. The Civil Rights Congress, believed to be a Communist-controlled group, was excluded by the NAACP from the meeting.

President Truman's Committee on Equality of Treatment and Opportunity in the Armed Forces, the Fahy Committee, reported that Negroes were still barred from 198 of 490 specialties in the Army, despite announced policy to the contrary. Negro soldiers were being trained in only 21 of the 106 training courses for enlisted men. However, segregation had been largely abandoned in the Army, Navy, Air Force and Marine Corps.

In July, in Korea, the Negro 24th Infantry Regiment recaptured the city of Yech'on after a 16-hour battle. The first break in the steady withdrawal in the face of the North Korean advance, it was the first U.S. victory in Korea.

Ralph Bunche received the Nobel Peace Prize for his Palestine mediation efforts. He was the first American Negro to receive this prize.

In the decade 1950 to 1960, the following Negroes served as alternate delegates to the U.N.: Marian Anderson, 1958–59; Robert L. Brokenburr, 1955–56; Archibald S. Carey, 1953–56; Zelma George, 1960; Edith Sampson, 1950–53; Channing H. Tobias, 1951-52.

Judge Andrew Howard, a Negro, was appointed to the Municipal Court for the District of Columbia by President Truman. Judge Emory Smith, a Negro, was also appointed by Truman to the Municipal Court of Washington, D.C., but he died shortly thereafter.

The American Medical Association seated its first Negro delegate.

Gwendolyn Brooks became the first Negro to win a Pulitzer Prize in poetry for her collection of poems, *Annie Allen.*

Jay S. Redding, a Negro, published a general study of the Negro in America, *They Came in Chains.*

Beetlecreek by William Demby, a Negro, was published. Set in the West Virginia coalfields of the author's youth, the story concerns an outcast of the white community who tries to become accepted by the Negro community. Through mishap and ill chance, he is falsely accused of betraying the Negroes, and is killed by a Negro gang. This story is at times a sort of *Intruder in the Dust* in reverse, and is probably one of the best of post-war Negro novels.

The Council on Harlem Theater was formed by four amateur community theater groups which combined to encourage Negro dramatists and actors, and to give them more exposure Off Broadway. The council also encouraged the showing of Negro plays in lodge halls, school auditoriums, etc. Among these new Negro plays were Julian Mayfield's *The Other Foot,* Ossie Davis' *Alice in Wonderland,* Lofton Mitchell's *The Bancroft Dynasty.*

The Apollo Theater on 125th St. in Harlem sponsored two white plays with all-Negro casts: *The Detective Story,* in which Sidney Poitier had his first major role, and *Rain.* Both productions were commercial and artistic failures.

Louis Armstrong visited Europe, and in nine countries armed guards had to protect him from being trampled by enthusiastic listeners.

Althea Gibson, on Oct. 26, was the first Negro accepted for competition for the National Tennis Championship, at Forest Hills, New York.

The first Negro hired to play professional basketball in the National Basketball Association was Ed "Chuck" Cooper. Signed by the Boston Celtics, he played for the next 6 years. In the same year, Nat "Sweetwater" Clifton joined the New York Knickerbockers of the NBA.

1951

In the case of MCKISSICK V. CARMICHAEL, the University of North Carolina Law School was opened to Negroes by court order.

The University of North Carolina admitted its first Negro student.

Oregon law forbade discrimination on account of race, color, religion or national origin at vocational, professional or trade schools, chartered or licensed under any state statute.

A Washington, D.C., Municipal Court of Appeals ruled segregation in restaurants illegal.

The New York City Council forbade discrimination in city-assisted housing developments.

President Truman established a Committee on Government Contract Compliance to combat discrimination against Negroes in private companies doing business with the Federal Government.

Four of the original Trenton Six were freed after a new trial, but two men, Collis English and Ralph Cooper, were again convicted and sentenced to death. The NAACP, which had been handling the defense, appealed the verdict. The four acquitted were Horace Wilson, John McKenzie, McKinley Forrest and James Thorpe.

When a Chicago Negro bus driver, Harvey E. Clark, a veteran, tried to move into a Cicero, Ill., apartment building, violence erupted. Windows were smashed, the Negro's furniture dumped out the window and burned. On the night of July 12, a mob of 3,500 gathered and rioted. Gov. Adlai Stevenson called out the National Guard, and 450 guardsmen and 200 Cicero and Cook County police quelled the disorder; 72 persons were arrested, 60 were charged, 17 people were hospitalized. On July 16, the Illinois NAACP announced that the apartment building was now Negro-owned and would be rented to both Negro and white veterans.

On Dec. 25, Harry Moore, an NAACP executive secretary for Florida, and his wife, were killed by a bomb placed under his home. Both were active in voter registration.

A delegation of American Negroes, headed by Paul Robeson and William L. Patterson, petitioned the U.S., charging the Government with a policy of genocide against Negroes in America.

The last all-Negro army unit, the 24th Infantry Regiment, was deactivated.

The Congressional Medal of Honor was awarded to Pfc. William Thompson of Brooklyn for heroism in Korea. Thompson, a Negro, manned a machinegun and single-handedly fought off the enemy during a withdrawal operation.

Ralph Bunche, the American Negro diplomat, was appointed Under Secretary for the U.N.

Between this year and the following, Channing H. Tobias

was alternate U.S. delegate to the U.N. Previous to this appointment he had served as a minister, professor at Payne College, chairman of the NAACP board of directors, and as a director of the Phelps-Stokes Fund. He had received the Spingarn Medal in 1948.

Carver National Monument, the first national park honoring a Negro, was opened in Joplin, Mo.

Go Tell It on the Mountain, an autobiographical novel by Negro author James Baldwin, was published. It was Baldwin's first and perhaps best novel.

Boy at the Window, an autobiographical novel by Owen Dodson, a Negro, was published.

We Fished All Night, by Negro novelist Willard Motley, was published. The novel dealt with lower-class life in Chicago.

Roy Campanella, of the the Brooklyn Dodgers, received the National League's Most Valuable Player Award. Campanella, a Negro, also won the award in 1953 and 1955.

Althea Gibson, a Negro, and Darlene Hard won the tennis singles and doubles championships at Wimbledon.

Jersey Joe Walcott, a Negro, was heavyweight boxing champion from 1951–52.

Sugar Ray Robinson held the middleweight boxing championship.

From 1951 to 1952, and 1952 through 1954, and again 1954 through 1955, Jimmy Carter, a Negro, was the lightweight boxing champion.

Johnny Bratton, a Negro lost the welterweight boxing championship to Kid Gavilan, a Cuban Negro, who held the title through 1954.

1952

The total Negro income for this year was $11.4 billion. The total white income was $194.1 billion.

The median incomes of white and Negro wage and salary earners were as follows: male, white $3,507, female $1,976; Negro male $2,038, female $814.

Unemployment rates were: white male, 2.2%, female 2.9%; Negro male 4.5%, female 4.8%.

The NAACP continued to expand. It opened a permanent regional office for the Southeast U.S. in Birmingham, Ala.

In the case of GRAY V. UNIVERSITY OF TENNESSEE, the University of Tennessee was ordered to admit Negroes to its graduate, professional and special schools. The first Negro was admitted the same year.

The NAACP succeeded in gaining admission of Negroes into the Nursing School of Louisiana State University, but legal attempts to desegregate the University of Florida Graduate Schools failed.

The NAACP succeeded in desegregating the public schools of southern Illinois.

NACCP lawyers brought five school desegregation cases before the Supreme Court. They involved segregation in South Carolina; Topeka, Kan.; Prince Edward County, Va.; a suburb of Wilmington, Del., and the District of Columbia. Four of the cases were appealed from lower court decisions upholding school segregation, but the Delaware case was being appealed by the state after a ruling against segregation. These cases culminated in the famous 1954 Supreme Court decision.

Through legal action, the NAACP opened certain public housing projects in Detroit, San Francisco, Long Branch, N.J., Sacramento and Richmond, Calif. However, none of the legal actions led to a court ruling on the general subject of open housing. For various reasons, in each individual case, specific housing projects were opened to Negroes or enjoined not to deny housing solely because of race.

The NAACP offered legal assistance to a white family in Omaha, Neb., that had moved into a Negro neighborhood, an act that gained national publicity.

The NAACP activity desegregated the Philco Corp., and prevailed upon the UAW to incorporate an antidiscrimination clause in the contract between the United Auto Workers and the Pressed Metals Corp.

The NAACP also in this year defended the rights of Negro workers on the B&O Railroad. Contrary to the provisions of the Railway Labor Act, the Brotherhood of Railway Clerks had sought to force Negro workers to join a Jim Crow local.

The result of the court case was that the Negroes were denied membership in the white local, but they did not have to join the Negro local.

The NAACP conducted an extensive study throughout this year on segregation on the railroads, in preparation for a hearing before the Interstate Commerce Commission.

As a result of an NAACP suit filed in Federal District Court, a swimming pool in Kansas City was desegregated. In Louisville, Ky., as a result of a suit in the Federal District Court, a municipal golf course was desegregated. However, the Supreme Court refused to review a case in which Negroes were denied admission on certain days of the week to a Miami, Fla., municipal golf course.

Through litigation the NAACP desegregated Ford's Theater in Baltimore, after 6 years of picketing.

NAACP lobbying resulted in hearings in the Senate Rules Committee on an anti-filibuster resolution. On Jan. 29, the Senate Rules Committee reported out Senate Resolution 203, a weak anti-filibuster measure. It provided for a 2/3 vote for cloture.

The NAACP came to the aid of several Negroes arrested and tried for rape and murder. In one of the most prominent it secured the acquittal of James Wright, a Scottsboro boy, who had been accused of the rape of a 13-year-old girl in Albany, N.Y. In another case, the NAACP secured the reversal of the conviction of Collis English and Ralph Cooper, the two remaining members of the Trenton Six.

A civil rights bill was prevented from coming to the floor of Congress throughout the year.

Tuskegee Institute reported that for the first time in the 71 years records had been kept, there were no lynchings.

In 12 Southern states 28%, or about 1,200,000, Negroes of voting age were registered to vote.

The Republican Party platform said: "We condemn bigots who inject class, racial and religious prejudice into public and political matters. Bigotry is un-American and a danger to the Republic. We deplore the duplicity and insincerity of the party in power in racial and religious matters. Although they have been in office as a majority party for many years, they have not kept, nor do they intend to keep their promises. The Republican Party will not mislead, exploit or attempt to confuse minority groups for political purposes. All American citizens are entitled to full, impartial enforcement of Federal laws relating to their civil rights. We believe that it is the primary responsibility of each state to order and control its own domestic institutions, and this power reserved to the states is essential to the maintenance of our Federal Republic. However, we believe that the Federal government should take supplemental action within its constitutional jurisdiction to oppose discrimination against race, religion or national origin." The platform called for appointments to office without regard to race, etc., anti-lynch action, elimination of poll taxes, an end to segregation in Washington, D.C., and fair employment practices.

The Democratic Party platform read: "We will continue our efforts to eradicate discrimination based on race, religion or national origin. . . . We favor Federal legislation effectively to secure these rights to everyone: (1) the right to equal opportunity for employment; (2) the right to security of persons; (3) the right to full and equal participation in the nation's political life, free from arbitrary restraints. We also favor legislation to perfect existing Federal civil right statutes and to strengthen the administrative machinery for the protection of civil rights."

The Socialist Party platform held: "Complete political, economic and social equality, regardless of race, religion or national origin, must be established. Equality can be achieved only after the ending of segregation practices. Segregation must be abolished in all public or public-supported institutions, in housing and in the armed services."

The Progressive Party platform said: "The war program of the bipartisans has been accompanied by the intensification of racist acts and practices against the Negro people, the Mexican-American people, the Puerto Rican people and the Jewish people. . . . The terror weapon of the bomb is turned upon the Negro people in an attempt to stem the rising militancy of their struggle for full equality and freedom. Both bombs, violence and terror will not halt the Negro people in their march to full liberation. Nor will they be put off by the pious repetition of platform promises by the two old parties which have shamelessly betrayed their pledges of anti-lynch and anti-poll tax legislation and an FEPC."

Charlotta A. Bass, a Negro, editor and publisher of the *Californian Eagle,* received the nomination of the Progressive Party for Vice President.

Only 21% of the Negroes who voted in this year voted for Dwight D. Eisenhower. He was remembered as a man who had testified against President Truman's move to end segregation in the Army.

On Nov. 28, an NAACP delegation met with President-elect Eisenhower. He claimed that he opposed Federal aid to segregated school systems, although he would not dictate to Southerners how to run their schools.

Ralph Ellison's *The Invisible Man* was published.

Jay S. Redding's psychological study of the effects of racism on the American Negro was published as *On Being Negro in America.*

The following American Negro athletes won gold medals at the Helsinki Olympics: Alice Coachman, women's high jump; Andrew Stanfield, 200-meter dash; Mal Whitfield, 800-meter run (an Olympic record); Harrison Dillard, 110-meter hurdles (an Olympic record); Jerome Biffle, running broad jump; Dillard and Stanfield for the 400-meter relay; Floyd Patterson, middleweight boxing; Catherine Hardy, Mae Faggs and Barbara Jones, woman's 400-meter relay. Negroes also won 4 silver and 2 bronze Olympic medals.

Larry Doby, a Negro baseball player with the Cleveland Indians, was the American League home-run champion in this year, and again in 1954.

From this year through 1961, Archie Moore, a Negro, was light heavyweight boxing champion.

1953

The total Negro income was $12.7 billion, as compared to $202.7 billion for whites.

The median family income for whites was $4,392; for Negroes, 2,461.

President Eisenhower's Administration ended segregation in schools on military bases, and of civilian employees in the

Navy shore establishments. The Administration also ended segregation in the Veterans Administration hospitals.

The Justice Department took action to implement a Supreme Court ruling forbidding segregation in Washington, D.C., restaurants.

Partly as a result of NAACP lobbying, the U.S. Attorney General turned down two candidates for U.S. District Attorney because they were segregationists, John Lee Smith of Texas and State Senator Warren Gill of Oregon.

The Commissioners of the District of Columbia issued an order abolishing segregation in several district agencies. Segregation was maintained, however, in the fire department, the recreation board and some welfare agencies.

The NAACP planned to initiate a 10-year Fight for Freedom to do away with all racial discrimination by 1963, the 100th anniversary of the Emancipation Proclamation.

The Supreme Court called for reargument in the five school segregation cases first heard by the Court in 1942. An NAACP task force of 100 lawyers, political scientists, sociologists, historians and other experts was formed to do the necessary research.

Through the efforts of the NAACP, a Negro was admitted as an undergraduate to Louisiana State University.

The NAACP filed a comprehensive complaint with the ICC asking for an order banning segregation of interstate passengers. This was the culmination of more than a year of investigation and research work. Although the Supreme Court had ruled in 1946 that state segregation laws could not be applied to interstate travelers, segregation still persisted.

On the recommendation of the NAACP, the Pennsylvania Department of Labor denied the use of migrant labor to one grower who the NAACP had discovered treated his workers unfairly. Also, a program of inspection of labor camps was announced.

Through the efforts of the NAACP skilled jobs were opened to Negroes by the Fisher Body Division and the Electromotive Diesel Division of General Motors.

During a strike by the International Ladies Garment Workers Union against the Bernstein-Mittleman Co. in Wilmington, Del., the NAACP worked among the Negro strike-breakers to convince them not to cross the picket lines.

Hulan Jack, a Negro New York State Assemblyman for 13 years, was elected Borough President of Manhattan. Jack, the first Negro to gain such a post, ran against another Negro, the Republican candidate, Elmer Carter. Tammany Hall had previously selected a white politician but at a late date switched to Jack.

The NAACP came to the defense of Negroes convicted of various crimes. In the most prominent case, it secured the reversal of the conviction of Mack Ingram. A North Carolina farmer had been convicted of "assault by leering" at a white girl. The Trenton Six case ended when Ralph Cooper, whose conviction had previously been reversed, entered a plea of no defense and made a confession incriminating himself and his co-defendants, four of whom had already been freed, and one of whom had died in prison from a heart attack. It was felt that Cooper had been forced to do this to gain his freedom.

The NAACP tried unsuccessfully to have civil rights put on the agenda of a top-level conference between President Eisenhower and Republican Congressional leaders.

Congress remained inactive on civil rights in this year. Only one civil rights bill was reported out of committee, and no action resulted. The House Appropriations Committee reduced funds for Howard University, the Freedmen's Hospital and the public housing program. In the Senate, an attempt to secure a new cloture rule to facilitate stopping filibusters was defeated. The House Labor Committee refused to hold hearings on a Fair Employment Practices Commission bill.

In Chicago and Cleveland, violence flared when Negroes attempted to move into white neighborhoods. In Chicago, police maintained a 24-hour vigil to protect Negroes.

In this year the NAACP pressured the U.S. delegation to the U.N. to support a U.N. Commission Study that condemned South Africa's racial policies. The U.S. indicated it would not vote approval of the report since it considered this a matter of domestic jurisdiction. The NAACP also aided Abdullahi Issa of Somaliland, who wished to adress the U.N.

as a representative of the Somali Youth League of the Territory of Somaliland. His visa expired before he could appear at the U.N., but the NAACP negotiated with the U.S. Government and Issa was permitted to re-enter the country to present his plea.

Gov. James F. Byrnes of South Carolina was a member of the U.S. delegation to the U.N. The NAACP and other liberal groups unsuccessfully protested his appointment on the ground that he held racist views. When Byrnes was designated the delegation's spokesman on human rights, NAACP protests were successful. Rep. Frances Bolton of Ohio was appointed human-rights spokesman.

Joseph H. Jackson, a Negro, became president of the National Baptist Convention. He inaugurated a program of developing land in Liberia to finance Baptist missionaries in Africa.

Maude Martha, an autobiographical novel by Gwendolyn Brooks, a Negro, about growing up in Chicago's South Side was published.

Take a Giant Step by Louis Peterson, a Negro had a run of 76 performances on Broadway. It dealt with adolescence and was a critical success.

1954

The total Negro income was $12.5 billion, compared to $203.6 billion for whites.

The median family income for whites was $4,339; for Negroes, $2,410.

The NAACP held a Freedom Fulfillment Conference to formally launch the Fight for Freedom campaign. Its goal was total elimination of discrimination by January, 1963, the centennial of the Emancipation Proclamation. President Eisenhower addressed the conference, endorsing the "ideal of equality among all men."

On May 17, in BROWN V. THE BOARD OF EDUCATION the Supreme Court, by a 9-0 decision, ruled that school segregation was unconstitutional since "separate educational facilities are inherently unequal." Chief Justice Warren wrote the opinion. Thurgood Marshall was the chief of the NAACP legal team which also included Robert L. Carter, Jack Greenberg, Louis Redding, James Nabrit, George E. C. Hayes,

Spottswood Robinson, 3d. Kenneth Clark was prominent in the research into the social and psychological effects of segregation. Over $100,000 was spent in this legal campaign, begun in 1950.

In the fall following the Supreme Court ruling, 8 states (Arkansas, Maryland, Missouri, West Virginia, Delaware, Arizona, New Mexico, Kansas) and the District of Columbia at least partially desegregated their school systems. A total of 150 school districts was affected. The school desegregation ruling did not entirely dispose of the four desegregation cases upon which the May 17 ruling was based. The Supreme Court ordered further reargument on what kind of decree the court should issue. On Nov. 15, the NAACP filed its brief, stating that the Court should require desegregation by September 1955.

School desegregation rulings set off a flurry of NAACP activity ranging from the petitioning of local school boards by local branches to desegregate, to the filing of suits to gain admission in previously all-white schools.

In HAWKINS V. BOARD OF CONTROL, the Supreme Court ruled that the University of Florida should admit a Negro student, regardless of any "public mischief" it might cause, or any other excuse for delay.

The AFL Convention endorsed the 1954 Supreme Court decision on desegregation.

As a result of the Supreme Court school desegregation ruling, very many racist groups sprang up in the South—the American States Rights Association, Southerners in Alabama, National Association for the Advancement and Protection of the White Race, Florida States Rights, Inc., and White Citizens Councils, among others.

The White Citizens Councils (WCC) were the most significant and influential of the organizations created to fight desegregation and civil rights. The first WCC was formed on July 11, 1954, in Indianola, Miss., in the Delta region. In a matter of weeks, the councils spread throughout the South and even into the border states. In October, a statewide association was formed uniting the local councils of Mississippi. It claimed 80,000 members. The councils strove for respectability, invariably enrolling the most prominent townspeople.

Proposed Constitutional amendments to set aside the Supreme Court's school desegregation decisions, introduced by Senator Eastland and Rep. John Bell Williams, both of Mississippi, died in committee.

The expenditures per pupil in Southern public schools for instruction (salaries, books, teaching supplies) were: North Carolina: white, $132.46; Negro $124.85. Florida: white, $175.92; Negro, $160.61. Alabama: white, $111.99, Negro, $105.02. Mississippi: white, $98.15; Negro, $43.17. Arkansas: white, $99.08; Negro $71.78. Louisiana: white, $165.08; Negro, $122.07.

On Sept. 18, President Eisenhower desegregated the Washington, D.C., fire department.

President Eisenhower nominated a Chicago Negro, J. Ernest Wilkins, to be Assistant Secretary of Labor. Wilkins often represented Labor Secretary James P. Mitchell at weekly Cabinet meetings.

President Eisenhower refused to urge civil rights action by Congress. He withheld support from a civil rights amendment to the Taft-Hartley Act. The House Committee on Interstate and Foreign Commerce approved by a vote of 19 to 7 a bill to end segregation in interstate travel. However, the Administration-controlled House Rules Committee refused to let the bill come to the floor for a vote.

In 1952, the NAACP had begun investigating and gathering information on segregation in interstate commerce. In 1953 it had brought an omnibus suit before the Interstate Commerce Commission, and in 1954 an ICC trial examiner recommended the commission issue an order abolishing segregation on railway coaches and in waiting rooms.

Two bills on fair employment practices were introduced in Congress. Illinois Senator Dirksen's bill, because it lacked enforcement powers, was opposed by civil rights groups. It died in committee. The second, with enforcement powers, was reported favorably out of the Senate Labor Committee, but it was never taken up by the Senate. It was sponsored by Senator Ives of New York and Senator Humphrey of Minnesota.

Vice President Nixon served as chairman of the Committee on Government Contracts, which was to assure the elimination of job discrimination by employers working under Government contracts. Two of the major complaints sent to it by the NAACP, involving the Capital Transit Co. and the Chesapeake and Potomac Telephone Co., were not acted upon. In general, the committee refused to condemn flagrant instances of job discrimination.

In this year the Housing and Home Finance Agency still gave Federal backing to programs for the development of segregated communities.

The NAACP was successful in opening public housing projects to Negroes in San Francisco; Camden and Elizabeth, N.J., and Detroit and Hamtramck, Mich.

The Navy desegregated the last of its yards in Charleston, S.C., by doing away with separate restaurants, fountains and washrooms.

The Defense Department reported that, as of Aug. 31, 1954, no all-Negro units existed in the armed services. Army schools in the Canal Zone were integrated, as well as mainland schools on military bases that were separate and operated in part by local authorities. In one case, at Fort Belvoir where local educational officials operated the base school and refused to integrate, the Federal Government took over control of the school and integrated it. However, a school built for Navy men's children at Bainbridge, Md., denied admission to Negroes with the support of top naval authorities in Washington.

Harvey Higley, head of the Veterans Administration, announced desegregation of VA hospitals begun the previous year had been completed. However, the NAACP found segregation practices in the New Orleans and Roanoke (Va.) veterans' hospital.

Despite protests from Negro organizations, the Department of Health, Education and Welfare reaffirmed its policy of giving Federal funds to segregated hospitals.

Public recreational facilities in Atlanta, Ga.; Houston, Tex.; Louisville, Ky.; and Nashville, Tenn., and the Oklahoma State Parks System were desegregated.

Charles C. Diggs, a Negro, was elected to the House of Representatives from Detroit, Mich.

From this year through 1959, Charles H. Mahoney served

as a permanent member of the U.S. delegation to the U.N. He was the first Negro permanent member.

Dr. Theodore K. Lawless, a Negro and a recognized authority on dermatology, won the Spingarn Medal.

Benjamin O. Davis Jr. became the first Negro general in the Air Force.

Youngblood, an autobiographical novel by John Oliver Killens, a Negro, was published. The novel is a social chronicle of the Black Belt in southeast Georgia where Killens grew up. It is in a sense of fictionalized continuation of W. E. B. Du Bois' *Souls of Black Folk.*

House of Flowers, by Truman Capote, starring the Negro singers Pearl Bailey and Diahann Carrol, was produced on Broadway.

Mrs. Patterson, by Charles Sebree and Greer Johnson, Negro playwrights, ran 101 performances at the National Theater. It was a quasi-fantasy about growing up in the rural South.

In Splendid Error, by the Negro playwright William Branch, was produced Off Broadway in New York City.

Eartha Kitt, Negro singer and actress, appeared in the movie version of *New Faces.* She has since become a successful nightclub and TV entertainer. Her other movies include *Anna Lucasta, The March of the Hawk* and *Synanon.*

Willie Mays, a Negro baseball player with the New York Giants, was the National League's batting champion with an average of .345. He was also voted the league's Most Valuable Player.

From 1954 through 1955 and in 1956, Johnny Saxton, a Negro, was welterweight boxing champion of the world.

There were 725,311 Negroes in Cuba, 12.4% of the population. Oriente Province contained the greatest number of Negroes and mestizos, 46.7%

D. "WITH ALL DELIBERATE SPEED"

By January 1969, a Federal survey showed that 15 years after the Supreme Court's unanimous decision in Oliver Brown et al v. Board of Education of Topeka, almost 80 per cent of the Negro children were still attending all-Negro schools and while the dual system has persisted in many areas of the South, there has been a vast increase in de facto segregation in the North.

1955

The urban Negro population in representative major American cities was: Chicago, 18%; Detroit, 22%; Los Angeles, 11.3%; New York, 12.2%.

Total Negro income was $13.1 billion, compared to $222 billion for whites.

Median family income for whites was $4,605; for non-whites, $2,549.

The first nationally significant direct action on the part of a Negro community took place on Dec. 1. Rosa Parks, a Negro, boarded the Cleveland Avenue bus in Montgomery, Ala., and took a vacant seat in the front of the bus. She refused to give her seat to a white man, and was arrested. Other Negro women organized and called for a boycott of the city buses. The next day a meeting of local Negro leaders, chaired by the Rev. L. Roy Bennett, decided to call a bus boycott for the following Monday, Dec. 5. Martin Luther King, Jr. pastor of the Dexter Avenue Baptist Church, accepted the job of seeing that the Negro community of over 50,000 was informed of the boycott. Normally 75% of the Montgomery bus riders were Negro, and the boycott was carried out with startling unanimity. On Monday evening, at a mass meeting King was elected president of the Boycott Committee of the Montgomery Improvement Association (MIA). Rev. Ralph Abernathy was put in charge of negotiating with city officials. The MIA did not originally demand an end to segregated seating, and for this reason the local NAACP refused to support the boycott at its inception. Negro demands were: (1) courteous treatment of Negro riders; (2) seating to be on a first-come first-served basis, with Negroes filling up the back of the bus and moving toward the front, whites filling up the front and moving

540

toward the rear, (3) Negro drivers for Negro routes. City officials broke off negotiations, however, and the Mayor and his subordinates publicly joined the White Citizens Council. The boycott went on into 1956, and on Feb. 26, 1956, King and almost 100 other Negroes were indicted on a charge of conspiring to conduct an illegal boycott. The NAACP finally supported them, defended the case in a Federal court, and had the bus segregation ordinance declared unconstitutional.

The Interstate Commerce Commission, in response to the omnibus suit filed with it by the NAACP, outlawed segregated buses and waiting rooms for interstate passengers. Carriers were given until Jan. 10, 1956, to comply.

In two cases taken to the Supreme Court by the NAACP, the Court affirmed that segregation in public recreation was barred by the 14th Amendment, and opened the Atlanta municipal golf course to Negroes.

On May 31, the Supreme Court handed down its guidelines for school desegregation. Local boards were to draw up their own plans "with all deliberate speed." This disappointed the NAACP, which had argued for a specific time limit.

This year 326 school districts desegregated. Before massive resistance to integration began in the South, Hoxie, Ark., provided an example of peaceful integration. After desegregation was complete, outside agitators of White Citizens Councils tried to create racial antagonism. A *Life* magazine story spotlighting the town, "Integration at Work," led to increased tension. The school board, however, refused to segregate. FBI officers were sent, and the U.S. Court of Appeals for the 8th Circuit in BREWER V. HOXIE SCHOOL BOARD upheld the right of the board to obtain injunctions against those who sought to interfere with its plan. The school remained open and integrated.

Public school desegregation continued with good results in Oklahoma, Kansas, Missouri, Delaware, Maryland, West Virginia and Texas. Beginnings were made in Arkansas, Tennessee and Kentucky. Georgia, Virginia, Louisiana, Alabama, Mississippi, South Carolina and North Carolina were definitely committed to fight integration.

The NAACP filed 33 desegregation petitions with local school boards in North Carolina, 15 in South Carolina, 13 in Alabama, 7 in Georgia and 6 in Mississippi, to no avail.

To preserve school segregation the Alabama Legislature passed the Engelhardt school "placement" bill. It also passed a bill providing a license fee of $100 for anyone soliciting NAACP memberships, and a tax of $5 on each membership. The bill applied only to Wilcox County, 79% Negro, with no registered Negro voters.

The Georgia Board of Education adopted a resolution revoking the license of any teacher who taught mixed classes or belonged to the NAACP. The resolution was rescinded, however, under pressure from the NAACP and popular opinion.

To delay integration, the Legal Education Advisory Committee of Mississippi recommended a 6-point program: (1) make champerty or encouraging litigation a violation of law and require out-of-state lawyers to be "cleared" by the Mississippi bar; (2) repeal the compulsory school attendance law; (3) abolish common-law marriages; (4) strengthen the libel law; (5) create an Authority for Maintenance of Racial Segregation with a staff and funds; (6) enact a statute providing punishment for persons interfering with individual rights according to state where done under the auspices of Federal law. (This was directed at FBI officers investigating Constitutional violations in the August, 1955, primary.)

Lynching returned to the South. Mississippi accounted for three: Rev. George W. Lee at Belzoni, Lamar Smith at Brookhaven, and Emmett Till near Money. In Humphreys County, Miss., Gus Courts and Rev. George W. Lee led a voter registration drive. They convinced about 400 of the 16,012 Negroes in the county to register. Violence, intimidation and economic pressure followed. Lee was lynched. By December, 1955, only Gus Courts' name remained on the registration lists. There were 7,013 whites in the county. On Nov. 25, Courts was the victim of an assassination attempt. The White Citizens Council of Mississippi inaugurated a campaign of economic pressure. Negroes who sought to vote or filed petitions for school desegregation were fired from their jobs or denied credit. In response, the NAACP raised $300,-000, including a $20,000 NAACP contribution, for deposit in the Negro-owned Tri-State Bank of Memphis. This money was used to aid victims of racist economic pressure. As a result of the terror tactics practiced by white Mississippians, the number of registered Negroes was reduced from 22,000 to 8,000 in less than a year.

The 84th Congress failed to enact any civil rights legislation, despite the fact that nearly 100 bills and amendments were introduced. The House Judiciary Committee reported favorably on a bill introduced by Emmanuel Celler, Representative of New York, and the Senate Judiciary Committee reported favorably on a bill of Senator Lehman of New York. No action was taken on either bill.

The House Committee on Education and Labor rejected an amendment to the Federal Aid to School Construction Bill, offered by Rep. Adam Clayton Powell Jr. to deny funds to segregated schools.

The House Armed Services Committee reported favorably on a bill to permit Governors to request the assignment of draftees or volunteers to the National Guard instead of the Reserves. Adam Clayton Powell Jr. introduced an amendment requiring such National Guard units to be desegregated. The amendment passed. At a press conference, President Eisenhower denounced the Powell amendment as "extraneous," and it was eliminated in a new bill passed by both the House and Senate at the end of July.

In a bill setting up a standard system of absentee voting, a provision was included to repeal the wartime exemption of servicemen from registering and paying the poll tax. In effect, the bill subjected Negro ex-servicemen to the normal voting disabilities that a Negro faced in the South.

The President's Committee on Government Contracts, chaired by Vice President Richard Nixon, was successful in obtaining the hiring of Negro operators by the Capital Transit Co.

The NAACP, with the cooperation of the Committee on Government Contracts and the CIO Oil Workers Union, made hiring Negroes in the oil refining industry possible.

A. Philip Randolph and Willard S. Townsend, both Negroes, were elected vice presidents of the AFL-CIO.

Congress passed a public housing bill. However, it rejected an amendment offered by Adam Clayton Powell Jr. that would have denied Federal funds to segregated projects.

The Housing and Home Finance Agency approved a program advanced by the National Association of Home Builders that set a 10% quota on housing for Negroes.

In view of its failure to find enough support for Federal open-housing legislation, the NAACP began lobbying for state laws. New York forbade discrimination in any housing constructed with FHA or Veterans Administration assistance. Jurisdiction of enforcement was given to the State Commission against Discrimination. This was the Metcalf-Baker Law; a similar bill failed in Illinois. New Jersey passed a law forbidding racial or religious discrimination in the granting of mortgages.

Robert Weaver was appointed State Rent Commissioner, the first Negro to hold Cabinet rank in New York State.

The NAACP succeeded in winning flat bans against segregation in public housing in Detroit and St. Louis from U.S. District Court Judges.

NAACP membership numbered 309,000.

Walter White, executive secretary of the NAACP since 1931, died. Roy Wilkins was chosen as White's successor. Since 1939, the NAACP had actually been two organizations: the NAACP itself, headed by Walter White and now Roy Wilkins, and the NAACP Legal Defense and Education Fund, headed by Thurgood Marshall. In 1952, the Legal Defense and Education Fund moved to separate headquarters, and in 1955 the interlocking directorate was ended. This may have been done purely for tax reasons. Because the NAACP maintained a Washington lobby, contributions to it could not be tax-exempt; but contributions to the Legal Defense and Education Fund as a separate body became tax-deductable. There were other indications that the split also took place because of disagreements in the organization; a portion of the membership desired a strategy of more direct action rather than long court battles.

Marian Anderson was the first Negro to sing at the Metropolitan Opera House in New York City. She appeared in Verdi's *The Masked Ball*.

Trouble in Mind, by Alice Childress, a Negro playwright, was produced Off Broadway in New York City.

The rise of rock-and-roll music marked the first experience of white teen-agers in large numbers with Negro blues.

Willie Mays, Negro baseball player with the New York Giants, was the National League home-run champion. He won this title again in 1962, 1964 and 1965.

Sugar Ray Robinson was middleweight boxing champion from 1955 through 1957 and again from 1958 through 1960.

Wallace Bud Smith, a Negro, was the lightweight boxing champion.

1956

Total Negro income was $14.4 billion, compared to $240 billion for whites.

The median family income for whites was $4,993; for nonwhites, $2,628.

As of October, 797 school districts had been desegregated since May, 1954. There were 319,184 Negroes attending these newly desegregated schools, while 2,400,000 Southern Negro school children attended segregated schools. There were no desegregated districts in Alabama, Florida, Georgia, Louisiana, Mississippi, North Carolina, South Carolina and Virginia.

An additional 200 school districts were desegregated in this year.

Negro students were kept from enrolling in school by a white mob in Mansfield, Tex.

In Sturgis, Ky., the National Guard was called out to disperse a mob that tried to prevent school integration.

Leading citizens in Clinton, Tenn., formed a posse to break up an anti-integration mob. The school remained open and integrated, and an all-white Southern jury found 6 white rioters guilty. However, in 1958, the integrated high school was blown up.

Sen. Harry Byrd of Virginia called for "massive resistance" to school desegregation, and 101 Southern Congressmen signed the Southern Manifesto against school integration. Senators Kefauver and Gore of Tennessee and Sen. Lyndon B. Johnson of Texas did not sign it. The manifesto called the Supreme Court decision a "clear abuse of judicial power" that was being exploited by "outside agitators." It accused the Justices of substituting "naked power for established law."

The White Citizens Councils claimed membership of 300,-000. The councils became particularly powerful in Mississippi, Louisiana and Alabama. They participated actively in politics, screening, endorsing, denouncing and campaigning for segregationist candidates. They also challenged and intimidated Negro voters or would-be registrants. In Grant Parish, La., the local council removed 90% of the registered Negroes from the voting lists.

Autherine Lucy, a Negro, was admitted to the University of Alabama under court order. As rioting flared, she was removed by the university. When she sued for reinstatement, she was permanently expelled for making "outrageous" charges in her suit. Appeals to the Federal Government for help were to no avail, and she eventually dropped her case.

The State of Alabama found the NAACP in contempt when it refused to open its books to state officials. The association was fined $100,000 and a court injunction prohibited it from operating in the state. The NAACP remained inactive in Alabama for the next two years.

Negro singer Nat King Cole was attacked by a group of whites while performing in a Birmingham, Ala., theater.

The home of a Birmingham, Ala., Negro leader, Rev. F. L. Shuttlesworth, was dynamited.

White racists established the United Southern Employees Association in North Carolina. Its aims included: (1) the end of the AFL-CIO in the South; (2) passage of laws for sterilization of those supporting integration to avoid "mongrelized" offspring; (3) reversal of the 1954 Supreme Court decision. The organization never established permanent roots.

On the issue of school integration, the Republican Party platform stated that the party "accepts the decision" and that desegregation should be brought about "with all deliberate speed."

The Democratic Party platform was less straightforward than its presidential candidate, Adlai Stevenson, desired. It said only that the decision brought "consequences of vast importance." An amendment pledging to carry out the Court's ruling was overwhelmingly defeated, and the final plank rejected the use of force "to interfere with the orderly determination of these matters by the courts." Both Presidential candidates, Eisenhower and Stevenson, said that they would not use troops to enforce a court integration order.

Only 1,238,038 Southern Negroes, or 25% of the voting population were registered to vote, compared to 1,008,614, or 20%, in 1952.

Almost 40% of Negro voters supported President Eisenhower, an increase of 19% over 1952. This was partly a reflection of the 1954 Supreme Court school desegregation ruling by a court led by an Eisenhower appointee, Earl Warren.

The Civil Rights Act of 1957 was first proposed in this year by President Eisenhower, but without the provision that the Justice Department could bring suit on behalf of Negroes denied the right to vote. Attorney General Herbert Brownell Jr. had failed to convince President Eisenhower to accept the provision. Not until the Presidential campaign was well under way did Eisenhower come out in support of Brownell's enforcement provision. The bill passed the House and reached the Senate on June 20, 1957.

Martin Luther King Jr. and almost 100 other Negroes were indicted on a charge of conspiring to conduct an illegal boycott in Montgomery, Ala. On March 22, King was sentenced to prison, but the case was settled by payment of a $500 fine. Shortly thereafter, the Supreme Court refused to review a similar case that originated in Columbia, S.C. The Court of Appeals in the case had ruled bus segregation unconstitutional, and it was widely thought that the Supreme Court had thus recognized the unconstitutionality of bus segregation. A dozen Southern cities promptly desegregated their buses. Actually, the Supreme Court had declined to review the case because it had to be retried. One outcome of the original confusion, however, was that the Montgomery bus company announced it was dropping its segregation seating policy. City officials then stated that they would arrest any driver who permitted integrated seating. Segregation continued, as did the boycott, with the company operating at a deficit. On May 11, Robert Carter, legal counsel for the NAACP, argued the case before the Federal District Court. On June 4, the court ruled against segregated seating. The case then went to the Supreme Court where on Nov. 13, the Court ruled that segregation on buses was unconstitutional. The city of Montgomery announced compliance, and in a mass meeting on Dec. 21 Montgomery Negroes agreed to end the boycott.

In May, Negroes began a bus boycott in Tallahassee, Fla.

In December, 21 Negroes in Birmingham, Ala., who defied Jim Crow bus laws were arrested.

On Jan. 10, an Interstate Commerce Commission ruling forbidding the segregation of interstate passengers took effect. Compliance in the South was uneven, but the Southern Railroad, the Louisville & Nashville and others removed the signs "white" and "colored" from their waiting rooms.

The Civil Aeronautics Board banned the use of Federal fun 's for building segregated airport facilities. When Jackson, Miss., refused to comply, funds earmarked for the renovation of the Municipal Airport were withheld.

By this year, 11 Southern cities had desegrated municipal golf courses, and the cities of Baltimore, Tulsa, Oklahoma City and San Antonio, Beaumont and Austin, Tex. had completely desegrated municipal parks.

Militant South, by Negro historian John Hope Franklin, was published.

Giovanni's Room, by the Negro writer James Baldwin, was published.

Gwendolyn Brooks, the Negro poet, published *Bronzeville Boys and Girls.*

Sammy Davis Jr., a Negro, was an immediate success in his first Broadway show, *Mr. Wonderful.*

At the Melbourne Olympics, the following American Negro athletes won gold medals: Charles Jenkins, 400-meter run; Lee Calhoun, 110-meter hurdles; Charles Dumas, high jump, an Olympic record; Gregory Bell, running broad jump; Ira Murchison, 400-meter relay; Lou Jones and Charles Jenkins, 1,600-meter relay; Milton Campbell, decathlon; Mildred McDaniel, women's high jump, an Olympic record. Negroes also won 3 silver and 2 bronze medals in the Olympics.

Don Newcombe, a Negro baseball player with the Brooklyn Dodgers, won the National League's Most Valuable Player and the Cy Young Awards.

Hank Aaron, a Negro baseball player for the Milwaukee

Braves, was the National League batting champion. He won this award again in 1959.

From this year through 1959, and again from 1960 through 1962, Floyd Patterson, a Negro, was the heavyweight boxing champion.

From this year through 1962, Joe Brown, a Negro, was the lightweight boxing champion.

1957

Total Negro income was $15.3 billion, compared to $248 billion for whites.

The median family income for whites was $5,166; for nonwhites, $2,764.

There were 14 Negro banks, with total assets of $46,-789,607.

The median of school years completed for people age 25-29 were: Male: white, 12.3 years; Negro, 9.4 years. Female: white, 12.3 years; Negro, 10.3 years.

Civil rights organizations staged a Prayer Pilgrimage; 27,-000 people assembled in Washington, D.C., on May 17.

Little Rock, Ark., was considered a "new South" city, with a moderate middle class and an enlightened Mayor, Woodrow Wilson Mann. Arkansas had integration at the university level, and Gov. Orval Faubus had never used race as a political issue. In fact, his election had been considered a liberal victory. The courts had approved an integration plan submitted by the Little Rock School Board, and it was to begin with the admission of a few Negro children to Central High School, on Tuesday, Sept. 3, 1957. On Monday night, in a totally unexpected move, Governor Faubus announced that he was posting National Guardsmen outside the school "to preserve order." On Tuesday, on the advice of the school board, no Negroes appeared. On Wednesday, nine Negro children tried to enter the school. They were turned away by the guardsmen and subjected to abuse from mob. Although President Eisenhower did not react to the posting of the Guardsmen, FBI agents were in Little Rock. In a reply to Governor Faubus' objections to integration, President Eisenhower said, "The Federal Constitution will be upheld by me by every legal means at my command." On

Sept. 9 the FBI presented a 400-page report to Federal District Judge Davies, who asked the U.S. Government to enter the case as a friend of the court. The Government promptly did so, and asked the judge to enjoin Governor Faubus from preventing integration. A hearing was set for 10 days later. Meanwhile, the guardsmen remained. On Sept. 20 Judge Davies granted the injunction against Governor Faubus. When school opened on Monday, Sept. 23, the Guardsmen were gone and nine Negro children went into the school. However, a mob of about 1,000 whites had gathered outside the school. While city police maintained order for a time, the situation threatened to turn into a violent riot, as whites advocated going into the school, dragging the "niggers" out and lynching them. At noon, city authorities ordered the Negro children out of the school. They left, and Daisy Bates, president of the Arkansas NAACP, said they "will not be out there again until they have the assurance of the President of the U.S. that they will be protected from the mob." The mob remained in front of the school on Tuesday, and no Negroes tried to enter the school. On Wednesday, President Eisenhower sent 1,000 members of the 101st Airborne Division into Little Rock, in addition to placing 10,000 Arkansas National Guardsmen on Federal service that morning. The nine Negroes, six girls and three boys, entered Central High School, and the mob was dispersed. The paratroopers left by the end of November, but a reduced number of federalized Guardsmen remained on duty until the end of the school year. On Oct. 3, fewer than 60 students participated in a walkout designed to protest the integration. Governor Faubus tried his best to maintain turmoil after the walkout; his charge the following week that paratroopers invaded the girls' dressing rooms was wholly unsubstantiated.

North Carolina began token desegregation in the cities of Greensboro, Winston-Salem and Charlotte.

Tennessee announced that desegregation of its 6 state colleges was to take effect in the fall of 1958.

In this year 38 school districts were desegregated.

A white South Carolina woman of an old and respected family had her house bombed because she wrote a mild article advocating a moderate approach to integration.

In Birmingham, Ala., a Negro clergyman was brutally beaten after attempting to enroll Negro children in an all-white school.

To save the Civil Rights Act from burial in the Judiciary Committee, dominated by Southerners, the Republican leadership proposed to bypass the committee and put the bill directly on the Senate calendar. Democrats, including John F. Kennedy and Lyndon B. Johnson, voted against this maneuver, but enough Democratic liberals joined the Republicans to succeed in bypassing the committee. In the Senate, Southern Democrats attacked Title III, a provision allowing the Justice Department to sue on behalf of any civil right, including desegregation of schools. Senator Russell of Georgia said he doubted President Eisenhower actually understood the provision. On July 3, the President was supposed to have confirmed Senator Russell's view when he told reporters that "there were certain phrases I didn't understand." Title III was stricken by the Senate. The rest of the bill was passed easily in August, after the majority leader, Lyndon B. Johnson, convinced the Southern senators that they could not seriously oppose the right to vote. This Civil Rights Act of 1957 established a commission to secure facts, assess the need for further legislation, etc., to set up a civil rights division in the Department of Justice headed by an assistant attorney general, and protected the right to vote. The U.S. Code was amended to affirm the right to vote in all elections and to sit on a grand jury or petit jury, regardless of race, color or previous condition of servitude. Opponents of civil rights succeeded in attaching an amendment to the bill. This provided that in cases of criminal contempt arising under the Civil Rights Act, the judge might impose up to $300 fine or up to 45 days in prison without a jury trial.

Adam Clayton Powell Jr. introduced an amendment to an appropriations bill for hospital construction. The amendment, which was defeated, provided that no Federal funds would be used for segregated hospitals.

In Montgomery, Ala., the end of segregated seating on buses led to violence. Martin Luther King Jr.'s home was shot at, and a Negro woman bus rider was wounded by a sniper. On Jan. 10, bombs exploded in four Negro churches and in the homes of two ministers, one Negro and one white, who had fought segregation. City officials suspended bus service completely for a short time.

As a result of the Montgomery bus boycott, the Southern Christian Leadership Conference (SCLC) was organized by Martin Luther King Jr., Bayard Rustin and Stanley Levinson. Ella Baker, a former field secretary for the NAACP and later of the Urban League, joined SCLC to organize mass meetings. The interracial organization sought to coordinate the activities of all non-violent protest groups in the U.S. It was committed to the goals of full citizenship and "total integration" in American life.

The NAACP, working with the President's Committee on Government Contracts and the International Association of Machinists, succeeded in having Negroes admitted to apprenticeship programs, training programs and previously all-white job levels in the aircraft industry.

Negroes were admitted into the International Brotherhood of Electrical Workers in Cleveland, and the Bricklayers, Masons and Marble Masons Protective Association in Milwaukee, Wis. It was accomplished in the latter case only after the AFL-CIO president, George Meany, and the International union threatened to revoke its charter.

New York State passed a law prohibiting racial discrimination in the operation of labor-management apprentice programs subsidized by any state agency.

Oregon, Washington, Massachusetts and New Jersey passed laws forbidding discrimination in public housing; the Sharkey-Brown-Isaacs Bill outlawed discrimination in private housing in New York City, the first such law in the U.S.

The white city officials of Tuskegee, Ala., redrew the city lines to exclude all but 10 of the 400 registered Negro voters. The Negroes responded with a boycott of local merchants.

To counteract Negro voter registration drives, the Georgia Elections Revision Committee proposed a constitutional amendment to disqualify persons from voting upon conviction of a felony and other lesser offenses.

For the first time since 1944, NAACP membership declined. This was generally attributed to harassment by Southern whites in both an official and private capacity. Because of the activities of the NAACP, Southern states tried to destroy or hinder the association. Texas and Arkansas passed laws to force the disclosure of the names and addresses of members. When NAACP officials refused to turn over membership lists, several were arrested in those states. In Georgia, an NAACP official was jailed when he refused to disclose financial records. Virginia and Tennessee outlawed NAACP legal aid to victims of discrimination on the grounds that it constituted barratry, maintenance and champerty. By December, the NAACP was involved in 25 court cases in which its right to function was at issue. In two cases, WATKINS V. U.S. and SWEEZEY V. NEW HAMPSHIRE, the Supreme Court ruled that due process applied not only to court procedure but also to state and Federal legislative branches. For the NAACP this meant protection against legislation directed against them by Southern states, especially the investigation committees set up in Florida, Louisiana and Virginia. In May, the Supreme Court decided to review the $100,000 contempt fine levied by an Alabama court in 1956 when the NAACP refused to turn over membership lists.

W. Robert Ming, a Chicago lawyer, became the first Negro elected to head the National Veterans Organization, the American Veterans Committee.

Notes of a Native Son, a collection of essays by the Negro writer James Baldwin, was published.

The Broadway musical, *Jamaica,* starred Negro singer Lena Horne.

The Land Beyond the River, by Lofton Mitchell, a Negro, had a successful run in an off Broadway theater in New York.

Simply Heavenly, by Langston Hughes, a comedy based on his *Simple* stories, after a successful run Off Broadway moved to Broadway for 62 performances.

Geoffrey Holder narrated the U.S. Steel TV production of *The Bottled Imp.* Holder, a native of Trinidad, is also known as a choreographer, painter, costume designer and author. In 1955 he had his first New York art exhibit at the Barone Gallery, which led to a Guggenheim fellowship; he has had a book of novellas, *Black Gods, Green Islands,* published; he appeared in the Broadway play *House of Flowers* as a dancer.

Hank Aaron, of the Milwaukee Braves, a Negro, was voted the Most Valuable Player in the National League. In this year, in 1963 and again in 1966, Aaron was the home-run champion of the National League.

From this year until his retirement from professional football in 1966, Jimmy Brown, a Negro, was All-League fullback and broke every existing ground-gaining record in the National Football League.

From this year through 1959, Hogan Kid Bassey, a Negro, was the featherweight boxing champion.

Charles Sifford, the first Negro member of the Professional Golfers Association, won the Long Beach Open Golf Tournament, the first such tournament won by a Negro.

1958

Total Negro income was $15.9 billion, compared to $260 billion for whites.

The median family income for whites was $5,300; for non-whites, $2,711.

In March, the Negro unemployment rate was 14.4%, the highest it had been in 11 years. The white unemployment rate was 6.9%.

Despite a massive voter registration drive by the NAACP and other organizations, the increase in Southern Negro registration from 1956 to 1958 was slight because of Southern resistance in the form of violence, intimidation and law. Georgia instituted a reading test for registration that was so difficult the political editor of the *Atlanta Constitution* conceded that probably no one could pass it. In 8 Southern states, where precise figures were available, the number of Negroes registered to vote was 1,028,827, compared to 1,074,672 in 1956. The percentages of Negroes 21 and over registered to vote in Southern states were: Mississippi, 3.4%; South Carolina, 12.5%; Alabama, 20.5%; Virginia, 24.1%; Arkansas, 27.6%; Georgia, 30.4%; Louisiana, 31.2%; North Carolina, 36%; Texas, 36.8%; Florida, 39.1%; Tennessee, 72.3%. In 28 counties in Southern states with Negro populations ranging up to 82% of the total population, there was not 1 Negro voter.

The U.S. Civil Rights Commission conducted an investigation in Macon County, Ala. The county, home of Tuskegee Institute and a literate Negro population which comprised

85% of the total county population, had only 28% of the Negroes registered to vote. Witnesses told the commission of delaying tactics, unfair tests, etc. The commission subpoenaed the voting officials and their records, but the officials refused to produce their records and often refused to testify. A court order finally allowed inspection of their voting files. The difficulties in Macon County and elsewhere led to the Civil Rights Bill of 1960. The commission also held a hearing in Montgomery, Ala., on the denial of voting rights, and prepared to hold hearings on discrimination in housing in New York City.

The University of Florida, as a result of an NAACP suit, was desegregated.

By this year, 400,000 Negro students attended desegregated schools, as opposed to 350,000 in 1957. Also, by 1958, 790 of 2,890 Southern and border-state school districts had been desegregated; 2½ million Negro children remained in segregated schools.

On Oct. 25, approximately 10,000 students, Negro and white, led by A. Philip Randolph, Jackie Robinson and Harry Belafonte, participated in the Youth March for Integrated Schools in Washington, D.C. President Eisenhower refused to see a delegation of the marchers' leaders.

The Spingarn Medal was awarded to Daisy Bates, head of the Little Rock NAACP branch, and the 9 students who integrated Little Rock's high schools.

In the face of segregationist pressure, the Little Rock School Board, late in the school year, asked a Federal judge to suspend the integration plan for 2½ years. Judge Lemley granted the request. The case was appealed and on Aug. 28 the Supreme Court heard the case of COOPER V. AARON; Cooper was a school board member, Aaron a Negro pupil. On Sept. 12 the Court rejected Judge Lemley's order for the suspension of integration, attacked evasive schemes and ruled that public funds could not be used to support private schools. Governor Faubus then closed all high schools in Little Rock to prevent "violence and disorder." The schools remained closed throughout 1958-59 school year. The mood was militantly segregationist in Little Rock. The moderate Congressman Brooks Hays was defeated by segregationist T. Dale Alford. The Legislature passed school closing laws; three members of the school board took a pro-Faubus view. Then the three segregationists were removed from the board by a recall election, and a Federal court found the school closing law unconstitutional.

To fight school desegregation, the Georgia Legislature suspended the compulsory attendance law in the case of a child forced to attend school with a member of another race.

The Supreme Court school desegregation decision had sparked a temporary rebirth of the Ku Klux Klan. The Klan claimed 100,000 new members since 1954, and 500 new chapters. But the Klan did not gain much power for several reasons: (1) the historic lack of respectability; (2) the White Citizens Councils, which were both well organized and respectable in the South; (3) large numbers of competing Klan and splinter groups.

In Monroe, N.C., two Negro boys, aged 8 and 9, were sentenced to a reformatory because they had been kissed by a white girl playmate.

Robert Nix, a Negro, was elected to the House of Representatives from Philadelphia, Pa.

In the 85th Congress several attempts were made to pass legislation that would have damaged the cause of Negro civil rights. The Jenner-Butler Bill denied the Supreme Court the right to review cases involving the right to practice law before state courts. If this bill had passed, it would have allowed Southern states to prevent NAACP lawyers from handling civil rights litigation. The Smith States' Rights Bill said that in a conflict between state and Federal law, state law would be valid unless Congress had specifically directed that the Federal Government had pre-empted the field. The bill passed in the House but died in the Senate by a vote of 41 to 40.

Because the filibuster had long been used by Southern Senators to prevent civil rights legislation from coming to a vote, civil rights groups and liberal Congressmen tried for several years to change the cloture rule. On March 26, the Senate Rules Committee approved by a vote of 5 to 4 Senate Resolution 17, sponsored by Paul Douglas. It provided for cloture two days after filing a petition, by a two-thirds majority of Senators present and voting, or 15 days after filing by a simple majority.

On Jan. 21, a special 3-judge U.S. District Court, in NAACP v. PATTY, held unconstitutional the Virginia laws which defined NAACP-sponsored litigation as illegal barratry; on Dec. 15, the Supreme Court upheld the lower courts decision. In a similar case, when a Federal court had dismissed an NAACP suit on behalf of a Negro who refused to take a segregated seat on a Memphis bus, because the plaintiff had ridden the bus only once and that time for the purpose of bringing suit, the Supreme Court ordered the lower court to decide the case on its merits, declaring that a lawsuit could not be disregarded even if the suit arose from a contrived situation.

The Supreme Court voided the $100,000 fine imposed on the NAACP by an Alabama court for its refusal to disclose its membership lists. The case was remanded to the Alabama court for further adjudication.

NAACP membership was 334,543 in this year.

By the end of the year, the President's Commission on Government Contracts, chaired by Vice President Nixon, had 60 cases pending, some filed as far back as April, 1955. The NAACP charged that two U.S. Air Force representatives investigating a case for the committee attempted to intimidate the complainants. The NAACP found that the companies which the committee had investigated and reported as making satisfactory progress, such as Esso Standard Oil, had made extremely minor and peripheral changes.

Through the efforts of the NAACP, Anheuser-Busch Breweries adopted a policy of nondiscrimination and began hiring Negroes for nonunion jobs. At the same time, the Teamsters Union adopted a nondiscriminatory policy for membership. Negroes then could be hired for union jobs in the brewing industry.

Boeing Aircraft in Wichita and National Cash Register in Dayton, Ohio, opened apprentice training programs to Negroes.

At the merger convention of the AFL and CIO, a program had been announced to end segregation in the labor movement. By 1958, however, the Brotherhood of Railway and Steamship Clerks had defied an order of the New York State Commission Against Discrimination to merge two segregated locals in New York. The Brotherhood of Locomotive Firemen and Enginemen had successfully defended in the Federal Court of Appeals in Cincinnati the right to exclude Negroes from membership, and 13 unions had complaints filed against them with the President's Committee on Government Contracts.

In MING V. HORGAN, the Superior Court of Sacramento, Calif., ruled that the developers of FHA-aided dwellings might not discriminate in the sale of such dwellings.

As a result of NAACP campaigns, public housing projects were desegregated in Erie, Pa., and Trenton N.J.

The three states—New York, Colorado and Michigan—in which open housing bills were introduced failed to pass such legislation.

The NAACP Youth Council conducted a sit-down campaign in Oklahoma City, Okla., that resulted in the desegregation of 39 lunch counters. In Wichita, Kans., after 4 days of sit-ins, the Dockum Drugstore chain began to serve Negroes throughout the state.

Ella Baker set up the Southern Christian Leadership Conference office in Atlanta, Ga., and became its first full-time executive secretary.

Martin Luther King Jr., Negro leader of SCLC, was stabbed in the chest by a Negro woman while autographing books in Harlem.

From this year through 1966, Dorothy I. Height served as a member of New York State's Social Welfare Board; long active in women's organizations, she was later president of the National Council of Negro Women.

Jay S. Redding's novel, *The Lonesome Road*, was published.

Eartha Kitt, Sammy Davis Jr., Frederick O'Neal and Rex Ingram, all Negroes, starred in the film version of *Anna Lucasta*.

In this year and in 1959, Ernie Banks, a Negro baseball player, with the Chicago Cubs, won the National League's Most Valuable Player award. In 1958 and 1960, he was the home-run champion of the league.

Virgil Akins, a Negro, was the welterweight boxing champion.

1959

Total Negro income was $17.4 billion, compared to $283 billion for whites.

The median family income for whites was $5,643; for non-whites $2,917.

There were 272,541 Negro farm operators in the U.S. The peak was 926,000 in 1920, 267,000 of whom were in the South. Of all Negro farmers 24% grew tobacco, and cotton remained the most important crop.

Voter registration campaigns that had been going on for more than 10 years in the face of heavy white opposition began to have an effect on local politics. In Tennessee, Negroes were elected to the Nashville and Oak Ridge city councils. Negroes were elected to several North Carolina city councils, among them was Mrs. J. J. Hannibal, the first Negro to be elected to public office in Kinston, N.C. In Virginia, State Senator Haddock, a white moderate, received the support of Negro voters, and won against the Byrd machine candidate in the July primary. In Mississippi, two archsegregationists were beaten in local elections in Hinds County.

A major voter registration drive was conducted in Memphis, where 15,000 Negroes were added to the voting roles.

Set up by the 1957 Civil Rights Act, by April of 1959 the Civil Rights Commission had on file 291 voting complaints from the South, including 119 from Alabama, 95 from Louisiana and 41 from Mississippi.

The Civil Rights Commission report of July 31 pointed out the "consistent denial of equal protection of the law as regards voting in 6 Alabama counties." The commission's report showed how whites were allowed to register, although making the same mistakes as Negroes who were refused.

In Louisiana, State Senator Rainach led a campaign to remove Negroes from the voting rolls. In Washington Parish, for example, 1,377 out of 1,517 Negroes were dropped from the list.

When the Civil Rights Commission went to Louisiana to investigate the prevention of Negroes registering to vote, the state attorney general secured an injunction prohibiting the commission from operating. The injunction was upheld by a

3-judge Federal Court, but the commission appealed to the Supreme Court.

The population of Fayette County in western Tennessee was 68.9% Negro, but only 17 Negroes voted between 1952 and 1959, according to the Justice Department. In the spring, the Fayette County Civic and Welfare League was organized to register Negroes by Memphis lawyer J. F. Estes. By the winter of 1959, Negro landowners who had registered to vote began to be refused crop loans for the coming season.

The Civil Rights Commission had to be renewed by the end of the first session of Congress or it would go out of existence. On Sept. 16, the last day of the session, an amendment was tacked onto a security appropriations bill which extended the life of the commission for two years and gave it funds for one year.

The White Citizens Councils achieved their greatest political victory in Mississippi, when in this year Ross Barnett was elected Governor. He was reputed to be a Council member. Whether he was or not, the Councils worked closely with the candidate to build a strong political machine.

The first reported lynching since 1955 occurred in Poplarville, Miss., when Mack Charles Parker, charged with the rape of a young white mother, was taken from jail 48 hours before his trial. On April 25, at the request of Governor Coleman, the FBI entered the case and conducted an extensive investigation. Its findings were submitted to a county grand jury in November, which refused to consider the evidence or acknowledge that a lynching had occurred within its jurisdiction. The county prosecutor dismissed the evidence as hearsay. On Nov. 5, the attorney general announced that the FBI findings would be submitted to a Federal grand jury by a U.S. District Attorney.

In May, Roy Wilkins suspended Robert Williams as president of the Monroe, N.C., branch of the NAACP when he advocated meeting "violence with violence" and "lynching with lynching."

A law passed in Arkansas making it illegal for state agencies to employ a member of the NAACP, was declared unconstitutional by the U.S. District Court.

In Louisiana, a U.S. District Court enjoined enforcement

of a state law that required NAACP branches to give their membership lists to the Louisiana Secretary of State.

Rep. Emmanuel Celler of New York, attempted to restore Title III, a provision which had been deleted from the 1957 Civil Rights Act. Title III allowed the Attorney General to seek injunctions on behalf of people denied civil rights. The Celler bill also provided for an extension of the Civil Rights Commission, and penalties for persons who obstructed school desegregation. The House Judiciary Committee deleted the provisions that would have provided means of enforcement.

The median of school years completed by people age 25 to 29 were: Male: white, 12.5; nonwhite, 10.9. Female: white, 12.4; nonwhite 11.0.

This year 19 school districts were desegregated.

On April 18, Roy Wilkins, A. Philip Randolph, Martin Luther King Jr., Daisy Bates, leader of the Little Rock integration campaign, Jackie Robinson and Harry Belafonte led 26,000 high school and college students in a second Youth March for Integrated Schools in Washington, D.C.

By the end of the year, five states—Alabama, Georgia, Louisiana, Mississippi and South Carolina—had not begun even token desegregation. In Prince Edward County, Va., the school board abolished the public school system rather than follow a court desegregation order.

In 17 border and Southern states and the District of Columbia, of a total of 3,000,000 Negro school-age children, only 182,100 were attending classes with white children.

In North Carolina, only 34 Negro pupils attended school with whites.

Georgia passed several laws to maintain school segregation. One authorized the Governor to close any school ordered integrated. Another allowed credit on the state income tax for contributions to segregated private schools. The Governor was authorized to pay the fees and expenses of counsel in school desegregation court cases. A bill aimed at the NAACP permitted suits against organizations rather than individuals, as the law had previously provided.

In the summer the newly elected Little Rock Board of Education decided to reopen the Little Rock schools, again on an integrated basis. City police maintained order as three Negro students entered Central High School, and three Negro students entered Hall High School. The mobs and the tension gradually faded, and token desegregation had taken place.

The Landrum-Griffin Act authorized Negro workers to sue for the abolition of auxiliary locals.

A. Philip Randolph criticized the AFL-CIO leadership at the National Convention for not having eliminated discrimination against Negroes. Later in 1961 Randolph was publicly censured by the executive committee, and blamed by AFL-CIO president George Meany for having created the Negro antagonism toward organized labor.

The "sit-in" campaign begun in 1958 grew. Negro and white college students desegregated eating facilities, mainly near college campuses in St. Louis, Chicago and Bloomington, Ind.

Miscegenation laws were repealed in California, Idaho and Nevada.

California passed a civil rights bill prohibiting discrimination in business establishments, business and vocational schools and professional groups. California also passed a law prohibiting discrimination in publicly assisted housing.

Oregon enlarged its antidiscrimination housing laws to include private housing.

The Urban Renewal Administration rescinded its quota system. Previously, privately built FHA 221 housing for relocation tenants had occupancy restricted by race percentage quotas.

A Raisin in the Sun, a play by Lorraine Hansberry, a Negro, became a landmark in Broadway history. Beside a Negro cast, it was produced and directed by Negroes Dave Cogan and Lloyd Richards. Jesse Shipps had been the last Negro to direct a Broadway play, *Abyssinia*, in 1907.

John Oliver Killens wrote the original screenplay for the movie, *Odds Against Tomorrow*, starring Harry Belafonte, Robert Ryan and Ed Begley.

Dorothy Dandridge, a Negro, made one of her most successful film appearances in *Porgy and Bess*, co-starring with Sidney Poitier. She had similar success in 1962 in *Carmen*

Jones with Harry Belafonte, Pearl Bailey and Diahann Carroll.

Odetta, a Negro folksinger, gave her first major concert at Town Hall. In 1960 she was the featured singer at the Newport Folk Festival.

Elgin Baylor, a Negro twice All-American, was named the Most Valuable Player in the basketball All-Star game.

From this year through 1965, Wilt Chamberlain, a Negro, was the National Basketball Association scoring champion.

From this year through 1963, Davy Moore, a Negro, was featherweight boxing champion.

1960

U.S. Census: There were 18,871,831 Negroes in the U.S., representing 10.5% of the population.

For the first time, more than half the nation's Negroes lived outside the Deep South.

For the first time, a Northern state, New York, had a higher Negro population than any Southern state.

The percentage of Negroes in the total population in each region in the U.S. was: Northeast, 16%; North Central, 18.3%; South, 59%; West, 5.8%.

Between 1950 and 1960, the intercensal migration of nonwhites was: 541,000 nonwhites moved to the Northeast; 558,-000 nonwhites moved to the North Central States; 332,000 nonwhites moved to the West; 1,457,000 nonwhites moved away from the South.

Of all Southern Negroes 58% lived in cities. In the North 96% of Negroes were urban, and in the West, 93%.

The percentage of the population of Negroes in selected metropolitan areas was: Baltimore, 21.9%; Boston, 3%; Chicago, 14.4%; Cleveland, 14.9%; Detroit, 14.9%; Los Angeles, 6.9%; New York, 10.5%; Philadelphia, 15.5%; St. Louis, 14.3%; Washington, D.C., 24.3%.

The life expectancy of male whites was 67.4 years; of Negroes, 61.1 years; of female whites, 74.1 years; of female Negroes 66.3 years.

The infant mortality rate per 1,000 live births was: white, 22.9; Negro, 43.2

One out of 3 Negro married women above 14 years of age

was divorced or separated. For white women the ratio was 1 out of 5.

Of Negro families with children under 18, 21% had female heads; the rate for whites was 6%.

Total executions under civil authority were 56: 35 Negroes and 21 whites. This included charges of murder, 26 Negroes and 18 whites; of rape, 7 Negroes and 1 white.

Total Negro income was $19.7 billion, as compared to $300 billion for whites.

The median income of white and nonwhite wage and salary workers by sex was: male—white, $5,137; Negro, $3,075; female—white, $2,537; Negro, $1,276.

Of all Negroes 75% earned less than the white average yearly income of $5,981.

Percentage of employed Negroes in relation to total employed by occupation in different parts of the U.S. in 1960:

	Northeast	North Central	South	West
Males:				
Professional, technical, etc.	3.6	3.0	2.8	4.5
Managers, officials, proprietors	2.7	1.8	1.4	2.3
Clerical	8.9	6.8	2.9	7.2
Craftsmen, foremen, etc.	11.5	11.0	8.6	12.9
Service, exclusive of private household	15.6	15.0	12.7	17.8
Laborers, except farm & mine workers	15.2	17.6	23.1	18.2
Farmers & farm managers	0.1	0.2	7.1	0.5
Farm laborers and foremen	0.8	0.7	11.4	2.3
Females:				
Professional, technical	8.4	6.8	7.5	7.5
Managers, officials, proprietors	0.9	1.1	1.0	1.3
Clerical	12.6	12.5	3.5	13.3
Private household workers	24.8	22.0	45.0	28.0

Negroes made up approximately 2.5% of all self-employed business men in the U.S.

The number of employed Negro workers in selected professions per 10,000 Negro population was: physicians and surgeons, 2%; dentists, 1.1%; lawyers, 1.1%; college professors, 1.9%; teachers, 16.4%; musicians and music teachers, 3%; clergymen, 7.4%; social workers, 3%; pharmacists, 1%.

Unemployment rates were: white male, 4.8%, and female 5.3%; nonwhite male, 10.7%, and female, 9.5%.

Of the Negro population, 38%, or approximately 1.5 million families, were home owners. In the North, 10.4% of the homes owned were substandard and 14.6% overcrowded. For whites the substandard figure was 3.6% and for overcrowded housing, 7.1%. In the South, 29.8% of homes owned by Negroes were substandard as opposed to 5.5% for whites, and 22.8% of Negro homes were overcrowded as opposed to 8.5% for whites.

Approximately 28% of Negroes of voting age in the South were registered to vote compared to between 60-70% of Northern Negroes. The percentages of Negroes of voting age registered to vote in the South were: Texas, 32%; Arkansas, 30%; Louisiana, 22%; Mississippi, 4%; Alabama, 14%; Tennessee, 59%; Virginia, 19%; North Carolina, 25%; South Carolina, 11%; Georgia, 22%; Florida, 26%.

The Civil Rights Act was signed by President Eisenhower on May 6. It authorized judges to appoint referees to aid Negroes in registering and voting, and also provided criminal penalties for bombing and mob action designed to obstruct court orders. Persons registered by referees were eligible to vote only in Federal elections.

The NAACP conducted major voter registration drives throughout the South, especially in big cities such as Jacksonville, Tampa, Tallahassee, Savannah, Nashville, Memphis and Little Rock. In some areas—Haywood County, Tenn., for example—Negroes registered for the first time since Reconstruction.

In Fayette County, Tenn., Negro tenant farmers who attempted to register were evicted by white landlords. Local wholesalers refused to deliver goods to local Negro store owners. In response, Tent City, 13 tents in an open field housing up to 100 dispossessed Negro families, was set up. Aid was contributed by a variety of sources. The Federal Government, using the new Civil Rights Act, stepped in with injunctions that forbade local officials to block Negro registration. Landlords were also told that if they proceeded with evictions, they would have to prove in court that the evictions were not attempts to interfere with voting rights. By the end of the year approximately 1,000 Negroes had registered and voted.

In a unanimous decision in U.S. v. RAINES, the Supreme Court upheld the Lousiana Federal Court ruling that the names of 1,377 Negro voters be returned to the voting lists in Washington Parish. A White Citizens Council drive had brought about the removal of the names under a Louisiana law that permitted any two voters to challenge the right to vote of a third.

The Democratic Party platform said: "The peaceful demonstrations for first-class citizenship which have recently taken place in many parts of this country are a signal to all of us to make good at long last the guarantees of our Constitution. The time has come to assure equal access for all Americans to all areas of community life, including voting booths, school rooms, jobs, housing and public facilities. The Democratic Administration which takes office next January will therefore use the full powers provided in the Civil Rights Acts of 1957 and 1960 to secure for all Americans the right to vote. . . . We will support whatever action is necessary to eliminate literacy tests and the payment of poll taxes as requirements for voting. A new Democratic Administration will also use its full powers, legal and moral, to ensure the beginning of good-faith compliance with the Constitutional requirement that racial discrimination be ended in public education. We believe that every school district affected by the Supreme Court's school desegregation decision should submit a plan providing for at least first step compliance by 1963, the 100th Anniversary of the Emancipation Proclamation. For this, and for the protection of all other Constitutional rights of Americans, the Attorney General should be empowered and directed to file civil injunction suits in Federal courts to prevent the denial of any civil rights on grounds of race, creed or color." The platform also supported establishment of a Fair Employment Practice Commission, the strengthening of the President's Commission on Civil Rights, and the ending of discrimination.

The Republican Party platform read: "This nation was created to give expression, validity and purpose to our spiritual heritage, the supreme worth of the individual. In such a nation, a nation dedicated to the proposition that all men are created equal, racial discrimination has no place. It can hardly be reconciled with the Constitution that guarantees equal protection under law to all persons. In a deeper sense, too, it is immoral and unjust. As to those matters within reach of political action and leadership, we pledge ourselves to its eradication." The platform further pledged: "Continued vigorous enforcement of the civil rights laws to guarantee the right to vote to all citizens in all areas of the country," completion of six grades of school as an adequate literacy test for voting, support of school desegregation court orders, support of "legislation to authorize the Attorney General to bring actions for school desegregation in the name of the U.S. in appropriate cases, as when economic coercion or threat of physical harm is used to deter persons from going to court to establish their rights."

The Socialist Party platform supported legislation "requiring the Federal Government to initiate legal action on behalf of school integration, voting rights, or any other civil right"; "adoption of the principle that only integrated institutions shall qualify for Federal funds"; depriving states of representation in Congress in proportion to the number of citizens that they deprive of the right to vote because of race; ending *de facto* segregation in Northern schools as well as *de jure* segregation in the South; open-occupancy legislation, FEPC legislation, "nonviolent mobilization of Negroes and whites for a direct challenge to Jim Crow wherever it exists."

The Negro vote was a crucial factor in this year's elections. Both parties campaigned actively for the Negro vote; in the last days of the campaign Martin Luther King Jr. was arrested in Atlanta for taking part in a sit-in. John F. Kennedy, the Democratic Presidential candidate, called Mrs. King to express his concern, and sent his brother Robert to talk to the judge who had sentenced King. The next day King was set free. Kennedy aides widely publicized this event. In Illinois, which Kennedy won by only 9,000 votes, approximately 250,000 Negroes voted for him. Michigan was won by Kennedy by 67,000 votes, with 250,000 of his votes coming from Negroes. South Carolina was won by 10,000 votes, and Kennedy received approximately 40,000 Negro votes. In 1956, Eisenhower had carried Nashville's three Negro wards by 3,258 to 2,861. In this election, Kennedy won them by 5,710 to 2,529. The largely Negro 6th A.D. in Brooklyn, N.Y., was carried by Stevenson by 13,754 to 8,973 in 1956. Kennedy won it by 22,777 to 5,808. An estimated 70% of the Negro vote went to Democrats.

The National States Rights Party (NSRP), an anti-Negro, anti-Semitic, organization, nominated Orval Faubus for the Presidency of the U.S. Although Faubus declined the nomination, the NSRP polled 28,952 votes in Arkansas and 169,572 in Louisiana, a total of 214,549 votes.

Mississippi ratified five constitutional amendments. One made the public school system a "permissive" rather than "mandatory" function. This meant that state and Federal courts could not require schools that had been closed to avoid integration to reopen, because the state was no longer required to operate a public school system. The Legislature also passed a law giving local school boards the power to close schools to "preserve the public peace."

This year saw the rapid spread of the sit-in. The idea caught on when, on Feb. 1, four Negro college students from North Carolina A&T sat at a Woolworth lunch counter in Greensboro, N.C., and refused to move when they were denied service. The sit-in spread to some 50 Southern towns. Eating facilities were desegregated in 108 Southern and border cities. The sit-ins led to wade-ins at segregated beaches, read-ins at segregated libraries, kneel-ins at segregated churches, etc. By September 1961, over 70,000 Negro and white students had taken part in sit-ins. About 3,600 students had been arrested. Over 141 students and 58 faculty members had been expelled by colleges for their part in such protests. The NAACP legal staff defended over 1,600 students who had been arrested in 12 Southern states for sit-in activities.

The students who had begun the sit-in in Woolworth's in Greensboro, N.C., ran into strong white opposition. Needing adult aid, they appealed to George Simpkins, president of the local branch of the NAACP. Simpkins called the New York office of the Congress of Racial Equality. CORE sent Len

Holt to Greensboro, N.C, to conduct sessions in the techniques of nonviolent direct action by simulating conditions protesters would have to face. Martin Luther King Jr. also came to Greensboro, as did Herbert Wright, youth secretary of the NAACP.

Twelve days after the Greensboro incident, 40 students from Fisk University sat in at a Nashville Woolworth lunch counter. After 4 days, 76 students were in jail, and the local NAACP pledged support. The house of the Negro attorney who defended the students, Z. Alexander Looby, was bombed, but by early May, 4 theaters and 6 lunch counters had been desegregated. Part of this success was because other Negroes supported the students and began a full-scale boycott of white merchants. Nashville political leaders and businessmen had to negotiate with the Negro community, and on May 10 Negroes entered 6 downtown Nashville stores and were served along with white customers.

A sit-in demonstration in Chattanooga, Tenn., on Feb. 23 led to a race riot.

The first sit-in demonstration in the Deep South was in the Montgomery, Ala., courthouse, by Alabama State College Students. The Alabama State Board of Education expelled 9 students for participation.

San Antonio, Tex., integrated lunch counters on March 16. It was the first large Southern city to do so.

Ella Baker, executive secretary of the Southern Christian Leadership Conference, asked that SCLC support be given to the sit-in campaign. King agreed, and $800 was provided. On April 15, at Shaw University, the SCLC sponsored a meeting of 200 students, 126 of them from the South. At this meeting the Student Non-Violent Coordinating Committee (SNCC) was formed. Ed King was selected temporary administrative secretary. It was decided that SNCC would retain close ties with SCLC, but would remain independent of it.

In May, SNCC met at Atlanta University. Martin Luther King Jr. and Ella Baker attended, as did Len Holt from CORE and observers from the National Student Association. Marion Barry was elected chairman, and it was decided to open an office, hire a secretary, raise money and, attempt to coordinate student activities throughout the South. In

October, at a conference of several hundred delegates in Atlanta, SNCC was formally established. The organization consisted of a delegate from each of 16 Southern states and Washington, D.C. There is no membership in SNCC *per se,* because it is, as it is named, a coordinating committee.

Kneel-in demonstrations in white Atlanta churches by 20 Negro and white students were held. As a result, acid was thrown at Lonnie King, a protest leader.

Ten days of sit-in demonstrations led to a race riot in Jacksonville, Fla., in which 50 people were injured and both white and Negro demonstrators were beaten.

Wade-ins by Negroes at a beach in Biloxi, Miss., ended in a race riot in which 10 Negroes were wounded by gunfire.

On Oct. 17, four national chain stores announced integration of lunch counters in about 150 stores in 112 cities in North Carolia, Virginia, West Virginia, Kentucky, Texas, Tennessee, Missouri, Maryland, Florida and Oklahoma.

The "selective patronage movement" of boycotts organized by 400 Negro ministers forced the hiring of Negroes in Philadelphia. At Sun Oil, Gulf Oil, Tastee Baking and Pepsi-Cola, approximately 600 Negroes were hired for white-collar jobs.

South Carolina was the scene of increasingly militant Negro activity and corresponding white reaction. In Orangeburg, tear gas and water hoses were used against approximately 1,000 demonstrating Negroes, 388 of whom were arrested, tried and fined.

The Negro American Labor Council was founded by A. Philip Randolph as a result of AFL-CIO recalcitrance on discriminatory practices. Cleveland Robinson, long a Negro labor leader, became its president in 1966.

In BATES V. LITTLE ROCK, the Supreme Court reversed the conviction of Daisy Bates, leader of the Little Rock desegregation movement, for refusing to furnish to city officials the NAACP membership lists. The unanimous opinion of the Court was that the city desired the lists to infringe on the freedoms of speech and peaceable assembly.

In the beginning of the year, Judge J. Skelly Wright of the U.S. District Court ordered New Orleans officials to submit a school integration plan by May 16. When they failed to do so, he formulated his own plan but granted delay of execution until Nov. 14. On Nov. 6, the Louisiana Legislature met to pass a series of statutes designed to prevent integration. Judge Wright immediately declared them unconstitutional. When the school board voted to comply with the order, Shelby Jackson ordered schools closed, and the Legislature suspended the school board creating a legislative committee to take charge of schools. The New Orleans School Board refused to recognize the committee. The Legislature then ordered state police to make sure schools were closed on Monday, Nov. 14. On the 14th, however, U.S. deputy marshals, with the cooperation of New Orleans police, escorted 5 first-grade Negro girls to 2 white schools. White parents boycotted the schools, stoned Negroes and clashed with police. A Negro family involved in the desegregation was forced to leave town. By the end of December, the Negro children attended schools that were almost entirely empty.

For Negroes 25 years and over, the percentages of those completing a number of school years were:

Number of school years attended	Males in %	Females in %
None	6.4	4.2
1-4 years	21.9	15.6
5-7 years	23.9	24.5
8 years	12.3	13.4
1-3 years of high school	17.3	20.0
4 years of high school	17.3	14.3
1-3 years of college	4.1	4.1
4 years of college	2.8	3.3
Median averages	7.7	8.6

Of Negroes between the ages of 14 and 15, 90% were enrolled in schools as opposed to 94.5% of whites. Between the ages of 16 and 17, 73% of the Negroes and 82% of the whites were enrolled; between the ages of 18 and 19, 38% of the Negroes and 43% of the whites, and between the ages of 20 and 24, 11% of Negro males and 21% of white males.

The number of school districts desegregated in this year was 17.

Four Southern states—South Carolina, Georgia, Alabama and Mississippi—had not undertaken any school integration. Houston, Tex., schools desegregated (Houston had had the largest segregated school system in the nation), and more Negroes attended integrated schools in Little Rock.

The new Clinton (Tenn.) High School opened peacefully. The old high school had been destroyed by dynamite in October, 1958, when integration was originally attempted.

Negroes were admitted to previously all-white schools in Chapel Hill, Durham and Raleigh, N.C., without incident.

In New Rochelle, N.Y., the first challenge to *de facto* school segregation was made. Housing segregation and gerrymandering of school board zones had created all-Negro and all-white schools. Since the local NAACP did not act on the demands of Negro parents, they themselves hired Paul Zuber, a Negro attorney from New York City. Zuber filed a lawsuit for open enrollment, and the Lincoln School case was won in 1961.

Roi Ottley, Negro journalist and author died at the age of 54. He wrote *New World a-Coming* in 1943 and *Black Odyssey* in 1948.

The Bean Eaters, a book of poetry by Negro Gwendolyn Brooks, was published.

From this year through 1965, LeRoi Jones, a Negro, edited *Yugen,* a prominent Beat poetry magazine.

Shadows, a film directed by John Cassavetes, depicted the problems of the Negro in certain parts of New York City.

Camilla Williams, Negro operatic soprano and winner of the Marian Anderson Award in 1943 and 1944, gave a special performance at the White House.

Chubby Checker, a Negro singer, born Ernest Evans in Philadelphia, set America off on a new dance craze when he introduced "The Twist," a multi-million dollar record.

At the Rome Olympics, the following American Negroes won gold medals: Lee Calhoun, 110-meter hurdles; John Thomas, high jump; Ralph Boston, running broad jump, an Olympic record; Otis Davis, 600-meter relay; Rafer Johnson, decathlon, Olympic record; Cassius Clay, light heavyweight boxing; Wilma Rudolph, 100-meter dash, Olympic record, and 200-meter dash. The women's 400-meter relay consisted of 4 Negroes: Martha Johnson, Lucinda Williams, Barbara Jones and Wilma Rudolph. Their victory set an Olympic and world record. Negroes also won 3 silver and 2 bronze medals.

Benny Kid Paret, a Negro, was welterweight boxing champion for 1960-61 and again for 1961-62.

1961

The median income of white and Negro wage and salary workers by sex was: male white, $5,287; female white $2,538; Negro male, $3,015; Negro female, $1,302.

President John F. Kennedy created the President's Committee on Equal Employment Opportunity and appointed Vice President Lyndon B. Johnson chairman.

The NAACP had 1,494 branches, with 388,334 members.

In December, over 700 demonstrators against segregation and discrimination, including Martin Luther King Jr., were arrested in Albany, Ga.

Arrested students in Rock Hill, S.C., refused to pay fines and asked for jail sentences instead, beginning the jail-in movements sponsored by SNCC.

After a riot at the University of Georgia on Jan. 11, two Negro students were suspended. A Federal Court order obtained their reinstatement on Jan. 16.

The Supreme Court reversed convictions of 16 sit-in demonstrators arrested in Baton Rouge, La.

A Freedom Ride campaign was begun by 13 CORE members, headed by James Farmer, and later joined by SNCC. An integrated group set out from Washington, D.C., on May 4 for a bus ride through the South to test compliance with integration orders of the Interstate Commerce Commission and Federal courts. They were attacked at several stops. After an attack in Montgomery, Ala., on May 20, Attorney General Robert Kennedy sent 600 U.S. marshals. Governor Patterson declared martial law and called out the National Guard. In Jackson, Miss., 27 of the Freedom Riders were arrested.

In September, the ICC forbade segregation on buses and in terminal facilities of interstate commerce.

In this year, Minnesota, New Hampshire, New Jersey, New York and Pennsylvania passed laws barring discrimination in private housing. Colorado, Connecticut, Massachusetts and Oregon already had such laws.

Augustus Hawkins, a Negro, was elected to the U.S. House of Representatives from California. He was re-elected in 1962, 1964 and 1966.

Adam Clayton Powell Jr., Negro of New York, became chairman of the Education and Labor Committee of the House of Representatives.

The American Dental Association directed all its societies to remove from their by-laws any discriminatory provisions in membership requirements. However, the Committee to End Discrimination of the association reported in 1965 that most Negro dentists in the 11 Southern states were still not able to join the ADA.

In the Lincoln School case, Federal District Court Judge Irving A. Kaufman ruled against the *de facto* segregation of Lincoln School in New Rochelle, N. Y. He ordered the Board of Education to present plans for desegregation.

Atlanta, Dallas, Memphis, Tampa and Galveston desegregated their schools peacefully. By the end of the year only Mississippi, Alabama and South Carolina had admitted no Negroes to white schools.

A group of American black nationalists demonstrated in favor of Patrice Lumumba, the dead Premier of the Congo, disrupting a U.N. debate.

There were 51 Black Muslim temples and missions in the U.S.

Whitney Young became executive director of the National Urban League.

Robert Weaver, a Negro, became Administrator of the Federal Housing and Home Finance Agency, the highest post held by an American Negro up to that time.

Thurgood Marshall was appointed to the U.S. Circuit Court of Appeals by President Kennedy.

James B. Parsons, a Negro, was appointed to Federal District Court. He was the first Negro to be a Federal District judge in the continental U.S.

Clifton R. Wharton, a Negro, became U.S. Ambassador to Norway. He was formerly Minister to Rumania, having been appointed in 1957.

Fred Moore became the first Negro sentry to guard the

Tomb of the Unknown Soldier in Arlington National Cemetery.

Reconstruction After the Civil War, by the Negro historian John Hope Franklin, was published.

James Baldwin's second book of essays, *Nobody Knows my Name,* equaled his first in all respects. Edmund Wilson reviewed it for the *New Yorker* magazine, and called Baldwin the best Negro writer ever produced in the U.S.

Night Song, a novel by John A. William, a Negro, was published. It is based loosely on the life of Charlie Parker.

Preface to a 20-Volume Suicide Note by LeRoi Jones, a Negro, was published. A collection of his early poetry, it has little about politics or social consciousness.

Purlie Victorious by Negro playwright Ossie Davis opened on Broadway.

Godfrey Cambridge, a Negro, won the Obie Award for best actor in Genêt's *The Blacks.* Cambridge is also known for numerous other acting roles, TV and public appearances.

Diana Sands, the Negro actress, appeared in the film version of *A Raisin in the Sun.*

Dick Gregory, a Negro, began his career as a comedian in the Chicago Playboy Club.

Alvin Ailey, a Negro, started the Alvin Ailey American Dance Theater. Ailey has toured in Europe and acted and danced as an individual in the U.S.

Roberto Clemente, a Puerto Rican Negro with the Pittsburgh Pirates, was National League batting champion.

Orlando Cepeda, a Puerto Rican Negro with the San Francisco Giants, was the National League home-run champion.

Bill Russell, a Negro, won the President's Trophy of the National Basketball Association as the most valuable player in professional basketball in this year and in 1962 and 1963.

Harold Johnson, a Negro, was light heavyweight boxing champion through 1963.

Emile Griffith, a Negro, was welterweight boxing champion in 1961, again from 1962 through 1963, and then from 1963 through 1967.

1962

The President's Committee on Equal Employment Opportunities ordered desegregation of Southern paper mills.

Almost 5% of all Negroes were employed by the Federal Government, representing 13% of all Federal employees.

In November, President Kennedy issued an executive order forbidding racial or religious discrimination in federally financed housing.

From this year through 1965, many states enacted civil rights legislation. Massachusetts, Indiana and Oklahoma enacted school desegregation laws. California and Oklahoma required that Negro history be taught. Arizona, Iowa, Maine, Kansas, Maryland, Montana, Missouri, Nebraska, Nevada, New Hampshire, Utah, Wyoming and the District of Columbia passed fair employment practice legislation. Indiana, Maine, Ohio, Rhode Island, Wisconsin enacted fair housing laws. Arizona, Missouri, Nevada and Utah barred discrimination in public accommodations.

Alaska passed an open-occupancy law.

In June, President Kennedy appointed the President's Committee on Equal Opportunity in the Armed Forces. The following year, when the committee's report was submitted, Secretary of Defense Robert MacNamara issued a policy statement directing military commanders to oppose discriminatory practices affecting military personnel and their dependents, both on and off military bases.

Percentages of Negroes as officers and enlisted men for each military service were: Army: officers, 3.2%, enlisted men, 12.2%. Air Force: officers, 1.2%, enlisted personnel, 9.2%. Navy: officers, 0.3%, enlisted personnel, 5.2%. Marines: officers, 0.2%; enlisted personnel 7.6%.

The Navy announced the assignment of the first Negro to command a U.S. warship—Lt. Cmdr. Samuel L. Gravely, to destroyer escort *U.S.S. Falgout.*

Marjorie Lawson, a Negro lawyer and Federal adviser, was appointed a judge for the District of Columbia by President Kennedy.

Edward R. Dudley, a Negro, was elected Borough President

of Manhattan. He had served as Minister to Liberia from 1948 through 1953.

There were 9 Negroes in the Legislature in Illinois, 9 in Michigan, 11 in Pennsylvania, 6 in New York, 6 in Missouri, 4 in Maryland, 3 in California and 1 in Georgia. The Georgia legislator was elected from Atlanta as a State Senator. He was the first Negro elected to the Georgia Legislature in over 90 years.

In the Albany Movement, Martin Luther King Jr. and SNCC, CORE and NAACP members joined in a campaign against segregation and discrimination in the Georgia city of Albany.

Supreme Court Justice Hugo Black ruled that the University of Mississippi had to admit James Meredith, a Negro Air Force veteran, who had applied 14 months before. Gov. Ross Barnett, on radio and TV, defied the Federal court order and promised to go to jail if necessary to prevent integration of the state university. He personally denied Meredith entrance, overruling the Board of Higher Education, which had agreed to accept the court order. Barnett was found guilty of civil contempt of Federal court and ordered to purge himself of contempt or pay $10,000 a day and face arrest. U.S. marshals escorted Meredith to the University of Mississippi on Sept. 30. Rioting broke out on the campus, resulting in the death of 2 persons and the injury of 100, and the calling up of 12,000 Federal troops, and National Guardsmen. Meredith was admitted, but 300 troops remained on the campus until July, 1963.

In 17 Southern and border states and Washington, D.C., 246,988 Negro pupils, or 7.6% of all Negro pupils, attended integrated classes.

Johnny Mathis was listed by *Ebony* as one of the 35 U.S. Negro millionaires, the only entertainer in this group. Mathis was born in 1935 in San Francisco, and was a star track athlete at San Francisco State College. Discovered as a singer in 1955, Mathis quickly became one of the most popular singers of the late 1950's and early 1960's.

Another Country by James Baldwin was published. The novel chronicles Negro-white relations with several sets of characters all living in Manhattan. It was a critical failure but a financial success.

A Different Drummer, a novel by Negro William Melvin Kelly, was published. It was highly praised and concerns the rejection by Negro farmers in a small town of white Southern paternalism.

The novel *Let No Man Write My Epitaph,* by Negro Willard Motley, was published.

A Ballad of Remembrance, by a Negro, Robert Hayden, was published. This was his third collection of verse.

The well-known Negro actor James Earl Jones received the Daniel Blum Theater Award.

Moon on a Rainbow Shawl by Errol John, a Negro playwright, opened off-Broadway in New York City.

Maury Wills, a Negro baseball player with the Los Angeles Dodgers, was voted the National League's most valuable player. In an Associated Press poll, he was named Athlete of the Year by American sportswriters.

Tommy Davis, also with the Dodgers was National League batting champion in this year and in 1963.

Sonny Liston, a Negro, was heavyweight boxing champion through 1964.

1963

Negroes owned or controlled 13 banks and about 50 life insurance companies and 34 federally insured savings and loan associations. The combined assets of these institutions was $764 million, or 0.12% of the total assets of such institutions in the U.S. The average Negro bank was one-fifth as large as the average bank in the country. It had $5.6 million in assets, compared to the average of $25.8 million.

In August, about 250,000 people took part in the March on Washington led by A. Philip Randolph and Bayard Rustin. About 60,000 of the participants were white. Martin Luther King Jr. said on the steps of the Lincoln Memorial: "I have a dream that one day this nation will rise up and live out the true meaning of its creed: 'We hold these truths to be self-evident; that all men are created equal.'"

Although the AFL-CIO had passed resolutions favoring Negro rights, its executive council refused to endorse the 1963 March on Washington.

Howard Jenkins Jr., a Negro, after serving in the Department of Labor since 1956, was appointed to the National Labor Relations Board.

In the fall term, 9.2% of Negro public school students in the South and border states were attending classes on an integrated basis.

In this year there were over 10,000 racial demonstrations, such as sit-ins and pray-ins, and over 5,000 American Negroes were arrested for their part in them.

In his inaugural address, Gov. George Wallace of Alabama said, "I draw the line in the dust and toss the gauntlet before the feet of tyranny and I say segregation now, segregation tomorrow, segregation forever."

Because of pressure from President Kennedy two Negro students were registered at the University of Alabama, despite protests by Governor Wallace. Soon after, President Kennedy became the first American President to say that segregation was morally wrong.

In April, Martin Luther King Jr. announced a drive against discrimination in Birmingham, Ala. The campaign which began with sit-ins, soon involved confrontations between demonstrators and Police Chief Eugene "Bull" Connor, and led to the arrest of King and his followers. On May 1, King called Birmingham school children into the campaign. On May 10, the Negro leader announced an agreement with the Senior Citizens Committee, composed of top business and professional men of the city, providing for desegregation of lunch counters, rest rooms, etc., the hiring and upgrading of Negro workers, release of the demonstrators (2,400 had been arrested) and establishment of a bi-racial committee. The agreement was denounced by "Bull" Connor and the Ku Klux Klan. Bombing of Rev. A. D. King's home and the Gaston Motel headquarters of the campaign set off a riot by thousands of Negroes for most of the night of May 11. About 50 people were injured.

A bomb thrown into the 16 St. Baptist Church in Birmingham, Ala., killed 4 children and injured 21 people. Later the same day, 2 Negro youths were killed in Birmingham, 1 by a policeman.

William L. Moore, a white postman from Baltimore, was

shot to death in April near Attalla, Ala., on a 1-man march through the South to protest racial segregation.

There were demonstrations in Savannah, Ga., in June, July and August. On June 12, 3,000 demonstrators marched, demanding desegregation of movie theaters, restaurants, hotels, motels and bowling alleys. On June 14, the Savannah Chamber of Commerce urged businesses to serve the public without regard to race, creed or color. On July 11, police used tear gas and fire hoses to turn back a march of 2,000 Negroes on police headquarters. The marchers were protesting the arrest of over 100 demonstrators the previous day, including their leader, Hosea Williams. In riots stemming from the demonstration and the police action to break it up, 2 Negroes were shot and 70 persons arrested. On Aug. 2, two committees representing 100 businessmen and civic leaders agreed to begin desegregation of hotels, motels, bowling alleys and some theaters, and on Oct. 1, Negro leaders agreed to a 60-day ban on street demonstrations. However, several groups of Negro demonstrators refused to recognize the agreement, because it did not provide for the release from jail of Hosea Williams and because restaurants were not included in the desegregation.

In June, a desegregation campaign in Cambridge, Md., led to open confrontations between Negroes and whites, resulting in several injuries. The violence continued until National Guard troops arrived and martial law was declared. Despite a truce between Negro leader Gloria Richardson and white Mayor Calvin W. Mowbray, arranged by Attorney General Robert Kennedy, limited martial law was required for a year.

In Mississippi, where White Citizens Councils were most powerful (they received more than $160,000 in public funds), the councils were the moving force behind the defeat of ex-Gov. J. P. Coleman in the gubernatorial election. Coleman was a moderate on segregation, and the councils backed Lt. Gov. Paul Johnson, who won by a landslide.

SNCC workers organized a mass voter registration campaign in Greenwood, Miss. which comedian Dick Gregory joined. Armed officers with dogs tried to prevent registration. The Justice Department asked Federal courts to enjoin harassment of would-be-voters.

In demonstrations led by Medgar Evers against segregation

in Jackson, Miss., 700 persons, including NAACP secretary
Roy Wilkins, were arrested. On June 12, Medgar Evers was
shot to death outside his home in Jackson. On the day Evers
was buried, President Kennedy sent to Congress a bill guaranteeing equal rights in public accommodations and giving the
Attorney General power to sue for enforcement of the 14th
and 15th Amendments. The bill also forbade discrimination in
state programs receiving Federal aid, in labor unions, in
employment and in voting.

Police in Danville, Va., broke up a demonstration, injuring
50 demonstrators. Over 300 were arrested in the next 2
months.

In the case of GANTT v. CLEMSON AGRICULTURAL COLLEGE
OF SOUTH CAROLINA, it was decided that Clemson College
must admit Harvey Gantt, a Negro. South Carolina was the
last state to maintain an all-white college and university
system.

In Detroit, 200,000 persons marched in opposition to
discrimination.

In June, 3,000 students boycotted Boston public schools to
protest *de facto* segregation.

In Chicago, 220,000 Negro children, about half the total
school enrollment, boycotted schools to protest *de facto* segregation and the policies of Supt. Benjamin C. Willis. The boycott symbolized the shift of the civil rights movement from
the South to the North, causing a hardening of Northern white
attitudes and decline in the popularity of President Kennedy.
In Chicago, Detroit, New York and Cleveland, whites began
to organize to protect "neighborhood schools" and white
neighborhoods. The PAT in New York was one such group.

California, Michigan and Washington passed open-occupancy laws.

In October and November in New York City, the Community Council on Housing led by Jesse Gray began rent
strikes against slum-lords. The courts would not order eviction
of striking tenants on the ground that the landlords were not
entitled to rent until they repaired their buildings.

A Gallup poll found that 21% of whites thought demonstrations helped the Negroes. This figure dropped to 10% in
1964. According to the Gallup poll, 72% of Negroes were for

demonstrations. In 1964, the poll found 55% of Negroes were in favor of demonstrations.

A Harris poll found that 91% of the Negroes questioned approved of the NAACP; 59% approved of CORE.

Carl T. Rowan, a Negro journalist, was appointed Ambassador to Finland. He served also as deputy assistant Secretary of State, U.N. alternate delegate and director of the U.S. Information Agency (1964).

The Emancipation Proclamation by Negro historian John Hope Franklin was published.

In his essay *The Fire Next Time*, James Baldwin, a Negro, wrote of the civil rights movement and the racial tensions in the U.S. which he felt made violence inevitable.

LeRoi Jones, a Negro, wrote *Blues People*, a non-fiction study of Negro blues music and the way in which it reflects the Negro experience in the U.S. It is considered by many to be his best work. Jones also edited *The Moderns,* an anthology of short stories, mostly by white Beat authors.

Sissie by John A. Williams, a Negro, was published. It portrays successive generations of a Negro family in the rural South and then in the urban North.

And Then We Heard Thunder, a novel by John Oliver Killens, a Negro, was published. Largely autobiographical, it is about discrimination in the Army during World War II. It was very well received and was nominated for the Pulitzer prize.

Walk in Darkness by Negro playwright William Hairston and *Tamborines to Glory* by Langston Hughes opened off-Broadway in New York City.

Sidney Poitier was awarded an Oscar for best actor of the year for his portrayal of a Negro who befriends an order of nuns in *Lilies of the Field*.

Claudia McNeil, a Negro actress, who has appeared in movies, Broadway plays and TV, was nominated for an Emmy award for her role in "Express Stop from Lenox Ave." on the CBS-TV series, *The Nurses*.

Andre Watts, a Negro, made his debut as a concert pianist at the age of 16, when he substituted for Glenn Gould with the New York Philharmonic under Leonard Bernstein at Philharmonic Hall. He was greeted with great critical acclaim.

Elston Howard, a Negro baseball player with the New York Yankees, was named the American League's Most Valuable Player.

Willie McCovey, a Negro baseball player with the San Francisco Giants, was the National League's home-run champion.

1964

The Civil Rights Act of 1964 forbade discrimination in public accommodations and employment. It allowed the Attorney General to institute suits and to deny Federal funds to local agencies which practiced discrimination. During debate on the bill, the U.S. Senate imposed cloture for the first time on a civil rights bill to end a Southern filibuster. President Johnson signed the bill on July 2.

The Civil Rights Act was contested almost immediately in the cases of KATZENBACH V. MCCLUNG and HEART OF ATLANTA V. U.S. Both were defended by the Attorney General's office, and the Supreme Court upheld the validity of the act's non-discrimination clauses for restaurants and motels, respectively.

In Mississippi, civil rights workers Michael H. Schwerner, and Andrew Goodman, whites, and James E. Chaney, Negro, were murdered by local whites.

In the case of HAMILTON V. ALABAMA, the Supreme Court reversed a conviction for contempt of court of Mary Hamilton. The conviction stemmed from her refusal to answer questions of an Alabama state prosecutor who addressed her as "Mary" instead of using courtesy title as was common with whites.

Rev. K. L. Buford and Stanley Smith were elected to the Tuskegee City Council, the first Negroes elected to public office in Alabama in the 20th century.

A court order opened the public schools of Prince Edward County, Va., after they had been closed for 5 years to avoid integration. However, in 1967, the educational system was essentially still segregated, the whites in private schools and the Negroes in public schools.

A school boycott by Negroes in New York kept 464,000 students out of class in a February demonstration and

267,000 in a March demonstration. In Cleveland a school boycott involved 68,000 pupils, about 86% of the Negro students. Cincinnati's school boycott involved 26,455 pupils, and Chicago had a school boycott involving 172,350 pupils. The Boston school boycott involved 20,000 pupils.

In 17 Southern states and Indiana and Wyoming, existing laws prohibited marriage between whites and Negroes.

Desegregation and actual Negro-white attendance in southern schools was as follows:

State	% of districts desegregated	%of Negro attendance with whites
Florida	31.3	2.65
Louisiana	4.5	1.12
Texas	33.8	7.26
Oklahoma	82.6	31.7
Arkansas	10.5	0.811
Mississippi	2.7	0.02
Alabama	6.7	0.032
Georgia	6.1	0.377
South Carolina	14.8	0.10
North Carolina	49.1	1.41
Tennessee	43.3	5.33
Missouri	95.8	44.1
Kentucky	99.4	62.5
Virginia	63.3	5.07
West Virginia	100.0	88.1
Maryland	100.0	51.7
Delaware	100.0	57.8
Washington, D.C.	100.00	86.0

Lemuel A. Penn, a Washington Negro school administrator, was shot and killed as he drove through Georgia, returning from Army Reserve duty at Fort Benning, Ga.

At the end of March, rioting broke out between Negroes and whites in Jacksonville, Fla. Whites and Negroes were injured, and over 200 Negroes arrested. Rioting Negro students and bystanders had stoned police, firemen, newsmen and school officials outside the Negro high school when police arrived to search the building after a bomb threat. About 12 to 15 Negroes attacked a 54-year-old white man in a mixed neighborhood. A bi-racial committee tried to ease tension.

In a riot in Harlem in July, 1 person was killed, 140 injured and 500 arrested. It was set off by the killing of a 15-year-old

Negro boy by an off-duty policeman. Molotov cocktails were used by Negroes in their attacks on white-owned stores and on policemen.

As a result of the Harlem riots, violence spread through the Borough of Brooklyn.

A riot in Rochester, N.Y., began on July 24 when policemen arrested a Negro man for allegedly molesting a Negro woman at a street dance. The rumor spread that the arrest had involved police brutality. In the ensuing riot 5 people were killed (3 in the crash of an official observation helicopter) and 750 people were arrested for looting, rioting and unlawful possession of firearms. About 75% of those arrested were Negroes. Governor Rockefeller sent National Guardsmen to restore order.

A riot in Jersey City, N.J., in August was touched off by a Negro's objection to police treatment of a Negro woman being arrested on a charge of drunkenness. The riot was characterized by attacks on police and looting of stores. About 450 policemen were used to control the rioters. By the evening of Aug. 5, the city was comparatively quiet.

A race riot erupted in Paterson, N.J., in August, when teen-age Negroes threw rocks at police cars. On the second night approximately 100 civilians were involved.

Fighting broke out between approximately 200 whites and Negroes at a Keansburg, N.J., amusement park. A police car and police garage were burned by white youths, according to the police report; four Negroes and 11 whites were arrested.

Rioting began in Dixmoor, a Chicago suburb, on Aug. 16 after a rumor spread about an attack by the white owner of a liquor store on a Negro woman who was accused of shoplifting a bottle of gin. Nearly 1,000 Negroes clashed with 225 state troopers and other policemen; 31 Negroes were arrested. About 50 persons, mostly white, were injured. The liquor store was looted, 2 houses were set on fire and 50 cars were damaged. The next day the liquor store was set on fire, and police who tried to disperse the crowd of 100 Negroes were met with gunfire. Tear gas and dogs were used to restore order.

A riot in Philadelphia began with the arrest of a Negro man for blocking traffic. Rumors of police brutality spread rapidly, even though the arresting officer was a Negro; 2 persons were killed and several hundred injured.

After the summer riots, a split occurred in the civil rights movement when Roy Wilkins of the NAACP spoke of "criminal elements" in the demonstrations.

Malcolm X resigned from the Black Muslims and formed the Organization for Afro-American Unity to promote self-defense and coordination with newly independent African nations, Negro control of communities and Negro conversion to the Moslem faith.

Of the 92,869 persons arrested on Federal charges in 1963 and 1964, parolees, probationers and serious state violators arrested under Fugitive Felon Act, 71.5% were white, and 28.5% were nonwhite.

In response to the violence of the summer, President Johnson expanded the War on Poverty and appointed Sargent Shriver as head of the Office of Economic Opportunity (OEO). In 1968 he appointed Aileen C. Hernandez, a Negro and an expert on labor education, to the Equal Employment Opportunity Commission.

Jean Noble, a Negro educator, headed the OEO committee which planned the Girls' Job Corps.

In July, as a result of numerous NAACP suits, the National Labor Relations Board refused to recognize unions that admitted members according to race.

The 24th Amendment to the Constitution eliminated the poll tax requirement for voting in Federal elections.

In the case of ANDERSON v. MARTIN, it was decided that racial designations of candidates might not appear on the ballot.

Approximately 38% of Negroes of voting age in the South were registered to vote, compared to 60% or 70% of Northern Negroes. The percentage of voting age Negroes registered by states was: Alabama, 21.6%; Arkansas 43.5%; Florida, 51.1%; Georgia, 39.1%; Louisiana, 31.6%; Mississippi, 6.7%; North Carolina, 45%; South Carolina, 34.2%; Tennessee, 67.2%; Texas, 57.7%; Virginia, 27.7%.

Approximately 1,000 volunteers were involved in the Mississippi Summer Project organized by COFO (Council of

Federated Organizations, representing SNCC, CORE, SCLC and NAACP) to register Negro voters. There were 1,000 arrests, 35 shooting incidents, 30 buildings bombed, 35 churches burned, 80 people beaten and at least 6 murders during the period of the campaign.

Gov. George Wallace of Alabama won 34% of the Democratic Presidential primary vote in Wisconsin, 30% in Indiana and 43% in Maryland. He appealed to the "backlash" among white working-class voters against civil rights movements.

The Freedom Democratic Party was founded in Mississippi in April. It was "open to all Democrats in Mississippi of voting age, regardless of race, creed or color." In August, the Freedom Party sent a delegation to the Democratic National Convention in Atlantic City, demanding to be seated instead of the regular Mississippi Democrats. They failed in this attempt, but they did receive an offer for 2 of their members to be admitted to the convention as delegates-at-large with full voting rights, and they forced the imposition of loyalty oaths on the regular Mississippi delegation. The delegation refused the offer of 2 at-large seats. Instead, they staged sit-ins in the seats of the Mississippi delegation, which had been vacated by delegates refusing to take the loyalty oath.

The Democratic Party platform said: "The Civil Rights Act of 1964 deserves and requires full observance by every American, and fair, effective enforcement if there is any default. Ending discrimination based on race, age, sex, or national origin demands not only equal opportunity, but the opportunity to be equal. We are concerned not only with people's rights to be free, but also with their ability to use their freedom."

The Republican Party platform read: "The [Democratic] administration has exploited interracial tensions by extravagant campaign promises without fulfillment, playing on the just aspirations of the minority groups, encouraging disorderly and lawless elements, and ineffectually administering the laws." The party platform pledged: "Full implementation and faithful execution of the Civil Rights Act of 1964, and all other civil rights statutes, to assure equal rights and opportunities guaranteed by the Constitution to every citizen"; "improvements of civil rights statutes adequate to changing needs of our times"; "such additional administrative or legislative

actions as may be required to end the denial for whatever unlawful reason, of the right to vote." It also said the party
intended to help assure equal opportunity and a good education for all, while opposing Federally sponsored "inverse
discrimination," whether by the shifting of jobs or the abandonment of neighborhood schools for reason of race. The
platform further pledged "to open avenues of peaceful progress in solving racial controversies while discouraging lawlessness and violence."

The Socialist Workers platform said that the party supported "independent Negro political action of the type manifested in the call for a Freedom Now Party." The party was
for: "Full economic, social and political equality for the
Negro people, and for all other minority groups. Solidarity
with mass actions aimed at securing these rights as exemplified
in the rent strikes, school boycotts, picketing of construction
sites, public demonstrations and sit-ins. Uphold the right of
self-defense against white supremacists' violence." The Socialist Workers advocated compensation of minorities for
disadvantages they had suffered, and the teaching of Negro
and African history in schools.

Nearly 6 million Negroes voted for the Democratic Presidential ticket, largely because the Republican candidate, Barry
Goldwater, had voted against the Civil Rights Bill of 1964 as
a Senator from Arizona. The total Negro vote for Democrats
was estimated at 95%.

John Conyers Jr., a Negro, was elected to the U.S. House
of Representatives from the 1st District in Michigan. He was
re-elected in 1966 by 85% of the vote of his district.

Constance Baker Motley, a Negro NAACP lawyer, was
elected to the New York State Senate in a special election in
February. She was the first Negro woman to hold this
position.

J. Raymond Jones, a Negro, was elected New York City
Democratic leader.

In the election of this year, California voters supported 2-1
a proposition guaranteeing the right to sell or lease or decline
to sell or lease property. They thus nullified California's open-
occupancy law, the Rumford Act.

The American Medical Association voted unanimously for

a resolution that it was "unalterably opposed to the denial of membership, privileges and responsibilities in the county medical societies, and state medical associations to any duly licensed physician because of race, color, religion, ethnic affiliation, or national origin."

Martin Luther King Jr. received the Nobel Prize for Peace on Dec. 10 in Oslo, Norway.

In this year and 1965, Franklin H. Williams, a Negro lawyer, was U.S. Representative to the Economic and Social Council of the UN. He was later Ambassador to Ghana.

Carl T. Rowan, the Negro Ambassador to Finland, was named by President Johnson to head the U.S. Information Agency. Rowan thus became the first Negro to sit on the National Security Council.

A Bent House, a novel, and *Cages*, a book of verse, were published by the Negro writer Owen Dodson.

A collection of short stories, *Dancers on the Shore* by William Melvin Kelley, a Negro, was published. Some of these stories deal with racial themes, and all prove Kelley to be an accomplished short-story writer.

Ralph Ellison, a Negro, published a collection of short articles and essays, *Shadow and Act*.

Dutchman, an absurdist one-act play, similar to works by Ionesco, was produced. It brought the playwright, LeRoi Jones, a Negro, to immediate prominence. It is a parable showing how the white man seduces and exploits the Negro, both physically and psychologically. Jones' second collection of verse, *The Dead Lecturer*, was published in this year. His poetry now included racial themes and reflected his increasingly anti-white philosophy.

Blues for Mr. Charley by a Negro, James Baldwin, ran on Broadway at the ANTA Theater and was moderately successful.

The Broadway play, *The Sign in Sidney Brustein's Window* by Lorraine Hansberry, a Negro, showed her assimilationist attitudes in that it was exclusively concerned with whites and their problems.

Golden Boy, starring the Negro entertainer Sammy Davis Jr., was produced on Broadway.

Adrienne Kennedy, a Negro and a member of the Actors Studio, was praised for her performance in Martin Duberman's play *In White America*. In this year, her allegorical play *Funnyhouse of a Negro* opened at the Cricket Theater in New York City and was praised by the critics.

Frank Silvera, a Negro actor-director-producer whose movies include *Hombre* and *Mutiny on the Bounty* and who played Nat Turner in the off-Broadway production of *Black Moses,* produced and directed his first Broadway play, *The Amen Corner.*

A Negro, Geraldine McCullough, won the George D. Widener Gold Medal at the Pennsylvania Academy of Fine Arts Exhibition. Her abstract sculpture *Phoenix* was done in welded steel and copper.

The following American Negroes won gold medals at the Tokyo Olympics: Robert Hayes, 100-meter dash; Henry Carr, 200-meter dash; Hayes Jones, 110-meter hurdles; Paul Drayton and Robert Hayes, 400-meter relay, an Olympic and world record; Wyomia Tyus, women's 100-meter dash. Negroes also won 5 silver medals and 2 bronze medals.

Arthur Ashe Jr. became the first Negro named to the American Davis Cup Team. In 1968 Ashe became the top ranked American tennis player when he won the National Open and the Men's Singles Tournament at Forest Hills, N.Y.

In this year and again in 1965, Roberto Clemente of the Pittsburgh Pirates, a Puerto Rican Negro, was the National League batting champion. Clemente won the league's Most Valuable Player award in 1966.

In this year and again in 1965, Tony Oliva of the Minnesota Twins, a Cuban Negro, was the American League's batting champion.

Lennie Moore, a Negro football player with the Baltimore Colts, was the National Football League's scoring leader.

Oscar Robertson, a Negro, won the President's trophy of the National Basketball Association as the most valuable player in professional basketball.

Muhammed Ali (Cassius Clay) won the heavyweight boxing championship.

1965

President Johnson in a speech at Howard University on June 4 pledged himself to fight for full equality for Negroes: "Freedom is not enough. You do not wipe away the scars of centuries by saying now you're free to go where you want and do as you desire and choose the leaders you please. You do not take a person who for years has been hobbled by chains and liberate him, bring him up to the starting line of a race and then say you're free to compete with all the others, and still justly believe that you have been completely fair."

Social Security Administration figures listed nonwhites as 34% of the poor in the U.S. They represented 30% of the rural poor and 31% of the urban poor.

President Johnson on March 15 called a joint session of Congress to pass a voting rights bill, saying "[We] must overcome the crippling legacy of bigotry and injustice. And We Shall Overcome." Passed five months later the Voting Rights Act of 1965 eliminated all qualifying tests for registration which abridged the rights to vote on the basis of race or color. The Attorney General was given the power to determine the purposes of such tests and to take legal action against local boards of elections.

In 25 states commissions had been established to combat discrimination.

On March 7, a massive march from Selma to Montgomery, Ala., was led by Martin Luther King Jr. and John Lewis of SNCC. The march was in protest against the killing of Jimmie Lee Jackson and the arrest of about 1,000 demonstrators in the voter registration campaign in Selma. About 500 marchers took part. On Edmund Pettus Bridge in Selma they were halted by 200 state troopers and sheriff's deputies with tear gas, clubs and whips. The filming of this scene on TV sent thousands of whites and Negroes to Selma to join the march. Later three white Unitarian ministers were beaten. One of them, Rev. James J. Reeb, died. On March 21, the second Selma to Montgomery march began under protection of the Alabama National Guard, federalized by President Johnson after Governor Wallace refused to guarantee the safety of the marchers. Four days later, 40,000 rallied in Montgomery, Ala.

Despite NAACP disapproval, Martin Luther King Jr. called for a national boycott of Alabama products and an end to Federal aid to the state.

On March 25, Viola Liuzzo, a 39-year-old white civil rights worker from Detroit, Mich., was shot and killed on Highway 80 by Klan members after the rally in Montgomery, Ala.

Jonathan Daniels was killed and Robert F. Morrisroe wounded by a shotgun fired by a special deputy sheriff in Haynesville, Ala. Daniels, an Episcopal seminary student from Massachusetts, and Morrisroe, a Roman Catholic priest from Chicago, were white civil rights workers in Lowndes County, Ala.

From January to July, Bogalusa, La., was the site of KKK activities and Negro demonstrations led by CORE, and was marked by frequent violence between whites and Negroes.

In April, Martin Luther King Jr. led a civil rights march from Roxbury to Boston Common in Massachusetts.

On Feb. 21, Malcolm X was assassinated during a rally at the Audubon Ballroom in New York City.

In August, rioting in Watts, a suburb of Los Angeles, was set off by the arrest of 21-year-old Marquette Frye, an unemployed Negro, for drunken driving. For 5 days, beginning Aug. 11, Negroes looted, attacked whites and police, burned buildings and controlled the streets until they were subdued by 13,000 National Guardsmen called out on Friday, Aug. 13. In all, 34 persons were killed, 1,032 injured, 4,000 arrested. Property damage was estimated at $40 million, and 200 businesses were totally destroyed and 700 were heavily damaged. An 8-man commission headed by former CIA head John A. McCone investigated the riot.

In a riot in Chicago's West Side on Aug. 12-14, about 80 persons were injured and 140 arrested. Disorder broke out when a Negro woman was killed by a fire engine from an all-white fire station. 500 Chicago policemen subdued the disorder which involved 1,000 people at its height.

Negro mobs smashed store windows and burned a car in North Philadelphia on Aug. 16.

In April, the Federal Government set the fall of 1967 as the final deadline for the beginning of integration in school systems trying to obtain Federal aid.

Of Federal Government employees 13% were Negroes. They included 13% in the Department of Defense, 16% in the Post Office, 25% in the Veterans Administration, 14% in the Treasury Department, 20% in the Department of Health, Education and Welfare, 34% in the General Services Administration, 13% in the Department of Commerce, 11% in the Department of State, 21% in the Department of Labor.

Thurgood Marshall became Solicitor General of the U.S.

Hobart Taylor Jr., a Negro, was appointed a director of the Export-Import Bank.

Samuel Clifford Adams Jr., a Negro, was appointed Overseas Director of the Agency for International Development. He had previously worked on many government educational programs in Africa and Southeast Asia.

Bennetta B. Washington, a Negro educator, became the Director of the Women's Job Corps in the Office of Economic Opportunity.

James M. Nabrit Jr., a Negro, was appointed as U.S. Ambassador to the U.N.

Patricia R. Harris became the first Negro woman appointed to an ambassadorial post abroad when she was made Ambassador to Luxembourg.

Maj. Gen. Benjamin O. Davis Jr., was named a lieutenant general in the U.S. Air Force. This was the highest rank yet obtained by a Negro in the armed services.

Constance Baker Motley, a Negro, was elected Borough President of Manhattan in New York City, the highest elective post ever held by a Negro woman.

Pope Paul VI appointed Rev. Harold Robert Perry auxiliary bishop of the New Orleans Archdiocese. He thus became the first American Negro Roman Catholic bishop in the 20th century.

The Autobiography of Malcolm X was published. In it he explained his conversion to the Muslim faith and his ideas of a new black nationalism.

John Oliver Killens, a Negro, published a documentary account of the civil rights movement in the South, entitled *The Black Man's Burden.*

John A. Williams, a Negro, published a record of his

travels in the U.S., *This Is My Country, Too*. In this book and in a TV documentary that he wrote in 1964, *Journey to Nigeria*, he affirmed that his real roots were in the U.S and not in Africa.

Manchild in the Promised Land by Claude Brown, a Negro, was published. An autobiography, the book gives a graphic account of Brown's life as a child and young man in Harlem.

LeRoi Jones' first novel, *System of Dante's Hell*, was published. A Negro, Jones uses his experience in Newark's ghetto for the story.

The novel *A Drop of Patience* by William Melvin Kelley, a Negro, tells the story of a blind Negro jazz musician.

The Catacombs by William Demby, a Negro, was published. Largely autobiographical, the novel tells of the international film colony in Rome of which Demby was a part.

The Amen Corner by James Baldwin was produced at the Barrymore Theater on Broadway.

The Toilet and *The Slave,* 2 one-act plays by LeRoi Jones opened off-Broadway. Jones in this year founded the Black Arts Repertory Theater. It was closed down when its parent organization, HARYOU, discovered a cache of guns in the basement.

Quincy Jones, a Negro, wrote the musical score for the movie *The Pawnbroker*.

Jane White, Negro actress, won an Obie for her performance as Princess Navara in Joseph Papp's production of *Love's Labors Lost*.

James Brown, Negro singer and the leading exponent of the big beat and soul music, grossed over $1 million and in 1966 was ranked second in the Billboard Campus Popularity Poll, behind Bob Dylan. Brown was born in Augusta, Ga., and originally trained to be a boxer. In 1968 he performed to a capacity audience at Yankee Stadium in New York City.

Zoilo Versalles, a Negro baseball player with the Minnesota Twins, was named the Most Valuable Player in the American League.

Gale Sayers, a Negro professional football player for the Chicago Bears, in his rookie year broke the NFL touchdown record and was chosen Rookie of the Year.

1966

In the U.S. 47% of all Negroes lived in the South and 53% in all other states. Negroes made up 26% of the population of cities with 1,000,000 or more people; 20% in cities with 250,000 to 1,000,000 people; 12% in cities with under 250,000 people; 4% of the population of suburbs and 10% in other areas.

The percentage of families of incomes of $7,000 or more was: Negroes, 28%; white 55%. The percent distribution of family income was: under $3,000, Negroes 32%, whites 13%; $3,000-$4,999, Negroes 24%, whites 14%; $5,000-$6,999, Negroes 17%, whites 19%; $7,000-$9,999, Negroes 16%, whites 25%; $10,000-$14,999, Negroes 9%, whites 20%; $15,000 and over, Negroes 3%, whites 10%. Median income: Negro, $4,481; white, $7,517.

Negroes constituted 11% of the total employed population. Some representative percentages by occupations were: professional and technical, 6%; teachers except college, 10%; clerical, 6%; sales, 3%; craftsmen and foremen, 6%; private household workers, 42%; protective services, 5%; waiters, cooks, bartenders, 16%; farmers and farm workers, 13%.

Despite Title VII of the Civil Rights Act of 1964, the following industries had unions which practiced discrimination: railroads, steamships, paper and pulp manufacturing, chemicals and oil refining, printing, skilled metal trades, tobacco manufacturing, Great Lakes shipping, building and construction, and various craft industries.

The white unemployment rate was 3.3%; the nonwhite unemployment rate was 7.3%.

In the school year 1966-67, an average of 15.9% of the Negro students in 11 Southern states attended integrated schools. The figures for individual states were: Texas, 44.9%; Arkansas, 15.1%; Louisiana, 3.4%; Mississippi, 2.5%; Alabama, 4.4%; Tennessee, 28.6%; Georgia, 8.8%; Florida, 22.3%; South Carolina, 5.6%; North Carolina, 15.4%; Virginia, 25.3%.

An average of 52.8% of Negroes of voting age were registered in 11 Southern states at the end of the summer. The figures for individual states were: Texas, 61.6%; Arkansas, 59.7%; Louisiana, 47.1%; Mississippi, 32.9%; Alabama,

51.2%; Tennessee, 71.7%; Georgia, 47.2%; Florida, 60.9%; South Carolina, 51.4%; North Carolina, 51%; Virginia, 46.9%.

Kivie Kaplan of Boston became president of the NAACP.

Floyd B. McKissick succeeded James Farmer as national director of CORE.

In May, Stokely Carmichael became the new head of SNCC.

Stokely Carmichael of SNCC and Floyd McKissick of CORE began to champion Black Power.

In June, President Johnson held a White House Conference on Civil Rights. It was boycotted by SNCC and attacked by CORE.

In July, at the NAACP Convention, Roy Wilkins, the executive secretary, said of Black Power: "We of the NAACP will have none of this. . . . It is the ranging of race against race on the irrelevant basis of skin color. It is the father of hatred and mother of violence." Subsequently, the National Urban League underlined its dedication to an "interracial approach" to the solution of the Negro's problems. In July of 1968, however, Whitney Young, director of the National Urban League opposed Wilkins at the annual convention of CORE. He said that he now believed strongly in Black Power because it emphasized "self-determination, pride, self-respect and participation and control of one's destiny and community affairs."

CORE, at its annual convention, resolved that "Black Power is not hatred. It is a means to bring Black Americans into the covenant of brotherhood. . . . it is a unified Black Voice reflecting racial pride in the tradition of our heterogeneous nation."

Sen. Robert F. Kennedy announced the formation of two corporations: the Bedford Stuyvesant Renewal and Rehabilitation Corp., and the Development and Services Corp.; the first was to be headed by Civil Court Judge Thomas R. Jones and would be composed of community leaders.

On Jan. 3, Sammy Younge Jr., a 22-year-old black College student, was murdered for attempting to use a white restroom at a Texaco service station in Tuskegee, Ala.

Vernon Dahmer, a Negro civil rights leader, was killed by a fire bomb in Hattiesburg, Miss., on Jan. 10 when night riders attacked his home and grocery store. His wife and daughter were also injured. Dahmer had announced on radio the day before that he would collect poll taxes and pay them for Negro voters. He was a former president of the local chapter of the NAACP.

James Meredith was the victim in June, of an assassination attempt on Highway 51 near Hernando, Miss., as he was marching to dramatize a voter registration drive. The march was resumed by Martin Luther King Jr., Floyd McKissick, Stokely Carmichael and other civil rights workers. It ended in a rally of 30,000 people at Jackson, Miss.

Julian Bond, a Negro, was denied his seat in the Georgia House of Representatives because of his opposition to the war in Vietnam. The Supreme Court ruled unanimously that Bond's constitutional rights of free speech had been violated when he was deprived of his seat. State Rep. George L. Smith said the Court decision left the House no alternative but to seat Bond.

On Sept. 10, in Atlanta, Ga., rioting broke out when police shot and wounded a Negro car-theft suspect. Mayor Ivan Allen was toppled from the roof of a car as he tried to calm the crowd, and 2 Negroes and 2 white policemen were shot. Stokely Carmichael and other SNCC members were arrested on the charge of inciting the riot.

A Kentucky civil rights law banned discrimination in public accommodations.

In an open housing march in Chicago, Martin Luther King Jr. was stoned by white Chicagoans. National Guardsmen protected Negro and white marchers in Cicero, Ill. This was part of a Southern Christian Leadership Conference campaign in Chicago announced by King in January.

On Chicago's West Side, roving gangs of Negroes began looting and tossing Molotov cocktails at police cars. The disturbances were set off by the turning off of fire hydrants by police. Even with the aid of Martin Luther King Jr., 1,000 policemen were unable to control a mob of 5,000 Negroes at the height of the riot on July 14. Some of the rioters were armed. On July 15, 4,000 National Guardsmen were called up by Gov. Otto Kerner. In 3 nights of rioting 2 Negroes were killed, 57 persons injured and 282 arrested.

In Waukegan, Ill., roving bands of Negro youths attacked cars and stores with rocks and Molotov cocktails on the night of Aug. 28. Over 60 youths, mostly Negroes, were arrested. The violence was set off the previous day when a Negro policeman attempted to arrest a Negro youth for allegedly attacking him with a bottle.

In a riot in Lansing, Mich., on Aug. 7 and 8, 31 persons were arrested and 11 injured during hit-and-run attacks by bands of Negro and white youths.

In Benton Harbor, Mich., on Aug. 28, gangs of Negro youths roamed the streets, throwing rocks at automobiles and stores. About 400 to 500 persons were involved, and 2 white youths shot and wounded a Negro, who later died.

Floyd J. McCree, a Negro, took office as Mayor of Flint, Mich.

A riot began in Omaha, Neb., with the breaking into of several stores in the Negro area and the gathering of a crowd of about 200. In 3 nights of violence 122 Negroes were arrested. New violence, fires, looting and vandalism broke out and continued for several days. As a result of these riots 24 adults and 7 youths were arrested.

In the East New York section of Brooklyn, N.Y., 2 persons were killed and 29 arrested in racial violence in July.

Percy Sutton, a Negro, became Borough President of Manhattan.

During a riot in the Hough section of Cleveland, July 18-20, Gov. James Rhodes declared a state of emergency and called out National Guard troops; 1,600 National Guardsmen helped police control the rioting. In 2 nights, 2 Negroes were killed and about 24 injured. Bands of Negroes still roved the streets as late as July 20. Between 45 and 50 fires were set, and approximately 150 persons were arrested. In all, 4 Negroes were killed and over 40 persons injured; 2,000 guardsmen were required to put down the disorders.

A riot in the Negro ghetto of Dayton, Ohio, on Sept. 1 and 2 was set off by the fatal shooting of a Negro man, presumably by whites in a passing car. Besides the Negro man killed, about 30 persons were injured and 130 arrests were made. Most of the violence consisted of smashing store windows and looting.

Robert C. Henry, a Negro, took office as Mayor of Springfield, Ohio.

Edward W. Brooke, a Negro Republican, was elected to the U.S. Senate from Massachusetts. He was the first Negro Senator since Reconstruction.

Robert Weaver became Secretary of Housing and Urban Development, the first Negro Cabinet member.

Andrew Felton Brimmer, a Negro and a prominent econo·mist, was named to the Federal Reserve Board.

Constance Baker Motley was appointed the first woman Federal judge.

A Negro, Pfc. Milton L. Olive, of the 503rd Infantry, 173rd Airborne Brigade, was posthumously awarded the Congressional Medal of Honor. Olive threw his body over a grenade, thus saving the lives of his fellow soldiers.

At the UNESCO-sponsored First World Festival of Negro Arts held in Dakar, Senegal, the following American Negroes won first prizes: Robert Hayden, poetry; Kenneth B. Clark, social science; William Majors, engraving; Mahalia Jackson, recordings; Louis Armstrong, jazz; Abbey Lincoln and Ivan Dixon, acting. LeRoi Jones, Louis Lomax, Ralph Ellison and Robert Weaver won second prizes.

Home, a collection of essays by LeRoi Jones, was published. It reflects his increasing militancy and hatred of whites.

James Baldwin wrote a collection of short stories, *Going to See the Man*. In 1968, his longest and least successful novel, *Tell Me How Long the Train's Been Gone* appeared.

In this year, two plays by Douglas Turner Ward, a Negro, were produced: *Happy Ending* and *Day of Absence*. They made up a double bill of one-act plays which had both critical and financial success, despite the newspaper strike in New York City. Both are satirical comedies directed against whites.

Who's Got His Own by a Negro, Ronald Milner, opened off-Broadway.

Bill Cosby, Negro actor, won the Emmy award as the best actor in a TV series. Cosby won the award again in 1967 and

1968. Born in Philadelphia and a star athlete in track, field
and football at Temple University, Cosby entered show business as a comedian. After establishing his reputation as a
nightclub comic, he was offered a role in the NBC-TV series
I Spy. Cosby thus became one of the first Negroes to star in
a TV series.

Ena Hartman, Negro actress, appeared in a major role in
the movie *The Girl Nobody Knew.*

The successful young Negro concert pianist Andre Watts
appeared as the principal soloist in the Philharmonic Stra-
vinsky Festival in New York City.

Emmet Ashford became the first Negro umpire in the
major leagues.

Bill Russell, the basketball star, became the first Negro to
coach a major league sports team, the Boston Celtics of the
National Basketball Association.

Frank Robinson, a Negro baseball player with the Baltimore Orioles, was the American League batting and home-run
champion, and was named the league's Most Valuable Player.

Mattie Alou, a Dominican Negro baseball player with the
Pittsburgh Pirates, was National League batting champion.

Emile Griffith, a Negro, won the middleweight boxing
championship.

1967

Negro employment in 9 representative metropolitan areas:

| | Negroes | | Rate of | |
	% of total population	% of total employment	Unemployment Total	Negroes
Atlanta	23.	15.2	2.6	15.5
Chicago	14.	13.5	2.8	x)
Cleveland	13.	11.2	3.1	15.5
Kansas City	11.2	8.9	4.1	x)
Los Angeles	7.6	6.9	4.4	10.7
New Orleans	30.7	20.1	4.0	10.0
New York	11.5	10.1	4.0	8.0
San Francisco	8.5	8.0	4.3	12.0
Washington, D.C.	25.	22.0	2.1	8.14

*) No figures given

Divided in different groups of employment in 9 representative metropolitan areas:

	Negro employment in % among		
	White collar jobs	Blue collar jobs	Craftsmen's jobs
Atlanta	2.3	33.8	6.4
Chicago	4.7	24.7	7.1
Cleveland	3.2	21.5	5.0
Kansas City	2.1	17.6	5.3
Los Angeles	2.8	14.5	4.1
New Orleans	3.0	44.8	10.2
New York	5.7	22.3	5.8
San Francisco	3.0	17.7	4.5
Washington, D.C.	8.4	51.9	10.7

The Urban Coalition was formed at a meeting in Washington of 22 business, labor, civil rights, city government, education and religious leaders on July 31, for the purpose of urging the commitment of greater resources to U.S. domestic problems. Among those present were Mayor John Lindsay of New York, David Rockefeller, Bayard Rustin, Whitney Young, I. W. Abel and Walter Reuther.

In August, the Urban Coalition held a convocation in Washington of over 800 mayors, business, labor, church and civil rights leaders to call on government to "reorder national priorities" and provide an emergency work program to provide jobs in cities.

The Ford Motor Co., Michigan Bell Telephone Co., and Chrysler Corp. were making an effort to provide jobs in the Detroit area for the employment of Negroes. Ford announced 6,500 job openings and sent recruiters into the ghetto to hire the hard-core unemployed.

Average weekly expenditures were: Food: Negroes, $18.62; whites, $21.49. Alcoholic beverages: Negroes, $0.81; whites, $0.97. Tobacco: Negroes, $1.21; whites, $1.55. Household supplies: Negroes, $0.99; whites, $1.30. Average annual expenditures were: Household operations (rent, repairs, laundry, cleaning, etc.): Negroes, $907.69; whites, $1,276.54. Clothing: Negroes, $446.09; whites, $534.22. Transportation, including cars: Negroes, $458.27; whites, $820.15. Recreation: Negroes, $130.34; whites, $214.40. Education: Negroes,

$28.26; whites, $57.43. Medical care: Negroes, $182.42; whites, $361.57. Personal care, including hair care: Negroes, $133.48; whites, $149.66.

In February, President Johnson asked Congress to pass a civil rights bill to bar discrimination in the sale and rental of housing, to stop interference with the exercise of civil rights and to end discrimination in the selection of juries.

Martin Luther King Jr. announced that he would work against the Vietnam war because he believed it had become the major obstacle to progress in the area of civil rights.

Rep. Adam Clayton Powell Jr., Democrat of New York and a Negro, was deprived of his chairmanship of the House Education and Labor Committee. He lost his seat in the House of Representatives, pending investigation of his qualifications, by a 364-64 vote of the House on Jan. 10. In March the House voted to exclude Powell from the 90th Congress by a vote of 248-176 tentative vote, and a 307-116 confirming vote. The grounds for exclusion were misuse of public funds and defiance of New York Courts in action stemming from a defamation suit against him.

President Johnson named Thurgood Marshall to the Supreme Court. Marshall was the first Negro ever to serve on the Supreme Court of the U.S.

Gene Roberts, of the *New York Times*, reported that the civil rights movement had collapsed in most communities of the South because of a decline in contributions to civil rights organizations, a shift of volunteers to the anti-poverty program, and anti-war protests and a shift of some rights funds to the North. The decline began after the Selma to Montgomery March in the spring of 1965. The Black Power movement accelerated the decline along with disputes over the role of whites in SNCC and CORE.

On June 21, 12 men and 4 women, members of a Negro revolutionary group, the Revolutionary Action Movement (RAM), were arrested on charges of plotting to murder moderate civil rights leaders such as Roy Wilkins and Whitney Young.

CORE voted in its national convention in July to drop the word "multiracial" from its constitutional provision on membership. By 1968 CORE had 70,000 members and offices in 33 states.

On July 20, 400 persons, representing 45 groups in 36 cities, attended a conference on Black Power in Newark, N.J. Some of those attending were former CORE leader James Farmer, Ron Karenga, SNCC chairman H. Rap Brown, and Rev. Jesse Jackson of SCLC.

In February, an explosion in his truck killed Wharlest Jackson, treasurer of the Natchez (Miss.) NAACP. The explosion was believed to have been caused by a delayed action bomb. Jackson had recently been upgraded in his job at the Armstrong Tire & Rubber Co. over a white man.

A Federal jury of white Mississippians convicted 7 men for participating in a KKK conspiracy to murder 3 civil rights workers in Mississippi in 1964; 8 were acquitted and no verdict was reached on 3. Among the convicted were Cecil R. Price, chief deputy sheriff of Neshoba County, and Sam H. Bowers, Imperial Wizard of the White Knights of the Ku Klux Klan. The convictions were said to be the first in a civil rights slaying in Mississippi. On Dec. 29, 2 were sentenced to 10-year terms, the maximum penalty under the law; 2 others to 6 years; the rest to 3-year terms.

Robert G. Clark became the first Negro elected to the Mississippi Legislature in the 20th century. In addition, 5 other Negroes won county level posts in Mississippi, and 16 won local posts.

It was announced that integrated law firms would be formed during the summer in Nashville, Memphis, Atlanta, Birmingham, Little Rock, and Charlotte, N.C.

Demonstrations by Negro students at Fisk University in Nashville, Tenn., were set off by reports of the arrest of a Negro student by a white policeman for drunkenness. The night before Stokely Carmichael had urged the students to take over the school administration. Negro rioters fired rifles at passing cars, stoned police and set stores on fire.

The first legal Negro-white marriage in Tennessee took place on July 21 in Nashville between Herman McDaniel Jr., 29-year-old Negro, and Joyce Christine Prescott, a 34-year-old white woman.

With fines up to $1,000 and imprisonment up to 5 years, inter-marriage was forbidden in 17 states, including Delaware, Missouri and Oklahoma; since World War II, 14 states west of the Mississippi had repealed such laws.

Rioting in Tampa, Fla., began after a policeman shot and killed a Negro burglary suspect. In three nights of violence, 15 persons were injured and over 80 arrested; 500 National Guardsmen and 150 police were required to put down the disturbances.

Rioting in Atlanta was set off by the arrest of Stokely Carmichael for failing to move on at request of the police. A petition signed by 700 residents of the Negro district of Atlanta asked "outsiders" (presumably Stokely Carmichael and other members of SNCC) to leave. They said: "We do not endorse nor condone, nor do we want riots in our community. We do not want our people shot, killed, or our children hurt. We do not want our community burned down. We condemn those persons who have come into our community, not to correct our grievances but to cause riots and turmoil in our community."

H. Rap Brown, national chairman of SNCC, was wounded by shotgun fire in Cambridge, Md., after he had urged a crowd of 400 Negroes to "burn this town down if this town don't turn around and grant the demands of Negroes." Brown was later arrested in Washington on charges of inciting riots and arson in Cambridge, Md. On July 27, Brown urged Washington Negroes to "get you some guns." He said, "The white man is your enemy. You got to destroy your enemy."

600 Negroes completed a 10-day march from Bogalusa, La., to Baton Rouge to protest discrimination in employment. In Baton Rouge, 2,200 National Guardsmen and police watched their rally.

On Nov. 2, violence began in Winston-Salem, N.C., after the funeral of a Negro killed by a policeman. At least 16 persons were injured and 51 arrested. Arrests totaled 250 by Nov. 5. To control the 500 Negro youths who were smashing windows, looting, sniping and setting fires 1,000 National Guardsmen were called out.

Bands of Negro youths set fires, smashed store windows and assaulted pedestrians in the Hunters Point section of San Francisco.

Violence broke out in the Hough section of Cleveland. 4 persons were arrested and 1 was injured. Store fronts were smashed, and at least 3 stores were looted.

Carl B. Stokes, a Negro Democrat, was elected Mayor of Cleveland, Ohio.

Rioting in Cincinnati began when roving bands of vandals threw bricks, rocks and fire bombs; 3 newsmen were beaten, some stores were looted. At its peak, the riots involved 1,000 Negro youths. Damage was estimated at over $1 million. Of 63 injuries reported, 56 were to whites; 484 people were arrested.

There was rioting in Toledo, Ohio, from July 24 to July 26.

A riot was started by Roxbury, Mass. Negro women as a demonstration over city welfare procedures. Over 100 persons were arrested and scores injured in 5 nights of violence.

Violence erupted in Newark, N.J., on July 13, when a Negro taxi driver was arrested on charges of assaulting a policeman. A crowd gathered to protest the arrest. The riots lasted 6 days and resulted in 23 deaths. (2 whites and 21 Negroes), 1,200 injuries and 1,300 arrests. The riots were reported to have caused over $10 million in business damages, almost a fifth in looted liquor, according to the Newark Economic Development Office.

Violence in Plainfield, N.J., started on July 14 with looting by gangs of Negro youths. Violence ended on July 19, with National Guardsmen making a house-to-house weapons search of Negro homes without warrants, under a declaration of a state of emergency by Governor Hughes. A policeman was killed in this rioting.

The death of a Negro soldier found hanged in a cell where he was being held on charges of being AWOL set off violence and vandalism in Cairo, Ill., on July 17 and 100 National Guardsmen were called to put down disorders, which ran from July 17 through July 19.

Violence in Minneapolis on July 19 through July 21 was set off by anger at the interference by a white policeman in a street fight between 2 Negro women over a wig.

Bands of Negro youths began throwing stones, smashing windows and setting fires in Buffalo on the night of June 27. About 300 persons were involved, 15 were arrested. On June 28, over 1,500 Negroes rioted; over 40 were wounded. Several white persons walking or driving through the Negro area were beaten. There were 46 arrests. The disturbances resulted in 68 wounded, 205 arrests, 24 fires and damage of $100,000.

The Vincent Astor Foundation announced a $1 million grant for parks and playgrounds in the Bedford Stuyvesant section of Brooklyn, under control of the corporation organized in December by Sen. Robert F. Kennedy and the Central Brooklyn Coordination Council.

A $7 million Federal grant was awarded to create jobs and train youths in the Bedford Stuyvesant section of Brooklyn.

Sporadic vandalism by groups of Negro youths occurred in Syracuse, N.Y. Nearly 100 persons were arrested.

In Detroit, on July 23, a riot began with a police raid on a speakeasy in the Negro section, and the arrest of between 70 and 80 persons. Rumors of police brutality spread. Negroes began to break windows and loot. They were joined by whites in the looting on the second day. By Aug. 6 there were 43 dead, over 1,250 fires, about 2,000 injuries and about 7,200 arrests. Over 14,000 paratroopers, National Guardsmen and state and local police were required to bring the city under control. Machine guns and tanks were used by the troops. The Kerner Commission on Civil Disorders estimated damage at $44 million.

On Aug. 2, Vice President Humphrey in a speech in Detroit called for a "Marshall Plan" of aid for the impoverished areas of cities.

On July 24 and 25, shooting, arson and looting in Grand Rapids, Mich., resulted in about 400 injuries.

Violence on July 24 and 25 in South Bend, Ind., resulted in the calling of 1,000 National Guardsmen, the injury of 9 persons and the arrest of about 30.

On Nov. 7, Richard C. Hatcher, a Negro, was elected the first Negro Mayor of Gary, Ind.

Violence in Chicago erupted on July 26 and 27, and resulted in the arrest of 57 persons.

Violence in East St. Louis, Ill., began Sept. 10, after a speech by H. Rap Brown, in which he told Negroes that America was on the eve of a revolution. The violence ended three nights later.

Rioting began in Milwaukee on July 30. By Aug. 2, the

toll was three dead, 100 injured, 541 arrested and $200,000 worth of damage.

Racial violence broke out in New Haven, Conn., on Aug. 19. Arrests in the first 2 nights reached 215. By Aug. 24, 350 persons had been arrested, most of them Negroes and Puerto Ricans. Scores were injured, none of them seriously.

President Johnson announced the formation of a Special Advisory Commission on Civil Disorders on July 27, to investigate racial disorders and to recommend remedial action. Gov. Otto Kerner of Illinois was appointed chairman, and Mayor John Lindsay of New York was made vice chairman.

A Negro boycott of the 1968 Olympics was proposed by Harry Edwards, a 24-year-old Negro teacher at San Jose State College in California.

There were 113 predominantly Negro colleges and universities in the U.S.

Gloria Gaston, a Negro and former liaison officer for the Peace Corps, was the Human Resource Development officer for the bureau of Latin America in the Agency for International Development.

Maj. Robert H. Lawrence Jr. of the Air Force, a Negro, was selected for the U.S. space program. He was the first Negro to qualify as an astronaut. He was among 4 chosen to be the crew of a manned orbiting laboratory.

Dem by William Melvin Kelley was published. The novel deals exclusively with white upper middle-class society and the bankruptcy of its values.

The Man Who Cried I Am by John A. Williams, a Negro, was published. It deals in part with Negro expatriates in Europe and with a forthcoming race war in which the Negroes are exterminated.

Sippi, a novel of Negro life in Mississippi since the 1954 Supreme Court Decision, was published. It was written by John Oliver Killens, a Negro.

Tales, a collection of short stories by LeRoi Jones, was published.

Pearl Bailey and Cab Calloway, world renowned Negro entertainers, were the stars of an all-Negro cast of *Hello, Dolly*, the musical version of Thornton Wilder's *The Matchmaker*.

Leslie Uggams, the young Negro actress and singer, starred in the Broadway musical *Hallelujah Baby*.

Arthur Ashe, a Negro, was U.S. clay court tennis champion. He and Charles Pasarell won the indoor doubles tennis championship.

Roberto Clemente, a Puerto Rican Negro baseball player with the Pittsburgh Pirates, was the National League's batting champion.

Hank Aaron, a Negro baseball player with the Atlanta Braves, was the National League homerun champion.

Orlando Cepeda, a Puerto Rican Negro baseball player with the St. Louis Cardinals, was the National League's Most Valuable Player.

Wilt Chamberlain, a Negro, was named the Most Valuable Player of the National Basketball Association.

1968

A special commission appointed by Governor Hughes of New Jersey concluded in its report, issued Feb. 10, that Newark police, state police and National Guardsmen used "excessive and unjustified force" against Negroes in putting down the riot of the previous summer, and that innocent bystanders had been killed by "indiscriminate" shooting.

On Feb. 29, the President's National Advisory Commission on Civil Disorders reported that the U.S. was "moving towards two societies, one black, one white, separate and unequal." It blamed riots of recent years mainly on "white racism." It recommended massive programs of job creation, training, removal of discrimination, revamping of welfare systems, Federal and private housing, improved methods of riot control through training programs for police and National Guardsmen, and greater efficiency in the processing and trial of rioters arrested. President Johnson was silent on the report; most civil rights leaders expressed approval of it one year later.

100 representatives of 35 colleges and universities, and 7 major school systems, met at Yale University in a symposium of studies on "black experience," which could be or should be added to academic curricula. Speakers included Ford Foundation president McGeorge Bundy, Ron Katenga, etc.

The Ford Foundation granted $3.2 million to various anti-poverty groups. $520,000 went to the Negro Industrial and Economic Union of Cleveland, a consulting agency for Negro businessmen, founded by Jim Brown, John Wooten and other prominent Negroes. The Bedford-Stuyvesant Development and Services Corp. received $400,000.

The heads of 18 building trades unions, meeting in Bal Harbour, Fla., assured the Department of Labor that they would actively recruit Negro membership and try to prevent discrimination by their local unions.

Violence began on Feb. 5 at Orangeburg, S.C., where several hundred Negro students of S.C. State College and Claflin College marched through the streets after protesting the segregation of a bowling alley. The riots continued, and on Feb. 8, three students were killed and 40 wounded. The Justice Department soon brought suits to desegregate the bowling alley as well as the Orangeburg Hospital.

On March 28, a riot began in Memphis Tenn., with a march led by Martin Luther King Jr., in support of a strike by city garbage collectors. 150 Negroes broke away from the march and began smashing windows, looting and attacking police. About 150 buildings were set on fire. 4,000 National Guardsmen were called in. One person was killed, a 16-year old looter. 50 or more persons were injured, and 300 persons were arrested.

Martin Luther King Jr. was assassinated in Memphis, Tenn. on April 4.

Rev. Ralph D. Abernathy became head of the Southern Christian Leadership Conference on the death of Martin Luther King Jr.

Rioting erupted in 125 U.S. cities after the assassination of King (from April 4 - 11). 68,887 troops were called up to curb the violence. At least 46 people were killed, all but 5 Negroes. Over 3,500 people were injured. More than $45 million worth of property was lost by fire or looting, and over 20,000 arrests were made. The biggest riots were in Washington, D.C., Baltimore, Chicago, and Pittsburgh. In Washington, D.C., 7 people were killed, 1,166 injured, 7,370 arrested; over 711 fires were set, and $15 million worth of insured damage was done. 15,000 troops were required to control the violence. In Baltimore 6 were killed, about 900 injured, over 5,500 arrested. More than 250 fires were set, and property damage was estimated at $10 million. In Chicago, 11 people were killed, about 1,000 injured, and 2,000 arrested. Property damage was over $10 million, and 1,000 people were left homeless by fire. In Pittsburgh, there were over 500 fires, 1,300 arrests, and damage of over one million dollar. In Kansas City, Mo., 5 Negroes and 2 police-men were killed in a gun battle between Negroes and police and National Guardsmen. In Detroit, 2 looters were killed and 23 persons were injured.

Violence broke out in Salisbury, Md., when hundreds of Negroes protested the death of a Negro deaf-mute burglary suspect shot by police. On the night of May 18, burning, looting and smashing of stores and cars with rocks lasted three hours. Rioting continued the next night, when an esti-mated one thousand Negroes were involved. The National Guard was called out by Gov. Spiro T. Agnew.

In Louisville, Ky., violence broke out on May 27, after a rally to protest reinstatement of a policeman accused of brutality in arresting a Negro. Two nights later, 2 persons were killed, and looting and fires broke out and continued through May 30. The number arrested was estimated at over 350.

On April 10, the House of Representatives passed and sent to President Johnson a civil rights bill containing a ban on racial discrimination in housing. The following day Presi-dent Johnson signed the Civil Rights Act of 1968, ending discrimination in 80% of sales and rentals of apartments and homes. It exempted rooming houses occupied by their owners and having four or fewer units, and single-family homes not sold or rented through a broker.

Ralph D. Abernathy presented a list of demands to govern-ment officials in Washington in preparation for the Poor People's Campaign planned originally by Martin Luther King Jr.

On May 2, the Poor People's March to Washington began in Memphis, Tenn., led by Ralph D. Abernathy. Ten days later the Poor People's Campaign was officially opened in Washington, D.C., with a Mother's Day March and a rally addressed by Mrs. Martin Luther King Jr. The following day Resurrection City, USA, was dedicated by Abernathy to shelter 3,000 participants in the Poor People's Campaign in Washington.

Over 50,000 participated in the "Solidarity Day" March of the Poor People's Campaign on June 19. They marched from the Washington Monument to the Lincoln Memorial. About one-half of the marchers were white.

On June 24, police closed down Resurrection City, after its camping permit had expired. Dismantling crews followed and cleared the city in less than 90 minutes. Almost no resistance was met. Ralph D. Abernathy and 300 of his followers were arrested after they marched to the Capitol in violation of laws against such demonstrations. A 9 p.m. to 5:30 a.m. curfew was imposed on the city by Mayor Walter Washington, a Negro. Abernathy received a 20-day jail sentence for leading the protest demonstration. He had entered a plea of no contest to the charge of unlawful assembly. Most of the others arrested with Abernathy received sentences of 10-15 days. The mule train, the symbol of the Poor People's Campaign, which left Marks, Miss., on May 13, arrived in Washington, but attracted little attention.

There are approximately 22 million Negroes representing 11% of the total population of the U.S. (The term non-white is often used in census reports. Of the total non-white population, 92% is Negro.)

As of 1968, the life expectancy of non-whites was at age 25, 43.1 additional years (for whites, 48.6); at age 35, 34.4 additional years (for whites, 39.1); at age 45, 26.4 additional years (for whites 30).

There were in this year 126 births per 1,000 non-white women aged 15-44. There were 86 births per 1,000 white women of the same ages.

As of 1968, the maternal mortality rate per 1,000 live births was more than three times as great for non-whites as for whites; .7 to .2. The infant mortality rate at less than one month old was 24.8 for non-whites, 15.6 for whites. The infant mortality rate at one month to one year was 14 for non-whites, 5 for whites.

52% of the Negro population live in the South, 40% in the North (18% in the Northeast and 22% in the North Central states), and 8% in the West.

Negroes constitute 12% of the population of metropolitan areas, and 20% of the population of central cities. In central cities, in metropolitan areas of 1 million or more, Negroes comprise 25% of the population of the central city. Negroes account for 5% of the suburban population.

The National Commission on Urban Problems forecasts that the number of Negroes in central cities will double by 1985.

As of 1968, Negroes constituted 39.4% (4.6 million) of the persons in poverty areas, although they were only 10.6% of the nation's population, 16 years of age and over. About ½ of all urban Negroes lived in poverty areas, compared with about 1/10 of the urban whites.

Of non-white families 69.1% are headed by husband and wife (88.9% for whites). Of non-white families, 26.4% are headed by a female (8.9% for whites).

Fortune Magazine reported that the Negro market represents $30 billion a year before taxes.

The median Negro family income is $4,939 as compared to $8,318 for whites. In the Northeast, it is $5,764, as compared to $8,746. In the North Central states it is $6,540 as compared to $8,414. In the South it is $3,992 as compared to $7,448 for whites. In the West it is $6,590 as compared to $8,901 for whites.

In 1968, 8.3 million non-whites lived below the poverty level (of $3,335 annual income for a non-farm family of 4), compared to 17.6 million whites. The non-white figure represents 35% of the non-white population. The figure for whites is only 10%.

In the previous year approximately 1 million non-whites rose above poverty levels.

There are 4.3 million non-whites employed as white collar workers, craftsmen and operatives. This marked the first time that more than ½ of all non-white workers held these jobs. Between 1960 and 1967, employment of non-whites in these occupations increased 47%. It increased only 16% for whites.

As of 1968, Negroes represented approximately 16.5% of the AFL-CIO membership. Negroes, however, participated in only 2.7% of union controlled apprenticeship programs.

Occupation distribution of nonwhites was as follows in 1968:

Occupation	Number of employed in 1000	Change in % to 1960-1967
Professional and Technical	592	+ 30
Managers, officials, proprietors	209	+ 6
Clerical	899	+ 23
Sales	138	+ 2
Craftsmen and foremen	617	+ 13
Operatives	1,882	+ 14
Service workers (except private households)	1,519	+ 23
Private household workers	835	— 23
Nonfarm laborers	899	— 2
Farmers and farm workers	423	— 31

8 Negroes served on the U.S. Mission to the United Nations in 1968, and 1 American Negro served on the U.N. Staff.

There were 320,000 Negroes employed in the Civil Service, representing 13.9% of the total.

There were 19 Negro Foreign Service officers and 38 Negro Foreign Service reserve officers.

As of 1968, 7 Negroes were U.S. Ambassadors.

In March, 1968, 312,000 or 9% of the men serving in the Armed Forces were Negro. Negroes represented 2% of all officers. In September, Frederick E. Davison was made a Brigadier General in the Army. He was the third Negro to be made a general in the Armed Forces.

According to Pentagon figures, Negroes made up 9.8% of the servicemen in Vietnam, 20% of combat troops, 25% of elite units such as paratroopers, and 14.1% of those killed in action.

The number of Negroes on draft boards increased from 278 in 1967 to 820 in 1968. They still constitute less than 5% of the total members. According to a study, two Southern states have no Negro members on draft boards at all.

There were 22 Negroes in the U.S. Military Academy, 15 Negroes in the U.S. Naval Academy, and 6 Negroes in the U.S. Air Force Academy.

The reenlistment rate of Negroes in the Army was three times that of whites.

The National Business League estimates that there are 50,000 Negro-owned or Negro controlled businesses.

The American College of Surgeons has somewhat more than 100 Negro members.

As of 1968, there were 236 Negroes on the editorial staffs of the 300 newspapers belonging to the AP Managing Editors Association. This total included 119 reporters.

The combined circulation of the Negro press and magazines was 3,500,000. The leader was *Ebony,* with a subscription of a million copies per month.

As of 1968, there were approximately 400 Negro members of Actor's Equity, which has jurisdiction over performers on the legitimate stage.

The three major TV networks, ABC, CBS and NBC, present 13 weekly series which regularly feature or star Negro actors and actresses.

There are 100 Negro-oriented radio stations in the U.S. which did a business of $28 million in 1967. Only five, however, are owned by Negroes.

As of 1968, 53% of the players of the National Basketball Association were Negroes; 27.7% of the players of the National Football League were Negroes; 29.2% of the players of the American Football League were Negroes; 33.4% of the players of the National and American Leagues in baseball were Negroes.

For the second quarter of 1968, figures show that 597,000 non-whites are unemployed, or 6.8%. The unemployment rate for non-whites is 3.8% for men 20 years or over; 6.2% for females 20 years and over, and 25.9% for both sexes aged 16 to 19 years.

As of 1968, the unemployment rate for non-whites in the 20 largest metropolitan areas of the U.S. was 7.6% (222,000 people). The rate for whites was 3.7 (332,000).

Over 4% of employed Negroes hold two jobs. It is about the same percentage for whites who hold two jobs.

62% of the non-whites not in the labor force as of 1968 expressed a desire to work, while the corresponding figure for whites was 55%.

3.4 million non-whites received welfare (14%) as compared to 5 million whites (3%).

The median number of years of schooling for non-whites is 12.2. For whites it is 12.6. 58% of young, non-white adults are high-school graduates.

In the last school year (1967-68), 14% of Negro students in 11 Southern states attended racially integrated schools, an increase of 1.5% over the previous years. 300 to 500 Southern city school districts maintained segregated schools.

There are 113 Negro institutions of higher education in the U.S.

An estimated 3% of the nation's medical students are Negro.

The membership of the NAACP is 427,000.

Founded in 1966, the National Welfare Rights Organization had over one hundred chapters in various cities. While non-racial in principle, its present membership of over 30,000 consists mostly of poor Negro women. Avoiding ideological controversies, the aims of the organization are practical: to mobilize public assistance for specific demands of poor people. The national leader is George A. Wiley (born in 1930), a chemist with a Ph.D. from Cornell University, who was in 1964 an associate national director of CORE.

3,072,000 Negroes are registered to vote in the South. In the 1968 Presidential election the Census Bureau reported that 51.4% of the registered non-whites voted, compared with 44% in 1964. This is the opposite of the national trend which shows a decline in voter participation.

At the Democratic National Convention, a Negro's name was placed in nomination for President. A Negro was also proposed for the Vice Presidency. There were 212 Negro delegates to the Convention.

As of 1968, there were 11 Negro federal judges in the U.S. courts.

In 1968, 107 Negroes served in the high echelons of government policy-making bodies, including a cabinet member, members of the Agency for International Development, the Office of Economic Opportunity, the Federal Reserve Board, Assistant and Deputy Assistant Secretaries of Cabinet departments, the Atomic Energy Commission, and the Import-Export Bank.

As of November, 1968, there were 79 Negro state representatives and 18 Negro state senators.

There were seven Negro mayors in the U.S. in 1968.

1,702 Negroes held elective or appointive positions in state, municipal and county agencies. Since 1965 about 385 Negroes have been elected to public office in the South.

As of December, 1968, there were seven Negro members of the House of Representatives, and one Negro Senator.

In a speech given on October 1 at Stanford University, Eldridge Cleaver said: "For all these hundreds of years, black people have had the thrust of their hearts against racism, because racism has been what has been murdering them. So black people oppose racism. The Black Panther Party opposes it, and we would hope that everyone can oppose it whether it's black or white. Because it will do us no good."

The *New York Times* concluded a report on the status of the Negro with the following statement: "Some officials believe that the statistical advances made by Negroes may have been more than offset by the hardening of attitudes and the polarization of whites and Negroes throughout the nation, as found by the National Advisory Commission on Civil Disorders." [January 12, 1969].

*   *

*

"One year later"—a study by the Urban America and the Urban Coalition, which was a follow-up of the "Kerner Report" of the President's National Advisory Commission on Civil Disorders, came in February 1969 to following conclusion: *"We are a year closer to two societies—black and white, increasingly separate and scarcely less unequal."*

Bibliography of Bibliographies

General Reference Guides:

Printed Materials

Bibliographic Index. A cumulative bibliography of bibliographies. Boston: The H. W. Wilson, *see* numbers. *See* NEGRO and other entries.

Carman, Harry James: *A guide to the principal sources for American civilization, 1800-1900, in the city of New York:* Printed materials. New York, 1962. *See* esp.: Part VIII Ethnic groups — The Negro, bibliography, 234ff.

Winchell, Constance M.: *Guide to Reference Books.* 8th Ed., Chicago, 1967. *See* NEGRO, and other entries.

Manuscripts

Carman, Harry James: *A guide to the principal sources for American cvilization, 1800--1900, in the City of New York:* Manuscripts. New York, 1960. Name index. *See* esp.: Part VIII. Ethnic groups, Negro. pp. 200-7.

U. S. Library of Congress: *The National Union Catalog of Manuscript Collections, 1966.* . . . Washington, 1967. Guide to nearly 126 repositories in the U.S. (1966) and published since 1959. It has been published by the Library of Congress since 1963. *See* NEGROES and other entries in an excellent subject and name index.

See Philip M. Hamer: *A guide to archives and manuscripts in the United States* (below).

Library Collections

American Library Directory: *A classified list of libraries in the United States and Canada . . .,* compiled biennially by Eleanor F. Steiner-Prag. 25th Ed., New York, 1967. Useful with *Subject Collections* (below).

Hamer, Philip M., ed.: *A Guide to Archives and Manuscripts in the United States.* New Haven, 1961.

Kruzas, Anthony T., ed.: *Directory of Special Libraries and Information Centers*. Detroit, Mich., 1967. *See* NEGRO and other entries in index.

Subject Collections: *A guide to special book collections and subject emphases as reported by university, college, public, and special libraries in the United States and Canada*. 3rd Ed., Rev. & Enl., New York, 1967. *See* NEGRO and other appropriate subject headings. Includes some references to MSS collections and a helpful group of collections. Source works are on page viii of the Introduction.

Printed Catalogues or Inventories
of Manuscript and Book Collections

California, University, Bancroft Library: *Catalogue of printed books*. Boston, 1964. 22 vols. *See* NEGROES (v. 14, 596-603); SLAVERY (v. 19, 165-181); and other subject entries.

California, University, University at Los Angeles, Library: *Guide to special collections*. Los Angeles, 1958. 76pp. (Its Occasional paper, no. 7).

Columbia University Library: *Manuscript collection in the Columbia University libraries; a descriptive list*. New York, 1959. 104pp. Entry No. 107 — Gumby, L. S. Alexander, Gumby Collection on the American Negro, 1800? — 1952. Material largely from 1910-50; large collection of clippings in subject groupings.

Duke University, Durham, N. C., Library: *Guide to the manuscript collection*. . . . 1939; rev. & enl. guide, 1947.

Fisk University, Nashville, Tenn., Library: *American missionary association archives*. . . . Nashville, 1947. 6 leaves.

Fisk University, Nashville, Tenn., Library: *Charles Waddell Chesnutt Collection*. A list of manuscripts, published works and related items. . . . Nashville, 1954. 32pp.

Hampton Institute, Hampton, Va., Collis P. Huntington Library: *A classified catalogue of the Negro collection* . . . compiled by Mentor A. Howe and Roscoe E. Lewis. Hampton, Va., 1940. 255pp. Author and title index.

Harvard University, Cambridge, Mass., Libraries: *Catalogue of the Peabody Museum of Archaeology and Ethnology* . . .: Subjects. Boston, 1963. 22 vols. *See* NEGROES [general] (v. 15, 78-97); NEGROES — American (v. 15, 97-131), and other subject entries.

Harvard University, Library: *Widener library shelf list*. Cambridge, Mass., 1966. *See* Volume 7, *Bibliography*, NEGROES — bibliography.

Howard University, Washington, D. C., Founders library. Moorland foundation: *A catalogue of books in the Moorland foundation*. . . . Washington, D.C., 1939. 499pp. Primarily a title catalogue, includes a selected list of uncatalogued pamphlets.

Illinois. State historical library, Springfield: *Manuscripts in the Illinois State Historical*. . . . Springfield, see numbers. *See* esp. no. 2 (1964), references to SLAVERY, and a long entry under CIVIL WAR. Author and subject index.

Michigan, University. Ann Arbor: *Michigan historical collections, Guide to manuscripts in the Michigan historical collections* Ann Arbor, 1963. 315pp. Subject and name index. *See* esp. NEGRO and SLAVERY and other subject entries.

New York Public Library. Schomburg Collection of Negro Literature: *Calendar of the manuscripts in the Schomburg Collection of Negro literature*. . . . Compiled by the historical records survey, Works projects administration. New York City, 1942 [3?]. 3 parts. Xerox copy of original in Schomburg Collection. Unpublished? Includes addenda; subject and name index.

New York Public Library. Schomburg Collection of Negro Literature: *Dictionary Catalogue of the Schomburg collection of Negro literature and history*. Boston, 1962. 9 vols. Two volume supplement issued in 1967.

New York (State). School of industrial and labor relations, Ithaca: *Library catalogue*. . . . Boston, 1967. 12 vols. *See* esp. NEGRO (v. 8, 60-82) and other subject entries.

Ohio State Archaeological and Historical Society. Library: *Guide to the manuscript collections*. . . . Columbus, 1953. 153pp. Descriptions of MSS holdings inadequate, but there is some material here, esp. SLAVERY, ABOLITIONISTS.

Syracuse University, Syracuse, N.Y., Library: *Manuscript register series* (no. 1, 1963 —   ). Each issue is an inventory of particular MSS in the library. *See* esp., no. 7 (Oct. 1964) — William Stanley Braithwaite.

Texas. Southern University, Houston, Library: . . . *Catalogue, Heartman Negro collection*. . . . Houston, 1955?. 325pp. [and] . . . *Recent additions to the Heartman Negro collection*. 1955. Arranged by Dewey Decimal classification. Newspaper, pamphlet and broadside dates from 1762-1900.

West Virginia, University, Library: *Guide to manuscripts and archives in the West Virginia collection.* Morgantown, 1958; a second volume, 1965. [W. Va. Univ. Bulletin. ser. 59, no. 10-1; ser. 65, no. 12-1.] Subject and name index.
See also, Edgar T. Thompson (below).

Wilberforce University, Wilberforce, Ohio, Carnegie Library: *The Benjamin William Arnett papers* [1838-1906]. . . . Wilberforce, Ohio, 1958. 18pp. Material largely relates to the African Methodist Episcopal Church.

Wilberforce University, Wilberforce, Ohio, Carnegie Library: *The Levi Jenkins Coppin Collection.* . . . Wilberforce, Ohio, 1957. 17pp.

Compiled Bibliographies and Indexes

to Periodical Publications

(since circa 1949)

Freedomways: A quarterly review of the Negro freedom movement. New York, 1961 + current. Frequent bibliographic essays, esp. by Ernest Kaiser, and briefly-annotated "Recent Books" section, covers the Negro in U. S. and other sections of the world. Two essays by Mr. Kaiser, who is on staff of the Schomburg Collection of New York Public Library, are excellent starting points for assessment and historiography of reference and research materials on the Negro, and should be consulted initially. *See* his, "The Negro Heritage Library and its critics," in Winter 1967 (pp. 64-74); and "Recently published Negro reference and research tools," in Fall 1966 (pp. 358-368). The latter article which offers criticism of works *in this list* is marked with asterisk (*).

Index to Select Periodicals. Annual cumulation. 1950 + current. A compilation of Negro periodicals begun by Charlotte W. Lytle of Hallie Q. Brown Library of Central State University, Wilberforce, Ohio. Following a first volume of decennial cumulation (1950/59), periodicals received by the Schomburg Collection of the New York Public Library were added to the compilation. It is arranged by topics and names, and lists articles from 11 current Negro periodicals in its last annual accumulation (1965). It is not annotated, but there is a lengthy listing of book reviews. The *Index* was designed to continue *A Guide to Negro periodical literature,* which had begun publication in 1941, and was interrupted by World War II.

Journal of Negro Education. In its numbers *passim.;* see esp., E. H. West, cited below. Not only education references.

* Miller, Elizabeth, W.: *The Negro in America; a bibliography....* Cambridge, Mass., 1966. 190pp. States that the period covered begins after the Supreme Court decision of 1954 and ends with the passage of the Voting Rights Bill of August 1965. Includes older references. Author index only.

Myrdal, Gunnar: *An American Dilemma. The Negro Problem and Modern Democracy.* New York, 1944; reissued in 1962. 1483pp. Bibliography: pp.1144-1180. Considerable source material and bibliography is to be found in the multi-volume Carnegie-Myrdal study of the Negro in America, which is the basis of the published work. The unpublished MSS are at the Schomburg Collection of the New York Public Library.

* *The Negro in Print; Bibliographic survey.* Bi-monthly. May 1965 + current. Originally designed to cover current materials from about 1960 forward, this listing soon included all periods, esp. coverage of special topical issues. Coverage was to survey "adult and juvenile, fiction and nonfiction, bound and unbound" publications. Special issues have concentrated on Negro history, books for young readers, housing, Negro in Armed Forces, and civil rights, among others.

New York Public Library: *Books about Negro life for children* [by] Augusta Baker, storytelling specialist, Office of Children's services. Revised, New York, 1966.

* Salk, Erwin A., compiler and editor: *A layman's guide to Negro History.* New, enlarged Ed., New York, McGraw-Hill Book Co., 1967. 196pp. This excellent guide is not only for the layman, but for the scholar also. Its format has been significantly altered from the 1st ed. of 1966, and although this is an improvement, there is still no index. Includes a section for children's books.

* Spangler, Earl: *Bibliography of Negro history; selected and annotated entries, general and Minnesota.* Minneapolis, 1963. 101pp. Subject and title index.

Thompson, Edgar T. and Alma M. Thompson: *Race and region, a descriptive bibliography compiled with special reference to the relations between whites and Negroes in the United States.* Chapel Hill, 1949. 194pp. Lists material found in the libraries of Duke University, University of North Carolina, and North Carolina College.

* Welsch, Edwin K.: *The Negro in the United States; a research guide.* Bloomington, 1965. 142pp. Bibliographical essays di-

622   BIBLIOGRAPHY

vided topically: historical and sociological background, the arts, etc. Bibliographical index of works cited.

* Work, Monroe Nathan: *A Bibliography of the Negro in Africa and America.* 1928; reprinted 1965. A work which represented the life-long enterprise of Work, who was Director of Records and Research at the Tuskegee Institute. Its 17,000 entries remain a primary bibliographic source. It is divided into three parts; the first, the Negro in Africa; the second, the Negro in North America; the last, the Negro in the Caribbean and Latin America. Includes not only books and periodical listings, but also a large number of pamphlets and fugitive papers.
See also, *Bibliographic Index,* in General Reference Guides: Printed Materials, above.

Recently published, but unevaluated bibliographies
in current books and pamphlets

Pages in brackets following entry refer to bibliographic sections

Alexander, Richard D. and others: *Management of racial integration in business; special report to management.* . . . New York, 1964. 147pp. [139-147, annotated].

Aptheker, Herbert: *Essays in the history of the American Negro.* New York, 1964. [pp.211-216].

Blake, Elias: "Color prejudice and the education of low income Negroes in the North and West," *Journal of Negro Education* 34 (Summer 1965), [pp.297-9].

Bontemps, Arna W., and Jack Conroy: *Anyplace but here.* New York, 1966. [pp.349-60]. (A revised and expanded version of *They Seek a City.*)

Buni, Andrew: *The Negro in Virginia politics, 1902-1965.* Charlottesville, Va., 1967. [pp.271-85].

California library association, Young adult librarians' round table: *American Negro in contemporary society; an annotated booklist.* The Association, 1966. 26pp.

Comitas, Labros: *Carribbeana 1900-1965: A topical bibliography.* Seattle, Wash., 1968. 930pp. Published for the Research Institute for the Study of Man.

Countryman, Vern, ed.: Conference on discrimination and the law, University of Chicago, 1963. *Discrimination and the law* [papers]. Chicago, 1965. 170pp. [pp.145-152; relevant cases, pp.153-163].

Courlander, Harold: *Negro folk music, U. S. A.* New York, 1963. 324pp. [pp.299-301; discography, pp.302-312].

Franklin, John Hope: *From slavery to freedom: a history of Negro Americans.* 3rd ed., New York, 1967. [pp.653-86, annotated].

Franklin, John Hope and Isidore Starr, eds.: *Negro in twentieth century America: a reader on the struggle for civil rights.* New York, 1967. [pp.539-42, annotated].

Graham, Hugh Davis: *Crisis in print; desegregation and the press in Tennessee.* Nashville, Tenn., 1967. [pp.317-28, annotated].

Jann, Janheinz: *Bibliography of neo-African literature from Africa, America, and the Caribbean.* New York, 1965. 359pp. [North America, pp.210-335].

Jewish social studies (periodical), Negro-Jewish relations in the United States: *Papers and proceedings of a conference convened by the Conference on Jewish social studies.* New York, Citadel, 1966). [pp.67-71].

Joann Carmen, Sister: *Study of race relations, a teaching unit.* National Catholic conference for interracial justice, 1965. [pp.52-70].

Koblitz, Minnie W.: *Negro in schoolroom literature; resource materials for the teacher of kindergarten through the sixth grade.* Center for urban education, 1967. 67pp., annotated.

McPheeters, Annie L.: *Negro progress in Atlantic, Georgia, 1950-1960; a selective bibliography on human relations from four Atlanta newspapers.* Atlanta, West Hunter branch, Atlanta public library, 1964. 55pp. [The Atlanta Constitution, Atlanta Daily World, The Atlanta Inquirer, and The Atlanta Journal].

Meier, August and Elliott M. Rudwick: *From plantation to ghetto; an interpretative history of the American Negroes.* New York, 1966. 280pp. [pp.253-267. Lists chiefly secondary sources which are readily available to the general reader and college student].

Meltzer, Milton: *Thaddeus Stevens and the fight for Negro rights.* New York, 1967. [pp.221-224].

Millender, Dharathula H.: *Real Negroes, honest settings; children's and young people's Negro life and history.* American federation of teachers, AFL-CIO, 1967. 28pp.

Nichols, Charles Harold: *Many thousand gone, the ex-slaves' account of their bondage and freedom.* (Studies in American literature and history, 1). Leiden, E. J. Brill, 1963, 229pp. [213-24].

Northwood, Lawrence King and Ernest A. T. Bart: *Urban deseg-regation; Negro pioneers and their white neighbors.* Seattle, Wash., 1965. 131pp. [pp.121-131].

Osofsky, Gilbert: *Burden of race; a documentary history of Negro-white relations in America.* New York, 1967. [pp.637-41, annotated].

Pease, William H. and Jane H. Pease: *Black utopia: Negro com-munal experiments in America.* Madison, Wisc., State His-torical Socitey of Wisconsin, 1963. [pp.191-200, MSS and annotations].

Reimers, David M.: *White Protestantism and the Negro.* New York, 1965. 236pp. [223-227, annotated].

Rollins, Charlemae Hill: *Famous American Negro poets.* New York, 1965. 95pp. (Famous biographies for young people.)

Strickland, Arvarh E.: *History of the Chicago urban league.* Urbana, Ill., 1966. 286pp. [pp.265-272].

Wagner, Jean: *Les poetes nègres des Etats-Unis: le sentiment racial et religieux dans la poésie de P. L. Dunbar à L. Hughes (1890-1940)*. Paris, Librairie Istra, 1963. 637pp. [pp.601-619; discography, pp.619-20].

Waskow, Arthur I.: *From Race Riot to Sit-In: 1919 and the 1960s.* A study in the connections between conflict and vio-lence. New York, 1966. 380pp. [pp.355-66; see also, "Preface"].

Waynick, Capus M., and others, eds.: *North Carolina and the Negro.* Mayors' cooperating committee, 1964. [pp.271-287].

West, E. H.: "Summary of research during 1964 related to the Negro and Negro education," *Journal of Negro Education* 35 (Winter 1966). [pp.62-72, lists 80 dissertations, with anno-tation].

———, "Summary of research during 1965 related to the Negro and Negro education," *Journal of Negro Education* 36 (Winter 1967). [pp.58-69].

Williams, Daniel T. and Carolyn L. Redden: *Black Muslims in the United States; a selected bibliography.* Tuskegee, Ala:, Tuskegee Institute, Hollis Burke Frissell Library, 1964. 19pp.

INDEX

The figures indicate the year under which the subject or name appears in the book.
Biographies of Negroes are to be found mostly in the year of their birth.

cotton growing in German colonies in, 1900
European penetration of, 1880
exploitation of, 1770
Garvey and, 1911
  united states of Africa advocated, 1922
  See also Garvey, Marcus
revived interest in, 1934
Russia and, 1935
slaves imported from
  cost of slaves, 1746
  expeditions (1859-1862), 1859
  first cargo of, 1502
  New England sources of, 1676
  principal U.S. sources, 1720
  prohibited, 1807
  survival rate, 1748
  treaty to bar, 1823
  See also Importation of slaves
in slave trade, 1621; see also Slave trade
African Baptist Church, founded in Alabama, 1839
  Boston, 1809
  in Philadelphia, 1809
  in Virginia, 1776
African Communities League, 1887
African Company, 1821
African Congregational Church, 1840
African Education Society, 1832
African Episcopal Church, 1787
  membership of, 1824
African Free School, 1805
  additional building for, 1820
  attendance of, 1824
  for boys, 1829
  Colored Grammar School No.1 founded by, 1835
  founded, 1787
African Methodism introduced in Africa, 1834
African Methodist Episcopal Book Concern, 1834
African Methodist Episcopal Church (AME Church)
bishops of
  R. Allen, see Allen, Bishop Richard
  S. Bean, 1827
  J. M. Brown, 1817
  M. Brown, see Brown, Reverend Morris
  J.W. Gaines (1888), 1840
  Gregg, 1926
  J.W. Loguen (1869), 1841
  D. Payne, see Payne, Bishop Daniel A.
  B.T. Tanner, 1835
  H. McTurner, 1834
founded
  in Philadelphia, 1828
  in San Francisco, 1854
  membership of, 1880
  missionary work of, 1827
  property owned by, 1876
  publication of, 1847
  schools founded by, 1864, 1881, 1885
  standing of, 1836
  Vesey joins, 1767
African Methodist Episcopal Church Magazine, 1841
African Methodist Episcopal Zion Church (AMEZ Church), 1820

bishops of
  W.H. Brooks, 1909
  G.W. Clinton (1896), 1959
  J.W. Hood, 1831
  C. Rush, 1828, 1840
  Varick, see Varick, Bishop James
  first educational effort of, 1817
  founded, 1750
    in Boston, 1838
    in New York, 1801, 1821
  membership of, 1870
  schools founded by, 1879
African Missionary Society, 1822
African Observer, The (journal), 1826
African Orthodox Church, 1926
African Presbyterian Church
  first, 1807
  founded, 1807
African School Association founded, 1840
African Sentinel and Journal of Liberty, The (newspaper), 1831
African Society, 1720
African Supply Association, 1859
African Union, 1821
Africanus, S.M., 1849
Afro-American Council
  militancy of, 1906
  B.T. Washington in, 1905, 1906
Afro-American Female Intelligence Society, 1832
Afro-American Flat Janitors Union, 1926
Afro-American League founded (1887), 1856
Afro-American Magazine (magazine), 1859
Afro-American Spokesman (magazine), 1859
Afro-American studies, advocated, 1875
Afro-American Unity, 1925
  founded, 1964
Afro-Cuban music, 1947; see also Music
Aggravated assault in South, 1867
Agricultural Adjustment Administration (AAA)
  benefits derived from, 1937
  effects on agriculture of, 1933
Agriculture
  cost of slaves and, 1832
  Depression and, 1930
  effects of AAA on, 1933
  in Florida, 1565
  migrations and disorganization in, 1921

slavery necessary in, 1833
slaves in, 1850
B.T. Washington's interest in, 1864
  See also Cotton; Farm workers; Farmers; Farms; Rice; Sugar; Tobacco; Wheat
Ailey, Alvin, 1961
Air Force
  desegregated, 1950
  expansion of Negro pilot training by, 1943
  first Negro general in, 1954
  first Negro squadron in, 1941
  Negro officers and enlisted men in, 1949, 1962
  Negroes in service units of, 1942

Air Force Officers Training School, 1943
Aitken, George, 1936
Akins, Virgil, 1958
Al Hajj Malik al-Shabbaz, see Malcolm X
Alabama
  admitted as slave state, 1819
    readmission of, 1868
  adopts 13th Amendment, 1865
  anti-lynching bills in, 1919
  assembly forbidden in, 1832
  banks established in, 1890
  bombings in, 1956, 1957, 1963
  boycotts in
    of merchants, 1957
    on products from, 1965
    public transportation, 1904
  churches founded in, 1839, 1867, 1880
  colleges founded in, 1866
  Democratic control of, 1874
  demonstrations in, 1929, 1963
    sit-ins, 1960
  elections in
    Negro vote, 1940
    voter intimidation, 1892
  first Negroes holding public office in 1964
  freedmen in, 1830, 1860
    laws on, 1865
  Freedom Ride in, 1961
  housing desegregated in, 1950
  KKK in, 1871
  laws of
    on curfew, 1909
    on freedmen, 1865
    on instruction, 1832
    on intermarriage, 1872, 1877
    on interracial fornication, 1882
    on killing or maiming, 1819
    on licenses for teaching, 1833
    literacy test for voting, 1946
    on NAACP, 1958
    on preaching, 1832
    on prisoners, 1876, 1884
    on reapportionment, 1957
    on school desegregation, 1955
    on school segregation, 1868
    on segregated housing, 1950
    segregated public transportation, 1891, 1906, 1955
    on whipping and branding, 1827
  march in, 1965
  Maroons in, 1672
  migration from, 1880, 1890, 1900
  Negro policemen in, 1930
  Negro population
    in black belt, 1880
    in cities, 1900, 1940
  Negro schools founded in, 1858, 1867, 1868
  Negro troops in Civil War and, 1864
  public transportation in
    boycott on, 1904
    resistance to desegregation of, 1957
    segregated, 1891, 1906, 1955, 1956
  Reconstruction of, 1865, 1867
  relief rates in, 1935
  riots in, 1956
    race, 1941, 1943, 1946
  schools in
    expenditures for, 1954